WEBSTER'S
DICTIONARY

WEBSTER'S DICTIONARY

THOMAS NELSON PUBLISHERS
Nashville

Published in Nashville, Tennessee, by Thomas Nelson, Publishers and distributed in Canada by Lawson Falle, Ltd., Cam-
bridge, Ontario.

Library of Congress Cataloging-in-Publication Data

Webster's dictionary of the English language. — New rev. ed.
    p.   cm.
  ISBN 0-8407-4805-1 (pb)
  I. Thomas Nelson Publishers.
PE1628.W55634   1991
423—dc20   91–4696
                                 CIP

A

A, a, *n.* 1. first letter of the English alphabet. 2. best grade.

a, *indef. art.* 1. one. 2. any single.

ab'a·cus, *n.* calculating device using sliding beads.

a·baft', *adj., adv., Nautical.* nearer the stern.

a·ban'don, *v.t.* 1. leave permanently. 2. give up. —*n.* 3. freedom from self-restraint. —**a·ban'don·ment,** *n.*

a·ban'doned, *adj.* 1. left or given up permanently. 2. without self-restraint; shameless.

a·base', *v.t.,* **abased, abasing.** degrade, humble. —**a·base'ment,** *n.*

a·bash', *v.t.* embarrass; shame. —**a·bashed',** *adj.* —**a·bash'ed·ly,** *adv.*

a·bate', *v.t., v.i.,* **abated, abating.** lessen, diminish. —**a·bate'ment,** *n.*

ab·at·toir (ab'ət twahr), *n.* slaughterhouse.

ab·bé (ab bā'), *n. French.* abbot; priest.

ab'bess, *n.* nun directing a convent.

ab'bey, *n., pl.* **ab'beys.** monastery or convent.

ab'bot, *n.* monk directing a monastery.

ab·bre'vi·ate", *v.t.,* **-ated, -ating.** shorten to essentials. —**ab·bre'vi·a'tion,** *n.*

ab'di·cate", *v.t.,* **-cated, -cating.** give up, as office or power. —**ab''di·ca'tion,** *n.*

ab'do·men, *n.* 1. part of the human body between the chest and hip. 2. part of an animal body in a similar location. —**ab·dom'in·al,** *adj.*

ab·duct', *v.t.* carry away, esp. by force. —**ab·duc'tion,** *n.* —**ab·duc'tor,** *n.*

a·beam', *adv., adj.,* across a ship or boat.

a·bed', *adv.* in bed.

ab''er·ra'tion, *n.* deviation from what is considered normal.

a·bet', *v.t.,* **abetted, abetting.** aid or encourage. —**a·bet'tor, a·bet'ter,** *n.*

a·bey'ance, *n.* suspension of activity.

ab·hor', *v.t.,* **abhorred, abhorring.** regard with horror or disgust. —**ab·hor'rence,** *n.* —**ab·hor'rent,** *adj.*

a·bide', *v.,* **abode** or **abided, abiding.** *v.i.* 1. remain. 2. dwell. —*v.t.* 3. wait for. 4. *Informal.* tolerate.

a·bid'ing, *adj.* enduring; steadfast.

a·bil'i·ty, *n., pl.* **-ties.** 1. power. 2. talent; aptitude.

ab'ject, *adj.* 1. downcast. 2. contemptible. —**ab·ject'ly,** *adv.*

ab·jec'tion, *n.* abject state.

ab·jure', *v.t.* **-jured, -juring.** renounce formally. —**ab''ju·ra'tion,** *n.*

ab'la·tive, *n.* grammatical case of origin, means, location, etc. —**ab'la·tive,** *adj.*

a·blaze', *adv., adj.* afire.

a'ble, *adj.,* **abler, ablest.** 1. with the power to do a certain thing. 2. competent. —**a'bly,** *adv.*

ab·lu'tion, *n.* washing; cleansing.

ab'ne·gate, *v.t.,* **-gated, -gating.** deny or renounce for oneself. —**ab''ne·ga'tion,** *n.*

ab·nor'mal, *adj.* not normal. —**ab''nor·mal'i·ty,** *n.*

a·board', *adv.* 1. onto a ship, train, etc. —*prep.* 2. on a ship, train, etc.; on board.

a·bode', *n.* 1. home; dwelling. 2. brief term of residence.

a·bol'ish, *v.t.* do away with. —**ab''o·li'tion,** *n.*

ab''o·li'tion·ist, *n.* favorer of the abolition of something.

A bomb, *n.* atomic bomb.

a·bom'in·a·ble, *adj.* disgusting; loathsome. —**a·bom'in·a·bly,** *adj.*

a·bom'in·ate", *v.t.,* **-nated, -nating.** hate or loathe. —**a·bom''in·a'tion,** *n.*

ab''o·rig'i·nal, *adj.* 1. primitive; original. —*n.* 2. aborigine.

a''bo·rig'in·e, *n.* original inhabitant, esp. a savage.

a·bor'tion, *n.* 1. termination of pregnancy before full development of a fetus. 2. wretched piece of work. —**a·bor'tion·ist,** *n.*

a·bor'tive, *adj.* (of a hope or attempt) frustrated at an early stage.

a·bound', *v.i.* to have or offer something in abundance.

a·bout', *prep.* 1. concerning; regarding. 2. around. 3. near by. 4. on the point of. —*adv.* 5. nearly; approximately. 6. in all directions. 7. in the opposite direction.

a·bove', *prep.* 1. higher than. 2. greater than. —*adv., adj.* 3. to or in a higher place. 4. in a previous part of a text.

a·bove'board", *adj., adv.* without deception or disguise.

a·brade', *v.t.,* **-braded, -brading.** scrape or rub. —**a·bra'sion,** *n.* —**a·bra'sive,** *adj., n.*

a·breast', *adv., adj.* 1. alongside. 2. side by side.

a·bridge', *v.t.,* **-bridged, -bridging.** shorten; abbreviate. —**a·bridg'ment,** *n.*

a·broad', *adv., adj.* 1. outside one's own country. 2. outdoors. 3. over a broad area.

ab'ro·gate", *v.t.,* **-gated, -gating.** end or revoke, as a law. —**ab''ro·ga'tion,** *n.*

ab·rupt', *adj.* 1. sudden. 2. steep. —**ab·rupt'ly,** *adv.* —**ab·rupt'ness,** *n.*

ab'scess, *n.* area filled with pus.

abscond

2

ab·scond', *v.i.* leave secretly and hurriedly.

ab·sent, *adj.* (ab'sənt) not present. —*v.t.* (ab sent') remove. —**ab'sence,** *n.* —**ab'sent·ly,** *adv.*

ab''sen·tee', *n.* absent person. —**ab''sen·tee'ism,** *n.*

ab'sent-mind'ed, *adj.* 1. not paying attention. 2. forgetful.

ab'so·lute, *adj.* 1. perfect. 2. pure; unqualified. 3. unrestricted. —*n.* 4. that which is perfect, pure, or unmodified. —**ab''so·lute'ly,** *adv.*

ab·solve', *v.t.,* -**solved, -solving.** free from blame or guilt. —**ab''so·lu'tion,** *n.*

ab·sorb', *v.t.* 1. take in, as a fluid. 2. get the attention of; fascinate. —**ab·sorb'ent,** *adj., n.* —**ab·sorp'tive,** *adj.* —**ab·sorp'tion,** *n.*

ab·stain', *v.i.* refrain. —**ab·sten'tion, ab'sti·nence,** *n.* —**ab'sti·nent,** *adj.*

ab·ste'mi·ous, *adj.* abstaining from excess.

ab·stract, *adj.* (ab'strakt) 1. reduced to essentials. 2. non-material; non-specific. —*n.* 3. summary; abridgment. —*v.t.* (ab strakt') 4. remove, esp. in a theft. 5. summarize; abridge. 6. cause attention to wander. —**ab·strac'tion,** *n.*

ab·struse', *adj.* hard to understand.

ab·surd', *adj.* nonsensical. —**ab·surd'ly,** *adv.* —**ab·surd'i·ty, ab·surd'ness,** *n.*

a·bun'dance, *n.* great supply. —**a·bun'dant,** *adj.* —**a·bun'dant·ly,** *adv.*

a·buse', *v.t.,* -**bused, -busing,** *n. v.t.* (ə byōoz') 1. use or treat wrongly. —*n.* (ə byōos') 2. wrong use or treatment. 3. insult. —**a·bus'ive,** *adj.*

a·but', *v.i.,* -**butted, -butting.** meet at an edge or end; border.

a·but'ment, *n.* construction touching or helping to support another construction.

a·bys'mal, *adj.* measureless in depth; bottomless.

a·byss', *n.* 1. great depth; chasm. 2. hell.

a·ca'cia, *n.* tropical plant with white or yellow flowers.

ac''a·dem'ic, *adj.* 1. pertaining to scholarship. 2. unconnected with actuality; theoretical.

a·cad'e·my, *n.* 1. school. 2. cultural organization. —**a·ca''de·mi'cian,** *n.*

ac·cede', *v.i.,* -**ceded, -ceding.** consent.

ac·cel'er·ate'', *v.,* -**ated, -ating.** *v.t., v.i.* increase in speed. —**ac·cel''er·a'tion,** *n.*

ac·cel'er·a''tor, *n.* vehicle speed control.

ac·cent, *n.* (ak'sent) 1. emphasis. 2. national or regional manner of pronouncing. —*v.t.* (ak sent') 3. emphasize; stress.

ac·cen'tu·ate'', *v.t.,* -**ated, -ating.** emphasize; stress. —**ac·centu·a'tion,** *n.*

ac·cept', *v.t.* 1. receive or take willingly. 2. agree to. —**ac·cept'a·ble,** *adj.* —**ac·cept'a·bly,** *adv.* —**ac·cept''a·bil'i·ty,** *n.* —**ac·cept'ance,** *n.*

ac'cess, *n.* 1. means or way of approach. 2. right of approach. 3. outburst; attack.

ac·ces'si·ble, *adj.* readily approached or reached. —**ac·ces''si·bil'i·ty,** *n.*

ac·ces'sion, *n.* 1. increase or addition. 2. assumption of office or position.

ac·ces'so·ry, *n., pl.* -**ries.** 1. additional working part, decorative object, etc. 2. companion in a crime.

ac'ci·dent, *n.* unexpected event, usually undesirable. —**ac''ci·den'tal,** *adj.* —**ac''ci·den'tal·ly,** *adv.*

ac·claim', *v.t.* 1. applaud; cheer. —*n.* 2. applause. —**ac''cla·ma'tion,** *n.*

ac·cli·mate'', *v.t.,* -**ated, -ating.** accustom to a new environment. Also, **ac·clim'a·tize''.**

ac·cliv'i·ty, *n., pl.* -**ties.** upward slope.

ac·com'mo·date'', *v.t.,* -**dated, -dating.** 1. provide with food, lodging, etc. 2. adjust to existing conditions. 3. help with a loan, favor, etc. —**ac·com''mo·da'tion,** *n.* —**ac·com'mo·dat''ing,** *adj.*

ac·com''mo·da'tions, *n., pl.* lodgings, esp. temporary ones.

ac·com'pa·ni·ment, *n.* 1. something used with another thing; accessory. 2. music used to supplement that of a singer, soloist, etc.

ac·com'pa·nist, *n.* player of a musical accompaniment.

ac·com'pa·ny, *v.t.,* -**nied, -nying.** 1. travel with. 2. provide a musical accompaniment for.

ac·com'plice, *n.* associate in crime.

ac·com'plish, *v.t.* succeed in doing. —**ac·com'plish·ment,** *n.*

ac·com'plished, *adj.* 1. completed. 2. highly skilled.

ac·cord', *v.t.* 1. grant, as a favor. 2. cause to be in agreement or harmony. —*v.i.* 3. be in agreement or harmony. —*n.* 4. agreement; harmony. 5. consent. —**ac·cord'ance,** *n.* —**ac·cord'ant,** *adj.*

ac·cord'ing, *adj., adv.* 1. in accordance. 2. **according to, a.** in accordance with. **b.** as stated by.

ac·cord'ing·ly, *adv.* 1. as is indicated or prescribed. 2. therefore.

ac·cor'di·on, *n.* reed instrument with keyboard and bellows. —**ac·cor'di·on·ist,** *n.*

ac·cost', *v.t.* approach and catch the attention of.

ac·count', *v.t.* 1. regard as. —*v.i.* 2. **account for, a.** explain or interpret. **b.** justify. **c.** be condemned or punished for. —*n.* 3. story; narrative. 4. explanation. 5. justification. 6. importance. 7. set of business transactions involving one client or customer. **8.** business record.

ac·count'a·ble, *adj.* answerable; responsible.

ac·count'ing, *n.* keeping or interpretation of business accounts. —**ac·count' ant,** *n.* —**ac·count'an·cy,** *n.*

ac·cou'ter·ment, *n.* piece of clothing or equipment carried on the person.

ac·cred'it, *v.t.* **1.** certify as competent or valid. **2.** attribute. —**ac·cred''it·a'tion,** *n.*

ac·cre'tion, *n.* growth, esp. by accumulation.

ac·crue', *v.i.* be added, esp. in a regular way. —**ac·cru'al,** *n.*

ac·cu'mu·late, *v.,* **-lated, -lating.** *v.t., v.i.* gather; collect. —**ac·cu''mu·la' tion,** *n.* —**ac·cu'mu·la''tive,** *adj.* —**ac· cu'mu·la''tor,** *n.*

ac'cu·rate, *adj.* correct; truthful. —**ac' cu·ra·cy, ac'cu·rate·ness,** *n.*

ac·curs'ed, *adj.* **1.** under a curse. **2.** damnable.

ac·cu'sa·tive, *n.* grammatical case for direct object of verb. —**ac·cu'sa·tive,** *adj.*

ac·cuse', *v.t.,* **-cused, -cusing.** denounce; blame. —**ac·cus'er,** *n.* —**ac''cu·sa' tion,** *n.*

ac·cus'tom, *v.t.* cause to become used to something.

ac·cus'tomed, *adj.* usual; customary.

ace, *n.* **1.** playing card with one pip. **2.** leading expert.

a·cer'bi·ty, *n.* harshness of temper or speech.

ac'e·tate'', *n.* fibre or fabric derived from cellulose.

a·cet'y·lene, *n.* highly inflammable gas.

ache, *v.i.,* **ached, aching,** *v.i.* **1.** suffer dull pain. —*n.* **2.** dull pain.

a·chieve', *v.t.,* **-chieved, -chieving.** succeed in reaching, finishing, or fulfilling. —**a·chieve'ment,** *n.*

ac'id, *n.* **1.** chemical compound reacting with base to form salt. **2.** sour substance. —*adj.* **4.** pertaining to acids. **5.** sour. —**a·cid'i·ty,** *n.*

a·cid'u·lous, *adj.* containing or suggesting acid.

ac·knowl'edge, *v.t.,* **-edged, -edging. 1.** admit as true or valid. **2.** show appreciation or gratitude for. —**ac·knowl' edg·ment,** *n.*

ac'me, *n.* summit.

ac'ne, *n.* skin complaint.

ac'o·lyte, *n.* priest's assistant; altar boy.

a'corn, *n.* nut of an oak tree.

a·cous'tic, *adj.* pertaining to transmission or reception of sound through air, etc. Also **a·cous'ti·cal.** —**a·cous'ti· cal·ly,** *adv.*

a·cous'tics, *n.* **1.** *sing.* science of transmission of sound through air, etc. **2.** *pl.* acoustic properties.

ac·quaint', *v.t.* **1.** make known. **2.** make familiar. —**ac·quain'tance,** *n.*

ac''qui·esce', *v.i.,* **-esced, -escing.** consent or comply. —**ac''qui·es'cence,** *n.* —**ac''qui·es'cent,** *adj.*

ac·quire', *v.t.,* **-quired, -quiring.** obtain; get.

ac''qui·si'tion, *n.* **1.** act or instance of acquiring. **2.** something acquired.

ac·quis'i·tive, *adj.* **1.** pertaining to acquisition. **2.** greedy, grasping.

ac·quit', *v.t.,* **-quitted, -quitting. 1.** release from blame or detention. **2.** conduct; behave. —**ac·quit'tal,** *n.*

a'cre, *n.* land area equal to 43,560 square feet or 4,047 square meters. —**a'cre· age,** *n.*

ac'rid, *adj.* harsh and bitter.

ac''ri·mo''ny, *n.* harshness of manner or expression. —**ac''ri·mo'ni·ous,** *adj.*

ac'ro·bat'', *n.* gymnastic entertainer, esp. one performing high above the ground. —**ac'ro·bat'ic,** *adj.*

ac''ro·nym, *n.* word formed from the initial letters of a phrase or title, as *NASA.*

a·cross', *prep.* **1.** from one side to the other of. **2.** on the other side. —*adv.* **3.** from one side to the other.

act, *n.* **1.** something done. **2.** law. **3.** one of the main divisions of a play, etc. —*v.i.* **4.** do something. **5.** conduct oneself. **6.** have an effect on something. **7.** perform in a play or plays.

act'ing, *n.* **1.** the profession of one who performs in plays. —*adj.* **2.** performing a specified function for the time being.

ac'tion, *n.* **1.** state of being active. **2.** something done. **3.** *Informal.* interesting activity. **4.** combat. **5.** lawsuit.

ac'ti·vate'', *v.t.,* **-vated, -vating.** cause to be active. —**ac''ti·va'tion,** *n.*

ac'tive, *adj.* **1.** performing actions. **2.** having an effect. **3.** *Grammar.* pertaining to verbs whose subjects act rather than being acted on. —**ac'tive·ly,** *adv.*

ac·tiv'i·ty, *n., pl.* **-ties.** action, esp. one of a number performed in a sequence.

ac'tor, *n.* man performing in plays. Also *fem.,* **ac'tress.**

ac'tu·al, *adj.* **1.** really existing. **2.** presently existing. —**ac''tu·al'i·ty,** *n.*

ac'tu·al·ly *adv.* **1.** really. **2.** presently. **3.** in fact; nevertheless.

ac'tu·ar'y, *n., pl.* **-aries.** mathematician for an insurance company. —**ac''tu·ar' i·al,** *adj.*

ac'tu·ate', *v.t.,* **-ated, -ating.** cause to act.

a·cu'men, *n.* sharpness of mind.

a·cute', *adj.* **1.** sharp. **2.** mentally keen. **3.** highly sensitive or perceptive. **4.** severely threatening or distressing. —**a· cute'ly,** *adv.* —**a·cute'ness,** *n.*

ad'age, *n.* old saying.

a·da′gio (ə dah′jō), *adj., Music.* slow.

ad′a·mant, *adj.* unyielding.

a·dapt′, *v.t.* change to suit conditions. —**a·dapt′a·ble,** *adj.* —**a″dap·ta′tion,** *n.*

add, *v.t.* 1. joint to another or others. 2. compute as a total. —*v.i.* 3. constitute an addition. —**ad·di′tion,** *n.* —**ad·di′tion·al,** *adj.* —**ad·di′tion·al·ly,** *adv.*

ad·dict′, *v.t* (ə dikt′) 1. make dependent on a drug, etc. —*n.* (a′ dikt) 2. addicted person. —**ad·dic′tion,** *n.*

ad′dle, *v.t.,* **-dled, -dling.** confuse; muddle.

ad·dress′ (ə dres′, or, for 2, ad′res), *n.* 1. speech; oration. 2. location of a business, residence, etc. 3. skill. —*v.t.* 4. speak to formally. 5. direct as a message. 6. apply. —**ad″dres·see′,** *n.*

ad·duce′, *v.t.,* **-duced, -ducing.** offer as a reason, proof, or example.

ad′e·noid″, *n.* normal growth in the throat behind the nose.

a·dept′, *adj.* (ə dept′) 1. skilled. —*n.* (a′ dept) 2. skilled person; expert.

ad′e·quate, *adj.* suitable or sufficient. —**ad′e·quate·ly,** *adv.* —**ad′e·qua·cy,** *n.*

ad·here′, *v.i.,* **-hered, -hering.** 1. cling. 2. be loyal or obedient. —**ad·her′ent,** *adj.* —**ad·her′ence, ad·he′sion,** *n.* —**ad·he′sive,** *adj., n.*

ad″-hoc″ *adj.* for one special purpose.

a·dieu′ (ə dyoE′, a dyœ′), *interj., n., pl.* **-dieux.** *French.* goodbye.

ad′i·pose″, *adj.* fatty.

ad·ja′cent, *adj.* near or adjoining.

ad′jec·tive, *n.* word qualifying a noun. —**ad″jec·tiv′al,** *adj.*

ad·join′, *v.t.* be next to.

ad·journ′, *v.t.* 1. suspend operations of (a meeting, court, etc.). —*v.i.* 2. suspend operations. —**ad·journ′ment,** *n.*

ad·judge′, *v.t.,* **-judged, -judging.** 1. decide or declare formally. 2. award by legal process.

ad·jud′i·cate″, *v.t.,* **-cated, -cating.** pass judgment regarding. —**ad·jud″i·ca′tion,** *n.*

ad′junct, *n.* something added.

ad·jure′, *v.t.,* **-jured, -juring.** 1. command formally. 2. request solemnly.

ad·just′, *v.t.* 1. cause to fit or function properly. 2. settle. —*v.i.* 3. adapt oneself. —**ad·just′a·ble,** *adj.* —**ad·just′er, ad·just′or,** *n.* —**ad·just′ment,** *n.*

ad′ju·tant, *n.* assistant to military commander.

ad″-lib′, *v.,* **-libbed, -libbing.** *Informal.* improvise while talking.

ad·min′is·ter, *v.t.* 1. direct or manage. 2. give, esp. according to prescribed rules.

ad·min″is·tra′tion, *n.* 1. act or process of administering. 2. term of office. 3. officials directing or managing. —**ad·**min′is·tra″tive, *adj.* —**ad·min′is·tra″tor,** *n.*

ad′mi·ral, *n.* naval officer of the highest rank.

ad′mi·ral·ty, *n., pl.* **-ies.** naval administrative department.

ad·mire′, *v.t.,* **-mired, -miring.** regard with great respect or pleasure. —**ad′mir·a·ble,** *adj.* —**ad″mi·ra′tion,** *n.* —**ad·mir′er,** *n.*

ad·mis′si·ble, *adj.* 1. proper for admission. 2. allowable.

ad·mis′sion, *n.* 1. act or instance of admitting. 2. confession. 3. permission for one to enter a theater, etc.

ad·mit′, *v.t.,* **-mitted, -mitting.** 1. allow to enter. 2. confess or concede. —**ad·mit′tance,** *n.*

ad·mix′ture, *n.* something added to a mixture.

ad·mon′ish, *v.t.* 1. urge, esp. as a warning. 2. reproach. —**ad″mo·ni′tion,** *n.* —**ad·mon′i·to″ry,** *adj.*

a·do′, *n.* fussy talk or action.

a·do′be, *n.* dried, unfired brick.

ad″o·les′cence, *n.* youth between puberty and physical maturity. —**ad″o·les′cent,** *adj., n.*

a·dopt′, *v.t.* take as one's own. —**a·dop′tion,** *n.*

a·dore′, *v.t.,* **-dored, -doring.** worship. —**a″do·ra′tion,** *n.* —**a·dor′a·ble,** *adj.*

a·dorn′, *v.t.* decorate. —**a·dorn′ment,** *n.*

a·dren′a·lin, *n.* hormone promoting vigorous bodily action.

a·drift′, *adj., adv.* drifting.

a·droit′, *adj.* clever. —**a·droit′ly,** *adv.* —**a·droit′ness,** *n.*

ad″u·la′tion, *n.* excessive praise or respect.

a·dult′, *n.* 1. physically mature person or animal. —*adj.* 2. physically mature. —**a·dult′hood,** *n.*

a·dul′ter·ate″, *v.t.,* **-ated, -ating.** add undesirable ingredients to. —**a·dul′ter·a′tion,** *n.*

a·dul′ter·er, *n.* committer of adultery. Also, *fem.,* **a·dul′ter·ess.**

a·dul′ter·y, *n., pl.* **-ies.** *n.* infidelity of a spouse. —**a·dul′ter·ous,** *adj.*

ad·vance′, *v.,* **-vanced, -vancing,** *n., adj. v.t.* 1. move forward. 2. suggest for consideration. 3. pay before earned. —*v.i.* 4. move forward. —*n.* 5. motion forward. 6. act intended to secure favor or friendship. 7. improvement. 8. sum to be repaid in money or work. 9. promotion. —*adj.* 10. early. —**ad·vance′ment,** *n.*

ad·van′tage, *n.* 1. more favorable situation. 2. benefit. —**ad″van·ta′geous,** *adj.*

ad′vent, 1. arrival. 2. **Advent, a.** coming of Christ. **b.** period before Christmas.

ad″ven·ti′tious, *adj.* coming or happening by accident.

ad·ven′ture, *n., v.,* **-tured, -turing.** *n.* 1.

risky undertaking. 2. thrilling or exciting experience. —*v.t.* undertake with risk. —*v.i.* 4. seek adventures. —**ad·ven'tur·er,** *n.* —**ad·ven'tur·ous,** *adj.*

ad'verb, *n. Grammar.* word modifying a verb. —**ad·ver'bi·al,** *adj.*

ad'ver·sar''y, *n., pl.* **-saries.** opponent or enemy.

ad·verse', *adj.* opposing or unfavorable. —**ad·verse'ly,** *adv.*

ad·ver'si·ty, *n., pl.* **-ties.** difficulty or misfortune.

ad·vert', *v.i.* refer.

ad'ver·tise, *v.,* **-tised, -tising.** *v.t.* 1. call attention to in order to elicit a public response. —*v.i.* 2. request something publicly. —**ad'ver·tis''er,** *n.* —**ad''ver·tise'ment,** *n.* —**ad'ver·tis''ing,** *n.*

ad·vice', *n.* 1. opinion urging choice or rejection of a course of action. 2. piece of information.

ad·vis'a·ble, *adj.* to be advised; desirable. —**ad·vis''a·bil'i·ty,** *n.*

ad·vise', *v.t.,* **-vised, -vising.** 1. urge to choose or reject a course of action. 2. recommend. 3. give information. —**ad·vis'er, ad·vis'or,** *n.* —**ad·vi'so·ry,** *adj.*

ad·vise'ment, *n.* thought; consideration.

ad·vo·cate, *n.* (ad'və kət) 1. person arguing one side of a dispute, esp. a lawyer. —*v.t.* (ad'vo kāt'') 2. to argue in favor of. —**ad''vo·ca·cy,** *n.*

adz, *n.* long-handled tool for dressing wood. Also **adze.**

ae·gis, (ē'jis), *n.* sponsorship.

ae'on (ē'on), *n.* extremely long time.

aer'ate, *v.t.,* **-ated, -ating.** expose to air.

aer'i·al, *adj.* 1. in or of the air. 2. pertaining to aviation. —*n.* 3. antenna for sending or receiving radio waves.

ae·ro''bics, *n.* exercises to strengthen circulation and respiration.

aer''o·dy·nam'ics, *n.* study of the dynamics of gases in motion. —**aer''o·dy·nam'ic,** *adj.*

aer''o·nau'tics, *n.* science of flying. —**aer''o·nau'ti·cal,** *adj.*

aer''o·sol, *n.* liquid applied by spraying from a pressurized container.

aer'o·space'', *n.* all space, including the earth's atmosphere.

aes·thete (es'thēt''), *n.* person sensitive to art or beauty.

aes·thet'ic (es thet'ik), *adj.* 1. pertaining to beauty. 2. sensitive to art or beauty. —*n.* 3. aesthetics, study of art or beauty.

a·far', *adv.* at a great distance.

af·fa'ble, *adj.* cordial; pleasant. —**af''fa·bil'i·ty,** *n.*

af·fair', *n.* 1. business matter. 2. event. 3. amorous relationship.

af·fect', *v.t.* 1. have influence on. 2. move emotionally. 3. make an affectation of.

af''fec·ta'tion, *n.* pretentious mannerism.

af·fect'ed, *adj.* 1. characterized by affectation. 2. moved emotionally.

af·fect'ing, *adj.* emotionally moving.

af·fec'tion, *adj.* 1. love. 2. sickness.

af·fec'tion·ate, *adj.* loving.

af''fi·da'vit, *n.* sworn written statement.

af·fil·i·ate, *v.t.,* **-ated, -ating,** *n. v.t.* (əf fil'ē āt'') 1. combine, as independent businesses for mutual benefit. —*n.* (əf fil'ē ət) 2. affiliated business, etc. —**af·fil'i·a'tion,** *n.*

af·fin'i·ty, *n., pl.* **-ties.** 1. attraction. 2. similarity.

af·firm', *v.t.* 1. state emphatically. 2. confirm; ratify. —**af''fir·ma'tion,** *n.* —**af·fir'ma·tive,** *adj.*

af·fix', *v.t.* attach.

af·flict', *v.t.* trouble. —**af·flic'tion,** *n.*

af'flu·ent, *adj.* prosperous. —**af'flu·ence,** *n.*

af·ford', *v.t.* 1. have enough money or other resources. 2. supply; provide.

af·fray', *n.* fight.

af·front', *v.t.* 1. insult or challenge openly. —*n.* 2. open insult or challenge.

a·fire', *adv., adj.* on fire. Also **a·flame'.**

a·float', *adv., adj.* floating.

a·foot', *adv., adj.* 1. on foot. 2. in action or in progress.

a·fore'said, *adj.* previously said.

a·fraid', *adj.* 1. full of fear. 2. unable because of fear. 3. regretful, as because of inability.

a·fresh', *adv.* from the beginning again.

aft, *adv., adj. Nautical.* toward or at the stern.

af'ter, *prep.* 1. behind. 2. later than. 3. lower in rank or importance. 4. in search or pursuit of. 5. in imitation of. —*adv.* 6. behind. 7. later.

af'ter·ef·fect'', *n.* later consequence.

af'ter·math'', *n.* consequence, usually unfavorable.

af''ter·noon', *n.* period after noon and before evening.

af'ter·thought'', *n.* belated thought.

af'ter·ward, *adv.* later. Also, **af'ter·wards.**

a·gain', *adv.* 1. once more. 2. besides.

a·gainst', *prep.* 1. toward or into contact with. 2. opposed or hostile to.

age, *n., v.,* **aged, aging.** *n.* 1. remoteness in time of birth or origin. 2. distinctive period of history, geology, etc. 3. **of age,** legally mature. —*v.t.* 4. bring or allow to come to ripeness or maturity. —*v.i.* 5. become old.

a'ged, *adj.* 1. of a specified age. 2. **the aged,** old people.

age''is·m, *n.* discrimination against the elderly.

age'less, *adj.* unaffected by time or age.

a′gen·cy, *n., pl.* **-cies. 1.** office handling business for others. **2.** government office. **3.** active force. **4.** means.

a·gen′da (ə jen′də), *n., pl.* business matters to be dealt with.

a′gent, *n.* **1.** person handling business for others. **2.** government official. **3.** active force or substance.

ag·glom·er·ate, *v.,* **-ated, -ating.,** *n., adj. v.t., v.i.* (a glom′ər āt) **1.** gather into a mass. —*n.* (a glom′ər ət) **2.** mass of miscellaneous things. —*adj.* **3.** gathered into a mass. —**ag·glom″er·a′tion,** *n.*

ag·gran′dize, *v.t.,* **-dized, -dizing.** increase in power, status, wealth, etc. —**ag·gran′dize·ment,** *n.*

ag′gra·vate″, *v.t.,* **-vated, -vating. 1.** make worse. **2.** annoy. —**ag″gra·va′tion,** *n.*

ag·gre·gate, *v.,* **-gated, -gating,** *adj., n. v.t., v.i.* (ag′gre gāt″) **1.** collect or gather. —*adj.* (ag′gre gət) **2.** total; collective. —*n.* **3.** sum; total. —**ag″gre·ga′tion,** *n.*

ag·gres′sion, *n.* hostile act or policy. —**ag·gres′sor,** *n.*

ag·gres′sive, *adj.* **1.** disposed to commit aggressions. **2.** forceful, as in business.

ag·grieve′, *v.t.,* **-grieved, -grieving.** wrong or offend seriously.

a·ghast′, *adj.* horrified.

a′gile, *adj.* nimble; deft. —**a·gil′i·ty,** *n.*

a′gi·tate″, *v.t.,* **-tated, -tating. 1.** shake violently. **2.** disturb emotionally. —**a″gi·ta′tion,** *n.*

a·glow′, *adj., adv.* glowing.

ag·nos′tic, *n.* person regarding the existence of God as unknowable.

a·go′, *adj., adv.* in the past.

a·gog′, *adj.* eager and excited.

ag′o·nize, *v.t.,* **-nized, -nizing.** put in agony.

ag′o·ny, *n., pl.* **-ies.** intense suffering.

a·grar′i·an, *adj.* pertaining to farming or the country.

a·gree′, *v.* **agreed, agreeing.** *v.i.* **1.** consent or promise. **2.** be of the same opinion. **3.** be harmonious or in accord. **4.** match exactly. —*v.t.* **5.** concede as true. —**a·gree′ment,** *n.*

a·gree′a·ble, *adj.* **1.** pleasant. **2.** reacting favorably. —**a·gree′a·bly,** *adv.*

ag′ri·cul″ture, *n.* science or occupation of farming. —**ag″ri·cul′tur·al,** *adj.*

a·ground′, *adj., adv.* (of a ship) in water too shallow for floating.

a·head′, *adv., adj.* **1.** in front. **2.** with an advantage over competitors.

aid, *n., v.* help.

aide-de-camp, *n., pl.* **aides-de-camp.** assistant military officer.

AIDS, acquired immune deficiency syndrome.

ail, *v.t.* distress or sicken. —**ail′ment,** *n.*

ail′er·on, *n.* an airplane wing that controls rolling.

aim, *v.t.* **1.** point, as for shooting. **2.** intend. —*v.i.* **3.** point a gun, etc. —*n.* **4.** act of pointing a gun, etc. **5.** intention or goal.

aim′less, *adj.* without a goal or purpose.

ain′t, *v.i., Dialect.* am, is, or are not.

air, *n.* **1.** gas compound surrounding the earth. **2.** appearance as derived from action, facial expression, etc. **3.** song or melody. **4. airs,** affectations. —*v.t.* **5.** ventilate.

air′borne″, *adj.* flying.

air conditioning, treatment of air to control purity, temperature, and humidity. —**air conditioner,** *n.* —**air′con·di″tion,** *v.t.*

air′craft, *n., pl.* **-craft.** flying craft.

air′field″, *n.* field for taxiing, takeoff, and landing of airplanes.

air force, flying fighting force.

air′line, *n.* company operating regularly scheduled aircraft flights. —**air′lin″er,** *n.*

air′plane, *n.* heavier-than-air flying craft with wings.

air′port″, *n.* airfield with terminal, storage, and service buildings.

air′ship″, *n.* lighter-than-air flying craft.

air′tight″, *adj.* **1.** preventing passage of air. **2.** unable to be disproven, as an argument.

air′y, *adj.,* **airer, airiest. 1.** open to air or breeze. **2.** loftily situated. **3.** impermanent as air. **4.** flippant; thoughtless. —**air′i·ly,** *adv.* —**air′i·ness,** *n.*

aisle (īl), *n.* **1.** passageway, esp. among seats as in a theater. **2.** a division of a church, esp. between pillars.

a·jar′, *adj., adv.* partly open, as a door.

a·kim′bo, *adj., adv.* with hands on hips and elbows out.

a·kin′, *adj.* **1.** of the same family. **2.** of the same sort.

à la carte, with each dish ordered and paid for separately.

a·lac′ri·ty, *n.* willing readiness.

à la mode, **1.** in fashion. **2.** with ice cream.

a·larm′, *n.* **1.** emergency signal. **2.** occasion for fear. **3.** fear. —*v.t.* **4.** startle or frighten.

a·las′, *interj.* (exclamation of regret).

al·be′it, *conj.* even though.

al·bi′no, *n., pl.* **-nos.** person or animal without skin pigmentation.

al′bum, *n.* **1.** blank book for mounting photographs, stamps, etc. **2.** blank book for sketching. **3.** booklike container for phonograph records.

al·bu′men, *n.* egg white or similar substance.

al′che·my, *n.* pre-scientific chemistry. —**al′che·mist,** *n.*

al′co·hol″, *n.* colorless liquid used as fuel, intoxicant, etc.

al″co·hol′ic, *adj.* 1. pertaining to alcohol. —*n.* 2. person addicted to alcohol.

al′cove, *n.* place set back from a larger adjoining space.

al′der, *n.* small tree of the birch family.

al′der·man, *n.* city ward representative.

ale, *n.* strong beerlike drink.

a·lert′, *adj.* 1. watchful. —*v.t., n.* 2. alarm. —**a·lert′ly,** *adv.* —**a·lert′ness,** *n.*

al″fal′fa, *n.* fodder plant.

al·gae (al′jē), *n. pl.; sing.* **al′ga.** one-celled water plants.

al′ge·bra, *n.* mathematical system based on symbols, not numbers. —**al″ge·bra′ic,** *adj.*

al′i·as, *adv.* 1. otherwise known as. —*n.* 2. assumed name.

al′i·bi, *n., pl.* -bis. legal plea of absence from the scene of a crime.

al′i·en, *adj.* 1. from outside; foreign. —*n.* 2. foreigner.

al′i·en·ate″, *v.t.,* -ated, -ating. 1. deprive someone of. 2. act so as to lose the friendship of. —**al″i·en·a′tion,** *n.*

al′i·en·ist, *n.* specialist in mental illness.

a·light′, *v.i.* 1. descend, as from a vehicle or animal. —*adv., adj.* 2. lighted. 3. afire.

a·lign (ə līn′), *v.t.* line up. —**a·lign′ment,** *n.*

a·like′, *adj.* 1. of the same kind or form. —*adv.* 2. in the same way.

al″i·men′ta·ry, *adj.* pertaining to food or nourishment.

al′i·mo″ny, *n.* allowance paid to a divorced wife by her former husband.

a·live′, *adj.* 1. living. 2. vigorous or lively. 3. teeming.

al′ka·li″, *n., pl.* -lis. acid-neutralizing chemical. —**al′ka·line″,** *adj.*

al′ka·loid″, *n.* bitter, alkali-containing chemical.

all, *adj.* 1. every. 2. the whole of. —*n., pron.* 3. everything or everybody. —*adv.* 4. entirely.

Al′lah, *n.* Muslim name for God.

al·lay′, *v.t.* calm or soothe.

al·lege′, *v.t.,* -leged, -leging. assert, esp. without proof. —**al″le·ga′tion,** *n.* —**al·leg′ed·ly,** *adv.*

al·le′giance, *n.* loyalty.

al′le·go″ry, *n., pl.* -ies. story or display using symbols. —**al″le·gor′i·cal,** *adj.*

al′ler·gy, *n., pl.* -gies. excessive sensitivity to some substance. —**al·ler′gic,** *adj.*

al·le′vi·ate, *v.t.,* -ated, -ating. relieve; mitigate. —**al·le′vi·a″tion,** *n.*

al′ley, *n., pl.* -leys. 1. narrow service street. 2. garden walk.

al·li′ance, *n.* 1. combination of independent nations, etc. 2. treaty for such a combination. 3. organization or club. 4. marriage.

al·lied′, *adj.* 1. joined in an alliance. 2. closely related.

al″li·ga′tor, *n.* broad-snouted reptile of the southeastern U.S.

al·lit″er·a′tion, *n.* use of the same sound to start several succeeding words.

al″lo·cate″, *v.t.,* -cated, -cating. assign or allot. —**al″lo·ca′tion,** *n.*

al·lot′, *v.t.,* -lotted, -lotting. 1. distribute to sharing parties. 2. assign. —**al·lot′ment,** *n.*

all′-out′, *adj.* without reservation; total.

al·low′, *v.t.* 1. permit. 2. give or grant. 3. grant to be true. —**al·low′a·ble,** *adj.* —**al·low′ance,** *n.*

al·loy, *v.t.* (ə loi′) 1. mix. 2. weaken; dilute. —*n.* (al′loi) 3. metal or metals with admixtures.

all′spice″, *n.* spice made from a West Indian berry.

al·lude′, *v.i.,* -luded, -luding. make reference to. —**al·lu′sion,** *n.* —**al·lu′sive,** *adj.*

al·lure′, *v.t.,* -lured, -luring, *n. v.t.* 1. attract temptingly. —*n.* 2. quality of attraction or temptation. —**al·lure′ment,** *n.*

al·lu′vi·um, *n.* soil deposited by moving water. —**al·lu′vi·al,** *adj.*

al·ly′, *v.,* -lied, -lying, *n., pl.* -lies. *v.t., v.i.* 1. unite for a common purpose. —*n.* 2. person, country, etc. joined in an alliance.

alma mater, one's college or secondary school.

al′ma·nac″, *n.* annual publication including a calendar and diverse useful information.

al·might′y, *adj.* 1. totally powerful. —*n.* 2. the Almighty, God.

al′mond, *n.* edible nut from a tree.

al′most, *adv.* nearly.

alms (ahms), *n., pl.* alms. charitable gift or money.

a·loft′, *adv., adj.* up high.

a·lone′, *adj. adv.* 1. by oneself or itself. 2. only.

a·long′, *prep.* 1. in the lengthwise direction of. —*adv.* 2. together with another or others. 3. steadily forward or into the future.

a·long′side″, *prep.* 1. beside. —*adv.* 2. to or at the side.

a·loof″, *adv.* 1. at some distance. —*adj.* 2. showing no interest or concern. —**a·loof′ness,** *n.*

a·loud′, *adv.* 1. in the normal volume of voice. 2. loudly.

al′pha·bet″, *n.* all the letters of a language in a customary order. —**al″pha·bet′i·cal,** *adj.* —**al′pha·bet·ize″,** *v.t.*

al·read′y, *adv.* 1. before a stated time. 2. so soon.

al′so, *adv.* additionally.

al′tar, *n.* block or table used for religious ceremonies.

al′ter, *v.t., v.i.* change. —**al″ter·a′tion,** *n.*

al″ter·ca′tion, *n.* quarrel; dispute.

al·ter·nate, *v., -nated, -nating, adj., n.*
v.i. (ahl′tər nāt″) **1.** act, appear, etc. in
turns. —*v.t.* **2.** employ in turns. —*adj.*
(ahl′tər nət) **3.** acting, appearing, etc.
in turns. —*n.* **4.** someone or something
that acts, appears, etc. in turns. —**al″
ter·na′tion,** *n.*

al·ter′na·tive″, *n.* **1.** other choice.
—*adj.* **2.** available as another choice.

al·though′, *conj.* even though.

al·tim′e·ter, *n.* gauge for measuring altitude.

al′ti·tude, *n.* height, esp. when considerable.

al′to, *n., pl.* -tos. **1.** musical range between soprano and tenor. **2.** singer, instrument or part with this range.

al″to·geth′er, *adv.* **1.** completely. **2.** in
general.

al′tru·ism, *n.* concern for others, not
oneself. —**al″tru·is′tic,** *adj.* —**al′tru·
ist,** *n.*

al′um, *n.* astringent used in medicine.

a·lu′mi·num, *n.* lightweight metal.

a·lum′nus, *n., pl.* -ni. school graduate.
Also, *fem.,* **a·lum′na,** *pl.* -nae.

al′ways, *adv.* **1.** all of one's life. **2.** forever. **3.** continually.

am, *v.,* first person present singular indicative of *be.*

a·mal′gam, *n.* a mixture.

a·mal′gam·ate″, *v., -ated, -ating. v.t.,
v.i.* form a combination or mixture.
—**a·mal″ga·ma′tion,** *n.*

a·mass′, *v.t.* gather.

am·a·teur, *n.* **1.** non-professional participant. **2.** lover of an art. —*adj.* **3.** by or
for non-professional participants.

am′a·teur″ish, *adj.* without professional
competence.

am′a·to″ry, *adj.* pertaining to love or
sex.

a·maze′, *v.t., -mazed, -mazing.* stun with
surprise. —**a·maz′ing,** *adj.* —**a·maze′
ment,** *n.*

am·bas′sa·dor, *n.* senior diplomat.
—**am·bas″sa·do′ri·al,** *adj.* —**am·bas′
sa·dor·ship″,** *n.*

am′ber, *n.* **1.** fossil resin. —*adj.* **2.**
yellow-brown.

am′ber·gris″, *n.* whale secretion used for
perfume.

am″bi·dex′trous, *adj.* equally able with
both hands. —**am″bi·dex·ter′i·ty,** *n.*

am′bi·ence, *n.* quality or mood of an environment. Also **am′bi·ance.** —**am′
bi·ent,** *adj.*

am·big′u·ous, *adj.* having more than
one possible meaning. —**am″bi·gu′i·
ty,** *n.*

am·bi′tion, *n.* **1.** strong desire for success. **2.** thing whose attainment is
strongly desired. —**am·bi′tious,** *adj.*

am′ble, *v.i., -bled, -bling, n. v.i.* **1.** move
easily and slowly. —*n.* **2.** easy, slow
walk.

am·bro′sia, *n.* divine food.

am′bu·lance, *n.* vehicle for the sick.

am′bu·la·to″ry, *adj.* able to walk.

am′bush, *n.* **1.** concealment for attackers.
2. attack from a concealed position.
—*v.t.* **3.** attack from a concealed position.

a·mel′io·rate″, *v.t., -rated, -rating.* improve. —**a·mel″io·ra′tion,** *n.*

a·men′, *interj.* so be it.

a·men′a·ble, *adj.* agreeable.

a·mend′, *v.t.* **1.** alter. **2.** improve. —*n.* **3.**
amends, compensation for damage, in-
jury, etc. —**a·mend′ment,** *n.*

a·men′i·ty, *n., pl.* -ties. something agreeable or polite.

A·mer′i·ca′na, *n., pl.* literature, artifacts, etc. having to do with U.S. history or culture.

A·mer′i·can·ism, *n.* **1.** partiality to
things identified with the U.S. **2.** something characteristic of the U.S.

am′e·thyst, *n.* **1.** violet quartz or corun-
dum. **2.** shade of violet.

a′mi·a·ble, *adj.* creating friendly feelings. —**a′mi·a·bly,** *adj.* —**a″mi·a·bil′
i·ty,** *n.*

a′mi·ca·ble, *adj.* without hostility or resentment. —**a′mi·ca·bly,** *adv.*

a·mid′, *prep.* among. Also, **a·midst′.**

a·miss′, *adj.* **1.** not right. —*adv.* **2.** not in
the right way.

am′i·ty, *n.* friendship.

am·mo′nia, *n.* pungent, water-soluble
gas.

am″mu·ni′tion, *n.* projectiles, together
with their charges of gunpowder, etc.
fired esp. from guns.

am·ne′sia, *n.* loss of memory.

am′nes·ty, *n., pl.* -ties. general pardon
by a government, esp. for political
crimes.

a·mok′, *adv.* amuck.

a·mong′, *prep.* **1.** surrounded closely by.
2. in the company or society of. Also,
a·mongst′.

a·mor′al, *adj.* without a sense of right or
wrong.

am′or·ous, *adj.* expressing love, esp. sexual love.

a·mor′phous, *adj.* shapeless or formless.

a′mor·tize″, *v.t., -tized, -tizing.* pay off
gradually. —**am″or·ti·za′tion,** *n.*

a·mount′, *n.* **1.** total. **2.** quantity. —*v.i.*
3. add up.

a·mour′, *n.* love affair.

am′pere, *n.* unit for measuring electric
current. —**am′per·age,** *n.*

am·phib′i·an, *n.* **1.** animal able to live
on land and water. —*adj.* **2.** Also,
am·phib′i·ous. able to live on land and
water.

am′phi·the″a·ter, *n.* arena or stadium
with tiers of seats surrounding the central area. Also, **am′phi·the″a·tre.**

am′ple, *adj.*, ampler, amplest. 1. copious. 2. sufficient. —am′ply, *adv.*

am′pli·fy″, *v.t.*, -fied, -fying. 1. increase in size. 2. increase in strength, as an electronic signal. —am′pli·fi″er, *n.* —am″pli·fi·ca′tion, *n.*

am′pli·tude″, *n.* 1. breadth or extent. 2. abundance.

am′pu·tate″, *v.t.*, -tated, -tating. remove, as a limb of a body. —am″pu·ta′tion, *n.* —am″pu·tee′, *n.*

a·muck′, *adv.* in a condition of murderous insanity.

am′u·let, *n.* magical charm worn on the person.

a·muse′, *v.t.*, -mused, -musing. 1. be funny to. 2. entertain. —a·muse′ment, *n.*

an, *indef. art.* variant of *a*, used when the following word begins with a vowel.

a·nach′ron·ism, *n.* something outside its proper historical period. —a·nach″ron·is′tic, *adj.*

an′a·gram″, *n.* word formed from the letters spelling another word.

a′nal, *adj.* pertaining to the anus.

an″a·log, *n.* represented by physical variables.

a·nal′o·gy, *n., pl.* -gies. *n.* comparison of an unfamiliar thing to a more familiar one. —a·nal′o·gous, *adj.*

a·nal′y·sis, *n., pl.* -ses. 1. separation into component parts. 2. summary of such a separation. 3. psychoanalysis. —an′a·lyst, *n.* —an″a·lyt′ic, an″a·lyt′ic·al, *adj.* —an′a·lyze″, *v.t.*

an·ar·chy, *n.* 1. society without rulers. 2. political or organizational chaos. —an′ar·chism″, *n.* —an′ar·chist, *n.*

a·nath′e·ma, *n.* 1. solemn curse. 2. something hated and despised.

a·nat′o·my, *n.* 1. study of the composition of animals and plants. 2. composition of an animal or plant. —an″a·tom′i·cal, *adj.*

an″ces·tor, *n.* forebear; one from whom a person descends. Also, *fem.* an″ces·tress. —an″ces·try, *n.*

an″chor, *n.* 1. device for mooring a ship or boat. —*v.i.* 2. to secure by anchor.

an·cho″vy, *n., pl.* -vies. tiny, salty, herringlike fish.

an′cient, *adj.* 1. of the oldest period of human history. 2. very old. —*n.* 3. person, esp. an author or philosopher, of the ancient period. 4. very old person.

and, *conj.* 1. along with. 2. *Informal.* used in place of the infinitive *to*.

and′i′ron″, *n.* horizontal iron support for firewood, used in pairs.

an′ec·dote″, *n.* true short story.

a·ne′mi·a, *n.* shortage of hemoglobin or red cells in the blood. —a·ne′mic, *adj.*

an″es·the′sia, *n.* lack of sensation induced by a gas or drug. —an″es·thet′ic, *adj.*, *n.* —an·es′the·tize″, *v.t.*

a·new′, *adv.* once more.

an′gel, *n.* messenger or attendant of God. —an·gel′ic, *adj.*

an′ger, *n.* 1. strong annoyance. —*v.t.* 2. make angry.

an·gi′na pec′to·ris, painful heart condition.

an′gle, *n., v.i.*, -gled, gling. *n.* 1. divergence of two lines or surfaces that meet. —*v.i.* 2. fish. 3. *Informal.* use stratagems for personal gain. —an′gler, *n.*

an′gle·worm″, *n.* earthworm.

An′gli·can, *n.* 1. member of the Church of England or churches in communion with it, e.g. the Episcopal Church. —*adj.* 2. pertaining to the Church of England or churches in communion with it. —An′gli·can·ism, *n.*

An′glo-Sax′on, *n.* 1. person descended from the Angles and Saxons in England. 2. person of English ancestry. —*adj.* 3. pertaining to or characteristic of the Anglo-Saxons.

an′gry, *adj.* -grier, -griest. 1. seriously annoyed. 2. suggesting human anger by action, appearance, etc. —an′gri·ly, *adv.*

an′guish, *n.* intense suffering.

an′gu·lar, *adj.* 1. having angles. 2. conspicuous for angles. —an″gu·lar′i·ty, *n.*

an′i·line, *n.* benzene derivative used for dyes.

an″i·mad·vert′, *v.i.* comment disapprovingly. —an″i·mad·ver′sion, *n.*

an′i·mal, *n.* 1. living thing other than a plant or bacterium. 2. any such thing other than a human being. —*adj.* 3. pertaining to animals.

an·i·mate, *v.t.*, -mated, -mating, *adj.* *v.t.* (an′ə māt) 1. give life to. 2. make lively. —*adj.* (an′ə mət) 3. having life. —an″i·ma′tion, *n.*

an″i·mos′i·ty, *n., pl.* -ties. hostility. Also, an′i·mus.

an′i·seed″, *n.* aromatic seed of the anise plant.

an′kle, *n.* joint between the foot and the leg.

an′nals, *n., pl.* historical records.

an·nex, *v.t.* (ən neks′) 1. join to a larger existing part. —*n.* (an′neks) 2. a part so joined. —an″nex·a′tion, *n.*

an·ni′hil·ate″, *v.t.*, -ated, -ating. destroy utterly. —an·ni″hil·a′tion, *n.*

an″ni·ver′sar·y, *n., pl.* -ries. same day of the year as that on which something occurred.

an′no·tate″, *v.t.*, -tated, -tating. explain or elaborate with notes. —an″no·ta′tion. *n.*

an·nounce′, *v.t.*, -nounced, -nouncing. make known, esp. publicly. —an·noun′cer, *n.* —an·nounce′ment, *n.*

an·noy', *v.t.* trouble, esp. so as to provoke dislike. —**an·noy'ance**, *n.*

an'nu·al, *adj.* 1. yearly. 2. living only one year, as a plant. —*n.* 3. something published once a year. 4. annual plant. —**an'nu·al·ly**, *adv.*

an·nu'i·ty, *n.*, *pl.* **-ties.** annual income bought from an insurance company.

an·nul', *v.t.*, **-nulled, -nulling.** make legally void. —**an·nul'ment**, *n.*

An·nun''ci·a'tion, *n.* announcement to the Virgin Mary or the impending birth of Christ; celebrated March 25.

an'o·dyne, *n.* pain reliever.

a·noint', *v.t.* put oil, etc. on as part of a ceremony of consecration. —**a·noint'ment**, *n.*

a·nom'a·ly, *n.*, *pl.* **-lies.** something inconsistent or abnormal. —**a·nom'a·lous**, *adj.*

a·non', *adv.* soon.

a·non'y·mous, *adj.* written or spoken by someone whose name is unknown or unpublished. —**an''o·nym'i·ty**, *n.*

an·oth'er, *adj.* 1. one more. 2. different. —*n.* 3. one more. 4. a different one.

an'swer, *n.* 1. reply to a question. 2. solution to a problem. 3. action provoked by something competing. —*v.t.* 4. reply to. —*v.i.* 5. give an answer. 6. be matching or well-suited. 7. be accountable or responsible.

an'swer·a·ble, *adj.* 1. able to be answered. 2. accountable; responsible.

ant, *n.* small social insect.

an·tag'o·nism, *n.* hostility. —**an·tag'o·nist**, *n.* —**an·tag''o·nis'tic**, *adj.* —**an·tag'o·nize''**, *v.t.*

Ant·arc'tic, *n.* 1. southernmost zone of the earth. —*adj.* 2. pertaining to this zone.

an''te·ce'dent, *adj.* 1. coming before. —*n.* 2. something coming before.

an''te·date'', *v.t.*, **-dated, -dating.** precede in time.

an''te·di·lu'vi·an, *adj.* 1. before the Flood. 2. from remotest antiquity.

an'te·lope'', *n.* deerlike animal.

an·ten''na, *n.*, *pl.* **—nae** (for one), **—nas** (for 2). 1. feeler on the head of an insect. 2. aerial; conductor for sending or receiving radio waves.

an·te'ri·or, *adj.* 1. previous. 2. at the front end.

an'te·room'', *n.* room preceding a major room.

an'them, *n.* hymnlike song.

an·thol'o·gy, *n.* book of literary selections.

an'thra·cite'', *n.* hard coal.

an'thro·poid'', *adj.* 1. resembling humanity. —*n.* 2. anthropoid animal.

an''thro·pol'o·gy, *n.* study of mankind. —**an''thro·pol'o·gist**, *n.*

an''ti·bi·ot'ic, *n.* substance for destroying or weakening microorganisms.

an''ti·bod''y, *n.*, *pl.* **-ies.** blood ingredient that fights foreign substances, e.g. bacteria.

an'tic, *n.* ridiculous or peculiar action.

an·tic'i·pate'', *v.t.*, **-pated, -pating.** 1. look forward to, esp. with pleasure. 2. use forethought to deal with. 3. predict. —**an·tic''i·pa'tion**, *n.*

an''ti·cli'max, *n.* disappointment of increasing expectations. —**an''ti·cli·mac'tic**, *adj.*

an''ti·dote'', *n.* substance to counteract a poison.

an''ti·his'ta·mine, *n.* substance to counteract allergic reaction.

an·tip'a·thy, *n.*, *pl.* **-thies.** dislike. —**an·tip''a·thet'ic**, *adj.*

an''ti·quar'i·an, *n.* student of antiquities.

an·ti·quar'y, *n.*, *pl.* **-quaries.** *n.* collector or student of antiquities.

an''ti·quat''ed, *adj.* obsolete.

an·tique', *n.* 1. old manufactured object, esp. a valuable one. —*adj.* 2. ancient.

an·tiq'ui·ty, *n.*, *pl.* **-ties.** 1. ancient times. 2. something antique.

an''ti·sep'tic, *n.* 1. substance for destroying harmful bacteria. —*adj.* 2. destroying harmful bacteria.

an''ti·so'cial, *adj.* 1. hostile to society. 2. shunning society.

an·tith'e·sis, *n.*, *pl.* **-ses.** direct opposite. —**an''ti·thet'i·cal**, *adj.*

an''ti·tox'in, *n.* substance for counteracting plant, animal, or bacterial toxin.

ant'ler, *n.* horn of a deer, moose, etc.

an'to·nym'', *n.* word meaning the opposite.

a'nus, *n.* opening at lower end of alimentary canal.

an'vil, *n.* object on which iron, etc. is rested while being hammered.

anx·i·e·ty, *n.*, *pl.* **-ies.** 1. fear of possible harm. 2. eagerness to act. —**anx'ious**, *adj.* —**anx'ious·ly**, *adv.*

an'y, *adj.* 1. someone, as readily as all others. 2. every. —*n.* 3. any person or persons.

an'y·bod''y, *pron.* some one person, as readily as all others. Also, **an'y·one''.**

an'y·how'', *adv.* 1. in any way. 2. whatever the situation is. Also, **an'y·way''.**

an'y·thing'', *pron.* 1. some one thing, as readily as all others. —*n.* 2. something, whatever or how much it may be.

an'y·where'', *adv.* in or into any place. Also, **an'y·place''.**

a·or'ta, *n.*, *pl.* **-as, -ae.** blood vessel from the heart. —**a·or'tic**, *adj.*

a·part', *adv.* 1. to pieces. 2. separately.

a·part·heid', *n.* racial segregation, esp. in the Union of South Africa.

a·part'ment, *n.* series of rooms forming a separate dwelling in a building.

a'pa·thy, *n.* lack of feeling or emotion. —**a''pa·thet'ic**, *adj.* —**a''pa·thet'ic·al·ly**, *adv.*

ape, *n., v.t.* **aped, aping.** *n.* **1.** large animal of the monkey family. —*v.t.* **2.** imitate.

ap·er·ture, *n.* opening.

a′pex, *n.* peak.

aph′o·rism, *n.* brief statement of a truth. —**aph″o·ris′tic,** *adj.*

aph″ro·dis′i·ac, *n.* drug promoting sexual excitement.

a′pi·ar″y, *n., pl.* **-ries.** bee farm.

a·piece′, *adv.* for each.

a·plomb′, *n.* self-possession.

A·poc′a·lypse, *n.* revelation to St. John the Apostle. —**A·poc″a·lyp′tic,** *adj.*

A·poc′ry·pha, *n., pl.* Biblical books not accepted by Protestants and Jews.

a·poc′ry·phal, *adj.* highly dubious.

ap′o·gee″, *n.* furthest distance of a satellite from its planet.

a·pol″o·get′ic, *adj.* confessing oneself to be at fault.

a·pol″o·gize″, *v.i.,* **-gized, -gizing.** confess oneself to be at fault and seek forgiveness.

a·pol′o·gy, *n., pl.* **-gies. 1.** confession of a fault in search of forgiveness. **2.** statement defending one's actions, etc.

ap′o·plex″y, *n.* bursting of blood vessel with consequent loss of bodily function. —**ap″o·plec′tic,** *adj.*

a·pos′tate″, *n.* renouncer of one's professed faith, etc. —**a·pos′ta·sy,** *n.*

a·pos′tle, *n.* **1.** one of the twelve disciples of Christ sent to preach. **2.** preacher of a new faith. —**a″pos·tol′ic,** *adj.*

a·pos′tro·phe, *n.* **1.** a sign, ′, used to indicate possessives, omitted letters, plurals involving numerals or initials, etc. **2.** remark made to or as if to some individual in the course of a speech, etc.

a·pos′tro·phize″, *v.t.* **1.** spell with an apostrophe. **2.** address in an apostrophe.

a·poth′e·car″y, *n., pl.* **-ies.** druggist.

ap·pall′, *v.t.* put in a state of horror or fear. Also **ap·pal′.** —**ap·pall′ing,** *adj.*

ap″pa·ra′tus, *n.* **1.** instruments, etc. required for an experiment, job, etc. **2.** organizational structure.

ap·par′el, *n.* **1.** clothes. —*v.t.* **2.** clothe.

ap·par′ent, *adj.* **1.** clear; obvious. **2.** as judged from appearances. —**ap·par′ent·ly,** *adv.*

ap″pa·ri′tion, *n.* ghost or phantom.

ap·peal′, *n.* **1.** request for help, mercy, etc. **2.** request for reconsideration. **3.** attractiveness. —*v.t.* **4.** request to have reconsidered. —*v.i.* **5.** make an appeal. **6.** have appeal.

ap·pear′, *v.i.* **1.** come into sight. **2.** seem. —**ap·pear′ance,** *n.*

ap·pease′, *v.t.,* **-peased, -peasing.** satisfy when hostile or demanding. —**ap·pease′ment,** *n.*

ap·pel′lant, *n.* person who appeals, esp. in law.

ap·pel′late, *adj.* handling appeals, as a court.

ap″pel·la′tion, *n.* name given to something or someone.

ap·pend′, *v.t.* add; join. —**ap·pend′age,** *n.*

ap″pen·dec′to·my, *n., pl.* **-ies.** surgical removal of an appendix.

ap·pen″di·ci′tis, *n.* inflammation of the appendix.

ap·pen′dix, *n., pl.* **-dixes, -dices. 1.** supplementary portion at the end of a book, etc. **2.** blind branch of the intestine.

ap′per·tain′, *v.i.* belong.

ap′pe·tite′, *n.* desire, as for food. —**ap′pe·tiz″er,** *n.* —**ap′pe·tiz″ing,** *adj.*

ap·plaud′, *v.t.* show approval of, as by applause.

ap·plause′, *n.* **1.** indications of approval of a dramatic performance, etc. **2.** public recognition and approval.

ap″ple, *n.* common, crisp fruit, generally red or green.

ap·pli′ance, *n.* machine, etc., esp. for home use.

ap′pli·ca·ble, *adj.* able to be applied.

ap·ply′, *v.,* **-plied, -plying.** *v.t.* **1.** place, as on an object or surface. **2.** put to use, as a theory or rule. **3.** devote to a task. —*v.i.* **4.** make a formal request. **5.** be relevant. —**ap″pli·ca′tion,** *n.* —**ap′pli·cant,** *n.*

ap·point′, *v.t.* **1.** choose and designate. **2.** provide; furnish. —**ap·poin′tive,** *adj.* —**ap·point″ee′,** *n.*

ap·point′ment, *n.* **1.** meeting at a stated time. **2.** selection, as for public office. **3.** provision or furnishing.

ap·por′tion, *v.t.* divide into shares. —**ap·por′tion·ment,** *n.*

ap′po·site, *adj.* appropriate.

ap·praise′, *v.t.,* **-praised, -praising.** estimate the value of. —**ap·prais′er,** *n.* —**ap·prais′al,** *n.*

ap·pre·ci·a·ble, *adj.* **1.** sufficient to be noted. **2.** worthy of note; considerable.

ap·pre′ci·ate″, *v.,* **-ated, -ating.** *v.t.* **1.** be grateful for. **2.** value truly. —*v.i.* **3.** gain in value. —**ap·pre″ci·a′tion,** *n.* —**ap·pre′ci·a·tive,** *adj.*

ap′pre·hend″, *v.t.* **1.** fear. **2.** understand. **3.** capture and arrest. —**ap″pre·hen′sion,** *n.*

ap″pre·hen′sive, *adj.* fearful.

ap·pren′tice, *n., v.t.* **-ticed, -ticing.** *n.* **1.** assistant learning a trade. —*v.t.* **2.** enroll as an apprentice. —**ap·pren′tice·ship″,** *n.*

ap·prise′, *v.t.,* **-prised, -prising.** inform; notify. Also, **ap·prize′.**

ap·proach′, *v.t.* **1.** come close to. **2.** propose business to. —*v.i.* **3.** come close. —*n.* **4.** act or instance of coming close. **5.** way of coming close. **6.** manner of taking action.

ap·proach′a·ble, *adj.* willing to be talked with.

ap″pro·ba′tion, *n.* approval.

ap·pro·pri·ate, *adj., v.t.* **-ated, -ating.** *adj.* (əp pro′pri ət) 1. useful or proper. —*v.t.* (ap pro′pri āt″) 2. reserve for a purpose, as money. 3. take for oneself. —**ap·pro′pri·a′tion,** *n.*

ap·prove, *v.,* **-proved, -proving.** *v.t.* 1. state to be good or suitable. 2. think favorably of. —*v.i.* 3. regard favorably. —**ap·prov′al,** *n.*

ap·prox·i·mate, *adj., v.t.* **-ated, -ating.** *adj.* (ap prox′i mət) 1. reasonably accurate but not precise. —*v.t.* (ap prox′i māt″) 2. amount to as an approximate figure, etc. —**ap·prox′i·mate·ly,** *adv.* —**ap·prox″i·ma′tion,** *n.*

ap·pur′te·nance, *n.* additional device or feature; accessory.

a′pri·cot″, *n.* orange-colored peachlike fruit.

A′pril, *n.* fourth month.

a′pron, *n.* covering worn over a dress or trouser front when working.

ap·ro·pos (ap″rə pō), *adv.* 1. apropos of, with regard to. 2. at the right time. —*adj.* 3. to the point; relevant.

apt, *adj.* 1. displaying a tendency. 2. likely. 3. able; intelligent. —**apt′ly,** *adv.* —**apt′ness,** *n.*

ap′ti·tude″, *n.* talent or ability.

aq″ua·ma·rine′, *n.* pale bluish-green.

a·quar′i·um, *n.* tank, bowl, etc., usually with glass walls, used for displaying live fish, etc.

a·quat′ic, *adj.* of the water.

aq′ue·duct, *n.* engineering structure for conducting water.

a′que·ous, *adj.* like, of, or created by water.

aq′ui·line″, *adj.* pertaining to or suggesting eagles.

ar′a·ble, *adj.* good for producing crops.

ar′bit·er, *n.* judge of controversial matters.

ar′bi·trar″y, *adj.* 1. unreasonable or unjustified. 2. admitting no discussion or complaint. 3. chosen at random as a basis for discussion. —**ar″bi·trar′i·ly,** *adv.*

ar′bi·trate″, *v.t.* **-trated, -trating.** 1. adjudicate after hearing disputants. 2. submit for adjudication. —**ar″bi·tra′tion,** *n.* —**ar′bi·tra″tor,** *n.*

ar′bor, *n.* shaded walk or garden.

ar·bo′re·al, *adj.* of or inhabiting trees.

ar·bu′tus, *n.* 1. shrub with dark green leaves and red berries. 2. trailing plant with white or pink blossoms.

arc, *n.* 1. segment of a circle. 2. light formed by electricity jumping between electrodes.

ar·cade′, *n.* 1. row of arches. 2. covered walk, esp. one between shops.

arch, *n.* 1. curved structure resisting compressive forces. —*v.i.* 2. bend as an arch does. —*adj.* 3. chief. 4. cheerfully mischievous. —**arch′way″,** *n.*

ar·cha′ic, *adj.* 1. out of date. 2. ancient.

arch·an·gel (ark′ān″jəl), *n.* chief angel.

arch′bi′shop, *n.* superior bishop.

arch·duke′, *n.* Austrian royal prince. Also fem., **arch′duch′ess.**

ar″che·ol′o·gy, *n.* study of acient cultures through their artifacts. —**ar″che·ol′o·gist,** *n.* —**ar″che·o·log′i·cal,** *adj.* Also **archaeologist.**

arch′er, *n.* user of a bow and arrow. —**arch′er·y,** *n.*

ar″chi·pel′a·go, *n., pl.* **-gos, -goes.** 1. group of closely spaced islands. 2. area of water surrounding and within such a group.

ar′chi·tect″, *n.* designer of buildings.

ar′chi·tec″ture, *n.* art of designing buildings. —**ar″chi·tec′tur·al,** *adj.*

ar·chives, *n., pl.* official records.

Arc′tic, *n.* 1. northernmost zone of the earth. —*adj.* 2. pertaining to this zone.

ar′dent, *adj.* eager. —**ar′dent·ly,** *adv.*

ar′dor, *n.* eagerness; zeal.

ar′du·ous, *adj.* difficult or tedious.

are, *v.* present indicative plural of *be.*

ar′e·a, *n.* 1. surface measure. 2. region.

area code, three-digit code used in telephoning outside one's own area.

a·re′na, *n.* large space for athletic contests and spectators.

ar′gon, *n.* chemical element, an inert gas.

ar′go·sy, *n., pl.* **-sies.** *Poetic.* large merchant ship or merchant fleet.

ar′gue, *v.,* **-gued, -guing.** *v.i.* 1. express a difference or differences of opinion. 2. offer reasons for or against something. —*v.t.* 3. present as true or valid. 4. express differences of opinion over. —**ar′gu·ment,** *n.* —**ar″gu·men·ta′tion,** *n.*

ar″gu·men′ta·tive, *adj.* given to argument or quarreling.

a′ri·a, *n.* song, as in an opera.

a′rid, *adj.* dry. —**a·rid′i·ty,** *n.*

a·rise′, *v.i.,* **arose, arisen, arising.** 1. get up. 2. happen.

ar″is·toc′ra·cy, *n., pl.* **-cies.** 1. government by a small hereditary or select class. 2. such a class. —**a·ris′to·crat,** *n.* —**a·ris″to·crat′ic,** *adj.*

a·rith′me·tic, *n.* calculation with numerals. —**ar″ith·met′i·cal,** *adj.*

ark, *n.* 1. vessel of Noah. 2. wooden chest.

arm, *n.* 1. upper human limb. 2. anything suggesting this by form, position, or function. 3. weapon. 4. **arms,** the military profession. —*v.t.* 5. equip with weapons.

ar·ma′da, *n.* fleet of fighting ships or airplanes.

Ar″ma·ged′don, *n.* major decisive battle.

arm″a·ment, *n.* weapons with which a ship, airplane, etc. is equipped.

arm′chair″, *n.* chair with arm supports.

arm′ful″, *n., pl.* **-fuls.** amount that can be held in one or both arms.

ar′mi·stice, *n.* suspension of hostilities; truce.

ar′mor, *n.* material, usually metal, protecting against weapons and missiles. —**ar′mored**, *adj.*

ar′mor·y, *n., pl.* **-ies.** 1. building for military activities and equipment storage. 2. place for storing weapons.

arm′pit″, *n.* area beneath the arm at the shoulder.

ar′my, *n., pl.* **-mies.** 1. land military force. 2. large number of persons.

a·ro′ma, *n.* scent; odor. —**ar″o·mat′ic**, *adj.*

a·round′, *prep.* 1. on all sides of. 2. in any or all areas of. —*adv.* 3. on all sides. 4. in any or all areas. 5. *Informal.* **a.** nearby. **b.** idly or aimlessly.

a·rouse′, *v.t.*, **aroused, arousing.** 1. awaken. 2. call into activity. —**a·rous′al**, *n.*

ar·raign′, *v.t.* 1. bring to court as a defendant. 2. accuse. —**ar·raign′ment**, *n.*

ar·range′, *v.*, **-ranged, -ranging.** *v.t.* 1. put in order. —*v.t., v.i.* 2. plan; prepare. —**ar·range′ment**, *n.*

ar′rant, *adj.* utter; downright.

ar·ray′, *v.t.* 1. arrange. 2. dress. —*n.* 3. order or arrangement. 4. clothing.

ar·rears′, *n., pl.* things overdue, esp. payments.

ar·rest′, *v.t.* 1. seize because of the commission of a crime. 2. stop. —*n.* 3. act or instance of arresting. 4. state of being arrested.

ar·rive′, *v.i.* 1. come to a place. 2. happen. —**ar·riv′al**, *n.*

ar′ro·gant, *adj.* proud and insolent. —**ar′ro·gant·ly**, *adv.* —**ar′ro·gance**, *n.*

ar′ro·gate″, *v.t.*, **-gated, -gating.** claim or seize unjustly. —**ar″ro·ga′tion**, *n.*

ar′row, *n.* missile shot from a bow.

ar·roy′o, *n., pl.* **-os.** *Southwest U.S.* gully.

ar′se·nal, *n.* place for making or storing weapons.

ar′se·nic, *n.* silvery-white poisonous chemical element.

ar′son, *n.* crime of burning buildings, etc. —**ar′son·ist**, *n.*

art, *n.* 1. activity of creating things that arouse the emotions through one or more senses. 2. things so created. 3. skill or profession. 4. cunning.

ar′ter·y, *n., pl.* **-ies.** 1. major blood vessel. 2. main line of travel or communication. —**ar·te′ri·al**, *adj.*

artesian well, well whose opening is lower than the head of water supplying it.

art′ful, *adj.* cunning.

ar·thri′tis, *n.* inflammation of a joint of the body. —**ar·thrit′ic**, *adj.*

ar′ti·choke, *n.* edible flower head of thistlelike plant.

ar′ti·cle, *n.* 1. object for use. 2. writing on a factual subject. 3. *Grammar.* **a, an,** or **the.**

ar·tic·u·late, *adj., v.*, **-lated, -lating.** *adj.* (ahr tik′yo͞o lat) 1. readily understood. 2. able in speech. 3. jointed. —*v.t.* (ahr tik′yo͞o lāt″) 4. express clearly. 5. arrange in a clear and orderly manner. 6. assemble with joints. —*v.i.* 7. speak clearly. —**ar·tic″u·la′tion**, *n.*

ar′ti·fice, *n.* 1. cunning. 2. cunning action.

ar·tif′i·cer, *n.* craftsman.

ar″ti·fi′cial, *adj.* 1. manufactured, esp. in imitation. 2. contrived or affected. —**ar″ti·fi′cial·ly**, *adv.* —**ar″ti·fi·ci·al′i·ty**, *n.*

ar·til′ler·y, *n.* 1. guns or other devices for shooting large missiles. 2. army branch handling such devices.

ar′ti·san, *n.* craftsman.

art′ist, *n.* practitioner of an art. —**ar·tist′ic**, *adj.* —**ar′tist·ry**, *n.*

art′less, *adj.* unaffected; natural.

art″y, *adj.*, **-ier, -iest.** feigning artistic sensitivity.

as, *adv.* 1. equally. 2. for example. 3. if and when. —*conj.* 4. equally to. 5. in the manner that. 6. while. 7. because; since. 8. though. —*pron.* 9. that. —*prep.* 10. in the guise of.

as·bes′tos, *n.* fibrous mineral used in fireproofing.

as·cen′an·cy, *n.* domination. Also, **as·cen′den·cy.**

as·cend′, *v.t., v.i.* climb or rise. —**as·cent′**, *n.* —**as·cen′dent**, *adj.*

As·cen′sion, *n.* ascent of Christ into heaven, celebrated 40 days after Easter.

as′cer·tain, *v.t.* find out.

as·cet′ic, *adj.* 1. without pleasure or self-indulgence. —*n.* 2. one who lives an ascetic life. —**as·cet′i·cism**, *n.*

as·cribe′, *v.t.*, **-scribed, -scribing.** relate to a supposed cause. —**as·crip′tion**, *n.*

a·sep′sis, *n.* absence of disease producing germs. —**a·sep′tic**, *adj.*

ash, *n., pl.* **ashes.** 1. remainder of something not fully burnt. 2. tree of the olive family. —**ash′tray″**, *n.*

a·shamed′, *adj.* feeling shame.

a·shore′, *adj., adv.* on or onto the shore.

a·side′, *adv.* 1. at or to the side. 2. apart. 3. in reserve.

as′i·nine″, *adj.* silly. —**as″i·nin′ity**, *n.*

ask, *v.t.* 1. seek to know. 2. seek information of. 3. seek, as a favor. 4. invite. —*v.i.* 5. seek a favor, information, etc.

a·skance', *adv.* with suspicion or disapproval.

a·skew', *adv., adj.* slanted or twisted out of position.

a·sleep', *adj., adv.* in or into a state of sleep.

as·par'a·gus, *n.* plant with edible shoots.

a"spar·tame, *n.* a synthetic sweetener.

as'pect, *n.* 1. way of interpreting or understanding something. 2. appearance or manner. 3. face or side toward a certain direction.

as'pen, *n.* type of poplar tree.

as·per'i·ty, *n., pl.* -ties. roughness of manner or speech.

as·per'sion, *n.* hostile or accusing remark.

as'phalt, *n.* black tarlike material.

as·phyx'i·ate", *v.t.,* -ated, -ating. harm through deprivation of oxygen. —**as·phyx"i·a'tion**, *n.*

as·pire', *v.i.,* -pired, -piring. have ambitious intentions. —**as"pi·ra'tion**, *n.* —**as·pir'ant**, *n.*

as'pi·rin, *n.* white crystalline drug used to relieve minor pain and fever.

ass, *n.* 1. donkey. 2. silly person.

as·sail', *v.t.* attack. —**as·sail'ant**, *n.*

as·sas'sin, *n.* murderer, esp. of a statesman. —**as·sas'sin·ate"**, *v.t.* —**as·sas"sin·a'tion**, *n.*

as·sault', *n., v.t.* attack.

as·say', *n.* 1. chemical evaluation, as of an ore. —*v.t.* 2. perform an assay upon.

as·sem'ble, *v.t., v.i.,* -bled, -bling. gather. —**as·sem'blage**, **as·sem'bly**, *n.*

as·sent', *v.i.* 1. agree; consent. —*n.* 2. agreement; consent.

as·sert', *v.t.* 1. declare. 2. claim. 3. assert oneself, present one's claims, demands, etc. boldly. —**as·ser'tion**, *n.* —**as·ser'tive**, *adj.*

as·sess', *v.t.* evaluate. —**as·sess'ment**, **as·ses'sor**, *n.*

as'set, *n.* something contributing to a profit or advantage.

as·sid'u·ous, *adj.* devoted to a task. —**as·sid'u·ous·ly**, *adv.* —**as"si·du'i·ty**, *n.*

as·sign', *v.t.* 1. give out as a task or responsibility. 2. appoint. 3. transfer possession or enjoyment of. —*n.* 4. *Law.* person to whom possession or enjoyment of something is transferred. —**as·sign'ment**, *n.* —**as·sign'a·ble**, *adj.* —**as·sign·ee'**, *n.*

as·sim'i·late", *v.t.,* -ated, -ating. 1. absorb. 2. make like some larger entity. —**as·sim"i·la'tion**, *n.*

as·sist', *v.t.* help in a task or occupation. —**as·sist'ant**, *n.* —**as·sist'ance**, *n.*

as·so·ci·ate, *v.,* -ated, -ating, *adj., n. v.t., v.i.* (əs so'shē āt) 1. join in a social or business relationship. —*v.t.* 2. connect in one's mind. —*adj.* (əs so'shē ət)

3. joined in a social or business relationship. —*n.* 4. someone or something so joined. —**as·so"ci·a'tion**, *n.*

as·sort', *v.t.* classify. —**as·sort'ment**, *n.*

as·sort'ed, *adj.* 1. of various kinds. 2. classified.

as·suage (əs swāj'), *v.t.,* -suaged, -suaging. relieve, as suffering.

as·sume', *v.t.,* -sumed, -suming. 1. suppose without knowing. 2. take upon oneself. 3. take or receive from another. 4. begin to cultivate, as a role or affectation. 5. feign.

as·sump'tion, *n.* 1. act or instance of assuming. 2. **the Assumption**, ascent of the Virgin Mary to heaven, celebrated August 15.

as·sure', *v.t.,* -sured, -suring. 1. state emphatically. 2. convince. 3. make certain or safe. 4. reassure. —**as·sur'ance**, *n.* —**as·sured'**, *adj.*

as'ter, *n.* daisylike flower.

as'ter·isk, *n.* a sign, used for footnote references, etc. in print.

a·stern', *adv., Nautical.* backwards.

as'ter·oid", *n.* small planetlike body between Mars and Jupiter.

asth'ma, *n.* respiratory disorder. —**asth·mat'ic**, *adj., n.*

a·stig'ma·tism, *n.* eye defect which causes imperfect focusing. —**a"stig·mat'ic**, *adj.*

a·stir', *adj., adv.* full of diverse action.

as·ton'ish, *v.t.* surprise greatly. —**as·ton'ish·ment**, *n.*

as·tound', *v.t.* surprise very greatly.

a·stray', *adv., adj.* away from guidance or control.

a·stride', *prep., adv., adj.* straddling.

a·strin"gent, *adj.* 1. constrictive, styptic. —*n.* 2. substance which causes contraction of body tissues.

as·trol'o·gy, *n.* study of stars and planets as influences on events. —**as"tro·log'i·cal**, *adj.* —**as·trol'o·ger**, *n.*

as'tro·naut", *n.* person exploring or traveling through outer space.

as"tro·nom'i·cal, *adj.* 1. pertaining to astronomy. 2. fantastic, as a number of quantity.

as·tron'o·my, *n.* study of planets, stars, etc. and space. —**as·tron'o·mer**, *n.*

as·tute', *adj.* shrewd. —**as·tute'ness**, *n.*

a·sun'der, *adv., adj.* in parts.

a·sy'lum, *n.* home for persons needing protection, e.g., the insane.

at, *prep.* in, on, or near (used to specify time, place, or rate.)

a'the·ism, *n.* belief that no god exists. —**a'the·ist**, *n.* —**a"the·is'tic**, *adj.*

ath'lete", *n.* a person who engages in athletics.

ath·let'ics, *n., pl.* sports involving vigorous bodily exercise. —**ath·let'ic**, *adj.*

a·thwart', *adv., prep.* from side to side.

at'las, *n.* book of maps.

at′mos·phere″, *n.* 1. air closest to the earth. 2. prevailing mood. —**at″mos·pher′ic**, *adj.*

at′oll, *n.* ring of coral islands or reefs.

a′tom, *n.* smallest unit constituting a distinct chemical element. —**a·tom′ic**, *adj.*

atomic bomb, bomb acting through atomic energy created by fission. Also, **atom bomb**.

atomic energy, energy created through fission or fusion of the nuclei of certain atoms.

at′om·iz″er, *n.* device creating a fine spray.

a·tone′, *v.i.,* **atoned, atoning**. make right or show regret for a wrong one has done. —**a·tone′ment**, *n.*

a·top′, *prep., adv.* on top of.

a·tro′cious, *adj.* 1. vicious; outrageous. 2. wretchedly bad. —**a·troc′i·ty**, *n.*

a″tro·phy, *n.* 1. a wasting away. —*v.i., v.t.* 2. to waste away.

at·tach′, *v.t.* 1. fasten to something. 2. bind by ties of affection. 3. assume legal possession of, as to settle a bad debt. —**at·tach′ment**, *n.*

at″ta·ché′, *n.* special member of an embassy staff.

at·tack′, *v.t.* 1. act against with physical violence, harsh words, etc. 2. commence to solve, work out, etc. with vigor. —*n.* 5. act or manner of attacking.

at·tain′, *n.* arrive at. —**at·tain′a·ble**, *adj.* —**at·tain′ment**, *n.*

at·tar′, *n.* scent extracted from flowers.

at·tempt′, *v.t., n.* try.

at·tend′, *v.t.* 1. be present at. 2. accompany. 3. care for. —*v.i.* 4. be present at a meeting, etc. 5. give heed. —**at·ten′dance**, *n.*

at·tend′ant, *n.* 1. minor assistant. —*adj.* 2. accompanying.

at·ten′tion, *n.* 1. heed. 2. care, esp. medical care.

at·ten′tive, *adj.* paying heed or care. —**at·ten′tive·ly**, *adv.*

at·ten′u·ate″, *v.t.,* -ated, -ating. 1. thin. 2. weaken or dilute. —**at·ten″u·a′tion**, *n.*

at·test′, *v.t.* bear witness; certify. —**at″tes·ta′tion**, *n.*

at″tic, *n.* unfinished floor space beneath the roof of a house.

at·tire′, *v.t.,* -tired, -tiring, *n. v.t.* 1. dress, esp. showily. —*n.* 2. clothes, esp. showy ones.

at′ti·tude″, *n.* 1. opinion or feeling. 2. posture.

at·tor′ney, *n., pl.* -eys. lawyer.

at·tract′, *v.t.* 1. pull towards oneself. 2. draw by evoking interest, allure, etc. in. —**at·trac′tive**, *adj.* —**at·trac′tive·ly**, *adv.* —**at·trac′tive·ness**, *n.* —**at·trac′tion**, *n.*

at·trib·ute′, *v.t.,* -uted, -uting, *n. v.t.* (ət trib′yo͞ot) 1. name something as the cause for. —*n.* (at′trib yo͞ot) 2. distinguishing quality or feature. —**at″tri·bu′tion**, *n.*

at·tri′tion, *n.* wearing-down.

at·tune′, *v.t.* -tuned, -tuning. put in harmony.

au′burn, *n.* reddish-brown.

auc′tion, *n.* 1. public sale to the highest bidder for each item. —*v.t.* 2. sell at an auction. —**auc″tion·eer′**, *n.*

au·da′cious, *adj.* daring. —**au·da′ci·ty**, *n.*

au′di·ble, *adj.* able to be heard. —**au′di·bly**, *adv.* —**au″di·bil′i·ty**, *n.*

au′di·ence, *n.* 1. group attending a play, concert, lecture, etc. 2. persons reached by a book, etc. 3. formal interview.

au′di·o″, *adj.* pertaining to electronic reproduction of sound.

au′dit, *v.t.* 1. examine financial accounts. —*n.* 2. examination of financial accounts. —**au′dit·or**, *n.*

au·di′tion, *n.* 1. trial of ability for an actor, musician, etc. —*v.t.* 2. give an audition to. —*v.i.* 3. perform at an audition.

au″di·to′ri·um, *n.* room for an audience.

au′di·to″ry, *adj.* pertaining to hearing.

au′ger, *n.* drill.

aught, *n., Archaic.* 1. anything. 2. zero. —*adv.* 3. in any way.

aug·ment′, *v.t.* add to. —**aug″men·ta′tion**, *n.*

au·gur (ah′gər), *v.t.* 1. predict. —*n.* 2. prophet. —**au′gu·ry** (ah′gyo͞o rē), *n.*

au·gust, *adj.* 1. (ə gust′) grand; majestic. —*n.* 2. **August** (ah′gəst), eighth month.

aunt, *n.* sister of a father or mother, or wife of an uncle.

au′ra, *n.* quality emanating from a particular place or person.

au′ral, *adj.* pertaining to hearing.

au′re·ole″, *n.* halo.

au re·voir (ō″rə vwahr′), *French.* until I see you again; goodbye.

au′ri·cle, *n.* 1. outer ear. 2. upper chamber of the heart. —**au·ric′u·lar**, *adj.*

au·rif′er·ous, *adj.* gold-bearing.

aus·pice, *n., usually pl.* sponsorship.

aus·pi′cious, *adj.* favorable; promising.

aus·tere′, *adj.* 1. severe in manner. 2. characterized by abstention. —**aus·ter′i·ty**, *n.*

au·then′tic, *adj.* true or genuine. —**au″then·ti′ci·ty**, *n.*

au·then′ti·cate″, *v.t.,* -ated, -ating. prove the authenticity of. —**au·then″ti·ca′tion**, *n.*

au′thor, *n.* creator, esp. of a written work. Also, *fem.,* **au′thor·ess**. —**au′thor·ship″**, *n.*

au·thor″i·tar′i·an, *adj.* characterized by excessive show or use of authority. —**au·thor″i·tar′i·an·ism**, *n.*

au·thor'i·ta"tive, *adj.* **1.** confirmed by competent authority. **2.** having authority.

au·thor'i·ty, *n., pl.* **-ties. 1.** official power. **2.** person having such power. **3.** proof for a statement. **4.** expert. **5. the authorities,** persons with legal power.

au'thor·ize, *v.t.,* **-ized, -izing.** give official consent to. —**au"thor·i·za'tion,** *n.*

au'to, *n.* automobile.

au"to·bi·og'ra·phy, *n., pl.* **-ies.** story of one's own life. —**au"to·bi·o·gra'phi·cal,** *adj.*

au·toc'ra·cy, *n., pl.* **-cies.** government by one absolute ruler. —**au'to·crat,** *n.* —**au"to·crat'ic,** *adj.*

au'to·graph", *n.* one's name in one's handwriting.

au'to·mat", *n.* restaurant with coin-operated serving machines.

au"to·mat'ic, *adj.* controlled by machinery, etc. rather than humans. —**au"to·mat'ic·al·ly,** *adv.*

au"to·ma"tion, *n.* replacement of human beings as controlling elements by automatic devices.

au·tom'a·ton", *n., pl.* **-ta.** manlike self-controlled machine; robot.

au"to·mo·bile", *n.* self-propelled passenger vehicle.

au"to·mo'tive, *adj.* pertaining to self-propelled road vehicles.

au·ton'o·my, *n.* self-government. —**au·ton'o·mous,** *adj.*

au'top"sy, *n., pl.* **-sies.** examination of a corpse to determine the cause of death.

au'tumn, *n.* season between summer and winter. —**au·tum'nal,** *adj.*

aux·il'ia·ry, *adj., n., pl.* **-ries.** *adj.* **1.** serving to assist. **2.** supplementary. —*n.* **3.** something that assists or supplements. **4.** verb used in connection with the principal verb of a sentence.

a·vail', *v.t.* **1. avail oneself,** take advantage. —*v.i.* **2.** be of help or use. —*n.* **3.** advantage or benefit.

a·vail'a·ble, *adj.* able to be used or acquired. —**a·vail"a·bil'i·ty,** *n.*

av'a·lanche", *n.* sudden descent down a slope of a mass of snow, rock, etc.

av'a·rice, *n.* greed. —**av"a·ri'cious,** *adj.*

a·vast', *interj. Nautical.* stop.

a·venge', *v.t.,* **avenged, avenging.** take revenge for. —**a·veng'er,** *n.*

av'e·nue", *n.* **1.** major street. **2.** approach road.

av'er·age, *n., adj., v.,* **-aged, -aging.** *n.* **1.** number representing the sum of a group of added figures divided by the number of figures. —*adj.* **2.** typical. **3.** revealed by an average. —*v.t.* **4.** find the average of. —*v.i.* **5.** form an average.

a·verse', *adj.* opposed; reluctant. —**a·verse'ly,** *adv.*

a·ver'sion, *n.* strong dislike.

a·vert', *v.t.* **1.** prevent. **2.** turn away, as the eyes.

a'vi·ar"y, *n., pl.* **-ries.** place for captive birds.

a"vi·a'tion, *n.* practice of flying aircraft.

a'vi·a"tor, *n.* person who flies aircraft. Also, *fem.,* **a"vi·a'trix.**

a'vid, *adj.* eager. —**a·vid'i·ty,** *n.*

a"vo·ca'do, *n., pl.* **-dos.** pear-shaped tropical fruit.

av"o·ca'tion, *n.* spare-time pursuit; hobby.

a·void', *v.t.* keep oneself away or safe from. —**a·void'a·ble,** *adj.* —**a·void'ance,** *n*

av"oir·du·pois', *n.* system of weights using a pound of 16 ounces.

a·vow', *v.t.* confess. —**a·vow'al,** *n.* —**a·vowed',** *adj.*

a·wait', *v.t.* wait for.

a·wake', *v.,* **awoke** or **awaked, awaking.** *adj. v.t., v.i.* **1.** Also, **a·wak'en,** wake. —*adj.* **2.** not asleep.

a·ward', *v.t.* **1.** bestow, as a prize, favor, etc. —*n.* **2.** something awarded.

a·ware', *adj.* conscious or perceptive. —**a·ware'ness,** *n.*

a·wash', *adj., adv.* just below water level; flooded.

a·way', *adv.* **1.** to or in another place or direction. **2.** from a place. **3.** out of one's possession. **4.** continuously. —*adj.* **5.** absent. **6.** at a specified distance.

awe, *n., v.t.,* **awed, awing.** *n.* **1.** overwhelming respect, reverence, etc. —*v.t.* **2.** fill with awe. —**awe'some,** *adj.*

aw'ful, *adj.* **1.** bad. **2.** awe-inspiring.

aw'ful·ly, *adv.* **1.** in an awful manner. **2.** *Informal.* very.

a·while', *adv.* for a while.

awk'ward, *adj.* **1.** clumsy. **2.** embarrassing. **3.** dangerous or difficult. —**awk'ward·ly,** *adv.* —**awk'ward·ness,** *n.*

awl, *n.* pointed tool.

awn'ing, *n.* device for shading windows, porches, etc. usually made of canvas.

a·wry', *adv., adj.* **1.** twisted. **2.** not right.

ax, *n., pl.* **axes.** broad-bladed chopping tool. Also, **axe.**

ax'i·om, *n.* statement accepted as a basic truth. —**ax"i·o·mat'ic,** *adj.*

ax'is, *n., pl.* **axes.** line on which something is centered or rotates. —**ax'i·al,** *adj.*

ax'le, *n.* shaft on which a wheel turns.

ay"a·tol'lah, *n.* Shi'ite Muslim religious leader.

aye (ī), *adv., n.* yes, esp. in voting.

a·zal'ea, *n.* flowering shrub.

az'ure, *n.* sky blue.

B

B, b, *n.* 1. second letter of the English alphabet. 2. second-best grade.

bab′ble, *v.,* **-bled, -bling,** *n.* *v.t.,* *v.i.* 1. speak unclearly or meaninglessly. —*n.* 2. unclear or meaningless spoken words or sounds. —**bab′bler,** *n.*

babe, *n.* baby.

ba·boon′, *n.* large monkey.

ba′by, *n., pl.* **-bies,** *v.t.,* **-bied, -bving.** *n.* 1. very young child. 2. infantile person. —*v.t.* 3. treat with excessive care or indulgence. —**ba′by·ish,** *adj.* —**ba′by·hood,** *n.*

bac′ca·lau′re·ate, *n.* bachelor's degree.

bach′e·lor, *n.* 1. unmarried man. 2. person holding the lowest academic degree. —**bach′e·lor·hood″,** *n.*

ba·cil·lus (bə sil′ləs), *n., pl.* **bacilli** (bə sil′ī). rod-shaped bacterium.

back, *n.* 1. part of a person opposite the face. 2. uppermost part of an animal. 3. side of an object opposite that usually faced; rear. 4. spine. —*adj.* 5. at the rear. 6. related to the past. —*adv.* 7. toward the rear. 8. into the past. 9. in return. —*v.t.* 10. sponsor; support. —*v.t.,* *v.i.* 11. move backwards. —**back′er,** *n.* —**back′ing,** *n.*

back′bite″, *v.t.,* *v.i.* slander, esp. someone absent. —**back′bit″er,** *n.*

back′bone′, *n.* 1. spine. 2. strength of character.

back′fire′, *v.i.* 1. fire prematurely, as an engine. 2. have adverse results, as a plan. —*n.* 3. premature firing of an engine.

back′ground′, *n.* 1. area at the rear of a scene. 2. information generally useful in a given situation. 3. origin, experience or environment.

back′lash′, *n.* sudden or sharp reaction.

back′log″, *n.* accumulation.

back′slide″, *v.i.,* **-slid, -slidden** or **-slid, -sliding.** forget good resolutions. —**back′slid″er,** *n.*

back talk, *Informal.* insolent reply.

back′ward, *adv.* Also, **back′wards.** 1. toward the rear. 2. back foremost. 3. toward the past. —*adj.* 4. toward the rear or the past. 5. not sufficiently advanced. —**back′ward·ly,** *adv.* —**back′ward·ness,** *n.*

back′woods′, *n., pl.* region of sparsely settled forest. —**back′woods′man,** *n.*

ba′con, *n.* cured meat from the back and sides of a hog.

bac·ter′i·a, *n., pl.* of **bacterium.** microscopic vegetable organism. —**bac·te′ri·al,** *adj.* —**bac·te′ri·al·ly,** *adv.*

bac·te″ri·ol′o·gy, *n.* study of bacteria. —**bac·te″ri·ol·og′i·cal,** *adj.* —**bac·te″ri·ol·o·gist,** *n.*

bad, *adj.,* **worse,** *n.,* *v.t.* *adj.* 1. unfavorable evil, or unacceptable. —*n.* 2. condition or realm of that which is bad. —*v.t.* 3. Also, **bade.** Past tense of **bid.** —**bad′ly,** *adv.* —**bad′ness,** *n.*

badge, *n.* object worn as a symbol of authority or distinction.

bad′ger, *n.* 1. burrowing animal. —*v.t.* 2. torment.

bad·i·nage (bad″ə nahzh′), *n.* teasing conversation.

bad′min·ton, *n.* game played with rackets.

baf′fle, *v.t.,* **-fled, -fling,** *n.* *v.t.* 1. confuse. —*n.* 2. passage made to divert or stop sound, light, etc. —**baf′fling,** *adj.* —**baf′fling·ly,** *adv.*

bag, *n.,* *v.,* **bagged, bagging.** *n.* 1. flexible container open at one end. 2. purse. 3. suitcase. —*v.t.* 4. put into bags. 5. kill. esp. in sport. —*v.i.* 6. bulge.

bag′gage, *n.* containers for things taken on a journey.

bag′gy, *adj.* irregularly bulging. —**bag′gi·ness,** *n.*

bag′pipe″, *n., often pl.* reed musical instrument played with air under pressure in a bag. —**bag′pip″er,** *n.*

bail, *n.,* *v.* *n.* 1. security for temporary release of a prisoner. 2. suspension handle. —*v.t.* 3. have released temporarily by putting up security. 4. empty of water with a vessel. —*v.i.* 5. bail out, escape by parachute. —**bail′a·ble,** *adj.*

bail′iff, *n.* 1. deputy sheriff. 2. officer keeping order in a court.

bail′i·wick, *n.* 1. area of a bailiff's authority. 2. any area of authority or competence.

bait, *n.* 1. something used as an attraction in trapping or fishing. —*v.t.* 2. supply with bait. 3. harass, as with dogs.

bake, *v.,* **′ked, baking.** *v.t.,* *v.i.* cook or harden with dry heat. —**bak′er,** *n.*

bak′er·y, *n., pl.* **-eries.** 1. place for baking food made with flour, etc. 2. place where such food is sold.

bal′ance, *n.,* *v.,* **-anced, -ancing.** *n.* 1. state of rest due to equal leverage around a point or line. 2. state of harmony, stability, etc. 3. weighing device. 4. remainder from a subtraction. —*v.t.* 5. put in balance. 6. compare or contrast. 7. review, as accounts. —*v.i.* 8. come into or be in balance.

bal′co·ny, *n., pl.* **-nies.** 1. floor area projecting from a building. 2. interior floor area overlooking a lower floor.

bald, *n.* 1. without hair. 2. without disguise or mitigation. —**bald'ly**, *adv.* —**bald'ness**, *n.*

bale, *n., v.t.* **baled**, **baling**. *n.* **1.** large compressed or tied bundle. —*v.t.* **2.** make into bales.

bale'ful, *adj.* hostile; evil. —**bale'ful·ly**, *adv.* —**bale'ful·ness**, *n.*

balk (bawk), *v.i.* **1.** refuse to act. **2.** be daunted. —*v.t.* **3.** obstruct. —*n.* **4.** obstruction. —**balk'y**, *adj.*

ball, *n.* **1.** evenly rounded object; sphere. **2.** game or games played with such a solid. **3.** an entertainment of dancing. —*v.t.* **4.** form into spheres.

bal'lad, *n.* **1.** narrative song or poem. **2.** sentimental song.

bal'last, *n.* **1.** weighty material used for stability. —*v.t.* **2.** supply with ballast.

ball bearing, machinery bearing rotating on steel balls.

bal''le·ri'na, *n.* leading female ballet dancer.

bal·let (bal lā'), *n.* entertainment by dancers, esp. one acting out a story.

bal·lis'tics, *n.* study of the motion and behavior of projectiles. —**bal·lis'tic**, *adj.*

bal·loon', *n.* **1.** baglike lighter-than-air vehicle with no engine or steering mechanism. —*v.i.* **2.** travel in balloons. —**bal·loon'ist**, *n.*

bal'lot, *n.* **1.** paper for indicating a vote. **2.** collective vote for a candidate, proposal, etc.

ball'room, *n.* room for social dancing.

bal'ly·hoo'', *n. Informal.* ostentatious publicity.

balm (bahm), *n.* **1.** healing or soothing substance. **2.** anything that heals or soothes.

balm'y, *adj.*, **balmier**, **balmiest**. soothing or refreshing. —**balm'i·ness**, *n.*

bal·sa (bawl'sa), *n.* lightweight wood of a tropical American tree, used for model-making, etc.

bal'sam, *n.* aromatic resin from certain trees. —**bal·sam'ic**, *adj.*

bal'us·ter, *n.* columnlike support for a railing.

bal'us·trade'', *n.* railing supported by balusters.

bam·boo'', *n.* tall tropical grass with hollow woodlike stems.

bam·boo'zle, *v.t. Informal.* mystify or cheat.

ban, *v.t.*, **banned**, **banning**, *n. v.t.* **1.** forbid. —*n.* **2.** act or instance of forbidding.

ba'nal, *adj.* boringly ordinary. —**ba·nal'i·ty**, *n.*

ba·nan'a, *n.* **1.** treelike tropical plant. **2.** fruit from this plant.

band, *n.* **1.** strip of binding material. **2.** stripe. **3.** group of wind and percussion musicians. **4.** informal group, esp. of

armed persons. —*v.t.* **5.** mark with bands. —*v.i.* **6.** gather or unite. —**band'mas''ter**, *n.* —**bands'man**, *n.* —**band'stand''**, *n.*

band'age, *n., v.t.*, **-aged**, **-aging**, *n.* **1.** strip of cloth, etc., esp. for covering a wound. —*v.t.* **2.** tie with a bandage.

ban·dan'na, *n.* printed cloth for the head or neck. Also, **ban·dan'a**.

ban'dit, *n.* armed robber. —**ban'dit·ry**, *n.*

band'wag''on, *n.* **1.** wagon for the musicians in a circus parade. **2.** obviously winning side of a controversy.

ban'dy, *v.t.*, **-died**, **-dying**, *adj. v.t.* **1.** exchange rapidly, as words. **2.** send back and forth rapidly, as a tennis ball. —*adj.* **3.** bowed, as legs.

bane, *n.* evil or destructive influence.

bane'ful, *adj.* destructive. —**bane'ful·ly**, *adv.* —**bane'ful·ness**, *n.*

bang, *n.* **1.** loud noise, as from an explosion or collision. **2.** Often, **bangs**, short hair across the forehead. —*v.i.* **3.** make a loud noise. **4.** strike.

ban'gle, *n.* decorative band for the wrist or ankle.

ban'ish, *v.t.* drive away; exile. —**ban'ish·ment**, *n.*

ban'ister, *n.* stair railing.

ban'jo, *n.* plucked stringed instrument with circular body. —**ban'jo·ist**, *n.*

bank, *n.* **1.** shore of a river or lake. **2.** slope. **3.** long mound. **4.** tilt, as a vehicle or its supporting surface at a turn. **5.** organization for the saving and lending of money. —*v.t.* **6.** heap up. **7.** tilt while turning. **8.** put into a bank. **9.** cover partly, as a fire. —*v.i.* **10.** have a bank account.

bank'er, *n.* proprietor or officer of a bank.

bank'ing, *n.* **1.** operation of a bank or banks. —*adj.* **2.** pertaining to the activities of banks.

bank'rupt'', *adj.* **1.** unable to pay debts. **2.** without resources. —*n.* **3.** bankrupt person. —*v.t.* **4.** make bankrupt. —**bank'rupt·cy**, *n.*

ban'ner, *n.* flag.

banns, *n., pl.* notice of a marriage to be performed. Also, **bans**.

ban'quet, *n., v.i.*, **-queted**, **-queting**. *n.* **1.** formal dinner or luncheon. —*v.i.* **2.** participate in a banquet. —**ban'quet·er**, *n.*

ban'tam, *n.* **1.** small fowl. —*adj.* **2.** miniature; tiny.

ban'ter, *n.* **1.** teasing. —*v.i.* **2.** exchange teasing remarks. —**ban'ter·er**, *n.*

bap'tism, *n.* rite of initiation, as into a church. —**bap·tis'mal**, *adj.*

Bap'tist, *n.* Protestant baptized by immersion in water.

bap'tize, *v.t.*, **-ized**, **-izing**. initiate into a church, esp. by sprinkling with or immersion in water.

bar, *n., v.t.,* **barred, barring,** *prep. n.* **1.** long round object, used in an enclosure as a lever, etc. **2.** stripe. **3.** obstruction. **4.** drinking place. **5.** counter for serving drinks. **6.** division of a musical composition. **7.** legal profession. —*v.t.* **8.** secure with a bar. **9.** exclude. **10.** obstruct. —*prep.* **11.** except for.

barb, *n.* **1.** sharp projection. —*v.t.* **2.** furnish with barbs.

bar·bar·i·an (bahr ber'ē ən), *n.* uncivilized person; savage. —**bar·bar'i·an·ism,** *n.*

bar·bar·ic (bahr ber'ik), *adj.* typical of or suggesting barbarians. —**bar·bar'i·cal·ly,** *adv.*

bar'bar·ism, *n.* barbaric act or state.

bar·bar·i·ty (bahr ber'ə tē), *n., pl.* **-ities.** **1.** cruelty. **2.** barbaric state.

bar·bar·ous (bahr'bə rəs), *adj.* **1.** cruel. **2.** uncivilized. —**bar'bar·ous·ly,** *adv.* —**bar'bar·ous·ness,** *n.*

bar'be·cue, *n.* **1.** to cook outdoors over an open fire. **2.** fireplace or grill used for cooking outdoors. **3.** meal cooked over an open fire. **4.** meat cooked and basted with sauce.

barbed, *adj.* **1.** having sharp projections. **2.** harsh, as a remark; caustic.

bar·bi·tu·rate (bahr bi'tshə rət), *n.* sedative.

bard, *n.* **1.** Celtic poet. **2.** any minstrel or poet. —**bard'ic,** *adj.*

bare, *adj., barer, barest, v.t.,* **bared baring.** *adj.* **1.** uncovered or unconcealed. **2.** unfurnished. **3.** mere. —*v.t.* **4.** strip of covering or concealment. —**bare'ness,** *n.*

bare'back'', *adv., adj.* without a saddle.

bare'faced'', *adj.* **1.** shameless. **2.** with an uncovered face.

bare'ly, *adv.* **1.** by the smallest possible amount. **2.** nakedly.

bar'gain, *n.* **1.** business agreement. **2.** advantageous purchase. —*v.i.* **3.** reach or attempt to reach a business agreement. —**bar'gain·er,** *n.*

barge, *n., v.,* **barged, barging.** *n.* **1.** slow freight-carrying boat. **2.** ceremonial boat carrying royalty, etc. —*v.t.* **3.** carry by barge. —*v.i.* **4.** barge in, *Informal.* intrude. —**barge'man,** *n.*

bar'i·tone'', *n.* **1.** musical range between tenor and bass. **2.** singer, instrument or part with this range.

bark, *n.* **1.** short utterance of a dog. **2.** covering of the stem of a tree or shrub. **3.** sailing vessel square-rigged on all but the last of three or more masts. —*v.t.* **4.** utter in a barklike tone. **5.** utter a bark. **6.** strip bark from. **7.** skin by accident.

bar'ley, *n.* grass with edible grain.

barn, *n.* building for crop storage, keeping of cows, etc. —**barn'yard'',** *n.*

bar'na·cle, *n.* shellfish that clings to ship bottoms, etc.

ba·rom'e·ter, *n.* device for measuring atmospheric pressure and thus foretelling weather changes. —**bar''o·met'ric, bar''o·met'ri·cal,** *adj.*

bar'on, *n.* low-ranking noble. Also, *fem.,* **bar'on·ess.** —**bar'on·age,** *n.* —**ba·ro'ni·al,** *adj.*

Ba·roque', *n.* florid style in architecture, etc. in the 17th century. Also, **ba·roque'.**

bar'rack, *n.* **1.** Usually, **barracks, dormitory for soldiers.** —*v.t.* **2.** house in barracks.

bar·ra·cu·da (bar''rə kōō'də), *n., pl.* **-da, -das.** pikelike tropical fish.

bar·rage (bar rahzh'), *n.* defensive barrier of artillery fire, captive balloons, etc.

bar'rel, *n., v.,* **-reled, -reling.** *n.* **1.** container, usually wood, with circular ends and bulging sides. **2.** measure of about 31 gallons. —*v.t.* **3.** put into barrels. —*v.i.* **4.** *Informal.* move at high speed.

bar'ren, *adj.* **1.** unable to support plant life. **2.** unable to bear children. **3.** profitless. —**bar'ren·ness,** *n.*

bar'ri·cade'', *n., v.t.,* **-caded, -cading.** *n.* **1.** obstruction, as to military advance. —*v.t.* **2.** defend or shut off with a barricade.

bar'ri·er, *n.* obstruction.

bar'ter, *n., v.t., v.i.* trade with goods or services alone.

ba·salt (bə sahlt', bā'sahlt), *n.* dark volcanic rock. —**ba·sal'tic,** *adj.*

base, *n., v.t.,* **based, basing,** *adj. n.* **1.** part on which a thing rests or stands. **2.** basis. **3.** principal ingredient. **4.** center of military operations. —*v.t.* **5.** give a basis or foundation to. —*adj.* **6.** contemptible. **7.** inferior, as a metal. —**base'ly,** *adv.* —**base'ness,** *n.*

base'ball'', *n.* **1.** game played in a diamond-shaped field with a batted ball. **2.** ball used in this game.

base'less, *adj.* unfounded in fact.

base'ment, *n.* **1.** lowermost part of a building. **2.** cellar.

bash, *v.t. Informal.* hit, as with a club.

bash'ful, *adj.* shy. —**bash'ful·ly,** *adv.* —**bash'ful·ness,** *n.*

bas'ic, *adj.* **1.** most important or significant; essential. —*n.* **2.** basics, most important or significant features. —**bas'i·cal·ly,** *adv.*

bas·il (baz'əl), *n.* herb of the mint family.

ba'sin, *n.* **1.** shallow bowl for liquids. **2.** pool. **3.** area drained by a river.

ba'sis, *n., pl.* **-ses.** **1.** something on which a thing depends. **2.** main ingredient.

bask, *v.i.* **1.** lie in warmth. **2.** enjoy favor, etc.

bas'ket, *n.* container of woven wood, wire, etc.

bas′ket·ball″, *n*. 1. game in which a ball is tossed over a hoop into a suspended net. 2. ball used in this game.

bass, *n*. 1. (bās) lowermost musical range. 2. singer, instrument, or part with this range. 3. (bas), *pl*. **basses**, **bass**. spiny-finned edible fish.

bas″si·net′, *n*. basketlike bed for a baby.

bas·soon′, *n*. bass woodwind. **—bas·soon′ist**, *n*.

bas′tard, *n*. 1. person born out of wedlock. 2. *Informal*. harsh or malicious person. *—adj*. 3. born out of wedlock. 4. not authentic. **—bas′tard·y**, *n*.

baste, *v.t.*, **basted, basting**. 1. sew temporarily. 2. cover with juices, etc. while cooking. **—bast′ing**, *n*.

bat, *n.*, *v.*, **batted, batting**. *n*. 1. club used for striking a ball, as in baseball or cricket. 2. nocturnal flying mammal. *—v.t.* 3. hit with a bat. *—v.i.* 4. have a turn batting.

batch, *n*. quantity of material prepared or gathered at one time.

bath, *n.*, *pl*. **baths**. 1. complete washing or immersion. 2. liquid for immersion or washing. **—bath′room″**, *n*. **—bath′tub″**, *n*.

bathe, *n.*, **bathed, bathing**. *n.i*. 1. take a bath. 2. go swimming, esp. in an ocean or lake. *—v.t.* 3. give a bath to. **—bath′er**, *n*.

ba′thos, *n*. 1. ridiculous anticlimax. 2. insincere sentimentality.

bath′robe, *n*. robe used before and after bathing.

ba·ton′, *n*. staff used for directing musicians, as a badge of office, etc.

bat·tal′ion, *n*. subdivision of a military division.

bat′ten, *n*. 1. thin strip of wood. *—v.t.* 2. secure or cover with battens. *—v.i.* 3. thrive.

bat′ter, *v.t.* 1. hit or attack repeatedly. *—n*. 2. person who bats. 3. cake mixture.

bat′ter·y, *n.*, *pl*. **-ies**. *n*. 1. device for storing electricity. 2. group of cannon used together. 3. group of any machines, etc. used together. 4. *Law*. illegal beating.

bat′ting, *n*. fiber packed in sheets.

bat′tle, *n.*, *v.*, **-tled, -tling**. *n*. 1. major military encounter. 2. warfare. *—v.t.*, *v.i.* 3. fight. **—bat′tle·field″**, *n*.

bat′tle·ment″, *n*. defensive wall with openings for shooting.

bat′tle·ship″, *n*. warship with heavy guns and armor.

bau′ble, *n*. trinket.

bawd′y, *adj.*, **-ier, -iest**. obscene. **—bawd′i·ness**, *n*.

bawl, *v.i.* 1. yell. 2. weep loudly.

bay, *n*. 1. distinct area of a wall. 2. broad inlet, esp. of a sea. 3. **at bay**, a. unable to escape. b. unable to attack. *—v.i.* 4. give prolonged howls.

bay′o·net″, *n.*, *v.t.*, **-netted, -netting**. *n*. 1. sharp thrusting weapon attached to a gun muzzle. *—v.t.* 2. stab with a bayonet.

bay′ou, *n*. marshy area of a river or lake, esp. in Louisiana.

bay window, window jutting from a building, esp. a window with its own foundations.

ba·zaar′, *n*. 1. Near Eastern salesplace. 2. temporary sale, esp. for charity.

be, *v.i.*, **was** or **were**, **been**, **being**. 1. exist: often refers to an adjective describing the subject. 2. occur. 3. continue. 4. (Used variously as an auxiliary verb).

beach, *n*. 1. flat shore, esp. a sandy one. *—v.t.* 2. haul onto a beach.

beach′comb″er, *n*. seaside scavenger.

bea′con, *n*. 1. signal light. 2. navigational radio station.

bead, *n*. 1. small decorative ball. 2. small drop. 3. **draw a bead on**, take aim at.

bead′y, *adj.*, **-ier, -iest**. beadlike; small and shiny.

beak, *n*. 1. pointed mouth, esp. of a bird. 2. projection suggesting this.

beam, *n*. 1. horizontal structural member. 2. shaft of light 3. steady radio or radar signal. 4. width of a ship. *—v.t.* 5. send as a radio or radar beam. *—v.i.* 6. shine. 7. smile kindly.

bean, *n*. any of various edible seeds.

bear, *v.t.* 1. carry. 2. endure. 3. suffer. 4. give birth to. 5. produce. *—v.i.* 6. head or move in a stated direction. 7. **bear with**, be patient with. *—n*. 8. large shaggy mammal. 9. speculator in the fall of stock prices. **—bear′er**, *n*. **—bear′a·ble**, *adj*.

beard, *n*. 1. hair on the lower jaw, etc. *—v.t.* 2. intrude upon and confront. **—beard′ed**, *adj*.

bear′ing, *n*. 1. posture or attitude. 2. support for a rotating part. 3. **bearings**, orientation.

beast, *n*. 1. large animal. 2. cruel or uncouth person.

beast′ly, *adj.*, **-lier, -liest**. nasty. **—beast′li·ness**, *n*.

beat, *v.*, **beat, beaten, beating**, *n*. *v.t.* 1. hit with force. 2. win against. 3. move vigorously back and forth, as arms or wings. *—v.i.* 4. throb, as the heart. *—n*. 5. marked rhythm. 6. unit of such a rhythm. 7. regular round, as that of a policeman.

be″a·tif′ic, *adj*. 1. blissful. 2. imparting blessings.

beat′ing, *n*. 1. act or instance of hitting, esp. a person or animal. 2. defeat.

beau, *n.*, *pl*. **beaus, beaux**. suitor.

beau′ti·ful, *adj*. having beauty. Also, **beau′te·ous**. **—beau′ti·ful·ly**, *adv*.

beau′ti·fy″, *v.t.*, **-fied, -fying**. make beautiful. **—beau″ti·fi·ca′tion**, *n*.

beau′ty, *n.*, *pl*. **-ties**. 1. quality sensed in

that which is in perfect harmony. 2. beautiful woman.

bea′ver, *n.* broad-tailed, dam-building rodent.

be·calm′, *v.t.* halt from a lack of wind in sails.

be·cause′, *conj.* 1. for the reason that. 2. **because of**, as a result of.

beck′on, *v.i.* 1. make a summoning gesture. —*v.t.* 2. summon with a gesture.

be·come′, *v.,* **-came, -come, -coming.** *v.i.* 1. come to be as specified. —*v.t.* 2. be suitable to.

be·com′ing, *adj.* 1. suitable; seemly. 2. attractively appropriate, as clothing. —**be·com′ing·ly**, *adv.*

bed, *n., v.,* **bedded, bedding.** *n.* 1. object to lie upon. 2. **to bed**, to rest in a lying position. 3. **into bed**, beneath the upper bedclothes of a bed. 4. layer of rock, etc. 5. layer of surface soil, as for flowers. 6. foundation for machinery. 7. bottom of a body of water. —*v.t.* 8. put into a bed. —*v.i.* 9. go to or into bed. —**bed′cov′er**, *n.* —**bed′fel′low**, *n.* —**bed′room′′**, *n.* —**bed′side′′**, *n., adj.* —**bed′spread′′**, *n.* —**bed′spring′′**, *n.* —**bed′time′′**, *n.*

be·daz′zle, *v.t.,* **-zled, -zling.** dazzle; amaze.

bed′clothes′′, *n., pl.* sheets, covers, etc. for a bed.

bed′ding, *n.* all movable objects used with a bed.

be·dev′il, *v.t.,* **-iled, -iling.** harass; torment. —**be·dev′il·ment**, *n.*

bed′lam, *n.* chaotic situation.

be′′drag′gle, *v.t.,* **-gled, -gling.** soil as by dragging through mud.

bed′rid′′den, *adj.* confined to bed by permanent illness or feebleness. Also, **bed′fast′′**.

bed′rock′′, *n.* uppermost layer of solid rock.

bed′stead′′, *n.* framework for bedding.

bee, *n.* 1. four-winged, pollen-gathering insect. 2. social meeting for joint work or competition. —**bee′hive′′**, *n.* —**bee′keep′′er**, *n.* —**bee′keep′′ing**, *n.* —**bees′wax′′**, *n.*

beech, *n.* hardwood tree.

beef, *n., pl.* **beeves** or **beefs.** 1. meat from cows, steers, etc. 2. any such animal. —**beef′steak′′**, *n.*

beef′y, *adj.* **-ier, -iest.** muscular; brawny.

bee′line′′, *n.* straight route.

beer, *n.* 1. drink of fermented malt, hops, etc. 2. any of various soft drinks made from plants.

beet, *n.* plant with an edible root.

beet′le, *n.* 1. insect with hard wings. 2. large mallet. —*adj.* 3. Also, **beet′ling.** overhanging. —**bee′tle-browed′′**, *adj.*

be·fall′, *v.i.,* **-fell, -fallen.** happen.

be·fit′, *v.t.,* **-fitted, -fitting.** be suitable to. —**be·fit′ting**, *adj.* —**be·fit′ting·ly**, *adv.*

be·fore′, *prep.* 1. at an earlier time than. 2. in front of. 3. in preference to. —*adv.* 4. at an earlier time. 5. in front. —*conj.* 6. earlier than the time that something happens. 7. rather than.

be·fore′hand′′, *adv.* 1. in advance. —*adj.* 2. ahead of time.

be·foul′, *v.t.* make foul.

be·friend′, *v.t.* act as a friend to.

beg, *v.,* **begged, begging.** *v.t., v.i.* ask as a favor.

beg′gar, *n.* 1. person who asks strangers for his livelihood. —*v.t.* 2. impoverish. 3. render inadequate, esp. any description of a thing. —**beg′gar·y**, *n.*

beg′gar·ly, *adj.* miserably inadequate.

be·gin′, *v.,* **began, begun.** *v.t., v.i.* start commence. —**be·gin′ning**, *n.*

be·gin′ner, *n.* 1. person who begins. 2. completely inexperienced person.

be·grudge′, *v.t.,* **-grudged, -grudging.** resent another's having or receiving. —**be·grudg′ing·ly**, *adv.*

be·guile′, *v.t.,* **-guiled, -guiling.** 1. charm. 2. while away pleasantly. —**be·guile′ment**, *n.*

be·half′, *n.* **in** or **on behalf of, a.** in the name of. **b.** in support of.

be·have′, *v.,* **-haved, -having.** *v.i.* 1. conduct oneself properly —*v.t.* 2. conduct in a specified way. 3. conduct properly. —**be·hav′ior**, *n.*

be·hest′, *n.* command; urging.

be·hind′, *prep.* 1. at the rear of. 2. at or to the far side of. 3. too late or slow for. 4. in defense or support of. 5. concealed by. —*adv.* 6. at the rear. 7. into a state of lateness or slowness.

be·hold′, *v.t.,* **-held, -held, -holding.** see; look at. —**be·hold′er**, *n.*

be·hold′en, *adj.* indebted.

be·hoove′, *v.t.,* **-hooved -hooving.** obligate.

be′ing, *n.* 1. existence. 2. essential nature. 3. something alive.

be·la′bor, *v.t.* attack by or as if by beating.

be·lat′ed, *adj.* later than expected or desirable. —**be·lat′ed·ly**, *adv.*

belch, *v.i.* 1. emit stomach gas through the mouth. —*v.t.* 2. emit violently, as smoke. —*n.* 3. act or instance of belching.

be·lea′guer, *v.t.* harass, as by a siege.

bel·fry (bel′frē), *n., pl.* **fries.** tower or turret for bells.

be·lie′, *v.t.,* **-lied, -lying.** 1. represent deceptively. 2. prove as false.

be·lieve′, *v.,* **-lieved, -lieving.** *v.t.* 1. accept as true or truthful. 2. guess to be so. —*v.i.* 3. have faith. 4. accept the existence of something. —**be·lief′**, *n.* —**be·liev′er**, *n.* —**be·liev′able**, *adj.*

be·lit′tle, *v.t.,* **-tled, -tling.** treat as of minor importance. —**be·lit′tle·ment**, *n.*

bell, *n.* **1.** hollow instrument, usually metal, that sounds when struck. **2.** something having the characteristic flared shape of this. **3.** *Nautical.* half-hour unit of time.

belle, *n.* attractive woman.

belles'-let'tres, *n., pl.* literature as an art.

bel'li·cose'', *adj.* warlike. —**bel'li·cos''i·ty,** *n.*

bel·lig'er·ent, *adj.* **1.** eager to fight. **2.** at war. —*n.* **3.** nation, etc. at war. —**bel·lig'er·ence, bel'lig'er·en·cy,** *n.*

bel'low, *v.t., n.* **1.** shout or roar. *n.* **2. bellows,** device for pumping air to a hearth.

bel'ly, *n., pl.* **-lies,** *v.i.,* **-lied, lying.** *n.* **1.** stomach. **2.** human abdomen. **3.** animal's underside. —*v.i.* **4.** swell.

be·long', *v.i.* **1.** be property. **2.** be a member, citizen, etc. of something. **3.** be appropriate.

be·long'ings, *n., pl.* possessions.

be·lov'ed, *adj.* **1.** loved. —*n.* **2.** loved one.

be·low', *prep.* **1.** lower than; under. **2.** inferior in worth or amount to. —*adv., adj.* **3.** to or in some lower place. **4.** later, as in a book. **5.** *Nautical.* on or to a lower deck.

belt, *n.* **1.** strap worn around the waist, over the chest, etc. **2.** long, narrow region, road, c'c. **3.** strap for driving machinery. **4.** *Informal.* violent blow. —*v.t.* **5.** *Informal.* **a.** hit violently. **b.** sing emphatically.

be·moan', *v.t.* lament.

be·muse', *v.t.,* **-mused, -musing.** put in a thoughtful or bewildered frame of mind.

bench, *n.* **1.** broad seat or stool. **2.** massive worktable. **3.** judge's seat. **4. the bench,** jurisprudence. —*v.t.* **5.** put on a bench.

bend, *v.,* **bent, bending,** *n. v.t.* **1.** form as a curved or angled shape, esp. by force. **2.** bow or stoop. **3.** submit oneself. —*n.* **4.** bent section. **5.** curve, as in a road or river.

be·neath', *prep.* **1.** under. **2.** unworthy of. —*adj., adv.* **3.** underneath.

ben''e·dic'tion, *n.* blessing.

ben''e·fac'tion, *n.* act or instance of charity.

ben'e·fac''tor, *n.* conferrer of benefactions. Also, *fem.,* **ben'e·fac''tress.**

be·nef'i·cent, *adj.* doing good. —**be·nef'i·cence,** *n.* —**be·nef'i·cent·ly,** *adv.*

ben''e·fi'cial, *adj.* useful; advantageous. —**be''ne·fi'cial·ly,** *adv.*

ben''e·fi'ci·ar·y, *n., pl.* **-aries.** enjoyer of a benefit.

ben'e·fit, *n., v.t.,* **-fitted, -fitting.** *n.* **1.** advantage. **2.** entertainment to raise

funds for charity, etc. **3.** payment from insurance, etc. —*v.t.* **4.** be of advantage to.

be·nev'o·lent, *adj.* kindly; well-intentioned. —**be·nev'o·lent·ly,** *adv.* —**be·nev'o·lence,** *n.*

be·night'ed, *adj.* **1.** lacking enlightenment. **2.** hampered or surrounded by darkness.

be·nign', *adj.* **1.** friendly; well-intentioned. **2.** *Medicine.* not malignant. —**be·nign'ly,** *adv.* —**be·nig'ni·ty,** *n.*

be·nig'nant, *adj.* **1.** benevolent. **2.** beneficial.

be·queath', *v.t.* transfer to heirs. —**be·quest',** *n.*

be·rate', *v.t.* **-rated, -rating.** scold.

be·reave', *v.t.,* **-reft, -reaving. 1.** leave sorrowful, esp. by dying. **2.** deprive; strip. —**be·reave'ment,** *n.*

be·ret (bə rā'), *n.* soft, flat, visorless cloth cap.

berm, *n.* earth embankment. Also, **berme.**

ber'ry, *n., pl.* **-ries. 1.** juicy cover for a seed or seeds. **2.** dried seed of a coffee plant, etc.

ber·serk', *adv., adj.* in violent frenzy.

berth, *n.* **1.** shelflike bed. **2.** job. **3.** ship's mooring place.

ber'yl, *n.* class of hard stone: includes emeralds and aquamarines.

be·seech', *v.t.,* **-sought,** or **-seeched, seeching.** request earnestly. —**be·seech'ing·ly,** *adv.*

be·set', *v.t.,* **-set, -setting.** harass.

be·set'ting, *adj.* obsessive, as a sin.

be·side', *prep.* **1.** at the side of. **2.** compared with. **3.** added to. **4.** irrelevant to.

be·sides', *adv.* **1.** in addition; else. —*prep.* **2.** in addition to; other than.

be·siege', *v.t.,* **-sieged, -sieging. 1.** lay siege to. **2.** distract repeatedly.

be·smirch', *v.t.* mark or soil.

be·speak', *v.t.,* **-spoke, -spoken** or **-spoke, speaking. 1.** speak for ahead of time; reserve. **2.** be eloquent of; reveal.

best, *adj.* **1.** superlative of *good.* **2.** major; greater. —*adv.* **3.** superlative of *well.* **4.** that which is best. **5.** one's utmost.

bes'ti·al, *adj.* savage. —**bes''ti·al'i·ty,** *n.*

be·stir', *v.t.,* **-stirred, -stirring.** rouse to action.

best man, groom's ring bearer at a wedding.

be·stow', *v.t.* give or grant. —**be·stow'al,** *n.*

bet, *n., v.,* **betted, betting.** *n.* **1.** guess on the unpredictable outcome of an event, made to gain money, etc. **2.** money, etc. put up to back one's guess. **3.** possible guess or action regarding an unpredictable matter. —*v.t.* **4.** put up to

back one's bet. 5. guess in betting.
—*v.i.* 6. make a bet.

be·tray′, *v.t.* 1. be treacherous to. 2. reveal, as a secret. 3. seduce with a false promise of marriage. 4. reveal involuntarily. —be·tray′al, *n.*

be·troth′al, *n.* engagement to marry.

be·trothed′, *n.* fiancé or fiancée.

bet′ter, *adj.* 1. comparative of *good.* 2. major; greater. —*adv.* 3. comparative of *well.* —*n.* 4. social superior. 5. that which is better. 6. Also, **bet′tor,** person who bets.

bet′ter·ment, *n.* improvement.

be·tween′, *prep.* 1. with two specified persons or things, one on each side. 2. involving or relating two persons or things. 3. as a result of two specified causes. 4. from either one of, in choosing. 5. as a secret shared by two persons.

bev′el, *n.* 1. outer edge formed as a diagonal. —*v.t.* 2. form as such a diagonal.

bev′er·age, *n.* something to drink other than water.

be·ware′, *v.,* -wared, -waring. *v.i.* 1. be cautious. —*v.t.* 2. be cautious of.

be·wil′der, *v.t.* confuse, esp. with surprise. —be·wil′der·ment, *n.*

be·witch′, *v.t.* 1. cast a spell on. 2. charm with delight.

be·yond′, *prep.* 1. on the far side of. 2. too late or advanced for. 3. outside the power or domain of. 4. after; past. —*adv.* 5. further away.

bi·an′nu·al, *adj.* twice a year. —bi·an′nu·al·ly, *adv.*

bib, *n.* apronlike cloth to catch dribbles.

bib′li·og′ra·phy, *n., pl.* -phies. list of books, articles, etc. used, recommended, or in existence. —bib′li·og′ra·pher, *n.* —bib′li·o·graph′i·cal, *adj.*

bi·cam′er·al, *adj.* composed of two legislative chambers.

bi·car′bo·nate, *n.* chemical compound releasing carbon dioxide when mixed with acid.

bick′er, *v.i.* quarrel about trifles. —bick′er·er, *n.*

bi′cy·cle, *n.* two-wheeled vehicle for a balancing rider. —bi′cy·clist, bi′cy·cler, *n.*

bid, *n., v.,* bid, bad or (for 4 and 6) bade, bid or (for 4 and 6) bidden, bidding. *n.* 1. offer for an auctioned item. 2. offer to fulfill a contract for a stated sum. 3. attempt to gain victory, favor, notice, etc. —*v.t.* 4. command or ask. 5. offer for an auctioned item. 6. express, esp. a goodbye. —*v.i.* 7. make a bid. —bid′der, *n.*

bier, *n.* support for a coffin.

bi·fo′′cals, *n., pl.* spectacles whose lenses have two areas apiece, each with two focuses.

big, *adj.,* bigger, biggest. 1. great in size or amount. 2. full-grown. 3. elder. 4. important. —big′ness, *n.*

big′a·my, *n.* marriage to two spouses in a single period. —big′a·mous, *adj.* —big′a·mist, *n.*

big′ot, *n.* person with strong, intolerant, unreasoning attitudes. —big′ot·ry, *n.* —big′ot·ed, *adj.*

bike, *n. Informal.* bicycle.

bi·lat′er·al, *adj.* 1. involving two sides or factions. 2. reciprocal; mutual. —bi·lat′er·al·ly, *adv.*

bi·lin′gual, *adj.* 1. familiar with two languages. 2. expressed in two languages.

bil′ious, *adj.* ill-tempered.

bilk, *v.t.* cheat.

bill, *n.* 1. itemized list or statement. 2. written request for payment. 3. printed announcement. 4. piece of paper currency. 5. beak of a bird. —*v.t.* request payment from in writing.

bill′board′′, *n.* large board for advertising posters.

bil′let, *n.* 1. job; position. 2. order to house a soldier. 3. accommodation obtained with such an order. —*v.t.* 4. house with such an order.

bil′′let-doux′, *n., pl.* billets-doux. love letter.

bill′fold′′, *n.* wallet.

bil′liards, *n.* game using hard balls propelled by a cue.

bil′ling, *n.* public listing of entertainers on a program.

bil′lion, *n.* 1. *U.S.* thousand million. 2. *Great Britain.* million million. —bil′lionth, *adj.*

bill of fare, menu.

bil′low, *n.* 1. swelling mass, as of water or smoke. —*v.i.* 2. appear in billows. —bil′low·y, *adj.*

bi·month′ly, *adj.* every two months.

bin, *n.* large container for loose storage or display.

bi′′na·ry, *adj.* of or pertaining to the mathematical base 2.

bind, *v.,* bound, binding. *v.t.* 1. tie or fasten together. 2. obligate. 3. reinforce, as with tape. —*v.i.* 4. stick fast or together. —bind′er, *n.* —bind′ing, *n.*

bin′na·cle, *n.* housing for a ship's compass.

bin·oc′u·lar, *n.* 1. binoculars, twin telescopelike glasses, one for each eye. —*adj.* 2. pertaining to both eyes.

bi′′o·chem′is·try, *n.* study of life processes as an aspect of chemistry.

bi′′o·de·grad′able, *adj.* readily decomposed by bacteria.

bi·og′ra·phy, *n., pl.* phies. story of a person's life or career. —bi′′o·graph′i·cal, *adj.* —bi·og′ra·pher, *n.*

bi·ol′o·gy, *n.* study of animals and

plants. —bi''o·log'i·cal, adj. —bi·ol'o·gist, n.

bi·o''nics, n. the study of living systems for application to mechanical or electronic systems.

bi''o·phys'ics, n. study of biological phenomena as related to physics. —bi''o·phys'i·cal, adj. —bi''o·phys'i·cist, n.

bi'ped, n. two-footed animal.

birch, n. hardwood tree with smooth bark.

bird, n. warm-blooded, feathered, flying animal.

bird's-eye, adj. taken from high above, as a view.

birth, n. 1. emergence from a womb, egg, etc. 2. heredity. 3. origin or beginning. —birth'mark'', n. —birth'place'', n. —birth'rate'', n. —birth'right'', n.

birth'day'', n. anniversary of one's birth.

bis'cuit, n., pl. -cuits, -cuit. 1. small, hard-baked cookie or cracker. 2. breadlike lump eaten esp. with gravy.

bi'sect, v.t. divide in two parts, esp. equal ones.

bish'op, n. 1. clergyman overseeing a number of local churches or parishes. 2. chessman moving diagonally an unlimited number of squares. —bish'op·ric, n.

bi'son, n. shaggy, large North American mammal.

bit, n. 1. small piece or amount. 2. boring tool. 3. metal mouthpiece for controlling a horse. 4. (computers) one binary digit or piece of data.

bitch, n. 1. female dog. 2. Informal. disagreeable woman. —bitch'y, adj.

bite, v., bit, bitten, biting, n. v.t. 1. close one's jaws firmly upon. 2. cut or eat into. —v.i. 3. make a biting motion. —n. 4. wound from being bitten. 5. snack. 6. ability to wound or disturb one's feelings.

bit'ing, adj. wounding to the feelings. —bit'ing·ly, adv.

bit'ter, adj. 1. harsh-tasting. 2. causing much suffering. 3. extremely resentful. —bit'ter·ly, adv. —bit'ter·ness, n.

bit'ter·sweet'', adj. causing both sadness and pleasure.

bituminous coal, soft coal, yielding tar when burned.

bi'valve'', n. mollusk with two hinged shells.

biv'ou·ac, n., v.i., -acked, -acking. n. 1. temporary encampment. —v.i. 2. camp in a bivouac.

bi·week'ly, adj., adv. every two weeks.

bi·zarre', adj. odd; grotesque.

blab, v., blabbed, blabbing, n. v.t., v.i. 1. reveal, as a secret. —v.i., n. 2. chatter.

black, n. 1. perfectly dark color, opposite to white in shading. 2. something that is black, e.g. clothes. 3. person of central African descent; negro. —adj. 4.

of the color black. 5. negro. 6. dejected or sullen. 7. evil. —black'ness, n.

black'ball'', v.t. exclude or prevent from being a member.

black belt, belt denoting highest skill in karate or judo.

black'ber''ry, n., pl. ries. dark berry of various types of bramble.

black'bird'', n. bird whose male has black plumage.

black'board'', n. board of slate or other material for writing on with chalk.

black'en, v.t. 1. make black. 2. defame. —v.i. 3. become black.

black eye, 1. discoloration around the eye from a blow. 2. something causing disrepute.

black'jack'', n. 1. small, flexible club. 2. card game.

black'list'', n. 1. list of persons out of favor. —v.t. 2. put on such a list.

black'mail'', n. 1. extortion by threats, esp. to reveal harmful information. —v.t. 2. practice blackmail on. —black'mail''er, n.

black mark, something unfavorable recorded against one.

black market, unlawful system for selling legally restricted goods. —black marketeer.

black'out'', n. 1. putting-out of lights, as in a play or during an air raid. 2. sudden loss of consciousness.

black sheep, disreputable member, esp. of a family.

black'smith'', n. person who forges iron by hand.

blad'der, n. 1. sac for collecting and discharging body fluids. 2. any of various bags for air or liquid.

blade, n. 1. metal part with a cutting edge or point. 2. leaf, esp. of grass.

blame, v.t., blamed, blaming, n. v.t. 1. accuse for a fault. 2. put the responsibility for on someone. 3. fail to sympathize with or understand. —n. 4. responsibility. —blame'less, adj. —blame'less·ly, adv. —blame'less·ness, n. —blame'wor''thy, adj.

blanch, v.t., v.i. turn pale or white.

blan'dish, v.t. flatter or coax. —blan'dish·ment, n.

blank, adj. 1. free of marks, as paper. 2. without thought, expression, etc. 3. unmitigated. —n. 4. blank piece of paper. 5. blank space. 6. cartridge without a missile. 7. lapse of awareness. —blank'ly, adv. —blank'ness, n.

blank'et, n. 1. warm bedcover. 2. broad or thick cover. —v.t. 3. cover or obscure, as if with a blanket. —adv. 4. covering all or many possibilities.

blare, v., blared, blaring, n. v.i., v.t. 1. sound loudly and harshly. —n. 2. loud, harsh sound. 3. ostentation.

blar'ney, n. wheedling, flattering talk.

bla·sé', adj. bored from over-familiarity.

blas·pheme', *v.t.*, **-phemed, -pheming.** speak sacrilegiously of. **—blas·phem'er,***n.* **—blas'phem·y,** *n.* **—blas'phem·ous,** *adj.*

blast, *v.t.* **1.** shatter, as with lightning or explosives. **2.** criticize harshly. **—v.i. 3.** blow violently. **—n. 4.** explosion or explosive force. **5.** violent rush of air. **6.** loud sound, as on a trumpet.

blast furnace, furnace for smelting iron, using a blast of air for draft.

blast'off", *n.* departure of a rocket.

bla'tant, *adj.* shamelessly obvious. **—bla'tant·ly,** *adv.* **—bla'tan·cy,** *n.*

blaze, *v.,* **blazed, blazing,** *n. v.t.* **1.** indicate the route of, esp. by cutting the bark of trees. **—v.i. 2.** burn brightly. **—n. 3.** bright fire. **4.** brilliant display. **5.** cut made on tree bark in blazing a trail.

blaz'er, *n.* jacket in a solid color, often with the badge of a school, etc.

bleach, *v.t., v.i.* **1.** make or become light in color. **—n. 2.** something used for bleaching.

bleach'ers, *n., pl.* tiers of benches for spectators.

bleak, *adj.* **1.** barren and gloomy. **2.** unpromising; without hope. **—bleak'ly,** *adv.* **—bleak'ness,** *n.*

blear'y, *adj.,* **-ier, -iest.** blurred, as the eyes.

bleat, *v.i.* **1.** utter a light cry, as a goat or calf. **—n. 2.** cry made by such an animal.

bleed, *v.,* **bled, bleeding,** *v.i.* **1.** lose blood. **2.** feel sympathetic grief. **—v.t. 3.** cause to lose blood. **4.** practice embezzlement or extortion upon.

blem'ish, *n.* **1.** skin flaw. **2.** flaw or defacement. **—v.t. 3.** make or form a blemish upon.

blench, *v.i.* **1.** become pale. **2.** flinch.

blend, *v.,* **blended, blending,** *n. v.t.* **1.** mix. **2.** shade into each other. **—v.i. 3.** mix. **4.** harmonize. **—n. 5.** mixture. **—blend'er,** *n.*

bless, *v.t.,* **blessed, blessing. 1.** invoke divine favor for. **2.** approve heartily. **3.** confer happiness upon. **—bles'sed,** *adj.* **—bles'sed·ly,** *adv.* **—bles'sed·ness,** *n.*

bles'sing, *n.* **1.** invocation of divine favor. **2.** approval. **3.** favorable event or circumstance.

blight, *n.* **1.** plant disease. **2.** deterioration. **3.** source of deterioration. **—v.t. 4.** put a blight on.

blimp, *n.* lighter-than-air vehicle without a rigid frame.

blind, *adj.* **1.** without eyesight. **2.** without perception. **3.** closed at the end or rear. **4.** hidden. **5.** beyond human reason or control. **—n. 6.** device for shutting out light or view. **7.** deceptive ruse. **—v.t. 8.** make blind. **—blind'ly,** *adv.* **—blind'ness,** *n.*

blind'fold", *n.* **1.** device to prevent a per-

son temporarily from seeing. **—v.t. 2.** put a blindfold on.

blink, *v.i.* **1.** wink repeatedly. **2.** go on and off repeatedly, as a light. **—v.t. 3.** cause to blink.

bliss, *n.* intense, tranquil happiness. **—bliss'ful,** *adj.*

blis'ter, *n.* **1.** raised area of skin enclosing watery matter. **2.** anything similar in form. **3.** form blisters on. **—v.i. 4.** become blistered.

blithe, *adj.* cheerful. **—blithe'ly,** *adv.* **—blithe'ness,** *n.*

blitz, *n.* sudden, massive attack.

bliz'zard, *n.* heavy storm of snow and wind.

bloat, *v.t.* swell abnormally.

blob, *n.* small, round form.

bloc, *n.* group of organizations or persons united in a common interest.

block, *n.* **1.** thick, short piece of material. **2.** auctioneer's platform. **3.** Also, **blockage,** obstruction. **4.** urban area bounded by streets. **—v.t. 5.** obstruct.

block·ade', *n.,* *v.t.,* **-aded, -ading.** *n.* **1.** barrier to navigation, created by warships, etc. **—v.t. 2.** impose such a barrier on.

block'head", *n.* stupid person.

block'house", *n.* fortified retreat.

blond, *adj.* **1.** having light hair and skin. **—n. 2.** blond person. Also, *fem.,* **blonde.**

blood, *n.* **1.** fluid in the arteries of animals. **2.** lineage. **3.** temperament. **4.** kinship. **5.** bloodshed. **—blood'less,** *adj.*

blood'curd"ling, *adj.* horrifying.

blood'hound", *n.* large hound tracking by scent.

blood'shed", *n.* killing.

blood'shot", *adj.* reddened from broken veins, as the eyes.

blood'thirst"y, *adj.* eager to kill. **—blood'thirst"i·ness,** *n.*

blood'y, *adj.,* **-ier, -iest. 1.** covered with blood. **2.** involving much bloodshed.

bloom, *v.i.* **1.** put forth flowers. **2.** be full of health or youth. **—n. 3.** flower. **4.** period or state of flowering.

blos'som, *n.* **1.** flower, esp. of a fruit. **—v.i. 2.** put forth blossoms.

blot, *n., v.,* **blotted, blotting.** *n.* **1.** stain, as from ink. **2.** something that mars or discredits. **—v.t. 3.** stain. **4.** efface. **5.** dry, as writing in ink. **—v.i. 6.** make blots.

blotch, *n.* **1.** skin discoloration. **—v.t. 2.** mark with blotches. **—blotch'y,** *adj.*

blot'ter, *n.* **1.** sheet for blotting up excess ink. **2.** log of events, esp. in a police station.

blouse, *n.* loose shirt.

blow, *v.,* **blew, blown, blowing,** *n. v.i.* **1.** move, as wind. **2.** exhale with force. **3.** **blow over, a.** pass by, as a storm. **b.**

cease to be troublesome, as a scandal.
—*v.t.* 4. drive with wind or breath. 5.
cause to sound with the breath, as a
horn. 6. **blow up, a.** inflate. **b.** explode. **c.** enlarge. —*n.* 7. stroke, as
with a fist or club. 8. saddening shock.
—**blow'er,** *n.*

blow'out", *n.* break of an automobile
tire.

blow'torch", *n.* lamp for burning or
melting.

blub'ber, *n.* 1. whale fat. —*v.i.* 2. weep
noisily. —**blub'ber·y,** *adj.* —**blub'ber·
er,** *n.*

blud'geon, *n.* 1. short club. —*v.t.* 2. beat
with a bludgeon. 3. coerce.

blue, *n.* 1. primary color, that of a clear
sky. 2. **blues, a.** jazz tune with a slow
tempo, and words, and a certain har-
monic pattern. **b.** mental depression.
—*adj.* 3. of the color blue. 4. sad.

blue'ber"ry, *n., pl.* **-ries.** shrub with
blue-black berries.

blue'blood", *n.* person of distinguished
ancestry. —**blue'blood"ed,** *adj.*

blue'-col'lar, *adj.* pertaining to manual
workers.

blue'jay", *n.* blue North American bird.

blue law, law restricting commerce or recreation on a quasi-religious basis.

blue'print", *n.* 1. photographic reproduction of a measured drawing, appearing
as white on blue. 2. any plan or project. —*v.t.* 3. reproduce or present as a
blueprint.

blue'stock"ing, *n.* female pedant.

bluff, *v.t.* 1. deceive with an air of frank-
ness or assurance. —*adj.* 2. frank or
abrupt in manner. 3. rising steeply.
—*n.* 4. steep cliff or ridge. 5. act or instance of bluffing.

blun'der, *n.* 1. avoidable error. —*v.i.* 2.
make such an error. 3. move unthinkingly or awkwardly. —**blun'der·er,** *n.*

blunt, *adj.* 1. with a dull edge. 2.
plain-sp⌐ken. —*v.t.* 3. dull the edge
of. —**blunt'ly,** *adv.* —**blunt'ness,** *n.*

blur, *v.,* **blurred, blurring,** *n. v.t.* 1. cause
to lose sharpness or clarity. —*v.i.* 2.
become indistinct. —*n.* 3. something
that blurs; smear. 4. indistinct image or
impression. —**blur'ry,** *adj.* —**blur'ri·
ness,** *n.*

blurt, *v.t.* say impulsively.

blush, *v.i.* 1. become red in the face with
embarrassment or anger. 2. be
ashamed. —*n.* 3. redness in the face. 4.
pink tone.

blus'ter, *v.i.* 1. roar, as the wind. 2. pretend rage, bravery, etc. —*n.* 3. pretense of rage, bravery, etc. —**blus'ter·
er,** *n.*

boar, *n.* 1. ungelded male pig. 2. wild
hog.

board, *n.* 1. long, flat piece of wood. 2.
sheet of fibrous material. 3. meals as

part of one's accommodations. 4. administrative group. 5. **on board,** on or
onto a ship, airplane, train, etc. —*v.t.*
6. go on or onto, as a ship. 7. pay for
the accommodations, with meals, of.
—*v.i.* 8. live as a boarder. —**board'er,**
n.

boarding house, house offering lodgings
with board.

boast, *v.i.* 1. talk to excess about one's
merits or accomplishments. —*n.* 2.
boasting remark. 3. something boasted
about. —**boast'er,** *n.* —**boast'ful,** *adj.*
—**boast'ful·ly,** *adv.* —**boast'ful·ness,**
n.

boat, *n.* 1. small vessel or craft. 2. loosely, any ship. 3. container with curved
sides converging at the ends. —*v.i.* 4.
travel in a boat, esp. for recreation.
—**boat'man,** *n.*

boat·swain (bō'sən), *n.* petty officer in
charge of a deck crew.

bob, *v.,* **bobbed, bobbing,** *n. v.t.* 1. cut in
a short hairdo. —*v.i.* 2. sink, then rise
again quickly. —*n.* 3. short hairdo. 4.
quick sinking and rising movement. 5.
weight hung from a line or pendulum.

bob'sled", *n.,* **sledded, sledding.** *n.*
1. long high-speed sled. —*v.i.* 2. ride in
such a sled.

bock, *n.* dark beer.

bode, *v.t.,* **boded, boding. bode ill** or
well; foretell bad or good events.

bod'i·ly, *adj.* 1. pertaining to the body.
—*adv.* 2. physically.

bod'y, *n., pl.* **-ies.** *n.* 1. physical part of a
man or animal. 2. corpse. 3. part of a
vehicle that encloses passengers or
freight. 4. distinct area of water or
land. 5. object in outer space. 6. group
or organization. 7. richness or flavor.

bod'y·guard", *n.* person or group protecting against attack.

bog, *n., v.* **bogged, bogging.** *n.* 1. marshy
or spongy area. —*v.t., v.i.* 2. sink into
a bog. 3. slow or halt, as in accomplishing something. —**bog'gy,** *adj.*

bog'gle, *v.i.,* **-gled, -gling.** hesitate.

bo'gus, *adj.* false.

bo'gy·man", *n., pl.* **-men.** imaginary demon. Also **bo'gey·man".**

boil, *v.t.* 1. heat in water that bubbles
from being heated. 2. heat to bubbling.
—*v.i.* 3. be heated in either of these
ways. 4. seethe, as with rage. —*n.* 5.
enough heat for boiling. 6. inflamed,
pus-filled swelling.

boil'er, *n.* 1. container for boiling things.
2. container for making steam or heating water.

bois'ter·ous, *adj.* 1. rowdy. 2. stormy.
—**bois'ter·ous·ly,** *adv.*

bold, *adj.* 1. daring. 2. presumptuous. 3.
conspicuous. —**bold'ly,** *adv.* —**bold'
ness,** *n.*

bo·lo'gna, *n.* smoked sausage.

bol'ster, *n*. **1.** long pillow. —*v.t.* **2.** prop up.

bolt, *n*. **1.** fastener with a thread; screw. **2.** sliding device for securing a door, etc. **3.** arrow for a crossbow. **4.** stroke of lightning. **5.** sudden dash. **6.** roll, as of cloth. —*v.t.* **7.** fasten or secure with a bolt. **8.** swallow hastily. —*v.i.* **9.** flee or start suddenly.

bomb, *n*. **1.** explosive or incendiary device. —*v.t.* **2.** destroy or attack with bombs.

bom·bard', *v.t.* **1.** attack with bombs or shells. **2.** direct atomic particles against the nuclei of. —**bom·bard'ment**, *n*.

bom''bar·dier', *n*. person who bombs from an airplane.

bom'bast, *n*. grandiose, empty language. —**bom·bas'tic**, *adj*.

bomb'er, *n*. **1.** military plane for dropping bombs. **2.** person who plants bombs.

bomb'shell'', *n*. **1.** bomb. **2.** someone or something sensational.

bona fide (boʹnə fīdʺ, boʹnə fēʹdä) in good faith.

bo·nan'za, *n*. source of prosperity.

bon'bon'', *n*. piece of candy.

bond, *n*. **1.** something that binds. **2.** business obligation. **3.** certificate of money lent at interest to an organization. **4.** monetary guarantee from a bailed prisoner, employee, etc.

bond'age, *n*. servitude.

bone, *n*., *v.t.*, **boned, boning**, *n*. **1.** part of a skeleton. —*v.t.* **2.** remove the bones from.

bon'fire'', *n*. large outdoor fire.

bon mot (bâwʺ mōʹ), *pl*. **bons mots**. witty or pithy remark.

bon'net, *n*. woman's cloth hat with a chin strap.

bo'nus, *n*., *pl*. **-nuses**. payment in addition to that customary.

bon voyage (bâw vwah yahjʹ) good journey: said to someone departing.

bon'y, *adj*., **-ier, -iest**. with bones much in evidence. —**bon'i·ness**, *n*.

boo, *interj*., *n*., *pl*. **boos**, *v.t.*, **booed, booing** *interj*., *n*. **1.** sound made to startle or show disapproval. —*v.t.* **2.** disapprove of with boos.

boo'by, *n*., *pl*. **-bies**. fool. Also, **boob**.

book, *n*. **1.** long piece of writing, etc., published or kept as a distinct entity. **2.** major subdivision of such a piece. **3.** libretto. **4. books**, business accounts. **5.** something suggesting a bound book in form. —*v.t.* **6.** record. **7.** make a reservation for. —**book'bind''er**, *n*. —**book'bind''ing**, *n*. —**book'case''**, *n*. —**book'keep''er**, *n*. —**book'keep''ing**, *n*. —**book'let**, *n*. —**book'shelf''**, *n*. —**book'shop''**, **book'store''**, *n*.

book'end'', *n*. device for holding books upright on a shelf.

book'mak''er, *n*. person who takes bets. Also, *Informal*, **book'ie**.

book'worm'', *n*. person fond of reading.

boom, *n*. **1.** loud, deep, hollow sound. **2.** spar hinged at one end. **3.** flurry of business or industrial activity. —*v.i.* **4.** make a booming noise. **5.** enjoy a boom, as a town or industry.

boom'er·ang'', *n*. **1.** Australian throwing stick that returns to the thrower. —*v.i.* **2.** be harmful to the originator, as a plot.

boon, *n*. favor or blessing.

boon'dog''gle, *n*. piece of meaningless, contrived work.

boor, *n*. uncouth person. —**boor'ish**, *adj*.

boost, *v.t.* **1.** lift from below. **2.** add to the power of. **3.** speak in praise of. —*n*. **4.** act or instance of boosting.

boot, *n*. **1.** shoe with tall sides. —*n*., *v.t.* **2.** kick. —*v.t.* **3.** (computers) to load operating system software.

booth, *n*. small shelter or enclosure.

boot'leg'', *v*., **-legged, -legging**, *adj*. *v.t.* **1.** make or sell unlawfully, esp. liquor. —*v.i.* **2.** act as a bootlegger. —*adj*. **3.** made or sold by bootleggers. —**boot'leg''ger**, *n*.

boo'ty, *n*., *pl*. **-ties**. plunder; spoils.

booze, *n*., *v.i.*, **boozed, boozing**. *Informal n*. **1.** liquor. —*v.i.* **2.** drink liquor heavily.

bo'rax, *n*. **1.** crystalline salt. **2.** *Informal*. cheap, showy furniture.

bor'der, *n*. **1.** edge. **2.** special area along an edge. **3.** political boundary. —*v.t.* **4.** give a border to. **5.** adjoin the edge of. —*v.i.* **6. border on, a.** adjoin. **b.** nearly belong to. —**bor'der·land''**, *n*. —**bor'der·line''**, *n*.

bore, *v*., **bored, boring**, *n*. *v.t.*, *v.i.* **1.** penetrate with a rotating movement. —*v.t.* **2.** dig by boring. **3.** weary by being uninteresting. **4.** cylindrical hollow, e.g. in the barrel of a cannon. **5.** uninteresting person or thing. **6.** petty annoyance. —**bore'dom**, *n*.

bor'ough, *n*. incorporated town.

bor'row, *v.t.* **1.** take and later return. **2.** take for use in one's own creative work. —**bor'row·er**, *n*.

bos'om, *n*. **1.** human breast, esp. as the seat of emotion. **2.** midst.

boss, *n*. **1.** employer or manager. **2.** rounded projection. —*v.t.* **3.** *Informal*. order or control firmly.

bos'sy, *adj*. *Informal*. domineering.

bo'sun, *n*. boatswain.

bot'a·ny, *n*. study of plants. —**bo·tan'i·cal**, **bo·tan'ic**, *adj*. —**bot'a·nist**, *n*.

botch, *v.t.* **1.** ruin, as work. —*n*. **2.** clumsy or ineffectual work.

both, *adj*., *pron*. **1.** one and the other. —*conj*., *adv*. **2.** equally.

both'er, *v.t.* **1.** annoy or worry. —*v.i.* **2.**

take the trouble to do something. —*n.*
3. source of annoyance or worry.
—**both'er·some**, *adj.*

bot'tle, *n., v.t.,* **-tled, -tling.** *n.* 1. container, usually glass and with a stoppable narrow outlet, for liquids and gases. 2. capacity of such a container, used as a measure. —*v.t.* 3. put into a bottle. —**bot'tler**, *n.*

bot'tle·neck'', *n.* obstruction to a flow of work.

bot'tom, *n.* 1. lowermost part. 2. ground under a body of water. 3. cause or meaning. —**bot'tom·less**, *adj.*

bou·doir', *n.* woman's private sitting room.

bough, *n.* limb of a tree.

bouil·lon (bool'yən), *n.* clear broth.

boul'der, *n.* large, rounded stone.

boul'e·vard'', *n.* major city street, often tree-lined.

bounce, *v.,* **bounced, bouncing,** *n.* *v.i.* 1. jump in a new direction after striking a hard surface. —*v.t.* 2. cause to jump in this way. —*n.* 3. act or instance of bouncing. 4. ability to bounce.

bound, *v.i.* 1. jump. 2. run with jumping steps. 3. bounce. —*v.t.* 4. adjoin or determine the boundaries of. —*n.* 5. act or instance of jumping or bouncing. 6. **bounds**, limits. —*adj.* 7. tied or joined. 8. obligated. 9. certain. 10. headed for a specified goal. —**bound'less**, *adj.*

bound'a·ry, *n., pl.* **-ries.** border of an area of land.

bou·quet', *n.* 1. bunch or arrangement of flowers. 2. aroma of wine.

bour·bon, (bər'bən), *n.* American whiskey made from corn mash.

bour·geois (boŏr'zhwah), *n., pl.* **-geois**, *adj.* *n.* 1. member of the bourgeoisie. —*adj.* 2. concerned with money, possessions, social conventions, etc. 3. pertaining to the bourgeoisie.

bour·geoi·sie (boŏr''zhwah zē'), *n., sing.* or *pl.* social class of merchants, businessmen, professionals, clerks, etc.; middle class.

bout, *n.* 1. fight or contest. 2. period or spell.

bou·tique (boō tēk'), *n.* small shop for fashionable goods.

bow (bō for 1-3, 6; bou for 4, 5, 7-9). *n.* 1. springy length of wood for shooting arrows. 2. length of wood for playing various stringed instruments. 3. Also, **bow knot**, knot with two loops. 4. front part of a ship, etc. 5. forward bend of the upper body as a mark of respect or acceptance. —*v.t.* 6. play with a bow. 7. cause to stoop, as beneath a burden. —*v.i.* 8. bend the upper body forward. 9. agree or submit.

bow'el, *n.* 1. intestine. 2. bowels, inner depths.

bowl, *n.* 1. deep, wide-topped container.

—*v.t.* 2. roll with an underhanded motion. —**bowl'er**, *n.*

bow'leg''ged, *adj.* with legs curved outward at the knees.

box, *n.* 1. container, usually rectangular and with a lid. 2. compartment suggesting this in form. 3. blow of the hand. —*v.t.* 4. put into a box. 5. have a fistfight with. —**box'er**, *n.*

boy, *n.* young male. —**boy'hood''**, *n.* —**boy'ish**, *adj.*

boy'cott, *n.* 1. refusal to deal or associate with a person or persons in order to coerce them. —*v.t.* 2. practice a boycott on.

brace, *v.t.,* **braced, bracing,** *n.* *v.t.* 1. stiffen. 2. prepare for an emotional shock. 3. stimulate. —*n.* 4. stiffening device. 5. pair. 6. hand tool for drilling with a bit.

brace'let, *n.* decorative armband.

brack'et, *n.* 1. brace for a corner. 2. horizontally projecting support. classification. —*v.t.* 4. support with brackets.

brad, *n.* thin, small-headed nail.

brag, *v.i.,* **bragged, bragging,** *n.* *v.i.* 1. boast. —*n.* 2. boasting talk. —**brag'ger, brag'gart**, *n.*

braid, *n.* 1. interweaving of three strands of fiber. —*v.t.* 2. make into a braid.

brain, *n.* 1. organ of thought, control of actions, etc. 2. **brains**, **a.** intelligence. **b.** cleverness. —**brain'y**, *adj.*

brain'storm'', *n. Informal.* sudden idea or impulse.

brain'wash'', *v.t.* change the attitudes or beliefs of through psychological conditioning.

braise, *v.t.* **braised, braising.** brown. then simmer, esp. meat.

brake, *n., v.,* **braked, braking.** *n.* 1. device for slowing or stopping machinery. —*v.t.,* *v.i.* 2. slow down or stop with a brake.

brake'man, *n.* assistant to a railroad conductor.

bram'ble, *n.* prickly shrub.

bran, *n.* grain husks separated from flour in milling.

branch, *n.* 1. woodlike extension from the body of a tree, etc. 2. anything derived or extending from a main body, system, etc. —*v.i.* 3. put forth branches. 4. extend as a branch.

brand, *n.* 1. identifying mark or symbol of a company's merchandise. 2. merchandise so identified. 3. identifying mark burned into hide or skin. 4. piece of burning wood. —*v.t.* 5. put a brand on.

bran'dish, *v.t.* wave, as a sword or club.

brand-new, *adj.* wholly new.

bran'dy, *n., pl.* **-dies,** *v.t.,* **-died, -dying.** *n.* 1. distilled grape or other wine. —*v.t.* 2. preserve in brandy.

brash, *adj.* 1. hot-headed. 2. noisy and uncouth. —**brash′ness,** *n.*

brass, *n.* 1. alloy of copper and zinc. 2. brasses, wind instruments of brass. 3. *Informal.* high military officers.

bras·siere′, *n.* supporter for women's breasts.

brat, *n.* ill-behaved child.

bra·va′do, *n.* false courage or confidence.

brave, *adj., n., v.t.,* **braved, braving.** *adj.* 1. courageous. 2. fine-looking. —*n.* 3. American Indian warrior. —*v.t.* 4. encounter defiantly. —**brave′ly,** *adv.* —**brav′er·y, brave′ness,** *n.*

bra′vo, *interj.* well done!

bra·vu′ra, *n.* brilliance or daring.

brawl, *v.i.* 1. fight noisily. —*n.* 2. noisy fight. —**brawl′er,** *n.*

brawn, *n.* muscular strength. —**brawn′y,** *adj.*

bray, *n.* 1. cry of a donkey. —*v.i.* 2. make this or a similar sound.

bra′zen, *adj.* 1. made of brass. 2. shameless. 3. strident. —**bra′zen·ly,** *adv.* —**bra′zen·ness,** *n.*

breach, *n.* 1. opening broken through. 2. violation. 3. rift, as in a friendship. —*v.t.* 4. make a breach in or through.

bread, *n.* 1. food of baked flour, water, etc. 2. livelihood. —*v.t.* 3. coat before cooking with bread crumbs.

breadth, *n.* 1. width. 2. range, as of knowledge.

bread′win″ner, *n.* sole support of a family.

break, *v.,* **broke, broken, breaking,** *n.* *v.t.* 1. force to divide into pieces. 2. put out of repair. 3. terminate. 4. violate. 5. end the effectiveness of. 6. reduce in health, wealth, rank, etc. —*v.i.* 7. force one's way. 8. end a relationship. 9. appear or begin suddenly. 10. pause in activity. 11. be broken. 12. **break down, a.** fail in health or operation. **b.** abandon self-restraint. —*n.* 13. act or instance of breaking. 14. stroke of luck or mercy. 15. pause in activity. 16. change. —**break′age,** *n.* —**break′a·ble,** *adj.*

break″danc·ing, *n.* style of dancing characterized by acrobatic spins and robotic movement.

break′down″, *n.* 1. failure of health or operation. 2. detailed analysis.

break′er, *n.* 1. wave that breaks on the shore. 2. device or person that breaks.

break′fast, *n.* morning meal.

break′neck″, *adj.* reckless, as speed.

break′through″, *n.* 1. act or instance of forcing a way against opposition. 2. major accomplishment or discovery.

break′wa″ter, *n.* wall for breaking the force of waves.

breast, *n.* 1. upper forward part of the body. 2. this part regarded as the seat of the emotions. 3. woman's milk-secreting gland. —*v.t.* 4. oppose or head into forcefully. —**breast′bone″,** *n.* —**breast′-feed″,** *v.t.*

breath, *n.* 1. air going into and out of the lungs. 2. manner of breathing. 3. ability to breathe readily. —**breath′less,** *adj.* —**breath′less·ly,** *adv.* —**breath′y,** *adj.*

breathe, *v.,* **breathed, breathing.** *v.i.* 1. move air into and out of the lungs. —*v.t.* 2. speak or sing, esp. quietly.

breath′tak″ing, *adj.* astonishing or exciting.

breech, *n.* 1. buttocks. 2. loaded end of a gun. 3. **breeches,** trousers.

breed, *v.,* **bred, breeding,** *n. v.t.* 1. give birth to. 2. raise, as animals. 3. be a source of. —*v.i.* 4. give birth to offspring. 5. emerge or proliferate. —*n.* 6. strain, as of animals. 7. type, esp. of person. —**breed′er,** *n.*

breed′ing, *n.* 1. act of one who breeds. 2. manners or character.

breeze, *n., v.i.,* **breezed, breezing.** *n.* 1. light wind. —*v.i.* 2. become a breeze. 3. move briskly or jauntily. —**breez′y,** *adj.*

breth′ren, *n. Archaic.* 1. brothers. 2. monks.

brev′i·ty, *n.* briefness.

brew, *v.t.* 1. make by fermenting malt and hops, as beer. 2. make by any of various means, as beverages or other liquids. 3. plot. —*v.i.* 4. begin to appear or take shape. —*n.* 5. something brewed. —**brew′er,** *n.*

brew′er·y, *n., pl.* **-ies.** place for brewing malt beverages.

briar, *n.* brier.

bribe, *v.t.,* **bribed, bribing,** *n. v.t.* 1. pay to abuse a position of trust. —*n.* 2. payment offered for this. —**brib′er·y,** *n.*

bric′-a-brac″, *n.* miscellaneous decorative objects.

brick, *n.* 1. oblong object of baked or unbaked clay, etc., used in construction. 2. oblong object of any material. —*v.t.* 3. enclose or cover with brickwork. —**brick′lay″er,** *n.* —**brick′work″,** *n.*

bride, *n.* woman at the time of her wedding. —**brid′al,** *adj.* —**brides′maid″,** *n.*

bride′groom″, *n.* man at the time of his wedding.

bridge, *n., v.t.,* **bridged, bridging.** *n.* 1. structure for crossing a stream, valley, etc. 2. any of various connecting structures, etc. 3. control post of a ship. 4. card game for four players. —*v.t.* 5. cross with or as with a bridge.

bridge′head″, *n.* fortified position of invaders.

bri′dle, *n., v.t.,* **-dled, -dling.** *n.* 1. harness for a horse's head. 2. means of restraint. —*v.t.* 3. put a bridle on. 4. restrain.

brief, *adj.* 1. short or concise. —*n.* 2. legal summary. —*v.t.* 3. supply with useful information. —**brief′ly,** *adv.* —**brief′ness,** *n.* —**brief′ing,** *n.*

brief′case″, *n.* handle-held case for business papers.

bri′er, *n.* thorny bush.

brig, *n.* 1. two-masted square-rigged ship. 2. navy or marine prison.

bri·gade′, *n.* 1. military unit formed of battalions. 2. pseudo-military organization.

brig′a·dier general, military officer between a colonel and a major general. Also, **brig″a·dier′.**

bright, *adj.* 1. shedding or reflecting much light. 2. intelligent or mentally active. 3. cheerful. 4. promising. —**bright′ly,** *adv.* —**bright′ness,** *n.* —**bright′en,** *v.t., v.i.*

bril′liant, *adj.* very bright. —**bril′liant·ly,** *adv.* —**bril′liance, bril′lian·cy,** *n.*

brim, *n., v.i.,* **brimmed, brimming.** *n.* 1. rim. —*v.i.* 2. run or run over with liquid.

brin′dled, *adj.* gray or tawny with darker spots. Also **brin′dle.**

brine, *n.* salty water.

bring, *v.t.,* **brought, bringing.** 1. carry or escort to a place. 2. cause as a consequence. 3. **bring about,** cause. 4. **bring out,** make apparent. 5. **bring up,** raise, as children.

brink, *n.* edge or verge.

brisk, *adj.* 1. lively or abrupt. 2. forceful, as the wind. —**brisk′ly,** *adv.* —**brisk′ness,** *n.*

bris′ket, *n.* breast meat.

bris′tle, *n., v.i.,* **-tled, -tling.** *n.* 1. stiff hair, as on a pig. 2. fiber on the head of a brush. —*v.i.* 3. stand up stiffly. 4. be tense with annoyance, etc.

brit′tle, *adj.* easily shattered. —**brit′tle·ness,** *n.*

broach, *v.t.* bring forth as a subject of discussion.

broad, *adj.* 1. wide. 2. diverse. 3. not strict. 4. not detailed. —**broad′ly,** *adv.* —**broad′ness,** *n.* —**broad′en,** *v.t., v.i.*

broad′cast″, *v.t.,* **-cast,** or (for 1) **-casted, -casting** *n. v.t.* 1. send by radio or television. 2. scatter widely. —*n.* 3. radio or television program. —**broad′cast″er,** *n.*

broad′-mind″ed, *adj.* not strict or opinionated. —**broad″-mind′ed·ly,** *adv.* —**broad″-mind′ed·ness,** *n.*

bro·chure′, *n.* pamphlet.

brogue, *n.* Irish accent, esp. in speaking English.

broil, *v.t.* cook with direct heat from a fire, etc. —**broil′er,** *n.*

broke, *adj. Informal.* without money; bankrupt.

brok′en, *adj.* 1. past participle of *break,*

used adjectivally. 2. deprived of spirit, health, etc. 3. badly pronounced, as by a foreigner. 4. discontinuous. —**brok′en·ly,** *adv.*

brok′er, *n.* agent for buying and selling. —**brok′er·age,** *n.*

bron′co, *n., pl.* **-cos.** wild or half-wild horse of the West. Also, **bron′cho.**

bron′to·saur″us, *n.* large herbivorous dinosaur.

bronze, *n., v.t.* **bronzed, bronzing.** *n.* 1. alloy of copper and tin. 2. reddish-brown. —*v.t.* 3. color like or coat with bronze.

brooch, *n.* large ornamental pin.

brood, *n.* 1. group of children or baby chickens. —*v.i.* 2. worry or sulk at length.

brook, *n.* 1. small stream. —*v.t.* 2. endure.

broom, *n.* bundle of straws, etc. attached to a stick and used for sweeping. —**broom′stick″,** *n.*

broth, *n.* soup from boiled meat.

broth′el, *n.* house of prostitution.

broth′er, *n.* 1. son of one's father. 2. fellow-human as an object of love, etc. 3. fellow-member of a religious order, lodge, etc. —**broth′er·hood,** *n.* —**broth′er·ly,** *adj.*

broth′er-in-law″, *n., pl.* **broth′ers-in-law″.** 1. brother of a spouse. 2. husband of a sister or sister-in-law.

brow, *n.* 1. eyebrow. 2. forehead. 3. edge of a cliff.

brow′beat″, *v.t.,* **-beat, -beaten, -beating.** bully,

brown, *n.* 1. color combining red, yellow, and black. —*v.t., v.i.* 2. make or become brown.

browse, *v.i.,* **browsed, browsing.** look idly through things for sale. —**brows′er,** *n.*

bruise, *v.,* **bruised, bruising,** *n. v.t.* 1. injure the skin or surface of with a blow or pressure. 2. hurt, as the feelings. —*v.i.* 3. become bruised. —*n.* 4. mark made by bruising.

brunch, *n. Informal.* meal part-breakfast, part-lunch.

bru·net′, *n.* person with dark hair, esp. when with dark eyes. Also, *fem.,* **bru·nette′.**

brunt, *n.* shock, as of an attack.

brush, *n.* 1. device for cleaning, painting, etc. consisting of bristles on a handle. 2. act or instance of brushing. 3. something suggesting a brush in form. 4. Also, **brush′wood″,** underbrush. —*v.t.* 5. remove′or apply with a brush. 6. apply a brush to. 7. graze lightly in passing.

brush′off″, *n. Informal.* tactless act of dismissing or ignoring someone.

brusque, *adj.* abrupt in manner. —**brusque′ly,** *adv.* —**brusque′ness,** *n.*

bru'tal, *adj.* extremely cruel or harsh. —**bru·tal'i·ty**, *n.*

bru'tal·ize, *v.t.*, **-ized**, **-izing**. 1. make brutal. 2. treat brutally. —**bru''tal·i·za'tion**, *n.*

brute, *adj.* 1. beastlike, esp. in force or lack of intelligence. —*n.* 2. beast. 3. brutal person. —**brut'ish**, *adj.*

bub'ble, *n., v.i.*, **-bled**, **-bling**. *n.* 1. void or body of gas surrounded by a liquid. 2. something bubblelike in roundness and thinness. 3. something insubstantial. —**bub'bly**, *adj.* —*v.i.* 4. give off bubbles.

buc''ca·neer', *n.* pirate, esp. in the Caribbean Sea.

buck, *n.* 1. grown male deer, goat, etc. 2. act or instance of bucking. 3. *Informal.* dollar. —*v.t.* 4. oppose with force. —*v.i.* 5. rear upward, as a horse.

buck'et, *n.* open watertight container.

buck'le, *n., v.*, **-led**, **-ling**. *n.* 1. fastener for two ends of a belt, etc. —*v.t.* 2. fasten with a buckle. 3. cause to bulge or bend, as sheet metal. —*v.i.* 4. bulge or bend.

buck'tooth'', *n.* projecting front tooth. —**buck'toothed'**, *adj.*

buck'wheat'', *n.* wheat with triangular seeds.

bu·col'ic, *adj.* pastoral; serene and countrylike.

bud, *n., v.i.*, **budded**, **budding**. *n.* 1. swelling from which a flower, leaf, etc. grows. —*v.i.* 2. put forth such swellings.

budge, *v.*, **budged**, **budging**. *v.t., v.i.* move by or because of force.

budg'et, *n.* 1. allotment of money, time, etc. for various purposes. —*v.t.* 2. submit to a budget. —**budg'et·ar''y**, *adj.*

buff, *n.* 1. dull tan color. —*v.t.* 2. polish with a soft surface.

buf''fa·lo'', *n., pl.* **-loes**. 1. any of various wild oxen. 2. American bison.

buf'fer, *n.* something that prevents or lessens the shocks of collision.

buf·fet (bəf fā'), *n.* 1. sideboard. 2. meal for eaters helping themselves.

buf·foon', *n.* clownish person. —**buf·foon'er·y**, *n.*

bug, *n., v.t.* **bugged**, **bug·ging**. *n.* 1. insect. 2. (computers) an error in programming. *v.t.* 3. *Informal.* **a.** plant listening devices in. **b.** pester.

bug'gy, *n., pl.* **-gies**. 1. light one-horse carriage. 2. baby carriage.

bu'gle, *n.* trumpetlike brass instrument. —**bu'gler**, *n.*

build, *v.*, **built**, **building**, *n. v.t.* 1. assemble, as a structure. 2. found or base. 3. bring into being or develop. —*v.i.* 4. establish or base something. 5. accumulate. —*n.* 6. frame of the body. —**build'er**, *n.*

build'ing, *n.* habitable construction.

built'-in', *adj.* integral or inherent.

built'-up', *adj.* made from a number of parts.

bulb, *n.* 1. any of various underground plant stems, roots, or buds. 2. something swelling toward the end. —**bulb'ous**, *adj.*

bulge, *n., v.i.*, **bulged**, **bulging**. *n.* 1. swelling. —*v.i.* 2. swell.

bulk, *n.* 1. size or weight. 2. greater or principal part. —*v.i.* 3. be massive or important. —*adj.* 4. shipped without containers. —**bulk'y**, *adj.*

bull, *n.* 1. male ox, elephant, etc. 2. speculator in the rise of stock prices. 3. papal decree. —**bull'ish**, *adj.*

bull'dog'', *n.* small, heavy-built fighting dog.

bull'doze'', *v.t.*, **-dozed**, **-dozing**. 1. push or level earth. 2. *Informal.* force with aggressiveness. —**bull'doz·er**, *n.*

bul'let, *n.* pointed projectile from a firearm. —**bul'let-proof''**, *adj.*

bul'le·tin, *n.* 1. announcement, esp. of news. 2. official publication.

bul'lion, *n.* ingots of precious metal.

bulls'eye'', *n.* 1. center of a target. 2. direct hit.

bul'ly, *n., pl.* **-lies**, *v.t.*, **-lied**, **-lying**. *n.* 1. person who injures or threatens weaker persons. —*v.t.* 2. act as a bully toward.

bul'wark, *n.* defensive wall or barrier.

bum, *n., v.*, **bummed**, **bumming**. *n.* 1. poor person who refuses to work. —*v.i.* 2. live as a bum. —*v.t.* 3. obtain by begging.

bum'ble·bee'', *n.* yellow-and-black bee.

bump, *v.t.* 1. collide with, esp. not violently. —*v.i.* 2. move over a bumpy surface. 3. **bump into**, **a.** collide with. **b.** *Informal.* meet by chance. —*n.* 4. act or instance of bumping or of being bumped. 5. surface unevenness or swelling. —**bump'y**, *adj.*

bump'er, *n.* 1. device to receive the shock of collisions. —*adj.* 2. especially abundant, as a crop.

bump'tious, *adj.* annoyingly self-assertive. —**bump'tious·ly**, *adv.*

bun, *n.* small baked roll.

bunch, *n.* 1. small cluster. 2. *Informal.* group of persons. —*v.t., v.i.* 3. gather into a bunch.

bun'dle, *n., v.t.*, **-dled**, **-dling**. *n.* 1. group of things bound or wrapped together. —*v.t.* 2. make into a bundle.

bun'ga·low'', *n.* one-storied cottage.

bun'gle, *v.*, **-gled**, **-gling**, *n. v.t., v.i.* 1. do or act stupidly. —*n.* 2. act or instance of bungling. —**bun'gler**, *n.*

bun'ion, *n.* inflamed swelling at the joint of the big toe.

bunk, *n.* 1. flat frame serving as a bed, esp. in barracks, camps, or ships. 2. *Informal.* false statements. —*v.i.* 3. sleep in a bunk. —**bunk'house''**, *n.*

bunk'er, *n.* 1. storage space for coal, etc.

2. underground shelter against bombs or shells.

bun'ny, *n., pl.* **-nies.** *Informal.* rabbit.

bun'ting, *n.* cloth for making flags or flaglike decorations.

buoy, *n.* 1. floating signal or marker. 2. life preserver. *v.t.* 3. lift up, as the spirits. 4. keep afloat.

buoy'ant, *adj.* cheerful or optimistic. —**buoy'an·cy,** *n.*

bur, *n.* 1. seed capsule with sharp, clinging extensions. 2. burr.

bur'den, *n.* 1. heavy load. 2. theme. 3. chorus or refrain. —*v.t.* 4. put a load upon. —**bur'den·some,** *adj.*

bu'reau, *n., pl.* **-reaus, -reaux.** 1. official agency or department. 2. chest of drawers.

bu·reau·cra·cy, (byōo rah'krə sē), *n., pl.* **-cies.** 1. government by officials. 2. government departments as a source of political power, obstruction to progress, etc. —**bu'reau·crat",** *n.* —**bu" reau·crat'ic,** *adj.*

bur'glar, *n.* person who breaks into buildings, esp. to steal. —**bur'gla·ry,** *n.* —**bur'glar·ize",** *v.t.*

bur'i·al, *n.* burying of the dead.

bur'lap, *n.* coarse jute or hemp cloth.

bur·lesque", *n., v.t.,* **-lesqued, -lesquing.** *n.* 1. sexually allusive vaudeville. 2. satirical parody. —*v.t.* 3. make the subject of a burlesque.

bur'ly, *adj.,* **-lier, -liest.** big and strong. —**bur'li·ness,** *n.*

burn, *v.,* **burned.** or **burnt, burning.** *v.t.* 1. use as fuel. 2. damage with heat. 3. create or finish with fire or intense heat. 4. damage with acids, etc. —*v.i.* 5. be on fire. 6. give out light or heat. 7. be damaged by heat. 8. be full of eagerness or passion. —*n.* 9. burned place. —**burn'a·ble,** *adj.*

burn'er, *n.* device for applying intense heat.

bur'nish, *v.t.* rub to a polish.

burn"out", *n.* lethargy resulting from excess stress.

burp, *Informal. n., v.i.* 1. belch. —*v.t.* 2. cause to burp.

burr, *n.* 1. rough edge on cut metal. 2. rough trilling of the sound *r*, as by a Scot.

bur'row, *n.* 1. hole of a digging animal. —*v.i.* 2. dig deep holes. 3. hide in or as if in a burrow.

burst, *v.,* **burst, bursting,** *n. v.i.* 1. be torn apart, as from pressure. 2. make a sudden and vehement beginning into song, tears, etc. 3. cause to be torn apart. —*n.* 4. act or instance of bursting. 5. sudden show of energy. 6. volley of shots.

bury, *v.t.,* **-ied, -ying.** 1. put under earth or other material. 2. entomb. 3. put out of sight or notice. 4. immerse, as in work.

bus, *n., pl.* **-es, -ses,** *v.t.* **-ed** or **-sed, -ing** or **-sing.** *n.* 1. vehicle for many passengers. 2. (computers) a circuit for connecting two components. —*v.t.* 3. transport by bus.

bush, *n.* 1. low, spreading woody plant. 2. land overgrown with bushes. —**bush'y,** *adj.*

bush'el, *n.* dry measure of 4 pecks or 32 quarts.

bus'i·ly, *adv.* in a busy manner.

busi'ness, *n.* 1. type of work or commerce. 2. duty or task. 3. rightful concern. 4. commerce. 5. event or affair. 6. **mean business,** have earnest intentions. —**busi'ness·man,** *n.* —**busi'ness· wom"an,** *n.*

busi'ness·like", *adj.* efficient.

bust, *n.* 1. head, neck, and upper part of the chest. 2. sculpture of these parts. 3. *Informal.* **a.** failure. **b.** bankruptcy. —*v.t., v.i.* 4. *Informal.* break or burst.

bus'tle, *n., v.i.,* **-tled, -tling.** *n.* 1. activity, as of a crowd. —*v.i.* 2. move hurriedly.

bus'y, *adj.,* **-ier, -iest,** *v.t.,* **-ied, -ying.** *adj.* 1. with much to do. 2. in action or use. 3. full of distracting elements, as a decoration. —*v.t.* 4. cause to be busy. —**bus'y·ness,** *n.*

bus'y·bod"y, *n., pl.* **-ies.** gossipy or meddlesome person.

but, *prep.* 1. except for. —*conj.* 2. and yet. 3. on the other hand. —*adv.* 4. only; merely. 5. just; only.

butch'er, *n.* 1. slaughterer or seller of meat. —*v.t.* 2. slaughter. —**butch'er·y,** *n.*

but'ler, *n.* head male house servant.

butt, *n.* 1. thick end. 2. remnant of a smoked cigarette or cigar. 3. target. 4. act or instance of butting. —*v.t.* 5. ram with the head. 6. join without overlapping.

butte, *n.* steep hill isolated in flat land.

but'ter, *n.* 1. solid product made from churned cream. —*v.t.* 2. spread with butter. 3. **butter up,** *Informal.* ingratiate oneself with. —**but'ter·fat",** *n.*

but'ter·fly", *n., pl.* **-flies.** slender-bodied four-winged insect.

but'ter·milk", *n.* liquid remaining after butter is made of cream.

but'ter·scotch", *n.* candy of brown sugar, butter, etc.

but'tocks, *n., pl.* part on which one sits.

but'ton, *n.* 1. broad object passed through holes or loops in cloth as a fastener. 2. object pushed to operate a control mechanism. 3. large badge with a slogan, etc. —*v.t., v.i.* 4. fasten with buttons. —**but'ton·hole",** *n.*

but'tress, *n.* 1. heavy mass resisting a thrust, as that of an arch. —*v.t.* 2. give stability or support to.

bux'om, *adj.* attractively plump.

buy, *v.t.,* **bought, buying,** *n. v.t.* **1.** get in return for money. **2.** *Informal.* accept as true or wise. —*n.* **3.** *Informal.* something cheap at the price. —**buy′er,** *n.*

buzz, *v.i.* **1.** make a deep, rough hum. —*n.* **2.** hum of this sort. —**buzz′er,** *n.*

buz′zard, *n.* **1.** type of slow hawk. **2.** type of vulture.

by, *prep.* **1.** close to. **2.** past. **3.** a multiplier or other dimension being. **4.** in measures or units of. **5.** after. **6.** during the time of day or night. **7.** not later than. **8.** through the agency of. **9.** according to. **10.** by way of, **a.** past or through. **b.** as a means or form of. **11.** in readiness. **12.** aside. **13.** past. —**by′stand″er,** *n.*

by′gone″, *adj.* in the past.

by′gones″, *n., pl.* past events.

by′law″, *n.* rule for an organization's internal affairs.

by′pass″, *n.* route, etc. serving as an alternate way between two points.

by′-prod″uct, *n.* product incidental to a main one. Also, **by′prod″uct.**

byte, *n.* (computers) a group of eight bits of data.

C

C, c, *n.* **1.** third letter of the English alphabet. **2.** third best grade. **3.** centigrade.

cab, *n.* **1.** chauffeured vehicle for hire. **2.** shelter for the operator of a locomotive, etc.

ca·bal′, *n.* **1.** group of intriguers. **2.** intrigue of such a group.

cab·a·ret (kab″ə rā′), *n.* restaurant with musical entertainment.

cab′bage, *n.* vegetable with a head of thick leaves.

cab′in, *n.* **1.** primitive house. **2.** passenger room on a ship. **3.** passenger space in an airplane.

cab′i·net, *n.* **1.** boxlike piece of furniture. **2.** body of officials reporting to a head of state. —**cab′i·net·mak″er,** *n.* —**cab′i·net·work″,** *n.*

ca′ble, *n., v.t.,* **-bled, -bling.** *n.* **1.** heavy rope. **2.** heavy electric wire. **3.** cablegram. —*v.t.* **4.** send a cablegram to.

ca′ble·gram″, *n.* transoceanic telegraph message.

ca·boose′, *n.* car for the conductor and brakemen of a freight train.

cache. (kash), *n., v.t.,* **cached, caching.** *n.* **1.** hiding place, esp. for food and supplies. **2.** goods hidden in such a place. —*v.t.* **3.** put in a cache.

cack′le, *v.i.,* **-led, -ling,** *n. v.i.* **1.** make henlike noises. —*n.* **2.** henlike noise. **3.** *Informal.* busy, meaningless talk.

ca·coph′o·ny, *n., pl.* **-nies.** harsh, disagreeable sound. —**ca·coph′o·nous,** *adj.*

cac′tus, *n., pl.* **-tuses, -ti.** prickly desert plant.

cad, *n.* violator of a gentlemanly code. —**cad′dish,** *adj.*

ca·dav′er, *n.* corpse. —**ca·dav′er·ous,** *adj.*

cad′die, *n.* person who carries a golfer's clubs. Also, **cad′dy.**

ca′dence, *n.* **1.** rise and fall of a speaking voice. **2.** marching rhythm. **3.** end of a musical phrase.

ca·det′, *n.* **1.** military student. **2.** trainee.

cadge, *v.,* **cadged, cadging.** *v.t., v.i.* **1.** beg. —*v.t.* **2.** get by begging. —**cadg′er,** *n.*

ca′dre, *n.* organizational nucleus, esp. of military officers.

ca·fe (ka fā′), *n.* small restaurant. Also, **ca·fé′.**

caf″e·te′ri·a, *n.* self-service restaurant.

caf·feine′, *n.* stimulant in coffee or tea. Also, **caf·fein′.**

cage, *n. v.t.,* **caged, caging.** *n.* **1.** open-work structure for confinement. **2.** openwork structure of any kind. —*v.t.* **3.** confine in a cage.

ca·hoots′, *Informal.* **in cahoots with,** in a conspiracy with.

cais′son, *n.* **1.** watertight chamber for work under water. **2.** ammunition wagon.

ca·jole′, *v.t.,* **-joled, -joling.** coax or wheedle. —**ca·jol′er·y,** *n.*

cake, *n., v.,* **caked, caking.** *n.* **1.** sweetened piece of baked dough. **2.** flat piece of food, fried or baked. **3.** piece of soap. —*v.t., v.i.* **4.** cover with or form a solid crust.

ca·lam′i·ty, *n., pl.* **-ties.** disaster. —**ca·lam′i·tous,** *adj.*

cal′cu·late″, *v.,* **-lated, -lation.** *v.t.* **1.** ascertain through rational means. **2.** plan methodically. —*v.i.* **3.** reckon. **4.** rely. —**cal′cu·la″tor,** *n.* —**cal″cu·la′tion,** *n.* —**cal′cu·la·ble,** *adj.*

cal′cu·lat″ed, *adj.* intended to produce the actual result.

cal′cu·lat″ing, *adj.* scheming.

cal′cu·lus, *n.* method used in higher mathematics.

cal′dron, *n.* large kettle.

cal′en·dar, *n.* **1.** printed object or device for determining the day of the month, etc. **2.** system for reckoning the years. **3.** schedule of agenda.

cal′en·der, *n.* **1.** machine for giving a smooth finish. —*v.t.* **2.** smooth in a calender.

calf, *n., pl.* **calves.** *n.* **1.** young cow or bull. **2.** fleshy part of the lower leg. —**calf′skin″,** *n.*

cal′i·ber, *n.* 1. diameter of a bullet, gun bore, etc. 2. quality of character. Also, **cal′i·bre.**

cal′i·brate″, *v.t.*, **-brated, -brating.** 1. establish the scale of measurements of. 2. determine the caliber of. —**cal″i·bra′tion,** *n.*

cal′i·co″, *n., pl.* **-coes, -cos.** printed cotton.

cal′i·per, *n.* device for measuring outside or inside diameters. Also, **cal′i·pers.**

cal″is·then′ics, *n. pl.* athletic exercises.

calk, *v.t.* caulk.

call, *v.t.* 1. utter loudly. 2. summon. 3. name or describe. 4. telephone. 5. awaken. —*v.i.* 6. make an order or request. 7. impose a demand. 8. make a visit. 9. cry, as an animal. 10. shout. —*n.* 11. act or instance of calling. 12. urge or appeal. —**call′er,** *n.*

cal·lig″ra·phy′, *n.* handwriting, penmanship, often ornamental.

call′ing, *n.* vocation.

cal·li′o·pe″, *n.* organ of s ㅁam whistles.

cal′lous, *adj.* insensitive to the sufferings of others. —**cal′lous·ly,** *adv.* —**cal′lous·ness,** *cal·los′i·ty,* *n.*

cal′low, *adj.* immature or inexperienced. —**cal′low·ness,** *n.*

cal′lus, *n., pl.* **-luses.** hard thickening on the skin.

calm, *adj.* 1. without strong emotion. 2. undisturbed. —*n.* 3. state of quiet. —*v.t.* 4. make quiet or tranquil. —**calm′ly,** *adv.* —**calm′ness,** *n.*

cal′o·rie, *n.* unit of heat measurement.

cal′um·ny, *n., pl.* **-nies.** slander.

cam, *n.* rotating machine part producing reciprocating motion.

ca″ma·ra′de·rie, *n.* cheerful companionship.

cam′ber, *n.* shallow upward curve.

cam′bric, *n.* fine linen or cotton.

cam′cor·der, *n.* combined portable video camera and recorder.

cam′el, *n.* desert animal storing water in one or two humps.

cam′e·o, *n., pl.* **-os.** gem of contrasting layers of stone.

cam′er·a, *n.* 1. boxlike device for taking photographs, shooting movie film, etc. 2. optical device for copying a view. —**cam′er·a·man,** *n.*

cam·ou·flage (kam′ə flahzh″) *n., v.t.* **-flaged, -flaging.** *n.* 1. paintwork, etc. making something hard to see or interpret. —*v.t.* 2. apply camouflage to.

camp, *n.* 1. temporary residence in the open. 2. recreation area in the country. —*v.i.* 3. establish or live in a camp. —**camp′fire″,** *n.* —**camp′site″,** *n.* —**camp′er,** *n.*

cam·paign′, *n.* 1. series of operations to attain a planned goal. —*v.i.* 2. act in a campaign. —**cam·paign′er,** *n.*

cam′phor, *n.* aromatic crystalline substance.

cam′pus, *n., pl.* **-puses.** 1. open area of lawn and trees, esp. the grounds of a school. 2. academic community.

can, *v.i.,* past tense **could** for 1 and 2, **canned, canning** for 3, *n. v.i.* 1. be able or know how to. 2. have the right to. 3. preserve in sealed cans or jars. —*n.* 4. metal container sealed to preserve food, etc. 5. cylindrical container, esp. of sheet metal. —**can′ner,** *n.*

ca·nal′, *n.* artificial waterway.

ca·nard′, *n.* rumour, esp. a malicious one.

ca·nar′y, *n., pl.* **-ies.** yellow songbird.

can′cel, *v.t.,* **-celed, -celing.** 1. cover with marks, esp. in order to invalidate. 2. invalidate or terminate. 3. *Math.* remove from both sides of an equation. —**can″cel·la′tion,** *n.*

can′cer, *n.* spreading malignant tumor. —**can′cer·ous,** *adj.*

can″de·la′brum, *n., pl.* **-bra.** branched candlestick.

can′did, *adj.* 1. frank. 2. unposed, as a snapshot. —**can′did·ly,** *adv.* —**can′dor, can′did·ness,** *n.*

can′di·date″, *n.* competitor for public office, an honor, etc. —**can′di·da·cy,** *n.*

can′dle, *n., v.t.,* **-dled, -dling.** *n.* 1. cylinder of wax, etc. with a central wick for burning. —*v.t.* 2. inspect against a light, as eggs.

can′dle·stick″, *n.* holder for candles.

can′dy, *n., pl.* **-dies,** *v.t.,* **-died, -dying.** *n.* 1. flavored sweet. —*v.t.* 2. cook in sugar. 3. form into sugar crystals.

cane, *n., v.t.,* **caned, caning.** *n.* 1. hollow, jointed plant stalk. 2. stick held while walking. —*v.t.* 3. stretch with split rattan, as a chair seat. 4. beat with a cane.

ca′nine, *adj.* 1. pertaining to dogs. 2. pertaining to wolves or foxes. —*n.* 3. dog, wolf, or fox. 4. sharp human tooth.

can′is·ter, *n.* small storage can used in a kitchen.

can′ker, *n.* ulcerous sore.

can′ner·y, *n., pl.* **-ries.** plant for canning food.

can′ni·bal, *n.* person or animal that eats its own kind. —**can′ni·bal·ism,** *n.*

can′ni·bal·ize″, *v.t.,* **-ized, -izing.** strip in order to reuse parts.

can′non, *n., pl.* **-nons, -non.** heavy gun.

can″non·ade′, *n.* continuous firing of cannon.

can·not′, *v.i.* can not.

can′ny, *adj.,* **-nier, -niest.** shrewd. —**can′ni·ly,** *adv.* —**can′ni·ness,** *n.*

ca·noe (kə nōō′) *n., v.i.,* **-noed, -noing.** *n.* 1. narrow paddled boat. —*v.i.* 2. travel by canoe.

can′on, *n.* 1. basic principle or law. 2. church official. 3. official list of writings. —**ca·non′i·cal,** *adj.*

can′on·ize″, *v.t.,* **-ized, -izing.** declare to be a saint. —**can″on·i·za′tion,** *n.*

can'o·py, *n., pl.* -pies. 1. light, rooflike covering supported by poles. 2. rooflike projection, as over a window.

cant, *n.* 1. hypocritical jargon. 2. slang or jargon of a group. —*v.t., v.i.* 3. slant.

can·tan'ker·ous, *adj.* ill-tempered.

can·ta'ta, *n.* setting of a narrative for chorus.

can·teen', *n.* 1. portable container for water. 2. recreation center, as for soldiers.

can'ter, *n.* easy gallop.

can'ti·le''ver, *n.* 1. projecting structural member secured at one end. —*v.t.* 2. support with or treat as a cantilever.

can'to, *n., pl.* -tos. division of a long poem.

can'tor, *n.* singer at a Jewish service.

can'vas, *n.* 1. tightly woven heavy cloth of hemp, cotton, etc. 2. painting on canvas.

can'vass, *v.t., v.i.* solicit for votes, opinions, sales orders, etc.

cap, *n., v.t.,* capped, capping. *n.* 1. soft, close-fitting hat. 2. anything for capping. —*v.t.* 3. cover the upper end of.

ca'pa·ble, *adj.* 1. competent. 2. capable of, with the ability, personality, etc. for. —ca''pa·bil'i·ty, *n.* —ca'pa·bly, *adv.*

ca·pa'cious, *adj.* spacious.

ca·pac'i·ty, *n., pl.* -ties. 1. ability to contain a quantity of material, number of persons, etc. 2. amount that can be produced. 3. role or function. 4. capability.

cape, *n.* 1. cloak. 2. projection of land seaward

ca'per, *v.i.* 1. leap about playfully. —*n.* 2. playful leap.

cap'il·lar''y, *adj.* pertaining to the attraction of liquids in narrow tubes to above normal levels.

cap'i·tal, *n.* 1. location of a national or state government. 2. money for investing or lending. 3. upper feature of a column or pier. 4. letter of the form used to begin a sentence or proper name. —*adj.* 5. excellent. 6. large, as letters. 7. pertaining to the death penalty.

cap'i·tal·ism, *n.* economic system based on investment or lending at interest of privately owned money. —cap'i·tal·ist, *n.* —cap''i·tal·is'tic, *adj.*

cap'i·tal·ize'', *v.,* -ized, -izing. *v.t.* 1. spell with an initial capital. 2. use as or change into capital (2). 3. furnish with capital (2). —*v.i.* 4. capitalize on, exploit. —cap''i·tal·i·za'tion, *n.*

cap'i·tol, *n.* legislative building.

ca·pit'u·late, *v.i.,* -lated, -lating. cease to fight or resist. —ca·pit''u·la'tion, *n.*

ca·price', *n.* whim or whimsy. —ca·pri'cious, *adj.*

cap'size, *v.,* -sized, -sizing. *v.t., v.i.* overturn, as a boat.

cap'stan, *n.* upright drum for winding cables.

cap'sule, *n.* sealed container.

cap'tain, *n.* 1. military or naval officer. 2. master of a ship. 3. leader. —cap'tain·cy, *n.*

cap'tion, *n.* title, explanation, etc. for a printed picture.

cap'tious, *adj.* argumentative or fault-finding. —cap'tious·ly, *adv.* —cap'tious·ness, *n.*

cap'ti·vate'', *v.t.,* -vated, -vating. fascinate, as with charm. —cap''ti·va'tion, *n.*

cap'tive, *n.* captured person or animal. —cap·tiv'i·ty, *n.*

cap'tor, *n.* person who takes a captive.

cap'ture, *v.t.,* -tured, -turing. *n. v.t.* 1. prevent from fleeing, fighting, etc. by force. 2. express through art or speech. —*n.* 3. act or instance of capturing.

car, *n.* 1. automobile. 2. wheeled vehicle of any kind. 3. elevator compartment.

ca·rafe', *n.* bottle for serving beverages, usually water or wine.

car'a·mel, *n.* 1. burnt sugar, used as a flavor or color. 2. type of candy.

car'at, *n.* 1. unit of 200 milligrams for weighing gems. 2. karat.

car'a·van'', *n.* group of travelers, beasts of burden, etc. in a desert.

car'bine, *n.* 1. short-barreled rifle. 2. light automatic military rifle.

car''bo·hy'drate, *n.* starch or sugar.

car'bon, *n.* nonmetallic element found in organic compounds.

car'bun·cle, *n.* 1. subcutaneous inflammation. 2. type of gem.

car'bu·ret''or, *n.* device for making explosive mixtures of air and gasoline.

car'cass, *n.* 1. dead animal body. 2. rough frame or shell, as of a building.

card, *n.* 1. stiff paper bearing writing, etc. 2. one of such papers used in games. 3. postcard. 4. cards, game played with cards.

card'board'', *n.* thick, papery sheeting.

car'di·ac'', *adj.* pertaining to the heart.

car'di·gan, *n.* sweater buttoning in front.

car'di·nal, *n.* 1. Roman Catholic ecclesiastic second to the pope. 2. red American songbird. 3. cardinal number. —*adv.* 4. primary.

cardinal number, basic number, as 1, 2, 3, etc.

car'di·o·gram'', *n.* electrocardiogram. —car'di·o·graph'', *n.*

car''di·ol'o·gy, *n.* branch of medicine concerned with the heart.

care, *n., v.,* cared, caring. *n.* 1. responsibility. 2. charge or protection. 3. cautionor heed. 4. worry. —*v.i.* 5. have responsibility. 6. feel liking or de-

careful

sire. 7. feel affection. 8. feel concern.
—*v.t.* 9. have as a subject of concern.

care'ful, *adj.* 1. cautious. 2. with attention to accuracy.

care'less, *adj.* not properly careful.

ca·ress', *v.t.* 1. touch lightly and affectionately. —*n.* 2. gesture or touch indicating affection.

car'go, *n., pl.* **-goes, -gos.** freight.

car'i·ca·ture'', *n., v.t.,* **-tured, -turing.** *n.* 1. exaggerated rendering of a person's peculiarities. —*v.t.* 2. render in caricature. —**car'i·ca·tur''ist,** *n.*

car'ies, *n.* decay of teeth or bones.

car'il·lon, *n.* set of bells tuned to a scale. —**car''il·lon·neur',** *n.*

car'mine, *n.* purplish red or crimson.

car'nage, *n.* slaughter.

car'nal, *adj.* pertaining to the body or its appetites.

car'ni·val, *n.* 1. time of merrymaking before Lent. 2. fair with entertainments.

car'ni·vore'', *n.* flesh-eating animal or plant. —**car·niv'o·rous,** *adj.*

car'ol, *n., v.,* **-oled, -oling.** *n.* 1. song of praise, esp. at Christmas. —*v.i., v.t.* 2. sing exuberantly. —**car'ol·er, car'ol·ler,** *n.*

ca·rouse', *v.i.,* **-roused, -rousing,** *n. v.i.* 1. drink together boisterously. —*n.* 2. Also, **ca·rous'al,** period of carousing.

ca''rou·sel', *n.* carrousel.

carp, *v.i., n., pl.* **carp** or **carps.** *v.i.* 1. find fault unjustly. —*n.* 2. edible fresh-water fish. —**carp'er,** *n.*

car'pen·ter, *n.* builder in wood. —**car'pen·try,** *n.*

car'pet, *n.* 1. cloth floor covering. —*v.t.* 2. cover with or as if with a carpet. —**car'pet·ing,** *n.*

car'port'', *n.* open-ended shelter for an automobile.

car'riage, *n.* 1. large animal-drawn passenger vehicle. 2. any of various moving and carrying devices. 3. posture.

car'ri·er, *n.* 1. thing or person that carries. 2. aircraft carrier.

car'ri·on, *n.* dead, decaying flesh.

car'rot, *n.* vegetable with an edible orange root.

car'rou·sel, *n.* merry-go-round.

car'ry, *v.,* **-ried, -rying.** *v.t.* 1. support or suspend. 2. take the weight of and move. 3. transmit. 4. win or attain. 5. prosecute or develop. —*v.i.* 6. be transmitted.

cart, *n.* 1. small wagon. —*v.t.* 2. transport in a small wagon.

car·tel', *n.* monopolistic association of businesses.

car'ti·lage, *n.* tough, elastic skeletal tissue.

car'ton, *n.* cardboard box.

car·toon', *n.* 1. amusing or satirical drawing. 2. motion picture of such drawings. 3. artist's design for a fresco, tapestry, etc. —**car·toon'ist,** *n.*

car'tridge, *n.* 1. unit of ammunition for a handgun, rifle, etc. 2. any unit loaded or fitted into a machine.

cart'wheel'', *n.* sidewise handspring.

carve, *v.t.,* **carved, carving.** 1. form by cutting parts from. 2. cut into parts, as meat. —**carv'er,** *n.* —**carv'ing,** *n.*

cas·cade', *n., v.i.,* **-caded, -cading.** *n.* 1. chain of shallow waterfalls. —*v.i.* 2. fallin or as if in a cascade.

case, *n., v.t.,* **cased, casing.** *n.* 1. box. 2. instance. 3. predicament. 4. rational argument. 5. form of a noun, etc. that shows its role in a sentence. —*v.t.* 6. put in a case.

case'ment, *n.* window hinged on one side.

cash, *n.* 1. money as opposed to checks, etc. 2. money or check given in payment. —*v.t.* 3. exchange for money, as a check or coupon.

cash·ier', *n.* 1. person in charge of cash in a bank, etc. —*v.t.* 2. dismiss, as from the military.

cas'ing, *n.* outer cover.

ca·si'no, *n., pl.* **-nos.** 1. place for dances, entertainments, etc. 2. place for gambling.

cask, *n.* barrel for liquids.

cas'ket, *n.* 1. box for jewels, etc. 2. ornate coffin.

cas'se·role'', *n.* 1. dish for baking. 2. food baked in such a dish.

cas·sette'', *n.* a compact, ready-to-use case containing audio or video tape.

cas'sock, *n.* clergyman's long, loose garment.

cast, *v.t.,* **cast, casting,** *n, v.t.* 1. throw. 2. directs or project. 3. form in a mold. —*n.* 4. act or instance of casting. 5. something formed in a mold. 6. casing of a broken limb. 7. group performing a play, etc. 8. air or appearance.

cast'a·way'', *n.* shipwrecked person.

caste, *n.,* rigid social division, esp. in India.

cast'er, *n.* 1. small wheel supporting a furniture leg, etc. 2. table pitcher for vinegar, etc. Also, **cast'or.**

cas'ti·gate'', *v.t.,* **-gated, -gating.** rebuke severely. —**cas''ti·ga'tion,** *n.* —**cas'ti·ga''tor,** *n.*

cast'ing, *n.* something cast in a mold.

cas'tle, *n.* 1. heavily fortified residence. 2. chess rook.

cast'-off'', *adj.* discarded.

cas'trate, *v.t.,* **-trated, -trating.** remove the testicles of. —**cas·tra'tion,** *n.*

cas'u·al, *adj.* 1. occurring by chance. 2. not regular. 3. informal. 4. relaxed. —**cas'u·al·ly,** *adv.* —**cas'u·al·ness,** *n.*

cas'u·al·ty, *n., pl.* **-ties.** 1. victim of an accident or military action. 2. serious accident.

cas'u·ist·ry, *n., pl.* **-tries.** sophistry. —**cas'u·ist,** *n.*

cat, *n.* 1. small, furry, four-footed animal. 2. any feline.

cat'a·clysm, *n.* sudden, drastic change. —**cat"a·clys'mic**, *adj.*

cat'a·comb", *n.* underground passage with burial places.

cat'a·log", *n., v.t.,* **-loged, -loging.** *n.* **1.** list of things acquired, to be sold, etc. —*v.t.* **2.** list in a catalog. Also, **cat'a·logue"**.

cat'a·lyst, *n.* something that affects the speed of a chemical reaction without being altered in the process. —**cat'a·lyt'ic**, *adj.*

cat"a·ma·ran', *n.* boat with two parallel hulls.

cat'a·pult", *n.* **1.** machine for hurling missiles, launching airplanes, etc. —*v.t.* **2.** hurl or launch from or as if from a catapult.

cat'a·ract", *n.* **1.** large waterfall. **2.** opacity in the eye causing blindness.

ca·tarrh', *n.* inflammation of mucous membranes in the nose or throat.

ca·tas'tro·phe, *n.* major disaster. —**cat"a·stroph'ic**, *adj.*

cat'call", *n.* shrill noise expressing contempt.

catch, *v.,* **caught, catching,** *n. v.t.* **1.** capture or seize. **2.** discover or surprise. **3.** be infected with. —*v.i.* **4.** become caught or entangled. **5.** take or retain hold. —*n.* **6.** act or instance of catching. **7.** number of things caught, esp. fish. **8.** something for catching hold. **9.** desirable spouse or acquaintance. **10.** *Informal.* drawback. **catch'er**, *n.*

catch'all", *n.* place, category, etc. for miscellaneous things.

catch'ing, *adj.* **1.** contagious. **2.** attractive.

catch'up, *n.* ketchup.

catch'y, *adj.* **-ier, -iest.** memorable, as a tune.

cat·e·chism (kat'ə kism), *n.* set of questions and answers, esp. on religious doctrine.

cat'e·chize", *v.t.,* **-chized, -chizing.** question in detail. Also, **cat'e·chise"**.

cat"e·gor'i·cal, *adj.* **1.** pertaining to categories. **2.** specific, as a statement. —**cat"e·gor'i·cal·ly**, *adv.*

cat'e·go·rize", *v.t.,* **-rized, -rizing.** put into categories.

cat'e·go"ry, *n., pl.* **ries.** classification.

ca'ter, *v.i.* **1.** supply food, drink, tableware, etc. to parties for a fee. **2.** be overly accommodating. —**ca'ter·er**, *n.*

cat'er·cor"nered, *adj., adv.* on diagonally opposite corners. Also, **cat'er·cor"ner**.

cat'er·pil'lar, *n.* crawling larva of a butterfly, moth, etc.

cat'gut", *n.* tough string made from dried intestines of sheep, etc.

ca·thar'sis, *n.* purging, esp. of morbid emotions.

ca·thar'tic, *n.* **1.** medicine for clearing the bowels. —*adj.* **2.** pertaining to cathartics. **3.** pertaining to a catharsis.

ca·the'dral, *n.* church in which a bishop normally officiates.

cath'o·lic, *adj.* **1.** universal. **2.** **Catholic,** pertaining to the Roman Catholic Church. —*n.* **3.** **Catholic,** member of the Roman Catholic Church. —**cath"o·lic'i·ty**, *n.* —**Ca·thol'i·cism**, *n.*

cat'nap", *n., v.i.,* **-napped, -napping.** *n.* **1.** brief nap. —*v.i.* **2.** take such a nap.

cat's'-paw", *n.* person used by another as a tool.

cat'sup, *n.* ketchup.

cat'tle, *n., pl.* cows, bulls, etc. —**cat'tle·man**, *n.*

cat'walk", *n.* narrow elevated walk, esp. for industrial workers.

cau'cus, *n., v.i.,* **-cused** or **-cussed, -cusing** or **-cussing.** *n.* **1.** business meeting of political leaders. —*v.i.* **2.** meet in a caucus.

caul'dron, *n.* caldron.

cau'li·flow"er, *n.* edible white head of a vegetable of the cabbage family.

caulk, *v.t.* make watertight, esp. a seam.

cau'sal, *adj.* pertaining to or involving the relation of cause and effect. —**cau·sal'i·ty**, *n.*

cause, *n., v.t.,* **caused, causing.** *n.* **1.** something to which a later event or condition is attributed. **2.** reason or motivation. **3.** goal or purpose, esp. political or religious. **4.** case for advocacy. —*v.t.* **5.** be the cause of. —**caus'er**, *n.* —**caus'a·tive**, *adj.*

cause'way", *n.* raised roadway.

caus'tic, *adj.* **1.** burning. **2.** bitterly sarcastic.

cau'ter·ize", *v.t.,* **-ized, -izing.** *Medicine.* burn or sear, as the flesh of a wound, to seal it. —**cau"ter·i·za'tion**, *n.*

cau'tion, *n.* **1.** care, as to avoid danger. **2.** warning. —*v.t.* **3.** warn. —**cau'tion·ar"y**, *adj.*

cau'tious, *adj.* careful to avoid danger.

cav'al·cade", *n.* procession, esp. on horseback.

cav"a·lier', *n.* **1.** horseman, esp. a knight. **2.** gallant. —*adj.* **3.** casual. **4.** arrogant.

cav'al·ry, *n., pl.* **-ries.** *n.* **1.** fighting force on horseback. **2.** fighting force in motor vehicles. —**cav'al·ry·man**, *n.*

cave, *n., v.,* **caved, caving.** *n.* **1.** covered opening in the earth. —*v.i., v.t.,* **2. cave in,** collapse. —**cave'-in"**, *n.*

cav'ern, *n.* spacious cave. —**cav'ern·ous**, *adj.*

cav'i·ar", *n.* roe, esp. that of sturgeon. Also, **cav'i·are"**.

cav'il, *n., v.i.,* **-iled, -iling.** quibble. —**cav'il·er, cav'il·ler**, *n.*

cav'i·ty, *n., pl.* **-ities.** hollow place.

ca·vort', *v.i.* frolic.

cay·enne', *n.* extremely hot red pepper.

cay·use', *n.* small cowboy horse.

cease, *v.,* ceased, ceasing. *v.i., v.t., n.* stop, —cease'less, *adj.*

ce'dar, *n.* type of fragrant pine.

cede, *v.t.,* ceded, ceding. yield possession of.

ceil'ing, *n.* 1. structure or surface forming the upper part of a room, etc. 2. upper limit.

cel'e·brate", *v.,* -brated, -brating. *v.t.* 1. perform ritually. 2. mark or commemorate with festivity. 3. do honor to. —*v.i.* 4. have festivities. —cel"e·bra'tion, *n.* —cel'e·brant, *n.* —cel'e·brat"ed, *adj.*

ce·leb'ri·ty, *n., pl.* -ties, 1. fame. 2. currently famous person.

ce·ler'i·ty, *n.* swiftness.

cel'er·y, *n.* plant with edible leaf stalks.

ce·les'tial, *adj.* pertaining to heaven or outer space.

cel'i·bate", *n.* 1. unmarried person. 2. sexually abstinent person. —*adj.* 3. pertaining to celibates or celibacy. —cel'i·ba·cy, *n.*

cell, *n.* 1. unit of protoplasm. 2. unit of space. 3. habitable space in a prison, monastery, etc. 4. electric battery. 5. local unit of an organization. —celled, *adj.* —cel'lu·lar, *adj.*

cel'lar, *n.* 1. basement. 2. storage space totally or partly underneath a building. 3. collection of wine.

cel·lo (tshel'lō), *n., pl.* -los. large bowed stringed instrument. —cel'list, *n.*

cel'lo·phane", *n.* transparent wrapping material.

Cel'lu·loid", *n. Trademark.* plastic made from nitrocellulose and camphor.

Cel'sius, *adj.* centigrade.

ce·ment', *n.* 1. mixture of burned lime and clay, used for building. 2. adhesive substance. —*v.t.* 3. join with cement. 4. cover with cement.

cem'e·ter"y, *n., pl.* -ies. area of land for burying the dead.

cen'sor, *n.* 1. person who eliminates unauthorized material from writings, etc. 2. official who criticizes the state of government, society, etc. —cen'sor·ship", *n.*

cen·so'ri·ous, *adj.* given to harsh criticism.

cen'sure, *n., v.t.,* -sured, -suring. rebuke or condemnation. —*v.t.* 2. rebuke or condemn.

cen'sus, *n.* counting and analysis of population, etc.

cent, *n.* hundredth part of a dollar.

cen'taur", *n. Greek Mythology.* creature with the body of a horse and the head and trunk of a man.

cen"te·nar'i·an, *n.* person 100 years old.

cen'te·nar"y, *adj., n., pl.* -ies. centennial.

cen·ten'ni·al, *adj.* 1. pertaining to or marking a period of 100 years. —*n.* 2. hundredth anniversary. 3. celebration of such an anniversary.

cen'ter, *n.* 1. point or area equidistant from all outer points. 2. place of concentration. 3. area of political moderation. —*v.t.* 4. put or concentrate at a center.

cen'ti·grade", *adj.* pertaining to a system of temperature measurement in which the range between the freezing and boiling points of water is 100 degrees; Celsius.

cen'ti·gram", *n.* hundredth part of a gram. Also, cen'ti·gramme".

cen'ti·me"ter, *n.* hundredth part of a meter. Also, cen'ti·me"tre.

cen'ti·pede", *n.* many-legged crawling insect.

cen'tral, *adj.* 1. located at the center. 2. accessible from all points. 3. fundamental; basic. —cen'tral·ly, *adv.*

cen'tral·ize", *v.t.,* -ized, -izing. 1. unite under or control from a single authority. 2. place at a center. —cen"tral·i·za'tion, *n.*

cen·trif'u·gal force, force tending to pull a mass away from a point around which it moves.

cen·trip'e·tal force, force tending to pull a mass toward a point around which it moves.

cen'tu·ry, *n., pl.* -ries. 1. period of 100 years. 2. such a period as a unit, reckoned from A.D. 1.

ce·ram'ic, *n.* 1. ceramics, making of objects from baked clay or similar materials. 2. object so made. —*adj.* 3. pertaining to ceramics. 4. made as a ceramic.

ce're·al, *n.* 1. grain used as food. 2. food manufactured from such grain. —*adj.* 3. pertaining to grain.

cer·e'bral, *adj.* reasoned rather than felt.

cer"e·mo'ni·al, *adj.* 1. formal. —*n.* 2. ceremony.

cer'e·mo"ny, *n., pl.* -nies. 1. ordered set of actions for a formal occasion. 2. formality. —cer"e·mo'ni·ous, *adj.*

cer'tain, *adj.* 1. without doubt. 2. without error. 3. inevitable. 4. unspecified. —cer'tain·ly, *adv.* —cer'tain·ty, *n.*

cer·tif'i·cate, *n.* document that certifies.

cer'ti·fy", *v.t.,* -fied, -fying. 1. declare formally to be competent, valid, true, etc. 2. issue a certificate to. —cer"ti·fi·ca'tion, *n.*

cer'ti·tude", *n.* inevitability.

ces·sa'tion, *n.* stop.

ces'sion, *n.* act or instance of ceding.

cess'pool", *n.* receptacle for plumbing wastes.

chafe, *v.,* chafed, chafing. *v.t.* 1. wear by rubbing. 2. warm by rubbing, as the skin. —*v.i.* 3. become restless and annoyed.

chaff, *n.* **1.** waste from threshed grain. **2.** worthless stuff. —*n. v.i.* **3.** banter.

chafing dish, metal dish with a heating lamp underneath.

cha·grin', *n., v.t.,* **-grined, -grining.** *n.* **1.** embarrassment at failure or disappointment. —*v.t.* **2.** cause chagrin in.

chain, *n.* **1.** flexible length formed of connected pieces. **2.** related series of events, arguments, etc. **3. chains,** bondage. —*v.t.* **4.** fasten with a chain.

chain reaction, series of reactions each caused by one immediately previous.

chair, *n.* **1.** seat with a back. **2.** official post or position, esp. a chairmanship of professorship. **3.** chairman. —*v.t.* **4.** preside over as chairman.

chair'man, *n.* person who presides over a meeting. —**chair'man·ship''**, *n.* Also, **chair'per''son.**

chaise longue, *pl.* **chaise longues.** daybed with a chairlike back at one end. Also, **chaise lounge.**

cha·let (sha lā'), *n.* Swiss farmhouse with a low, jutting roof.

chal'ice, *n.* wine goblet used in religious communions.

chalk, *n.* **1.** soft white limestone. **2.** white or dyed stonelike material for writing on blackboards. —*v.t.* **3.** write or mark with chalk. —**chalk'y,** *adj.*

chal'lenge, *v.t.,* **-lenged, -lenging,** *n. v.t.* **1.** call upon to fight, compete, or act bravely. **2.** demand identification of. **3.** demand proof from or for. **4.** reject as a juror. —*n.* **5.** act or instance of challenging. **6.** demand for one's best effort. —**chal'leng·er,** *n.*

cham'ber, *n.* **1.** room, esp. a bedroom. **2.** enclosed space, as in a machine, gun, or part of the body. **3.** legislative or official body. **4. chambers,** judge's office. —**cham'bered,** *adj.* —**cham'ber·maid'',** *n.*

chamber music, music written for small groups and intended for home entertaining.

cha·me·le·on (kə mē'lē ən), *n.* lizard able to change the color of its skin.

cham·ois (sham'ē), *n.* **1.** small European mountain antelope. **2.** Also, **cham'my,** soft leather of a chamois or other animal, used for polishing.

champ, *v.t., v.i.* bite or chew noisily.

cham·pagne (sham pān'), *n.* sparkling white wine, originally from northern France.

cham'pi·on, *n.* **1.** person who fights in another's behalf. **2.** athlete winning or getting first place in a series of competitions. **3.** advocate of a cause. —*v.t.* **4.** defend or advocate. —**cham'pi·on·ship'',** *n.*

chance, *n., adj., v.,* **chanced, chancing.** *n.* **1.** possibility of becoming, doing, or getting something desired. **2.** the un-predictable. **3.** unpredictable event. **4.** risk. **5.** lottery ticket. —*adj.* **6.** accidental. —*v.t.* **7.** risk. —*v.i.* **8.** transpire or come by accident.

chan'cel, *n.* area of a church around the altar.

chan'cel·lor, *n.* high government or academic official. —**chan'cel·lor·ship''**, *n.*

chanc'y, *adj.,* **-ier, -iest.** risky or uncertain.

chan''de·lier', *n.* lighting fixture suspended from a ceiling.

chand'ler, *n.* supplier, esp. to ships. —**chand'ler·ry,** *n.*

change, *v.,* **changed, changing,** *n. v.t.* **1.** make into a different form. **2.** give up one for the other, as articles of clothing, vehicles, etc. **3.** give lower denominations of money in exchange for. —*v.i.* **4.** become different. **5.** leave one vehicle for another. —*n.* **6.** act or instance of changing. **7.** variety. **8.** money returned from that offered in payment. **9.** money in small denominations, esp. coins. —**change'less,** *adj.* —**change'a·ble,** *adj.*

chan'nel, *n., v.t.,* **-neled, -neling.** *n.* **1.** deeper part of a watercourse. **2.** body of water linking two larger ones. **3.** groove. **4.** *Television and radio.* frequency band. **5. channels,** offices in an official sequence for a given purpose. —*v.t.* **6.** send through or as through a channel. **7.** make grooves in.

chant, *n.* **1.** sung liturgical music. **2.** heavily rhythmical song or speech. —*v.t.* **3.** sing or utter in a chant.

chan'tey, *n., pl.* **-teys.** rhythmical work song of a sailor. Also, **chan'ty.**

cha·os (kā'os), *n.* utter disorder. —**cha·ot'ic,** *adj.*

chap, *v.,* **chapped** or **chapt, chapping.** *v.t., v.i.* roughen or crack, as the skin or lips.

chap'el, *n.* **1.** minor church. **2.** private church, as in a school or house.

chap·er·on (shap'ə rōn), *n., v.t.,* **-oned, -oning.** *n.* **1.** person who accompanies young unmarried persons to ensure propriety. —*v.t.* **2.** accompany as a chaperon. Also, **chap'er·one''.**

chap'lain, *n.* **1.** clergyman employed by an institution, military force, etc. **2.** clergyman attached to a chapel.

chaps, *n., pl.* leather legging worn by cowboys.

chap'ter, *n.* **1.** division of a book. **2.** local branch of an association. **3.** council of a religious community.

char, *v.,* **charred, charring.** *v.t., v.i.* **1.** burn on the surface. **2.** burn to charcoal.

char'ac·ter, *n.* **1.** personality. **2.** moral strength. **3.** person as judged by his actions. 4. eccentric or conspicuous person. 5. reputation. 6. person in a work of fiction. 7. any symbol used in forming writing.

char″ac·ter·is′tic, *adj.* 1. typical. —*n.* 2. typical or distinguishing quality. —**char″ac·ter·is′tic·al·ly,** *adv.*

char′ac·ter·ize″, *v.t.,* **-ized, -izing.** 1. attribute or give characteristics to. 2. be characteristic of. —**char″ac·ter·i·za′ tion,** *n.*

cha·rade′, *n.* pantomime offering clues to guessing a secret word.

char′coal″, *n.* wood partially burned in the absence of air.

charge, *v.,* **charged, charging,** *n. v.t.* 1. supply or load. 2. electrify. 3. accuse. 4. make responsible. 5. ask as a price or fee. 6. enter as a debt. 7. attack with swift movement. 8. require payment. 9. move swiftly in an attack. —*n.* 10. act or instance of charging. 11. that with which something is charged. 12. care or responsibility. 13. object of one's care or responsibility. —**charge′ a·ble,** *adj.*

char′i·ot, *n.* two-wheeled horse-drawn vehicle. —**char″i·o·teer′,** *n.*

cha·ris·ma (kə riz′mə), *n.* quality of leadership derived from the personality. —**char″is·mat′ic,** *adj.*

char′i·ta·ble, *adj.* 1. kindly. 2. generous. 3. pertaining to charities.

char′i·ty, *n., pl.* **-ties.** 1. love for mankind. 2. generosity to the needy. 3. organization for helping the needy. 4. kindness in judging others.

char·la·tan (shahr′lə tən), *n.* perpetrator of frauds. —**char′la·tan·ism, char′la· tan·ry,** *n.*

charm, *n.* 1. attractive or delightful quality. 2. trinket. 3. magic spell. —*v.t.* 4. exercise charm or a charm upon. —**charm′er,** *n.* —**charm′ing,** *adj.*

chart, *n.* 1. map, esp. for navigation. 2. graph or table. —*v.t.* 3. make a chart of. 4. map or plan.

char′ter, *n.* 1. license or franchise. 2. statement of fundamental organizational principles. 3. hire of a vehicle. —*v.t.* 4. grant a charter to. 5. hire, as for a trip.

char′y, *adj.,* **-ier, -iest.** 1. cautious. 2. sparing.

chase, *v.,* **chased, chasing,** *n. v.t.* 1. go after to overtake or capture. 2. drive away. 3. hunt. 4. engrave, as metal. —*v.i.* 5. *Informal.* rush. —*n.* 6. pursuit. 7. hunting of game.

chasm (kas′m), *n.* abyss.

chas·sis (chas′ē, chas′ē), *n., pl.* **-sis.** frame and running gear of an automobile, not including the engine.

chaste, *adj.* 1. pure, esp. of sexual desire or activity. 2. tastefully restrained. —**chas′ti·ty,** *n.*

chas′ten, *v.t.* correct or subdue, esp. by punishment or scolding.

chas·tise′, *v.t.,* **-tised, -tising.** punish or scold.

chat, *n.,* *v.i.,* **chatted, chatting.** *n.* 1. light, informal conversation. —*v.i.* 2. have such a conversation.

cha·teau′, *n., pl.* **-teaux, -teaus.** castle or country house in France. Also, **châ· teau′.**

chat′tel, *n.* piece of movable personal property.

chat′ter, *v.i.* 1. make rapid sounds with the voice. 2. talk foolishly. 3. make rapid clashing sounds, as the teeth of a chilled person. —*n.* 4. chattering noise. 5. foolish talk.

chauf·feur′, *n.* person hired to drive an automobile.

chau′vin·ism, *n.* fanatical devotion to one's country, etc. —**chau′vin·ist,** *n.* —**chau″vin·is′tic,** *adj.*

cheap, *adj.* 1. low in price. 2. low in worth. 3. despicable. 4. *Informal.* stingy. —*adv.* 5. at low cost. —**cheap′ly,** *adv.* —**cheap′ness,** *n.* —**cheap′en,** *v.t., v.i.*

cheat, *v.t.* 1. deceive, esp. for money. 2. evade. —*v.i.* 3. be deceptive. —*n.* 4. deception. 5. deceiver.

check, *n.* 1. precaution. 2. inspection. 3. halt or frustration. 4. identification slip. 5. document transferring money. 6. bill, as in a restaurant. 7. square in a checkered pattern. 8. *Chess.* danger to a king. —*v.t.* 9. halt or restrain. 10. verify or investigate. 11. place with another for shipment or storage. —**check′ book″,** *n.* —**check′room″,** *n.*

check′er, *n.* 1. person or thing that checks. 2. **checkers, a.** pattern of squares in alternating colors. **b.** game played on a board with this pattern. 3. disk used in playing checkers. —**check′ er·board″,** *n.*

check′mate″, *n.,* **-mated, -mating** *n.* 1. *Chess.* inevitable capture of a king. 2. total defeat or ruin. —*v.t.* 3. impose a checkmate on.

check′up″, *n.* medical examination.

ched′dar, *n.* hard cheese, often sharp.

cheek, *n.* 1. side of the face below the eye. 2. impudence.

cheer, *n.* 1. happiness. 2. shout of delight, encouragement, etc. 3. food and entertainment. —*v.i.* 4. shout cheers. 5. become less unhappy. —*v.t.* 6. encourage, etc. with cheers. 7. make less unhappy. —**cheer′ful,** *adj.* —**cheer′less,** *adj.*

cheese, *n.* food made from milk curds.

cheese′burg″er, *n.* hamburger cooked with cheese.

cheese′cake″, *n.* cake made with cheese.

cheese′cloth″, *n.* loosely woven cotton.

chef, *n.* cook, esp. a supervising cook.

chem′i·cal, *adj.* 1. pertaining to, or produced or operated by, chemistry. —*n.* 2. substance produced by or used in chemistry. —**chem′i·cal·ly,** *adv.*

che·mise′, *n.* loose-fitting woman's dress or slip.

chem′is·try, *n.* study of substances and their production or conversion. —**chem′ist,** *n.*

che·nille′, *n.* fabric woven from a soft, tufted yarn.

cher′ish, *v.t.* regard as dear or precious.

cher′ry, *n., pl.* **-ries.** tree bearing a small, red fruit.

cher′ub, *n., pl.* **-ubs, -ubim.** angel often shown as a chubby, winged child. —**che·ru′bic,** *adj.*

chess, *n.* game played on a checkerboard with 16 pieces on each of two sides. —**chess′board″,** *n.* —**chess′man,** *n.*

chest, *n.* 1. any of various boxlike containers for storage. 2. part of the body within the ribs.

chest′nut, *n.* tree of the beech family with an edible nut.

chev′ron, *n.* sign like a V or inverted V, used for military insignia, heraldry, etc.

chew, *v.t.* reduce with the teeth, as for swallowing. —**chew′y,** *adj.*

Chi·an·ti (kē ahn′tē), *n.* dry red table wine.

chic, *n.* elegance; smartness.

chi·can′er·y, *n., pl.* **-ries.** trickery.

chi·ca″no, *n., fem.* —**a.** a person of Mexican descent.

chick, *n.* young bird, esp. a chicken.

chick′en, *n.* hen or rooster.

chick′en-heart″ed, *adj.* cowardly.

chicken pox, contagious virus disease of children.

chick′pea″, *n.* edible seed of a bushy plant.

chic′o·ry, *n.* plant with leaves used in salad and roots used as a coffee substitute.

chide, *v.,* **chided** or **chid, chided** or **chid** or **chidden, chiding.** *v.t., v.i.* scold; rebuke.

chief, *n.* 1. principal person. —*adj.* 2. main. —**chief′ly,** *adv.*

chief′tain, *n.* leader of a tribe or clan.

chif·fo·nier (shif′ə nēr′), *n.* chest of drawers. Also, **chif″fon·ier′.**

Chi·hua·hua (tshi wa′wa), *n.* small dog.

child, *n., pl.* **children.** 1. human before puberty. 2. offspring. —**child′birth″,** *n.* —**child′hood″,** *n.* —**child′less,** *adj.* —**child′like″,** *adj.*

child′ish, *adj.* characteristic of children, esp. as regards behavior or judgment.

chil′i, *n.* dish of beef, red pepper, etc. Also, **chili con car′ne.**

chill, *n.* 1. perceptible cold. 2. shiver from cold. —*adj.* 3. chilly. —*v.t.* 4. cause to be cold. —*v.i.* 5. become cold.

chill′y, *adj.,* **-ier, -iest.** cold.

chime, *n., v.,* **chimed, chiming.** *n.* 1. bell, esp. in a clock. 2. **chimes,** tuned bells. —*v.t., v.i.* 3. sound with chimes.

chi·me′ra (kî mē′rə), *n.* fantastic, imaginary thing. —**chi·mer′i·cal,** *adj.*

chim′ney, *n., pl.* **-nies.** passage for smoke or heat.

chim″pan·zee′, *n.* medium-sized ape.

chin, *n.* part of the face at the lower jaw.

chi′na, *n.* 1. porcelain. 2. vitrified earthenware. 3. dishes, etc. Also, **chi′na·ware.**

chink, *n.* 1. narrow crack. 2. clinking sound.

chintz, *n.* printed cotton, usually glazed.

chip, *n., v.,* **-ped, -ping.** *n.* 1. small cut or broken piece. 2. token used in gambling, etc. 3. (computers) the basic component of miniaturized electronic circuitry. —*v.t.* 4. knock chips from. —*v.i.* 5. break into chips.

chip′munk″, *n.* small North American squirrel.

chip′per, *adj.* lively in spirit.

chi·rop·o·dy (kī rop′ə dē), *n.* podiatry. —**chi·rop′o·dist,** *n.*

chi·ro·prac·tic (kī″rə prak′tik), *n.* treatment of illness through manipulation of the joints. —**chi′ro·prac″tor,** *n.*

chirp, *v.i.* make short, shrill, birdlike noises.

chis′el, *n., v.t.,* **-eled** or **-eling.** *n.* 1. cutting tool driven at one end. —*v.t.* 2. cut with a chisel. —*v.i.* 3. *Informal.* cheat, esp. on small matters. —**chis′el·er,** *n.*

chit′chat″, *n.* light conversation or gossip.

chit′ter·lings, *n., pl.* small intestines of pigs as a food. Also, **chit′lins, chit′lings.**

chiv′al·ry, *n.* 1. medieval institution of knighthood. 2. courage, gallantry, etc. —**chiv·al′ric,** *adj.* —**chiv′al·rous,** *adj.*

chlo·rine (klō′rēn), *n.* greenish chemical used for disinfection. —**chlo′ri·nate″,** *v.t.*

chlo′ro·form″, *n.* 1. volatile liquid anaesthetic. —*v.t.* 2. kill or anaesthetize with chloroform.

chlo′ro·phyll, *n.* green substance in plants. Also, **chlo′ro·phyl.**

chock, *n.* 1. wedge stopping wheels from rolling. —*v.t.* 2. stop with chocks.

chock′-full′, *adj.* absolutely full.

choc′o·late, *n.* 1. dark-brown substance made from or flavored with cacao seeds. 2. reddish brown.

choice, *n., adj.,* **choicer, choicest.** *n.* 1. fact or instance of choosing. 2. thing chosen. —*adj.* 3. superior in quality.

choir (kwîr), *n.* 1. chorus, esp. one singing religious music. **2.** part of a church for such a chorus.

choke, *v.,* **choked, chocking,** *n. v.t.* **1.** cut off the breath of. **2.** clog. —*v.i.* **3.** suffer from the cutting-off of breath. —*n.* **4.** act, instance, or sound of choking.

cho·les·ter·ol (kə les'tə rōl''), *n.* solid found in bile, etc.

choose, *v.,* **chose, chosen, choosing.** *v.t.* **1.** decide upon as best to take, do, etc. —*v.i.* **2.** make a choice.

choos'y, *adj.,* **-ier, -iest.** *Informal.* taking great care or trouble over purchases, etc. Also, **choos'ey.**

chop, *v.,* **chopped, chopping,** *n. v.t., v.i.* **1.** cut with small blows. —*n.* **2.** small cutting blow. **3.** meat cut from the rib, shoulder, or loin. **4.** small, distinct waves of water. **5. chops,** mouth and lower cheeks. —**chop'per,** *n.* —**chop'py,** *adj.*

chop'sticks'', *n., pl.* twin sticks used in eating, esp. in the Far East.

chop su'ey, quasi-Chinese food of meat, bean sprouts, etc.

chor·al (kōr'əl), *adj.* pertaining to or for a chorus.

cho·rale', *n.* **1.** hymn tune. **2.** choral composition. **3.** chorus or choir.

chord (kōrd), *n.* **1.** combination of musical tones. **2.** straight line intercepting an arc at two points.

chore, *n.* routine or hard task.

chor·e·og·ra·phy (kōr''ē ahg'rə fē), *n.* art of planning or executing ballets or dances. —**chor''e·o·graph'ic,** *adj.* —**chor'e·o·graph'',** *v.t.* —**chor''e·og'ra·pher,** *n.*

chor'tle, *v.,* **-tled, -tling.** *v.i., v.t.* speak with chuckles.

cho·rus (kō'rəs), *n.* **1.** singing group. **2.** composition for such a group. **3.** repeated part of a song composed in stanzas. **4.** unison. —*v.t.* **5.** utter in chorus.

chow, *n.* **1.** medium-sized dog. **2.** *Informal.* food.

chow'der, *n.* soup of milk, clams, fish, etc.

chow mein, quasi-Chinese dish of fried noodles, meat, bean sprouts, etc.

chris'ten, *v.t.* **1.** baptize. **2.** name formally. —**chris'ten·ing,** *n.*

Chris'ten·dom, *n.* Christian part of the world or of humanity.

Chris'tian, *n.* **1.** believer in Christ. —*adj.* **2.** pertaining to believers in Christ or to their churches. **3.** consistent with the teachings of Christ, esp. regarding charity or salvation. —**Chris''ti·an'i·ty,** *n.*

Christian name, name given to a person, as at baptism.

Christ'mas, *n.* celebration of the birth of Christ, usually December 25.

chro·mat'ic, *adj.* **1.** pertaining to color.

2. *Music.* composed of semitones, as a scale.

chrome, *n., adj., v.t.,* **chromed, chroming.** *n.* **1.** chromium or a chromium alloy. —*adj.* **2.** made with chromium. —*n.* **3.** plate with chrome.

chro'mi·um, *n.* corrosion-resistant metallic element.

chro'mo·some'', *n.* gene-bearing body.

chron'ic, *adj.* **1.** long-lasting or recurrent. **2.** suffering from a chronic ailment. —**chron'i·cal·ly,** *adv.*

chron'i·cle, *n., v.t.,* **-cled, -cling.** *n.* **1.** chronological record. —*v.t.* **2.** put into such a record. —**chron'i·cler,** *n.*

chro·nol'o·gy, *n., pl.* **-gies. 1.** measurement of time. **2.** recording of events in order of occurrence. **3.** dating of events. —**chron''o·log'i·cal,** *adj.*

chro·nom'e·ter, *n.* highly accurate timepiece.

chrys'a·lis, *n.* pupa or cocoon of a butterfly.

chrys·an'the·mum, *n.* showy late-blooming flower.

chub'by, *adj.,* **-bier, -biest.** plump.

chuck, *v.t.* **1.** toss. **2.** tap, esp. under the chin. —*n.* **3.** neck and shoulder cut of beef. **4.** act or instance of chucking.

chuck'le, *v.i.,* **-led, -ling,** *n. v.i.* **1.** laugh softly. —*n.* **2.** soft laugh.

chug, *n., v.i.,* **chugged, chugging.** *n.* **1.** sound of an engine exhaust. —*v.i.* **2.** move with chugs.

chum, *n. Informal.* friend. **chum'my,** *adj.*

chump, *n. Informal.* person with bad judgment.

chunk, *n.* thick fragment.

chunk'y, *adj.,* **-ier, -iest.** short and thick.

church, *n.* **1.** religious organization. **2.** religious building. **3.** whole community of Christians. —**church'go''er,** *n.* —**church'ly,** *adj.* —**church'man,** *n.*

church'yard'', *n.* grounds of a church, esp. when used as a cemetery.

churl, *n.* surly, ill-mannered person. —**churl'ish,** *adj.*

churn, *n.* **1.** device for shaking cream to form butter. —*v.t., v.i.* **2.** stir or shake.

chute (shōōt), *n.* slide for transferring materials, etc.

chut'ney, *n.* Indian relish.

chutz·pah (khōōtz'pah), *n. Yiddish.* impudence; audacity. Also, **chutz'pa.**

ci·ca·da (si kā'də), *n.* large insect making a shrill rasping sound; often called a locust.

ci'der, *n.* apple juice.

ci·gar', *n.,* roll of tobacco leaves for smoking.

cig''a·rette', *n.* roll of tobacco in paper for smoking.

cinch, *n.* **1.** *Informal.* something easy. **2.** strap for securing a saddle.

cin'der, *n.* ash.

cin′e·ma, *n.* motion picture or pictures. —**cin″e·mat′ic,** *adj.*

cin′na·mon, *n.* East Indian spice.

ci′pher, *n.* 1. code. 2. zero.

cir′ca, *prep.* around; used in dating.

cir′cle, *n., v.t.,* **-cled, -cling.** *n.* 1. closed two-dimensional curve with one center. 2. something formed like such a curve. 3. group of friends, persons with common interests, etc. —*v.t.* 4. go around in a circle.

cir′cuit, *n.* 1. continuous path of movement. 2. regular round of professional visits. 3. path of an electric current.

cir·cu′i·tous, *adj.* roundabout.

cir′cuit·ry, *n.* components of an electrical circuit.

cir′cu·lar, *adj.* 1. shaped like a circle. —*n.* 2. pamphlet, etc. for general distribution.

cir′cu·lar·ize″, *v.t.,* **-ized, -izing.** 1. solicit from or notify by means of circulars. 2. make circular.

cir′cu·late″, *v.,* **-ated, -ating.** *v.i.* 1. move in a closed, continuous path. 2. move from person to person or place to place. —*v.t.* 3. cause to move in either of these ways. —**cir′cu·la·to″ry,** *adj.*

cir″cu·la′tion, *n.* 1. act or instance of circulating. 2. normal movement of blood. 3. readership of a periodical.

cir′cum·cise″, *v.t.,* **-cised, -cising.** cut away the foreskin of. —**cir′cum·ci′sion,** *n.*

cir″cum·fer·ence, *n.* dimension along the line of a circle. —**cir·cum′fer·en″tial,** *adj.*

cir″cum·lo·cu′tion, *n.* wordy, evasive speech.

cir″cum·nav′i·gate, *v.t.,* **-gated, gating.** sail or fly entirely around.

cir′cum·scribe″, *v.t.,* **-scribed, -scribing.** 1. draw a circle around. 2. confine.

cir′cum·spect″, *adj.* cautious. —**cir″cum·spec′tion,** *n.*

cir′cum·stance″, *n.* 1. accompanying condition. 2. chance. 3. **circumstances,** state of material welfare.

cir″cum·stan′tial, *adj.* 1. pertaining to circumstances or circumstance. 2. pertaining to legal evidence implying but not proving something. 3. detailed.

cir′cum·vent″, *v.t.* prevent or overcome with cunning. —**cir″cum·ven′tion,** *n.*

cir′cus, *n.* 1. traveling show of animals, acrobats, etc. 2. ancient show of human and animal combats, etc.

cir′rus, *n.* feathery cloud formation.

cis′tern, *n.* tank for water storage.

cit′a·del, *n.* fortress, esp. in a city.

cite, *v.t.,* **cited, citing.** 1. mention as a scholarly authority. 2. mention as an example. 3. mention officially as meritorious. 4. summon before a court. —**ci·ta′tion,** *n.*

cit′i·zen, *n.* member of a state or other political entity. —**cit′i·zen·ry,** *n.* —**cit′i·zen·ship″,** *n.*

cit′ron, *n.* lemonlike fruit whose rind is candied.

cit″ron·el′la, *n.* oil used to repel mosquitoes, etc.

citrus, *adj.* of or pertaining to lemons, oranges, limes, etc. —**cit′ric,** *adj.*

cit′y, *n., pl.* **-ies.** 1. large community. 2. government of such a community.

civ′ic, *adj.* pertaining to cities or their citizens.

civ′ics, *n., pl.* study of the relation of citizens to political entities.

civ′il, *adj.* 1. not military or religious. 2. polite. —**ci·vil′i·ty** *n.*

civil engineering, engineering of public works or the like. —**civil engineer.**

ci·vil′ian, *n.* person outside any military or police organization.

civ″i·li·za′tion, *n.* 1. lawful, orderly state of society. 2. society characterized by order. 3. civilized part of the world.

civ′i·lize″, *v.t.,* **-ized, -izing.** cause to adopt civilization.

civil service, non-military, non-police government service. —**civil servant.**

civil war, war between factions of the same nation.

clad, *adj.* dressed.

claim, *v.t.* 1. designate for oneself. 2. assert as true. 3. require. —*n.* 4. act or instance of claiming. 5. something claimed. —**claim′ant, claim′er,** *n.*

clair·voy′ance, *n.* sensitivity to things not usually seen, esp. the supernatural. —**clair·voy′ant,** *adj., n.*

clam, *n.* bivalve mollusk.

clam′ber, *v.i.* climb laboriously.

clam′my, *adj.,* **-mier, -miest.** cold and moist.

clam′or, *n.* 1. loud outcry. —*v.i.* 2. make such an outcry, as in demanding or complaining. —**clam′or·ous,** *adj.*

clamp, *n.* 1. mechanical device for holding things together. —*v.t.* 2. fasten with a clamp.

clan, *n.* group of families with a common ancestor. —**clans′man,** *n.*

clan·des′tine, *adj.* secret; stealthy.

clang, *n.* loud ringing noise.

clang′or, *n.* clanging, as of bells.

clank, *n.* dull metallic sound.

clan′nish, *adj.* sociable together but excluding others.

clap, *v.t.* 1. strike together, as the palms of the hands. —*v.i.* 2. clap the palms together. —*n.* 3. sound of clapping. 4. act or instance of clapping.

clap·board (klə′bərd), *n.* board used as a siding for buildings.

clap′per, *n.* object for striking a bell.

claque, *n.* group for the purpose of applauding a performer, esp. for pay.

clar'et, *n.* dry red table wine.

clar'i·fy'', *v.t.*, -fied, -fying. make clear. —**clar''i·fi·ca'tion**, *n.*

clar''i·net', *n.* reed woodwind instrument. —**clar''i·net'ist**, *n.*

clar'i·ty, *n.* clearness, esp. to the understanding.

clash, *v.i.* 1. strike together violently. 2. be in violent disagreement. —*n.* 3. act or instance of clashing.

clasp, *n.* 1. folding fastener. 2. embrace. 3. grasp, as of the hand. —*v.t.* 4. hold with or in a clasp.

class, *n.* 1. category or grade. 2. social or economic level. 3. *Informal.* stylishness. 4. group of students taught or graduating together. —*v.t.* 5. classify. —**class'less**, *adj.* —**class'mate''**, *n.* —**class'room''**, *n.*

clas'sic, *adj.* 1. excellent of its kind. 2. completely typical. 3. harmonious. 4. pertaining to Greco-Roman antiquity or art. —*n.* 5. something excellent of its kind. 6. Greek or Roman author.

clas'si·cal, *adj.* 1. pertaining to Greco-Roman antiquity or art. 2. *Music.* serious and of permanent value. 3. traditional.

clas'si·cism, *n.* adherence to forms or principles deemed classic. —**clas'si·cist**, *n.*

clas'si·fy'', *v.t.*, -fied, -fying. 1. put into meaningful categories. 2. designate officially as secret. —**clas''si·fi·ca'tion**, *n.*

clat'ter, *n.* 1. loud rattling noise. —*v.i.* 2. make a clatter. —*v.t.* 3. cause to clatter.

clause, *n.* 1. unit of a sentence. 2. unit of a document.

claus''tro·pho'bi·a, *n.* morbid fear of enclosure. —**claus''tro·pho'bic**, *adj.*

clav'i·chord'', *n.* pianolike keyboard instrument.

clav'i·cle, *n.* collarbone.

claw, *n.* 1. hooked paw or foot. —*v.t.*, *v.i.* 2. scratch or grasp with or as with a claw.

clay, *n.* earth in a readily molded state.

clean, *adj.* 1. free of dirt, germs, impurities, etc. 2. keeping things clean. 3. irreproachable. 4. thorough. —*v.t.* 5. make clean. —**clean'er**, *n.* —**clean'up''**, *n.*

clean·ly (klen'lē) *adj.*, -lier, -liest. free of or avoiding dirt, etc. —**clean'li·ness**, *n.*

cleanse, *v.t.*, cleansed, cleansing. make clean.

clear, *adj.* 1. perfectlytransparent. 2. lucid. 3. unambiguous. 4. obvious. 5. unobstructed. 6. free of blame, danger, debt, etc. —*adv.* 7. clearly. —*v.t.* 8. make clear. 9. pass without colliding with. 10. net a profit of. —**clear'ly**, *adv.* —**clear'ness**, *n.*

clear'ance, *n.* 1. space between two obstructions. 2. official approval to proceed.

clear'ing, *n.* forest area free of trees.

cleat, *n.* object attached to a surface to improve traction, give reinforcement, etc.

cleave, *v.*, cleaved or (for 1) cleft or clove, cleaved or (for 1) cleft or cloven, cleaving. *v.t.*, *v.i.* 1. split. —*v.i.* 2. adhere or be faithful. —**cleav'er**, *n.* —**cleav'age**, *n.*

clef, *n. Music.* symbol establishing pitch.

cleft, *n.* narrow opening; crack.

clem'ent, *n.* 1. merciful. 2. mild, as the weather. —**clem'en·cy**, *n.*

clench, *v.t.* press or bind firmly together.

cler'gy, *n.*, *pl.* -gies. priests, ministers, and other religious leaders. —**cler'gy·man**, *n.*

cler'i·cal, *adj.* 1. pertaining to clerks. 2. pertaining to clergy.

clerk, *n.* 1. record keeper. 2. retail employee.

clev'er, *adj.* able in understanding, contriving, etc. —**clev'er·ly**, *adv.* —**clev'er·ness**, *n.*

cli·ché, *n.* trite metaphor or phrase.

click, *n.* 1. sharp noise from striking, buckling, etc. —*v.t.*, *v.i.* 2. move with a click.

cli'ent, *n.* person who buys professional services.

cli''en·tele', *n.* clients of a professional man, merchant, etc.

cliff, *n.* abrupt rise of land.

cli·mac'ter·ic, *n.* critical period of life, esp. in middle age.

cli'mate, *n.* characteristic weather. —**cli·mat'ic**, *adj.*

cli'max, *n.* point of greatest interest, emotion, tension, etc. —**cli·mac'tic**, *adj.*

climb, *v.t.* 1. move upward upon or within. —*v.i.* 2. climb something. 3. grow or become higher. —*n.* 4. act or instance of climbing. 5. something climbed. —**climb'er**, *n.*

clinch, *v.t.* 1. establish firmly. 2. bend to secure firmly, as a driven nail. —*n.* 3. act or instance of clinching.

cling, *v.i.*, clung, clinging. 1. hold firmly. 2. stay close.

clin'ic, *n.* 1. session of medical treatment as a form of instruction. 2. association of medical specialists. 3. place for treating outpatients.

clin'i·cal, *adj.* 1. pertaining to clinics. 2. pertaining to medical education and treatment involving actual cases. 3. impersonally analytical.

clink, *n.* 1. high, muted ringing. —*v.i.* 2. make such a sound. —*v.t.* 3. strike so as to make such a sound.

clink'er, *n.* lump of coal ash, etc.

clip, *v.*, clipped, clipping. *v.t.* 1. cut, as with scissors. 2. fasten. 3. *Informal.* hit sharply. —*v.i.* **4.** move swiftly. —*n.* **5.** fastener. **6.** *Informal.* sharp blow.

clip'per, *n.* **1.** fast sailing vessel. **2.** **clippers,** device for cutting hair.

clip'ping, *n.* article cut from a periodical.

clique, *n.* exclusive social group. —**cliqu'ish,** *adj.*

cloak, *n.* **1.** long, loose garment worn over the shoulders. —*v.t.* **2.** cover with a cloak. **3.** obscure.

clob'ber, *v.t. Informal.* beat.

clock, *n.* **1.** machine for measuring time. **2.** narrow sock ornament. —*v.t.* **3.** time. —**clock'work'',** *n., adj.*

clock'wise'', *adv., adj.* as the hands of a clock move, i.e. from left to right through 12 o'clock.

clod, *n.* **1.** lump of earth. **2.** *Informal.* stupid person.

clog, *v.,* **clogged, clogging,** *n. v.t.* **1.** stop flow through; choke. —*v.i.* **2.** become stopped up. —*n.* **3.** act or instance of clogging. **4.** thick-soled shoe.

clois'ter, *n.* **1.** covered walk in a monastery, etc. **2.** monastic institution.

clone, *n., v.* (biology) a genetic duplicate of an organism.

close, *v.,* **closed, closing,** *adj.,* **closer, closest,** *n. v.t.* (klōz) **1.** block or fill, as with a door. **2.** move so as to block or fill. **3.** deny public access to. **4.** conclude. —*v.i.* **5.** become closed. —*n.* **6.** conclusion. —*adj.* (klōs) **7.** near; not far. **.8.** confined. **9.** intimate. **10.** stuffy. **11.** careful. **12.** secretive. —**close'ly,** *adv.* —**close'ness,** *n.* —**clo'sure,** *n.*

clos'et, *n.* **1.** small storage room. —*v.t.* **2.** put in a small room for privacy.

close'-up'', *n.* photograph at close range.

clot, *n., v.i.,* **clotted, clotting,** *n.* **1.** lump, esp. of coagulated blood. —*v.i.* **2.** form a clot.

cloth, *n., pl.* **cloths. 1.** material of interwoven fibers. **2.** piece of such material. **3. the cloth,** the clergy.

clothe, *v.t.,* **clothed, clothing. 1.** put clothes on. **2.** give clothes to.

clothes, *n., pl.* things to cover the human body. Also, **cloth'ing.**

cloud, *n.* **1.** mass of vapor in the sky. **2.** mass of airborne material. **3.** something marring happiness, reputation, etc. —*v.t.* **4.** make indistinct, as from vapor. **5.** mar. —*v.i.* **6.** become cloudy. —**cloud'less,** *adj.* ⁺—**cloud'y,** *adj.*

cloud'burst'', *n.* sudden, violent rainstorm.

clout, *n.* **1.** blow. —*v.t.* **2.** hit.

clove, *n.* **1.** tropical spice.· **2.** section of a head of garlic, etc.

clo'ven, *adj.* divided or split.

clo'ver, *n.* three-leafed herb.

clo'ver-leaf'', *n.* system of curved ramps between roads crossing at different grades.

clown, *n.* **1.** entertainer with funny antics. —*v.i.* **2.** act like a clown.

cloy'ing, *adj.* repulsively sweet, sentimental, etc.

club, *n., v.* **clubbed, clubbing.** *n.* **1.** stick, etc. for striking blows. **2.** similar object used in exercises or sports. **3.** social group. **4.** suit of playing cards. —*v.t.* **5.** strike with a club. —*v.i.* **6.** unite for a purpose. —**club'foot'',** *n.* —**club'house'',** *n.*

cluck, *n.* **1.** henlike sound. —*v.i.* **2.** make such a sound.

clue, *n.* **1.** indication of the solution to a puzzle.

clump, *n.* cluster, as of trees.

clum'sy, *adj.,* **-sier, -siest.** without skill or care. —**clum'si·ly,** *adv.* —**clum'si·ness,** *n.*

clus'ter, *n.* **1.** loose group. —*v.t., v.i.* **2.** gather in a group.

clutch, *v.t., v.i.* **1.** grasp violently. —*n.* **2.** grasp. **3. clutches,** unrightful possession or power. **4.** device for engaging a machine with its mover.

clut'ter, *v.t.* **1.** fill with unwanted things. —*n.* **2.** disorderly accumulation.

coach, *n.* **1.** enclosed horse-drawn carriage. **2.** bus. **3.** railroad passenger car. **4.** trainer, as in sports or performing arts. —*v.t.* **5.** train, rehearse, or prompt. —**coach'man,** *n.*

co·ag'u·late'', *v.,* **-ated, -ating.** *v.i., v.t.* turn from a liquid to a semi-solid. —**co·ag''u·la'tion,** *n.* —**co·ag'u·lant,** *n.*

coal, *n.* **1.** combustible mineral. **2.** ember. —*v.t.* **3.** supply with coal.

co''a·lesce', *v.i.,* **-lesced, lescing.** unite. —**co''a·les'cence,** *n.*

co''a·li'tion, *n.* act of uniting for a specific purpose.

coal oil, kerosene.

coarse, *adj.* **1.** composed of large grains, fibers, etc. **2.** roughly made. **3.** unrefined, as manners or language. —**coarse'ly,** *adv.* —**coarse'ness,** *n.* —**coars'en,** *v.t., v.i.*

coast, *n.* **1.** land by a sea, etc. —*v.i.* **2.** move by gravity or momentum. **3.** sail along a coast. —**coast'al,** *adj.* —**coast'line'',** *n.*

coast'er, *n.* **1.** person or thing that coasts. **2.** mat or stand for wet glasses. **3.** ship on a coastal run.

coat, *n.* **1.** cold-weather garment. **2.** jacket. **3.** Also, **coat'ing,** layer of material. —*v.t.* **4.** cover with a coat.

coat of arms, *Heraldry.* arms of a person, state, etc.

coax, *v.t.,* persuade with flattery or wheedling.

co·ax'i·al, *adj.* having a common axis.

cob, *n.* corncob.

cob'ble, *v.t.,* **-bled, -bling.** *n.* **1.** repair, as shoes. **2.** assemble clumsily. —*n.* **3.**

Also, **cob'ble·stone''**, large pebble used for paving.

cob'bler, *n.* 1. person who cobbles. 2. fruit-filled pastry.

co'bra, *n.* poisonous Asian and African snake.

cob'web'', *n.* web of a spider.

co·caine', *n.* narcotic from a tropical plant.

cock, *n.* 1. rooster. 2. faucet. —*v.t.* 3. tilt. 4. make ready for firing, as a gun.

cock·ade', *n.* hat badge or ribbon.

cock'a·too'', *n.* crested East Indian parrot.

cocker spaniel, small, droopy-eared spaniel.

cock'eyed'', *adj. Informal.* awry; wrong.

cock'le, *n.* edible shellfish.

cock'ney, *n., pl.* **-nies.** 1. native of London's East End. 2. dialect of such a native.

cock'pit'', *n.* 1. place for a cockfight. 2. space for an airplane crew.

cock'roach'', *n.* crawling insect found in buildings.

cock'sure'', *adj.* foolishly self-assured.

cock'tail'', *n.* 1. mixed alcoholic drink. 2. mixed appetizer.

cock'y, *adj.,* **-ier, -iest.** *Informal.* showily self-assured.

co'coa, *n.* drink made from roasted cacao powder.

co'co·nut, *n.* fruit of a palm tree, whose flesh and juice are consumed. Also, **co'coa·nut.**

co·coon', *n.* case of certain insect pupas, made of a thread.

cod, *n., pl.* **cod, cods.** edible northern saltwater fish. Also, **cod'fish''.**

cod'dle, *v.t.,* **-dled, -dling.** 1. cook in water just below boiling. 2. take excessive care of; pamper.

code, *n., v.t.,* **coded, coding.** *n.* 1. set of laws or principles. 2. formula for secret messages. 3. formula for transcription by telegraph, wigwag, etc. —*v.t.* put into code.

co'deine, *n.* pain reliever derived from opium. Also, **co'dein.**

cod'i·cil, *n.* appendix to a will.

cod'i·fy'', *v.t.,* **-fied, -fying.** put into systematic form, esp. in writing. —**cod''i·fi·ca'tion,** *n.*

co'-ed'', *n. Informal.* woman in a coeducational school. Also, **co'ed''.**

co·ed''u·ca'tion, *n.* enrollment of men and women in the same school. —**co·ed''u·ca'tion·al,** *adj.*

co''ef·fi'cient, *n.* multiplier.

co·erce', *v.t.,* **-erced, -ercing.** compel by force or threats. —**co·er'cion,** *n.*

co·e'val, *adj.* at or of the same age.

co''ex·ist', *v.i.* 1. exist together. 2. live

together without dispute. —**co''ex·ist'ence,** *n.*

cof'fee, *n.* drink made from the roasted seed of a tropical shrub.

cof'fer, *n.* chest for valuables.

cof'fin, *n.* burial chest.

cog, *n.* gear tooth.

co·gent, (kō'jənt), *adj.* forcefully convincing, as an argument. —**co'gen·cy,** *n.*

cog'i·tate'', *v.,* **-tated, -tating.** *v.t., v.i.* ponder. —**cog''i·ta'tion,** *n.* —**cog'i·ta''tor,** *n.*

co·gnac (kon'yak), *n.* a French brandy.

cog'nate'', *adj.* 1. related. —*n.* 2. someone or something related.

cog·ni'tion, *n.* knowledge or perception. —**cog'ni·tive,** *adj.*

cog'ni·zance, *n.* official notice. —**cog'ni·zant,** *adj.*

cog·no'men, *n.* nickname.

cog'wheel'', *n.* gear wheel, esp. in a clock, toy, etc.

co·hab'it, *v.i.* live together, esp. out of wedlock. —**co·hab''i·ta'tion,** *n.*

co·here', *v.i.,* **-hered, -hering.** 1. stick together. 2. be rationally connected. —**co·her'ent,** *adj.* —**co·her'ence,** *n.*

co·he'sion, *n.* tendency of particles, etc. to hold together. —**co·he'sive,** *adj.*

coif'fure', *n.* hair style.

coil, *n.* 1. spiral or helix. —*v.t., v.i.* 2. wind into a coil.

coin, *n.* 1. piece of metal used as money. 2. metal money. —*v.t.* 3. stamp as money. 4. invent as a new expression. —**coin'age,** *n.*

co''in·cide', *v.i.,* **-cided, -ciding.** 1. happen at the same time. 2. be in the same space. 3. be in agreement. —**co·in'cidence,** *n.* —**co·in''ci·den'tal, co·in'ci·dent,** *adj.*

co·i'tus, *n.* sexual intercourse. Also, **co·i'tion,** *n.*

coke, *n.* fuel derived from coal.

col'an·der, *n.* large strainer.

cold, *adj.* 1. having a temperature lower than normal or working temperature. 2. having a relatively low temperature. 3. feeling a lack of warmth. 4. unemotional. 5. hostilely unexpressive. 6. *Informal.* **a.** unprepared. **b.** unconscious. **c.** fully memorized. —*n.* 7. cold conditions, weather, etc. 8. illness associated with cold weather. —**cold'ly,** *adv.* —**cold'ness,** *n.*

cold'blood''ed, *adj.* 1. having blood the temperature of the environment. 2. without emotion, conscience, etc.

cold war, prolonged hostile situation without fighting.

cole'slaw'', *n.* salad of shredded raw cabbage.

col'ic, *n.* abdominal cramp.

col·lab'o·rate'', *v.i.,* **-rated, -rating.** 1. work together, as on a project. 2. assist the invaders of one's country. —col·lab″o·ra′tion, *n.* —col·lab′o·ra″tor, *n.* —col·lab″o·ra′tion·ist, *n.*

col·lapse′, *v.*, -lapsed, -lapsing, *n. v.i.* **1.** fall because of weakness. **2.** fold when not in use. **3.** fail suddenly in bodily or mental health. —*v.t.* **4.** cause to collapse. —*n.* **5.** act or instance of collapsing. —col·laps′i·ble, *adj.*

col′lar, *n.* **1.** band worn around the neck. **2.** band of material applied to a shaft, etc. —*v.t.* **3.** seize by the neck. **4.** put a collar on.

col′lar·bone″, *n.* bone between the breastbone and shoulder blade; clavicle.

col·lat′er·al, *n.* **1.** security for a loan. —*adj.* **2.** accompanying. **3.** related through a remote ancestor.

col′league, *n.* professional associate.

col·lect′, *v.t.*, *v.i.* **1.** gather together. —*v.t.* **2.** acquire to enjoy permanently. **3.** enforce payment of. —*adv.*, *adj.* **4.** with the receiver paying the charges. —col·lect′a·ble, col·lect′i·ble, *adj.*, *n.* —col·lect′or, *n.* —col·lec′tion, *n.*

col·lect′ed, *adj.* with one's emotions under control.

col·lec′tive, *adj.* **1.** involving cooperation. —*n.* **2.** collective enterprise or workplace. —col·lec′tive·ly, *adv.*

col·lec′tiv·ism, *n.* adoption of collective working methods. —col·lec′tiv·ist, *n.*, *adj.* —col·lec′tiv·ize″, *v.t.*

col′lege, *n.* **1.** generalized institution of higher learning. **2.** specialized school. **3.** official organization. —col·le′giate, *adj.*

col·lide′, *v.i.*, -lided, -liding. strike against another or each other while moving. —col·li′sion, *n.*

col′lie, *n.* large, long-haired dog.

col·lo′qui·al, *adj.* pertaining to or used in informal conversation only. —col·lo′qui·al·ism, *n.*

col′lo·quy, *n.*, *pl.* -quies. discussion.

col·lu′sion, *n.* unlawful conspiracy. —col·lu′sive, *adj.*

co·logne′, *n.* perfumed toilet water.

co′lon, *n.* **1.** part of the large intestine. **2.** punctuation mark written thus:.

colo·nel (kər′nəl), *n.* military officer between a lieutenant colonel and a brigadier general. —colo′nel·cy, *n.*

col′o·nize, *v.*, -nized, -nizing. *v.t.* **1.** establish colonies in. —*v.i.* **2.** settle in or as a colony.

col″on·nade′, *n.* row of columns, esp. before a porch.

col′o·ny, *n.*, *pl.* -nies. **1.** region in the possession of a foreign nation. **2.** community of settlers. **3.** group of social insects, etc. —co·lon′i·al, *adj.*, *n.* —col′on·ist, *n.*

col′or, *n.* **1.** property deriving from specific wavelengths of light. **2.** pigment. **3.** vividness. **4.** colors, **a.** national flag. **b.** uniform, badge, etc. distinctively colored. —*v.t.* **5.** give color to. —*v.i.* **6.** blush. —col″or·a′tion, *n.* —col′or·ful, *adj.* —col′or·ing, *n.*

col″or·a·tu′ra, *n.* soprano capable of brilliant effects.

col′ored, *n.* Negro; black.

col′or·less, *adj.* not vivid.

co·los′sal, *adj.* gigantic; enormous.

co·los′sus, *n.*, *pl.* -si -suses. something gigantic.

colt, *n.* young male horse.

col′umn, *n.* **1.** narrow, upright structural support. **2.** stack of printed or written lines read together. **3.** regular series of articles by a journalist. **4.** file of troops. —col′um·nist, *n.*

co′ma, *n.* pathological unconsciousness. —co′ma·tose″, *adj.*

comb, *n.* **1.** pronged device for arranging the hair or other fibers. **2.** crest of a rooster, etc. **3.** honeycomb. —*v.t.* **4.** use a comb on. **5.** search exhaustively.

com·bat, *n.*, *v.t.*, -bated, -bating. *n.* (kom′bat) **1.** battle. —*v.t.* (kəm bat′) **2.** fight or oppose. —com·bat′ant, *n.*, *adj.* —com·bat′ive, *adj.*

com″bi·na′tion, *n.* **1.** act or instance of combining. **2.** group of successive settings of a lock dial that open the lock.

com·bine′, *v.t.*, *v.i.* (kəm bīn′) **1.** join together. —*n.* (kom′bīn) **2.** machine that harvests and threshes grain. **3.** syndicate.

com′bo, *n.*, *pl.* -bos. *Jazz.* small instrumental group.

com·bus′tion, *n.* act of burning. —com·bus′ti·ble, *adj.*

come, *v.i.*, came, come, coming, *interj.* *v.i.* **1.** move to this place. **2.** attend; be present. **3.** occur; happen. —*interj.* **4.** be truthful, reasonable, etc.

co·me′di·an, *n.* humorous performer. Also, *fem.*, co·me″di·enne′.

com′e·dy, *n.*, *pl.* -dies. **1.** drama with a happy ending. **2.** amusing situation.

come′ly, *adj.*, -lier, -liest. physically attractive.

co·mes′ti·ble, *n.*, *adj.* edible.

com′et, *n.* cloud of fine dust in orbit around the sun.

com′fort, *n.* **1.** feeling of physical well-being. **2.** consolation. —*v.t.* **3.** console or reassure.

com′fort·a·ble, *adj.* **1.** enjoying comfort. **2.** promoting comfort. —com′fort·a·bly, *adv.*

com′fort·er, *n.* **1.** source of comfort. **2.** quilt.

com′ic, *adj.* **1.** Also, com′i·cal, amusing. **2.** pertaining to comedy. **3.** comics, comic strip. —*n.* **4.** comedian. —com′i·cal·ly, *adv.*

com'ing, *adj.* **1.** on the way. **2.** destined for preeminence. —*n.* **3.** approach or arrival.

com'ma, *n.* a mark, used especially to separate phrases or clauses in a sentence.

com·mand', *v.t.* **1.** order or direct. **2.** have authority over. **3.** have the use or enjoyment of. **4.** overlook. —*n.* **5.** order. **6.** authority or control.

com'man·dant", *n.* commanding officer.

com"man·deer', *v.t.* take control of by authority or force.

com·man'der, *n.* naval officer between a lieutenant commander and a captain in rank.

commander in chief, *n., pl.* **commander in chief.** supreme military commander.

com·mand'ment, *n.* order, esp. a standing one from a deity.

com·man'do, *n., pl.* **-dos, -does.** member of a raiding force.

com·mem'o·rate', *v.t.,* **-rated, -rating.** honor or preserve the memory of. —**com·mem"o·ra'tion,** *n.* —**com·mem'o·ra·tive,** *adj.*

com·mence', *v.,* **-menced, -mencing.** *v.t., v.i.* begin.

com·mence'ment, *n.* **1.** beginning. **2.** high-school graduation ceremony.

com·mend', *v.t.* **1.** praise. **2.** recommend. **3.** entrust. —**com·mend'a·ble,** *adj.* —**com"men·da'tion,** *n.* —**com·mend'a·to"ry,** *adj.*

com·men'su·ra·ble, *adj.* able to be measured or evaluated in the same way.

com·men'su·rate, *adj.* equal or in proportion.

com'ment, *n.* **1.** remark or remarks on something observed. **2.** opinion or explanation regarding something. —*v.i.* **3.** make a comment.

com'men·tar"y, *n., pl.* **-ries.** set of explanatory notes.

com'men·ta"tor, *n.* person who comments on current events.

com'merce, *n.* purchasing and sale of merchandise.

com·mer'cial, *adj.* **1.** pertaining to commerce. —*n.* **2.** television or radio advertisement.

com·mer'cial·ism, *n.* emphasis on ready mass saleability rather than on quality, taste, etc.

com·mer'cial·ize", *v.t.,* **-ized, -izing.** make, sell, etc. for maximum profit.

com·min'gle, *v.,* **-gled, -gling.** *v.t., v.i.* blend.

com·mis'er·ate", *v.i.* **-ated, -ating.** feel sympathetic sorrow. —**com·mis"er·a'tion,** *n.*

com"mis·sar'i·at, *n.* military department in charge of food.

com'mis·sar"y, *n., pl.* **-ries.** *n.* **1.** military food shop. **2.** factory canteen.

com·mis'sion, *n.* **1.** entrusted task. **2.** formal authorization. **3.** military officership. **4.** committee. **5.** salesman's percentage of the amount of a sale. —*v.t.* **6.** entrust or authorize. **7.** put in service, as a ship.

com·mis'sion·er, *n.* head of a municipal department or commission.

com·mit', *v.t.,* **-mitted, -mitting. 1.** obligate. **2.** state the position of in a controversy. **3.** do, esp. a crime. **4.** send for confinement. —**com·mit'ment,** *n.* —**com·mit'al,** *n.*

com·mit'tee, *n.* chosen group of persons with specified responsibilities. —**com·mit'tee·man,** *n.* —**com·mit'tee·wom"an,** *n.*

com·mode', *n.* **1.** chest of drawers. **2.** water closet.

com·mo'di·ous, *adj.* roomy.

com·mod'i·ty, *n., pl.* **-ties.** *Commerce.* material or article, as opposed to a service.

com'mo·dore", *n.* **1.** naval officer ranking between a captain and a rear admiral. **2.** head of a yacht squadron.

com'mon, *adj.* **1.** pertaining to many or to all. **2.** not unusual. **3.** low in rank or status. **4.** vulgar. —*n.* **5.** area of public land in a village. —**com'mon·ly,** *adv.*

com'mon·er, *n.* citizen not of the nobility.

common law, law based on custom and court decisions.

com'mon·place", *adj.* **1.** completely or tritely familiar. —*n.* **2.** something commonplace.

common sense, ordinary good judgment. —**com'mon-sense",** **com"mon·sen'si·cal,** *adj.*

com'mon·weal", *n.* general good.

com'mon·wealth", *n.* **1.** federation of states. **2.** state.

com·mo'tion, *n.* uproar.

com'mu·nal, *adj.* pertaining to or shared by a community or group.

com·mune', *v.i.,* **-muned, -muning.** *n.* *v.i.* (kə myōōn') **1.** be in intimate communication or sympathy. —*n.* (kom' yōōn) **2.** community sharing goods, responsibilities, etc.

com·mun'i·ca·ble, *adj.* **1.** able to be communicated. **2.** able to be transferred, as an illness.

com·mun'i·cant, *n.* partaker of the Eucharist.

com·mun'i·cate', *v.,* **-cated, -cating.** *v.t.* **1.** make understood to others. —*v.i.* **2.** exchange messages. **3.** be in communion. **4.** be connected, as rooms. —**com·mun"i·ca'tion,** *n.*

com·mun'i·ca·tive, *adj.* talkative or confiding.

com·mun'ion, *n.* **1.** state of intimacy. **2.** *Christianity.* sharing of bread and wine in remembrance of Christ. **3.** religious denomination.

com·mun″i·qué, *n.* official message or news release.

com·mu·nism, *n.* **1.** political theory demanding public ownership of economic resources. **2. Communism.** socialism derived from the theories of **Karl Marx.** —**com″mu·nis′tic**, *adj.* —**com′mu·nist**, *n., adj.*

com·mun′i·ty, *n., pl.* **-ties. 1.** town, etc. **2.** group with common interests, etc. **3.** sharing in common.

com·mute′, *v.*, **-muted, -muting.** *v.t.* **1.** altar, as a prison sentence. —*v.i.* **2.** travel regularly, as between home and work. —**com·mut′er**, *n.* —**com″mu·ta′tion**, *n.*

com·pact, *adj.* (kəm pakt′) **1.** occupying a minimal space. **2.** succinct. —*n.* (kom′pakt) **3.** small cosmetic case. **4.** small-bodied car. **5.** mutual agreement. —**com·pact′ly**, *adv.* —**com·pact′ness**, *n.*

com·pan′ion, *n.* **1.** person who keeps one company. **2.** one of a pair or set. —**com·pan′ion·ship″**, *n.*

com·pan′ion·a·ble, *adj.* willing to keep one company.

com·pan′ion·way″, *n.* stair in a ship.

com′pa·ny, *n., pl.* **-nies. 1.** fellowship; companionship. **2.** group of persons. **3.** group of persons assembled for social purposes. **4.** guests. **5.** business organization or association. **6.** military unit.

com′pa·ra·ble, *adj.* allowing comparison.

com·par′a·tive, *adj.* **1.** involving comparison. **2.** in comparison to other cases. —**com·par′a·tive·ly**, *adv.*

com·pare′, *v.*, **-pared, -paring,** *n. v.t.* **1.** examine for similarities and differences. **2.** regard or describe as similar. —*v.i.* **3.** be similar to, esp. in worth. —*n.* **4. beyond compare,** without equal.

com·par′i·son, *n.* **1.** act or instance of comparing. **2.** similarity.

com·part′ment, *n.* division of a larger space.

com′pass, *n.* **1.** instrument for establishing or indicating direction. **2.** scope. **3. compasses,** instrument for drawing circles.

com·pas′sion, *n.* sympathy, esp. with suffering or weakness. —**com·pas′sion·ate**, *adj.*

com·pat′i·ble, *adj.* **1.** content together. **2.** logically consistent. —**com·pat″i·bil′i·ty**, *n.*

com·pa′tri·ot, *n.* fellow national.

com·pel′, *v.t.*, **-pelled, -pelling.** force.

com·pen′di·um, *n., pl.* **-ums, -a.** detailed summary. —**com·pen′di·ous**, *adj.*

com·pen·sate″, *v.*, **-sated, -sating.** *v.t.* **1.** pay, as for work or damage. —*v.i.* **2.** serve to offset or make up for something else. —**com″pen·sa′tion**, *n.* —**com·pen′sa·to″ry**, *adj.*

com′pete, *v.i.*, **-peted, -peting.** act in rivalry. —**com″pe·ti′tion**, *n.* —**com·pet′i·tive**, *adj.* —**com·pet′i·tor**, *n.*

com·pe·tent, *adj.* **1.** normal in mental ability. **2.** able to work, etc. adequately. **3.** adequately done. **4.** legally authorized. —**com′pe·tent·ly**, *adv.* —**com′pe·tence, com′pe·ten·cy**, *n.*

com·pile′, *v.t.*, **piled, piling.** gather or publish together, as documents. —**com·pil′er**, *n.* —**com″pi·la′tion**, *n.*

com·pla′cen·cy, *n.* satisfaction, esp. with oneself. —**com·pla′cent**, *adj.*

com·plain′, *v.i.* **1.** discuss one's grievance with others. —*v.t.* **2.** state as a grievance. —**com·plain′er**, *n.*

com·plaint′, *n.* **1.** act or instance of complaining. **2.** wording in which one complains. **3.** distressing illness.

com·plai′sant, *adj.* willing or eager to please. —**com·plai′sance**, *n.*

com·ple·ment, *n.* (com′plə ment) **1.** something that completes. **2.** wholeness. —*v.t.* (com′plə ment″) **3.** complete. —**com″ple·men′ta·ry**, *adj.*

com·plete, *adj., v.t.*, **-pleted, -pleting.** *adj.* **1.** entire; with nothing missing. **2.** accomplished. **3.** utter. —*v.t.* **4.** perfect. **5.** finish. —**com·plete′ly**, *adv.* —**com·plete′ness**, *n.* —**com·ple′tion**, *n.*

com·plex, *adj.* (kəm pleks′) **1.** not readily analyzed or understood. —*n.* (kom′pleks) **2.** something complex. **3.** *Psychology.* **a.** group of impulses controlling behavior. **b.** obsessive attitude. —**com·plex′i·ty**, *n.*

com·plex′ion, *n.* color and texture of the skin.

com′pli·cate″, *v.t.*, **-cated, -cating. 1.** make difficult to do or understand. **2.** make unnecessarily complex. —**com″pli·ca′tion**, *n.*

com·plic′i·ty, *n., pl.* **-ties.** association, esp. in crime.

com·pli·ment, *n.* (kom′plə mənt) **1.** expression of praise. —*v.t.* (kom′plə ment″) **2.** pay a compliment to.

com″pli·men′tar·y, *adj.* **1.** serving as a compliment. **2.** granted free of charge.

com·ply′, *v.i.*, **-plied, -plying.** act as ordered or urged. —**com·pli′ance**, *n.* —**com·pli′ant**, *adj.*

com·po′nent, *n.* **1.** part of a whole. —*adj.* **2.** serving as a component.

com·port′, *v.t.* conduct or behave. —**com·port′ment**, *n.*

com·pose′, *v.t.*, **-posed, -posing. 1.** create or organize artistically. **2.** constitute. **3.** put in order. **4.** make calm.

com·posed′, *adj.* apparently calm.

com·pos′ite, *adj.* made of many constituents.

com″po·si′tion, *n.* 1. something composed. 2. method of composing. 3. nature, as of constituents or traits.

com′post, *n.* decayed matter for use as fertilizer.

com·po′sure, *n.* apparent calm.

com′pote″, *n.* dish of stewed fruits.

com·pound, *adj.* (kom′pownd) 1. not simple; complex. —*n.* 2. substance of mixed elements. 3. building enclosure. —*v.t.* (kəm pownd′) 4. mix or make by mixing. 5. permit unlawfully.

com″pre·hend′, *v.t.* 1. have a conception or understanding of. 2. include. —**com″pre·hen′sion**, *n.* —**com″pre·hen′si·ble**, *adj.*

com″pre·hen′sive, *adj.* including all or most elements. —**com″pre·hen′sive·ly**, *adv.* —**com″pre·hen′sive·ness**, *n.*

com·press, *v.t.* (kəm pres′) 1. press to lessen volume. 2. put under pressure. —*n.* (kahm′pres) 3. pad of cloth applied as an aid to medicine. —**com′pres′sion**, *n.* —**com·pres′sor**, *n.*

com·prise′, *v.t.*, **-prised, -prising.** 1. include. 2. consist of.

com′pro·mise″, *n., v.*, **-mised, -mising.** *n.* 1. expedient but not fully satisfactory agreement. 2. something with disparate elements. —*v.i.* 3. make a compromise. —*v.t.* 4. endanger in reputation, etc.

comp·trol′ler, *n.* financial manager.

com·pul′sion, *n.* act or instance of compelling. —**com·pul′sive**, *adj.* —**com·pul′so·ry**, *adj.*

com·punc′tion, *n.* uneasy, guilty feeling.

com·pute′, *v.t.*, **-puted, -puting.** determine by calculation. —**com″pu·ta′tion**, *n.*

com·put′er, *n.* electronic device for rapid calculation or data comparison. —**com·put′er·ize**, *v.t.* —**com·put″er·i·za′tion**, *n.*

com′rade″, *n.* 1. close friend. 2. associate. —**com′rade·ship″**, *n.*

comsat, *n.* artificial communications satellite.

con, *v.t.*, **conned, conning,** *adj., n. v.t.* 1. survey carefully. —*n.* 2. person or argument opposed. 3. *Nautical.* responsibility, as for guiding a ship.

con·cave′, *adj.* curving inward. —**con·cav′i·ty**, *n.*

con·ceal′, *v.t.* hide or keep secret. —**con·ceal′ment**, *n.*

con·cede′, *v.t.*, **-ceded, -ceding.** 1. admit as true. 2. acknowledge defeat in. 3. grant.

con·ceit′, *n.* 1. excessive pride. 2. fanciful idea or expression.

con·ceit′ed, *adj.* full of conceit.

con·ceive′, *v.*, **-ceived, -ceiving.** *v.i.* 1. form an idea. 2. become pregnant.

—*v.t.* 3. imagine as possible or true. 4. become pregnant with. —**con·ceiv′a·ble**, *adj.* —**con·ceiv′a·bly**, *adv.*

con′cen·trate″, *v.*, **-trated, -trating.** *n. v.t.* 1. focus. 2. increase in strength. —*v.i.* 3. focus attention or effort. —*n.* 4. something concentrated. —**con″cen·tra′tion**, *n.*

con·cen′tric, *adj.* having a common or identical center.

con′cept, *n.* idea of something possible. —**con·cep′tu·al**, *adj.*

con·cep′tion, *n.* act or instance of conceiving.

con·cern′, *v.t.* 1. be the business of. 2. cause care or anxiety in. 3. have as a subject. —*n.* 4. business or affair. 5. care or anxiety. 6. business organization. 7. importance.

con·cerned′, *adj.* 1. anxious. 2. interested. 3. engaged in political or social problems.

con·cern′ing, *prep.* on the subject of.

con′cert, *n.* 1. series of musical compositions performed at one time. 2. harmony.

con·cert′ed, *adj.* performed in an agreed manner.

con″cer·ti′na, *n.* small accordion.

con·cer′to (kən cher′tō), *n., pl.* **-tos, -ti.** orchestral composition, usually with soloists.

con·ces′sion, *n.* 1. act or instance of conceding. 2. something conceded.

con·ces′sion·aire″, *n.* person allowed to engage in trade on another's property.

con·cil′i·ate″, *v.t.*, **-ated, -ating.** pacify or appease. —**con·cil′i·a″tor**, *n.* —**con·cil′i·a·to″ry**, *adj.* —**con·cil″i·a′tion**, *n.*

con·cise′, *adj.* confined to essentials, as a piece of writing. —**con·cise′ly**, *adv.* —**con·cise′ness**, *n.*

con′clave, *n.* private meeting.

con·clude′, *v.*, **-cluded, -cluding.** *v.t.* 1. end. 2. reach an opinion or decision. —*v.i.* 3. bring a meeting, etc. to an end. —**con·clu′sion**, *n.*

con·clu′sive, *adj.* compelling a certain opinion or decision.

con·coct′, *v.t.* 1. make of varied ingredients. 2. devise. —**con·coc′tion**, *n.*

con·com′i·tant, *adj.* 1. accompanying. —*n.* 2. something concomitant. —**con·com′i·tant·ly**, *adv.*

con′cord, *n.* harmonious agreement.

con·cord′ance, *n.* list of occurrences in a book of certain words, etc.

con′course, *n.* 1. crowd. 2. space or hall for accommodating crowds.

con·crete′, *adj.* (kon krēt′) 1. real; material. 2. specific. —*n.* (kon′krēt) 3. material of cement and stone, etc. —*v.t., v.i.* 4. solidify. —**con·cre′tion**, *n.*

con·cu·bine″, *n.* wife of less than full status.

con"cu·pis'cence, *n.* lust. —con"cu·pis' cent, *adj.*

con·cur', *v.i.,* -curred, -curring. 1. agree. 2. cooperate. 3. coincide. —con·cur' rent, *adj.* —con·cur'rence, *n.*

con·cus'sion, *n.* 1. shock, as from a blow. 2. malfunctioning of the mind or body from a blow.

con·demn', *v.t.* 1. disapprove of strongly. 2. reject as unfit. 3. acquire by legal authority. 4. sentence, as to prison. —con"dem·na'tion, *n.*

con·dense', *v.,* -densed, -densing. *v.t., v.i.* 1. turn from a gas to a liquid. —*v.t.* 2. put in succinct form. —con" den·sa'tion, *n.* —con·dens'er, *n.*

con"de·scend', *v.i.* 1. show kindness or affability to an inferior. —*v.t.* 2. do with a good grace despite superior status. —con"de·scen'sion, *n.*

con'di·ment, *n.* flavor or seasoning.

con·di'tion, *n.* 1. state of health, repair, etc. 2. good state of health, etc. 3. something necessary or required. —*v.t.* 4. put in condition. 5. accustom.

con·di'tion·al, *adj.* subject to certain conditions.

con·dole', *v.i.,* -doled, -doling. express sorrowful sympathy. —con·dol'ence, *n.*

con"do·min'i·um, *n.* 1. multi-unit group of privately owned dwellings. 2. territory under a joint rule.

con·done', *v.t.,* -doned, -doning. fail to forbid or disapprove of.

con·duce', *v.i.,* -duced, -ducing. tend or lead. —con·duc'ive, *adj.*

con·duct', *v.t.* (kən dukt') 1. lead or direct. 2. transmit. 3. behave. —*n.* (kahn' dukt) 4. behavior.

con·duc'tor, *n.* 1. leader of a band or orchestra. 2. person in charge of a train, etc. 3. thing that transmits electricity, heat, etc.

con·duit (kahn'dit), *n.* channel for wiring or fluids.

cone, *n.* 1. solid generated by rotating an isosceles triangle around its centerline. 2. fruit of an evergreen.

con·fec'tion, *n.* food made with sugar. —con·fec'tion·er, *n.* —con·fec'tion·er·y, *n.*

con·fed'er·a·cy, *n., pl.* -cies. alliance.

con·fed'er·ate, *n., adj., v.,* -ated, -ating. *n.* (kən fed'ər ət) 1. ally or accomplice. —*adj.* 2. allied. —*v.t., v.t.* (kən fed'ər āt") 3. ally. —con·fed"er· a'tion, *n.*

con·fer', *v.,* -ferred, -ferring. *v.t.* 1. bestow. —*v.i.* 2. consult or discuss. —con·fer'ment, *n.* —con"fer·ence, *n.*

con·fess', *v.t.* 1. admit as true. 2. profess belief in. 3. hear the confession of.

con·fes'sion, *n.* 1. act or instance of confessing. 2. admission of sins by a penitent. 3. creed or sect.

con·fes'sion·al, *n.* place where a priest hears confessions.

con·fes'sor, *n.* priest who hears confessions.

con·fet'ti, *n.* finely chopped colored paper thrown about in celebration.

con'fi·dant", *n.* person in whom one confides. Also, *fem.,* con'fi·dante".

con·fide', *v.,* -fided, -fiding. *v.i.* 1. place trust, esp. by relating secrets. —*v.t.* 2. entrust to someone's care or hearing.

con'fi·dence, *n.* 1. trust. 2. self-assurance. —con'fi·dent, *adj.* —con'fi· dent·ly, *adv.*

con"fi·den'tial, *adj.* 1. to be kept a secret. 2. entrusted with secrets. —con" fi·den'tial·ly, *adv.*

con·fig"u·ra'tion, *n.* outline or contour.

con·fine, *v.t.,* -fined, -fining, *n.* *v.t.* (kənfīn') 1. keep within limits or boundaries. 2. keep as if a prisoner. —*n.* 3. confines (khan'fīnz), boundaries. —con·fine'ment, *n.*

con·firm', *v.t.* 1. certify as true. 2. approve formally. 3. admit fully to a church. —con"fir·ma'tion, *n.*

con'fis·cate, *v.t.,* -cated, -cating. seize by authority. —con"fis·ca'tion, *n.*

con"fla·gra'tion, *n.* fire causing major damage.

con·flict, *n.* (kahn'flikt) 1. fight. 2. disagreement. 3. emotional malaise or quandary. —*v.i.* (kən flikt') 4. be hostile or in disagreement.

con'flu·ence, *n.* place where two rivers, etc. meet.

con·form', *v.i.* 1. form one's appearance, manners, etc. according to prevailing standards. 2. act or be in accordance with a law, rule, etc. 3. be similar. —*v.t.* 4. cause to conform. —con·form'i·ty, *n.*

con·form'ist, *n.* person who conforms unquestioningly.

con·found', *v.t.* confuse.

con·front', *v.t.* 1. approach or face hostilely. 2. force to face. —con"fron·ta' tion, *n.*

con·fuse', *v.t.,* -fused, -fusing. 1. hamper in the powers of perception, analysis, decision, etc. 2. embarrass. 3. mistake for another. —con·fu'sion, *n.*

con·fute', *v.t.,* -futed, -futing. show as wrong. —con"fu·ta'tion, *n.*

con·geal', *v.t., v.i.* thicken or freeze. —con·geal'ment, *n.*

con·gen'i·al, *adj.* agreeable. —con·gen" i·al'i·ty, *n.*

con·gen'i·tal, *adj.* from the time of birth. —con·gen'i·tal·ly, *adv.*

con·gest', *v.t.* fill to excess. —con·ges' tion, *n.*

con·glom·er·ate, *v.,* -ated, -ating, *adj., n. v.t., v.i.* (kən glahm'ə rāt") 1. form into a mass. —*adj.* (kən glahm'ə rət) 2.

congratulate 52

formed as a mass. —*n.* **3.** mass of small elements. **4.** corporation composed of diverse subsidiaries. —**con·glom″er·a'tion,** *n.*

con·grat'u·late″, *v.t.,* **-lated, -lating.** show sympathetic pleasure, as for success or good luck. —**con·grat″u·la'tion,** *n.* —**con·grat'u·la·to″ry,** *adj.*

con'gre·gate″, *v.,* **-gated, -gating.** *v.t.,* *v.i.* gather into a group or assembly. —**con″gre·ga'tion,** *n.* —**con″gre·ga'tion·al,** *adj.*

con'gress, *n.* **1.** legislative body. **2.** former gathering. —**con·gres'sion·al,** *adj.*

Con'gress·man, *n.* member of the U.S. Congress, esp. the House of Representatives.

con'gru·ent, *adj.* in correspondence or harmony. —**con'gru·ence,** *n.*

con'gru·ous, *adj.* **1.** congruent. **2.** appropriate. —**con·gru'i·ty,** *n.*

con'ic, *adj.* **1.** Also, **con'i·cal,** cone-shaped. **2.** derived from a cone.

con'i·fer, *n.* tree or shrub bearing cones. —**co·nif'er·ous,** *adj.*

con·jec'ture, *n.,* *v.* **-tured, -turing.** *n.,* *v.t.,* *v.i.,* guess. —**con·jec'tur·al,** *adj.*

con·join', *v.t.,* *v.i.* join together.

con'ju·gal, *adj.* marital.

con'ju·gate″, *v.t.,* **-gated, -gating.** give the inflections of a verb. —**con″ju·ga'tion,** *n.*

con·junc'tion, *n.* **1.** union or combination. **2.** coincidence. **3.** word linking others in a sentence. —**con·junc'tive,** *adj.*

con·junc'ture, *n.* combination of events.

con·jure, *v.t.,* **-jured, -juring.** cause to appear as by magic. —**con'jur·er, con'jur·or,** *n.*

con·nect', *v.t.* **1.** join. —*v.i.* **2.** adjoin. —**con·nec'tor, con·nec'ter,** *n.* —**con·nec'tive,** *adj.* —**con·nec'tion,** *n.*

con·nive', *v.i.,* **-nived, -niving. 1.** conspire. **2.** permit crime, etc. to occur by ignoring it. —**con·niv'er,** *n.* —**con·niv'ance,** *n.*

con″nois·seur', *n.* person with refined knowledge.

con·note', *v.t.,* **-noted, -noting.** imply through wording, etc. —**con″no·ta'tion,** *n.*

con·nu'bi·al, *adj.* marital.

con'quer, *v.t.* overcome, as in war. —**con'quer·or,** *n.*

con'quest, *n.* **1.** act or instance of conquering. **2.** something conquered.

con″san·guin'i·ty, *adj.* blood relationship.

con'science, *n.* inner prompting to do good or repent evil. —**con″sci·en'tious,** *adj.*

con'scious, *adj.* **1.** aware of the surrounding world. **2.** aware of some specific thing. **3.** deliberate. —**con'scious·ness,** *n.*

con·script', *v.t.* (kən skript') **1.** enroll forcibly in an army, labor force, etc. —*n.* (kahn'skript) **2.** conscripted person. —**con·scrip'tion,** *n.*

con'se·crate″, *v.t.,* **-crated, -crating.** dedicate, as to deity. —**con″se·cra'tion,** *n.*

con·sec'u·tive, *adj.* one after the other. —**con·sec'u·tive'ly,** *adv.*

con·sen'sus, *n.* general agreement on a question.

con·sent', *n.* **1.** permission. **2.** agreement. —*v.i.* **3.** give permission.

con'se·quence″, *n.* **1.** result. **2.** importance.

con'se·quent, *adj.* resulting.

con″se·quen'tial, *adj.* **1.** important. **2.** consequent.

con·serv'a·tive, *n.* **1.** person skeptical of change. **2.** pertaining to conservatives. **3.** avoiding excesses. —**con·serv'a·tive·ly,** *adv.* —**con·serv'a·tism,** *n.*

con·ser'va·to″ry, *n.,* *pl.* **-ries. 1.** greenhouse. **2.** art or music school.

con·serve', *v.t.,* **-served, -serving.** keep from decaying, being squandered, etc. —**con″ser·va'tion,** *n.* —**con″ser·va'tion·ist,** *n.*

con·sid'er, *v.t.* **1.** think of the importance, implications, etc. of. **2.** regard; believe. **3.** be considerate of.

con·sid'er·a·ble, *adj.* rather important.

con·sid'er·ate, *adj.* respectful of the feelings of others.

con·sid″er·a'tion, *n.* **1.** state of being considerate. **2.** act of considering. **3.** something to be considered. **4.** fee.

con·sign', *n.* **1.** deliver. **2.** entrust. —**con·sign'ment,** *n.*

con·sist', *v.i.* **1.** be composed. **2.** have essential nature.

con·sis'ten·cy, *n.* **1.** agreement with something already done, stated, or implied. **2.** ability to hold together, as of a liquid. —**con·sis'tent,** *adj.* —**con·sis'tent·ly,** *adv.*

con·sole', *v.t.,* **-soled, -soling.** *n.* *v.t.* (kən sōl') **1.** soothe or cheer in grief or annoyance. —*n.* (kahn'sōl) **2.** television set, etc. standing on the floor. **3.** instrument panel. —**con″so·la'tion,** *n.*

con·sol'i·date″, *v.,* **-dated, -dating.** *v.t.,* *v.i.* unite into a solid; whole. —**con·sol″i·da'tion,** *n.*

con'som·mé″, *n.* soup based on a clear meat broth.

con'so·nant, *adj.* **1.** in harmony. —*n.* **2.** speech sound other than a vowel. —**con'so·nance,** *n.*

con·sort, *v.i.* (kən sort') **1.** be in company or association. —*n.* (kahn'sort) **2.** spouse of a sovereign.

con·sor'ti·um, *n.,* *pl.* **-tia.** international business alliance.

con·spic'u·ous, *adj.* **1.** readily observed. **2.** compelling observation. —**con·spic'**

u·ous'ly, *adv.* —con·spic'u·ous·ness, *n.*

con·spire', *v.t.,* -spired, -spiring. plan secretly as a group. —con·spir'a·cy, *n.* —con·spir'a·tor, *n.*

con'sta·ble, *n.* policeman. —con·stab'u·lar''y, *n.*

con'stant, *adj.* 1. continual. 2. faithful. —*n.* 3. unvarying element. —con'stant·ly, *adv.* —con'stan·cy, *n.*

con''stel·la'tion, *n.* pattern of stars.

con''ster·na'tion, *n.* horrified shock.

con'sti·pate'', *v.t.,* -pated, -pating. impair the movement of the bowels. —con''sti·pa'tion, *n.*

con·stit'u·ent, *adj.* 1. forming an essential part. 2. electing. —*n.* 3. voter. 4. constituent thing. —con·stit'u·en·cy, *n.*

con'sti·tute'', *v.t.,* -tuted, -tuting. 1. combine to form. 2. be tantamount to.

con''sti·tu'tion, *n.* 1. act or instance of constituting. 2. fundamental law. 3. body, esp. as regards health.

con''sti·tu'tion·al, *adj.* 1. pertaining to a constitution. 2. permitted by a constitution. 3. pertaining to health. —*n.* 4. health-promoting walk.

con·strain', *v.t.* 1. compel. 2. restrain. —con·straint', *n.*

con·strict', *v.t.* force to be narrow. —con·stric'tion, *n.*

con·struct', *v.t.* build. —con·struc'tor, *n.* —con·struc'tion, *n.*

con·struc'tive, *adj.* useful or helpful.

con·strue', *v.t.,* -strued, -struing. interpret.

con'sul, *n.* government agent in a foreign city who assists his nationals there. —con'sul·ar, *adj.* —con'sul·ate, *n.*

con·sult', *v.t.* 1. seek advice or information from. —*v.i.* 2. discuss business matters. —con''sul·ta'tion, *n.*

con·sul'tant, *n.* 1. person who is consulted. 2. person who seeks advice.

con·sume', *v.t.,* -sumed, -suming. 1. use up in the process of living, etc. 2. destroy, as by fire.

con·sum'er, *n.* person who uses goods or services for himself rather than in business.

con·sum·mate, *adj., v.t.* -mated, -mating. *adj.* (kǝn sum'ǝt) 1. perfect. —*v.t.* (kahn sǝm āt') 2. complete, esp. the state of marriage by sexual intercourse. —con''sum·ma'tion, *n.*

con·sump'tion, *n.* 1. act or instance of consuming. 2. tuberculosis of the lungs. —con·sump'tive, *adj.*

con'tact, *n.* 1. touch. 2. communication. 3. connection.

con·ta'gious, *adj.* distributed by personal contact, as disease. —con·ta'gion, *n.*

con·tain', *n.* 1. enclose; include. 2. restrain. —con·tain'er, *n.*

con·tam'in·ate'', *v.t.,* -ated, -ating. spoil. the purity of. —con·tam''in·a'tion, *n.* —con·tam'in·ant, *n.*

con'tem·plate'', *v.t.,* -plated, -plating. 1. regard or think of intently. 2. anticipate. —con''tem·pla'tion, *n.* —con'tem'pla·tive, *adj.*

con·tem'po·rar''y, *adj., n., pl.* -ries, *adj.* 1. Also, con·tem''po·ra'ne·ous, of the same time. 2. modern. —*n.* 3. person or thing of the same age.

con·tempt', *n.* 1. disapproval involving a feeling of one's own superiority. 2. defiance, as of a court order. —con·tempt'i·ble, *adj.*

con·tend', *v.t.* 1. assert forcibly. —*v.i.* 2. fight or be in opposition. —con·tend'er, *n.*

con·tent, *n.* (kahn'tent) 1. something contained. 2. meaning or message. (kǝntent') 3. contentment. —*adj.* 4. satisfied. 5. willing. —*v.t.* 6. satisfy. —con·tent'ed, *adj.* —con·tent'ed·ly, *adv.* —con·tent'ed·ness, *n.*

con·ten'tious, *adj.* quarrelsome.

con·tent'ment, *n.* contented state.

con·test, *n.* (kahn'test) 1. competition or fight. —*v.i.* (kǝn test') 2. dispute. 3. fight to gain or hold. —con·test'ant, *n.*

con'text, *n.* circumstances giving exact meaning. —con·tex'tu·al, *adj.*

con·tig'u·ous, *adj.* 1. in touch. 2. adjacent. —con''ti·gu'i·ty, *n.*

con'ti·nent, *n.* 1. major land mass. 2. **the Continent,** European mainland. —*adj.* 3. sexually abstemious. —con''ti·nen'tal, *adj.* —con'ti·nence, *n.*

con·tin'gen·cy, *n., pl.* -cies. chance occurrence.

con·tin'gent, *adj.* 1. depending on chance. —*n.* 2. chance occurrence. 3. group of recruits.

con·tin'u·al, *adj.* 1. repeated without pause. 2. continuous. —con·tin'u·al·ly, *adv.*

con·tin'ue, *v.,* -ued, -uing. *v.t., v.i.* 1. not stop. 2. recommence. 3. extend. —*v.i.* 4. remain. —con·tin''u·a'tion, con·tin'u·ance, *n.*

con·tin'u·ous, *adj.* uninterrupted. —con·tin'u·ous·ly, *adv.* —con''tin·u'i·ty, *n.*

con·tort', *v.t.* twist out of shape. —con·tor'tion, *n.*

con'tour, *n.* outline of a form.

con'tra·band'', *n.* 1. goods unlawful to import or export. —*adj.* 2. constituting such goods.

con''tra·cep'tion, *n.* prevention of pregnancy. —con''tra·cep'tive, *adj., n.*

con·tract, *n.* (kahn'trakt) 1. formal business agreement. —*v.t.* (kǝn trakt') 2. undertake or establish by contract. 3. be afflicted with. 4. make smaller. —*v.i.* 5. make a contract. 6. become smaller. —con·trac'tion, *n.*

con·trac'tor, *n*. **1.** person who undertakes work by contract. **2.** builder.

con''tra·dict', *v.t.* **1.** declare to be falsely stated. **2.** declare to have not spoken the truth. **3.** be inconsistent with. —**con''tra·dic'tion**, *n*. —**con''tra·dic'to·ry**, *adj*.

con·tral'to, *n., pl.* **-tos.** lowest female singing voice.

con·trap'tion, *n. Informal.* gadget.

con·tra·ry, *n., pl.* **-ries,** *adj. n.* **1.** (kahn' trer ē) something opposite. —*adj.* **2.** opposite. **3.** (kǝn trer'ē) stubborn; perverse. —**con·trar'i·ly**, *adv*.

con·trast, *v.t.* (kǝn trast') **1.** show the differences of from another or others. —*v.i.* **2.** reveal differences from another or others. —*n.* (kahn'trast) **3.** act or instance or contrasting. **4.** something notably different.

con'tra·vene'', *v.t.*, **-vened, -vening.** act in violation of. —**con''tra·ven'tion**, *n*.

con·trib'ute, *v.*, **-uted, -uting.** *v.t., v.i.* give toward a desired total. —**con·trib'u·tor**, *n*. —**con''tri·bu'tion**, *n*. —**con·trib'u·to''ry**, *adj*.

con·trite', *adj.* repentant. —**con·trite'ness, con·tri'tion**, *n*.

con·trive', *v.t.*, **-trived, -triving. 1.** devise or invent. **2.** bring about. —**con·triv'ance**, *n*.

con·trol', *v.t.*, **-trolled, -trolling**, *n. v.t.* **1.** govern or direct. **2.** restrain. —*n.* **3.** ability to control. **4.** Often, **controls,** means of controlling. —**con·trol'la·ble**, *adj*.

con·trol'ler, *n.* financial manager.

con'tro·ver''sy, *n., pl.* **-sies.** earnest debate. —**con''tro·ver'sial**, *adj*.

con'tro·vert'', *v.t.* **1.** dispute. **2.** debate.

con·tu'me·ly, *n., pl.* **-lies.** scornful abuse.

con·tu'sion, *n.* bruise.

co·nun'drum, *n.* riddle answered with a pun.

con''ur·ba'tion, *n.* area of urban density resulting from unchecked growth.

con''va·lesce'', *v.i.*, **-lesced, -lescing.** become better after illness. —**con''va·les'cent**, *n., adj.* —**con''va·les'cence**, *n*.

con·vec'tion, *n.* movement of heated or cooled gases or liquids.

con·vene', *v.*, **-vened, -vening.** *v.i., v.t.* assemble in a meeting.

con·ven'ience, *n.* **1.** ease or handiness. **2.** something promoting this. —**con·ven'ient**, *adj*.

con'vent, *n.* community of nuns.

con·ven'tion, *n.* **1.** assembly of a political party, professional association, etc. **2.** something customary.

con·ven'tion·al, *adj.* **1.** ordinary. **2.** customary.

con·verge', *v.*, **-verged, -verging.** *v.t., or assertion.*

con·verge', *v.*, **-verged, -verging.** *v.t., v.i.* join by oblique movement. —**con·ver'gence**, *n.* —**con·ver'gent**, *adj*.

con·ver'sant, *adj.* familiar; skilled.

con''ver·sa'tion, *n.* **1.** informal talk. **2.** ability to carry on such talk. —**con''ver·sa'tion·al**, *adj.* —**con''ver·sa'tion·al·ist**, *n*.

con·verse, *v.i.*, **-versed, -versing,** *adj., n.* *v.i.* (kǝn vǝrs') **1.** carry on a conversation. —*adj.* (kahn'vǝrs) **2.** in reverse order or position. —*n.* **3.** something converse. —**con·verse'ly**, *adv*.

con·vert, *v.t.* (kǝn vǝrt') **1.** change from one thing or state to another. **2.** acquire a new religion. —*v.i.* **3.** be converted. —*n.* (kahn'vǝrt) **4.** person with a new religion. —**con·vert'er, con·vert'or**, *n.* —**con·vert'i·ble**, *adj*.

con·vex', *adj.* curving outward. —**con·vex'i·ty**, *n*.

con·vey', *v.t.* **1.** transport. **2.** transmit. **3.** succeed in expressing. —**con·vey'er, con·vey'or** *n.* —**con·vey'ance**, *n*.

con·vict, *v.t.* (kǝn vikt') **1.** find guilty. —*n.* (kahn'vikt) **2.** person found guilty.

con·vic'tion, *n.* **1.** act or instance of convicting or being convicted. **2.** strongly held belief.

con·vince', *v.t.*, **-vinced, -vincing.** cause to believe.

con·viv'i·al, *adj.* **1.** fond of company. **2.** festive.

con·voke', *v.t.*, **-voked, -voking.** call to an assembly. —**con'vo·ca''tion**, *n*.

con''vo·lu'tion, *n.* **1.** twist, fold, etc. **2.** formation of these.

con·voy, *n.* (kahn'voi) **1.** ships, etc. with a protective escort. **2.** protective escort. —*v.t.* (kǝn voi') **3.** escort protectively.

con·vulse', *v.t.*, **-vulsed, -vulsing. 1.** agitate. **2.** rack with laughter or anger. —**con·vul'sion**, *n.* —**con·vul'sive**, *adj*.

coo, *v.i.*, **cooed, cooing. 1.** make a dovelike sound. —*n.* **2.** dovelike sound.

cook, *v.t.* **1.** prepare (food) by heating. —*v.i.* **2.** act as a cook. **3.** become cooked or heated. —*n.* **4.** person who cooks. —**cook'er·y**, *n.* —**cook'book''**, *n*.

cook'ie, *n.* small baked sweet biscuit.

cool, *adj.* **1.** slightly cold; not warm. **2.** not adding to body heat. **3.** showing no emotion. **4.** unenthusiastic. —*n.* **5.** cool condition. —*v.t.* **6.** make cool. —*v.i.* **7.** become cool. —**cool'er**, *n.* —**cool'ly**, *adv.* —**cool'ness**, *n*.

cool'ie, *n.* Far Eastern unskilled laborer.

coon, *n.* raccoon. —**coon'skin''**, *n*.

coop, *n.* **1.** shelter for chickens, etc. —*v.t.* **2.** confine.

coop'er, *n.* barrel maker.

co''op'er·ate'', *v.i.*, **-ated, -ating.** act in harmony or together with others. Also, **co''-op'er·ate''.** —**co''op''er·a'tion**, *n*.

co"op'er·a·tive, *adj.* 1. willing to cooperate. 2. jointly owned by the users. —*n.* 3. cooperative store, apartment house, etc. Also, co"-op'er·a·tive.

co·or·di·nate, *adj., n., v.t.,* -nated, -nating. *adj.* (ko"or'də nət) 1. equal in importance. 2. pertaining to coordination. —*n.* 3. something coordinate. *v.t.* (ko"or'də nāt") 4. put in proper interaction. 5. make coordinate.

co"or'di·na"tion, *n.* 1. act or instance of coordinating. 2. proper interaction, esp. of the limbs or muscles.

cop, *n., v.t.,* copped, copping. *Informal. n.* 1. policeman. 2. arrest. —*v.t.* 3. seize.

cope, *v.i.,* coped, coping. attack and overcome a problem or emergency.

cop'ing, *n.* uppermost course of an unroofed masonry wall.

co'pi·ous, *adj.* abundant.

cop'per, *n.* reddish metallic element.

cop'per·head", *n.* poisonous North American snake.

copse, *n.* thicket. Also, cop'pice.

cop'u·late", *v.i.,* -lated, -lating. have sexual intercourse. —cop"u·la'tion, *n.*

cop'y, *n., pl.* -ies, *v.t.,* -ied, -ying. *n.* 1. imitation of an original. 2. individual published book. 3. words to be printed. —*v.t.* 4. make or be a copy of. —cop'y·ist, *n.*

cop'y·right", *n.* 1. exclusive right to publish a book or license its publication. —*v.t.* 2. obtain a copyright for.

co·quette', *n.* flirtatious woman.

cor'al, *n.* 1. hardened skeletons of a marine animal. 2. yellowish red.

cord, *n.* 1. strong string. 2. electric wire. 3. 128 cubic feet of chopped wood.

cor'dial, *adj.* 1. warmly friendly. —*n.* 2. liqueur. —cor'dial·ly, *adv.* —cor"di·al'i·ty, *n.*

cor'don, *n.* 1. circle of guards. —*v.t.* 2. put a cordon around.

cor'do·van, *n.* soft, dark leather.

cor'du·roy", *n.* 1. ribbed cotton. 2. felled tree trunks used as a paving.

core, *n., v.t.,* cored, coring. *n.* 1. central part or element. —*v.t.* 2. remove the core from.

cork, *n.* 1. bark of an oak tree. 2. stopper made of this bark. —*v.t.* 3. stop with a cork.

cork'screw", *n.* augerlike device for pulling corks.

corn, *n.* 1. American plant with kernels on a cob. 2. small hard seed of a cereal plant. 3. *Informal.* trite or sentimental art. 4. painful growth on the foot. —*v.t.* 5. pickle in brine. —corn'starch", *n.*

cor'ne·a, *n.* outer coating of the eyeball.

cor'ner, *n.* 1. angular junction. 2. intersection of two streets. 3. monopoly of a commodity or stock. —*v.t.* 4. trap in a corner. 5. get a monopoly on.

cor'ner·stone", *n.* stone at the corner of a building with its date, etc.

cor·net', *n.* trumpetlike musical instrument.

cor'nice, *n.* major horizontal molding on or at the top of a wall.

cor"nu·co'pi·a, *n.* hornlike container with fruits, flowers, etc. spilling from it.

cor'ol·lar"y, *n., pl.* -ies. statement deduced from one already proven.

cor'o·nar"y, *adj., n., pl.* -ies. *adj.* 1. pertaining to the arteries supplying the heart. —*n.* 2. coronary thrombosis.

cor"o·na'tion, *n.* installation of a monarch.

cor'o·ner, *n.* official who investigates suspicious deaths.

cor"o·net, *n.* crown of a noble.

cor'po·ral, *adj.* 1. bodily. —*n.* 2. lowest noncommissioned military officer.

cor'po·rate, *adj.* pertaining to organizations.

cor"po·ra'tion, *n.* 1. business organization existing as an entity apart from its members. 2. municipal government.

cor·po're·al, *adj.* physical.

corps (kor), *n., pl.* corps (korz). military branch.

corpse, *n.* dead body.

cor'pu·lence, *n.* fatness. —cor'pu·lent, *adj.*

cor·pus·cle (kor'pus əl), *n.* blood or lymph cell.

cor·ral', *n., v.t.,* -ralled, -ralling. *n.* 1. enclosure for cattle, horses, etc. —*v.t.* 2. enclose in a corral.

cor·rect', *adj.* 1. accurate. 2. according to rules. —*v.t.* 3. make correct. 4. punish. —cor·rect'ly, *adv.* —cor·rect'ness, *n.* —cor·rec'tion, *n.* —cor·rec'tive, *adj.*

cor·re·late", *v.,* -lated, -lating. *v.t.* 1. put into a mutual relationship. —*v.i.* 2. have a mutual relationship. —cor"re·la'tion, *n.* —cor·rel'a·tive, *adj.*

cor"re·spond", *v.i.* 1. write or exchange letters, news, etc. 2. match. —cor"re·spond'ence, *n.* —cor"re·spond'ent, *n.*

cor'ri·dor, *n.* narrow passageway.

cor·rob'o·rate", *v.t.,* -rated, -rating. support or confirm with evidence, etc. —cor·rob"o·ra'tion, *n.* —cor·rob'o·ra·tive, *adj.*

cor·rode', *v.,* -roded, -roding. *v.t., v.i.* decay, esp. by chemical action. —cor·ro'sion, *n.* —cor·ro'sive, *adj., n.*

cor'ru·gate", *v.,* -gated, -gating. *v.t., v.i.* bend into parallel ridges and furrows. —cor"ru·ga'tion, *n.*

cor·rupt', *adj.* 1. impure. 2. depraved. —*v.t.* 3. make corrupt. —*v.i.* 4. become corrupt. —cor·rupt'ly, *adv.* —cor·rupt'i·ble, *adj.* —cor·rup'tion, *n.*

cor·sage (kor sahʒ'), *n.* small bouquet for a party dress.

cor'set, *n*. garment for shaping the torso.

cor·tege', *n*. ceremonial procession. Also, **cor·tège'**.

cor''us·cate'', *v.i.*, **-cated, -cating.** glitter. —**cor''us·ca'tion**, *n*.

cos·met'ic, *n*. **1.** preparation applied to the body to improve its appearance. —*adj.* **2.** improving outer appearance.

cos'mic, *adj.* pertaining to the cosmos.

cos'mo·naut'', *n*. astronaut.

cos''mo·pol'i·tan, *n*. **1.** Also, **cos·mop'o·lite''**, person regarding the entire world as his home. —*adj.* **2.** characteristic of such persons.

cos'mos, *n*. the entire universe.

cost, *v.t.*, **cost, costing**, *n. v.t.* **1.** require or exact as specified. —*n.* **2.** something given up in exchange. **3.** loss; grief.

cost'ly, *adj.*, **-lier, -liest.** costing much.

cos'tume, *n.*, *v.t.*, **-tumed, -tuming**. *n*. **1.** dress, esp. of a special or unusual kind. —*v.t.* **2.** supply with such dress.

cot, *n*. narrow folding bed.

co·te·rie, *n*. small, exclusive group of friends.

cot'tage, *n*. small house. —**cot'tag·er**, *n*.

cot'ter pin'', split fastener passed through the things to be attached, then bent open.

cot'ton, *n*. fiber from a plant of the mallow family. —**cot'ton·y**, *adj.* —**cot'ton·seed**, *n*.

cot'ton·mouth'', *n*. water moccasin.

cot'ton·tail'', *n*. white-tailed American rabbit.

cot'ton·wood'', *n*. poplar with hairy seeds.

couch, *n*. **1.** bedlike article of furniture. —*v.t.* **2.** put into words.

cou'gar, *n*. tawny American wildcat.

cough, *n*. **1.** loud expulsion of breath from the lungs, as to clear the throat. —*v.i.* **2.** emit a cough. —*v.t.* **3.** expel with a cough.

coun'cil, *n*. body of legislators, advisors, etc. —**coun'cil·man, coun'cil·or, coun'cil·lor**, *n*.

coun'sel, *v.t.*, **-seled, seling**. *n. v.t.* **1.** advise. —*n.* **2.** legal representative. **3.** advice. —**coun'se·lor, coun'sel·lor**, *n*.

count, *v.t.* **1.** note one by one to get a total. **2.** include in a total or group. **3.** consider as being. —*v.i.* **4.** count numbers or items. **5.** be important. **6.** depend. —*n.* **7.** act or instance of counting. **8.** total. **9.** legal accusation. **10.** continental European nobleman equal to an earl.

count'down'', *n*. count of seconds in reverse order before an action.

coun'te·nance, *n.*, *v.t.*, **-nanced, -nancing**. *n*. **1.** face, esp. with regard to expression. **2.** approval. —*v.t.* **3.** approve.

count'er, *n*. **1.** person or thing that counts. **2.** tablelike surface for serving, displaying goods, etc. **3.** token used in games.

coun'ter, *v.i.* **1.** act in retaliation. —*v.t.* **2.** oppose. —*adj.* **3.** opposed. —*adv.* **4.** in opposition. —**coun''ter·act'**, *v.t.* —**coun'ter·at·tack''**, *v.t.*, *v.i.*, *n*. —**coun''ter·bal''ance**, *v.t.*, *n*. —**coun'' ter·clock'wise**, *adj.*, *adv.* —**coun''ter·rev''o·lu'tion**, *n*. —**coun''ter·rev''o·lu'tion·ar''y**, *adj.*, *n*. —**coun'ter·weight''**, *n.*, *v.t.*

coun'ter·feit'', *v.t.* **1.** imitate closely, esp. money. **2.** pretend. —*adj.* **3.** having been counterfeited. —*n.* **4.** something counterfeit. —**coun'ter·feit''er**, *n*.

coun'ter·mand'', *v.t.* cancel with a contrary order.

coun'ter·part'', *n*. **1.** similar person or thing. **2.** duplicate.

coun'ter·point'', *n. Music.* interaction of melodies.

coun'ter·sign'', *n*. **1.** reply to a password establishing identity. **2.** secret sign. **3.** confirming signature. —*v.t.* **4.** sign as a confirmation.

coun'ter·sink'', *v.t.*, **-sunk, -sinking**. **1.** drive or set flush with or below a surface. **2.** cut to receive the head of a countersunk part.

count'ess, *n*. wife of a count or earl.

count'less, *adj.* innumerable.

coun'try, *n.*, *pl.* **-tries**. **1.** rural area. **2.** land of which one is a citizen. **3.** region. —**coun'try·man**, *n*.

coun'try·side'', *n*. rural terrain.

coun'ty, *n*. **1.** political division of a U.S. state. **2.** political division of a European country.

coup (ko͞o), *n.*, *pl.* **coups** (ko͞oz). bold, adroit, successful act.

coup de grace (ko͞o''de grahs'), something putting an end to a miserable existence.

coupe (ko͞o pā'), *n*. two-door hard-top car.

cou'ple, *n.*, *v.*, **-pled, -pling**. *n*. pair. —*v.t.*, *v.i.* **2.** join one to another. —**coup'ling**, *n*.

coup'let, *n*. pair of verses that rhyme.

cou'pon, *n*. valuable certificate to be cut or detached from a bond, advertisement, etc.

cour'age, *n*. bravery or fortitude. —**cou·ra'geous**, *adj.*

cou'ri·er, *n*. messenger.

course, *n.*, *v.i.*, **coursed, coursing**. *n*. **1.** path or direction of a moving thing. **2.** natural progress or outcome. **3.** way of acting. **4.** phase of a meal. **5.** program of instruction in one subject. **6.** layer of stones, shingles, etc. in a building. —*v.i.* **7.** run or race.

court, *n*. **1.** Also, **court'yard**, area surrounded by buildings. **2.** agency for trying civil or criminal cases. **3.** group immediately attached to a sovereign. **4.** act of wooing. **5.** place to play ball games. —*v.t.* **6.** woo. **7.** ingratiate oneself with. **8.** seek to obtain. —*v.i.* **9.** engage in courtship. —**court'house''**, *n.* —**court'room''**, *n.*

cour'te·ous, *adj.* polite.

cour'te·san, *n.* prostitute.

cour'te·sy, *n., pl.* **-sies.** politeness.

cour'ti·er, *n.* member of a royal court.

court'ly, *adj.,* **-lier, -liest.** worthy of a royal court, esp. in manner.

court'-mar''tial, *n., pl.* **courts-martial,** *v.t.,* **-tialed, -tialing.** *n.* **1.** military court or trial. —*v.t.* **2.** try before such a court.

court'ship'', *n.* wooing.

cous'in, *n.* offspring of an uncle or aunt.

cove, *n.* small inlet or bay.

cov'e·nant, *n.* agreement.

cov'er, *v.t.* **1.** put a lid, shelter, etc. over. **2.** conceal. **3.** protect or shield. **4.** clothe. **5.** hold at bay with a gun, etc. **6.** investigate or watch. —*n.* **7.** something that covers. **9.** means of concealing actions, identity, etc. —**cov'er·age**, *n.* —**cov'er·ing**, *n.*

cov'er·let, *n.* bedspread.

cov'ert, *adj.* concealed. —**cov'ert·ly**, *adv.*

cov'er-up'', *n.* plot to conceal guilt or guilty actions.

cov'et, *v.t.* desire enviously. —**cov'et·ous**, *adj.*

cov'ey, *n., pl.* **-ies.** flock of quail or partridge.

cow, *n.* **1.** four-footed milk-giving bovine animal. **2.** female elephant, whale, etc. —*v.t.* **3.** intimidate. —**cow'hide''**, *n.*

cow'ard, *n.* person without courage. —**cow'ard·ly**, *adj., adv.* —**cow'ard·ice**, *n.*

cow'boy'', *n.* ranch worker. Also, **cow' hand''.**

cow'er, *v.i.* cringe.

cowl, *n.* hood or hooded cloak.

co'work''er, *n.* fellow worker.

cox·swain (kok'sən), *n.* steerer of a boat.

coy, *adj.* affectedly shy.

coy·o'te, *n.* small North American wolf.

co'zy, *adj.,* **-zier, -ziest.** snug and comfortable. —**coz'i·ly**, *adv.* —**coz'i·ness**, *n.*

crab, *n.* four-legged crustacean.

crab'ap'ple, *n.* small, sour apple

crab·bed, *n.* **1.** Also, **crab'by**, ill-tempered. **2.** hard to read.

crab'grass', *n.* grass regarded as a weed.

crack, *v.i., v.t.* **1.** break across abruptly. —*n.* **2.** act or instance of cracking. **3.** narrow break or opening.

crack'er, *n.* **1.** crisp wafer. **2.** firecracker.

crack'le, *v.i.,* **-led, -ling,** *n.* **1.** make rapid snapping sounds in bending. —*n.* **2.** irregular cracked pattern.

crack'pot'', *n. Informal.* person with delusions.

cra'dle, *n., v.t.,* **-dled, -dling.** *n.* **1.** rocking, high-sided bed for a baby. **2.** concave support, as for a boat. —*v.t.* **3.** place or rock in a cradle. **4.** support in or as in a cradle.

craft, *n., pl.* **crafts** (for 1 and 2), **craft** (for 3). *n.* **1.** cunning. **2.** skilled trade. **3.** vehicle for movement through water or air.

crafts'man, *n.* **1.** skilled handworker. **2.** skilled, conscientious worker of any kind. —**crafts'man·ship''**, *n.*

craft'y, *adj.,* **-ier, -iest.** cunning. —**craft' i·ly**, *adv.*

crag, *n.* abruptly rising rock formation. —**crag'gy**, *adj.*

cram, *v.,* **crammed, cramming.** *v.t.* **1.** pack tightly or excessively. —*v.i.* **2.** *Informal.* study in a hasty, superficial way.

cramp, *n.* **1.** painful muscular contraction. **2.** Often, **cramps,** abdominal spasms. —*v.t.* **3.** afflict with cramp. **4.** hamper or confine.

cran'ber''ry, *n., pl.* **-ries.** sour red berry from an evergreen.

crane, *n., v.t.,* **craned, craning.** *n.* **1.** long-legged, long-billed water bird. **2.** hoisting machine. —*v.t.* **3.** stretch and bend, as the neck.

cra'ni·um, *n., pl.* **-niums, -nia. 1.** bone covering the brain. **2.** skull. —**cra'ni· al**, *adj.*

crank, *n.* **1.** rotating device incorporating a lever. **2.** *Informal.* person with an ill temper or delusion. —*v.t.* **3.** move with a crank. —**crank'case''**, *n.* —**crank' shaft''**, *n.*

crank'y, *adj.,* **-ier, -iest.** ill-tempered. —**crank'i·ly**, *adv.*

cran'ny, *n., pl.* **-nies.** crevice.

craps, *n.* dice game. —**crap'shoot''er**, *n.*

crash, *n.* **1.** destructive collision, fall, etc. **2.** noise of this. **3.** business failure. **4.** coarse linen. —*v.i.* **5.** suffer a crash. —*v.t.* **6.** cause to have or produce a crash. **7.** batter one's way through.

crass, *adj.* stupid and coarse.

crate, *n., v.t.,* **crated, crating.** *n.* **1.** wooden shipping case. —*v.t.* **2.** pack in a crate.

cra'ter, *n.* pit in the ground made by volcanic eruption, meteors, bombs, etc.

cra·vat', *n.* necktie.

crave, *v.t.,* **craved, craving.** desire or request eagerly. —**crav'ing**, *n.*

cra'ven, *n.* **1.** coward. —*adj.* **2.** cowardly.

craw, *n.* **1.** sac in a bird's gullet. **2.** stomach.

crawl, *v.i.* **1.** move on several legs with the body horizontal. **2.** move slowly. **3.** feel as if crawled on. —*n.* **4.** crawling movement. **5.** swimming stroke.

cray'fish'', *n.* small lobsterlike crustcean. Also, **craw'fish''**.

cray'on, *n.* stick of pigmented material for making lines or tones.

craze, *v.*, **crazed, crazing**, *n.* *v.t.* 1. make insane. 2. cause to crack in random patterns. —*v.i.* 3. become crazed. —*n.* 4. fad.

cra'zy, *adj.*, **-zier, -ziest.** 1. insane. 2. rickety. —**cra'zi·ly**, *adv.*

creak, *v.t.* 1. make a squeak or groan from bending or rubbing. —*n.* 2. sound from such a cause. —**creak'y**, *adj.*

cream, *n.* 1. richer part of milk. 2. substance with a creamlike or salvelike consistency. 3. yellowish white. 4. finest part or element. —*v.t.* 5. make with cream. 6. beat to a creamlike consistency. —**cream'y**, *adj.*

cream'er, *n.* cream pitcher.

cream'er·y, *n.*, *pl.* **-ies.** place for processing or selling dairy products.

crease, *n.*, *v.t.*, **creased, creasing.** *n.* 1. ridge made by pressing. 2. furrow. —*v.t.* 3. make a crease or creases in.

cre·ate', *v.t.* **-hated, -hating.** 1. bring into existence. 2. bring about. —**cre·a'tion**, *n.*

cre·a'tive, *adj.* 1. pertaining to creation. 2. of an original mind; inventive. —**cre''a·tiv'i·ty**, *n.*

cre·a'tor, *n.* 1. person who creates. 2. **the Creator**, God.

cre'dence, *n.* belief, as in the truth of a statement.

cre·den'tials, *n.* documentation proving authority, identity, etc.

cred'i·ble, *adj.* able to be believed. —**cred''i·bil'i·ty**, *n.*

cred'it, *n.* 1. deference of payment. 2. money paid or owed to one. 3. praise or good reputation. 4. source of this. 5. acknowledgment for participation. 6. unit of academic accomplishment. —*v.t.* 7. believe. 8. give a credit or credits to.

cred'it·a·ble, *adj.* deserving of credit.

cred'i·tor, *n.* person to whom a debt is owed.

cre'do, *n.*, *pl.* **-dos.** creed.

cred'u·lous, *adj.* too ready to believe things. —**cre·du'li·ty**, *n.*

creed, *n.* formally stated belief.

creek, *n.* small stream.

creep, *v.i.*, **crept, creeping.** 1. crawl. 2. move stealthily. 3. grow along the ground.

cre'mate'', *v.t.*, **-mated, -mating.** burn at a funeral. —**cre·ma'tion**, *n.* —**cre'ma·to''ry**, **cre''ma·to'ri·um**, *n.*

Cre'ole, *n.* descendant of the original settlers of Louisiana.

cre'o·sote'', *n.* wood preservative distilled from wood or coal tar.

crepe, *n.* 1. thin, crinkled cloth. 2. rolled, filled pancake. Also, **crêpe.**

cre·scen'do, *adj.*, *n.*, *pl.* **-dos.** *adj.*, *adv.* 1. increasing in loudness. —*n.* 2. increase in loudness.

cres'cent, *n.* shape like that of a new moon.

crest, *n.* 1. uppermost edge or feature. 2. feature surmounting a heraldic escutcheon.

crest'fal''len, *adj.* abashed.

cre'tin, *n.* idiot suffering from a thyroid deficiency.

cre'tonne, *n.* heavy, printed upholstery or curtain material.

cre·vasse', *n.* crevice, esp. in a glacier.

crev'ice, *n.* deep, narrow gap.

crew, *n.* labor force, esp. on a ship. —**crew'man**, *n.*

crib, *n.*, *v.t.*, **cribbed, cribbing.** *n.* 1. small child's bed with high slatted sides. 2. receptacle for corn, animal fodder, etc. 3. stall for cattle. 4. *Informal.* aid to cheating in school. —*v.t.* 5. confine as in a crib. 6. *Informal.* copy dishonestly.

crib'bage, *n.* card game.

crick, *n.* cramp in the neck or back.

crick'et, *n.* 1. grasshopperlike insect. 2. game played with wide bats, esp. in England.

cri'er, *n.* maker of vocal announcements.

crime, *n.* violation of the law.

crim'in·al, *adj.* 1. pertaining to or guilty of crime. —*n.* 2. committer of crimes.

crim''in·ol'o·gy, *n.* study of crime. —**crim''in·ol'o·gist**, *n.*

crimp, *n.*, *v.t.* pleat.

crim'son, *n.* deep red.

cringe, *v.i.*, **cringed, cringing.** 1. crouch or draw back from fear. 2. behave servilely.

crin'kle, *v.* **-kled, -kling.** *v.t.*, *v.i.* 1. wrinkle. 2. rustle, as crisp paper. —**crin'kly**, *adj.*

crip'ple, *v.t.*, **-pled, -pling.** *n.* *v.t.* 1. deprive of the use of arms or legs. 2. render ineffective. —*n.* 3. crippled person.

cri'sis, *n.*, *pl.* **-ses.** point that determines a good or bad outcome.

crisp, *n.* 1. brittle. 2. clear; fresh. 3. briskly abrupt in manner.

criss'cross'', *n.* 1. pattern of crossed lines. —*adj.*, *adv.* 2. in this pattern. —*v.t.* 3. mark with this pattern. —*v.i.* 4. move in or bear this pattern.

cri·ter'i·on, *n.*, *pl.* **-ions, -ia.** basis for judgment.

crit'ic, *n.* person who evaluates good and bad qualities.

crit'i·cal, *adj.* 1. pertaining to critics. 2. pertaining to crises. 3. fault-finding. —**crit'i·cal·ly**, *adv.*

crit'i·cize'', *v.t.*, **-cized, -cizing. 1.** evaluate. **2.** find fault with. **—crit'i·cism**, *n.*

cri·tique', *n.* evaluation by a critic.

croak, *v.i.* **1.** make a deep froglike noise. **—n. 2.** croaking sound.

cro·chet (krō shā'), *v.t.*, **-cheted, -cheting.** make with a hooked needle and thread.

crock, *n.* earthenware vessel. **—crock'er·y,** *n.*

croc'o·dile'', *n.* large tropical river reptile.

cro'cus, *n., pl.* **-cuses.** early-blooming flower of the iris family.

crone, *n.* shriveled old woman.

cro'ny, *n., pl.* **-nies.** close friend.

crook, *n., v.,* **crooked, crooking. n. 1.** hooked staff. **2.** curve. **3.** *Informal.* thief. **—v.i., v.t., 4.** bend.

crook'ed, *adj.* **1.** full of bends. **2.** dishonest.

croon, *v.i., v.t.* sing or hum in low, sweet sounds. **—croon'er,** *n.*

crop, *n., v.t.,* **cropped, cropping. n. 1.** yield at a harvest. **2.** whip. **3.** craw of a bird. **—v.t. 4.** cut short.

cro·quet (krō kā'), *n.* lawn game with balls driven by mallets.

cro·quette', *n.* deep-fried piece of ground meat, etc.

cross, *n.* **1.** upright with a side-to-side beam used in Roman crucifixions. **2.** this form as a symbol of Christianity. **3.** modification of this symbolizing Christian saints, sects, etc. **4.** source of trouble or unhappiness. **5.** mixture of breeds. **—v.t. 6.** go across. **7.** thwart. **8.** mix with another breed. **—adj. 9.** ill-tempered. **—cross'road**'', *n.* **—cross' roads**'', *n., sing.* **—cross'wise**'', **cross' ways**'', *adv.* **—cross'ly,** *adv.*

cross'bow'', *n.* weapon with a short bow mounted on a guide for a type of arrow.

cross''**-ex·am'ine**, *v.t. Law.* examine after examination by an opposing attorney. Also, **cross''-ques'tion. —cross'' -ex·am'i·na''tion.** *n.*

cross'-eyed'', *adj.* with eyes not properly aligned.

cross'-ref'er·ence, *n.* reference to another part of a book. **—cross'-re·fer',** *v.i., v.t.*

crotch, *n.* **1.** place where a tree limb branches from a larger one. **2.** place where the legs meet.

crotch'et, *n.* eccentric whim or attitude. **—crotch'et·y,** *adj.*

crouch, *v.i., n.* stoop or squat.

croup, *n.* inflammation of respiratory passages.

crow, *v.i.,* **crowed.** or (for 1) **crew, crowed crowing**, *n. v.i.* **1.** cry like a rooster. **2.** boast or exult. **—n. 3.** crowing sound. **4.** shiny dark bird.

crow'bar'', *n.* heavy metal lever.

crowd, *n.* **1.** large, random group. **—v.t. 2.** fill with a crowd. **3.** force into a retricted space. **—v.i. 4.** push one's way. **5.** gather in a crowd.

crown, *n.* **1.** symbol of sovereignty. **2.** royalty as the head of state. **3.** upper part. **—v.t. 4.** give a crown to. **5.** reward or fulfill.

cru'cial, *adj.* **1.** decisive. **2.** trying. **—cru' cial·ly,** *adv.*

cru'ci·ble, *n.* melting pot.

cru'ci·fix'', *n.* image of the Christian cross.

cru'ci·fy'', *v.t.,* **-fied, -fying. 1.** nail to a cross as punishment. **2.** ruin the reputation, happiness, etc. of. **—cru''ci·fix' ion,** *n.*

crude, *adj.* **1.** unrefined or unfinished. **2.** boorish. **—crude'ly,** *adv.* **—crud'i·ty, crude'ness,** *n.*

cru'el, *adj.* **1.** causing suffering. **2.** desiring to cause suffering. **—cruel'ly,** *adv.* **—cru'el·ty,** *n.*

cru'et, *n.* small bottle for oil, vinegar, etc.

cruise, *v.,* **cruised, cruising,** *n. v.i.* **1.** travel slowly, as for recreation or inspection. **2.** move at normal speed, as a ship. **—v.t. 3.** cruise in or over. **—n. 4.** act or instance of cruising.

cruis'er, *n.* large, lightly armored warship.

crul'ler, *n.* piece of twisted deep-fried dough.

crumb, *n.* small fragment, esp. from dough.

crum'ble, *v.,* **-bled, -bling.** *v.t., v.i.* break or drop in pieces.

crum'ple, *v.,* **-pled, -pling.** *v.i., v.t.* collapse into wrinkles.

crunch, *v.t.* **1.** crush, chew, grind, etc. with a brittle sound. **—v.i. 2.** emit such a sound.

cru·sade', *n., v.i.,* **-saded, -sading.** *n.* **1.** Christian campaign to recover the tomb of Christ from the Muslims. **2.** idealistic campaign. **—v.i. 3.** engage in a crusade. **—cru·sad'er,** *n.*

crush, *v.t.* **1.** break or squeeze with pressure. **2.** reduce to helplessness or despair through an attack. **—v.i. 3.** become crushed. **—n. 4.** crowd. **5.** *Informal.* infatuation. **—crush'er,** *n.*

crust, *n.* **1.** hardened outer surface. **—v.t. 2.** cover with a crust. **—crust'y,** *adj.*

crus·ta'cean, *n.* sea animal with jointed feet and a hard outer shell.

crutch, *n.* prop for a lame person.

crux, *n., pl.* **cruxes, cruces.** decisive feature or aspect.

cry, *v.,* **cried, crying,** *n., pl.* **cries.** *v.i.* **1.** weep loudly. **2.** utter a call. **3.** ask for something loudly. **—v.t. 4.** announce in a shout. **—n. 5.** act or instance of crying.

crypt, *n.* underground church vault, esp. for burial.

cryp′tic, *adj.* defying interpretation.

cryp′to·gram″, *n.* code message.

cryp·tog′ra·phy, *n.* encoding and decoding of messages, etc. —**cryp·tog′ra·pher**, *n.*

crys′tal, *n.* 1. clear quartz. 2. geometrically formed fused mineral, sugar, etc. 3. brilliant glass or glassware. 4. window of a watch dial. —**crys′tal·line**, *adj.* —**crys′ta·lize″**, *v.t.*, *v.i.*

cub, *n.* young animal.

cub′by·hole″, *n.* small enclosure.

cube, *n.*, *v.t.*, **cubed, cubing.** 1. solid with six square sides. 2. *Math.* third power of a number. —*v.t.* 3. divide into cubes. 4. *Math.* multiply to the third power. —**cu′bic**, *adj.* —**cu′bic·al**, *adj.*

cu′bi·cle, *n.* small alcove.

cu′bit, *n.* measure of about 18 inches.

cuck′old, *n.* 1. husband of an unfaithful wife. —*v.t.* 2. make a cuckold of. —**cuck′old·ry**, *n.*

cuck′oo″, *n.* 1. bird with a two-note call. —*adj.* 2. *Informal.* crazy.

cu′cum″ber, *n.* long, green fruit used in salads or as pickles.

cud, *n.* food chewed by cows, etc. after regurgitation.

cud′dle, *v.*, **-dled, -dling.** *v.t.* 1. hold and caress. —*v.i.* 2. lie or curl up snugly.

cudg′el, *n.*, *v.t.*, **-eled, -eling.** *n.* 1. short club. —*v.t.* 2. beat with a cudgel.

cue, *n.*, *v.t.*, **cued, cuing** or **cueing.** *n.* 1. signal for speech or action. 2. stick used in billiards or pool. —*v.t.* 3. give a cue to.

cuff, *n.* 1. feature terminating a sleeve or trouser leg. 2. slap. —*v.t.* 3. slap.

cui·sine″, *n.* manner of cooking.

cul′-de-sac″, *n.* blind street with a turning circle at the end.

cu′li·nar″y, *adj.* pertaining to cooking.

cull, *v.t.* select.

cul′mi·nate″, *v.i.*, **-nated, -nating.** reach a final development. —**cul″mi·na′tion**, *n.*

cul′pa·ble, *adj.* at fault. —**cul″pa·bil′i·ty**, *n.*

cul′prit, *n.* 1. accused person. 2. guilty person.

cult, *n.* 1. religious sect. 2. religious practice or devotion. —**cult′ist**, *n.*

cul′ti·vate″, *v.t.*, **-vated, -vating.** 1. work on to grow crops. 2. develop, as personal qualities. 3. seek to make a friend or associate. —**cul′ti·va″tor**, *n.*

cul″ti·va′tion, *n.* 1. development of culture, manners, etc. 2. act or instance of cultivating.

cul′ture, *n.* 1. familiarity with the arts, etc. 2. society, esp. with regard to its art or technology. 3. development through special care. —**cul′tur·al**, *adj.*

cul′vert, *n.* drain under an embankment.

cum′ber·some, *adj.* heavy; burdensome.

cu′mu·la″tive, *adj.* increasing from additions.

cu′mu·lus, *n.*, *pl.* **-li.** dense cloud with domelike upper parts.

cun′ning, *adj.* 1. crafty; sly. 2. clever; skillful. —*n.* 3. craftiness; slyness. 4. skill.

cup, *n.*, *v.t.*, **cupped, cupping,** *n.* 1. small bowlike drinking utensil. 2. contents of a cup. —*v.t.* 3. form into a cuplike shape.

cup′board, *n.* storage cabinet, esp. for dishes or food.

cup′cake″, *n.* small cup-shaped cake.

Cu′pid, *n.* mythological god of love, represented as a naked boy with a bow and arrow.

cu·pid′i·ty, *n.* greed; avarice.

cu·po·la (kyōō′pə lə), *n.* windowed structure on top of a roof.

cur, *n.* mongrel dog.

cu·rate (kōōr′it), *n.* clergyman with a parish. —**cu″ra·cy**, *n.*

cu·ra′tor, *n.* custodian or director of a museum department.

curb, *n.* 1. Also, **curb′ing,** edge of a sidewalk. 2. wall at the top of a well. 3. border or framework. 4. something that restrains. —*v.t.* 5. check or restrain.

curd, *n.* coagulate milk substance, used esp. to make cheese.

cur′dle, *v.*, **-dled, dling.** *v.t.*, *v.i.* form into curds.

cure, *n.* 1. method of remedial treatment, esp. for disease. 2. recovery from disease. —*v.t.* 3. restore to health; heal. 4. preserve, as food.

cur′few, *n.* ban on being out late.

cu·ri·o (kyōōr′ē ō″), *n.* small beautiful or rare object.

cu·ri·ous (kyōōr′e əs), *adj.* 1. inquisitive. 2. odd. —**cu′ri·ous·ly**, *adv.* —**cu″ri·os′i·ty**, *n.*

curl, *v.t.*, *v.i.* 1. form into spiral shapes; coil. —*v.i.* 2. become curved, spiraled or undulated. 3. move in a curving direction. —*n.* 4. something with a curved or twisted form. —**curl′y**, *adj.*

cur′lew, *n.*, *pl.* **-lews** or **-lew.** shore bird with a downcurved beak.

curl′i·cue″, *n.* fancifully curved ornamental figure.

cur′rant, *n.* 1. small seedless raisin. 2. acid edible berry of a wild shrub.

cur′ren·cy, *n.* 1. money. 2. general acceptance or use.

cur′rent, *adj.* 1. happening in the present. 2. practiced or accepted. —*n.* 3. continuous movement of a fluid. 4. flow of electricity. —**cur′rent·ly**, *adv.*

cur·ric′u·lum, *n.*, *pl.* **-lums, -la.** program of studies. —**cur·ric′u·lar**, *adj.*

cur′ry, *n.*, *pl.* **-ries**, *v.t.*, **-ried, -rying.** *n.*

1. spicy condiment. 2. food made with this. —*v.t.* 3. brush, as a horse. 4. make with curry.

curse, *n., v.t.,* **cursed,** or **curst, cursing.** *n.* 1. prayer, etc. invoking harm to another. 2. blasphemy, etc. 3. source of constant trouble. —*v.t.* 4. make the object of a curse. —**curs'ed,** *adj.*

cur"sor, *n.* indicator on a computer monitor showing where the next input will appear.

cur'so·ry, *adj.* hasty or superficial.

curt, *adj.* rude; abrupt. —**curt'ly,** *adv.*

cur·tail', *v.t.* cut short. —**cur·tail'ment,** *n.*

cur'tain, *n.* cloth hanging before a window, theater stage, etc.

curt'sy, *n., pl.* **-sies,** *v.i.,* **-sied, sying.** *n.* 1. woman's bow in which the knees are bent. —*v.i.* 2. make such a bow. Also, **curt'sey.**

cur'va·ture, *n.* 1. curve. 2. degree of curving. 3. abnormal curve, as of the spine.

curve, *n., v.,* **curved, curving.** *n.* 1. continuous line continually changing direction. 2. anything formed along such a line. —*v.t., v.i.* 3. bend along a curve.

cush'ion, *n.* 1. soft pad for support. —*v.t.* 2. preserve from a shock, as from impact.

cusp, *n.* pointed projection.

cus'pid, *n.* single pointed tooth; canine tooth.

cus'pi·dor", *n.* spittoon.

cus'tard, *n.* sweet milk and egg mixture that sets after cooking.

cus'to·dy, *n., pl.* **-dies.** 1. guardianship; care. 2. legal restraint; imprisonment. —**cus·to'di·an,** *n.* —**cus·to'di·al,** *adj.*

cus'tom, *n.* 1. habitual practice or manner of thinking. 2. **customs,** revenue on foreign goods. —*adj.* 3. made to personal order. —**cus'tom·ar"y,** *adj.* —**cus'tom·ar'i·ly,** *adv.*

cus'to·mer, *n.* buyer; purchaser.

cut, *v.,* **cut, cutting,** *n. v.t.* 1. divide or penetrate with something sharp. 2. form with sharp tools. 3. terminate abruptly. 4. *Informal.* **a.** shun ostentatiously. **b.** be absent from. —*v.i.* 5. become cut. 6. swerve. —*n.* 7. wound from cutting. 8. act or instance of cutting. 9. wounding or snubbing remark. 10. illustration for printing.

cu·ta'ne·ous, *adj.* pertaining to the skin.

cute, *adj.,* **-ter, -test,** 1. attractive; pretty. 2. clever; shrewd.

cu'ti·cle, *n.* outer layer of skin.

cut'lass, *n.* short, heavy edged sword.

cut'ler·y, *n.* cutting tools, esp. for food.

cut'let, *n.* slice or patty food for frying or broiling.

cut'ter, *n.* 1. person or implement for cutting. 2. ship's boat with oars. 3. Coast Guard ship.

cy'a·nide", *n.* potassium- or sodium-based poisonous substance.

cy"ber·net'ics, *n.* study of human control systems and functions and of mechanical systems that can be used to replace them. —**cy"ber·net'ic,** *adj.*

cy'cla·mate", *n.* artificial sweetening agent.

cy'cle, *n., v.i.,* **-cled, -cling.** *n.* 1. repeated series. 2. repeated period of time. 3. two-wheeled vehicle. —*v.i.* 4. ride a cycle. —**cy'clic, cy'cli·cal,** *adj.* —**cy'clist,** *n.*

cy'clone, *n.* storm with rotating winds.

cy"clo·pe'dia, *n.* encyclopedia. Also, **cy"clo·pae'di·a.**

cy'clo·tron", *n.* machine for giving acceleration to charged particles by electric and magnetic forces.

cyl'in·der, *n.* 1. solid generated by a rectangle turned on its centerline. 2. expansion chamber in an engine. —**cy·lin'dri·cal,** *adj.*

cym·bal (sim'bəl), *n.* one of a pair of concave brass or bronze plates struck together.

cyn'ic, *n.* person who sees all actions as selfishly motivated. —**cyn'i·cal,** *adj.* —**cyn·i·cism** (sin'ə siz"əm), *n.*

cy'no·sure", *n.* center of attraction.

cy'press, *n.* scaly-leaved evergreen tree.

cyst, *n.* abnormal sac or growth, usually filled with fluid.

czar (zar), *n.* Slavic emperor. Also, fem., **cza·ri'na.**

D

D, d, *n.* 1. fourth letter of the English alphabet. 2. fourth-best grade.

dab, *v.,* **dabbed, dabbing,** *n. v.t.* 1. touch or apply lightly. —*n.* 2. small moist lump.

dab'ble, *v.i.,* **-bled, -bling.** 1. play in water. 2. be superficially active. —**dab'bler,** *n.*

daft, *adj.* 1. insane. 2. silly.

dag'ger, *n.* short pointed weapon.

dahl'ia, *n.* showy perennial flowering plant.

dai'ly, *adj., n., pl.* **-lies.** *adj.* 1. happening each day. —*n.* 2. daily periodical.

dain'ty, *adj.,* **-tier, -tiest,** *n., pl.* **-ties.** *adj.* 1. delicate; fine. —*n.* 2. delicacy. —**dain'ti·ly,** *adv.* —**dain'ti·ness,** *n.*

dair'y, *n. pl.* **-ies.** place where milk and milk products are produced. —**dair'y·man,** *n.*

da·is (dā'is), *n., pl.* **-ises.** raised platform.

dai'sy, *n., pl.* **-sies.** flower with a yellow diskshaped centre and white petals.

dale, *n.* valley.

dal'ly, *v.i.,* **-lied, -lying. 1.** play in a loving way. **2.** delay; waste time. **—dal'li·ance,** *n.*

dam, *n., v.t.,* **dammed, damming.** *n.* **1.** barrier to hold back water. **2.** female parent, esp. of quadrupeds. *—v.t.* **3.** obstruct, as with a dam.

dam'age, *n., v.t.,* **-aged, -aging.** *n.* **1.** injury. **2. damages,** compensation for injury. *—v.t.* **3.** injure; harm. **—dam'age·a·ble,** *adj.*

dam'ask, *n.* **1.** fabric woven in patterns. *—adj.* **2.** pink.

damn, *v.t.* condemn. **—dam'na·ble,** *adj.* **—dam·na'tion,** *n.*

damp, *adj.* **1.** moist. *—n.* **2.** moisture. *—v.t.* **3.** make moist. **4.** deaden, as a shock. **—damp'ness,** *n.*

damp'en, *v.t.* **1.** make damp. **2.** deaden or depress, as the spirits. *—v.i.* **3.** become damp.

damp'er, *n.* **1.** something that deadens or depresses. **2.** valve in a flue to regulate draft.

dam'sel, *n.* Archaic. girl.

dance, *v.,* **danced, dancing,** *n.* *v.i.* **1.** move one's body and feet in rhythm, esp. to music. *—v.t.* **2.** execute as a dance. **3.** cause to dance. *—n.* **4.** social gathering for dancing. **—dancer,** *n.*

dan·de·li'on, *n.* weedy plant with yellow flowers.

dan'druff, *n.* scales that form on the scalp and fall off.

dan'dy, *n. pl.,* **-dies,** *adj.,* **-dier, -diest.** *n.* **1.** man overly particular about his appearance. *—adj.* **2.** *Informal.* very good.

dan'ger, *n.* exposure to harm; risk. **—dan'ger·ous,** *adj.*

dan'gle, -gled, -gling. *v.i., v.t.* hang loosely.

dank, *adj.* unpleasantly moist.

dap'per, *adj.* **1.** neat. **2.** small and active.

dap'ple, *adj., n., v.,* **-pled, -pling.** *adj.* **1.** Also, **dap'pled,** spotted. *—n.* **2.** spot or marking. *—v.t.* **3.** mark with spots.

dare, *v.,* **dared, daring,** *n. v.i.* **1.** have the necessary courage or audacity. *—v.t., n.* **2.** challenge. **—dar'ling,** *adj., n.*

dark, *adj.* **1.** having little or no light. **2.** tending in color toward black. **3.** gloomy. **4.** ignorant. *—n.* **5.** absence of light. **—dark'en,** *v.t., v.i.* **—dark'ness,** *n.*

dar'ling, *n.* **1.** person dear to another. *—adj.* **2.** very dear; cherished.

darn, *v.t.* mend by weaving rows of stitches.

dart, *n.* **1.** small pointed missile usually thrown by hand. **2.** sudden motion. *—v.t., v.i.* **3.** move suddenly and swiftly.

dash, *v.t.* **1.** hurl violently. **2.** smash. **3.** frustrate. *—v.i.* **4.** rush; sprint. *—n.* **5.** small amount shaken from a bottle, etc. **6.** short race. **7.** punctuation mark (—) indicating a break.

dash'board'', *n.* instrument panel.

dash'ing, *adj.* **1.** lively. **2.** showy; stylish. **—dash'ing·ly,** *adv.*

das'tard, *n.* coward; sneak. **—das'tard·ly,** *adj.*

da''ta, *n. pl.* **1.** facts; figures. **2.** (computers) information stored in a memory.

da''ta·base, *n.* (computers) a structured file facilitating data access and manipulation.

date, *n., v.,* **dated, dating.** *n.* **1.** particular time. **2.** day of the month. **3.** appointment. **4.** sweet, fleshy fruit of a palm tree. *—v.t.* **5.** give a date to. *—v.i.* **6.** belong to a specific time.

dat'ed, *adj.* **1.** antiquated. **2.** showing a date.

daub, *v.t.* **1.** cover or smear with a soft, muddy substance. *—v.t., v.i.* **2.** paint clumsily. *—n.* **3.** something daubed. **—daub'er,** *n.*

daugh'ter, *n.* female child. **—daugh'ter·ly,** *adj.*

daugh'ter-in-law'', *n. pl.,* **daughters-in-law.** son's wife.

daunt, *v.t.* frighten; dishearten. **—daunt'less,** *adj.*

dav'en·port'', *n.* large couch.

daw'dle, *v.i.,* **-dled, -dling.** waste time. **—daw'dler,** *n.*

dawn, *v.i.* **1.** begin to grow light in the morning. *—n.* **2.** break of day.

day, *n.* **1.** period between sunrise and sunset. **2.** period of earth's rotation on its axis. **3.** era; period of time.

day'dream'', *n.* **1.** period of pleasant, dreamy thought. *—v.t.* **2.** have daydreams.

day'light'', *n.* **1.** light of day. **2.** openness.

day'time'', *n.* period between sunrise and sunset.

daze, *v.t.,* **dazed, dazing,** *n., v.t.* **1.** stun; bewilder. *—n.* **2.** stunned condition.

daz'zle, *v.t.,* **-zled, -zling. 1.** overwhelm with intense light. **2.** impress with brilliance.

dea'con, *n.* **1.** cleric just below a priest in rank. **2.** lay church officer. **—dea'con·ry,** *n.*

dead, *adj.* **1.** no longer alive. **2.** without life. **3.** obsolete. **4.** accurate; unerring. *—adj., adv.* **5.** straight. *—n.* **6. the dead,** persons no longer living. **—dead'en,** *v.t.*

dead'line'', *n.* latest time by which something must be completed.

dead'lock'', *n.* **1.** frustrated standstill. *—v.t., v.i.* **2.** bring or come to a deadlock.

dead'ly, *adj.* **-lier, -liest. 1.** likely to cause

death. 2. typical of death. —**dead′li·**
ness, *n.*

deaf, *adj.* incapable of hearing. —**deaf′**
ness, *n.* —**deaf′en,** *v.t.*

deal, *v.,* **dealt, dealing.** *n.* *v.t.* **1.** portion
out. **2.** administer, as a blow. —*v.i.* **3.**
do or have business. **4.** portion out
cards, etc. —*n.* **5.** business transaction
or agreement. —**deal′er,** *n.*

dean, *n.* **1.** college official who supervises
students or faculty. **2.** presiding cleric
in a cathedral.

dear, *adj.* **1.** beloved. **2.** expensive. —*n.*
3. beloved person. —**dear′ly,** *adv.*

dearth (dərth), *n.* scarcity; lack.

death, *n.* **1.** act of dying. **2.** state of being
dead. —**death′less,** *adj.* —**death′like″,**
adj. —**death′ly,** *adj., adv.*

de·ba′cle, *n.* ruinous collapse.

de·bar′, *v.t.,* **-barred, -barring.** exclude;
prohibit.

de·base′, *v.t.,* **-based, -basing.** lower in
value. —**de·base′ment,** *n.*

de·bate′, *v.* **-bated, -bating.** *n.* *v.t.* **1.** discuss; argue. **2.** consider. —*v.i.* **3.** take
part in discussion. —*n.* **4.** discussion of
opposing views. —**de·bat′a·ble,** *adj.*
—**de·bat′er,** *n.*

de·bauch′, *v.t.* **1.** corrupt; seduce. —*n.*
2. debauchery; seduction. —**de·bauch′**
er·y, *n.*

de·bil′i·tate, *v.t.,* **-tated, -tating.** weak-
en. —**de·bil″i·ta′tion,** *n.*

de·bil′i·ty, *n., pl.* **-ties.** weakness.

deb′it, *n.* **1.** recorded debt. —*v.t.* **2.**
charge with a debt.

deb″o·nair′, *adj.* **1.** courteous; pleasantly mannered. **2.** carefree.

de·bris′ (də brē′), *n.* rubbish; remains.

debt, *n.* **1.** something owed. **2.** condition
of owing. —**debt′or,** *n.*

de·but′ (dā byōō′), *n.* **1.** first public appearance. **2.** formal introduction into
society.

deb′u·tante″, *n.* girl making a society de-
but.

dec′ade, *n.* ten-year period.

dec′a·dence, *n.* decay; deterioration.
—**dec′a·dent,** *adj., n.*

dec″a·he′dron, *n., pl.* **-drons, -dra.**
tensided solid.

de·cal′, *n.* transfer of a picture or design
from paper to glass, wood, etc. Also,
de·cal″co·ma′ni·a.

Dec′a·logue″, *n.* Ten Commandments.
Also, **Dec′a·log″.**

de·camp′, *v.i.* **1.** break camp. **2.** depart
suddenly.

de·cant′, *v.t.* pour gently so as not to disturb sediment.

de·cant′er, *n.* ornamental bottle, esp. for
wine.

de·cap′i·tate″, *v.t.,* **-tated, -tating.** be-
head. —**de·cap″i·ta′tion,** *n.*

de·cath′lon, *n.* contest consisting of ten
track and field events.

de·cay′, *v.i., v.t.* **1.** deteriorate; rot. —*n.*
2. deterioration.

de·cease′, *n., v.i.* **-ceased, -ceasing.** *n.* **1.**
death. —*v.i.* **2.** die. —**de·ceased′,** *adj.,*
n.

de·ceit′, *n.* lying; fraud. —**de·ceit′ful,**
adj.

de·ceive′, *v.t.* **-ceived, -ceiving.** mislead.

De·cem′ber, *n.* twelfth and final month.

de′cent, *adj.* **1.** appropriate. **2.** not offensive to modesty. **3.** respectable. **4.** adequate. —**de′cent·ly,** *adv.* —**de′cen·cy,**
n.

de·cen′tral·ize″, *v.t.,* **-ized, -ising.** free
from dependency on a central authori-
ty, source, etc. —**de·cen″tral·i·za′**
tion, *n.*

de·cep′tion, *n.* **1.** act or instance of de-
ceiving. **2.** fraud. —**de·cep′tive,** *adj.*

de·cide′, *v.,* **-cided, -ciding.** *v.t.* **1.** reach
a decision regarding. —*v.i.* **2.** make a
judgment or choice.

de·cid′ed, *adj.* **1.** clear-cut. **2.** determined. —**de·cid′ed·ly,** *adv.*

de·cid′u·ous, *adj.* shedding leaves at a
particular season, as a tree or shrub.

dec′i·mal, *adj.* **1.** based on the number
ten. **2.** pertaining to fractions whose
denominators are ten or some power of
ten. —*n.* **3.** decimal fraction.

dec′i·mate″, *v.t.,* **-mated, -mating.** destroy a sizable number of.

de·ci′pher, *v.t.* determine the meaning
of.

de·ci′sion, *n.* **1.** choice or judgment. **2.**
emphasis; firmness.

de·ci′sive, *adj.* **1.** determining an outcome or conclusion. **2.** emphatic; firm.
—**de·ci′sive·ly,** *adv.* —**de·ci′sive·ness,**
n.

deck, *n.* **1.** floor of a ship, bridge, etc. **2.**
pack of playing cards. —*v.t.* **3.** adorn.

de·claim′, *v.i., v.t.,* speak or utter rhe-
torically. —**de″clam·a′tion,** *n.* —**de·**
clam′a·to″ry, *adj.*

de·clare′, *v.t.* **-clared, -claring.** **1.** make
known. **2.** say emphatically. —**de·clar′**
a·tive, de·clar′a·to″ry, *adj.* —**dec″la·**
ra′tion, *n.*

de·clen′sion, *n.* **1.** grammatical inflection
of nouns, pronouns, or adjectives. **2.**
decline.

de·cline′, *v.,* **-clined, -clining.** *n. v.t., v.i.*
1. bend or slope downward. **2.** deteriorate. **3.** refuse. —*v.i.* **4.** give grammatical inflections. —*n.* **5.** deterioration. **6.**
downward slope.

de·cliv′i·ty, *n., pl.* **-ties.** downward
slope.

de·code′, *v.t.* **-coded, -coding.** decipher
from code.

de″com·pose′, *v.,* **-posed, -posing.** *v.t.,*
v.i. **1.** break up into parts. **2.** decay.
—**de″com·po·si′tion,** *n.*

de·cor', *n.* style of decoration.

dec'o·rate'', *v.t.*, **-rated, -rating. 1.** adorn. **2.** give a medal to. **—dec'o·ra·tive,** *adj.* **—dec'o·ra''tor,** *n.* **—dec''o·ra'tion,** *n.*

dec'o·rous, *adj.* proper.

de·co'rum, *n.* propriety.

de·coy', *n.* **1.** artificial bird used as a lure in hunting. **2.** lure. —*v.t.* **3.** lure into a trap.

de·crease', *v.*, **-creased, -creasing,** *n. v.t., v.i.* **1.** gradually lessen. —*n.* **2.** lessening.

de·cree', *n., v.*, **-creed, -creeing.** *n.* **1.** edict. —*v.t.* **2.** ordain by decree.

de·crep'it, *adj.* worn by old age or long use. **—de·crep'i·tude'',** *n.*

de·cry', *v.t.*, **-cried, -crying.** denounce. **—de·cri'al,** *n.*

ded'i·cate'', *v.t.*, **-cated, -cating. 1.** set apart; devote. **2.** inscribe. **—ded''i·ca'tion,** *n.*

de·duce', *v.t.*, **-duced, -ducing.** infer; derive. **—de·duc'i·ble,** *adj.*

de·duct', *v.t.* subtract; take away. **—de·duct'i·ble,** *adj.*

de·duc'tion, *n.* **1.** act or result of reasoning from the general to the specific. **2.** amount deducted. **—de·duc'tive,** *adj.*

deed, *n.* **1.** something that is done; an act. **2.** legal conveyance esp. of land. —*v.t.* **3.** transfer by deed.

deem, *v.t., v.i.* believe; adjudge.

deep, *adj.* **1.** extending far downward or inward. **2.** difficult to understand. **3.** profound; serious. **4.** dark and rich, esp. a color. **5.** low in pitch. —*n.* **6.** deep place. —*adv.* **7.** far down. **—deep'en,** *v.t., v.i.* **—deep'ly,** *adv.*

deer, *n., pl.* **deer, deers.** ruminant animal, the male of which have antlers or horns.

de·face', *v.t.*, **-faced, -facing.** mar; disfigure. **—de·face'ment,** *n.*

de fac'to, actually existing but not lawfully authorized.

de·fame', *v.t.* **-famed, -faming.** attack the reputation of; slander. **—def''am·a'tion,** *n.* **—de·fam'a·to''ry,** *adj.*

de·fault', *n.* **1.** failure, esp. to pay a debt. —*v.t., v.i.* **2.** fail, esp. to pay, when required.

de·feat', *v.t.* **1.** overthrow; conquer. —*n.* **2.** act or instance of defeating.

de·feat'ist, *n.* person who accepts defeat. **—de·feat'ism,** *n.*

de'fe·cate'', *v.i.*, **-cated, -cating.** *v.i.* excrete waste from the bowels. **—def''e·ca'tion,** *n.*

de·fect', *n.* **1.** (dē'fekt, dē fekt') imperfection; fault. —*v.i.* (dē fekt') **2.** desert a cause, esp. to join another. **—de·fec'tive,** *adj.* **—de·fec'tion,** *n.* **—de·fec'tor,** *n.*

de·fend', *v.t.* **1.** protect; guard against attack. **2.** support with one's words. **—de·fend'er,** *n.*

de·fend'ant, *n. Law.* accused person.

de·fense', *n.* **1.** protection against attack. **2.** justification. **3.** *Law.* reply to a charge. **—de'fense·less,** *adj.* **—de·fen'si·ble,** *adj.*

de·fen'sive, *adj.* **1.** pertaining to defense. **2.** anxious to justify oneself. —*n.* **3.** situation of a defender.

de·fer', *v.*, **-ferred, -ferring.** *v.t., v.i.* **1.** postpone. —*v.i.* **2.** yield politely. **—de·fer'ment,** *n.* **—def'er·ence,** *n.* **—de''fer·en'tial,** *adj.*

de·fi'ance, *n.* open disregard of or bold resistance to authority. **—de·fi'ant,** *adj.*

de·fi'cien·cy, *n., pl.* **-cies.** lack; inadequate amount. **—de·fi'cient,** *adj.*

def'i·cit, *n.* deficiency, esp. of assets.

de·file', *v.*, **-filed, -filing.** *v.t.* **1.** desecrate. **2.** make filthy. —*v.i.* **3.** march in file. —*n.* **4.** narrow passage. **—de·file'ment,** *n.*

de·fine', *v.t.*, **-fined, -fining. 1.** state the meaning of. **2.** determine. **—def''i·ni'tion,** *n.* **—de·fin'a·ble,** *adj.*

def'i·nite, *adj.* **1.** exact. **2.** within precise limits. **—def'i·nite·ly,** *adv.*

de·fin'i·tive, *adj.* **1.** conclusive. **2.** defining.

de·flate', *v.*, **-flated, -flating.** *v.t., v.i.* **1.** collapse by releasing air. **2.** increase in purchasing power. **—de·fla'tion,** *n.* **—de·fla'tion·ar''y,** *adj.*

de·flect', *v.t., v.i.* turn from a course; swerve. **—de·flec'tion,** *n.*

de·form', *v.t.* **1.** mar the form of. **2.** make ugly. **—de''for·ma'tion,** *n.* **—de·form'i·ty,** *n.*

de·fraud', *v.t.* cheat; take rights or property of by fraud.

de·fray', *v.t.* pay, as expenses.

de·frost', *v.t., v.i.* free or be freed of ice.

deft, *adj.* skillful. **—deft'ly,** *adv.* **—deft'ness,** *n.*

de·funct', *adj.* no longer alive or in existence.

de·fy', *v.t.*, **-fied, -fying. 1.** openly resist. **2.** challenge.

de·gen·er·ate, *adj., n., v.*, **ated, ating.** *adj.* (dē jen'ər ət) **1.** deteriorated. **2.** depraved. *n.* **3.** depraved person. —*v.i.* (dē jen'ər āt) **4.** deteriorate. **—de·gen''er·a'tion,** *n.* **—de·gen'er·a·cy,** *n.* **—de·gen'er·a·tive,** *adj.*

de·grade', *v.t.*, **-graded, -grading.** reduce in quality or rank. **—de''gra·da'tion,** *n.*

de·gree', *n.* **1.** stage or point, as in a process. **2.** extent or intensity. **3.** title conferred by a college. **4.** unit of temperature. **5.** 360th of a circle.

de·hu'man·ize'', *v.t.*, **-ized, -izing.** deny human qualities to.

de·hy'drate, *v.*, **-drated, -drating.** *v.t. v.i.* remove or lose water. **—de''hy·dra'tion,** *n.*

de'i·fy'', *v.t.*, **-fied, -fying.** make a god of. —**de''i·fi·ca'tion,** *n.*

deign, *v.t., v.i.* condescend.

de'ism, *n.* belief that a god created the world but has had no control over it. —**de'ist,** *n.*

de'i·ty, *n., pl.* **-ties.** god or goddess

de·ject', *v.t.* dishearten. —**de·jec'tion,** *n.*

de·lay', *v.t.* 1. postpone. 2. hinder; make late. —*v.i.* 3. linger; procrastinate. —*n.* 4. act or instance of delaying.

de·lec'ta·ble, *adj.* delightful; delicious. —**de''lec·ta'tion,** *n.*

del·e·gate, *n., v.t.,* **-gated, -gating.** *n.* (del'ə gət) 1. representative. —*v.t.* (del'ə gāt) 2. send as arepresentative. 3. entrust to another, as authority. —**del''e·ga'tion,** *n.*

de·lete', *v.t.,* **-leted, -leting.** remove from a text. —**de·le'tion,** *n.*

del''e·te'ri·ous, *adj.* injurious to health;

de·lib·er·ate, *v.,* **-ated, -ating,** *adj. v.t., v.i.* (dē lib'ər ăt) 1. ponder. —*adj.* (dĕlib'ər ət) 2. intentional. 3. unhurried. —**de·lib'er·ate·ly,** *adv.* —**de·lib''er·a'tion,** *n.* —**de·lib'er·a·tive,** *adj.* —**de·lib'er·a''tor,** *n.*

del'i·ca·cy, *n., pl.* **-cies.** 1. fineness of quality. 2. choice food.

del'i·cate, *adj.* 1. fine in quality or texture. 2. easily damaged. 3. considerate; tactful. 4. functioning precisely. —**del'i·cate·ly,** *adv.*

del''i·ca·tes'sen, *n.* store selling food specialties.

de·li'cious, *adj.* 1. pleasing to taste. 2. delectable. —**de·li'cious·ly,** *adv.*

de·light', *v.t., v.i.* 1. give great pleasure. —*n.* 2. joy or great pleasure. —**de·light'ed,** *adj.* —**de·light'ful,** *adj.*

de·lin'e·ate'', *v.t.,* **-ated, -ating.** trace the outline of. —**de·lin''e·a'tion,** *n.*

de·lin'quent, *adj.* 1. neglectful of duty or law. 2. late, as a debt. —*n.* 3. delinquent person. —**de·lin'quen·cy,** *n.*

de·lir'i·um, *n.* temporary excited mental disorder. —**de·lir'i·ous,** *adj.*

de·liv'er, *v.t.* 1. set free or save. 2. hand over. 3. assist at the birth of. 4. present to an audience. 5. distribute. —**de·liv'er·ance,** *n.* —**de·liv'er·y,** *n.*

del·phin'i·um, *n.* tall blue garden flower.

del'ta, *n.* deposit of soil formed at a divided river mouth.

de·lude', *v.t.,* **-luded, -luding.** mislead.

del·uge (del'yŏōj), *n., v.t.,* **-uged, -uging.** *n.* 1. flood. 2. heavy rainfall. —*v.t.* 3. flood. 4. overwhelm.

de·lu'sion, *n.* false conception, esp. one persistent and opposed to reason. —**de·lu'sive,** *adj.*

de·luxe', *adj.* of specially fine quality.

delve, *v.i.,* **delved, delving.** dig.

dem'a·gogue'', *n.* unscrupulous player on popular emotion. Also, **dem'a·gog''.** —**dem'a·gog''y, dem'a·gogu''er·y,** *n.*

de·mand', *v.t.* 1. ask for boldly; claim as a right. 2. require. *v.i.* 3. make a demand. —*n.* 4. act or instance of demanding. 5. thing demanded. —**de·mand'ing,** *adj.*

de·mean', *v.t.* 1. debase; humble. 2. behave; conduct.

de·mean'or, *n.* behavior or conduct.

de·ment'ed, *adj.* mentally deranged.

de·mer'it, *n.* 1. fault. 2. mark against a person for a fault.

dem'i·god, *n.* 1. mythological being who is divine and human. 2. godlike human.

de·mil'i·tar·ize'', *v.t.,* **-ized, -izing.** free from military control. —**de·mil''i·tar·i·za'tion,** *n.*

de·mise', *n., v.t.,* **-mised, -mising.** *n.* 1. death. —*n., v.t.* 2. transfer by lease.

de·mo'bi·lize'', *v.t.,* **-lized, -lizing.** free from military service; disband. —**de·mo''bi·li·za'tion,** *n.*

de·moc'ra·cy, *n.* 1. government by the people. 2. country with such government. 3. social equality. —**dem'o·crat'',** *n.* —**dem''o·crat'ic,** *adj.* —**de·moc'ra·tize'',** *v.t.*

De·mo'crat, *n.* member of the Democratic party.

de·mol'ish, *v.t.* destroy. —**dem''o·li'tion,** *n.*

de'mon, *n.* 1. evil spirit; devil. 2. person regarded as evil. —**de·mon'ic, de·mo'ni·ac'', de''mo·ni'a·cal,** *adj.*

dem'on·strate'', *v.* **-strated, -strating.** *v.t.* 1. prove in detail. 2. explain by example. 3. reveal. —*v.i.* 4. call public attention to one's attitude. —**dem''on·stra'tion,** *n.* —**dem'on·stra''tor,** *n.* —**de·mon'stra·ble,** *adj.*

de·mon'stra·tive, *adj.* 1. self-expressive. 2. illustrative or explanatory. 3. conclusive.

de·mor'al·ize'', *v.t.,* **-ized, -izing.** lower the morale of. —**de·mor''al·i·za'tion,** *n.*

de·mote', *v.t.,* **-moted, -moting.** lower in rank. —**de·mo'tion,** *n.*

de·mur', *v.i.,* **-murred, -murring,** *n. v.i.* 1. object. —*n.* 2. objection.

de·mure', *adj.* modest; coy. —**de·mure'ly,** *adv.*

den, *n.* 1. cave of a wild animal. 2. vile place. 3. small, private room for a man.

de·ni'al, *n.* 1. refusal of consent. 2. contradiction. 3. refusal to believe.

den'i·grate'', *v.t.,* **-grated, -grating.** blacken or malign the character of. —**den''i·gra'tion,** *n.*

den'im, *n.* heavy twill cotton cloth.

den'i·zen, *n.* inhabitant.

de·nom'i·nate'', *v.t.,* **-nated, -nating.** name.

de·nom″i·na′tion, *n.* 1. name. 2. act of naming. 3. religious sect. —**de·nom″i·na′tion·al,** *adj.*

de·nom′i·na″tor, *n. Math.* term below the line in a fraction; divisor.

de·note′, *v.t.,* **-noted, -noting.** indicate; mean. —**de″no·ta′tion,** *n.*

de·noue·ment (dā nōō mähn′), *n. Literature.* resolution of a conflict.

de·nounce′, *v.t.,* **-nounced, -nouncing.** 1. accuse openly. 2. inform against. —**de·nounce′ment,** *n.*

dense, *adj.* 1. thick. 2. stupid. —**dense′ly,** *adv.* —**dense′ness,** *n.* —**den′si·ty,** *n.*

dent, *n.* 1. hollow area made by a blow. —*v.t., v.i.* 2. make or receive a dent.

den′tal, *adj.* pertaining to teeth or dentistry.

den′ti·frice, *n.* preparation used in brushing the teeth.

den′tist, *n.* doctor specializing in teeth and gums. —**den′tist·ry,** *n.*

den′ture, *n.* set of false teeth.

de·nude′, *v.t.,* **-nuded, -nuding.** strip. —**den″u·da′tion,** *n.*

de·nun″ci·a′tion, *n.* 1. condemnation. 2. accusation.

de·ny′, *v.t.,* **-nied, -nying.** 1. reject as untrue. 2. refuse to give or allow. 3. refuse something to.

de·o′dor·ant, *n.* 1. preparation for destroying odors. —*adj.* 2. destroying odors.

de·part′, *v.i.* 1. leave; go away. 2. die. —**de·par′ture,** *n.*

de·part′ment, *n.* 1. part or section. 2. field of activity. —**de·part″men′tal,** *adj.*

de·pend′, *v.i.* 1. look outside oneself for support, help, etc. 2. be according to conditions. —**de·pend′a·ble,** *adj.* —**de·pend′a·bly,** *adv.* —**de·pend″a·bil′i·ty,** *n.* —**de·pend′ent,** *adj., n.* —**de·pend′ence, de·pend′en·cy,** *n.*

de·pict′, *v.t.* 1. portray; delineate. 2. describe. —**de·pic′tion,** *n.*

de·plete′, *v.t.,* **-pleted, -pleting.** exhaust or reduce in amount. —**de·ple′tion,** *n.*

de·plore′, *v.t.,* **-plored, -ploring.** regret strongly. —**de·plor′a·ble,** *adj.*

de·pop′u·late″, *v.t.,* **-lated, -lating.** remove remove the population of. —**de·pop″u·la′tion,** *n.*

de·port′, *v.t.* expel from a country. —**de″por·ta′tion,** *n.*

de·port′ment *n.* conduct or behaviour.

de·pose′, *v.t.,* **-posed, -posing.** 1. remove from office or power. 2. testify. —**dep″o·si′tion,** *n.*

de·pos′it, *v.t.* 1. put in a bank, etc. 2. give in partial payment. 3. drop or cause to settle. 4. something deposited. —**de·pos′i·tor,** *n.*

de·pot (dē′pō), *n.* 1. bus or railroad station. 2. storage place for military supplies.

de·prave′, *v.t.* **-praved, -praving.** corrupt. —**de·prav′i·ty,** *n.*

dep′re·cate″, *v.t.,* **-cated, -cating.** 1. express disapproval of. 2. belittle. —**dep″re·ca′tion,** *n.* —**dep′re·ca·to″ry,** *adj.*

de·pre·ci·ate (dē prē′shē āt″), *v.,* **-ated, -ating.** *v.t., v.i.* 1. lessen in value or seeming importance. —*v.t.* 2. belittle. —**de·pre″ci·a′tion,** *n.*

dep″re·da′tion, *n.* robbery.

de·press′, *v.t.* 1. deject; sadden. 2. push down. 3. weaken. —**de·pressed′,** *adj.* —**de·press′ant,** *n.*

de·pres′sion, *n.* 1. act of depressing or being depressed. 2. depressed state. 3. period when business and employment decline. —**de·pres′sive,** *adj.*

de·prive′, *v.t.,* **-prived, -priving.** withhold from. —**de″pri·va′tion,** *n.*

depth, *n.* 1. distance downward or inward. 2. quality of being deep. 3. intensity or profundity. 4. profundity. 5. **depths,** deepest part.

dep″u·ta′tion, *n.* delegation.

dep′u·ty, *n., pl.* **-ties.** person appointed to act as a substitute for another.

de·rail′, *v.t., v.i.* run off the rails. —**de·rail′ment,** *n.*

de·range′, *v.t.,* **-ranged, -ranging.** 1. disturb the arrangement of. 2. make insane. —**de·range′ment,** *n.*

der′by, *n.* stiff hat with a round crown.

der′e·lict″, *adj.* 1. abandoned by its owner. 2. negligent. —*n.* 3. something abandoned, esp. a ship. 4. destitute person.

der″e·lic′tion, *n.* 1. negligence of a duty. 2. forsakenness.

de·ride′, *v.t.,* **-rided, -riding.** mock. —**de·ri′sion,** *n.* —**de·ri′sive,** *adj.*

de·rive′, *v.* **-rived, -riving.** *v.t.* 1. obtain from a source. 2. trace to or from a source. 3. deduce; infer. —*v.i.* 4. originate or be derived. —**der″i·va′tion,** *n.* —**de·riv′a·tive,** *adj., n.*

der′o·gate″, *v.,* **-gated, -gating,** *v.t., v.i.,* detract. —**der″o·ga′tion,** *n.* —**de·rog′a·to″ry,** *adj.*

der′rick, *n.* 1. crane for lifting and moving heavy objects. 2. tall framework over an oil well.

des·cant, *n.* 1. (des′kant) melody. —*v.i.* (des kant′) 2. sing. 3. discourse.

de·scend (di send′) *v.t.* 1. move down, along or through. —*v.i.* 2. move downward. 3. slope downward. 4. make a sudden attack, etc. 5. be derived from specified ancestors. —**des·cent′,** *n.* —**de·scen′dant,** *n.*

de·scribe′, *v.t.,* **-scribed, -scribing.** 1. give a conception or account of. 2. trace by movement. —**de·scrib′a·ble,** *adj.* —**de·scrip′tion,** *n.* —**de·scrip′tive,** *adj.*

de·scry′, *v.t.,* **-scried, -scrying.** perceive.

des'e·crate", *v.t.*, **-crated, -crating.** profane. **—des''e·cra'tion,** *n.*

de·seg're·gate", *v.*, **-gated, -gating.** *v.t.*, *v.i.* eliminate racial segregation in. **—de·seg're·ga'tion,** *n.*

de·sert', *v.t.* (de zɜrt') 1. abandon. 2. abscond from permanently, as duty. **—n.** 3. Often, **deserts,** something deserved. 4. (dez'ərt) wasteland, esp. a sandy one. **—adj.** 5. desolate; barren. **—de·sert'er,** *n.* **—de·ser'tion,** *n.*

de·serve', *v.*, **-served, -serving.** *v.t.* 1. have as a rightful outcome or reward. **—v.i.** 2. be worthy. **—de·serv'ing,** *adj., n.*

des'ic·cate", *v.*, **-cated, -cating.** *v.t.*, *v.i.* dry completely. **—des''ic·ca'tion,** *n.*

de·sign', *v.t.* 1. plan the form and making of. 2. contrive. 3. intend. **—n.** 4. plan or pattern. 5. designing of artistic objects. 6. scheme or intention.

des'ig·nate", *v.t.*, **-nated, -nating.** 1. specify; indicate. 2. name. 3. appoint. **—des''ig·na'tion,** *n.*

de·sign'er, *n.* 1. one who designs. **—adj.** 2. of or pertaining to clothing, etc. styled by a designer, as *designer jeans.*

de·sign'ing, *adj.* scheming.

de·sire', *v.* **-sired, -siring,** *n.* *v.t.* 1. long for. 2. request. **—v.i.** 3. have a desire. **—n.** 4. craving. 5. request. 6. lust. 7. thing desired. **—de·sir'a·ble,** *adj.* **—de·sir'a·bly,** *adv.* **—de·sir''a·bil'i·ty,** *n.* **—de·sir'ous,** *adj.*

de·sist', *v.i.* stop; cease.

desk, *n.* table with drawers used for writing.

des·o·late, *adj., v.* **-lated, -lating.** *adj.* (des'ə lit) 1. barren. 2. lonely. 3. uninhabited. **—v.t.** (des'ə lāt') 4. make barren. **—des''o·la'tion,** *n.*

de·spair', *v.i.* 1. lose hope. **—n.** 2. hopelessness.

des''per·a'do, *n., pl.* **-does, -dos.** reckless criminal.

des'per·ate, *adj.* 1. reckless due to despair. 2. having an urgent need. 3. very serious. 4. extreme or drastic. **—des''per·a'tion,** *n.*

des'pi·ca·ble, *adj.* contemptible. **—des'pi·ca·bly,** *adv.*

de·spise', *v.t.*, **-spised, -spising.** scorn; loathe.

de·spite', *prep.* in spite of.

de·spoil', *v.t.* rob; pillage.

de·spond', *v.i.* lose hope or courage. **—de·spond·en·cy, de·spond'ence,** *n.* **—de·spond'ent,** *adj.*

des'pot, *n.* tyrant or absolute ruler. **—des·pot'ic,** *adj.* **—des'pot·ism,** *n.*

des·sert', *n.* sweet course ending a meal.

des''ti·na'tion, *n.* place to be reached.

des'tine, *v.t.*, **-tined, -tining.** 1. intend. 2. predetermine.

des'tin·y, *n., pl.* **-nies.** 1. predetermined course of events. 2. rate.

des'ti·tute", *adj.* 1. deprived. 2. without means of existence. **—des''ti·tu'tion,** *n.*

de·stroy', *n.* 1. damage so as to eliminate. 2. kill.

de·stroy'er, *n.* 1. light, fast warship. 2. person or thing that destroys.

de·struc'tion, *n.* 1. act or instance of destroying. 2. agency by which one is destroyed. **—de·struct'i·ble,** *adj.* **—de·struc'tive,** *adj.*

des'ul·to''ry, *adj.* 1. random. 2. disconnected. **—des''ul·to'ri·ly,** *adv.*

de·tach', *v.t.* separate; disconnect. **—de·tach'a·ble,** *adj.*

de·tached', *adj.* 1. separate; not connected. 2. disinterested.

de·tach'ment, *n.* 1. state of being detached. 2. military unit on a special mission.

de·tail', *n.* 1. subordinate part or feature. 2. soldiers for a specific duty. **—v.t.** 3. make, plan, or relate the details of. 4. assign to a duty.

de·tain', *v.t.* 1. keep from going on; delay. 2. keep in custody. **—de·ten'tion,** *n.*

de·tect', *v.t.* discover. **—de·tec'tion,** *n.* **—de·tec'tor,** *n.* **—de·tect'a·ble, de·tect'i·ble,** *adj.*

de·tec'tive, *n.* investigator seeking private or hidden information.

de·tente (dā tahnt'), *n.* lessening of tension, esp. internationally.

de·ter', *v.t.*, **-terred, -terring.** discourage or prevent. **—de·ter'ment,** *n.* **—de·ter'rent,** *n.*

de·ter'gent, *adj.* 1. cleansing. **—n.** 2. preparation used for cleaning.

de·te'ri·o·rate", *v.*, **-rated, -rating.** *v.t.*, *v.i.* worsen. **—de·te''ri·o·ra'tion,** *n.*

de·ter''mi·na'tion, *n.* 1. act or instance of determining. 2. firmness of resolve. 3. firm intention.

de·ter'mine, *v.* **-mined, -mining.** *v.t.* 1. settle. 2. ascertain. 3. direct; impel. 4. set limits to. **—v.i.** 5. decide. **—de·ter'mi·na·ble,** *adj.* **—de·ter'mi·nate,** *adj.*

de·ter'mined, *adj.* showing determination.

de·test', *v.t.* hate. **—de·test'a·ble,** *adj.* **—de·test'a·bly,** *adv.* **—de''tes·ta'tion,** *n.*

de·throne', *v.t.*, **-throned, -throning.** remove from sovereign power.

det'o·nate", *v.*, **-nated, -nating.** *v.t.*, *v.i.* explode. **—det''o·na'tion,** *n.* **—det''o·na'tor,** *n.*

de'tour', *n.* 1. roundabout course. **—v.t.**, *v.i.* 2. go or route on a detour.

de·tract', *v.t.* 1. take away. **—v.i.** 2. take a desirable quality. **—de·trac'tion,** *n.*

det'ri·ment, *n.* 1. injury or loss. 2. something that causes injury or loss. **—det''ri·men'tal,** *adj.*

de·val'u·ate", *v.t.*, **-ated, ating.** lessen in

value. Also, **de·val'ue. —de·val"u·a' tion,** *n.*

dev'as·tate", *v.t.,* **-tated, -tating.** destroy everywhere. **—dev"as·ta'tion,** *n.*

de·vel'op, *v.t.* **1.** bring to maturity or completeness. **2.** elaborate. **3.** fall ill with. **4.** *Photography.* bring out the picture on. **—v.i. 5.** be developed. **—de·vel'op·ment,** *n.* **—de·vel"op· men'tal,** *adj.*

de·vi·ate, *v.i.,* **-ated, ating,** *adj., n. v.i.* (dē'vēăt") **1.** turn aside; digress. **—adj.** (dē'vē it") **2.** deviant. **—n. 3.** deviant person. **4.** sexual pervert. **—de"vi·a' tion,** *n.*

de·vice', *n.* **1.** tool, etc. **2.** plan. **3.** symbol or representation.

dev'il, *n., v.t.,* **-iled** or **-illed, -iling** or **-illing.** *n.* **1.** fiend of hell. **2. the Devil,** Satan. **3.** malicious or formidable person. **—v.t. 4.** torment. **—dev'il·ish,** *adj.* **—dev'il·ry, devil·try,** *n.*

de'vi·ous, *adj.* **1.** indirect; circuitous. **2.** shifty; not straightforward. **—de'vi· ous·ly,** *adv.*

de·vise', *v.t.,* **-vised, -vising,** *n. v.t.* **1.** contrive. **2.** bequath. **—n. 3.** bequest. **—de·vis'er,** *n.*

de·void', *adj.* empty of something specified.

de·volve', *v.,* **-volved, -volving.** *v.i., v.t.* pass to another, as a duty.

de·vote', *v.t.,* **-voted, -voting.** dedicate. **—de·vot'ed,** *adj.*

de"vo·tee', *n.* admirer or enthusiast.

de·vo'tion, *n.* **1.** dedication. **2.** devout act, esp. a prayer. **—de·vo'tion·al,** *adj.*

de·vour', *v.t.* **1.** eat hungrily. **2.** consume or take in greedily.

de·vout', *adj.* pious; very religious.

dew, *n.* moisture condensed at ground level. **—dew'drop",** *n.* **—dew'y,** *adj.*

dex'ter·ous, *adj.* skillful; cunning. Also, **dex'trous. —dex·ter'i·ty,** *n.*

dex'trose, *n.* type or sugar found in plants and animals.

di"a·be'tes, *n.* disease characterized by the body's inability to use sugar properly. **—di"a·be'tic,** *adj., n.*

di"a·bol'ic, *adj.* devilish. Also, **di"a·bol' i·cal.**

di'a·dem", *n.* crown.

di'ag·nose", *v.t.,* **-nosed, -nosing. 1.** make a diagnosis of. **2.** establish by diagnosis.

di"ag·no'sis, *n., pl.* **-ses.** determination of the nature of an illness or situation. **—di"ag·nos'tic,** *adj.*

di·ag'o·nal, *adj.* **1.** connecting two nonadjacent angles. **2.** oblique. **—n. 3.** something that is diagonal.

di'a·gram", *n., v.t.,* **-gramed, -graming.** *n.* **1.** chart or plan that explains something simply. **—v.t. 2.** make a diagram of. **—di"a·gram·mat'ic,** *adj.*

di'al, *n., v.t.,* **-aled** or **-aling.** *n.* **1.** disk or strip with a calibrated edge, as on a clock or gauge. **2.** disk turned to get radio frequencies, make telephone calls, etc. **—v.t. 3.** obtain or reach by turning a dial.

di'a·lect", *n.* variety of a language peculiar to a region or class. **—di"a·lec'tal,** *adj.*

di'a·logue", *n.* conversation between two or more people. Also, **di'a·log".**

di·am'e·ter, *n.* **1.** straight line passing through the centre of a circle. **2.** length of such a line. **—di"a·met'ri·cal,** *adj.*

di'a·mond, *n.* **1.** hard, transparent crystallization of carbon. **2.** parallelogram. **3. diamonds,** suit of playing cards. **4.** baseball field.

dia'per, *n.* **1.** piece of absorbent material that forms a baby's undercloth. **—v.t. 2.** put a diaper on.

di·a·phragm" (dī'ə fram"), *n.* **1.** muscular wall, esp. between the chest and abdomen. **2.** vibrating disk in a microphone etc. **3.** contraceptive device for women.

di"ar·rhe'a, *n.* intestinal disorder characterized by too frequent and too loose bowel movements.

di'a·ry, *n.* daily record of experiences. **—di'a·rist,** *n.*

di·as'to·le, *n.* normal rhythmic expansion of the heart. **—di"a·stol'ic,** *adj.*

di'a·tribe", *n.* bitter denunciation.

dice, *n. pl., sing.* **die,** *v.,* **diced, dicing.** *n.* **1.** small cubes marked on each side with one to six spots, used in games. **—v.i. 2.** play with dice. **—v.t. 3.** cut into small cubes.

di·chot'o·my, *n.* division into two parts.

dick'er, *v.i.* bargain.

dic'tate", *v.,* **-tated, -tating.** *v.t., v.i.* **1.** speak for preservation in writing. **2.** impose on others, as terms. **—dic·ta' tion,** *n.*

dic'ta·tor, *n.* de facto absolute ruler. **—dic'ta·tor·ship",** *n.* **—dic"ta·to'ri· al,** *adj.*

dic'tion, *n.* **1.** choice of words. **2.** enunciation.

dic'tion·ar"y, *n., pl.* **-ies.** book explaining the meanings, etc. of alphabetically listed words.

dic'tum, *n.* authoritive statement; pronouncement.

di·dac'tic, *adj.* intended for instruction. **—di·dac'ti·cism,** *n.*

die, *v.i.,* **died, dying,** *n. v.i.* **1.** cease to live. **2.** lose vigor or strength. **—n. 3.** shaping device.

di·er'e·sis, *n., pl.* **-ses.** mark placed over a vowel to show that it is pronounced separately.

die'sel, *n.* internal-combustion engine in which fuel is ignited by air compression. Also, **diesel engine.**

di'et, *n.* **1.** food normally eaten. **2.** selection of food for purposes of health. 3. legislature. —*v.i.* 4. be on a diet. —**di'e·tar''y**, *adj.* —**di''e·ti'tian, di''e·ti'cian,** *n.* —**di''e·tet'ic,** *adj.*

dif'fer, *v.i.* 1. be different. 2. disagree.

dif'fer·ence, *n.* 1. unlikeness. 2. disagreement. 3. amount after subtraction. —**dif'fer·ent,** *adj.* —**dif'fer·ent·ly,** *adv.*

dif''fer·en'tial, *adj.* 1. pertaining to difference. —*n.* 2. difference. 3. Also, **differential gear,** gear turning axles at individual speeds.

dif''fer·en'ti·ate', *v.,* -ated, -ating. *v.t.* 1. make unlike. 2. distinguish between or from another. —*v.i.* 3. make a distinction.

dif'fi·cult, *adj.* 1. hard to do or understand. 2. hard to deal with or satisfy. —**dif'fi·cul''ty,** *n.*

dif'fi·dent, *adj.* shy; self-conscious. —**dif'fi·dence,** *n.*

dif·frac'tion, *n.* breaking of light, sound, etc. into separate components.

dif·fuse', *v.* -fused, -fusing, *adj.* *v.t., v.i.* (dif fyo͞oz') 1. disseminate; spread. —*adj.* (dif fyoos') 2. not concentrated. 3. wordy. —**dif·fu'sion,** *n.*

dig, *v.,* dug, digging, *n.* *v.t.* 1. cut into or turn over. 2. form by digging. 3. discover or remove by or as if by digging. —*v.i.* 4. break up earth, etc. by digging. —*n.* 5. act or instance of digging. 6. taunting remark.

di·gest', *v.t.* (də jest') 1. transform food in the body so it is absorbable. 2. absorb mentally. —*n.* (dī'jest). 3. abridged and systematic collection of information; summary. —**di·gest'i·ble,** *adj.* —**di·ges'tion,** *n.* —**di·ges'tive,** *adj.*

dig'it, *n.* 1. finger or toe. 2. any Arabic figure: 0 to 9. —**dig'it·al,** *adj.*

dig''i·tal, *adj.* represented by numerals.

dig''i·tal'is, *n.* dried leaves or a plant, used as a heart stimulant.

dig'ni·fied'', *adj.* showing dignity; stately.

dig'ni·fy'', *v.t.,* -fied, -fying. honor; give dignity to.

dig'ni·tar''y, *n., pl.* -ies. eminent person, esp. because of rank.

di·gress', *v.i.* wander away from the main subject or purpose. —**di·gres'sion,** *n.* —**di·gres'sive,** *adj.*

dike, *n.* dam made to prevent flooding.

di·lap'i·dat''ed, *adj.* ruined; broken down. —**di·lap''i·da'tion,** *n.*

di·late', *v.,* -lated, -lating. *v.t., v.i.* 1. widen; expand. 2. speak at length. —**di·la'tion, dil''a·ta'tion,** *n.*

dil'a·to''ry, *adj.* delaying.

di·lem'ma, *n.* predicament requiring a puzzling choice between two alternatives.

dil''et·tante', *n., pl.* -tantes, -tanti. amateur, superficial artist, thinker, etc.

dil'i·gent, *adj.* hard-working. —**dil'i·gence,** *n.*

dill, *n.* plant with aromatic leaves and seeds used for flavoring.

di·lute', *v.t.,* -luted, -luting. water down; thin out. —**di·lu'tion,** *n.*

dim *adj.,* dimmer, dimmest, *v.,* dimmed, dimming. *adj.* 1. not bright; indistinct. 2. not clearly seeing or understanding. —*v.t., v.i.* 3. make or grow dim. —**dim'ly,** *adv.*

dime, *n.* ten-cent coin.

di·men'sion, *n.* 1. length, breadth, or height. 2. coordinate used in locating something in space and/or time. —**di·men'sion·al,** *adj.*

di·min'ish, *v.t., v.i.* lessen in size or importance. —**dim''i·nu'tion,** *n.*

di·min'u·tive, *adj.* 1. very small. —*n.* 2. suffix or variant modifying a word to indicate smallness.

dim'i·ty, *n.* thin woven cloth.

dim'ple, *n., v.,* -pled, -pling. *n.* 1. small, natural hollow, esp. on the cheek or chin. —*v.t., v.i.* 2. form dimples.

din, *n., v.t.,* dinned, dinning. *n.* 1. confused or continuous noise. —*v.t.* 2. repeat insistently.

dine, *v.,* dined, dining. *v.i.* 1. eat dinner. —*v.t.* 2. provide dinner for.

di'ner, *n.* 1. person eating. 2. railroad dining car. 3. restaurant resembling such a car.

din·ghy, *n.* small boat belonging to a larger boat.

din·gy (din'jē), *adj.,* -gier, -giest. dark; grimy. —**din'gi·ness,** *n.*

din'ner, *n.* main meal of the day.

di'no·saur'', *n.* large reptile of prehistoric times.

dint, *n.* 1. exertion. 2. dent.

di·o·cese (dī'ə sēs''), *n.* district under a bishop. —**di·oc'e·san,** *adj., n.*

dip, *v.,* dipped, dipping, *n.* *v.t.* 1. lower briefly and raise. 2. remove with a scoop. —*v.i.* 3. be dipped. 4. plunge abruptly. —*n.* 5. short swim or bath. 6. abrupt plunge or slope.

diph·thong (dif'thong, dip'thong), *n.* sound containing two vowels.

di·plo'ma, *n.* certificate conferring a degree.

di'plo·mat'', *n.* 1. official representing a state. 2. person of tact. —**di·plo'ma·cy,** *n.* —**dip''lo·mat'ic,** *adj.*

dip'per, *n.* 1. ladle. 2. **Dipper,** either of two constellations in the shape of a dipper.

dip''so·ma'ni·a, *n.* irresistible craving for alcohol. —**dip''so·ma'ni·ac'',** *n.*

dire, *adj.,* direr, direst. 1. Also, **dire'ful,** dreadful. 2. urgent.

di·rect', *adj.* 1. straight. 2. straightforward. 3. unbroken; continuous. 4.

faithful to an original. —*v.t.* **5.** guide.
6. supervise or command. **7.** address.
—**di·rect′ly,** *adv.* —**di·rect′ness,** *n.*
—**di·rec′tor,** *n.*

di·rec′tion, *n.* **1.** line toward a place,
point of the compass, etc. **2.** instruction. **3.** act, instance, or responsibility
of directing. —**di·rec′tion·al,** *adj.*

di·rec′tive, *n.* general order.

di·rec′to·ry, *n., pl.* **-ries.** book with
names, addresses, etc.

dirge, *n.* funeral song.

dir′i·gi·ble, *n.* maneuverable airship.

dirk, *n.* dagger.

dirt, *n.* **1.** any unclean substance; filth. **2.**
soil.

dirt′y, *adj.,* **-ier, -iest,** *v.,* **-ied, -ying.** *adj.*
1. not clean; soiled. **2.** indecent. —*v.t.,*
v.i. **3.** make or become dirty. —**dirt′i·**
ness, *n.* —**dirt′i·ly,** *adv.*

dis·a′ble, *v.t.,* **-bled, -bling.** make incapable or unfit. —**dis″a·bil′i·ty,** *n.*

dis″a·buse′, *v.t.,* **-bused, -busing.** rid of
false ideas; set right.

dis″ad·van′tage, *n.* **1.** unfavorable circumstance. **2.** injury or detriment.
—**dis″ad·van′taged,** *adj.* —**dis·ad″**
van·ta′geous, *adj.*

dis″af·fect′, *v.t.* make unfriendly; antag-
onize. —**dis″af·fec′tion,** *n.*

dis″a·gree′, *v.i.* **-greed, -greeing. 1.** fail
to agree. **2.** quarrel. —**dis″a·gree′**
ment, *n.*

dis″a·gree′a·ble, *adj.* not agreeable; unpleasant —**dis″a·gree′a·bly,** *adv.*

dis″ap·pear′, *v.i.* **1.** vanish. **2.** cease to
exist. —**dis″ap·pear′ance,** *n.*

dis″ap·point′, *v.t.* thwart the expectations
or hopes of.—**dis″ap·point′ment,** *n.*

dis″ap·prove′, *v.,* **-proved, -proving.**
v.t., v.i. not to approve. —**dis″ap·**
prov′al, *n.*

dis·arm′, *v.t.* **1.** take away or deprive of
weapons. **2.** make friendly. —*v.i.* **3.** reduce armed forces. —**dis·ar′ma·ment,**
n.

dis″ar·range′, *v.t.,* **-ranged, -ranging.**
put in disorder. —**dis″ar·range′ment,**
n.

dis″ar·ray′, *v.t.* **1.** throw into disorder.
—*n.* **2.** disorder; confusion.

dis·as′ter, *n.* cause of much damage.
—**dis·as′trous,** *adj.*

dis″a·vow′, *v.t.* disclaim knowledge of
or responsibility for. —**dis″a·vow′al,**
n.

dis·band′, *v.t., v.i.* break up, as an or-
ganisation. —**dis·band′ment,** *n.*

dis·bar′, *v.t.,* **-barred, -bar·ring.** expel
from the legal profession. —**dis·bar′**
ment, *n.*

dis·be′lieve′, *v.,* **-lieved, -lieving.** *v.t.,*
v.i. refuse to believe. —**dis″be·lief′,** *n.*

dis·burse′, *v.t.,* **-bursed, -bursing. 1.** pay
out. **2.** scatter. —**dis·burse′ment,** *n.*

disc, *n.* disk.

dis·card′, *v.t.* (dis kard′) **1.** throw away.
—*n.* (dis′kard) **2.** state of being thrown
away. **3.** something thrown away.

dis·cern′ (di sərn′), *v.t.* perceive; recognize; distinguish. —**dis·cern′i·ble,** *adj.*
—**dis·cern′ment,** *n.* —**dis·cern′ing,**
adj.

dis·charge′, *v.,* **-charged, -charging,** *n.*
v.t. (dis charg′) **1.** emit. **2.** shoot or
fire. **3.** unload. **4.** perform. **5.** release
or dismiss from service. —*v.i.* **6.** release a load, etc. —*n.* (dis′charj) **7.** act,
instance, or means of discharging. **8.**
something discharged.

dis·ci′ple, *n.* follower of a teacher or
teaching.

dis′ci·pline, *n., v.* **-plined, -plining.** *n.* **1.**
training that develops self-control. **2.**
punishment. **3.** set or system of rules
and regulations. **4.** branch of learning.
—*v.t.* **5.** train. **6.** punish. —**dis′ci·pli·**
na″ry, *adj.* —**dis′ci·pli·nar″i·an,** *n.*

dis·claim′, *v.t.* disown.

dis·claim′er, *n.* disavowal or renuncia-
tion.

dis·close′, *v.t.,* **-closed, -closing.** reveal
or uncover. —**dis·clo′sure,** *n.*

dis″co, *n.* **1.** discotheque; a club featuring dancing to rock music. **2.** a style of
dance music with a pronounced beat.

dis·col′or, *v.t., v.i.* fade or stain. —**dis·**
col″or·a′tion, *n.*

dis·com′fit, *v.t.* frustrate the plans of;
disconcert. —**dis·com′fi·ture,** *n.*

dis·com′fort, *n.* lack of comfort.

dis″con·cert′, *v.t.* upset; disarrange; per-
turb.

dis″con·nect′, *v.t.* finish the connection
of; separate. —**discon·nec′tion,** *n.*

dis·con′so·late, *adj.* unhappy; dejected.

dis″con·tent′, *adj.* **1.** Also, **dis″con·**
tent′ed, dissatisfied with something;
not content. —*n.* **2.** dissatisfaction;
lack of content.

dis″con·tin′ue, *v.,* **-ued, uing.** *v.t., v.i.*
stop. —**dis″con·tin′u·ance, dis″con·**
tin″u·a′tion, *n.*

dis′cord, *n.* **1.** lack of harmony. **2.** disagreement. —**dis·cord′ance,** *n.* —**dis·**
cord′ant, *adj.*

dis·co·thèque′ (dis″kō tek′), *n.* place
where people dance to recorded music.

dis′count, *n.* **1.** reduction in price. —*v.t.*
2. deduct from a bill. **3.** advance with
deduction or interest. **4.** sell at less
than the regular price. **5.** disregard.
—**dis·count′a·ble,** *adj.*

dis·cour′age, *v.t.,* **-aged, -aging.** hamper
or stop with predictions of failure, disapproval, etc. —**dis·cour′age·ment,**
n.

dis·course′, *n., v.i.,* **-coursed, -coursing.**
n. (dis′kors) **1.** conversation. **2.** essay
or lecture. —*v.i.* (dis kors′) **3.** converse.

dis·cour'te·sy, *n., pl.* **-sies.** lack of courtesy; rudeness. —**dis·cour'te·ous,** *adj.*

dis·cov'er, *v.t.* perceive for the first time. —**dis·cov'er·er,** *n.* —**dis·cov'er·y,** *n.* —**dis·cov'er·a·ble,** *adj.*

dis·cred'it, *v.t.* 1. cast doubt on. 2. injure the reputation of. —*n.* 4. state of being discredited.

dis·creet', *adj.* prudent. —**dis·creet'ly,** *adv.*

dis·crep'an·cy, *n.* inconsistency.

dis·crete', *adj.* separate; distinct.

dis·cre'tion, *n.* 1. prudence. 2. freedom of choice in actions. —**dis·cre'tion·ary",** *adj.*

dis·crim·i·nate, *v.i.,* **-nated, -nating,** *adj. v.i.* (dis krim ə nāt') 1. make careful distinctions. 2. show unjust favor or disfavor. —*adj.* (dis krim'ə nit) 3. making careful distinctions. —**dis·crim''i·na'tion,** *n.* —**dis·crim'i·nat"ing,** *adj.* —**dis·crim'i·na·to"ry,** *adj.*

dis·cur'sive, *adj.* rambling; wandering from topic to topic.

dis·cuss', *v.t.* talk or write about. —**dis·cus'sion,** *n.*

dis·dain', *v.t.* 1. scorn; despise. —*n.* 2. scorn. —**dis·dain'ful,** *adj.*

dis·ease', *n. v.t.,* **-eased, -easing.** *n.* 1. ailment; sickness. —*v.t.* 2. affect with sickness.

dis"em·bark', *v.i.* leave a ship or aircraft. —**dis"em·bar·ka'tion, dis"em·bark'ment,** *n.*

dis"em·bod'y, *v.t.,* **-ied, -ying.** free from the body. —**dis"em·bod'i·ment,** *n.*

dis"en·chant', *v.t.* destroy the enthusiasm of. —**dis"en·chant'ment,** *n.*

dis"en·gage', *v.,* **-gaged, -gaging.** *v.t., v.i.* disconnect. —**dis"en·gage'ment,** *n.*

dis·fa'vor, *n.* 1. disapproval. —*v.t.* 2. treat with disfavour.

dis·fig'ure, *v.t.,* **-ured, -uring.** mar. —**dis·fig'ure·ment,** *n.*

dis·fran'chise, *v.t.,* **-chised, -chising.** deprive of a right or privilege, esp. voting. Also, **dis"en·fran'chise.**

dis·gorge', *v.,* **-gorged, -gorging.** *v.t., v.i.* pour out.

dis·grace', *n., v.t.,* **-graced, -gracing.** *n.* 1. state or cause of shame. —*v.t.* 2. bring shame upon. —**dis·grace'ful,** *adj.*

dis·grun'tle, *v.t.,* **-tled, -tling.** make discontent or sulky.

dis·guise', *v.t.,* **-guised, -guising,** *n. v.t.* 1. render temporarily unrecognizable. 2. misrepresent. —*n.* 3. something that disguises. —**dis·guise'ment,** *n.*

dis·gust', *v.t.* 1. offend the good taste or senses of. —*n.* 2. sickening dislike.

dish, *n.* 1. shallow container for food. 2. food that is served.

dis·heart'en, *v.t.* discourage.

di·shev'el, *v.t.,* **-eled, -eling.** cause disarray in.

dis·hon'est, *adj.* not honest. —**dis·hon'est·ly,** *adv.* —**dis·hon'es·ty,** *n.*

dis·hon'or, *n.* 1. lack of respect; disgrace. —*v.t.* 2. disgrace. —**dis·hon'or·a·ble,** *adj.*

dis"il·lu'sion, *v.t.* free from illusion. —**dis"il·lu'sion·ment,** *n.*

dis"in·cline', *v.t.,* **-clined, -clining.** make unwilling or averse. —**dis·in"cli·na'tion,** *n.*

dis"in·fect', *v.t.* rid of infection. —**dis"in·fect'ant,** *n., adj.*

dis"in·her'it, *v.t.* deprive of inheritance.

dis·in'te·grate", *v.,* **-grated, -grating.** *v.t., v.i.* separate *v.t., v.i.* separate into elements. —**dis·in"te·gra'tion,** *n.*

dis·in'ter·est, *n.* indifference.

dis·in'ter·est·ed, *n.* 1. impartial. 2. indifferent.

dis·joint'ed, *adj.* 1. separated at the joints. 2. incoherent.

disk, *n.* 1. thin, flat, round object. 2. phonograph record.

disk·ette", *n.* (computers) a 5¼-inch flexible disk or a 3½-inch hard disk used for data storage.

dis·like', *v.t.,* **-liked, -liking,** *n. v.t.* 1. regard with aversion or distaste. —*n.* 2. aversion; distaste.

dis'lo·cate", *v.t.,* **-cated, -cating.** put out of the proper or customary place. —**dis"lo·ca'tion,** *n.*

dis·lodge', *v.t.,* **-lodged, -lodging.** force from a place. —**dis·lodg'ment,** *n.*

dis·loy'al, *adj.* not loyal; unfaithful. —**dis·loy'al·ty,** *n.*

dis'mal, *adj.* 1. gloomy; dreary. 2. causing dreariness or misery.

dis·man'tle, *v.t.,* **-tled, -tling.** 1. deprive or strip of equipment. 2. take apart.

dis·may', *v.t.* 1. dishearten. —*n.* 2. disheartenment.

dis·mem'ber, *v.t.* deprive of limbs. —**dis·mem'ber·ment,** *n.*

dis·miss', *v.t.* 1. direct or allow to leave. 2. discharge from employment. 3. put out of consideration. —**dis·mis'sal,** *n.*

dis·mount', *v.i.* 1. alight from a horse, bicycle, etc. —*v.t.* 2. take from a mounting. 3. dismantle.

dis"o·be'di·ent, *adj.* not obedient. —**dis"o·be'di·ence,** *n.* —**dis"o·bey',** *v.t.*

dis·or'der, *n.* 1. confusion. 2. ailment. 3. riot. —*v.t.* 4. create disorder in. —**dis·or'der·ly,** *adj.*

dis·or'gan·ize", *v.t.,* **-ized, -izing.** throw into confusion. —**dis·or"gan·i·za'tion,** *n.*

dis·own', *v.t.* repudiate.

dis·par'age, *v.t.,* **-aged, -aging.** belittle. —**dis·par'age·ment,** *n.*

dis′pa·rate, *adj.* distinct in kind. —**dis·par′i·ty,** *n.*

dis·pas′sion·ate, *adj.* impartial. —**dis·pas′sion·ate·ly,** *adv.*

dis·patch′, *v.t.* 1. send off. 2. kill. 3. transact quickly.—*n.* 4. sending-off. 5. killing. 6. promptness. 7. message. —**dis·patch′er,** *n.*

dis·pel′, *v.t.,* **-pelled, -pelling.** scatter; drive off.

dis·pen′sa·ry, *n., pl.* **-ries.** place where medical aid is given.

dis″pen·sa′tion, *n.* 1. act or instance of dispensing. 2. something dispensed. 3. release from obligation. 4. divine ordering of events.

dis·pense′, *v.,* **-pensed, -pensing.** *v.t.* 1. distribute. 2. prepare and give out as medicine. —*v.i.* 3. **dispense with,** a. forgo b. get rid of. —**dis·pen′sa·ble,** *adj.*

dis·perse′, *v.,* **-persed, -persing.** *v.t., v.i.* scatter. —**dis·per′sal, dis·per′sion,** *n.*

dis·place′, *v.t.,* **-placed, -placing.** 1. put out of place. 2. take the place of. —**dis·place′ment,** *n.*

dis·play′, *v.t., n.* exhibit.

dis·please′, *v.t.,* **-pleased, -pleasing.** offend. —**dis·pleas′ure,** *n.*

dis·pose′, *v.,* **-posed, -posing.** *v.t.* 1. arrange. 2. incline or make willing. —*v.i.* 3. rid oneself. —**dis·pos′a·ble,** *adj.* —**dis·pos′al,** *n.*

dis″po·si′tion,*n.* 1. temperament. 2. tendency. 3. arrangement. 4. settlement. 5. disposal.

dis″pos·sess′, *v.t.* deprive of possession. —**dis″pos·ses′sion,** *n.*

dis′pro·por′tion, *n.* lack of proportion. —**dis″pro·por′tion·ate,** *adj.*

dis·prove′, *v.t.,* **-proved, -proving.** prove false. —**dis·proof′,** *n.*

dis·pute′, *v.,* **-puted, -puting.** *n. v.i., v.t.* 1. argue. —*v.t.* 2. express doubt regarding. 3. oppose or fight. —*n.* 4. act or instance of disputing. 5. state of being disputed. —**dis·pu′tant,** *n., adj.* —**dis·put′a·ble,** *adj.* —**dis″pu·ta′tion,** *n.* —**dis″pu·ta′tious,** *adj.*

dis·qual′i·fy′, *v.t.,* **-fied, -fying.** make or declare unqualified. —**dis·qual′i·fi·ca′tion,** *n.*

dis·qui′et, *v.t.* 1. disturb; make uneasy. —*n.* 2. Also, **dis·qui′e·tude,** restlessness.

dis″qui·si′tion, *n.* formal discourse.

dis″re·gard′, *v.t.* 1. ignore. 2. treat with little or no respect. —*n.* 3. neglect. 4. lack of respect.

dis″re·pair′, *n.* impaired condition.

dis″re·pute′, *n.* bad reputation. —**dis·rep′u·ta·ble,** *adj.*

dis″re·spect′, *n.* lack of respect. —**dis″re·spect′ful,** *adj.*

dis·robe′, *v.,* **-robed, -robing.** *v.t., v.i.* undress.

dis·rupt′, *v.t., v.i.* 1. break up. 2. disturb. —**dis·rup′tion,** *n.* —**dis·rup′tive,** *adj.*

dis·sat′is·fy″, *v.t.,* **-fied, -fying.** fail to satisfy; displease. —**dis·sat″is·fac′tion,** *n.*

dis·sect′, *v.t.* 1. cut apart. 2. examine closely. —**dis·sec′tion,** *n.*

dis·sem′ble, *v.,* **-bled, -bling.** *v.t., v.i.* disguise. —**dis·sem′blance,** *n.* —**dis·sem′bler,** *n.*

dis·sem′i·nate″, *v.t.,* **-nated, -nating.** distribute widely. —**dis·sem″i·na′tion,** *n.*

dis·sen′sion, *n.* disagreement or quarreling.

dis·sent′, *v.i.* 1. disagree. —*n.* 2. disagreement. —**dis·sent′er,** *n.*

dis″ser·ta′tion, *n.* formal essay; thesis.

dis·sim′i·lar, *adj.* not similar. —**dis·sim″i·lar′i·ty,** *n.*

dis·sim′u·late″, *v.,* **-lated, -lating.** *v.t., v.i.* dissemble. —**dis·sim″u·la′tion,** *n.*

dis′si·pate″, *v.,* **-pated, -pating.** *v.t.* 1. scatter. 2. squander. —*v.i.* 3. live in extravagance or vice. —**dis″si·pa′tion,** *n.*

dis′si·pat″ed, *adj.* living in extravagance or vice.

dis·so′ci·ate″, *v.t.,* **-ated, -ating.** break the connection between.

dis′so·lute″, *adj.* dissipated. —**dis′so·lute″ly,** *adv.* —**dis″so·lu′tion,** *n.*

dis·solve′, *v.,* **-solved, -solving.** *v.t., v.i.* 1. melt; combine with a liquid. 2. terminate. 3. destroy. —**dis″so·lu·tion,** *n.*

dis′so·nance, *n.* musical discord. —**dis′so·nant,** *adj.*

dis·suade′, *v.t.,* **-suaded, -suading.** deter by persuasion. —**dis·sua′sion,** *n.*

dis′tance, *n.* 1. interval of space or time. 2. remoteness. 3. reserve; aloofness. —**dis′tant,** *adj.*

dis·taste′, *n.* dislike. —**dis·taste′ful,** *adj.*

dis·tem′per, *n.* infectious disease of dogs.

dis·tend′, *v.t., v.i.* expand. —**dis·ten′tion,** *n.*

dis·till′, *v.t.* 1. make or purify by evaporation and condensation. —*v.t.* 2. become distilled. —**dis·till′er,** *n.* —**dis·till′er·y,** *n.* —**dis″til·la′tion,** *n.*

dis·tinct′, *adj.* 1. individual. 2. clearly noticeable or understandable. —**dis·tinct′ly,** *adv.*

dis·tinc′tion, *n.* 1. act or instance of distinguishing. 2. difference. 3. eminence. 4. something that gives or betokens eminence.

dis·tinc′tive, *adj.* characteristic.

dis·tin′guish, *v.t.* 1. characterize as individual. 2. perceive. 3. make eminent or excellent. —**dis·tin′guish·a·ble,** *adj.* —**dis·tin′guished,** *adj.*

dis·tort′, *v.t.* 1. alter from a normal

shape. 2. corrupt the true meaning of. —dis·tor'tion, n.

dis·tract', v.t. 1. prevent from concentrating. 2. bewilder. —dis·trac'tion, n.

dis·tract'ed, adj. frantic. Also, dis·traught'.

dis·tress', n. 1. pain or need. 2. source of this. 3. danger. —v.t. 4. cause distress in.

dis·trib'ute, v.t., -uted, -uting. 1. give out in portions. 2. disperse. —dis''tri·bu'tion, n. —dis·trib'u·tor, n.

dis'trict, n. distinct geographical area.

dis·trust', n. 1. lack of trust. —v.t. 2. place no trust in. —dis·trust'ful, adj.

dis·turb', v.t. 1. end the quiet state of. 2. upset or trouble. 3. interrupt. —dis·turb'ance, n.

dis·use', n. absence of use.

ditch, n. channel dug in the ground.

dit'to, n., pl. -tos. 1. the same as before. 2. Also, ditto mark, a mark, '', used to indicate that the word or line above is repeated.

dit'ty, n., pl. -ties. simple tune.

di·ur'nal, adj. 1. daily. 2. pertaining to the day.

di·van', n. long, low couch.

dive, v.i., dived or dove, dived, diving, n. v.i. 1. fall intentionally. 2. descend below the water. 3. lose altitude quickly. —n. 4. act, instance, or form of diving. —div'er, n.

di·verge', v.i., -verged, -verging. 1. part in two or more directions. 2. become of unlike opinion, etc. —di·ver'gent, adj. —di·ver'gence, n.

di'vers, adj. Archaic. various.

di·verse', adj. 1. different. 2. various. —di·verse'ly, adv. —di·vers'i·ty, n.

di·ver'si·fy'', v.t., -fied, -fying. vary. —di·ver''si·fi·ca'tion, n.

di·vert', v.t. 1. turn aside from a path or course. 2. entertain; amuse. —di·ver'sion, n.

di·vest', v.t. 1. deprive or strip. 2. rid.

di·vide', v., -vided, -viding. v.t. 1. separate into parts or classes. 2. prevent from uniting. —v.i. 3. separate. —n. 4. line separating two drainage areas. —di·vid'er, n.

div'i·dend'', n. 1. number to be divided. 2. sum allotted to a stockholder.

di·vine', adj., v.t., -vined, -vining. adj. 1. godly or godlike. 2. religious. —v.t. 3. prophesy. 4. perceive intuitively. —div''i·na'tion, n.

di·vin'i·ty, n., pl. -ties. 1. deity. 2. theology.

di·vis'i·ble, adj. able to be divided, esp. evenly.

di·vi'sion, n. 1. act or instance of dividing. 2. element or component. 3. Math. process of determining the ratio of one number to another. 4. military unit.

di·vi'sive, adj. causing disunity.

di·vi'sor, n. Math. number used to divide another.

di·vorce', n., v.t., -vorced, -vorcing. n. 1. legal dissolution of a marriage. 2. conceptual separation. —v.t. 3. separate oneself from by a divorce. 4. separate by a divorce. 5. separate conceptually. —di·vorce'ment, n.

di·vor''cee', n. divorced woman.

di·vulge', v.t., -vulged, -vulging. reveal. —di·vulg'ence, n.

Dix'ie, n. southern part of the U.S.

diz'zy, adj., -zier, -ziest. 1. unsteady. 2. causing unsteadiness, as a height.

do, v., did, done, doing. v.t. 1. be at work upon or occupied with. 2. complete. 3. cause. —v.i. 4. act. 5. succeed in or accomplish something. 6. suffice. 7. happen.

doc'ile, adj. readily disciplined. —do·cil'i·ty, n.

dock, n. 1. place for ships between voyages. 2. pier or wharf. 3. fleshy part of an animal's tail. —v.t. 4. put into a dock. 5. deduct from the wages of. —v.i. 6. enter a dock.

dock'et, n. 1. list of agenda, esp. of a court. —v.t. 2. put on a docket.

doc'tor, n. 1. person who practices medicine, etc. 2. person with a high academic degree. —v.t. 3. Informal. heal or fix. —doc'tor·al, adj. —doc·tor·ate, n.

doc''tri·naire', adj. rigidly adhering to or following doctrine.

doc'trine, n. body of teaching, esp. in religion or politics. —doc'trin·al, adj.

doc'u·ment, n. 1. writing, etc. used as a proof. —v.t. 2. prove or support with documents. —doc''u·men·ta'tion, n.

doc''u·men'ta·ry, adj. n., pl. -ries. adj. 1. pertaining to documents. 2. serving as a record of events. —n. 3. film, etc. serving as a record of events.

dodge, v., dodged, dodging, n. v.t. 1. avoid by moving quickly. 2. evade by a trick. —v.i. 3. dodge something. —n. 4. act or instance of dodging. 5. trick.

doe, n. female or certain animals, as deer or rabbits.

doff, v.t. Archaic. remove, as a hat.

dog, n., v.t., dogged, dogging. n. 1. four-legged domestic animal. —v.t. 2. track; follow.

dog'ged, adj. stubborn in difficulty.

dog'ger·el, n. bad verse.

dog'ma, n. doctrine, esp. in religion, regarded as unquestionable.

dog·mat'ic, adj. 1. pertaining to or published as dogma. 2. offering personal opinions as dogma. —dog'ma·tism, n.

dog'wood'', n. tree with white or pink blossoms.

doi′ly, *n., pl.* **-lies.** small table mat, often of lace.

dol′drums, *n., pl.* **1.** equatorial region with little wind. **2.** period of depression or inactivity.

dole, *n., v.t.,* **doled, doling.** *n.* **1.** money, food, etc. given to the unemployed. —*v.t.* **2.** portion out sparingly.

dole′ful, *adj.* sad.

doll, *n.* toy shaped like a baby or other human being.

dol′lar, *n.* currency unit of the U.S., Canada, etc.

do·lor·ous, *adj.* sorrowful or painful.

dol′phin, *n.* aquatic mammal.

dolt, *n.* oaf. —**dolt′ish,** *adj.*

do·main′, *n.* **1.** territory of a ruler. **2.** area of influence or power.

dome, *n.* structure like an upcurved segment of a sphere.

do·mes′tic, *adj.* **1.** pertaining to the home. **2.** belonging to or originating in one's own country. **3.** tamed. —**do″mes·ti′ci·ty,** *n.*

do·mes′ti·cate″, *v.t.,* **-cated, -cating.** adapt to domestic conditions. —**do·mes″ti·ca′tion,** *n.*

dom′i·cile″, *n., v.t.,* **-ciled, -ciling.** *n.* **1.** residence. —*v.t.* **2.** house.

dom′i·nant, *adj.* prevailing. —**dom′i·nance,** *n.*

dom′i·nate″, *v.t.,* **-nated, -nating. 1.** master. **2.** be most conspicuous in. —**dom″i·na′tion,** *n.*

dom″i·neer′, *v.t., v.i.* tyrannize.

do·min′ion, *n.* **1.** sovereign power. **2.** territory reigned over or ruled by a sovereign.

dom′i·no, *n., pl.* **-noes. 1.** small plaque marked with spots. **2. dominoes,** a game played with these plaques. **3.** mask.

don, *n., v.t.,* **donned, donning.** *n.* **1.** title of respect for a Spanish gentleman. —*v.t.* **2.** *Archaic* put on, as clothes.

do′nate, *v.,* **-nated, -nating.** *v.t., v.i.* give, esp. in charity or friendship. —**do·na′tion,** *n.* —**do′nor,** *n.*

don′key, *n., pl.* **-keys.** domesticated ass.

doo′dle, *v.i.,* **-dled, -dling,** *n. v.i.* **1.** scribble or draw absentmindedly. —*n.* **2.** product of doodling.

doom, *n.* **1.** death or annihilation. **2.** fate. —*v.t.* **3.** predestine or sentence to death, damnation, etc.

door, *n.* **1.** movable partition for barring access. **2.** Also, **door′way″,** entrance. **3. out of doors,** outdoors.

dope, *n., v.t.,* **doped, doping.** *n.* **1.** *Informal.* **a.** habit-forming drug. **b.** fool. **c.** information. **2.** thick liquid used for industrial purposes. —*v.t.* **3.** *Informal.* drug.

dor′mant, *adj.* **1.** asleep or at rest. **2.** not active. —**dor′man·cy,** *n.*

dor′mer, *n.* window structure in a roof.

dor′mi·to″ry, *n., pl.* **-ries.** place for residents of an institution to sleep.

do′ry, *n., pl.* **-ries.** flat-bottomed rowboat used for fishing, etc.

dose, *n., v.t.,* **dosed, dosing.** *n.* **1.** amount of medicine taken at one time. —*v.t.* **2.** give medicine to. —**dos′age,** *n.*

dos·si·er (dos″sē a′), *n.* file of documents on one subject.

dot, *n., v.t.,* **dotted, dotting.** *n.* **1.** tiny round mark. —*v.t.* **2.** mark or make with dots.

dote, *v.i.,* **doted, doting. 1.** show excessive fondness. **2.** be senile. —**dot′ing,** *adj.* —**dot′age,** *n.*

dou′ble, *adj., adv., n., v.,* **-bled, -bling.** *adj.* **1.** twice as many or large as usual. **2.** intended for two. **3.** having two aspects. —*adv.* **4.** twice. —*n.* **5.** duplicate. —*v.t.* **6.** fold over. **7.** make twice as much or as many of. —*v.i.* **8.** fold in two. **9.** reverse one's direction. —**doub′ly,** *adv.*

dou′ble-cross′, *v.t. Informal.* cheat or betray.

doubt, *v.t.* **1.** be unsure or skeptical of. —*n.* **2.** uncertainty or distrust. **3.** something unsettled or uncertain. —**doubt′ful,** *adj.* —**doubt′less,** *adv.*

dough, *n.* pastry mixture of flour and water for baking. —**dough′y,** *adj.*

dough′nut″, *n.* deep-fried ring-shaped cake.

dour, *adj.* gloomily severe.

douse, *v.t.,* **doused, dousing.** plunge into or drench with liquid.

dove, *n.* cooing pigeonlike bird.

dove′tail″, *n.* **1.** interlocking carpentry joint. —*v.t.* **2.** join with dovetails.

dow′a·ger, *n.* widow endowed with a title or property.

dow′dy, *adj.,* **-dier, -diest.** plainly or untidily dressed, made up, etc.

dow′el, *n., v.t.,* **-eled, -eling.** *n.* **1.** round length of wood, used as a fastening between two joined pieces. —*v.t.* **2.** fasten with dowels.

down, *adv., adj.* **1.** to or at a lower place. **2.** to or in a lower condition, amount, etc. **3.** in writing. **4.** in advance. **5.** out of operation. —*adv.* **6.** to a later period. **7.** dejected. **8.** completed. —*prep.* **9.** descending along, through, etc. **10.** soft feathers or hair. —*v.t.* **11.** put down. —**down′stairs′,** *adv., adj., n.* —**down′ward, down′wards,** *adv.* —**down′y,** *adj.*

down′fall″, *n.* **1.** fall, as of snow. **2.** fall, as from power or eminence.

down′grade″, *v.t.,* **-graded, -grading,** *adv., adj, n. v.t.* **1.** demote. —*adv., adj.* **2.** downward. —*n.* **3.** downward slope.

down′heart′ed, *adj.* discouraged. —**down′heart′ed·ly,** *adv.*

75 drive

down'hill", adv., adj. downward.

down'pour", n. heavy rainstorm.

down'right", adj. 1. utter. —adv. 2. utterly.

down'stairs", adv. to or at a lower level.

down'-to-earth", adj. realistic.

down'town', adv., adj. toward or in the business district of a town.

down'trod'den. adj. oppressed.

dow'ry, n., pl. -ries. property bestowed on a bride by her family.

dox·ol'o·gy, n., pl. -gies. hymn of praise.

doze, v.i., dozed, dozing, n. v.i. 1. sleep lightly. —n. 2. light sleep.

doz'en, n., pl. -ens or (after a number) -en. group of twelve. —doz'enth, adj.

drab, n, adj., drabber, drabbest. n. 1. yellow-brown. —adj. 2. dreary. —drab'ly, adv. —drab'ness, n.

draft, n. 1. act or amount of drawing. 2. swallowing or inhalation. 3. current of air. 4. tentative version of writing. 5. order to pay. 6. selection for conscription. —v.t. 7. make a draft of. 8. conscript. —draft'ee, n. —draft'y, adj.

drafts'man, n. person who makes working drawings or sketches.

drag, v., dragged, dragging. v.t. 1. pull with effort. 2. search with a dragnet. —v.t. 3. move slowly or with effort. —n. 4. act or instance of dragging. 5. Informal. something or someone dreary or obstructive.

drag'net", n. 1. net for fishing up submerged objects. 2. methodical police search.

drag'on, n. mythical large reptile.

drag'on·fly", n. large, stiff-winged insect.

drain, n. 1. channel for carrying away liquids. 2. steady depletion. —v.t. 3. remove through a channel. 4. deplete steadily. —v.i. 5. be drained. —drain'age, n.

dram, n. 1. eighth part of an apothecary's ounce or fluid ounce. 2. small drink.

dra'ma, n. 1. play. 2. theater as an art. 3. sensational event. 4. emotionalism. —dram'a·tist, n. —dram'a·tize", v.t. —dra·mat'ic, adj.

drape, n., v., draped, draping. n. 1. cloth hanging or curtain. —v.t., v.i. 2. hang loosely or in folds. —drap'er·y, n.

dras'tic, adj. severe or extreme.

draught, n., v.t., adj. draft.

draw, v., drew, drawn, drawing, n. v.t. 1. pull, attract, or take in. 2. elicit or provoke. 3. receive. 4. sketch with a pencil, pen, etc. 5. Nautical. need a depth of. —v.i. 6. exert a pulling force. 7. move. 8. pass smoke, etc. readily. 9. make demands. 10. lessen in size. —n. 11. act or instance of drawing. 12. even final score. —draw'ing, n.

draw'back", n. lessening of advantage.

draw'bridge", n. bridge that can be lifted or pulled.

draw·er, n. (drah'ər) 1. person or thing that draws. (drôr) 2. sliding compartment in a piece of furniture. 3. drawers. underpants.

drawl, n. 1. slow speech. —v.t., v.i. 2. speak in a drawl.

drawn, adj. haggard.

dray, n. heavy freight wagon.

dread, n. 1. fearful anticipation. 2. awe. —adj. 3. awesome. —v.t. 4. anticipate fearfully.

dread'ful, adj. 1. very bad. 2. inspiring dread.

dream, n., v., dreamed or dreamt, dreaming. n. 1. succession of images appearing in sleep or reverie. 2. vision of something possible or desirable. —v.t. 3. imagine in a dream. —v.i. 4. have a dream. dream'er, n. —dream'less, adj. —dream'like", adj. —dream'y, adj.

drear'y, adj., -ier, -iest. causing sadness or boredom.

dredge, v., dredged, dredging, n. v.t. 1. dig, esp. under water. 2. coat with flour. —n. 3. digging device.

dregs, n., pl. sediment, as of wine.

drench, v.t. soak with falling liquid.

dress, v.t. 1. put clothing on. 2. prepare or finish. —v.i. 3. put on clothing. 4. wear formal clothing. —n. 5. clothing. 6. skirt. —dress'mak"er, n.

dres'ser, n. 1. person who dresses. 2. chest of drawers with a mirror.

dres'sing, n. 1. material applied to wounds, bruises, etc. 2. sauce for salad. 3. stuffing for fowl.

drib'ble, v., -bled, -bling, n. v.t. 1. let drip untidily. —n. 2. act or instance of dribbling.

dri'er, n. thing or substance for drying.

drift, v.i. 1. be carried by a current. 2. move or live aimlessly or passively. —n. 3. drifting motion. 4. force or gist, as of an argument. 5. pile of wind-driven snow.

drift'wood", n. wood weathered and driven ashore by the sea.

drill, n. 1. boring tool. 2. system of exercises. 3. seed-planting machine. 4. coarse fabric. —v.t. 5. bore with a drill. 6. train or exercise with a drill.

dri'ly, adv. in a dry manner.

drink, n., v., ＼nk, drunk, drinking. n. 1. liquid for swallowing. 2. alcoholic liquor. —v.t. 3. swallow as a drink. —v.i. 4. swallow liquid. 5. take alcoholic liquor. —drink'er, n.

drip, v., dripped, dripping, n. v.i. 1. fall in drops —v.t. 2. let liquid fall in drops. 3. let fall in drops. —n. 4. act, instance, or sound of dripping.

drive, v., drove, driven, driving, n. v.t. 1. force along. 2. compel 3. control, as a vehicle. 4. transport in a road vehicle.

drivel

76

—*v.i.* **5.** operate a road vehicle. **6.** advance forcefully. —*n.* **7.** forceful campaign. **8.** energy. **9.** motivation. **10.** pleasure trip in an automobile. **11.** road for pleasure driving. —**driv′er,** *n.* —**drive′way,** *n.* —**drive′-in″,** *adj., n.*

driv′el, *n., v.i.,* **-eled, -eling.** *n.* **1.** stupid, nonsensical utterance. —*v.i.* **2.** write or talk drivel.

driz′zle, *n., v.,* **-zled, -zling.** *n.* **1.** fine rain. —*v.i., v.t.* **2.** rain in fine drops.

droll, *adj.* **1.** oddly amusing. —*n.* **2.** oddly amusing person. —**drol′ly,** *adv.* —**droll′ness, drol′ler·y,** *n.*

drom′e·dar″y, *n., pl.* **-ies.** single-humped camel.

drone, *n., v.i.,* **droned, droning.** *n.* **1.** low hum. **2.** nonworking male bee. **3.** idler. —*v.i.* **4.** emit a drone.

drool, *v.i.* **1.** drip saliva. —*n.* **2.** saliva that drips.

droop, *v.i.* **1.** hang loosely. **2.** lose energy or hope. —*n.* **3.** act or instance of drooping. —**droop′y,** *adj.*

drop, *v.t.,* **dropped, dropping,** *n. v.t.* **1.** allow to fall. **2.** abandon. **3.** put down. —*v.i.* **4.** fall. —*n.* **5.** globule of liquid that falls or is about to fall. **6.** descent. **7.** small drink. —**drop′per,** *n.*

drop′sy, *n.* edema.

dross, *n.* **1.** waste on top of molten metal. **2.** waste matter.

drought, *n.* long dry spell. Also, **drouth.**

drove, *n.* group of driven cattle. —**drov′er,** *n.*

drown, *v.i., v.t.* **1.** suffocate in water. —*v.t.* **2.** flood.

drowse, *v.i.,* **drowsed, drowsing,** *n. v.i.* **1.** be close to sleep. —*n.* **2.** sleepy state. —**drows′y,** *adj.*

drub, *v.t.,* **drubbed, drubbing.** beat. —**drub′bing,** *n.*

drudge, *v.i.,* **drudged, drudging,** *n. v.i.* **1.** do dull, hard work. —*n.* **2.** a person who drudges. —**drudg′er·y,** *n.*

drug, *n., v.t.,* **drugged, drugging.** *n.* **1.** medicinal substance. **2.** narcotic, hallucinogen, etc. —*v.t.* **3.** stupefy with a drug. —**drug′gist,** *n.* —**drug′store″,** *n.*

drum, *n., v.* **drummed, drumming.** *n.* **1.** percussion musical instrument. **2.** eardrum. **3.** cylindrical object. —*v.i.* **4.** beat rhythmically. —*v.t.* **5.** play on a drum. —**drum′mer,** *n.* —**drum′stick″,** *n.*

drunk, *adj.* **1.** overcome by alcohol. —*n.* **2.** *Informal.* **a.** drunken person. **b.** alcoholic.

drunk′ard, *n.* alcoholic.

drunk′en, *adj.* drunk.

dry, *adj., v.,* **drier, driest,** *v.,* **dried, drying.** *adj.* **1.** free of moisture. **2.** thirsty. **3.** not sweet. **4.** not emotional or expressive. —*v.t.* **5.** free of moisture. —*v.i.*

6. become dry. —**dry′ly,** *adv.* —**dry′ness,** *n.*

dry′-clean″, *v.t.* clean with chemicals rather than water. —**dry cleaner,** *n.*

dry goods, cloth or things made of cloth.

du′al, *adj.* **1.** pertaining to two. **2.** twofold. —**du·al′i·ty,** *n.*

dub, *v.t.,* **dubbed, dubbing.** **1.** make a knight of. **2.** give a name to.

du′bi·ous, *adj.* doubtful.

du′cal, *adj.* pertaining to dukes.

duch′ess, *n.* woman equal in rank to a duke.

duch′y, *n., pl.* **-ies.** area ruled by a duke or duchess.

duck, *n.* **1.** flat-billed waterfowl. **2.** canvaslike cloth. —*v.i.* **3.** stoop or crouch to avoid a blow. —*v.t., v.i.* **4.** plunge into water breifly. —**duck′ling,** *n.*

duct, *n.* passage for fluids. —**duct′less,** *adj.*

duc′tile, *adj.* able to be stretched. —**duc·til′i·ty,** *n.*

dude, *n. Informal.* **1.** fancy dresser. **2.** man from the city.

due, *adj.* **1.** owed. **2.** proper. **3.** adequate. **4.** expected to arrive. —*adv.* **5.** directly. —*n.* **7.** something due.

du′el, *n., v.,* **-eled, -eling.** *n.* **1.** formal mortal combat between two persons. —*v.t., v.i.* **2.** fight in a duel. —**du′elist, duel′er.**

du·et′, *n.* **1.** musical composition for two. **2.** pair of musicians.

duke, *n.* nobleman next in rank to a prince. —**duke′dom,** *n.*

dull, *adj.* **1.** not vivid. **2.** not interesting. **3.** not intelligent. **4.** not sharp. —*v.t., v.i.* **5.** make or become dull. —**dul′ly,** *adv.* —**dull′ness, dul′ness,** *n.*

du′ly, *adv.* in a due manner.

dumb, *adj.* **1.** unable to speak or make sound. **2.** silent. **3.** *Informal.* stupid.

dumb′bell″, *n.* weight for exercising the arms.

dumb′found″, *v.t.* render speechless with astonishment. Also, **dum′found″.**

dumb″wait′er, *n.* **1.** hoist for food. **2.** small serving table.

dum′my, *n., pl.* **-ies,** *adj.* **1.** lifesized object in human form. **2.** imitation or mockup. —*adj.* **3.** serving as an imitation.

dump, *v.t.* **1.** throw or pour down and abandon. **2.** unload in a heap. —*n.* **3.** place for refuse. **4.** military storage place.

dump′ling, *n.* rounded piece of baked dough, sometimes with a fruit filling.

dump′ster, *n.* a large, metal bin for holding garbage until pick-up.

dump′y, *adj.,* **-ier, -iest** squat.

dun, *n., v.t.,* **dunned, dunning.** *n.* **1.** dull gray-brown. —*v.t.* **2.** attempt to recover a debt from.

dunce, *n.* poor learner.

dune, *n.* mound of wind-driven sand.

dung, *n.* manure. —**dung'heap",** **dung' hill,** *n.*

dun''ga·rees', *n., pl.* blue cotton work pants or overalls.

dun'geon, *n.* dark prison, as in a castle.

dunk, *v.t.* dip into a drink.

du'o, *n., pl.* -os. duet.

dupe, *v.t.,* duped, duping, *n. v.t.* 1. cheat. —*n.* 2. person who is cheated. —**dup'er,** *n.*

du'plex, *adj.* 1. double. —*n.* 2. two-floored apartment. 3. two-family house.

du·pli·cate, *v.t.,* -cated, -cating, *adj., n. v.t.* (dōō'pli kāt'') 1. imitate exactly. —*n.* (dōō'pli kət) 2. exact imitation. —*adj.* 3. serving as a duplicate. —**du'' pli·ca'tion,** *n.* —**du'pli·ca''tor,** *n.*

du·plic'i·ty, *n., pl.* -ties. deceit.

du'ra·ble, *adj.* long-lasting; sturdy. —**du' ra·bly,** *adv.* —**dura·bil'i·ty,** *n.*

du·ra'tion, *n.* period of existence.

du·ress', *n.* coercion.

dur'ing, *prep.* in or throughout the period of.

dusk, *n.* 1. darker part of twilight. 2. gloom. —**dusk'y,** *adj.*

dust, *n.* 1. powder, esp. of earth. 2. disintegrated human remains. —*v.t.* 3. remove dust from. 4. put powder on. —*v.i.* 5. remove dust from furniture, etc. —**dust'y,** *adj.*

du'te·ous, *adj.* dutiful.

du'ti·a·ble, *adj.* subject to customs duty.

du'ti·ful, *adj.* faithful to duty. —**du'ti· ful·ly,** *adv.*

du'ty, *n., pl.* -ties. 1. moral requirement. 2. requirement by authority. 3. action, conduct, etc. required by morality or authority. 4. tax on an import.

dwarf, *n., pl.* dwarfs, dwarves. *v.t.* 1. abnormally small living thing. —*v.t.* 2. make abnormally small. 3. make seem small.

dwell, *v.i.,* dwelled or dwelt, dwelling. 1. have one's habitation. 2. linger, as in speech or thought. —**dwel'ler,** *n.* —**dwel'ling,** *n.*

dwin'dle, *v.i.,* -dled, -dling. diminish.

dye, *n., v.t.,* dyed, dying. *n.* 1. stain for cloth, etc. —*v.t.* 2. stain with dye. —**dy'er,** *n.* —**dye'stuff,** *n.*·

dy·nam'ic, *adj.* 1. pertaining to motion. 2. vigorous, as a person. —**dy·nam'i· cal·ly,** *adv.* —**dy'na·mism,** *n.*

dy'na·mo'', *n., pl.* -mos. electrical generator.

dy'nas·ty, *n., pl.* -ties. succession of rulers in one family. —**dy·nas'tic,** *adj.*

dys'en·ter''y, *n.* intestinal inflammation.

dys·pep'si·a, *n.* indigestion. —**dys·pep' tic,** *adj., n.*

E

E, e, *n.* 1. fifth letter of the English alphabet. 2. fifth-best grade.

each, *adj.* 1. every one individually. —*adv.* 2. apiece.

ea'ger, *adj.* full of desire. —**ea'ger·ly,** *adv.* —**ea'ger·ness,** *n.*

ea'gle, *n.* large bird of prey.

ear, *n.* 1. part of the body for hearing. 2. grain-bearing part of a plant. —**ear' drum",** *n.* —**ear'muffs",** *n., pl.*

earl, *n.* British nobleman equal to a count. —**earl'dom,** *n.*

ear'ly, *adj., adv.,* -lier, -liest. 1. before the expected time. 2. in good time. 3. toward the beginning.

ear'mark'', *v.t.* note for the future.

earn, *v.t.* work or deserve to acquire. —**earn'ings,** *n., pl.*

ear'nest, *adj.* 1. sincere; serious. —*n.* 2. pledge. —**ear'nest·ly,** *adv.*

ear'ring'', *n.* ornament hung from an ear lobe.

ear'shot'', *n.* hearing distance.

earth, *n.* 1. this planet. 2. ground level. 3. regions below ground level. 4. soil. —**earth'en,** *adj.* —**earth'en·ware'',** *n.* —**earth'ly,** *adj.* —**earth'quake'',** *n.*

earth'ly, *adj.* pertaining to this world.

earth'worm'', *n.* worm living in soil.

earth'y, *adj.,* -ier, -iest. matter-of-fact.

ease, *n., v.t.,* eased, easing. *n.* 1. freedom from toil, pain, etc. —*v.t.* 2. make easy.

ea'sel, *n.* stand for a painting, etc.

east, *n.* 1. direction to the right of north. 2. eastern area. —*adj., adv.* 3. toward, in, or from the east. —**east'er·ly,** *adj.* —**east'ern,** *adj.* —**east'ern·er,** *n.* —**east'ward,** *adv., adj.* —**east'wards,** *adv.*

East'er, *n.* celebration of the resurrection of Christ.

eas'y, *adj.,* -ier, -iest. 1. not difficult. 2. free of pain, etc. —**eas'i·ly,** *adv.* —**eas' i·ness,** *n.*

eat, *v.t.,* ate, eaten, eating. 1. consume as food. 2. dissolve, erode, etc.

eaves, *n., pl.* projecting edge of a roof.

eaves'drop'', *v.i.,* -dropped, -dropping. overhear conversation, esp. intentionally.

ebb, *n.* 1. going-out of a tide. 2. decline or lessening. —*v.i.* 3. go out, as the tide. 4. decline or lessen.

eb'o·ny, *n.* 1. hard, dark wood. 2. very deep brown or black.

e·bul'lient, *adj.* 1. exuberant. 2. bubbling. —e·bul'lience, *n.*

ec·cen'tric, *adj.* 1. peculiar in manner. 2.
off center. —*n.* 3. eccentric person. 4.
eccentric machine part. —ec''cen·tric'
i·ty, *n.*

ec·cle''si·as'tic, *adj.* 1. Also, ec·cle''si·
as'ti·cal. pertaining to churches. —*n.*
2. clergyman.

ech·e·lon (esh'ǝ lon''), *n.* 1. formation of
troops, etc., each line being to the right
or left of that preceding it. 2. level of
responsibility.

ech'o, *n., pl.* -oes, *v.t.,* -oed, -oing. *n.* 1.
reflected sound. —*v.t.* 2. reflect as an
echo.

e·clair', *n.* custard-filled pastry.

e·clec'tic, *adj.* using those thought best,
regardless of source.

e·clipse', *n., v.t.,* -clipsed, -clipsing. *n.* 1.
obscuring of the sun or moon. —*v.t.* 2.
obscure.

e·clip'tic, *n.* apparent annual path of the
sun.

e·col'o·gy, *n., pl.* -gies. 1. study of the
relation of living things to their environment. 2. system permitting living
things to exist. —e'co·log'i·cal, *adj.*
—e·col'o·gist, *n.*

e''co·nom'i·cal, *adj.* thrifty.

e''co·nom'ics, *n.* 1. *sing.* study of
wealth. 2. *pl.* resources and demands
on wealth. —e''co·nom'ic, *adj.* —e·
con'o·mist, *n.*

e·con'o·my, *n., pl.* -mies. 1. thrift. 2.
system of producing and dividing
wealth. —e·con'o·mize'', *v.i.*

ec'sta·sy, *n., pl.* -sies. state of overwhelming emotion. —ec·stat'ic, *adj.,*
n.

ec''u·men'i·cal, *adj.* 1. universal. 2. promoting universal accord, esp. in religion.

ec'ze·ma, *n.* scaly skin disease.

ed'dy, *n., pl.* -dies, *v.i.,* -died, -dying. *n.*
1. turbulence of water or wind. —*v.i.*
2. move in an eddy.

edge, *n., v.,* edged, edging. *n.* 1. outer
limit. 2. sharp intersection. —*v.t.* 3.
border. —*v.i.* 4. sidle. —edge'wise'',
edge'ways'', *adv.* —edg'ing, *n.*

ed'i·ble, *adj.* suitable for eating. —ed''i·
bil'i·ty, *n.*

e'dict, *n.* decree.

ed'i·fice, *n.* building.

ed'i·fy'', *v.t.,* -fied, -fying. educate or
improve the mind of. —ed''i·fi·ca'
tion, *n.*

ed'it, *v.t.* prepare for publication or presentation. —ed'i·tor, *n.* —ed''i·tor'ial
n., adj.

e·di'tion, *n.* printing of a book.

ed''i·tor'i·al, *n.* 1. periodical's commen-
tary on public issues. —*adj.* 2. pertaining to editing.

ed'u·cate'', *v.t.* -cated, -cating. develop
the mind, knowledge or skill of. —ed''

u·ca'tion, *n.* —ed''u·ca'tion·al, *adj.*
—ed'u·ca''tor, *n.*

eel, *n.* long, snakelike fish.

ee'rie, *adj.,* -rier, -riest. wierd; uncanny.

ef·face', *v.t.,* -faced, -facing. eliminate
all trace of. —ef·face'ment, *n.*

ef·fect', *n.* 1. result. 2. influence. 3. effects, personal property. —*v.t.* 4.
cause. —ef·fect'ive, *adj.* —ef·fec'tu·
al, *adj.*

ef·fem'i·nate, *adj.* unmanly. —ef·fem'
i·na·cy, *n.*

ef''fer·vesce', *v.i.,* -vesced, -vescing.
bubble. —ef''fer·ves'cent, *adj.* —ef''
fer·ves'cence, *n.*

ef·fete', *adj.* decadent.

ef''fi·ca'cious, *adj.* producing the desired result. —ef'fi·ca·cy, *n.*

ef·fi'cient, *adj.* efficacious without
waste. —ef·fi'cient·ly, *adv.* —ef·fi'
cien·cy, *n.*

ef'fi·gy, *n., pl.* -gies. copy or image, esp.
in three dimensions.

ef'fort, *n.* 1. expenditure of strength,
thought, etc. 2. attempt.

ef·front'er·y, *n., pl.* -ies. impudence.

ef·fu'sion, *n.* outpouring of enthusiasm.
—ef·fu'sive, *adj.*

e·gal'i·tar''i·an, *adj.* believing that all
people should be equal.

egg'head'', *n. Informal.* intellectual.

egg'plant'', *n.* purple-skinned vegetable.

e'go, *n.* self. —e''go·cen'tric, *adj., n.*

e'go·ism, *n.* selfishness. —e'go·ist, *n.*
—e''go·is'tic, e''go·is'ti·cal, *adj.*

e'go·tism, *n.* self-conceit; vanity. —e'go·
tist'', *n.* —e''go·tis'tic, e''go·tis'ti·cal,
adj.

e·gre'gious, *adj.* conspicuous in a bad
way.

eight, *n.* seven plus one. —eighth, *adj.*

eight·een', *n.* seventeen plus one.

eight'y, *n.* eight times ten. —eight'i·eth,
adj.

ei·ther (ē'thǝr, ī'thǝr), *adj.* 1. one or the
other but not both. 2. each. —*pron.* 3.
one or the other. —*conj.* 4. (used to
emphasize choice). —*adj.* 5. as well.

e·ject', *v.t.* hurl or force out. —e·jec'
tion, *n.*

eke, *v.t.,* eked, eking. eke out, gain with
difficulty.

e·lab·o·rate, *adj., v.t.,* -rated, -rating.
adj. (ē lab'ǝ rǝt) 1. having many parts
or aspects. —*v.t.* (ē lab'ǝ rāt') 2. plan
in detail. —e·lab''o·ra'tion, *n.*

e·lapse', *v.i.,* -lapsed, -lapsing. pass, as
time.

e·las'tic, *adj.* able to recover from
stretching or bending. —*n.* elastic material or object. —e·las''tic'i·ty, *n.*

e·late', *v.t.,* -lated, -lating. raise in spirits.
—e·la'tion, *n.*

el'bow, *n.* joint halfway up the arm.
—*v.t., v.i.* push with the elbows.

el'der, *adj.* 1. senior. —*n.* 2. senior. 3.

shrub with red or purple berries. —**eld′ est**, *adj.* —**eld′er·ly**, *adj.*

e·lect′, *v.t.* 1. choose, esp. by a vote. —*adj.* 2. chosen. 3. elected to but not yet in public office. —**e·lec′tion**, *n.* —**e·lec′tor**, *n.* —**e·lec′tor·al**, *adj.* —**e·lec′tor·ate**, *n.* —**e·lec′tive**, *adj.*

e·lec″tric′i·ty, *n.* 1. property of motion in certain particles composing matter. 2. current created by such motion. —**e·lec′tric, e·lec′tri·cal**, *adj.* —**e·lec′ tri·fy″**, *v.t.*

e·lec′tro·cute″, *v.t.*, **-cuted, -cuting**. injure or kill with electricity. —**e·lec″ tro·cu′tion**, *n.*

e·lec′trode, *n.* object conducting electricity into or out of a battery, etc.

e·lec·trol′y·sis, *n.* decomposition of a material by the passage of electricity. —**e·lec″tro·lyt′ic**, *adj.*

e·lec″tro·mag′net, *n.* magnet operating through an electric current. —**e·lec″ tro·mag·net′ic**, *adj.*

e·lec′tron, *n.* negatively charged particle of an atom.

e·lec″tron′ics, *n.*, *sing.* study of the action of electrons and its application to technology. —**e·lec″tron′ic**, *adj.*

el′e·gant, *adj.* tasteful and dignified. —**el′e·gance**, *n.*

el′e·gy, *n.*, *pl.* **-gies**. poem of lament, esp. for the dead. —**el″e·gi′ac, el″e·gi′a· cal**, *adj.*

el′e·ment, *n.* 1. major or basic component. 2. natural environment. 3. elements, natural forces, esp. of weather. —**el″e·men′tal**, *adj.*

el″e·men′ta·ry, *n.* fundamental; rudimentary.

el′e·phant, *n.* large four-legged animal with a long prehensile nose.

el′e·vate″, *v.t.*, **-vated, -vating**. 1. raise to a greater height. 2. raise in rank, spirits, etc.

el″e·va′tion, *n.* 1. height. 2. drawing of one side of a building, etc., in its true dimensions.

el′e·va″tor, *n.* 1. cabinet or platform for raising or lowering persons or goods. 2. storage place for grain.

e·lev′en, *n.* ten plus one.

elf, *n.*, *pl.* **elves**. small fairy. —**elf′in, elf′ ish**, *adj.*

e·lic′it, *v.t.* draw forth, as a reaction or comment.

el′i·gi·ble, *adj.* suitable for choice. —**el″ i·gi·bil′i·ty**, *n.*

e·lim′i·nate″, *v.t.*, **-nated, -nating**. get rid of. —**e·lim″i·na′tion**, *n.*

e·lite′ (i lēt′), *n.* choice element. —**e·lit′ ism**, *n.*

e·lix′ir, *n.* medicine in a solution of alcohol.

elk, *n.*, *pl.* **elks, elk**. large mooselike deer.

el·lipse′, *n.* oval symmetrical about two axes. —**el·lip′ti·cal**, *adj.*

elm, *n.* tall deciduous tree.

el″o·cu′tion, *n.* public speaking.

e·lon′gate″, *v.t.*, *v.i.*, **-gated, -gating**. lengthen. —**e″lon·ga′tion**, *n.*

e·lope″, *v.i.*, **-loped, -loping**. flee, esp. in order to marry. —**e·lope′ment**, *n.*

e′lo·quent, *adj.* convincing in speech. —**e′lo·quence**, *n.*

else, *adj.* 1. other. 2. more. —*adv.* 3. otherwise.

else′where″, *adv.* somewhere else.

e·lu′ci·date″, *v.t.*, **-dated, -dating**. clarify; explain. —**e·lu″ci·da′tion**, *n.*

e·lude′, *v.t.*, **-luded, -luding**. escape or evade. —**e·lu′sive**, *adv.*

e·ma′ci·ate″, *v.t.*, **-ated, -ating**. make abnormally thin. —**e·ma″ci·a′tion**, *n.*

em′a·nate″, *v.i.*, **-nated, -nating**. come forth; issue. —**em″a·na′tion**, *n.*

e·man′ci·pate″, *v.t.*, **-pated, -pating**. free, as from bondage. —**e·man″ci· pa′tion**, *n.* —**e·man′ci·pa″tor**, *n.*

e·mas′cu·late″, *v.t.*, **-lated, -lating**. castrate.

em·balm′, *v.t.* preserve against decay after death.

em·bank′, *v.t.* support, strengthen, etc. with piled earth, etc. —**em·bank′ment**, *n.*

em·bar′go, *n.*, *pl.* **-goes**. *n.* ban on shipping or commerce.

em·bark′, *v.i.* 1. set forth, esp. on a ship. —*v.t.*, *v.i.* 2. board, esp. a ship. —**em″ bar·ka′tion**, *n.*

em·bar′rass, *v.t.* 1. make ashamed or self-conscious. 2. put at a loss for money. —**em·bar′rass·ment**, *n.*

em′bas·sy, *n.*, *pl.* **-sies**. permanent mission to a foreign government.

em·bed′, *v.t.*, **-bedded, -bedding**. sink and fix firmly.

em·bel′lish, *v.t.* decorate. —**em·bel′lish· ment**, *n.*

em′ber, *n.* red-hot piece of fuel.

em·bez′zle, *v.t.*, **-zled, -zling**. steal from an employer, client, etc. —**em·bez′ zler**, *n.* —**em·bez′zle·ment**, *n.*

em·bit′ter, *v.t.* make bitter.

em′blem, *n.* symbolic design. —**em″ blem·at′ic**, *adj.*

em·bod′y, *v.t.*, **-died, -dying**. 1. realize in bodily form. 2. incorporate. —**em· bod′i·ment**, *n.*

em·boss′, mark with raised designs or lettering.

em·brace′, *v.*, **-braced, -bracing**, *n.* *v.t.* 1. put the arms around. 2. accept readily. —*v.i.* 3. embrace each other. —*n.* 4. act or instance of embracing.

em·broi′der, *v.t.* decorate with applied colored yarns. —**em·broi′der·y**, *n.*

em′bry·o″, *n.*, *pl.* **-oes**. animal or plant in the first stage of development. —**em″bry·on′ic**, *adj.*

e·mend', v.t. correct; edit. —e''men·da'tion, n.

em'er·ald, n. vivid green gem.

e·merge', v.i., -merged, -merging. appear into notice. —e·mer'gence, n.

e·mer'gen·cy, n., pl. -cies. mishap demanding prompt action.

e·met'ic, adj. 1. causing vomiting. —n. 2. emetic substance.

em'i·grate'', v.i., -grated, -grating. leave one's country to settle elsewhere. —em''i·gra'tion, n. —em''i·grant, n., adj.

em'i·nent, adj. high in standing or rank. —em'i·nence, n. —em'i·nent·ly, adv.

em'is·sar''y, n., pl. -ies. person sent on a mission.

e·mit', v.t., -mitted, -mitting. send out or forth; discharge. —e·mis'sion, n.

e·mo'tion, n. 1. natural feelings and reactions. 2. specific feeling or reaction. —e·mo'tion·al, adj.

em'per·or, n. ruler of an empire.

em'pha·sis, n., pl. -ses. force or stress. —em·phat'ic, adj. —em'pha·size'', v.t.

em'pire, n. number of countries or regions under one monarch.

em·pir'i·cal, adj. derived from experience.

em·ploy', v.t. 1. hire or use. —n. 2. hire. —em·ploy'er, n. —em·ploy'ee, n. —em·ploy'ment, n.

em·po'ri·um, n., pl. -ums, -a. store with varied merchandise.

em·pow'er, v.t. give official power to.

em'press, n. woman married to or with the rank of an emperor.

emp'ty, adj., -tier, -tiest, v., -tied, -tying. adj. 1. lacking contents. —v.t. 2. make empty. —v.i. 3. become empty. —emp'ti·ness, n.

em'u·late'', v.t., -lated, -lating. imitate, esp. in excellence. —em''u·la'tion, n. —em'u·lous, adj.

e·mul'sion, n. mixture of two liquids made possible by addition of a third. —e·mul'si·fy'', v.t., v.i.

en·a'ble, v.t., -bled, -bling. make able.

en·act', v.t. 1. make into law. 2. represent in a play. —en·act'ment, n.

en·am'el, n., v.t., -eled or -elled, -eling or -elling. n. 1. glassy, fused coating. 2. hard, glossy paint. 3. exterior material of teeth. —v.t. 4. cover with enamel.

en·am'ored, adj. full of love.

en·camp', v.i., v.t. camp. —en·camp'ment, n.

en·case', v.t., -cased, -casing. enclose.

en·chant', v.t. 1. charm. 2. put a magic spell on. —en·chant'ment, n.

en·cir'cle, v.t., -cled, -cling. surround.

en·close', v.t., -closed, -closing. 1. surround. 2. put into a container, envelope, etc. —en·clo'sure, n.

en·com'pass, v.t. 1. surround. 2. include.

en·core' (ahn'kōr), interj. 1. again: request to a musician. —n. 2. repetition of a musical performance.

en·coun'ter, v.t. 1. happen to meet. 2. meet in combat. —n. 3. act or instance of encountering.

en·cour'age, v.t., -aged, -aging. give courage or resolution to. —en·cour'age·ment, n.

en·croach', v.i. trespass. —en·croach·ment, n.

en·cum'ber, v.t. burden or hinder. —en·cum'brance, n.

en·cy''clo·pe'di·a, n. reference work dealing at length with all areas of knowledge. Also, en·cy''clo·pae'di·a. —en·cy''clo·pe'dic, adj.

end, n. 1. far or final part. 2. result. 3. purpose. —v.t. 4. put an end to. —v.i. 5. come to an end. —end'less, adj.

en·dan'ger, v.t. put in danger.

en·dear', v.t. make dear. —en·dear'ing, adj. —en·dear'ment, n.

en·deav'or, v.t., n. attempt.

end'ing, n. conclusion.

end'most'', adj. farthest.

en·dorse', v.t., -dorsed, -dorsing. 1. write on the back of, esp. a signature. 2. approve. —en·dors'er, n. —en·dorse'ment, n.

en·dow', v.t. 1. provide with personal resources or qualities. 2. give money for. —en·dow'ment n.

en·dure', v., -dured, -during v.t. 1. tolerate. 2. suffer. —v.i. 3. survive. —en·dur'able,adj. —en·dur'ance, n.

en'e·my, n., pl. -mies. 1. person who wishes one harm. 2. hostile nation or military force.

en'er·gy, n., pl. -gies. 1. force able to produce motion, heat, light, etc. 2. vigor. —en''er·get'ic, adj.

en'er·vate'', v.t., -vated, -vating. deprive of vitality. —en''er·va'tion, n.

en·fee'ble, v.t., -bled, -bling. make feeble.

en·fold', v.t. wrap.

en·force', v.t., -forced, -forcing. administer forcefully, as a law. —en·force'ment, n.

en·gage', v.t., -gaged, -gaging. 1. commit. 2. commit to marriage. 3. hire. 4. hold or connect with. 5. meet and fight. —en·gage'ment, n.

en·gag'ing, adj. charming. —en·gag'ing·ly, adv.

en·gen'der, v.t. bring into being.

en'gine, n. 1. machine producing mechanical force, esp. by means of heat energy. 2. locomotive.

en''gi·neer', n. 1. person who designs systems or structures applying static or dynamic forces or various sources of energy. **2.** skilled operator of machines, etc. —**en′′gi·neer′ing,** *n.*

en·grave′, *v.t.,* **-graved, -graving.** form designs or letters with shallow cuts on wood, steel, etc. —**en·grav′er,** *n.* —**en·grav′ing,** *n.*

en·gross′, *v.t.* capture the attention of.

en·gulf′, *v.t.* swallow up; submerge.

en·hance′, *v.t.,* **-hanced, -hancing.** increase or improve.

e·nig′ma, *n., pl.* **-mas.** puzzle. —**e′′nig·mat′ic,** *adj.*

en·join′, *v.t.* forbid.

en·joy′, *v.t.* **1.** get pleasure from. **2.** have the benefit of. —**en·joy′a·ble,** *adj.* —**en·joy′ment,** *n.*

en·large′, *v.,* **-larged, -larging.** *v.t.* **1.** make larger. —*v.i.* **2.** become larger. —**en·large′ment,** *n.*

en·light′en, *v.t.* free of ignorance or wrong attitudes. —**en·light′en·ment,** *n.*

en·list′, *v.t., v.i.* enroll. —**en·list′ment,** *n.*

en·liv′en, *v.t.* make lively.

en′mi·ty, *n., pl.* **-ties.** hostility.

en·nui′, *n.* boredom.

e·nor′mi·ty, *n., pl.* **-ties. 1.** wickedness. **2.** outrage.

e·nor′mous, *adj.* beyond normal size or extent. —**e·nor′mous·ly,** *adv.*

e·nough′, *n., adj., adv. n.* **1.** as much as is wanted; sufficiency. —*adj.* **2.** adequate; sufficient. —*adv.* **3.** sufficiently.

en·quire′, *v.t., v.i.,* **-quired, -quiring.** inquire. —**en·quir′y,** *n.*

en·rage′, *v.t.,* **-raged, -raging.** put in a rage.

en·rich′, *v.t.* make rich or richer. —**en·rich′ment,** *n.*

en·roll′, *v.t.* name on a list or record. —**en·roll′ment,** *n.*

en route, on the way.

en·sconce′, *v.t.* put in a snug or secure place.

en·sem′ble, *n.* related group.

en·shrine′, *v.t.,* **-shrined, -shrining.** put in or as if in a shrine.

en′sign, *n.* **1.** flag, as on a ship. **2.** lowest commissioned naval officer.

en·slave′, *v.t.,* **-slaved, -slaving.** make a slave of. —**en·slave′ment,** *n.*

en·sue′, *v.i.,* **-sued, -suing.** follow, esp. as a consequence.

en·sure′, *v.t.,* **-sured, -suring.** make sure.

en·tail′, *v.t.* necessitate.

en·tan′gle, *v.t.,* **-gled, -gling.** trap or impede. —**en·tan′gle·ment,** *n.*

en′ter, *v.t.* **1.** go into. **2.** have enrolled in or admitted to something. **3.** list or record.

en′ter·prise′′, *n.* **1.** project with some risk. **2.** willingness to undertake such projects. —**en′ter·pris′′ing,** *adj.*

en′′ter·tain′, *v.t.* **1.** have as a guest. **2.** amuse. **3.** consider. —**en′′ter·tain′er,** *n.* —**en′′ter·tain′ment,** *n.*

en·thu′si·asm, *n.* intense approval, or favor. —**en·thu′si·ast,** *n.* —**en·thu′′si·as′tic,** *adj.*

en·tice′, *v.t.,* **-ticed, -ticing.** tempt, esp. deceitfully. —**en·tice′ment,** *n.*

en·tire′, *adj.* complete. —**en·tire′ly,** *adv.* —**en·tire′ty,** *n.*

en·ti′tle, *v.t.,* **-tled, -tling.** give a right or claim.

en′ti·ty, *n., pl.* **-ties.** one that exists.

en′′to·mol′o·gy, *n.* study of insects. —**en′′to·mol′o·gist,** *n.*

en·tou·rage (ahn′′tŏŏ rahzh′), *n.* followers of an important person.

en′trails, *n., pl.* internal organs, esp. viscera.

en·trance, *n., v.t.,* **-tranced, -trancing.** *n.* (in′trəns) **1.** way of entering. **2.** right to enter. **3.** act of entering. —*v.t.* (entrans′). **4.** fill with wonder.

en·trap′, *v.t.* catch, as if in a trap. —**en·trap′ment,** *n.*

en·treat′, *v.t., v.i.* ask earnestly. —**en·treat′y,** *n.*

en·tree (ahn trā′), *n.* main dinner course.

en·trench′, *v.t.* secure the position of.

en·tre·pre·neur (ahn′′trə prə nər′), *n.* undertaker of business ventures.

en·trust′, *v.t.* **1.** give to someone in trust. **2.** trust with something.

en′try, *n., pl.* **-tries. 1.** entrance. **2.** something noted. **3.** competitor.

e·nu′mer·ate′′, *v.t.,* **-ated, -ating. 1.** cite one by one. **2.** count. —**e·nu′′mer·a′tion,** *n.*

e·nun′ci·ate′′, *v.,* **-ated, -ating.** *v.t., v.i.* speak distinctly. —**e·nun′′ci·a′tion,** *n.*

en·vel′op, *v.i.* wrap up.

en′ve·lope′′, *n.* **1.** paper cover for letters, papers, etc. **2.** outer covering.

en·vi′ron·ment, *n.* **1.** surroundings. **2.** conditions. —**en·vi′′ron·men′tal,** *adj.*

en·vi′rons, *n., pl.* surrounding area.

en·vis′age, *v.t.,* **-aged, -aging.** visualize; contemplate.

en·vi′sion, *v.t.* contemplate as likely.

en′voy, *n.* diplomatic representative.

en′vy, *n., v.t.,* **-vied, -vying.** *n.* **1.** resentment over another's good luck. —*v.t.* **2.** feel envy toward. —**en′vi·a·ble,** *adj.* —**en′vi·ous,** *adj.*

e′on, *n.* very long period.

e·phem′er·al, *n.* short-lived.

ep′ic, *adj.* **1.** heroic. —*n.* **2.** poem about heroism.

ep′i·cure′, *n.* person with refined tastes, esp. for food and drink. —**ep′′i·cu·re′an,** *adj., n.*

ep′′i·dem′ic, *adj.* **1.** spreading through a community. —*n.* **2.** epidemic disease.

ep''i·der'mis, *n.* outer layer of skin. —**ep''i·der'mal, ep''i·der'mic,** *adj.*

ep'i·gram'', *n.* witty observation. —**ep'' i·gram·mat'ic,** *adj.*

ep'i·lep''sy, *n.* nervous disease with convulsions and unconsciousness. —**ep''i· lep·tic,** *adj., n.*

ep'i·logue'', *n.* final statement of a play, etc.

E·piph'a·ny, *n.* revelation of Jesus as the Christ, celebrated January 6.

e·pis'co·pal, *adj.* pertaining to or governed by a bishop.

ep'i·sode'', *n.* occurrence. —**ep''i·sod'ic,** *adj.*

e·pis'tle, *n.* letter; written message.

ep'i·taph'', *n.* inscription on a tomb.

ep'i·thet'', *n.* characterizing name.

e·pit'o·me'', *n., pl.* **-mes.** 1. summary. 2. typical example. —**e·pit'o·mize'',** *v.t.*

ep'och, *n.* distinct historical or geological period. —**ep'och·al,** *adj.*

eq'ua·ble, *adj.* emotionally steady.

e'qual, *adj., n., v.t.* **-qualed, -qualing.** *adj.* 1. of the same amount, rank, etc. 2. competent; adequate. —*n.* 3. equal person or thing. —*v.t.* 4. be equal to. —**e·qual'i·ty,** *n.* —**e'qual·ize'',** *v.t.*

e''qua·nim'i·ty, *n.* calm.

e·quate', *v.t.,* **-quated, -quating.** regard as equal. —**e·qua'tion,** *n.*

e·qua'tor, *n.* imaginary line bisecting the earth. —**e''qua·to'ri·al,** *adj.*

e''qui·dis'tant, *adj.* equally far.

e''qui·lat'er·al, *adj.* with equal sides.

e''qui·lib'ri·um, *n.* balance.

e'qui·nox'', *n.* time of equal day and night periods, marking the beginning of spring or autumn. —**e''qui·noc'ti·al,** *adj.*

e·quip', *v.t.,* **-quipped, -quipping.** furnish with what is necessary. —**e·quip'ment,** *n.*

e'qui·ta·ble, *adj.* just; fair. —**e'qui·ta·bly,** *adv.*

e'qui·ty, *n.* 1. fairness. 2. value of something in excess of money owed for it.

e·quiv'a·lent, *adj., n.* equal. —**e·quiv'a·lence,** *n.*

e·quiv'o·cal, *adj.* of doubtful meaning or nature.

e·quiv'o·cate, *v.i.,* **-cated, -cating.** speak equivocally. —**e·quiv''o·ca'tion,** *n.*

er'a, *n.* distinctive historical period.

e·rad'i·cate'', *v.t.,* **-cated, -cating.** eliminate by destroying. —**e·rad''i·ca'tion,** *n.*

e·rase', *v.t.,* **-rased, -rasing.** obliterate. —**e·ras'er,** *n.* —**e·ra'sure,** *n.*

e·rect', *adj.* 1. upright. —*v.t.* 2. build. —**e·rec'tion,** *n.*

er'mine, *n.* weasel with white winter fur.

e·rode', *v., v.t.* **-roded, -roding.** *v.t., v.i.* wash away or out. —**e·ro'sion,** *n.*

e·rot'ic, *adj.* pertaining to or arousing sexual desire. —**e·rot'i·cism,** *n.*

err, *v.i.* be in error.

er'rand, *n.* journey for some purpose.

er'rant, *adj.* wandering.

er·rat'ic, *adj.* unreliable.

er·rat'um, *n., pl.* **-a.** printing or writing error.

er·ro'ne·ous, *adj.* in error.

er'ror, *n.* mistaken belief or action.

erst'while'', *adj.* former.

er'u·dite'', *adj.* informed; scholarly. —**er''u·di'tion,** *n.*

e·rupt', *v.i.* break forth. —**e·rup'tion,** *n.*

es'ca·late'', *v.i.,* **-lated, -lating.** 1. rise on an escalator. 2. increase rapidly, as in intensity.

es'ca·la'tor, *n.* endless moving stair.

es'ca·pade'', *n.* reckless adventure.

es·cape', *v.,* **-caped, -caping,** *n. v.t., v.i.* 1. flee. —*v.t.* 2. evade the notice of. —*n.* 3. act or instance of escaping.

es·cap'ism, *n.* tendency to attempt to escape reality. —**es·cap'ist,** *n., adj.*

es·chew', *v.t.* shun; do without.

es·cort', *v.t.* (i skort') 1. take charge of and accompany. —*n.* (es'kort) 2. person or thing that escorts.

es'crow, *n. Law.* state of property that is temporarily held in trust for another.

es·cutch'eon, *n.* symbolic shield holding a coat of arms.

es''o·ter'ic, *adj.* reserved for an understanding few.

es·pe'cial, *adj.* special. —**es·pe'cial·ly,** *adv.*

es'pi·o·nage'', *n.* practice of spying.

es·pouse', *v.t.,* **-poused, -pousing.** 1. marry. 2. devote oneself to. —**es·pous'al,** *n.*

es·prit de corps (es prē'də kor'), morale of an organization.

es·py', *v.t.,* **-pied, -pying.** discern.

es·say', *n.* (es'sā) 1. writing on some theme. —*v.t.* (es sā') 2. attempt. —**es'say·ist,** *n.*

es'sence, *n.* 1. basic nature. 2. concentrated substance.

es·sen'tial, *adj.* 1. indispensable. —*n.* 2. something indispensable. —**es·sen'tial·ly,** *adv.*

es·tab'lish, *v.t.* 1. bring into being. 2. prove. —**es·tab'lish·ment,** *n.*

es·tate', *n.* 1. personal property. 2. grounds belonging to a house.

es·teem', *n.* 1. evaluation. —*v.t.* 2. deem. —**es'tim·a·ble,** *adj.*

es'thete'', *n.* aesthete.

es·thet'ics, *n.* aesthetics.

es·ti·mate, *n., v.t.,* **-mated, -mating.** *n.* (es'tə mət) 1. rough calculation or appraisal. —*v.t.* (es'tə māt'') 2. make an estimate of. —**esti·ma'tion,** *n.*

es·trange', *v.t.,* **-tranged, -tranging.** lose the affection of.

es'tu·ary, *n., pl.* **-ies.** tidal river mouth.

et cetera, and other persons or things. Abbreviated etc.

etch, *v.t.* make or mark by the corrosion of acid. —**etch′ing,** *n.*

e·ter′nal, *adj.* lasting or valid forever. —**e·ter′nal·ly,** *adv.* —**e·ter′ni·ty,** *n.*

e′ther, *n.* 1. upper part of the atmosphere. 2. volatile, flammable anaesthetic or solvent.

e·the′re·al, *adj.* 1. delicate. 2. unearthly.

eth′ics, *n.* 1. study of right and wrong in actions. 2. *pl.* **a.** Also, **eth′ic,** personal standards of right and wrong action. **b.** standards of conduct adopted by professionals. —**eth′i·cal,** *adj.*

eth′nic, *adj.* 1. pertaining to distinct nations or tribes. —*n.* 2. member of a minority national group. —**eth·nic′i·ty,** *n.*

et′i·quette, *n.* code of acceptable conduct.

e″ty·mol′o·gy, *n.* study of word origins.

Eu′cha·rist, *n.* 1. Holy Communion. 2. bread and wine used at Holy Communion. —**Eu′cha·ris′tic,** *adj.*

Eu·clid′e·an, *adj.* pertaining to traditional geometry. Also, **Eu·clid′i·an.**

eu·gen′ics, *n.* attempt to improve humanity by controlled mating. —**eu·gen′ic,** *adj.*

eu′lo·gy, *n.*, *pl.* **-gies.** praise in speech or writing. —**eu′lo·gize′,** *v.t.*

eu′nuch, *n.* castrated man.

eu′phe·mism, *n.* expression substituted for a less agreeable one. —**euphe·mis′tic,** *adj.*

eu·pho′ni·ous, *adj.* pleasant-sounding. —**eu′pho·ny,** *n.*

eu·pho′ri·a, *n.* sensation of well-being. —**eu·phor′ic,** *adj.*

eu·re′ka, *interj.* I have found it!

eu″tha·na′si·a, *n.* killing to prevent or end suffering.

e·vac′u·ate′, *v.t.*, **-ated, -ating.** 1. empty. 2. send to a place of security. —**e·vac″u·a′tion,** *n.* —**e·vac″u·ee′,** *n.*

e·vade′, *v.t.*, **-vaded, -vading.** avoid or escape from. —**e·va′sion,** *n.* —**e·va′sive,** *adj.*

e·val′u·ate″, *v.t.*, **-ated, -ating.** estimate the worth of. —**e·val″u·a′tion,** *n.*

e″van·gel′i·cal, *adj.* 1. pertaining to the New Testament. 2. emphasizing salvation through Jesus.

e·van′gel·ist, *n.* 1. author of a Gospel. 2. itinerant preacher. —**e·van′gel·ism,** *n.*

e·vap′o·rate″, *v.t.*, *v.i.*, **-rated, -rating.** turn into vapor. —**e·vap″o·ra′tion,** *n.*

eve, *n.* time just before.

e′ven, *adj.* 1. level or smooth. 2. unvarying. 3. equal. 4. divisible by two. 5. with nothing owed. —*adv.* 6. although improbable. 7. yet; still. —*v.t.* 8. make even. —**e′ven·ness,** *n.*

eve′ning, *n.* time between afternoon and night.

e·vent′, *n.* something that happens. —**e·vent′ful,** *adj.*

e·ven′tu·al, *adj.* at some future time. —**e·ven′tu·al·ly,** *adv.*

e·ven″tu·al′i·ty, *n.*, *pl.* **-ties.** possible occurrence.

ev′er, *adv.* at any time.

ev′er·green″, *adj.* 1. with green leaves all the year round. —*n.* 2. evergreen tree or plant.

ev″er·last′ing, *adj.* eternal or lifelong.

ev′er·y, *adj.* 1. each individual. 2. any possible. —**ev′er·y·one″,** *pron.* —**ev′er·y·thing″,** *n.*

ev′er·y·bod″y, *n.* every person.

ev′er·y·where″, *adv.* at or to every place.

e·vict′, *v.t.* drive out, as from rented lodgings. —**e·vic′tion,** *n.*

ev′i·dence, *n.*, *v.t.*, **-denced, -dencing.** 1. matter supporting an argument. —*v.t.* 2. make evident.

ev′i·dent, *adj.* obvious. —**ev′i·dent·ly,** *adv.*

e′vil, *adj.* 1. wrong or wicked. 2. injurious. —**e′vil·ly,** *adv.*

e·vince′, *v.t.*, **-vinced, -vincing.** make obvious.

e·voke′, *v.t.*, **-voked, -voking.** call forth. —**e·voc′a·tive,** *adj.* —**ev″o·ca′tion,** *n.*

e·volve′, *v.*, **-volved, -volving.** *v.t.*, *v.i.* develop gradually. —**ev″o·lu′tion,** *n.*

ex·ac·er·bate (eks as′ər bāt), *v.t.*, **-bated, -bating.** aggravate.

ex·act′, *adj.* 1. accurate. 2. precise. —*v.t.* 3. extort or demand. —**ex·act′ly,** *n.* —**ex·act′ing,** *adj.* —**ex·ac′tion,** *n.*

ex·ag′ger·ate″, *v.t.*, **-ated, -ating.** overstate the importance of. —**ex·ag″ger·a′tion,** *n.*

ex·alt′, *v.t.* 1. raise in status. 2. praise. —**ex″al·ta′tion,** *n.*

ex·am′ine, *v.t.*, **-ined, -ining.** 1. inspect. 2. test for knowledge. —**ex·am″i·na′tion,** *n.* —**ex·am′in·er,** *n.*

ex·am′ple, *n.* 1. sample. 2. illustrative instance.

ex·as′per·ate″, *v.t.*, **-ated, -ating.** anger or annoy seriously. —**ex·as″per·a′tion,** *n.*

ex′ca·vate″, *v.t.*, **-vated, -vating.** dig, as in or from earth. —**ex″ca·va′tion,** *n.*

ex·ceed′, *v.t.* 1. be in excess of. 2. surpass.

ex·ceed′ing·ly, *adv.* extremely.

ex·cel′, *v.*, **-celled, -celling.** *v.t.*, *v.i.* surpass.

ex′cel·lent, *adj.* among the finest of its kind. —**ex′cel·lent·ly,** *adv.* —**ex′cel·lence,** *n.*

ex·cept′, *prep.* 1. Also, **ex·cept′ing,** aside from. —*v.t.* 2. exclude or disregard. —**ex·cep′tion,** *n.*

ex·cep′tion·a·ble, *adj.* objectionable.

ex·cep'tion·al, *adj.* highly unusual. —ex·cep'tion·al·ly, *adv.*

ex'cerpt, *n.* quotation, esp. printed.

ex·cess', *n.* (ik ses', ek'ses'') 1. lack of self-restraint or moderation. 2. surplus. —*adj.* (ek'ses'') 3. surplus. —ex·ces'sive, *adj.*

ex·change', *v.t.,* -changed, -changing, *n. v.t.* 1. give in return for something else. —*n.* 2. act or instance of exchanging.

ex'cise, *n., v.t.,* -cised, -cising. *n.* (ek'sīz) 1. tax on merchandise. —*v.t.* (ik sīz') 2. cut out. —ex·ci'sion, *n.*

ex·cite', *v.t.,* -cited, -citing. 1. stimulate. 2. rouse emotionally. —ex·cit'a·ble, *adj.* —ex·cite'ment, *n.* —ex·cit'ed·ly, *adv.* —ex·cit'ing, *adj.*

ex·claim', *v.i., v.t.* shout or speak loudly and emotionally. —ex''cla·ma'tion, *n.*

ex·clude', *v.t.,* -cluded, -cluding. leave or keep out. —ex·clu'sion, *n.* —ex·clu'sive, *adj.*

ex·co'ri·ate'', *v.t.,* -ated, -ating. denounce bitterly. —ex·co''ri·a'tion, *n.*

ex'cre·ment, *n.* excreted matter.

ex·cres'cence, *n.* abnormal outgrowth.

ex·crete', *v.t.,* -creted, -creting. eliminate as waste from the body. —ex·cre'tion, *n.* —ex'cre·to''ry, *adj.*

ex·cru'ci·at''ing, *adj.* racking.

ex'cul·pate'', *v.t.,* -pated, -pating. prove guiltless. —ex''cul·pa'tion, *n.*

ex·cur'sion, *n.* short pleasure journey. —ex·cur'sion·ist, *n.*

ex·cuse', *v.t.,* -cused, -cusing, *n. v.t* (iks kyŏoz') 1. remove or mitigate the blame of or for. 2. forgive. 3. permit to leave. —*n.* (eks kyŏos') 4. something that excuses. —ex·cus'a·ble, *adj.* —ex·cus'a·bly, *adv.*

ex'e·crate'', *v.t.,* -crated, -crating. 1. denounce. 2. detest. —ex'e·cra·ble, *adj.*

ex'e·cute'', *v.t.,* -cuted, -cuting. 1. perform. 2. kill after condemnation. —ex''e·cu'tion, *n.* —ex''e·cu'tion·er, *n.*

ex·ec'u·tive, *adj.* 1. concerned with administration of laws, policies, etc. —*n.* 2. person in an executive capacity.

ex·ec'u·tor, *n.* person who administers a will. Also, *fem.,* ex·ec'u·trix.

ex·em'pla·ry, *adj.* serving as a good example.

ex·em'pli·fy'', *v.t.,* -fied, -fying. be an example of. —ex·em''pli·fi·ca'tion, *n.*

ex·empt', *v.t., adj.* free from an obligation. —ex·emp'tion, *n.*

ex'er·cise'', *n., v.,* -cised, -cising. *n.* 1. activity developing skill, knowledge, strength, etc. 2. performance. 3. exercises, ceremony. —*v.t.* 4. cause to do exercises. 5. put into effect.

ex·ert', *v.t.* put into action. —ex·er'tion, *n.*

ex·hale', *v.,* -haled, -haling. *v.t., v.i.* breathe out. —ex''ha·la'tion, *n.*

ex·haust', *v.t.* 1. empty; deplete. 2. tire thoroughly. —*n.* 3. waste gas, etc. from machinery. —ex·haus'tion, *n.*

ex·haus'tive, *adj.* omitting nothing.

ex·hib'it, *v.t., n.* display. —ex''hi·bi' tion, *n.* —ex·hib'i·tor, *n.*

ex''hi·bi'tion·ism, *n.* ostentation; self-display. —ex''hi·bi'tion·ist, *n.*

ex·hil'a·rate'', *v.t.,* -rated, -rating. 1. fill with delight. 2. stimulate. —ex·hil''a·ra'tion, *n.*

ex·hort', *v.t.* urge strongly. —ex''hor·ta' tion, *n.*

ex·hume', *v.t.,* -humed, -huming. dig up after burial. —ex''hu·ma'tion, *n.*

ex'i·gen·cy, *n., pl.* -cies. urgency. —ex'i·gent, *adj.*

ex'ile, *v.t.,* -iled, -iling. *n. v.t.* 1. banish from a country. —*n.* 2. state of banishment. 3. exiled person.

ex·ist', *v.i.* 1. have being. 2. be alive. —ex·ist'ence, *n.* —ex·ist'ent, *adj.*

ex'it, *n.* 1. departure. 2. means of departure.

ex of·fi·ci·o (eks ''ə fish'ē ō), by virtue of his or her office.

ex·on'er·ate'', *v.t.,* -ated, -ating. declare guiltless. —ex·on''er·a'tion, *n.*

ex·or'bi·tant, *adj.* beyond reason or moderation. —ex·or'bi·tance, *n.*

ex'or·cize'', *v.t.,* -cized, -cizing. expel with incantations. —ex'or·cism, *n.*

ex·ot'ic, *adj.* markedly foreign.

ex·pand', *v.t., v.i.* widen. —ex·pan'sion, *n.* —ex·pan'sive, *adj.*

ex·panse', *n.* broad, unbroken area.

ex·pa'ti·ate'', *v.i.,* -ated, -ating. talk or write at length.

ex·pa'tri·ate, *n.* person living outside his country.

ex·pect', *v.t.* 1. regard as going to happen. 2. regard as obligatory. —ex''pec·ta'tion, ex·pect'an·cy, *n.* —ex·pec' tant, *adj.*

ex·pec'to·rate'', *v.t., v.i.,* -rated, -rating. spit.

ex·pe'di·ent, *adj.* 1. useful on a given occasion. 2. determined by self-interest alone. —*n.* 3. something expedient. —ex·pe'di·en·cy, *n.*

ex'pe·dite'', *v.t.,* -dited, -diting. 1. make faster or easier. 2. do quickly.

ex''pe·di'tion, *n.* journey for exploration or invasion. —ex''pe·di'tion·ar''y, *adj.*

ex''pe·di'tious, *adj.* prompt.

ex·pel', *v.t.,* -pelled, -pelling. 1. oust. 2. emit.

ex·pend', *v.t.* 1. spend. 2. use up. —ex·pend'i·ture, *n.*

ex·pend'a·ble, *adj.* able or intended to be sacrificed, as in war.

ex·pense', *n.* 1. act or instance of spending. 2. cost.

ex·pen′sive, *adj.* high in price.

ex·per′i·ence, *n., v.t.,* **-enced, -encing.** *n* 1. something lived through. 2. knowledge from life, work, etc. —*v.t.* 3. have experience of.

ex·per′i·ment, *n.* 1. test establishing facts. —*v.i.* 2. engage in experiments. —**ex·per″i·men·ta′tion,** *n.* —**ex·per″i·men′tal,** *adj.*

ex′pert, *n.* 1. person with specialized knowledge or skill. —*adj.* 2. pertaining to such persons. —**ex′pert·ly,** *adv.* —**ex″per·tise′, ex′pert·ness,** *n.*

ex′pi·ate″, *v.t.,* **-ated, -ating.** atone for. —**ex″pi·a′tion,** *n.* —**ex′pi·a·to″ry,** *adj.*

ex·pire′, *v.i.,* **-pired, -piring.** 1. die. 2. cease to be in effect. 3. breathe out. —**ex″pi·ra′tion,** *n.*

ex·plain′, *v.t.* 1. make understandable or meaningful. 2. account for. —**ex″pla·na′tion,** *n.* —**ex·plan′a·to″ry,** *adj.*

ex′ple·tive, *n.* exclamation.

ex′pli·ca·ble, *adj.* able to be explained.

ex·plic′it, *adj.* 1. clear. 2. outspoken.

ex·plode′, *v.,* **-ploded, -ploding.** *v.t., v.i.* burst from internal pressure. —**ex·plo′sive,** *adj., n.* —**ex·plo′sion,** *n.*

ex·ploit′, *n.* (eks′ploit) 1. daring deed. —*v.t.* (iks ploit′) 2. take advantage of. —**ex″ploi·ta′tion,** *n.* —**ex·ploit′a·tive,** *adj.*

ex·plore′, *v.,* **-plored, -ploring.** *v.t., v.i.* investigate thoroughly. —**ex·plor′er,** *n.* —**ex″plo·ra′tion,** *n.* —**ex·plor′a·to″ry,** *adj.*

ex·po′nent, *n.* 1. expounder of a principle. 2. *Math.* number indicating how many times a quantity is to be multiplied by itself.

ex·port′, *v.t.* (ik sport′, eks′port) 1. ship out of the country. —*n.* (eks′port) 2. something exported.

ex·pose′, *v.t.,* **-posed, -posing.** 1. reveal. 2. make vulnerable. —**ex·pos′ure,** *n.*

ex″po·si′tion, *n.* 1. event presenting manufactures, processes, etc. to the public. 2. explanation.

ex post facto, retroactive; retroactively.

ex·pos′tu·late″, *v.i.,* **-lated, -lating.** argue in objection. —**ex·pos″tu·la′tion,** *n.*

ex·pound′, *v.t.* state or explain.

ex·press′, *v.t.* 1. communicate adequately. 2. squeeze. —*adj.* 3. precise; definite. —*n.* 4. vehicle on a fast, direct schedule. 5. agency for sending things. —**ex·press′ive,** *adj.*

ex·pres′sion, *n.* 1. means of expressing. 2. facial attitude. 3. revelation of feeling.

ex·pro′pri·ate″, *v.t.,* **-ated, -ating.** seize for public use.

ex·pul′sion, *n.* act or instance of being expelled.

ex·punge′, *v.t.,* **-punged, -punging.** erase.

ex′pur·gate″, *v.t.,* **-gated, -gating.** censor.

ex′qui·site, *adj.* of extreme refinement.

ex′tant′, *adj.* alive; present.

ex·tem″po·ra′ne·ous, *adj.* without prior preparation.

ex·tend′, *v.t.* 1. stretch or expand. 2. offer. —*v.i.* 3. be extended. —**ex·ten′sion,** *n.*

ex·ten′sive, *adj.* large in extent or scope.

ex·tent′, *n.* amount or degree of extending.

ex·ten′u·ate″, *v.t.,* **-ated, -ating.** prompt leniency for.

ex·te′ri·or, *adj.* 1. outer or outward. —*n.* 2. outside.

ex·ter′mi·nate″, *v.t.,* **-nated, -nating.** destroy wholly. —**ex·ter″mi·na′tion,** *n.* —**ex·ter′mi·na″tor,** *n.*

ex·ter′nal, *adj.* exterior; outward.

ex·tinct′, *adj.* no longer in existence.

ex·tinc′tion, *n.* dying-out or destruction.

ex·tin′guish, *v.t.* put out of existence, as a flame.

ex′tir·pate″, *v.t.,* **-pated, -pating.** uproot; exterminate.

ex·tol′, *v.t.,* **-tolled, -tolling.** praise highly.

ex·tort′, *v.t.* obtain by threats or force. —**ex·tor′tion,** *n.* —**ex·tor′tion·ist,** *n.* —**ex·tor′tion·ate,** *adj.*

ex′tra, *adj.* additional.

ex·tract′, *v.t.* (ik strakt′) 1. draw out. —*n.* (ek′strakt) 2. something extracted. —**ex·trac′tion,** *n.*

ex′tra·dite″, *v.t.,* **-dited, -diting.** surrender for prosecution to a foreign country. —**ex′tra·di″tion,** *n.*

ex·tra′ne·ous, *adj.* 1. from outside. 2. irrelevant.

ex·tra·or′di·nar″y, *adj.* 1. remarkable. 2. out of the ordinary.

ex·trav′a·gant, *adj.* beyond economy, reason, etc. —**ex·trav′a·gance,** *n.*

ex·treme′, *adj.* 1. farthest. 2. ultimate. 3. immoderate. —*n.* 4. farthest point, position, etc. —**ex·treme′ly,** *adv.*

ex·trem′i·ty, *n., pl.* **-ties.** *n.* 1. something extreme. 2. end. 3. extremities, hands and feet.

ex′tri·cate″, *v.t.,* **-cated, -cating.** free.

ex′tro·vert″, *n.* person oriented toward the outside world. —**ex″tro·ver′sion,** *n*

ex·u′ber·ant, *adj.* full of health and spirits. —**ex·u′ber·ance,** *n.*

ex·ude′, *v.,* **-uded, -uding.** *v.t., v.i.* 1. pass through the pores. 2. seem to radiate. —**exu·da′tion,** *n.*

ex·ult′, *v.i.* rejoice. —**ex″ul·ta′tion,** *n.*

eye, *n.* 1. organ of sight. 2. eyelike opening. 3. visual sensitivity. —**eye′brow″,**

n. —eye′ball″, n. —eye′lid″, n. —eye′
sight″, n.
eye′lash″, n. row of stiff hairs over the
eye.
eye′sore″, n. unpleasant sight.

F

F, f., n. 1. sixth letter of the English alphabet. 2. sixth-best grade.
fa′ble, n. 1. moralizing story. 2. legend.
fab′ric, n. cloth.
fab′ri·cate″, v.t., -cated, -cating. 1. assemble. 2. invent for deception. —fab″
ri·ca′tion, n.
fab′u·lous, adj. wonderful.
fa·cade, (fə sahd′), n. decorative building
front. Also, fa·çade′.
face, n., v., faced, facing. n. 1. front of
the human head. 2. main surface. 3.
outer appearance. —v.t. 4. confront.
—v.i. 5. look or be turned toward.
—fa′cial, adj.
fac′et, n. 1. plane surface of a gem, etc. 2.
aspect.
fa·ce′tious, adj. joking; impish; frivolous.
fac′ile, adj. revealing no effort.
fa·cil′i·tate″, v.t., -tated, -tating. make
easy.
fa·cil′i·ty, n., pl. -ties. 1. ease. 2. skill. 3.
facilities, equipment, staff, etc.
fac·sim′i·le, n. copy; reproduction.
fact, n. objective truth. —fac′tu·al, adj.
fac′tion, n. group promoting its own interests. —fac′tion·al, adj.
fac′tor, n. 1. influential thing. 2. quantity
multiplied by another.
fac′to·ry, n., pl. -ries. place of manufacture.
fac·to′tum, n. person who does odd
jobs.
fac′ul·ty, n., pl. -ties. 1. aptitude or ability. 2. teaching staff.
fad, n. brief fashion or whim.
fade, v., faded, fading. v.i. 1. lose color
or freshness. 2. disappear slowly.
fag, v.t., fagged, fagging. tire.
Fahr′en·heit″, adj. pertaining to a temperature scale with the freezing point
of water at 32 degrees and the boiling
point at 212 degrees.
fail, v.t. 1. attempt without success. 2.
not to do. 3. disappoint. —v.i. 4. have
no success. 5. die away. —fail′ing, n.
—fail′ure, n.
faint, adj. 1. weak. —n. 2. temporary loss
of consciousness. —v.i. 3. go into a
faint. —faint′ly, adv. —faint′ness, n.

fair, adj. 1. honest; just. 2. beautiful or
handsome. 3. light. 4. mediocre. 5.
sunny. 6. gathering for sales or display.
—fair′ly, adv.
fair′y, n., pl. -ies. creature with magic
powers.
faith, n. 1. belief; confidence. 2. loyalty.
3. religion. —faith′ful, adj. —faith′
less, adj.
fake, adj., n., v.t., faked, faking. adj. 1.
false. —n. 2. something false. —v.t. 3.
give a false appearance of. —fak′er, n.
fal′con, n. small hawk.
fall, v.i., fell, fallen, falling, n. v.i. 1. descend without support. —n. 2. act or
instance of falling. 3. autumn.
fal′la·cy, n., pl. -cies. instance of false
reasoning. —fal·la′cious, adj.
fal′li·ble, adj. capable of mistakes.
—fal″li·bil′i·ty, n.
fal′low, adj. unplanted.
false, adj., falser, falsest. 1. not true. 2.
untruthful or unfaithful. —false′ly,
adv. —false′hood″, n. —fal′si·fy″,
v.t. —fal′si·ty, n.
fal·set′to, n., pl. -tos. artificially high
voice.
fal′ter, v.i. act, speak, etc. hesitantly or
unsteadily.
fame, n. widespread reputation. —fa′
mous, famed, adj.
fa·mil′iar, adj. 1. well known. 2. well acquainted. —fa·mil′iar·ly, adv. —fa·
mil″i·ar′i·ty, n. —fa·mil′iar·ize″, v.t.
fam′i·ly, n., pl. -lies. 1. group of relatives. 2. group of related things. —fa·
mil′ial, adj.
fam′ine, n. severe food shortage.
fam′ish, v.t. starve.
fan, n., v.t., fanned, fanning. n. 1. device
for moving air. 2. Informal. devotee.
—v.t. 3. cool or move with a fan.
fa·nat′ic, n. irrational enthusiast or hater. —fa·nat′i·cal, adj. —fa·nat′i·
cism, n.
fan′ci·er, n. breeder of animals or plants.
fan′cy, adj., -cier, -ciest, n., v.t., -cied,
-cying. adj. 1. elaborate. —n. 2. imagination. 3. liking. —v.t. 6. take a liking
to. —fan′ci·ful, adj. —fan′ci·ly, adv.
fan′fare′, n. 1. introductory call of trum-
pets, etc. 2. publicity.
fang, n. long, pointed tooth.
fan·tas′tic, adj. odd and extravagant.
fan′ta·sy, n., pl. -sies. 1. imagination. 2.
something imagined.
far, adj., adv., farther, farthest. at or to a
great distance.
farce, n. ridiculous comedy. —far′ci·cal,
adj.
fare, n., v.i., fared, faring. n. 1. money
paid to travel. 2. food. —v.i. 3. pros-
per or succeed.
fare′well′, interj., n., adj. goodbye.
far′-fetched′, adj. implausible.

farm, *n*. **1**. place for raising plants or animals. —*v.t*. **2**. cultivate. —**farm′er**, *n*. —**farm′hand″**, *n*. —**farm′house″**, *n*. —**farm′yard″**, *n*.

far′-off′, *adj*. remote.

far′-reach′ing, *adj*. with extensive effects.

far′sight″ed, *adj*. **1**. provident. **2**. seeing distant objects better than close ones.

fas′ci·nate″, *v.t*., **-nated, -nating**. hold the entire attention of. —**fas″ci·na′tion**, *n*.

Fas′cism, *n*. authoritarian, militaristic system of government. —**Fas′cist**, *n*., *adj*. —**Fas·cis′tic**, *adj*.

fash′ion, *n*. **1**. manner of acting. **2**. prevailing style. —*v.t*. **2**. make. —**fash′ion·a·ble**, *adj*.

fast, *adj*. **1**. speedy. **2**. firm; fixed. —*adv*. **3**. firmly. —*v.i*. **4**. abstain from food or drink. —*n*. **5**. act or instance of fasting.

fast′en, *v.t*. attach; make secure. —**fas′ten·er**, *n*. —**fast′en·ing**, *n*.

fas·tid′i·ous, *adj*. not readily pleased. —**fas·tid′i·ous·ly**, *adv*.

fat, *adj*., **fatter, fattest**, *n*. *adj*. **1**. having much fat. —*n*. **2**. greasy material. —**fat′ness**, *n*. —**fat′ty**, *adj*.

fa′tal, *adj*. causing death or destruction. —**fa′tal·ly**, *adv*.

fa′tal·ism, *n*. **1**. belief in fate. **2**. resignation. —**fa′tal·ist**, *n*. —**fa″tal·is′tic**, *adj*. —**fa″tal·is′ti·cal·ly**, *adv*.

fa·tal′i·ty, *n*., *pl*. **-ties**. **1**. deadliness. **2**. death by accident.

fate, *n*. **1**. power determining events. **2**. death.

fa′ther, *n*. **1**. male parent. **2**. founder or originator. **3**. Christian priest. —**fa′ther·hood″**, *n*. —**fa′ther·ly**, *adj*.

fa′ther-in-law″, *n*., *pl*. **fathers-in-law**. father of a spouse.

fath′om, *n*. **1**. *Nautical*. unit of 6 linear feet. —*v.t*. **2**. probe to understand.

fa·tigue′, *n*., *v.t*., **-tigued, -tiguing**. *n*. **1**. weariness. **2**. **fatigues**, military work clothes. —*v.t*. **3**. tire thoroughly.

fat′ten, *v.t*. **1**. make fat. —*v.i*. **2**. become fat.

fat′ty, *adj*. containing fat.

fat′u·ous, *adj*. foolishly self-satisfied. —**fa·tu′i·ty**, *n*.

fau′cet, *n*. valve for running water; tap.

fault, *n*. defect. —**fault′y**, *adj*.

fau′na, *n*., *pl*. animals.

faux pas (fō′pah′), *pl*. **faux pas**. social mistake.

fa′vor, *n*. **1**. act of kindness. **2**. approval. —*v.t*. **3**. do a favor for. **4**. treat as a favorite. **5**. advocate or support. —**fa′vor·a·ble**, *adj*. —**fa′vor·ite**, *adj*., *n*.

fa′vor·it·ism, *n*. preferential treatment for favorites.

fawn, *v.i*. **1**. show servility. —*n*. **2**. young deer.

faze, *v.t*., **fazed, fazing**. daunt.

fear, *n*. **1**. desire to escape danger. **2**. awe. —*v.t*. **3**. have fear of. **4**. believe with regret. —**fear′ful**, *adj*. —**fear′less**, *adj*.

fea′si·ble, *adj*. able to be done; practical. —**fea″si·bil′i·ty**, *n*.

feast, *n*. **1**. religious festival. **2**. lavish meal. —*v.i*. **3**. have a feast.

feat, *n*. act of skill or daring.

feath′er, *n*. part of a bird's covering. —**feath′er·y**, *adj*.

fea′ture, *n*., *v.t*., **-tured, turing**. *n*. **1**. distinct aspect. **2**. **features**, face. —*v.t*. **4**. present as a feature.

Feb′ru·ar″y, *n*. second month.

fe′ces, *n*., *pl*. solid excrement. —**fe′cal**, *adj*.

feck′less, *adj*. **1**. ineffectual. **2**. irresponsible.

fe′cund, *adj*. fertile. —**fe·cun′di·ty**, *n*.

fed′er·al, *adj*. **1**. composed of federated states. **2**. pertaining to a federation.

fed″er·a′tion, *n*. union of states or organizations under a central government or authority.

fee, *n*. charge for services.

fee′ble, *adj*., **-bler, -blest**. without energy or force. —**fee′bly**, *adv*. —**fee′ble·ness**, *n*.

feed, *v*., **fed, feeding**, *n*. *v.t*. **1**. nourish with food. —*v.i*. **2**. eat. —*n*. **3**. animal food.

feed″back, *n*. **1**. noise caused by a microphone picking up its own amplified signal. **2**. reactions to an idea or course of action.

feel, *v*., **felt, feeling**, *n*. *v.t*. **1**. sense by touch. **2**. be aware of. **3**. believe. —*v.i*. **4**. be sensed as specified. —*n*. **5**. feeling; sensation. —**feel′ing**, *n*.

feign, *v.t*. pretend.

feint, *n*. **1**. false attack made as a diversion. —*v.i*. **2**. make a feint.

fe·lic′i·tate″, *v.t*., **-tated, -tating**. congratulate. —**fe·lic″i·ta′tion**, *n*.

fe·lic′i·tous, *adj*. appropriate. —**fe·lic′i·tous·ly**, *adv*.

fe·lic′i·ty, *n*., *pl*. **-ties**. happiness.

fe′line, *adj*. pertaining to the cat family.

fell, *v.t*. cause to fall.

fel′low, *n*. **1**. man. **2**. companion. —**fel′low·ship″**, *n*.

fel′on, *n*. committer of a major crime. —**fel′on·y**, *n*. —**fe·lo′ni·ous**, *adj*.

felt, *n*. fabric of compacted wool, etc.

fe′male, *adj*. **1**. pertaining to the sex bearing offspring. —*n*. **2**. someone or something female.

fem′i·nine, *adj*. characteristic of girls and women. —**fem″i·nin′i·ty**, *n*.

fence, *n*., *v*., **fenced, fencing**. *n*. **1**. light barrier. —*v.i*. **2**. fight with thrusting swords.

fend, *v.t*. drive or ward.

fend′er, *n*. cover for a wheel on a vehicle.

fer·ment, *v.t.* (fər ment') **1.** break down, as through bacterial action. —*v.i.* **2.** be broken down, as an organic substance. —*n.* (fər'ment) **3.** anticipatory excitement. —**fer''men·ta'tion**, *n.*

fern, *n.* fronded plant reproduced by spores.

fe·ro'cious, *adj.* savage. —**fe·ro'cious·ly**, *adv.* —**fe·roc'i·ty**, *n.*

fer'ret, *n.* **1.** weasellike animal. —*v.i.* **2.** hunt; search.

fer'rous, *adj.* pertaining to iron. Also, **fer'ric.**

fer'ry, *n., pl.* **-ries**, *v.t.,* **-ried**, **-rying.** *n.* **1.** Also, **fer'ry·boat''**, boat on a shuttle service. **2.** service running such a boat. —*v.t.* **3.** transport by or as by a ferry.

fer'tile, *adj.* yielding offspring, crops, etc. —**fer·til'i·ty**, *n.* —**fer'til·ize''**, *v.t.*

fer'vent, *adj.* passionate. Also, **fer'vid.** —**fer'vent·ly**, *adv.* —**fer'ven·cy**, **fer'vor**, *n.*

fes'ti·val, *n.* occasion of celebration or merrymaking. —**fes'tive**, *adj.* —**fes·tiv'i·ty**, *n.*

fes·toon', *n.* **1.** decorative hanging suspended between two supports. —*v.t.* **2.** drape.

fetch, *v.t.* **1.** get. **2.** summon.

fete (fāt), *n., v.t.,* **feted, feting.** *n.* **1.** festive entertainment. —*v.t.* **2.** honor with a fete. Also, **fête.**

fet'id, *adj.* evil-smelling.

fet'ish, *n.* subject of obsessive concern.

fet'ter, *n., v.t.* shackle or chain.

fet'tle, *n.* **in fine fettle,** in excellent state.

fe'tus, *n., pl.* **-tuses.** unborn young in its later state. —**fe'tal**, *adj.*

feud, *n.* murderous rivalry between families.

feu'dal·ism, *n.* system of serfs and overlords. —**feu'dal**, *adj.*

fe'ver, *n.* excess of body temperature. —**fe'ver·ish**, *adj.*

fe'ver blis'ter, *n.* a cold sore.

few, *adj., pron., n.* some but not many.

fi·an·cé (fē''ahn sā'), *n.* man engaged to be married. Also, *fem.,* **fi''an·cée'.**

fi·as'co, *n., pl.* **-coes, -cos.** ridiculous failure.

fi'at, *n.* decree.

fi'ber, *n.* long, thin piece of material. Also, **fi'bre.**

fick'le, *adj.* capricious and untrustworthy.

fic'tion, *n.* **1.** not factually true. **2.** novels, etc. —**fic'tion·al**, *adj.*

fic·ti'tious, *adj.* not factually true.

fid'dle, *n., v.i.,* **-dled, -dling.** *n.* **1.** violin. —*v.i.* **2.** play a fiddle. **3.** fumble. —**fid'dler**, *n.*

fi·del'i·ty, *n.* faithfulness.

fid'get, *v.i.* move or fumble nervously. —*n.* **2.** nervous state. —**fid'get·y**, *adj.*

fi·du'ci·ar''y, *adj., n., pl.* **-ies.** *adj.* **1.** pertaining to a trust. —*n.* **2.** trustee.

field, *n.* **1.** area of open land. **2.** area of work or knowledge.

fiend, *n.* **1.** evil spirit. **2.** vicious person. —**fiend'ish**, *adj.*

fierce, *adj.,* **fiercer, fiercest. 1.** savage. **2.** violent. —**fierce'ly**, *adv.*

fier'y, *adj.,* **-ier, -iest. 1.** covered or filled with fire. **2.** passionate.

fi·es'ta, *n.* festival in a Spanish-speaking region.

fife, *n.* small flute.

fif·teen', *n.* ten plus five. —**fif'teenth'**, *adj.*

fifth, *adj.* **1.** following the fourth. —*n.* **2.** fifth thing, person, or part.

fif'ty, *n., adj.* five times ten. —**fif'ti·eth**, *adj.*

fig, *n.* small, sweet tree fruit.

fight, *n., v.,* **fought, fighting.** *n.* **1.** dispute or competition with violence. **2.** angry argument. —*v.t.* **3.** make a fight against. —*v.i.* **4.** engage in a fight.

fig'ment, *n.* something merely imaginary.

fig'u·ra·tive, *adj.* using or forming a figure of speech.

fig'ure, *n., v.t.,* **-ured, -uring.** *n.* **1.** shape. **2.** numeral. **3.** sum. —*v.t., v.i.* **4.** calculate.

figure of speech, word or idiom not to be taken literally or in the usual way.

fil'a·ment, *n.* narrow thread or wire.

fil'bert, *n.* hazelnut.

filch, *v.t.* steal.

file, *n., v.t.,* **-filed, -filing.** *n.* **1.** group of documents. **2.** tool for rubbing. **3.** front-to-rear row. —*v.t.* **4.** preserve in a file. **5.** rub with a file.

fil'i·al, *adj.* pertaining to or appropriate in a son or daughter.

fil'i·bus''ter, *n.* meaningless speech hindering legislation.

fil'i·gree'', *n.* lace-like gold or silver wirework.

fill, *v.t.* **1.** cause to be completely occupied. **2.** satisfy the requirements of. —*v.i.* **3.** become full. —*n.* **4.** enough to fill.

fil·let (fil'ā), *n.* boneless lean cut of meat or fish.

fil'lip, *n.* stimulus.

film, *n.* **1.** thin coating. **2.** strip or sheet for registering photographic images. —*v.t.* **3.** make a motion picture or photograph of.

fil'ter, *n.* **1.** something screening out unwanted things. —*v.t., v.i.* **2.** pass through a filter. —*v.t.* **3.** exclude with a filter.

filth, *n.* foul matter. —**filth'y**, *adj.*

fin, *n.* bladelike extension.

fi'nal, *adj.* at the end. —**fi'nal·ly**, *adv.* —**fi·nal'i·ty**, *n.*

fi·na·le (fi na'lē), *n.* concluding feature.

fi′nal·ist, *n.* competitor in a final contest.

fi·nance (fi nans′, fī′nans), *n., v.t.,* **-nanced, -nancing.** *n.* 1. management of money. 2. **finances**, resources of money. —*v.t.* 3. lend or obtain money for. —**fi·nan′cial,** *adj.* —**fi″nan·cier′,** *n.*

find, *v.t.,* **found, finding,** *n. v.t.* 1. come upon by chance. 2. succeed in a search for. —*n.* 3. valuable discovery. —**find′er,** *n.* —**find′ing,** *n.*

fine, *adj.,* **finer, finest,** *n., v.t.,* **fined, fining.** *adj.* 1. in tiny pieces. 2. excellent. —*n.* 3. money penalty. —*v.t.* 4. impose a fine on. —**fine′ly,** *adv.* —**fine′ness,** *n.*

fin′er·y, *n.* fine costume.

fi·nesse′, *n.* skill, esp. in human relations.

fine″-tune″, *v.* to make minor adjustments.

fin′ger, *n.* extension of the hand.

fin′ick·y, *adj.* too particular or demanding. Also, **fin′i·cal, fin′ick·ing.**

fi′nis, *n., pl.* **-nises.** end; finish.

fin′ish, *v.t.* 1. bring to an end. 2. give a desired surface to. —*v.i.* 3. end an activity.

fi·nite (fī′nīt), *adj.* not endless.

fir, *n.* cone-bearing evergreen tree.

fire, *n., v.* **fired, firing.** *n.* 1. burning. 2. deep feeling. 3. discharge of guns. —*v.t.* 4. set fire to. 5. discharge, as of a gun. —**fire′proof″,** *adj.*

fire′arm″, *n.* weapon operated by explosives.

fire′crack″er, *n.* a firework.

fire′man, *n.* 1. person who extinguishes fires. 2. person who tends fires.

fire′trap″, *n.* building dangerous in fires.

fire′works″, *n., pl.* explosive and burning devices used in celebrations.

firm, *adj.* 1. unyielding. 2. steady. —*n.* 3. business organization. —**firm′ly,** *adv.* —**firm′ness,** *n.*

fir′ma·ment, *n.* heavens.

first, *adj., adv.* 1. at the very front or beginning. 2. before all others. —*n.* 3. first person or thing.

first′-hand′, *adj., adv.* without intermediaries.

fis′cal, *adj.* pertaining to income and expense; financial.

fish, *n., pl.* **fish,** *v.i. n.* 1. cold-blooded water animal, breathing with gills. —*v.i.* 2. attempt to catch fish. —**fish′er·man,** *n.*

fis′sion, *n.* splitting; cleaving. —**fis′sion·a·ble.** *adj.*

fis′sure, *n.* crack.

fist, *n.* ball of the hand and fingers for striking.

fit, *v.,* **fitted, fitting,** *adj.,* **fitter, fittest,** *n. v.i.* 1. be suitable, esp. in size. —*v.t.* 2. be suitable for. 3. cause to be suitable. —*adj.* 4. suitable. 5. healthy. —*n.* 6.

manner of fitting. 7. bodily seizure.

fit′ful, *adj.* intermittent; spasmodic. —**fit′ful·ly,** *adv.* —**fit′ful·ness,** *n.*

fit′ting, *adj.* suitable.

five, *adj., n.* four plus one.

fix, *v.t.,* **fixed, fixing.** 1. repair oradjust. 2. prepare. 3. establish firmly. —**fix′i·ty,** *n.*

fix·a′tion, *n.* psychological obsession.

fix′ture, *n.* attached piece of equipment.

fizz, *v.i.* **fizzed, fizzing,** *n. v.i.* 1. emit a buzzing bubbling sound. —*n.* 2. such a sound.

fiz′zle, *v.i.,* **-zled, -zling,** *n. v.i.* 1. fail. —*n.* 2. failure.

flab′by, *adj.,* **-bier, -biest.** fat, soft, and weak.

flac·cid (flak′sid) *adj.* flabby.

flag, *n., v.,* **flagged, flagging.** *n.* 1. emblem-bearing cloth. 2. Also, **flag′stone″,** flat paving stone. —*v.t.* 3. signal with a flag.

fla′grant, *adj.* outrageously evident. —**fla′grant·ly,** *adv.* —**fla′gran·cy,** *n.*

flail, *n.* 1. hand-held threshing device. —*v.t.* 2. beat or move in a flaillike manner.

flair, *n.* shrewd perceptiveness or talent.

flake, *n., v.,* **flaked, flaking.** *n.* 1. thin piece. —*v.i.* 2. fall off in flakes.

flam·boy′ant, *adj.* brashly ostentatious. —**flam·boy′ance,** *n.*

flame, *n., v.,* **flamed, flaming.** *n.* burning gas. —*v.i.* 2. be burned with flames.

fla·min′go, *n., pl.* **-gos.** pink tropical wading bird.

flam′ma·ble, *adj.* burnable.

flange, *n.* perpendicular edge.

flank, *n.* 1. side. —*v.t.* 2. be beside. 3. attack or get around the flank of.

flan′nel, *n.* loosely woven wool or cotton.

flap, *n., v.,* **flapped, flapping.** *n.* 1. hinged panel. 2. sound of flapping. —*v.t., v.i.* 3. move to and fro.

flare, *v.i.,* **flared, flaring,** *n. v.i.* 1. blaze. 2. curve outward. —*n.* 3. torchlike signal.

flash, *n.* 1. momentary bright light. 2. moment. —*v.i.* 3. emit a flash. —*v.t.* 4. cause to flash.

flash′light″, *n.* hand-held battery-operated light.

flash′y, *adj.,* **-ier, -iest.** showy. —**flash′i·ness,** *n.*

flask, *n.* bottle, often flat.

flat, *adj.,* **flatter, flattest** *n., adj.* 1. without rises or hollows. 2. absolute. 3. featureless. 4. *Music.* slightly low in pitch. —*n.* 5. apartment. 6. something flat. —**flat′ly,** *adv.* —**flat′ten,** *v.t., v.i.*

flat′ter, *v.t.* compliment, as in order to wheedle. —**flat′ter·y,** *n.*

flaunt, *v.t.* display proudly.

fla′vor, *n.* 1. taste. 2. Also, **fla′vor·ing,**

something giving a certain taste. —*v.t.*
3. add a flavor to.

flaw, *n.* shortcoming; fault. —**flaw'less,**
adj.

flax, *n.* threadlike plant fiber for linen.

flea, *n.* bloodsucking, wingless jumping
insect.

fleck, *n.* spot or flake.

fledg'ling, *n.* beginner at a profession,
etc.

flee, *v.,* **fled, fleeing.** *v.t., v.i.* escape;
run.

fleece, *n.* **1.** covering of a sheep, etc.
—*v.t.* **2.** cheat. —**fleec'y,** *adj.*

fleet, *n.* **1.** ships under one command.
—*adj.* **2.** swift.

fleet'ing, *adj.* passing quickly.

flesh, *n.* **1.** muscle tissue. **2.** soft part of a
plant. **3.** animal meat. —**flesh'y,** *adj.*

flex, *v.t., v.i.* bend. —**flex'i·ble,** *adj.*

flex''time, flex''i·time, *n.* system in
which work hours are flexible.

flick, *n.* **1.** quick, light motion. —*v.t.* **2.**
throw, etc. with such a motion.

flick'er, *v.i.* have a wavering light or appearance.

fli'er, *n.* **1.** aviator. **2.** advertising paper.

flight, *n.* **1.** act or instance of flying or
fleeing. **2.** stair between floors.

flight'y, *adj.,* **-ier, -iest.** overly emotional
or whimsical. —**flight'i·ness,** *n.*

flim'sy, *adj.,* **-ier, -iest.** readily torn or
broken. —**flim'si·ly,** *adv.*

flinch, *v.i.* hold back or retreat, as from a
blow.

fling, *v.t.,* **flung, flinging.** *n. v.t.* **1.** hurl.
—*n.* **2.** act or instance of flinging. **3.**
brief indulgence.

flint, *n.* spark-producing gray siliceous
rock. —**flint'y,** *adj.*

flip, *v.t.,* **flipped, flipping.** *n. v.t.* **1.** toss
jerkily. —*n.* **2.** act or instance of flip-
ping.

flip'pant, *adj.* cheerfully disrespectful.
—**flip'pan·cy,** *n.*

flip'per, *n.* flat limb for paddling.

flirt, *v.i.* **1.** make mild erotic advances. **2.**
consider something unseriously. —**flir-
ta'tion,** *n.* —**flir·ta'tious,** *adj.*

flit, *v.i.,* **flitted, flitting.** move quickly and
lightly.

float, *v.i.* **1.** be carried on water, etc. —*n.*
2. something that floats.

flock, *n.* **1.** group of sheep, etc. —*v.i.* **2.**
join in a flock.

flog, *v.t.,* **flogged, flogging.** whip.

flood, *n.* **1.** overflow, as of a river. —*v.t.,
v.i.* **2.** fill to excess.

flood'light'', *n.* lamp casting a directed
light.

floor, *n.* **1.** supporting interior surface. **2.**
bottom surface. **3.** right to speak.
—*v.t.* **4.** supply with a floor. —**floor'
ing,** *n.*

floor ex'er·cise'', *n.* tumbling maneuvers
performed on a mat in a competitive

gymnastics event.

flop, *v.,* **flopped, flopping.** *n. v.t., v.i.* **1.**
overturn heavily. —*v.i.* **2.** move clum-
sily. **3.** *Informal.* fail. —*n.* **4.** act or instance of flopping.

flo'ra, *n., pl.* plants.

flo'ral, *adj.* pertaining to flowers.

flor'id, *adj.* **1.** ruddy. **2.** gaudy.

flo'rist, *n.* flower merchant.

floss, *n.* soft down or twisted thread.
—**flos'sy,** *adj.*

flo·til'la, *n.* small fleet.

flounce, *v.i.,* **flounced, flouncing.** *n. v.i.*
1. move quickly and jerkily. —*n.* **2.** act
or instance of flouncing.

floun'der, *n.* **1.** edible flat fish. —*v.i.* **2.**
struggle.

flour, *n.* powdered grain, etc.

flour'ish, *v.i.* **1.** thrive. —*v.t.* **2.** wave.

flow, *v.i.* **1.** move steadily, as a liquid.
—*n.* **2.** act or instance of flowing.

flow'er, *n.* **1.** petaled seed-producing part
of a plant; blossom. —*v.i.* **2.** produce
blossoms. —**flow'er·y,** *adj.*

flu, *n.* influenza.

fluc'tu·ate'', *v.i.,* **-ated, -ating.** change
rate or quantity irregularly. —**fluc''tu·
a'tion,** *n.*

flue, *n.* passage for smoke, etc.

flu'ent, *adj.* speaking or writing readily.
—**flu'en·cy,** *n.*

fluff, *n.* soft fibrous material. —**fluff'y,**
adj.

flu'id, *adj.* **1.** flowing. —*n.* **2.** liquid or
gas.

fluke, *n.* **1.** barb. **2.** stroke of luck.

flume, *n.* chute carrying water.

flunk, *v.t., v.i. Informal.* fail at school.

flur'ry, *n., pl.* **-ries.** brief spells of activity, weather, etc.

flush, *v.t.* **1.** wash out. **2.** frighten from
cover. —*v.i.* **3.** be flushed. **4.** blush.
—*n.* **5.** act or instance of flushing.
—*adj.* **6.** even. **7.** wealthy.

flus'ter, *v.t.* confuse.

flute, *n.* **1.** high-pitched wind instrument.
2. Also **flut'ing,** longitudinal concavi-
ty. —**flut'ist,** *n.*

flut'ter, *v.t., v.i.* **1.** oscillate rapidly. —*n.*
2. excited state. —**flut'ter·y,** *adj.*

flux, *n.* **1.** fluid state. **2.** substance aiding
metal fusion.

fly, *v.,* **flew, flown, flying,** *n., pl.* **flies,**
v.i. **1.** move in the air. **2.** go quickly.
—*v.t.* **3.** cause to move in the air. **4.**
flee from. —*n.* **5.** two-winged insect.

flying colors, great success.

fly'wheel'', *n.* heavy wheel regulating a
machine by inertia.

foam, *n.* **1.** fine bubbles. —*v.i.* **2.** emit or
break into foam. —**foam'y,** *adj.*

fo'cus, *n., pl.* **-cuses, -ci,** *v.,* **-cused,
-cusing.** *n.* **1.** point of concentration.
2. state of sharpness or clarity. —*v.t.*
3. bring into focus.

fod′der, *n.* food for horses, cows, etc.

foe, *n.* enemy.

foe′tus, *n.* fetus.

fog, *n., v.,* **fogged, fogging.** *n.* **1.** water vapor obscuring vision. —*v.t., v.i.* **2.** obscure with fog. —**fog′gy,** *adj.*

fo′gy, *n., pl.* **-gies.** reactionary. Also, **fo′gey.**

foi′ble, *n.* weakness.

foil, *v.t.* **1.** frustrate. —*n.* **2.** thin metal sheeting. **3.** pointed sword. **4.** contrasting feature.

foist, *v.t.* get accepted by trickery.

fold, *v.t., v.i.* **1.** double over. **2.** wrap. —*n.* **3.** folded place.

fold′er, *n.* **1.** bent sheet for holding papers. **2.** folded, unbound pamphlet.

fol′i·age, *n.* leaves.

folk, *n.* **1.** folks, **a.** people. **b.** relatives. —*adj.* **2.** pertaining to ethnic groups. —**folk′lore″,** *n.*

folk′sy, *adj.,* **-sier, -siest.** *Informal.* characteristic of ordinary people.

fol′low, *v.t.* **1.** go after or along. **2.** happen after. **3.** conform to. **4.** learn from or understand. —*v.i.* **5.** go or happen after. **6.** be logically deductible.

fol′low·er, *n.* disciple or adherent.

fol′low·ing, *adj.* **1.** happening afterwards. —*prep.* **2.** after. —*n.* **3.** group of followers.

fol′ly, *n., pl.* **-lies.** mad or foolish thing or disposition.

fo·ment′, *v.t.* incite, as trouble.

fond, *adj.* full of affection. —**fond′ly,** *adv.* —**fond′ness,** *n.*

fon′dle, *v.t.,* **-dled, -dling.** handle fondly.

font, *n.* baptismal basin.

food, *n.* material that nourishes. —**food′stuff″,** *n.*

fool, *n.* **1.** person of bad judgment. —*v.t.* **2.** deceive. —*v.i.* **3.** act like a fool. —**fool′ish,** *adj.*

fool′hard″y, *adj.,* **-dier, -diest.** unwisely audacious.

fool′proof″, *adj.* proof against failure.

foot, *n.* **1.** extremity of a leg. **2.** lower-most feature; bottom; pedestal. **3.** unit of 12 inches. —**foot′hold″,** *n.* —**foot′step″,** *n.*

foot′ball″, *n.* **1.** game with a kicked ball. **2.** ball used.

foot′ing, *n.* **1.** support for a foot. **2.** basis.

foot′print, *n.* **1.** mark left by a foot. **2.** area required for an office machine.

fop, *n.* dressy, affected person. —**fop′pish,** *adj.*

for, *prep.* **1.** in favor of. **2.** in place of. **3.** in order to reach, etc. **4.** to be used, etc. by. **5.** during. **6.** obtaining in exchange. **7.** considering the nature of. —*conj.* **8.** because.

for′age, *v.i.,* **-aged, -aging,** *n.* search, as for food.

for′ay, *n.* plundering expedition.

for·bear′, *v.,* **-bore, -borne, -bearing.** *v.t.* **1.** refrain. —*v.i.* **2.** control oneself. —**for·bear′ance,** *n.*

for·bid′, *v.t.,* **-bade** or **-bad, -bidden, -bidding. 1.** give an order against. **2.** prevent.

for·bid′ding, *adj.* formidable or unapproachable.

force, *n., v.t.,* **forced, forcing.** *n.* **1.** agency influencing events. **2.** power. **3.** compulsion. **4.** organization or group. —*v.t.* **5.** compel. —**force′ful,** *adj.* —**for′ci·ble,** *adj.*

ford, *n.* **1.** wadeable part of a stream. —*v.t.* **2.** wade across.

fore, *adj., adv.* **1.** forward. —*n.* **2.** front.

fore·arm, *n.* (for′ahrm) **1.** arm between the elbow and wrist. —*v.t.* (for arm′) **2.** arm in advance.

fore′bear″, *n.* ancestor.

fore·bod′ing, *n.* premonition.

fore′cast′, *v.t.,* **-cast** or **-casted, -casting,** *n. v.t.* **1.** predict. —*n.* **2.** prediction.

fore·cas·tle (fōk′səl) *n.* upper forward part of a ship.

fore·close′, *v.t.,* **-closed, -closing.** deprive a mortgagor of the right of redeeming. —**fore·clos′ure,** *n.*

fore′fath″er, *n.* ancestor.

fore′fin″ger, *n.* finger nearest the thumb.

fore′front″, *n.* extreme forward position.

fore·gath′er, *v.i.* come together.

fore·go″ing, *adj.* preceding.

fore·gone′, *adj.* **1.** determined in advance. **2.** previous.

fore′ground″, *n.* area nearest the viewer.

fore′head, *n.* front of the head between the eyebrows and hair.

for′eign, *adj.* **1.** belonging to an area outside the country. **2.** not belonging where found. —**for′eign·er,** *n.*

fore′man, *n.* supervising worker.

fore′most″, *adj., adv.* first.

fore′noon″, *n.* morning after sunrise.

fo·ren′sic, *adj.* pertaining to legal proceedings or public debate.

fore″or·dain′, *v.t.* predestine. —**fore·or″di·na′tion,** *n.*

fore′run″ner, *n.* predecessor.

fore·see′, *v.t.,* **-saw, -seen, -seeing.** anticipate. —**fore·see′a·ble,** *adj.* —**fore′sight″,** *n.*

fore·shad′ow, *v.t.* hint at in advance.

for′est, *n.* area of trees. —**for″es·ta′tion,** *n.* —**for′est·ry,** *n.*

fore·stall′, *v.t.* prevent by early action.

fore·tell′, *v.t.,* **-told, -telling.** predict.

fore′thought″, *n.* planning, etc. in advance.

for·ev′er, *adv.* **1.** eternally. **2.** ceaselessly.

fore·warn′, *v.t.* warn beforehand.

fore′word″, *n.* book introduction.

for′feit, *v.t.* **1.** have taken away because of a misdeed, etc. —*n.* **2.** something forfeited. —*adj.* 3. forfeited. —**for'fei·ture,** *n.*

forge, *n., v.,* **forged, forging.** *n.* 1. place. for hammering hot metal. —*v.t.* 2. shape or assemble by hammering. 3. counterfeit. —*v.i.* 4. move against obstacles. —**forg'er,** *n.* —**forg'er·y,** *n.*

for·get', *v.t.,* **-got, -gotten, -getting.** 1. lose the memory of. 2. ignore. —**for·get'ful,** *adj.*

for·give', *v.t.,* **-gave, -given, -giving.** regard without ill will despite an offense. —**for·giv'a·ble,** *adj.* —**for·giv'ing·ly,** *adv.*

for·go', *v.t.,* **-went, -gone, -going.** do without.

fork, *n.* 1. pronged lifting instrument. 2. division into two branches from one. —*v.i.* 3. divide into two branches.

for·lorn', *adj.* forsaken. —**for·lorn'ly,** *adv.*

form, *n.* 1. outline or contour. 2. basic organizing principle. 3. information blank. —*v.t.* 4. give form to. 5. develop. —**for·ma'tion,** *n.* —**form'a·tive,** *adj.*

for'mal, *adj.* 1. emphasizing rules or customs. 2. explicit. 3. correct in manner. —**for'mal·ly,** *adv.* —**for·mal'i·ty,** *n.*

for'mat, *n.* basic design or plan.

for'mer, *adj.* 1. past. 2. being the first of two mentioned. —**for'mer·ly,** *adv.*

for'mi·da·ble, *adj.* 1. awe-inspiring. 2. difficult.

for'mu·la, *n., pl.* **-las, -lae.** 1. rule to be followed. 2. words to be uttered. 3. ingredients to be used. —**for'mu·late'',** *v.t.*

for'ni·cate'', *v.i.,* **-cated, -cating.** have illicit sexual intercourse. —**for''ni·ca'tion,** *n.* —**for'ni·ca''tor,** *n.*

for·sake', *v.t.,* **-sook, -saken, -saking.** 1. desert. 2. give up.

fort, *n.* 1. strongly fortified place. 2. army post.

for'te, *adj., adv. Music.* loud; loudly.

forte (fort), *n.* special ability.

forth, *adv.* 1. forward. 2. outward.

forth'com''ing, *adj.* soon to appear.

forth'right'', *adj.* frank.

forth''with', *adj.* without delay.

for'ti·fy'', *v.t.,* **-fied, -fying.** 1. make resistant to attack. 2. strengthen. —**for''ti·fi·ca'tion,** *n.*

for·tis'si·mo'', *adj., adv. Music.* with extreme loudness.

for'ti·tude'', *n.* persistent courage.

fort'night'', *n.* two-week period. —**fort'night''ly,** *adj., adv.*

for'tress, *n.* large fort.

for·tu'i·tous, *adj.* happening by chance.

for'tu·nate, *adj.* lucky. —**for'tu·nate·ly,** *adv.*

for'tune, *n.* 1. luck. 2. riches.

for'ty, *adj., n.* four times ten. —**for'ti·eth,** *adj.*

fo'rum, *n.* place for or occasion of public discussion.

for'ward, *adv.* 1. Also, **for'wards,** to the front. —*adj.* 2. at the front. 3. presumptious.

fos'sil, *n.* hardened or petrified plant or animal. —**fos'sil·ize'',** *v.t.*

fos'ter, *v.t.* 1. raise, as young. 2. promote. —*adj.* 3. in a family relationship of adoption rather than blood.

foul, *adj.* 1. dirty. 2. disgusting. 3. unethical. —*v.t.* 4. make foul. 5. obstruct or tangle. —*n.* 6. illicit act. —**foul'ly,** *adv.* —**foul'ness,** *n.*

found, *v.t.* establish.

found'er, *v.i.* 1. sink. 2. break down. —*n.* 3. person who founds.

found'ling, *n.* child abandoned by unknown parents.

foun'dry, *n., pl.* **-dries.** place for casting metal.

foun'tain, *n.* source of flowing water.

four, *adj., n.* three plus one. —**fourth,** *adj., n.*

four·teen', *adj., n.* ten plus four.

fowl, *n., pl.* **fowl.** 1. any bird. 2. domestic bird eaten as food.

fox, *n.* 1. small canine predatory animal. —*v.t.* 2. cheat; trick.

fox'y, *adj.* cunning.

foy'er, *n.* lobby, esp. of a theater.

fra'cas, *n.* brawl.

frac'tion, *n.* portion. —**frac'tion·al,** *adj.*

frac'tious, *adj.* rebellious.

frac'ture, *n., v.t., v.i.,* **-tured, -turing.** break.

frag'ile, *adj.* readily broken. —**fra·gil'i·ty,** *n.*

frag'ment, *n.* 1. broken or torn-away piece. —*v.t., v.i.* 2. break into pieces. —**frag'men·tar'y,** *adj.*

fra'grant, *adj.* sweet-smelling. —**fra'grance,** *n.*

frail, *adj.* 1. fragile. 2. weak, physically or morally. —**frail'ty,** *n.*

frame, *n., v.t.,* **framed, framing.** *n.* 1. open structure. 2. border. —*v.t.* 3. make a frame for. 4. put into words or concepts. —**frame'work'',** *n.*

franc, *n.* currency unit in French-speaking countries.

fran'chise, *n.* 1. right to vote. 2. right to do business.

frank, *adj.* 1. not deceitful or evasive. —*n.* 2. right to mail without postage. —**frank'ly,** *adv.* —**frank'ness,** *n.*

frank'furt·er, *n.* wiener.

fran'tic, *adj.* wild with emotion. —**fran'ti·cal·ly,** *adv.*

fra·ter'nal, *adj.* brotherly.

fra·ter'ni·ty, *n., pl.* **-ties.** male social organization.

frat'er·nize'', *v.i.,* **-ized, -izing.** be in friendly association.

fraud, *n.* 1. deceit for gain. 2. impostor.

—fraud′u·lent, *adj.* —fraud′u·lent·ly, *adv.* —fraud′u·lence, *n.*

fraught, *adj.* filled, as with some quality.

fray, *v.t., v.i.* 1. wear thin. —*n.* 2. fight.

fraz′zle, *v.t., v.i.*, -zled, -zling, *n. Informal.* fatigue.

freak, *n.* oddity, esp. of nature.

freck′le, *n.* brownish skin spot.

free, *adj.*, freer, freest, *adv., v.t.*, freed, freeing. *adj.* 1. not bound or controlled. 2. without charge. 3. without obstructions. —*adv.* 4. without charge. —*v.t.* 5. make free. —free′ly, *adv.* —free′dom, *n.*

free′hand″, *adj., adv.* without rulers, compasses, etc.

free′lance″, *n., v.i.*, -lanced. *n.* 1. person paid by the assignment. —*v.i.* 2. work as a freelance.

free′think″er, *n.* person without standard religious beliefs.

freeze, *v.*, froze, frozen, freezing, *n. v.t., v.i.* 1. harden from cold. —*v.i.* 2. suspend all visible motion. —*n.* 3. suspension of change.

freight, *n.* 1. merchandise, etc. in transit. —*v.t.* 2. load with freight.

freight′er, *n.* freight ship.

French horn, coiled wind instrument with a flaring bell.

fre·net′ic, *adj.* frantic.

fren′zy, *n., pl.* -zies. wild excitement. —fren′zied, *adj.*

fre′quen·cy, *n., pl.* -cies. number of occurrences in a given period.

fre·quent, *adj.* (frē′kwənt) 1. occurring often. —*v.t.* (frē kwent′) 2. be often present at. —fre′quent·ly, *adv.*

fresh, *adj.* 1. in good, new condition. 2. rested and energetic. 3. inexperienced. —fresh′ly, *adv.* —fresh′ness, *n.* —fresh′en, *v.t., v.i.*

fresh′et, *n.* flooded stream.

fresh′man, *n.* person in his first year, esp. in school or Congress.

fret, *v.*, fretted, fretting, *n. v.i.* 1. be anxious. —*v.t.* 2. fray or gnaw. —*n.* 3. state of anxiety. 4. repeated geometrical design. —fret′ful, *adj.* —fret′work″, *n.*

Freud′i·an, *adj.* 1. pertaining to the theories of Sigmund Freud. —*n.* 2. follower of Freud.

fri′a·ble, *adj.* readily crumbled.

fri′ar, *n.* monk.

fric′as·see″, *n., v.t.*, -seed, -seeing. *n.* 1. cut and stewed meat. —*v.t.* 2. make a fricassee of.

fric′tion, *n.* 1. rubbing. 2. resistance to sliding. 3. conflict; antagonism. —fric′tion·al, *adj.*

Fri′day, *n.* sixth day.

friend, *n.* 1. person who likes or is helpful to one. 2. supporter or sympathizer. —friend′less, *adj.* —friend′ly, *adj.* —friend′ship, *n.*

frieze, *n.* horizontal decorative band.

frig′ate, *n.* 1. sailing warship with one gun deck. 2. medium-sized modern warship.

fright, *n.* sudden fear. —fright′en, *v.t.* —fright′ful, *adj.*

frig′id, *adj.* 1. cold. 2. sexually unresponsive. —fri·gid′i·ty, *n.*

frill, *n.* 1. minor ornament. 2. something unnecessary. —fril′ly, *adj.*

fringe, *n., v.t.*, fringed, fringing. *n.* 1. border. 2. edging or parallel loose strands. —*v.t.* 3. supply or constitute a fringe for.

frisk, *v.i.* 1. gambol; frolic. —frisk′y, *adj.*

frit′ter, *v.t.* 1. waste gradually. —*n.* 2. fried cake.

friv′o·lous, *adj.* without proper seriousness. —friv′o·lous·ly, *adv.* —fri·vol′i·ty, *n.*

fro, *adv.* to and fro, away and back again.

frock, *n.* robe; dress.

frog, *n.* leaping amphibian.

fro′lic, *v.i.*, -icked, -icking, *n. v.i.* 1. romp. 2. make merry. —*n.* 3. occasion of frolicking. —frol′ick·er, *n.* —frol′ic·some, *adj.*

from, *prep.* 1. beginning or originating at. 2. with no opportunity or use of. 3. as unlike. 4. because of.

frond, *n.* branchlike leaf.

front, *n.* 1. foremost part or surface. 2. vertical side. 3. pretense; mask. 4. forward battle area. —*v.i.* 5. face. —front′age, *n.* —front′al, *adj.*

fron·tier′, *n.* outer limit. —fron′tiers′man, *n.*

fron′tis·piece″, *n.* illustration beginning a book.

frost, *n.* 1. frozen vapor. 2. freezing temperature. —*v.t.* 3. cover with frost. 4. cover with frosting. —frost′y, *adj.*

frost′bite″, *n.* injury to the body from freezing.

frost′ing, *n.* sweetened coating for a cake; icing.

froth, *n., v.i.* foam. —froth′y, *adj.*

fro′ward, *adj.* willful.

frown, *n.* 1. expression of displeasure. —*v.i.* 2. assume such an expression. 3. look with disapproval.

fru′gal, *adj.* 1. thrifty. 2. meager. —fru′gal·ly, *adv.* —fru·gal′i·ty, *n.*

fruit, *n.* 1. juicy, seedbearing growth. 2. reward of endeavor. —fruit′ful, *adj.* —fru·i′tion, *n.* —fruit′less, *adj.*

frump, *n.* dowdy woman. —frump′ish, frump′y, *adj.*

frus′trate″, *v.t.*, -trated, -trating. prevent from succeeding. —frus·tra′tion, *n.*

frus′tum, *n.* lower part of a severed cone.

fry, *v.t.* cook in a grease, directly over direct heat. —fry′er, *n.*

fuch·sia (fyōō'shə), *n.* shrub with pink-to-purple flowers.

fud'dle, *v.t.,* **-dled, -dling.** stupefy, as with liquor.

fudge, *n.* **1.** soft candy made of butter, milk, sugar and flavouring. —*v.i.* **2.** cheat.

fu'el, *n., v.,* **-eled** or **-elled, -eling** or **-elling.** *n.* **1.** substance for burning. —*v.t.* **2.** supply with fuel. —*v.i.* **3.** take on fuel.

fu'gi·tive, *n.* **1.** person who flees. —*adj.* **2.** fleeing. **3.** transitory.

ful'crum, *n.* support for a lever.

ful''fill', *v.t.,* **-filled, -filling. 1.** satisfy. **2.** accomplish. —**ful·fill'ment, ful·fil' ment,** *n.*

full, *adj.* **1.** completely occupied. **2.** complete. **3.** broad or ample. —*adv.* **4.** completely. **5.** directly. —**ful'ly,** *adv.* —**full'ness, ful'ness,** *n.*

full'-scale', *adj.* unreduced.

ful'some, *adj.* annoyingly excessive.

fum'ble, *v.,* **-bled, -bling,** *n. v.i.* **1.** grope. —*v.t.* **2.** handle clumsily. —*n.* **3.** act or instance of fumbling.

fume, *n., v.,* **fumed, fuming.** *n.* **1.** odor, smoke, etc. —*v.t.* **2.** treat with fumes. —*v.i.* **3.** show petulance. **4.** give off fumes.

fum'i·gate'', *v.t.,* **-gated, -gating.** expose to fumes, as to kill vermin. —**fum''i· ga'tion,** *n.*

fun, *n.* **1.** enjoyment. **2.** source of enjoyment.

func'tion, *n.* **1.** purpose. **2.** ceremony. —*v.i.* **3.** operate; work. —**func'tion·al,** *adj.*

func'tion·ar''y, *n., pl.* **-ries.** official.

fund, *n.* **1.** money for a purpose. **2. funds,** ready money.

fun''da·men'tal, *adj.* **1.** basic; essential. —*n.* **2.** something fundamental. —**fun''da·men'tal·ly,** *adv.*

fun''da·men'tal·ism, *n.* literal belief in a sacred text. Also, **Fun''da·men'tal· ism.** —**fun''da·men'tal·ist,** *n., adj.*

fu'ner·al, *n.* ceremony of farewell to the dead.

fu·ne're·al, *adj.* mournful; solemn.

fun'gus, *n., pl.* **-gi** or **-guses.** spore-reproduced plant without chlorophyll. —**fun'gous,** *adj.*

fun'nel, *n.* **1.** tapered channel used to help pouring. **2.** smokestack.

fun'ny, *adj.,* **-nier, -niest. 1.** comical. **2.** peculiar.

fur, *n.* thick animal hair with its hide. —**fur'ry,** *adj.*

fu'ri·ous, *adj.* **1.** wildly angry. **2.** wild. —**fu'ri·ous·ly,** *adv.*

furl, *v.t.* bundle up.

fur'long, *n.* eighth of a mile.

fur'lough, *n.* **1.** military leave of absence. —*v.t.* **2.** grant a furlough to.

fur'nace, *n.* heating chamber.

fur'nish, *v.t.* **1.** supply. **2.** put furniture in.

fur'nish·ings, *n. pl.* **1.** furniture and decorative objects. **2.** minor clothing, etc.

fur'ni·ture, *n.* tables, chairs, etc.

fu'ror, *n.* frenzied excitement.

fur'ri·er, *n.* dealer in furs.

fur'row, *n.* **1.** groove or wrinkle. —*v.t.* **2.** make furrows in.

fur'ther, *adv.* **1.** to a greater distance or extent. **2.** in addition. —*adj.* **3.** additional. **4.** farther. —*v.t.* **5.** promote. —**fur'ther·ance,** *n.*

fur'ther·more'', *adv.* in addition.

fur'thest, *adj.* **1.** most distant. —*adv.* **2.** to the greatest distance or extent.

fur'tive, *adj.* sneaking. —**fur'tive·ly,** *adv.*

fu'ry, *n., pl.* **-ries. 1.** extreme rage. **2.** violence.

fuse, *n., v.t.,* **fused, fusing.** *n.* **1.** Also, **fuze,** detonating device. **2.** device of fusible metal for preventing electrical overloads. —*v.t., v.i.* **3.** melt. —**fu'si· ble,** *adj.* —**fu'sion,** *n.*

fu'sil·lade'', *n.* discharge of massed guns.

fuss, *n.* **1.** unreasonable show of concern. —*v.i.* **2.** make a fuss. —**fus'sy,** *adj.*

fu'tile, *adj.* vain; useless. —**fu·til'i·ty,** *n.*

fu'ture, *n.* **1.** time to come. **2.** what will happen. **3.** promise of success.

fuzz, *n.* fine hair or fibres. —**fuz'zy,** *adj.*

G

G, g, *n.* seventh letter of the English alphabet.

gab, *v.i.,* **gabbed, gabbing,** *n.* chatter.

gab'ble, *v.,* **-bled, -bling,** *v.i., v.t. n.* babble.

ga'ble, *n.* wall area perpendicular to a roof ridge.

gadg'et, *n.* mechanical contrivance. —**gadg'et·ry,** *n.*

gaff, *n.* **1.** spar for the head of a fore-and-aft sail. **2.** hook for landing fish.

gaffe, *n.* social blunder.

gag, *n., v.,* **gagged, gagging,** *n.* **1.** device to prevent speech by stopping the mouth. **2.** joke. —*v.t.* **3.** silence with a gag. —*v.i.* **4.** retch.

gai'e·ty, *n., pl.* **-ties. 1.** quality of being gay. **2.** merrymaking.

gai'ly, *adv.* in a gay manner.

gain, *v.t.* **1.** acquire. **2.** reach. —*v.i.* **3.** profit. —*n.* **4.** profit. —**gain'ful,** *adj.*

gain''say', *v.t.,* **-said, -saying. 1.** deny. **2.** contract.

gait, *n.* manner of walking or running.

ga′la, *adj.* 1. festive. —*n.* 2. celebration.

ga′lax·y, *n., pl.* **-ies.** vast cluster of stars. —**ga·lac′tic,** *adj.*

gale, *n.* high wind.

gall, *n.* 1. liquid secreted by the liver. 2. *Informal.* impudence.

gal′lant, *adj.* 1. brave; high-spirited. 2. polite to women. —**gal′lant·ry,** *n.*

gal′lery, *n., pl.* **-ies.** 1. covered passage. 2. uppermost theater balcony. 3. place for the display of art.

gal′ley, *n., pl.* **-leys,** 1. rowed ship. 2. ship's kitchen.

gal′lon, *n.* liquid measure of 4 quarts or 128 fluid ounces.

gal′lop, *n.* 1. fastest gait of a horse. —*v.i.* 2. move at a gallop.

gal′lows, *n., pl.* **-lowses, -lows.** frame for hanging condemned persons.

gall′stone″, *n.* stony mass in the gall bladder.

ga·lore′, *adv.* in abundance.

ga·losh′, *n.* rubber or rubberized boot.

gal·van′ic, *adj.* pertaining to electric currents, esp. from batteries.

gal′va·nize″, *v.t.,* **-nized, -nizing.** 1. apply electricity to. 2. plate with zinc. 3. stimulate.

gam′bit, *n.* opening in chess involving a sacrifice.

gam′ble, *v.,* **-bled, -bling,** *n. v.i.* 1. stake money on the outcome of a game, race, etc. —*v.t.* 2. stake by gambling. —*n.* 3. risky undertaking. —**gam′bler,** *n.*

gam′bol, *v.i.,* **-boled** or **-bolled, -boling** or **-bolling,** *n.* romp.

game, *n., adj., v.i.,* **gamed, gaming.** *n.* 1. contest decided by skill or chance. 2. hunted animals or birds. 3. *Informal.* willing to meet a challenge. —*adj.* 3. open wide.

game′cock″, *n.* rooster used in cockfights.

gam′ut, *n.* 1. musical scale. 2. complete range.

gan′der, *n.* male goose.

gang, *n.* group of workers, criminals, etc. acting or associating together.

gan′gling, *adj.* awkwardly tall. Also, **gan′gly.**

gan′gli·on, *n., pl.* **-a, -ons.** mass of nerve cells.

gan′grene, *n.* decay of body tissue deprived of blood. —**gan′gre·nous,** *adj.*

gang′ster, *n.* member of a criminal gang.

gang′way″, *n.* 1. entrance to a ship. —*interj.* 2. clear the way!

gap, *n.* opening; hiatus.

gape, *v.i.,* **gaped, gaping.** 1. open the mouth wide. 2. stare with stupefied astonishment.

ga·rage′, *n.* place for keeping automobiles.

garb, *n.* clothing.

gar′bage, *n.* food refuse.

gar′ble, *v.t.,* **-bled, -bling.** confuse.

gar′den, *n.* 1. area for growing plants. —*v.i.* 2. work in a garden. —**gar′den·er,** *n.*

gar·de′ni·a, *n.* white fragrant flower.

gar·gan′tu·an, *adj.* gigantic.

gar′gle, *v.i.,* **-gled, -gling.** rinse the throat with liquid and air bubbles.

gar′goyle, *n.* fantastic waterspout.

gar′ish, *adj.* vulgarly showy.

gar′land, *n.* wreath.

gar′lic, *n.* strong-flavored material from a plant bulb.

gar′ment, *n.* article of clothing.

gar′net, *n.* deep-red gemstone.

gar′nish, *v.t.* 1. decorate. —*n.* 2. decoration.

gar″nish·ee′, *v.t.,* **-eed, -eeing.** *Law.* attach (money or property) to settle a bad debt.

gar′ret, *n.* attic.

gar′ri·son, *n.* 1. resident body of troops. —*v.t.* 2. station as a defensive force.

gar·rote′, *n., v.t.,* **-roted, -roting.** *n.* 1. device for strangling. —*v.t.* 2. kill with a garrote.

gar′ru·lous, *adj.* talkative. —**gar·ru′li·ty,** *n.*

gar′ter, *n.* band for holding up a stocking.

gas, *n., v.t.,* **gassed, gassing.** *n.* 1. expansive fluid. 2. *Informal.* gasoline. —*v.t.* 3. injure or kill with a gas. —**gas′e·ous,** *adj.* —**gas′sy,** *adj.*

gash, *n.* 1. long, deep cut. —*v.t.* 2. make a gash in.

gas′ket, *n.* seal against leakage.

gas′o·hol, *n.* a mixture of gasoline and alcohol.

gas′o·line″, *n.* engine fuel derived from petroleum. Also, **gas′o·lene″.**

gasp, *v.i.* 1. sudden, short breath. —*n.* 2. act or instance of gasping.

gas′tric, *adj.* pertaining to the stomach.

gas·tron′o·my, *n.* cooking as an art. —**gas″tro·nom′ic, gas″tro·nom′i·cal,** *adj.*

gate, *n.* 1. open-air door. 2. Also **gate′way″,** structure holding such a door.

gath′er, *v.t.* 1. bring together. 2. infer. —*v.i.* 3. come together. 4. increase. —**gath′er·ing,** *n.*

gauche (gōsh), *adj.* socially awkward.

gaud′y, *adj.,* **-ier, -iest.** bright and showy. —**gaud′i·ly,** *adv.*

gauge (gāj), *n., v.t.,* **gauged, gauging.** *n.* 1. measuring instrument. 2. standard measure. —*v.t.* 3. measure. 4. estimate the amount of. Also, **gage.**

gaunt, *adj.* lean; bony.

gaunt′let, *n.* 1. glove with a flaring cuff. 2. hazardous route.

gauze, *n.* loosely woven cloth. —**gauz′y,** *adj.*

gav'el, *n.* hammerlike noisemaker.

gawk, *v.i.* stare stupidly.

gay, *adj.* **1.** cheerful. —*n.*, *adj.* **2.** homosexual. —**gay''e·ty, gai''e·ty**, *n.* —**gay''ly**, *adv.*

gaze, *v.i.*, **gazed, gazing.** look steadily.

ga·zette', *n.* published official record.

gaz''et·teer', *n.* geographical reference work.

gear, *n.* **1.** Also, **gear'wheel''**, toothed machine wheel. **2.** mechanical assembly. **3.** equipment. —*v.t.* **4.** furnish with gears or a gear.

gel'a·tin, *n.* jellylike substance from bones or various vegetable substance. Also, **gel'a·tine.** —**ge·lat'i·nous**, *adj.*

geld, *v.t.*, **gelded, gelding.** castrate.

gel'id, *adj.* icy.

gem, *n.* jewel. Also, **gem'stone''.**

gen'der, *n.* classification into masculine, feminine, and neuter.

gene, *n.* entity by which hereditary characteristics are transmitted.

ge''ne·al'o·gy, *n.*, *pl.* **-gies.** study of ancestry. —**ge''ne·a·log'i·cal**, *adj.* —**ge''ne·al'o·gist**, *n.*

gen'er·al, *adj.* **1.** pertaining to a whole group. **2.** unspecific. **3.** common. —*n.* **4.** military officer ranking above a colonel. —**gen'er·al·ly**, *adv.*

gen''er·al'i·ty, *n.*, *pl.* **-ties.** statement supposed to be generally true.

gen'er·al·ize'', *v.i.*, **-ized, -izing.** infer or speak in generalities. —**gen''er·al·i·za'tion**, *n.*

gen'er·ate'', *v.t.*, **-ated, -ating.** bring into being. —**gen'er·a·tive**, *adj.*

gen''er·a'tion, *n.* **1.** group of persons of about the same age. **2.** period of about 30 years. **3.** production, esp. of electricity.

gen'er·a''tor, *n.* machine for producing electricity.

ge·ner'ic, *adj.* pertaining to a group. —**ge·ner'i·cal·ly**, *adv.*

gen'er·ous, *adj.* **1.** giving freely. **2.** ample. —**gen'er·ous·ly**, *adv.* —**gen''er·os'i·ty**, *n.*

ge·net'ics, *n.* study of heredity. —**ge·net'i·cal·ly**, *adv.* —**ge·net'ic**, *adj.* —**ge·net'i·cist**, *n.*

ge'ni·al, *adj.* warmly outgoing. —**ge''ni·al'i·ty**, *n.*

gen'i·tals, *n.*, *pl.* sexual organs. Also, **gen''i·ta'li·a.** —**gen'i·tal**, *adj.*

gen'ius, *n.* **1.** presiding spirit. **2.** great mental power. **3.** person with such powers.

gen'o·cide'', *n.* willful killing of a whole race or nation.

gen·teel', *adj.* overrefined. —**gen·til'ity** *n.*

gen'tile, *n.* **1.** non-Jew. —*adj.* **2.** non-Jewish.

gen'tle, *adj.* mild in manner or effect. —**gen'tly**, *adv.*

gen'tle·man, *n.* **1.** Also, *fem.*, **gen'tle·wom''an**, man of the upper class. **2.** well-mannered man.

gen'try, *n.* persons of the upper class.

gen'u·flect'', *v.i.* bend the knee in homage. —**gen''u·flec'tion**, *n.*

gen'u·ine, *adj.* **1.** true; real. **2.** sincere. —**gen'u·ine·ly**, *adv.* —**gen'u·ine·ness**, *n.*

ge'nus, *n.*, *pl.* **genera, genuses. 1.** type. **2.** *Biology.* distinctive group of plant or animal species.

ge·og'ra·phy, *n.*, *pl.* **-phies. 1.** study of the earth or its features. **2.** terrain. —**ge''o·graph'i·cal, ge''o·graph'ic**, *adj.* —**ge·og'ra·pher**, *n.*

ge·ol'o·gy, *n.* study of the earth's crust. —**ge''o·log'ic, ge''o·log'i·cal**, *adj.*

ge·om'e·try, *n.*, *pl.* **-tries.** study of points, lines, planes, and solids. —**ge''o·met'ric, ge''o·met'ri·cal**, *adj.*

ge''o·phys'ics, *n.* study of the effects of climate, etc. on the earth.

ger''i·at'rics, *n.* branch of medicine dealing with old age. —**ger''i·at'ric**, *adj.*

germ, *n.* **1.** disease-causing organism. **2.** origin.

ger·mane', *adj.* relevant.

ger'mi·cide'', *n.* destroyer of germs. —**ger''mi·ci'dal**, *adj.*

ger'mi·nate'', *v.*, **-nated, -nating.** *v.i.*, *v.t.* sprout. —**ger''mi·na'tion** *n.*

ger'ry·man''der, *vt.* manipulate election districts so as to favor one side.

ges'tate, *v.t.*, **-tated, -tating.** bear in the uterus. —**ges·ta'tion**, *n.*

ges·tic'u·late'', *v.i.*, **-lated, -lating.** make gestures. —**ges·ticu·la'tion**, *n.*

ges'ture, *v.i.*, **-tured, -turing.** *n.* *v.i.* **1.** move the hands, arms, etc. as a signal. —*n.* **2.** act or instance of gesturing. **3.** act intended to impress others.

get, *v.*, **got, gotten, getting.** —*v.t.* **1.** take or receive. **2.** cause to be or do. —*v.i.* **3.** become. **4.** go or arrive.

gey'ser, *n.* natural eruption of water or steam.

ghast'ly, *adj.*, **-lier, -liest. 1.** horrible. **2.** ghostlike. —**ghast'li·ness**, *n.*

gher'kin, *n.* small pickle.

ghet'to, *n.*, *pl.* **-tos, -toes.** neighborhood populated by particular minority ethnic group.

ghost, *n.* spirit from the dead. —**ghost'ly**, *adj.*

ghoul, *n.* **1.** robber of the dead. **2.** person morbidly fascinated by disasters. —**ghoul'ish**, *adj.*

GI, *n.*, *pl.* **GI's, GIs**, *adj.* *n.* enlisted man. —*adj.* **2.** government issue.

gi'ant, *n.* **1.** greatly oversized creature or thing. —*adj.* **2.** gigantic. Also, *fem.*, **gi'ant·ess.**

gib'ber (jib'ər), *v.i.* make incoherent utterances. —**gib'ber·ish**, *n.*

gibe. (jīb), *v.i.*, **gibed, gibing**, *n.* jeer.

97 glue

gib·let (jib'lit), *n.* internal organ of fowl.

gid'dy, *adj.*, -dier, -diest. 1. dizzy. 2. frivolous.

gift, *n.* 1. something given. 2. natural ability.

gift'ed, *adj.* intelligent or talented.

gi·gan'tic, *adj.* huge.

gig'gle, *v.i.*, -gled, -gling, *n. v.i.* 1. laugh in a quick, high-pitched way. —*n.* 2. act or instance of giggling.

gild, *v.t.*, gilded or gilt, gilding. cover with gold leaf. —gilt, *adj.*

gill, *n.* 1. (jil) quarter of a pint; 4 fluid ounces. 2. (gill) breathing apparatus of a fish, etc.

gim·crack (jim'krak"), *adj.* showy and cheap.

gim'let, *n.* small boring tool.

gim'mick, *n. Informal.* gadget.

gin, *n.*, *v.t.*, ginned, ginning. *n.* 1. distilled grain liquor. 2. cotton seed remover. —*v.t.* 3. process with a cotton gin.

gin'ger, *n.* tropical spice. —gin'ger·y, *adj.*

gin'ger·ly, *adj.* 1. cautious. —*adv.* 2. cautiously.

ging'ham, *n.* checked or striped cotton.

gi·raffe', *n.* long-necked, long-legged African animal.

gird, *v.t.*, girded or girt, girding. surround, as with a belt.

gird'er, *n.* major structural beam.

gir'dle, *n.*, *v.t.*, -dled, -dling. *n.* 1. woman's undergarment. 2. belt. —*v.t.* 3. encircle.

girl, *n.* young female. —girl'hood", *n.* —girl'ish, *adj.*

girth, *n.* circumference.

gist (jist), *n.* basic meaning or content.

give, *v.*, gave, given, giving, *n. v.t.* 1. transfer. 2. make a present of. 3. supply or afford. 4. concede. —*v.i.* 5. yield, as to force. —*n.* 6. compressibility. —giv'er, *n.*

giv'en, *adj.* 1. specified. 2. granted. 3. habituated.

gla'cial, *adj.* icy.

gla'cier, *n.* broad, moving mass of ice.

glad, *adj.*, gladder, gladdest. 1. happy. 2. quite willing. —glad'ly, *adv.* —glad'ness, *n.* —glad'den, *v.t.*, *v.i.*

glade, *n.* open space in a forest.

glad'i·a"tor, *n.* swordsman in ancient Roman contests.

glad"i·o'lus, *n.*, *pl.* -luses, -li. flower with spikes of funnel-shaped blossoms. Also, glad"i·o'la.

glam'or, *n.* mysterious charm. Also, glam'our. —glam'or·ous, *adj.* —glam'or·ize, *v.t.*

glance, *v.t.*, glanced, glancing, *n.*, *v.i.* 1. look briefly. 2. ricochet. —*n.* 3. act or instance of glancing.

gland, *n.* bodily organ that extracts and

processes elements in the blood. —glan'du·lar, *adj.*

glare, *n.*, *v.i.*, glared, glaring. *n.* 1. dazzling brightness. 2. furious look. —*v.i.* 3. cast a glare.

glar'ing, *adj.* 1. dazzlingly bright. 2. ostentatious; loud. 3. flagrant.

glass, *n.* 1. substance of fused silicates. 2. object of this substance. 3. object with a lens or lenses. 4. glasses, lenses in a frame, used to aid vision. —glass'ful, *n.* —glas'sy, *adj.*

glaze, *v.t.*, glazed, glazing, *n. v.t.* 1. fill with glass, as a window. 2. put a glassy coating on. —*v.i.* 3. become glassy. —*n.* 4. glassy coating.

gla'zier, *n.* person who glazes windows.

gleam, *n.* 1. beam of light. —*v.i.* 2. emit a gleam.

glean, *adj.* gather.

glee, *n.* joy. —glee'ful, *adj.*

glen, *n.* isolated, small valley.

glib, *adj.*, glibber, glibbest. unconvincingly ready with explanations. —glib'ly, *adv.* —glib'ness, *n.*

glide, *v.*, glided, gliding, *n. v.i.*, *v.t.* 1. slider —*n.* 2. act or instance of gliding.

glid'er, *n.* unpowered aircraft.

glim'mer, *n.*, *v.i.* gleam.

glimpse, *v.t.*, glimpsed, glimpsing, *n. v.t.* 1. see briefly or in part. —*n.* 2. act or instance of glimpsing.

glint, *v.i.*, *n.* gleam or glitter.

glis'ten, *v.i.* reflect with a dull shine.

glitch, *n.* (computers) a problem or error in a program.

glit'ter, *v.i.* 1. shine or reflect brightly. —*n.* 2. act or instance of glittering.

gloam'ing, *n.* evening twilight.

gloat, *v.i.* experience proud or malicious pleasure.

globe, *n.* 1. the earth. 2. model of the earth. 3. spherical object. —glob'al, *adj.*

glob'ule, *n.* tiny ball or drop. —glob'u·lar, *adj.*

gloom, *n.* 1. darkness. 2. sadness or dreariness. —gloom'y, *adj.*

glo"ri·fy', *v.t.*, -fied, -fying. 1. give glory to. 2. exaggerate the importance or worth of. —glo"ri·fi·ca'tion, *n.*

glo'ry, *n.*, *pl.* -ries, *v.i.*, -ried, -rying. *n.* 1. high honor. 2. splendor or splendid feature. —*v.i.* 3. take pride. —glo'ri·ous, *adj.*

gloss, *n.* 1. sheen. 2. explanation. —glos'sy, *adj.*

glos'sa·ry, *n.*, *pl.* -ries. list of terms with definitions.

glove, *n.* garment for the hand.

glow, *v.i.* 1. give off soft light or color. —*n.* 2. act or instance of glowing.

glow'er, *v.i.* stare threateningly.

glu'cose, *n.* sugar in fruit and honey.

glue, *n. v.t.*, glued, gluing. *n.* 1. adhesive

substance. —*v.t.* **2.** fasten with glue.

glum, *adj.,* **glummer, glummest.** gloomy; moody. —**glum'ly,** *adv.*

glut, *v.,* **glutted, glutting,** *n., v.i.* **1.** eat to excess. —*v.t.* **2.** satiate. **3.** oversupply. —*n.* **4.** act or instance of glutting.

glu·ti·nous, *adj.* sticky.

glut'ton, *n.* person who overeats. —**glut'ton·ous,** *adj.* —**glut'ton·y,** *n.*

gly'cer·in, *n.* liquid derived from fats and oils. Also, **gly'cer·ine.**

gnarled, *adj.* twisted or knotted, like a tree trunk.

gnash, *v.t.* grind together, as the teeth, with anger or frustration.

gnat, *n.* small, stinging insect.

gnaw, *v.t., v.i.* bite away gradually.

gnome, *n.* dwarf who guards treasure. —**gnom'ish,** *adj.*

go, *v.i.,* **went, going,** *n., pl.* **goes.** *v.i.* **1.** leave. **2.** operate. **3.** belong. **4.** become.

goad, *n., v.t.* prod.

goal, *n.* **1.** object to be reached or attained. **2.** *Sports.* area to be defended.

goat, *n.* horned, cud-chewing mammal.

goat·ee', *n.* small, pointed beard.

gob'ble, *v.,* **-bled, -bling,** *n. v.t.* **1.** eat greedily. —*v.i.* **2.** make turkeylike sounds. —*n.* **3.** sound of a turkey.

gob'ble·dy·gook'', *n. Informal.* jargon.

go'-be·tween'', *n.* arranger of bargains between others.

gob'let, *n.* stemmed, deep-bowled drinking vessel.

gob'lin, *n.* evil supernatural being.

god, *n.* **1.** one of the supreme beings. **2. God,** the Supreme Being. Also, *fem.,* **god'dess.** —**god'hood'',** *n.* —**god'less,** *adj.*

god'child'', *n.* child sponsored in religion by a godparent.

god'head'', *n.* **1.** godhood. **2. the Godhead,** God.

god'ly, *adj.,* **-lier, -liest.** devout. —**god'li·ness,** *n.*

god'par''ent, *n.* sponsor of a godchild. Also, *masc.,* **god'fa''ther,** *fem.,* **god'mother.**

god'send'', *n.* piece of good luck.

gog'gle, *v.i.,* **-gled, -gling,** *n. v.i.* **1.** stare with eyes bulging. —*n.* **2. goggles,** protective glasses.

go'ing, *adj.* **1.** current. **2.** operative. —*n.* **3.** departure. **4.** conditions.

goi'ter, *n.* enlargement of the thyroid gland. Also, **goi'tre.**

gold, *n.* soft, yellow, precious metallic element. —**gold'en,** *adj.*

gold'en·rod'', *n.* plant with tiny yellow flowers.

golden rule, do unto others as you would have others do unto you.

gold'fish'', *n.* small yellow-orange fish.

golf, *n.* outdoor game played with balls knocked from ground level with clubs. —**golf'er,** *n.*

go'nad, *n.* animal reproductive organ.

gon'do·la, *n.* **1.** one-oared Venetian boat. **2.** low-sided railroad freight car. **3.** airship cabin. —**gon''do·lier',** *n.*

gong, *n.* thin brass disk beaten to produce sound.

gon''or·rhe'a, *n.* a venereal disease.

good, *adj.,* **better, best,** *n. adj.* **1.** right; proper. **2.** kind. **3.** beneficial. —*n.* **5.** good purpose or result. **6. goods,** valuable objects or material.

good''bye', *interj.* **1.** (departing salutation). —*n.* **2.** saying of goodbye. Also, **good''by'.**

Good Friday, Friday before Easter.

good'ly, *adj.,* **-lier, -liest. 1.** considerable in amount. **2.** good. **3.** good-looking.

goof, *Informal. n.* **1.** blunderer. **2.** blunder. —**goof'y,** *adj.*

goose, *n., pl.* **geese.** web-footed duck-like bird.

go'pher, *n.* **1.** burrowing rodent. **2.** prairie squirrel.

gore, *n., v.t.,* **gored, goring.** *n.* **1.** blood. **2.** triangular segment. —*v.t.* **3.** pierce, as with a horn. —**gor'y,** *adj.*

gorge, *n., v.,* **gorged, gorging.** *n.* **1.** narrow canyon. **2.** gullet. —*v.t.* **3.** glut. —*v.i.* **4.** eat greedily.

gor'geous, *adj.* dazzlingly attractive.

go·ril'la, *n.* powerful manlike African ape.

Gos'pel, *n.* **1.** teachings of Jesus and the Apostles.

gos'sa·mer, *adj.* **1.** light and frail. —*n.* **2.** cobweb.

gos'sip, *n.* **1.** rumors and conjectures about others. **2.** person who originates or spreads these. —*v.i.* **3.** engage in gossip. —**gos'sip·y,** *adj.*

gouge, *n., v.t.,* **gouged, gouging.** *n.* **1.** chisel for cutting grooves. —*v.t.* **2.** cut out with a scooping motion.

gou'lash, *n.* stew seasoned with paprika.

gourd, *n.* decorative fruit of the squash or melon family.

gour·mand (gŏōr'mənd), *n.* heavy eater and drinker.

gour·met (gŏōr mā') *n.* connoisseur of food and drink.

gout, *n.* illness causing pain in the joints. —**gout'y,** *adj.*

gov'ern, *v.t.* **1.** have authority over. **2.** guide. **3.** determine.

gov'ern·ment, *n.* **1.** system for running a country. **2.** group in political control. —**gov''ern·men'tal,** *adj.*

gov'er·nor, *n.* **1.** supreme local official. **2.** device for controlling machinery speed. —**gov'er·nor·ship,** *n.*

gown, *n.* long outer garment.

grab, *v.t., v.i.,* **grabbed, grabbing,** *n.* snatch.

grace, *n., v.t.,* **graced, gracing.** *n.* 1. beauty of form, movement or manner. 2. kindness or favor. 3. prayer before a meal. —*v.t.* 4. add grace to, as by being present. —**grace′ful**, *adj.* —**grace′less**, *adj.*

gra′cious, *adj.* 1. charming in manner 2. kind. 3. discriminatingly luxurious.

grack′le, *n.* crowlike blackbird.

gra·da′tion, *n.* succession of increasing or decreasing amounts, etc.

grade, *n., v.t.,* **graded, grading.** *n.* 1. step in a progressive series. 2. Also, **gra′di·ent**, slope. —*v.t.* 3. assign a grade to. 4. give a level to, as a road.

grad′u·al, *adj.* in small amounts. —**grad′u·al·ly**, *adv.*

grad·u·ate, *v.,* **-ated, -ating,** *n., adj. v.t.* (grad′yoō ăt″) 1. leave after satisfying academic requirements. 2. certify as having satisfied requirements. 3. divide into grades. —*n.* (grad′yoō ət) 4. person who has graduated. —*adj.* 5. post-baccalaureate. —**grad″u·a′tion**, *n.*

graf·fi·to (grafē′tō), *n., pl.* **-ti.** writing or drawing by a passer-by.

graft, *n.* 1. transplant of organic material. 2. dishonest use of public funds. —*v.t.* 3. transplant. 4. obtain by graft.

grain, *n.* 1. hard seed, as of wheat. 2. hard particle. 3. pattern of fiber, as in wood.

gram, *n.* metric unit of weight, about 1/28 of an ounce. Also, **gramme**.

gram′mar, *n.* forms and arrangement of words. —**gram·mat′i·cal**, *adj.*

gran′a·ry, *n., pl.* **-ries.** place for storing grain.

grand, *adj.* 1. impressive. 2. illustrious. —**grand′ly**, *adv.* —**gran′deur**, *n.*

grand′child″, *n.* child of a son or daughter. Also, *masc.,* **grand′son″**, *fem.,* **grand′daugh″ter.**

gran·dil′o·quent, *adj.* pretentious in speech. —**gran·dil′o·quence**, *n.*

gran′di·ose″, *adj.* 1. full of grandeur. 2. pompous.

grand′par″ent, *n.* parent of a parent. Also, *masc.,* **grand′fa″ther,** *fem.,* **grand′moth″er.**

grand′stand″, *n.* stand for spectators at sporting events.

gran′ite, *n.* grainy igneous rock.

grant, *v.t.* 1. give. 2. admit. —*n.* 3. something granted.

gran′u·late″, *v.t.,* **-lated, -lating.** form as or in granules.

gran′ule, *n.* small particle —**gran′u·lar,** *adj.*

grape, *n.* small juicy fruit.

grape′fruit″, *n.* large, sharp-tasting citrus fruit.

graph, *n.* two-dimensional visual representation of interrelated data.

graph′ic, *adj.* 1. pertaining to two-dimensional visual art. 2. vividly realistic.

graph′ite, *n.* soft carbon used as a writing material or lubricant.

grap′ple, *v.,* **-pled, -pling.** *v.i.* 1. wrestle; struggle. —*v.t.* 2. grasp and hold.

grasp, *v.t.* 1. take hold of with the hand; clutch. 2. comprehend. —*v.i.* 3. make clutching motions. —*n.* 4. act or instance of grasping. 5. ability to grasp.

grasp′ing, *adj.* avaricious.

grass, *n.* 1. narrow-leafed green plant with seedlike fruit. —**gras′sy,** *adj.*

grass′hop″per, *n.* jumping, plant-eating insect.

grate, *v.,* **grated, grating,** *n. v.t.* 1. scrape into particles. 2. grind. —*v.i.* 3. grind or rasp. 4. be irritating. —*n.* 5. Also, **grat′ing,** framework of metal, etc. bars. —**grat′er,** *n.*

grate′ful, *adj.* 1. appreciative of favors. 2. welcome.

grat′i·fy″, *v.t.,* **-fied, -fying.** be pleasing to. —**grat″i·fi·ca′tion**, *n.*

gra′tis, *adj.* free of charge.

grat′i·tude″, *n.* appreciation for favors.

gra·tu′i·tous, *adj.* 1. gratis. 2. uncalled-for.

gra·tu′i·ty, *n., pl.* **-ties.** gift, esp. a tip.

grave, *adj.* 1. solemn. 2. important; serious. —*n.* 2. place of burial.

grav′el, *n.* mixture of stone fragments. —**grav′el·ly,** *adj.*

grav′i·tate″, *v.i.,* **-tated, -tating.** 1. move by gravity. 2. move or tend naturally. —**grav″i·ta′tion**, *n.* —**grav″i·ta′tion·al,** *adj.*

grav′i·ty, *n.* 1. seriousness. 2. pull toward the center of the earth.

gra′vy, *n., pl.* **-ies.** meat juice, or a sauce from this.

gray, *adj.* 1. mixed black and white. 2. dreary.

gray matter, 1. brain tissue. 2. *Informal.* intelligence.

graze, *v.,* **grazed, grazing.** *v.t. v.i.* 1. scrape in passing. —*v.i.* 2. feed on grasses.

grease, *n., v.t.,* **greased, greasing.** *n.* (grēs) 1. thick, fatty or oily substance. —*v.t.* (grēz) 2. coat or lubricate with grease. —**greas′y,** *adj.*

great, *adj.* 1. large. 2. eminent. —**great′ly,** *adv.*

greed, *n.* excessive passion for money, food, etc. —**greed′y,** *adj.*

green, *n.* 1. color of leaves and plants. 2. **greens,** leafy vegetables. —*adj.* 3. of the color green. 4. unripened or unprocessed.

green′er·y, *n.* plant life.

green′house″, *n.* glazed building for growing plants.

greet, *v.t.* 1. acknowledge meeting. 2. receive in a specified way. —**greet′ing**, *n.*

gre·gar′i·ous, *adj.* associating with others of one's kind.

gre·nade′, *n.* small hand bomb.

gren′a·dine″, *n.* pomegranate syrup.

grey, *adj.* gray.

grey′hound″, *n.* fast, slender hound.

grid, *n.* system of crisscrossed elements.

grid′dle, *n.* pan for cooking pancakes, etc.

grid′iron″, *n.* 1. broiling frame. 2. football field.

grid″lock, *n.* severe, urban traffic jam.

grief, *n.* 1. great unhappiness. 2. ruin; failure.

griev′ance, *n.* 1. cause for complaint. 2. complaint.

grieve, *v.,* **grieved, grieving.** *v.i* 1. suffer grief. —*v.t.* 2. cause grief to.

griev′ous, *adj.* 1. seriously injurious. 2. being in grief.

grill, *n.* 1. gridiron. 2. broiled dish. —*v.t.* 3. broil. 4. *Informal.* question severely.

grille, *n.* open screen; grating. —**grille′work″,** *n.*

grim, *adj.,* **grimmer, grimmest.** 1. harsh. 2. menacing. —**grim′ly** *adv.*

gri′mace, *n., v.i.,* **-maced, -macing.** *n.* 1. smirk, esp. of displeasure. —*v.i.* 2. give such a smirk.

grime, *n.* clinging dirt. —**grim′y** *adj.*

grin, *n., v.i.,* **grinned, grinning.** *n.* 1. broad, toothy smile. —*v.i.* 2. give such a smile.

grind, *v.t.,* **ground, grinding.** 1. wear down with pressure or friction. 2. turn the crank of. —**grind′er,** *n.*

grip, *v.t.,* **gripped, gripping,** *n. v.t.* 1. grasp firmly. —*n.* 2. firm grasp. 3. handle. 4. small piece of luggage.

gripe, *v.,* **griped, griping,** *n. v.t.* 1. produce pain in the bowels. —*v.i.* 2. *Informal.* complain. —*n.* 3. pain in the bowels. 4. *Informal.* complaint.

gris′ly, *adj.,* **-lier, -liest.** horrible.

grist, *n.* grain for grinding. —**grist′mill″,** *n.*

gris′tle, *n.* cartilage. —**gris′tly,** *adv.*

grit, *n., v.t.,* **gritted, gritting.** *n.* 1. rough, hard particles. 2. fortitude. —*v.t.* 3. grind together, as the teeth. —**grit′ty,** *adj.*

grits, *n. pl.* coarsely ground grain.

griz′zled, *adj.* with gray hair.

griz′zly, *adj.,* **-zlier, -zliest,** *n. adj.* 1. grayish. —*n.* 2. Also, **grizzly bear,** large, ferocious American bear.

groan, *n.* 1. deep utterance, as of pain. —*v.i.* 2. give such an utterance.

gro′cer, *n.* food merchant. —**gro′cer·y,** *n.*

grog′gy, *adj.,* **-gier, -giest.** befuddled.

groin, *n.* junction of the abdomen and thighs.

grom′met, *n.* eyelet.

groom, *n.* 1. man at his wedding. 2. tender of horses. —*v.t.* 3. comb, etc. to make tidy.

groove, *n., v.t.,* **grooved, grooving.** *n.* 1. long, shallow depression. —*v.t.* 2. make a groove in.

grope, *v.i.,* **groped, groping.** feel for something blindly.

gross, *adj.* 1. coarse. 2. flagrant. 3. before deductions. —*n.* 4. *pl.* **gross,** quantity of 144.

gro·tesque′, *adj.* fantastically distorted.

grot′to, *n., pl.* **-tos, -toes.** cave.

grouch, *v.i.* 1. sulk. —*n.* 2. sulky mood. 3. person who sulks. —**grouch′y,** *adj.*

ground, *n.* 1. solid surface of the earth. 2. earth. 3. **grounds, a.** basis **b.** land of an estate or institution. **c.** dregs of coffee, etc. —*v.t.* 4. instruct in rudiments.

ground′hog″, *n.* woodchuck.

ground′less, *adj.* without reason.

ground′work″, *n.* basic or preparatory work.

group, *n.* 1. number of persons or things considered together. *v.t., v.i.* 2. form into a group or groups.

grouse, *n., pl.* **grouse,** *v.i.,* **groused, grousing.** *n.* 1. plump game bird. —*v.i.* 2. complain.

grove, *n.* cluster of trees.

grov′el, *v.i.,* **-eled, -eling.** 1. crouch low or crawl. 2. behave servilely.

grow, *v.,* **grew, grown, growing.** *v.i.* 1. become. 2. develop. —*v.t.* 3. cause to live, as plants. —**grow′er,** *n.* —**growth,** *n.*

growl, *n.* 1. low, rumbling vocal noise. —*v.i.* 2. make such a noise.

grown′-up′, *adj., n.* adult.

grub, *v.,* **grubbed, grubbing,** *n. v.i., v.t.* 1. dig. —*n.* 2. beetle larva. 3. drudge. 4. *Informal.* food.

grub′by, *adj.,* **-bier, -biest.** nastily dirty.

grudge, *n., v.t.,* **grudged, grudging.** *n.* 1. long-held resentment. —*v.t.* 2. begrudge. —**grudg′ing·ly,** *adv.*

gru′el·ing, *adj.* exhausting; very tiring.

grue′some, *adj.* horrifying or loathsome.

gruff, *adj.* curt.

grum′ble, *v.i.,* **-bled, -bling,** complain in a suppressed manner.

grum′py, *adj.,* **-pier, -piest.** surly.

grunt, *n.* 1. throaty sound caused by exertion, etc. —*v.i.* 2. utter such a sound.

guar″an·tee′, *n., v.t.,* **-teed, -teeing.** *n.* 1. firm assurance. 2. promise to make good if necessary. —*v.t.* 3. assure with a guarantee. Also, **guar′an·ty.** —**guar′an·tor″.**

guard, *v.t., v.i.* 1. watch, esp. in order to protect or confine. —*n.* 2. person or group that guards. 3. protection. 4. protective device.

guard′ed, *adj.* cautious.

guard′i·an, *n.* 1. person who guards. 2.

person responsible for a minor or incompetent. —**guard'ian·ship''**, n.

gu''ber·na·to'ri·al, adj. pertaining to governors.

guer·ril'la, n. irregular soldier using surprise tactics.

guess, v.t. **1.** form an opinion about without knowing. —n. **2.** act or instance of guessing. —**guess'work''**, n.

guest, n. **1.** enjoyer of hospitality. **2.** customer of a hotel, etc.

guf·faw', n. **1.** raucous laugh. —v.i. **2.** emit such a laugh.

guide, v.t., **guided**, **guiding**, n. v.t. **1.** tell how to proceed. —n. **2.** person or thing that guides. —**guid'ance**, n.

guile, n. unscrupulous cunning.

guilt, n. **1.** responsibility for a wrong action. **2.** shame. —**guilt'y**, adj.

guin'ea pig, **1.** small, fat rodent. **2.** subject of an experiment.

guise, n. semblance.

gui·tar', n. six-stringed plucked instrument. —**gui·tar'ist**, n.

gulch, n. deep narrow ravine.

gulf, n. **1.** ocean area partly surrounded by land. **2.** wide deep void.

gull, n. light-colored soaring water bird.

gul'let, n. throat.

gul'li·ble, adj. credulous. —**gul''li·bil'i·ty**, n.

gul'ly, n., pl. **-lies.** narrow ravine.

gulp, v.t., v.i. **1.** swallow hastily. —n. **2.** act or instance of gulping.

gum, n., v.t., **gummed**, **gumming**. n. **1.** sticky, semisolid substance. **2.** area of flesh surrounding teeth. —v.t. **3.** stick with gum.

gump'tion, n. enterprise.

gun, n., v., **gunned**, **gunning**. n. **1.** weapon shooting a missile by means of an explosive charge. —v.t., v.i. **2.** hunt with a gun. —**gun'ner·y**, n.

gunk, n. Informal. viscous substance.

gun'ny, n. coarse cloth of jute or hemp.

gun'pow''der, n. explosive used in guns.

gun·wale (gun'l), n. upper edge of a ship's side.

gur'gle, v.i., **-gled**, **-gling**, n. v.i. **1.** emit a bubbling sound in flowing. —n. **2.** such a sound.

gu'ru, n. Hindu spiritual teacher.

gush, v.i. **1.** flow out abundantly. **2.** express oneself effusively. —n. **3.** act or instance of gushing. —**gush'y**, adj.

gus'set, n. triangular reinforcement.

gust, n. **1.** strong puff of air. **2.** sudden outburst. —**gust'y**, adj.

gus'ta·to''ry, adj. pertaining to the sense of taste.

gus'to, n. great enjoyment or vigor.

gut, n., v.t., **gutted**, **gutting**. n. **1.** intestine. **2.** **guts**, Informal. courage. —v.t. **3.** destroy the inside of.

gut'ter, n. **1.** channel for rain water. **2.** realm of sordidness. —v.t. **3.** splutter before being extinguished, as a candle.

gut'tur·al, adj. pertaining to or produced in the throat.

guy, n. **1.** Informal. male person. **2.** Also, **guy'wire''**, steadying wire.

guz'zle, v.i., v.t., **-zled**, **-zling**. drink greedily.

gym·na'si·um, n., pl. **-ums**, **-a**. place for physical exercise. Also, Informal, gym.

gym·nas'tics, n. pl. physical exercises. —**gym'nast**, n. —**gym·nas'tic**, adj.

gy''ne·col'o·gy, n. branch of medicine concerned with women's diseases. —**gy''ne·col'o·gist**, n.

gyp, n., v.t., **gypped**, **gypping**. Informal. swindle.

gyp'sum, n. sulfate of calcium, used to make plaster of Paris.

gy·rate', v.i., **-rated**, **-rating**. whirl. —**gy·ra'tion** n.

gy'ro·scope'', n. object maintaining its position by the inertia of a rapidly turned wheel. —**gy''ro·scop'ic**, adj.

H

H, h, n. eighth letter of the English alphabet.

hab'it, n. **1.** custom, esp. one hard to depart from. **2.** distinctive costume. —**ha·bit'u·al**, adj. —**ha·bit'u·ate''**, v.t.

hab'it·a·ble, adj. able to be lived in.

hab'i·tat'', n. usual area of habitation.

hab''i·ta'tion, n. home.

hack, v.i. v.t. **1.** chop roughly. —v.i. **2.** cough hoarsely. —n. **3.** artistic drudge.

hack''er, n. a computer enthusiast.

hack'saw'', n. frame-mounted metal-cutting saw.

had'dock, n., pl. **-dock**, **-docks**. Atlantic codlike fish.

Ha'des, n. hell. Also, **ha'des**.

haft, n. knife or ax handle.

hag, n. ugly old woman.

hag'gard, adj. weary-looking.

hag'gle, v.i., **-gled**, **-gling**. dispute over a price.

hail, v.t. **1.** greet loudly. **2.** shout to. **3.** welcome as desirable. **4.** shower heavily. —n. **5.** frozen rain in small balls. —**hail'stone''**, n.

hair, n. **1.** slender growth from the skin. **2.** these growths collectively. —**hair'y**, adj. —**hair'i·ness**, n.

hair'rais''ing, adj. terrifying.

hair'split"ting, *n.* making of trivial distinctions.

hal'cy"on, *adj.* idyllic.

hale, *adj., v.t.,* **haled, haling.** *adj.* 1. full of health and vigor. —*v.t.* 2. summon forcibly.

half, *n., pl.* **halves,** *adj., adv. n.* 1. one of two equal divisions. —*adj.* 2. being a half. —*adv.* 3. as far as a half.

half'-breed", *n.* child of parents from different races.

half'-heart'ed, *adj.* without enthusiasm or determination. —**half'-heart'ed·ly,** *adv.*

half'way', *adj., adv.* 1. at or to a midpoint. 2. to a partial extent.

half'wit", *n.* person of subnormal intelligence. —**half'-wit'ted,** *adj.*

hal"i·but, *n., pl.* **-but, -buts.** northern saltwater flatfish.

hal"i·to'sis, *n.* bad breath.

hall, *n.* 1. large room, as for meetings. 2. Also, **hall'way",** corridor or vestibule.

hal"le·lu'jah, *interj.* praise the Lord! Also, **hal"le·lu'iah.**

hal'low, *v.t.* sanctify.

Hal"low·een', *n.* eve of All Saints' Day, celebrated October 31. Also, **Hal"low·e'en'.**

hal·lu"ci·na'tion, *n.* deluded perceptions of a nonexistent sight, sound, etc. —**hal·lu'ci·nate",** *v.i.* —**hal·lu'ci·na·to"ry,** *adj.*

ha'lo, *n., pl.* **-los, -loes.** ring of light, as around the portrayed head of a holy person.

halt, *v.t., v.i., n.* stop.

hal'ter, *n.* line for securing an animal.

halve, *v.t.,* **halved, halving.** 1. divide into halves. 2. reduce by half.

ham, *n.* upper part of a hog's hind leg.

ham'bur"ger, *n.* sandwich of ground beef in a bun. Also, **ham'burg.**

ham'let, *n.* small village.

ham'mer, *n.* 1. device for beating or driving with blows. —*v.t., v.i.* 2. strike with repeated blows.

ham'mock, *n.* flexible bed suspended at the ends.

ham'per, *v.t.* 1. encumber. —*n.* 2. covered basket.

hand, *n.* 1. extremity of the arm. 2. active part. 3. hired worker. 4. handwriting. 5. side or direction. —*v.t.* 6. give with the hand. —**hand'ful,** *n.*

hand'ball", *n.* game with a thrown rubber ball.

hand'book", *n.* manual.

hand'clasp", *n.* handshake.

hand'gun", *n.* pistol.

hand'i·cap", *n., v.t.,* **-capped, -capping.** *n.* 1. hindrance. —*v.t.* 2. hinder.

hand'i·work", *n.* 1. work done by hand. 2. work done personally.

hand'ker·chief", *n.* small wiping cloth.

han'dle, *n., v.t.,* **-dled, -dling.** *n.* 1. something to be grasped. —*v.t.* 2. grasp, as in order to wield. 3. manage or dominate. 4. sell.

hand'out", *n.* 1. charitable gift. 2. news release.

hand'-pick', *v.t.* 1. pick by hand. 2. choose carefully and individually.

hand'shake", *n.* friendly gripping and shaking of another's hand.

hand'some", *adj.* 1. good-looking. 2. generous.

hands"-on", *adj.* practical; making actual use of, as *hands-on training.*

hand'writ"ing, *n.* freehand writing. —**hand'writ"ten,** *adj.*

hand'y, *adj.,* **-ier, -iest.** convenient. —**hand'i·ly,** *adv.* —**hand'i·ness,** *n.*

hand'y·man, *n.* man who does odd jobs.

hang, *v.,* **hung** or (for 2) **hanged, hanged,** *n. v.t.* 1. hold up from above. 2. kill by suspending from a rope around the neck. —*v.i.* 3. be hung or hanged. —**hang'man,** *n.*

hang'ar, *n.* aircraft shelter.

hang'dog", *adj.* abject.

han'ker, *v.i.* yearn.

Ha'nu·ka", *n. Judaism.* festival of the rededication of the Temple at Jerusalem. Also, **Ha'nuk·kah".**

hap"haz'ard, *adj.* 1. random. —*adv.* 2. by chance.

hap'less, *adj.* unlucky.

hap'pen, *v.i.* come about by chance. —**hap'pen·ing,** *n.*

hap'py, *adj.,* **-pier, -piest.** 1. feeling pleased. 2. fortunate. —**hap'pi·ly,** *adv.* —**hap'pi·ness,** *n.*

ha·rangue', *n., v.t.,* **-rangued, -ranguing.** *n.* 1. long vehement speech. —*v.t.* 2. deliver a harangue.

ha·rass', *v.t.* trouble persistently. —**ha·rass'ment,** *n.*

har'bin·ger, *n.* forerunner.

har'bor, *n.* 1. sheltered place for shipping. —*v.t.* 2. shelter.

hard, *adj.* 1. unyielding. 2. difficult. —*adv.* 3. energetically. —**hard'en,** *v.t., v.i.*

hard'-heart'ed, *adj.* callous.

hard'ly, *adv.* barely; scarcely.

hard'ship", *n.* something hard to endure.

hard"ware, *n.* 1. tools, fasteners, etc. 2. (computers) equipment, as microchips, disk drives, printers, etc.

har'dy, *adj.* **-dier, -diest.** *n.* 1. of much endurance. 2. vigorous. —**har'di·ly,** *adv.*

hare, *n.* rabbitlike mammal.

ha'rem, *n.* 1. women's quarters of a Muslim house. 2. its inhabitants.

hark, *v.i.* listen.

hark'en, *v.i.* hearken.

har'lot, *n.* prostitute.

harm, *n.* 1. injury. —*v.t.* 2. injure.

—**harm′ful**, *adj.* —**harm′ful·ly**, *adv.* —**harm′less**, *adj.* —**harm′less·ly**, *adv.*

har·mon′i·ca, *n.* mouth organ.

har′mo·ny, *n.* **1.** pleasant combination. **2.** agreement; accord. —**har·mo′ni·ous**, *adj.* —**har′mo·nize″**, *v.t., v.i.*

har′ness, *n.* **1.** straps, etc. on an animal that pulls or carries. —*v.t.* **2.** put a harness on. **3.** control the energy of.

harp, *n.* **1.** large plucked stringed instrument. —*v.i.* **2.** speak tediously. —**harp′ist**, *n.*

har·poon′, *n.* **1.** spear for whales, etc. —*v.t.* **2.** spear with a harpoon.

har′row, *n.* **1.** device for breaking and leveling plowed ground. —*v.t.* **2.** work on with a harrow. **3.** cause anxiety to.

har′ry, *v.t.*, **-ried, -rying.** harass.

harsh, *adj.* **1.** unpleasantly rough. **2.** severe. —**harsh′ly**, *adv.* —**harsh′ness**, *n.*

har′vest, *n.* **1.** occasion of gathering crops. **2.** crop gathered. —*v.t.* **3.** gather as a harvest. —**har′vest·er**, *n.*

hash, *v.t.* **1.** chop finely for cooking. —*n.* **2.** chopped mixture of meat and vegetables.

hasp, *n.* bolted fastening fitted over a shackle.

has′sle, *n., v.i.*, **-sled, -sling.** *Informal.* squabble.

has′sock, *n.* cushionlike seat.

haste, *n.* speed, esp. when excessive. —**hast′y**, *adj.* —**hast′i·ly**, *adv.*

has′ten, *v.t., v.i.* hurry.

hat, *n.* head garment, esp. a formal one.

hatch, *v.t.* **1.** bring forth from eggs. —*v.i.* **2.** open to release young. —*n.* **3.** Also, **hatch′way″**, opening serving as a door or window.

hatch′et, *n.* short-handled chopping tool.

hate, *v.t.*, **hated, hating**, *n. v.t.* **1.** dislike violently. *n.* **2.** Also, **hat′red**, feeling of hating.

hate′ful, *adj.* to be hated.

haugh′ty, *adj.*, **-tier, -tiest.** arrogant. —**haugh′ti·ness**, *n.* —**haugh′ti·ly**, *adv.*

haul, *v.t., v.i.* **1.** pull. —*n.* **2.** act or instance of hauling.

haunch, *n.* area from upper thigh to buttock.

haunt, *v.t.* **1.** be often present at. —*n.* **2.** favorite place or resort.

have, *v.t.*, **had, having. 1.** own or possess. **2.** acquire. **3.** experience or engage in. **4.** cause. **5.** be obliged.

ha′ven, *n.* place of shelter.

hav′oc, *n.* vast destruction.

hawk, *n.* **1.** bird of prey. —*v.t.* **2.** peddle.

haw′ser, *n.* mooring or towing rope.

hay, *n.* grass, etc. dried as fodder.

hay fever, allergy to pollen.

hay′wire″, *adv. Informal.* awry.

haz′ard, *n., v.t.* risk. —**haz′ard·ous**, *adj.*

haze, *n, v.t.*, **hazed, hazing.** *n.* **1.** light mist or vapor. —*v.t.* **2.** harass or humiliate, as in an initiation. —**haz′y**, *adj.* —**haz′i·ly**, *adv.*

haz′el, *n.* tree of the birch family. —**haz′el·nut″**, *n.*

he, *pron., pl.* **they**, *n., pl.* **he's.** *pron.* **1.** male person or animal mentioned. —*n.* **2.** male person or animal.

head, *n.* **1.** part of the body for thinking, eating, seeing, etc. **2.** director. **3.** uppermost or working feature. —*adj.* **4.** at or against the head. —*v.t.* **5.** direct. —*v.i.* **6.** direct oneself. —**head′ache″**, *n.*

head′ing, *n.* title or subtitle.

head′line″, *n.* title of a newspaper article.

head′long″, *adv., adj.* **1.** with the head first. **2.** at reckless speed.

head′-on′, *adj., adv.* with the front end or ends foremost.

head′quar″ters, *n., pl.* main center of command.

head′strong″, *adj.* willful and impulsive.

head′way″, *n.* forward motion.

head′y, *adj.*, **-ier, -iest.** intoxicating.

heal, *v.t.* **1.** return to health. **2.** make whole again.

health, *n.* **1.** well-being. **2.** condition of the body or mind. —**health′ful**, *adj.* —**health′y**, *adj.*

heap, *n.* **1.** loose pile. —*v.t.* **2.** pile up.

hear, *v.*, **heard, hearing.** *v.t.* **1.** perceive through the ears. **2.** understand from others. **3.** listen to. —**hear′ing**, *n.*

hear′ken, *v.i.* listen carefully.

hear′say″, *n.* rumor.

hearse, *n.* funeral car.

heart, *n.* **1.** organ that pumps blood. **2.** compassion orsensitivity. **3.** courage. **4.** enthusiasm. **5.** center. **6.** essence. —**heart′less**, *adj.*

heart′break″, *n.* great sorrow. —**heart′bro″ken**, *adj.*

heart′en, *v.t.* encourage.

heart′felt″, *adj.* deeply sincere.

hearth, *n.* floor of a fireplace, furnace.

heart′y, *adj.*, **-ier, -iest.** enthusiastic. —**heart′i·ly**, *adv.* —**heart′i·ness**, *n.*

heat, *n.* **1.** warmth. **2.** strong feeling. —*v.t., v.i.* **3.** warm. —**heat′er**, *n.*

hea′then, *n., pl.* **-thens, -then,** *adj. n.* **1.** person not Christian, Jewish, or Muslim. —*adj.* **2.** pertaining to such persons.

heave, *v.*, **heaved** or **hove, heaving.** *n. v.t.* **1.** lift, or lift and throw, with effort. —*v.i.* **2.** rise and fall in rhythm. —*n.* **3.** act or instance of heaving.

heav′en, *n.* **1.** heavens, sky. **2. Heaven,** dwelling of God, the angels, and the blessed. —**heav′en·ly**, *adj.*

heav′y, *adj.*, **-ier, -iest. 1.** with much weight. **2.** with much difficulty. —**heav′i·ly**, *adv.*

heav′y-hand′ed, *adj.* **1.** clumsy. **2.** tyrannical.

heck'le, v.t., **-led, -ling.** harass verbally.

hec'tare, n. area of 10,000 square meters.

hec'tic, adj. 1. feverish. 2. hasty and confused.

hedge, n., v., **hedged, hedging.** n. 1. barrier of close-growing shrubs. —v.t. 2. partition off with a hedge. —v.i. 3. refuse to commit oneself.

hedge'hog'', n. American porcupine.

he'don·ism, n. doctrine that pleasure is the highest good. —**he'don·ist,** n. —**he''do·nis'tic,** adj.

heed, v.t. 1. pay attention to. —n. 2. attention. —**heed'ful,** adj. —**heed'less,** adj.

heel, n. 1. rear of the foot. 2. something similar in form or location. —v.i., v.t. 3. lean; list.

heft, v.t. pick up in order to weigh.

heft'y, adj., **-ier, -iest.** 1. heavy. 2. large.

heif'er, n. young cow.

height, n. 1. dimension from bottom to top. 2. raised area. 3. highest point.

height'en, v.t. 1. make higher. —v.i. 2. increase.

hei'nous, adj. outrageously wicked.

heir, n. a person who inherits. Also, fem., **heir'ess.**

heir'loom'', n. family possession.

hel'i·cop''ter, n. aircraft flying by means of a propellerlike rotor.

he'li·um, n. light gaseous chemical element.

he'lix, n., pl. **-lixes, -lices.** rising curve. —**hel'i·cal,** adj.

hell, n. Also **Hell,** place of confinement for those not redeemed. —**hel'lish,** adj.

hel·lo', interj. (exclamation of greeting).

helm, n. means of steering a ship. —**helms'man,** n.

hel'met, n. protective head covering.

help, v.t. 1. assist. 2. rescue. 3. prevent or mitigate. —v.i. 4. be useful. —n. 5. assistance. 6. rescue. —**help'ful,** adj.

help'ing, n. portion of food.

help'less, adj. unable to act. —**help'less·ly,** adv. —**help'less·ness,** n.

help'mate'', n. helpful companion. Also, **help'meet''.**

hem, n., v.t., **hemmed, hemming.** n. 1. edge formed on a cloth. —v.t. 2. make a hem on.

hem'i·sphere'', n. 1. half a sphere. 2. half of the earth. —**hem''i·spher'i·cal,** adj.

hem'lock'', n. 1. pinelike evergreen. 2. poisonous plant related to parsley.

hem'or·rhage, n. massive loss of blood.

hemp, n. Asiatic plant used for rope and hashish.

hen, n. female bird, esp. a chicken.

hence, adv. 1. away. 2. from this time. 3. therefore.

hence'forth', adv. from now on.

hench'man, n. assistant villain.

her, pron. 1. objective of she. —adj. 2. pertaining to a female previously mentioned.

her'ald, n. 1. officer who announces. 2. signifier of what is to come. —v.t. 3. signify in advance.

her'ald·ry, n. study of coats of arms, etc. —**he·ral'dic,** adj.

herb (ərb), n. annual seed plant used in cookery or medicine. —**her·ba'cious,** adj. —**herb'age,** n. —**herb'al,** adj.

her''cu·le'an, adj. with immense effort.

herd, n. 1. group of cows, sheep, etc. 2. person who tends such a group. —v.i., v.t. 3. gather or move as a herd.

here, adv. 1. in or to this place. 2. now.

here·af'ter, adv. 1. after this. —n. 2. next world.

here'by', adv. by this means.

he·red'i·tar''y, adj. so by inheritance or heredity.

here·in', adv. in this.

here·of', adv. of or concerning this.

her'e·sy, n., pl. **-sies.** contradiction of a dogma. —**her'e·tic,** n. —**he·ret'i·cal,** adj.

here'to·fore'', adv. until now.

here·with', adv. 1. with this. 2. by this means.

her'it·age, n. traditions, etc. from predecessors.

her·met'ic, adj. airtight. Also, **her·met'i·cal.** —**her·met'i·cal·ly,** adv.

her'mit, n. person willingly living alone. —**her'mit·age** n.

her'ni·a, n. abdominal rupture.

he'ro, n., pl. **-roes.** 1. person of courage and accomplishment. 2. protagonist. Also, fem., **he'ro·ine.** —**he·ro'ic,** adj. —**he'ro·ism,** n.

he'ro·in, n. morphine-based narcotic.

her'on, n. wading bird.

her''pes, n. a viral infection causing sores.

her'ring, n. North Atlantic fish.

hers, pron. something belonging or pertaining to her.

her·self', pron. 1. intensive and reflexive of she. 2. her true self.

hertz, n. Physics. one cycle per second.

hes'i·tate'', v.i., **-tated, -tating.** 1. be unresolved. 2. pause briefly. 3. be reluctant. —**hes''i·ta'tion,** n. —**hes'i·tant,** adj.

het'er·o·dox'', adj. unorthodox. —**het'er·o·dox''y,** n.

het''er·o·ge'ne·ous, adj. 1. dissimilar. 2. of dissimilar components. —**het''er·o·ge·ne'i·ty,** n.

het''er·o·sex'u·al, adj. 1. attracted solely to the opposite sex. —n. 2. heterosexual person. —**het''er·o·sex''u·al'i·ty,** n.

hew, v.t., **hewed, hewed** or **hewn, hewing.** chop.

hex, v.t. 1. put an evil spell on. —n. 2. evil spell.

hex'a·gon", *n.* six-sided plane figure. —**hex·ag'o·nal**, *adj.*

hi·a'tus, *n., pl.* **-tuses, -tus.** interruption.

hi'ber·nate", *v.i.,* **-nated, -nating.** be dormant through winter. —**hi"ber·na'tion**, *n.*

hic'cup, *n., v.i.,* **-cuped, -cuping.** *n.* 1. sharp sound due to involuntary contraction of the diaphragm. —*v.i.* 2. emit such a sound. Also, **hic'cough.**

hick'o·ry, *n., pl.* **-ries.** tree of the walnut family.

hide, *v.,* **hid, hidden, hiding**, *n. v.t.* 1. keep from being seen. —*v.i.* 2. conceal oneself. —*n.* 3. animal skin.

hid'e·ous, *adj.* horribly ugly.

hi'er·ar"chy, *n., pl.* **-ies.** organization of higher officials.

hi"er·o·glyph'ic, *n.* picture representing a word or sound.

high, *adj.* 1. being or reaching far up. 2. of a specified height. 3. superior. 4. notably large in amount. —*adv.* 5. in or to a high place or situation. —**high'ly**, *adv.*

high'-flown", *adj.* pretentious, as speech.

high'-hand'ed, *adj.* overbearing. —**high'-hand'ed·ly**, *adv.* —**high'-hand'ed·ness**, *n.*

high'land, *n.* hilly or mountainous region.

high'light", *n.* 1. brilliant reflection. 2. salient fact. —*v.t.* 3. emphasize.

high'ness, *n.* 1. height. 2. **Highness**, title of respect for royalty.

high'-rise', *n.* multistoried building. Also, **high'rise".**

high'-strung', *adj.* nervous.

high'way", *n.* major road.

hi'jack", *v.t. Informal.* take in transit by robbery. —**hi'jack"er**, *n.*

hike, *v.i.,* **hiked, hiking**, *n. v.i.* 1. go for a long walk. —*n.* 2. long walk.

hi·lar'i·ous, *adj.* 1. merry. 2. very funny. —**hi·lar'i·ty**, *n.*

hill, *n.* distinctive area of rising ground. —**hill'y**, *adj.*

hil'lock, *n.* small hill.

hilt, *n.* handle of a sword, etc.

him, *pron.* objective of *he.*

him·self', *pron.* 1. intensive or reflexive of *him.* 2. his true self.

hind, *adj.,* **hinder, hindmost** or **hindermost.** *adj.* behind.

hin'der, *v.t.* 1. stop or slow down. —*adj.* 2. rear. —**hin'drance**, *n.*

hind'sight", *n.* belated perception.

hinge, *n., v.i.,* **hinged, hinging.** *n.* 1. support allowing the supported part to turn. —*v.i.* 2. depend.

hint, *n.* 1. something that allows an inference to be made. —*v.t.* 2. imply. —*v.i.* 3. make a hint.

hip, *n.* area around the upper leg joints.

hip'pie, *n., pl.* **-pies.** *Informal.* person alienated from conventional society.

hip"po·pot'a·mus, *n., pl.* **-muses, -mi.** large river-loving African mammal.

hire, *v.t.,* **hired, hiring**, *n. v.t.* 1. employ or use for wages or a fee. —*n.* 2. amount paid in hiring.

hire'ling, *n.* unscrupulous mercenary.

hir'sute, *adj.* hairy.

his, *pron.* 1. something belonging or pertaining to him. —*adj.* 2. pertaining to him.

hiss, *n.* 1. prolonged s-like sound. —*v.i.* 2. emit a hiss. —*v.t.* 3. hiss at to show disapproval.

his'to·ry, *n., pl.* **-ries.** 1. study of the past. 2. account of the past. 3. known or recorded past. 4. determining forces as inferred from past events. —**his·to'ri·an**, *n.* —**his·tor'ic, his·tor'i·cal**, *adj.*

hit, *v.,* **hit, hitting**, *n. v.t.* 1. come against or send something against with force. —*v.i.* 2. come by chance. 3. strike a blow. —*n.* 4. accurate discharge of a missile. 5. successful song, etc.

hitch, *v.t.* 1. tie or harness. —*n.* 2. simple knot. 3. obstacle or drawback.

hitch'hike", *v.i.,* **-hiked, -hiking.** solicit a free automobile ride.

hith'er, *adv.* 1. to this place. —*adj.* 2. nearer.

hith'er·to", *adv.* until now.

hive, *n.* 1. beehive. 2. **hives**, itchy skin condition.

hoard, *n.* 1. precious hidden accumulation. —*v.t.* 2. accumulate and secrete.

hoarse, *adj.* emitting or having a harsh, grating sound.

hoar'y, *adj.,* **-ier, -iest.** 1. gray-haired from age. 2. very old.

hoax, *n.* 1. fraud. —*v.t.* 2. perpetrate a hoax on.

hob'ble, *v.,* **-bled, -bling.** *v.i.* 1. limp. —*v.t.* 2. hamper.

hob'by, *n., pl.* **-bies.** spare-time activity. —**hob'by·ist**, *n.*

hob'nob", *v.i.,* **-nobbed, -nobbing.** be on social terms.

ho'bo, *n., pl.* **-bos, -boes.** migrant worker.

hock'ey, *n.* game played on ice with long, clublike sticks and a puck.

ho'cus-po'cus, *n.* 1. meaningless jargon. 2. trickery.

hod, *n.* 1. trough for bricks or mortar. 2. coal scuttle.

hodge'podge", *n.* random mixture.

hoe, *n., v.t.,* **hoed, hoeing.** *n.* 1. long-handled tool for loosening earth. —*v.t.* 2. dig with a hoe.

hog, *n.* 1. pig raised for meat. 2. *Informal.* greedy person.

hogs'head", *n.* 1. large cask. 2. measure of 63 liquid gallons.

hoi'pol·loi', the common people.

hoist, *v.t.* **1.** lift, as by a crane. —*n.* **2.** hoisting device.

hold, *v.,* **held, holding,** *n. v.t.* **1.** have in the hand. **2.** keep from moving or changing. **3.** embrace. **4.** contain. **5.** possess. **6.** carry on. **7.** consider. —*v.i.* **8.** remain firm or fixed. —*n.* **9.** act or instance of holding. **10.** means of holding. **11.** cargo space. —**hold′er,** *n.* —**hold′ing,** *n.*

hole, *n.* opening, esp. a deep one.

hol′i·day″, *n.* **1.** day specially celebrated. **2.** day of no work.

hol′i·ness, *n.* **1.** quality of being holy. **2.** **Holiness,** title of respect for a pope.

hol′low, *adj.* **1.** empty inside. **2.** worthless; vain. **3.** booming. —*v.t.* **4.** make hollow.

hol′ly, *n., pl.* **-lies.** evergreen shrub with red berries.

hol′ly·hock″, *n.* tall plant with showy flowers.

ho′lo·caust″, *n.* widely destructive fire.

hol′ster, *n.* pistol holder.

ho′ly, *adj.,* **-lier, -liest. 1.** dedicated to religion. **2.** spiritually pure.

Holy Communion, Christian ritual of bread and wine.

Holy Spirit, spirit of God. Also, **Holy Ghost.**

hom′age, *n.* reverent respect.

home, *n.* **1.** place of residence. **2.** one's own place. —*adv.* **3.** to one's home. **4.** into the proper place. —**home′land″,** *n.* —**home′ward,** *adv.*

home′ly, *adj.,* **-lier, -liest. 1.** commonplace. **2.** not handsome or beautiful.

home′sick″, *adj.* sad at being away from home.

home′work″, *n.* schoolwork done at home.

home′y, *adj.,* **-ier, -iest.** cozy.

hom′i·cide″, *n.* killing of one person by another. —**hom′i·cid′al,** *adj.*

hom′i·ly, *n., pl.* **-lies.** sermon or moral lecture.

ho″mo·ge′ne·ous, *adj.* of uniform composition or content. —**ho·mo″ge·ne′i·ty,** *n.*

ho·mog′e·nize″, *v.t.,* **-nized, -nizing.** make homogeneous.

hom′o·nym, *n.* word like another in pronunciation but not in other ways.

Ho′mo sa′pi·ens″, man.

ho″mo·sex′u·al, *adj.* **1.** sexually attracted to one's own sex. —*n.* **2.** homosexual person. —**ho″mo·sex″u·al′i·ty,** *n.*

hone, *v.t.,* **honed, hone.** bring to a fine, sharp edge.

hon′est, *adj.* **1.** without desire to steal, lie, etc. **2.** genuine. **3.** frank. —**hon′est·ly,** *adv.* —**hon′es·ty,** *n.*

hon′ey, *n., pl.* **-neys.** syrup made by bees from flowers.

hon′ey·comb″, *n.* **1.** structure with hex-

agonal cells made by bees to store honey. **2.** openwork geometrical pattern.

hon′ey·dew″ melon, *n.* sweet, green melon.

hon′ey·moon″, *n.* vacation of newly-weds. —**hon′ey·moon″er,** *n.*

hon′ey·suck″le, *n.* climbing plant with small, sweet blossoms.

hon′or, *n.* **1.** high respect. **2.** good reputation. **3.** integrity. **4.** chastity. **5.** conferred distinction. —*v.t.* **6.** hold in honor. **7.** confer distinction or praise on. **8.** accept as valid. —**hon′or·a·ble,** *adj.* —**hon′or·ar″y,** *adj.*

hon″or·if′ic, *adj.* conferring honor.

hood, *n.* **1.** cloth covering for the head and nape. **2.** engine cover of an automobile, etc.

hood′lum, *n.* violent criminal.

hood′wink″, *v.t.* cheat.

hoof, *n., pl.* **hoofs, hooves.** hard foot covering of a horse, etc.

hook, *n.* **1.** curved object for hanging or attaching things. —*v.t.* **2.** attach with a hook. —*v.i.* **3.** curve as a hook does.

hoop, *n.* circular band.

hoot, *n.* **1.** loud, shrill sound. —*v.i.* **2.** utter a hoot. —*v.t.* **3.** show scorn for by hooting.

hop, *v.i.,* **hopped, hopping,** *n. v.i.* **1.** jump on one foot or with both feet together. —*n.* **2.** act or instance of hopping.

hope, *n., v.,* **hoped, hoping.** *n.* **1.** belief that something good may happen. **2.** source or cause of such a belief. —*v.t., v.i.* **3.** entertain hopes. —**hope′ful,** *adj., n.* —**hope′less,** *adj.*

hop′per, *n.* funnel-like chute.

horde, *n., v.i.,* **horded, hording.** *n.* **1.** swarm; multitude. —*v.i.* **2.** gather in a horde.

ho·ri′zon, *n.* apparent edge of a scene.

ho′ri·zon′tal, *adj.* running across, like a featureless horizon. —**ho″ri·zon′tal·ly,** *adv.*

hor′mone″, *n.* substance influencing one part of the body but made in another. —**hor·mo′nal,** *adj.*

horn, *n.* **1.** hard, pointed protuberance from an animal head. **2.** substance of this. **3.** pointed projection. **4.** wind instrument. —**horn′y,** *adj.*

hor′net, *n.* yellow and black wasp.

hor′o·scope″, *n.* chart of zodiacal signs.

hor·ren′dous, *adj.* horrible.

hor′ri·ble, *adj.* **1.** causing horror. **2.** *Informal.* very bad. —**hor′ri·bly,** *adv.*

hor′rid, *adj.* **1.** causing horror. **2.** very unpleasant.

hor′ri·fy″, *v.t.,* **-fied, -fying.** fill with horror.

hor′ror, *n.* strong fear and disgust.

hors de com·bat (or″də kom ba′), out of action.

hors d'oeuvre (or derv'), *n., pl.* **hors d'oeuvres,** appetizer.

horse, *n.* 1. four-footed grass eating animal. 2. supporting frame. —**horse'back",** *adv., n.* —**horse'man, horse' wom"an,** *n.*

horse chestnut, large-leaved flowering tree.

horse'laugh", *n.* loud, open laugh.

horse'play", *n.* rough play.

horse'pow"er, *n.* unit of power equalling 33,000 foot-pounds/minute or 746 watts.

horse'rad"ish, *n.* plant with a pungent root used as a relish.

horse'shoe", *n.* iron reinforcement for a hoof in the form of an open loop.

hor'ti·cul"ture, *n.* gardening. —**hor"ti·cul'tur·al,** *adj.* —**hor"ti·cul'tur·ist,** *n.*

ho·san'na, *interj.* (exclamation of praise to God).

hose, *n., pl.* (for 1) **hoses,** (for 2) **hose.** 1. flexible tube for water, etc. 2. long stocking.

ho'sier·y, *n.* stockings.

hos"pice, *n.* facility for terminally ill persons.

hos'pi·ta·ble, *adj.* readily offering hospitality.

hos'pi·tal, *n.* place for healing. —**hos'pi·tal·ize",** *v.t.*

hos"pi·tal'i·ty, *n.* generosity and friendship toward visitors.

host, *n.* 1. Also, *fem.,* **hos'tess,** person who entertains guests. 2. organism supporting parasites. 3. multitude. 4. wafer eaten in Holy Communion.

hos'tage, *n.* prisoner kept to enforce demands.

hos'tel, *n.* institution providing lodgings.

hos'tile, *adj.* in a state of enmity. —**hos·til'i·ty,** *n.*

hot, *adj.,* **hotter, hottest.** 1. very warm. 2. very spicy. 3. intense, as in emotion. —**hot'ly,** *adv.*

hot'bed", *n.* 1. miniature greenhouse. 2. prolific source.

hot'-blood'ed, *adj.* impetuous.

ho·tel', *n.* place renting rooms and often serving food.

hot'-head'ed, *adj.* quick-tempered. —**hot'head",** *n.*

hot rod, standard automobile with a supercharged engine. —**hot rod'der.**

hound, *n.* 1. hunting dog. —*v.t.* 2. persecute.

hour, *n.* twenty-fourth of a day. —**hour'ly,** *adv., adj.*

house, *n., pl.* **houses,** *v.t.,* **housed, housing.** *n.* (hows) 1. building to live in. 2. family. 3. business firm. 4. legislative body. —*v.t.* (howz) 5. provide lodgings or shelter for.

house'fly", *n.* ordinary fly.

house'hold", *n.* inhabitants of a house.

house'hold"er, *n.* 1. head of a household. 2. owner of a house.

house'keep"er, *n.* person responsible for keeping a house in order.

house'wife", *n.* wife who runs a home.

hous·ing (howz'ing), *n.* 1. complex of dwellings. 2. provision of dwellings.

hov'er, *v.i.* 1. remain poised in the air. 2. linger near by. 3. waver.

how, *adv.* 1. in what way. 2. in what state. 3. for what reason. 4. to what extent.

how·ev'er, *adv.* 1. regardless of how. —*conj.* 2. nevertheless.

how'itz·er, *n.* short-barreled, high-trajectory cannon.

howl, *v.i.* 1. raise a loud, animal-like cry. 2. laugh uproariously. 3. complain bitterly. —*n.* 4. act or instance of howling.

hub, *n.* center of a wheel.

hub'bub, *n.* confusion; disorder.

huck'le·ber"ry, *n., pl.* **-ries.** dark blue shrub berry.

huck'ster, *n.* peddler.

hud'dle, *n., v.,* **-dled, -dling.** *n.* 1. close, irregular group. —*v.t., v.i.* 2. gather in a huddle.

hue, *n.* 1. color. 2. tint.

huff, *n.* mood of silent resentment. —**huf'fy,** *adj.*

hug, *v.,* **hugged, hugging,** *n. v.t., v.i.* 1. embrace. —*v.t.* 2. keep close to. —*n.* 3. embrace.

huge, *adj.* very large. —**huge'ness,** *n.* —**huge'ly,** *adv.*

hulk, *n.* hull of a ship deprived of masts, etc.

hulk'ing, *adj.* large and bulky.

hull, *n.* 1. shell of a seed, etc. 2. body of a ship. —*v.t.* 3. remove the hulls from.

hul'la·ba·loo", *n.* clamor.

hum, *v.,* **hummed, humming,** *n. v.i.* 1. make an inarticulate sound between closed lips. —*v.t.* 2. render by humming. —*n.* 3. low, continuous murmur.

hu'man, *adj.* 1. being a man, woman, or child. 2. characteristic of man. —**hu'man·ly,** *adv.* —**hu'man·kind",** *n.*

hu·mane', *adj.* 1. merciful. 2. civilizing.

hu'man·ism, *n.* intellectual movement centered around man. —**hu'man·ist,** *n.* —**hu'man·is'tic,** *adj.*

hu·man"i·tar'i·an, *n.* 1. philanthropist. —*adj.* 2. philanthropic. —**hu·man"i·tar'i·an·ism,** *n.*

hu·man'i·ty, *n.* 1. human beings collectively. 2. quality of being humane.

hum'ble, *adj.,* **-bler, -blest,** *v.t.,* **-bled, -bling.** *adj.* 1. unpretentious; unconceited. 2. low in rank. —*v.t.* 3. make humble. —**hum'bly,** *adv.*

hum'drum", *adj.* drearily ordinary.

hu'mid, *adj.* moist. —hu·mid'i·fy", *v.t.* —hu·mid'i·ty, *n.*

hu·mil'i·ate", *v.t.,* -ated, -ating. cause to feel shame. —hu·mil"i·a'tion, *n.*

hu·mil'i·ty, *n.* humble quality.

hum'ming·bird, *n.* tiny bird with fast-moving wings.

hu'mor, *n.* 1. mood. 2. comical quality. 3. bodily fluid. —hu'mor·ist, *n.* —hu'mor·ous, *adj.*

hump, *n.* high lump on a back of a camel.

hu'mus, *n.* soil with decayed leaf matter, etc.

hunch, *n.* 1. *Informal.* intuitive feeling. 2. hump.

hunch'back", *n.* person with a hump on the back. Also, hump'back".

hun'dred, *adj., n.* ten times ten. —hun'dredth, *adj.*

hun'dred·weight", *n. U.S.* 100 pounds.

hun'ger, *n.* 1. desire to eat. 2. deprivation of food. 3. strong desire. —*v.i.* 4. be hungry. —hun'gry, *adj.* —hun'gri·ly, *adv.*

hunk, *n. Informal.* large piece.

hunt, *v.t.* 1. pursue to kill or harass. —*v.i.* 2. hunt game. 3. search. —*n.* 4. act or instance of hunting. —hunt'er, hunts'man, *fem.* hunt'ress, *n.*

hur'dle, *n., v.t.,* -dled, -dling. *n.* 1. barrier to be leapt. —*v.t.* 2. leap over.

hurl, *n.* throw with force.

hur'ly-bur'ly, *n., pl.* -lies. turmoil.

hur·rah', *interj., n.* (shout of approval). Also hur·ray'.

hur'ri·cane", *n.* tropical cyclone.

hur'ry, *v.,* -ried, -rying, *v.i.* 1. move or act quickly. —*v.t.* 2. cause to hurry. —*n.* 3. reason for hurrying. 4. eagerness to hurry. —hur'ried·ly, *adv.*

hurt, *v.,* hurt, hurting, *v.t.* 1. damage; injure. 2. pain the feelings of. —*v.i.* 3. cause pain. 4. do harm. —*n.* 5. damage; injury. —hurt'ful, *adj.*

hur'tle, *v.i.,* -tled, -tling. move at high speed.

hus'band, *n.* 1. woman's spouse. —*v.t.* 2. manage economically.

hus'band·ry, *n.* 1. farming. 2. management.

hush, *n., v.t.* silence.

husk, *n.* 1. outer covering. —*v.t.* 2. remove the husk from.

hus'ky, *adj.* 1. hoarse. 2. robust.

hus'tle, *v.,* -tled, -tling, *n. v.t.* 1. jostle. 2. force roughly. —*v.i.* 3. move or act energetically. —*n.* 4. act or instance of hustling. 5. *Informal.* enterprise.

hut, *n.* small, crude dwelling.

hutch, *n.* 1. cupboard. 2. coop for rabbits, etc.

hy'a·cinth", *n.* bell-shaped flower of the lily family.

hy'brid, *n.* 1. offspring or product of mixed species or varieties. —hy'brid·ize", *v.t.*

hy·dran'ge·a, *n.* shrub with clusters of white, blue, or pink flowers.

hy'drant, *n.* valved pipe from a water main.

hy·drau'lic, *adj.* 1. operated by liquid pressure. —*n.* 2. hydraulics, study of the mechanical properties of liquids. —hy·drau'li·cal·ly, *adv.*

hy'dro·car'bon, *n.* compound of hydrogen and carbon.

hy"dro·e·lec'tric, *adj.* pertaining to electricity produced by water power.

hy'dro·gen, *n.* flammable gaseous element.

hy"dro·pho'bi·a, *n.* rabies.

hy'dro·plane", *n.* 1. seaplane. 2. motorboat with hydrofoils or a planing hull.

hy"dro·pon'ics, *n.* growing of plants in liquids.

hy·e'na, *n.* wolflike African or Asian animal.

hy'giene, *n.* 1. system of health preservation. 2. cleanliness. —hy"gi·en'ic, *adj.* —hy"gi·en'i·cal·ly, *adv.*

hymn, *n.* poem or song of praise, as to God. —hymn'book", hym'nal, *n.*

hype, *n.* exaggerated publicity.

hy·per'bo·le", *n.* exaggeration for rhetorical effect. —hy"per·bol'ic, *adj.*

hy"per·crit'i·cal, *adj.* over-critical.

hy"per·sen'si·tive, *adj.* too sensitive.

hy"per·ten'sion, *n.* excessive blood pressure.

hy'phen, *n.* dash, -, used to join words or syllables. —hy'phen·ate", *v.t.* —hy"phen·a'tion, *n.*

hyp·no'sis, *n., pl.* -ses. sleeplike, obedient condition induced by suggestion from another. —hyp·not'ic, *adj.* —hyp'no·tism, *n.* —hyp'no·tist, *n.* —hyp'no·tize", *v.t.*

hy"po·chon'dri·a, *n.* fear of imaginary illness. —hy"po·chon'dri·ac", *n., adj.*

hy·poc'ri·sy, *n., pl.* -sies. false pretension to virtue, affection, etc. —hy'po·crite, *n.* —hy"po·crit'i·cal, *adj.*

hy"po·der'mic, *adj.* 1. under the skin. —*n.* 2. hypodermic injection or injecting device. —hy"po·der'mi·cal·ly, *adv.*

hy·pot'e·nuse", *n.* side of a right triangle opposite the right angle.

hy·poth'e·sis, *n., pl.* -ses. unproved theory. —hy"po·thet'i·cal, *adj.*

hys·te'ri·a, *n.* 1. pathologically excitable condition. 2. Also, hys·ter'ics, outbreak of uncontrolled emotion. —hys·ter'i·cal, *adj.*

I

I, i, *n.* **1.** ninth letter of the English alphabet. —*pron.* **2. I** (first person singular as a subject).

ibid., in the same place: used in scholarly notes.

ice, *n., v.,* **iced, icing.** *n.* **1.** water frozen solid. **2.** frozen dessert. —*v.t.* **3.** put ice over or around. **4.** put icing over. —*v.i.* **5.** freeze or form ice. —**ice′box″,** *n.* —**ice′skate″,** *n.* —**ic′y,** *adj.*

ice′berg″, *n.* floating fragment from a polar icecap.

ice′cap″, *n.* polar mass of ice.

ich″thy·ol′o·gy, *n.* study of fish. —**ich″ thy·ol′o·gist,** *n.*

i′ci·cle, *n.* conical hanging mass of frozen water.

ic′ing, *n.* sweet cover for a cake.

i′con, *n.* religious image, esp. in an eastern church.

i·con′o·clast″, *n.* destroyer of long-held values. —**i·con″o·clas′tic,** *adj.*

i·de′a, *n.* image in the mind; conception.

i·de′al, *adj.* **1.** perfect. **2.** imaginary. —*n.* **3.** something perfect. —**i·de′al·ly,** *adv.* —**i·de′al·ize″,** *v.t.*

i·de′al·ism, *n.* conformity to or belief in ideals. —**i·de′al·ist,** *n.* —**i″de·al·is′ tic,** *adj.*

i·den′ti·cal, *adj.* exactly alike or the same. —**i·den′ti·cal·ly,** *adv.*

i·den′ti·fy″, *v.t.,* **-fied, -fying. 1.** establish the identity of. **2.** associate with another person or thing. —**i·den″ti·fi· ca′tion,** *n.*

i·den′ti·ty, *n., pl.* **-ties. 1.** state of being identical. **2.** individuality.

i″de·ol′o·gy, *n., pl.* **-gies.** political or social doctrine. —**i″de·o·log′i·cal,** *adj.*

id′i·om, *n.* **1.** dialect. **2.** combination of words with a nonliteral meaning. —**id″ i·o·mat′ic,** *adj.*

id″i·o·syn′cra·sy, *n., pl.* **-sies.** personal trait.

id′i·ot, *n.* feeble-minded person. —**id″i· ot′ic,** *adj.* —**id′i·o·cy,** *n.*

i′dle, *adj.,* **idler, idlest,** *v.i.,* **idled, idling.** *adj.* **1.** not at work or in use. **2.** lazy. **3.** frivolous. —*v.i.* **4.** be idle. —**id′ly,** *adv.* —**id′ler,** *n.*

i′dol, *n.* **1.** statue of a god. **2.** idealized person. —**i′dol·ize″,** *v.t.*

i·dol′a·try, *n., pl.* **-tries.** worship of idols. —**i·dol′a·ter,** *n.* —**i·dol′a·trous,** *adj.*

i′dyll, *n.* **1.** poem of pastoral life. **2.** beautiful episode. Also, **i′dyl.** —**i·dyl′ic,** *adj.*

i.e., that is.

if, *conj.* **1.** on condition that. **2.** supposing that. **3.** whether.

ig′loo, *n., pl.* **-loos.** domed Eskimo snow house.

ig′ne·ous, *adj.* resulting from intense heat.

ig·nite′, *v.,* **-nited, -niting.** *v.t.,* **1.** set on or catch fire. —*v.i.* **2.** catch fire. —**ig· ni′tion,** *n.*

ig·no′ble, *adj.* base; mean.

ig′no·min″y, *n.* shame. —**ig″no·min′i· ous,** *adj.*

ig″no·ra′mus, *n., pl.* **-muses.** ignorant person.

ig′no·rant, *adj.* **1.** uneducated. **2.** unaware. —**ig′no·rance,** *n.* —**ig′no·rant· ly,** *adv.*

ig·nore′, *v.t.,* **-nored, -noring.** take no heed of.

ill, *adj.,* worse, (for 1) worst, *adv.,* worse, worst, *n. adj.* **1.** bad. **2.** sick. —*adv.* **3.** badly. **4.** scarcely. —*n.* **5.** harm.

ill′-ad·vised′, *adj.* showing bad judgment.

il·le′gal, *adj.* unlawful. —**il·le′gal·ly,** *adv.* —**il″le·gal′i·ty,** *n.*

il·leg′i·ble, *adj.* unable to be read. —**il· leg″i·bil′i·ty,** *n.*

il″le·git′i·mate, *adj.* **1.** not legitimate. **2.** born out of wedlock. —**il″le·git′i·ma· cy,** *n.*

il·lic′it, *adj.* not allowed. —**il·lic′it·ly,** *adv.*

il·lit′er·ate, *adj.* **1.** unable to read. —*n.* **2.** illiterate person. —**il·lit′er·a·cy,** *n.*

ill′ness, *n.* sickness.

il·log′i·cal, *adj.* opposed to logic.

il·lu′mi·nate″, *v.t.,* **-nated, nating. 1.** Also, **il·lu′mine,** light up. **2.** elucidate. **3.** decorate with gold and color. —**il· lu″mi·na′tion,** *n.*

ill′-use′, *v.t.,* **-used, using.** abuse. —**ill′ use′, ill′-us′age,** *n.*

il·lu′sion, *n.* **1.** deceptive impression. **2.** false conception. —**il·lu′sive,** —**il·lu′ so·ry,** *adj.*

il′lus·trate″, *v.t.,* **-trated, -trating. 1.** explain with examples. **2.** add pictures to, as a narrative. —**il″lus·tra′tion,** *n.* —**il′ lus·tra″tor,** *n.* —**il·lus′tra·tive,** *adj.*

il·lus′tri·ous, *adj.* distinguished; famous.

ill will, hostility.

im′age, *n.* **1.** picture. **2.** popular conception. —**im′age·ry,** *n.*

i·mag′ine, *v.t.,* **-ined, -ining. 1.** create in the mind. **2.** suppose to exist. **3.** believe wrongly to exist. —**i·mag′in·a·ble,** *adj.* —**i·mag′in·a·bly,** *adv.* —**i·mag′ in·a″ry,** *adj.* —**i·mag″i·na′tion,** *n.* —**i·mag′i·na·tive,** *adj.*

im·bal′ance, *n.* lack of balance.

im′be·cile, *n.* idiot. —im″be·cil′ic, *adj.* —im″be·cil′i·ty, *n.*

im·bibe′, *v.,* -bibed, -bibing. *v.t., v.i.* drink.

im·bro·gli·o (im brōl′yō), *n., pl.* -os. confused situation.

im·bue′, *v.t.,* -bued, -buing. permeate.

im′i·tate″, *v.t.,* -tated, -tating. have the same characteristics as. —im″i·ta′tion, *n.* —im′i·ta″tor, *n.* —im′i·ta″tive, *adj.*

im·mac′u·late, *adj.* without dirt or sin. —im·mac′u·late·ly, *adv.*

im′ma·nent, *adj.* inherent. —im′ma·nent·ly, *adv.* —im′ma·nence, *n.*

im″ma·te′ri·al, *adj.* 1. irrelevant. 2. not composed of matter.

im″ma·ture, *n.* with an undeveloped character. —im″ma·tu′ri·ty, *n.*

im·meas′ur·a·ble, *adj.* not to be measured. —im·meas′ur·a·bly, *adv.*

im·me′di·ate, *adj.* 1. unseparated by anything else. 2. direct. —im·me′di·a·cy, *n.* —im·me′di·ate·ly, *adv.*

im″me·mo′ri·al, *adj.* from before memory.

im·mense′, *adj.* huge. —im·men′si·ty, *n.* —im·mense′ly, *adv.*

im·merse′, *v.t.,* -mersed, -mersing. bury completely, as in a liquid. —im·mer′sion, *n.*

im′mi·grate″, *v.i.,* -grated, -grating. enter a country to settle. —im′mi·grant, *n., adj.* —im″mi·gra′tion, *n.*

im′mi·nent, *adj.* soon to happen. —im′mi·nence, im′mi·nen·cy, *n.*

im·mo′bile, *adj.* fixed in place. —im″mo·bil′i·ty, *n.* —im·mo′bi·lize″, *v.t.*

im·mod′e·rate, *adj.* lacking moderation. —im·mod′e·rate·ly, *adv.*

im·mod′est, *adj.* lacking modesty. —im·mod′es·ty, *n.*

im′mo·late″, *v.t.,* -lated, -lating. kill as a sacrifice. —im″mo·la′tion, *n.*

im·mor′al, *adj.* not moral. —im″mo·ral′i·ty, *n.*

im·mor′tal, *adj.* 1. never to die. 2. never to be forgotten. —*n.* 3. immortal being. —im″mor·tal′i·ty, *n.* —im·mor′tal·ize″, *v.t.*

im·mov′a·ble, *adj.* fixed in place.

im·mune′, *adj.* proof against disease, etc. —im·mun′i·ty, *n.* —im′mu·nize″, *v.t.* —im″mu·ni·za′tion, *n.*

im·mu′ta·ble, *adj.* unchangeable. —im·mu″ta·bil′i·ty, *n.*

imp, *n.* small demon. —imp′ish, *adj.*

im·pact′, *n.* (im′pakt) 1. violent shock. —*v.t.* (im pakt′) 2. force against something else.

im·pair′, *v.t.* put out of order. —im·pair′ment, *n.*

im·pale′, *v.t.,* -paled, -paling. pierce and support with a sharpened pole, etc.

im·pal′pa·ble, *adj.* 1. imperceptible to the touch. 2. subtle.

im·pan′el, *v.t.,* -eled, -eling. enroll for or as a jury.

im·part′, *v.t.* reveal, as news.

im·par′tial, *adj.* unbiased. —im·par′tial·ly, *adv.* —im·par″ti·al′i·ty, *n.*

im·pas′sa·ble, *adj.* impossible to pass along or over.

im′passe, *n.* deadlock.

im·pas′sioned, *adj.* passionate.

im·pas′sive, *adj.* revealing no emotion. —im″pas·siv′i·ty, *n.*

im·pa′tient, *adj.* without patience. —im·pa′tience, *n.*

im·peach′, *n.* try for wrongdoing in office. —im·peach′ment, *n.*

im·pec′ca·ble, *adj.* flawless.

im″pe·cu′ni·ous, *adj.* penniless.

im·pede′, *v.t.,* -peded, -peding. hinder. —im·ped′ance, im·ped′i·ment, *n.*

im·ped″i·men′ta, *n., pl.* things to be carried along.

im·pel′, *v.t.,* -pelled, -pelling. 1. drive forward. 2. urge.

im·pend′, *v.i.* be about to happen.

im·pen′e·tra·ble, *adj.* impossible to penetrate.

im·pen′i·tent, *adj.* not repentant.

im·per′a·tive, *adj.* 1. vitally necessary. 2. pertaining to command.

im·per·cep′ti·ble, *adj.* impossible or difficult to perceive. —im″per·cep′ti·bly, *adv.*

im·per′fect, *adj.* 1. flawed; deficient. 2. pertaining to uncompleted or continuing action. —im·per′fect·ly, *adv.* —im″per·fec′tion, *n.*

im·pe′ri·al, *adj.* pertaining to empires or emperors.

im·pe′ri·al·ism, *n.* policy of creating or holding an empire. —im·pe′ri·al·ist, *n., adj.* —im·pe″ri·al·is′tic, *adj.*

im·per′il, *v.t.,* -iled, -iling. endanger.

im·pe′ri·ous, *adj.* imposing one's will on others. —im·pe′ri·ous·ly, *adv.*

im·per′ish·a·ble, *adj.* not perishable.

im·per′ma·nent, *adj.* not permanent.

im·per′me·a·ble, *adj.* impossible to seep through.

im·per′son·al, *adj.* pertaining to no individuals. —im·per′son·al·ly, *adv.*

im·per′son·ate″, *v.t.,* -ated, -ating. pretend to be, as in acting. —im·per″son·a′tion, *n.* —im·per′son·a″tor, *n.*

im·per′ti·nent, *adj.* insolent. —im·per′ti·nence, *n.*

im″per·turb′a·ble, *adj.* impossible to disturb visibly. —im″per·turb′a·bly, *adv.*

im·per′vi·ous, *adj.* impenetrable, esp. by moisture.

im·pet′u·ous, *adj.* hasty; rash. —im·pet″u·os′i·ty, *n.*

im'pe·tus, *n*. 1. force in motion. 2. motivation.

im·pi'e·ty, *n*. disrespect, esp. for God. —im'pi·ous, *adj*.

im·pinge', *v.i.*, -pinged, -pinging. 2. encroach. —im·pinge'ment, *n*.

im·plac'a·ble, *adj*. impossible to appease. —im·plac'a·bly, *adv*.

im·plant', *v.t.* fix or plant firmly.

im·plaus'i·ble, *adj*. not plausible.

im'ple·ment, *n*. 1. piece of equipment. —*v.t.* 2. put in effect. —im''ple·men·ta'tion, *n*.

im'pli·cate'', *v.t.*, -cated, -cating. reveal as party to a crime.

im''pli·ca'tion, *n*. act or instance of implying or implicating.

im·plic'it, *adj*. 1. implied. 2. absolute, as trust. —im·plic'it·ly, *adv*.

im·plore', *v.t.*, -plored, -ploring. plead earnestly with or for. —im·plor'ing·ly, *adv*.

im·ply', *v.t.*, -plied, -plying. suggest as existing or being so.

im''po·lite', *adj*. rude.

im·pol''i·tic, *adj*. unwise as giving offense.

im·pon'der·a·ble, *adj*. 1. immeasurable. —*n*. 2. something imponderable.

im·port', *v.t.* (im port') 1. bring into a country, esp. for sale. 2. signify. —*n*. (im'port) 3. something imported. 4. significance. —im·port'er, *n*. —im''por·ta'tion, *n*.

im·port'ant, *adj*. 1. of great significance. 2. of great power. —im·por'tance, *n*.

im''por·tune', *v.t.*, -tuned, -tuning. urge insistently. —im''por·tun'i·ty, *n*. —im·por'tu·nate, *adj*.

im·pose', *v.*, -posed, posing. *v.t.* 1. force to accept. —*v.i.* 2. take advantage. —im''po·si'tion, *n*.

im·pos'ing, *adj*. impressive. —im·pos'ing·ly, *adv*.

im·pos'si·ble, *adj*. 1. not possible. 2. totally unsuitable or disagreeable. —im·pos''si·bil'i·ty, *n*.

im'post, *n*. tax on imports.

im·pos'tor, *n*. person pretending to an identity, competence, etc. he does not have. —im·pos'ture, *n*.

im'po·tent, *adj*. 1. helpless. 2. without strength. 3. incapable of sexual intercourse. —im'po·tence, im'po·ten·cy, *n*.

im·pound', *v.t.* 1. seize and hold legally. 2. dam.

im·pov'er·ish, *v.t.* make poor. —im·pov'er·ish·ment, *n*.

im·prac'ti·ca·ble, (im prak'ti kə bl), *adj*. impossible to do.

im·prac'ti·cal, *adj*. not practical.

im''pre·ca'tion, *n*. curse.

im''pre·cise', *n*. not precise; vague. —im''pre·ci'sion, *n*.

im·preg'na·ble, *adj*. proof against attack.

im·preg'nate'', *v.t.*, -nated, -nating. 1. saturate. 2. make pregnant. —im'' preg·na'tion, *n*.

im·press', *v.t.* 1. command respectful attention. 2. print. 3. force into military service.

im·pres'sion, *n*. 1. mental effect. 2. vague idea. 3. pressed mark.

im·pres'sion·a·ble, *adj*. easily influenced.

im·pres'sive, *adj*. commanding respect. —im·pres'sive·ly, *adv*.

im·print, *v.t.* (im print') 1. affix or print as a mark. —*n*. (im'print) 2. imprinted mark. 3. effect.

im·pris'on, *v.t.* confine in prison. —im·pris'on·ment, *n*.

im·prob'a·ble, *adj*. unlikely. —im·prob''a·bil'i·ty, *n*.

im·promp'tu, *adj.*, *adv*. without preparation.

im·prop'er, *adj*. not proper. —im''pro·pri'e·ty, *n*.

im·prove', *v.*, -proved, -proving. make or become better. —im·prove'ment, *n*.

im·prov'i·dent, *adj*. not thrifty. —im·prov'i·dence, *n*.

im'pro·vise'', *v.*, -vised, -vising. *v.t.* 1. create at short notice or with what is available. —*v.i.* 2. perform extemporaneously. —im·prov''i·sa'tion, *n*.

im·pru'dent, *adj*. not prudent. —im·prud'ence, *n*.

im·pugn', *v.t.* oppose as false.

im'pulse, *n*. 1. surge of force. 2. sudden decision to act. —im·pul'sive, *adj*.

im·pu'ni·ty, *n*. freedom from punishment.

im·pure', *adj*. 1. adulterated. 2. immoral. —im·pur'i·ty, *n*.

im·pute', *v.t.*, -puted, -puting. attribute. —im''pu·ta'tion *n*.

in, *prep*. 1. surrounded or contained by. 2. during. 3. into. 4. subjected to. —*adv*. 5. to the inside.

in-, prefix meaning "not" or "lack of." **inaccurate, inadequate, inapplicable, inappropriate, inarticulate, incertitude, inclement, incoherent, incompetent, incongruous, inconsequential, inconsistent, inconspicuous, incontinent, incredible, incredulous, incurable, indecent, indecision, indefinite, indelicate, indigestible, indiscreet, indispensable, indistinct, indivisible, inedible, ineligible, inequitable, inexact, infallible, infertile, informal, infrequent, inhumane, inhumanity, inoffensive, insane, insatiable, insecure, insincere, insufficient, intemperate, intolerable, intransitive, invisible, involuntary, invulnerable.**

in ab·sen'ti·a in his, her, or their absence.

in''ad·vert'ent, *adj*. 1. unobservant. 2.

due to unawareness or oversight. —**in″ ad·vert′ent·ly,** *adv.* —**in″ad·vert′ence,** *n.*

in·al′i·en·a·ble, *adj.* not to be taken away.

in·ane′, *adj.* pointless; silly. —**in·an′i·ty,** *n.*

in″as·much′as 1. considering that. 2. to the extent that.

'in·au′gu·rate″, *v.t.,* **-rated, -rating.** begin formally in a term of office, service, etc. —**in·aug″u·ra′tion,** *n.* —**in·aug′u·ral,** *adj., n.*

in′board″, *adj., adv.* within a ship or aircraft.

in′born″, *adj.* present at birth; innate.

in′bred′, *adj.* 1. inborn. 2. resulting from inbreeding.

in′breed′, *v.,* **-bred, -breeding.** *v.t., v.i.* breed from closely related stocks.

in″can·des′cent, *adj.* glowing from heat. —**in″can·des′cence,** *n.*

in″can·ta′tion, *n.* formula producing a magic spell.

in″ca·pac′i·tate″, *v.t.,* **-tated, -tating.** make unable or incompetent. —**in″ca·pac′i·ty,** *n.*

in·car′cer·ate″, *v.t.,* **-ated, -ating.** imprison.

in·car′nate, *adj., v.t.,* **-nated, -nating.** *adj.* (in kahr′nət) 1. in fleshly, mortal form. —*v.t.* (in kahr′nāt) 2. create in incarnate form. —**in″car′na′tion,** *n.*

in·cen′di·ar″y, *adj., n., pl.* **-ies.** *adj.* 1. causing fires. —*n.* 2. incendiary bomb. 3. deliberate setter of fires.

in·cense, *n., v.t.,* **-censed, -censing.** *n.* (in′sens) 1. gum or resin giving off perfumed smoke. —*v.t.* (in sens′) 2. enrage.

in·cen′tive, *n.* motive.

in·cep′tion, *n.* beginning.

in·ces′sant, *adj.* never ceasing. —**in·ces′sant·ly,** *adv.*

in′cest, *n.* sexual relations between very close relatives. —**in·ces′tu·ous,** *adj.*

inch, *n.* 1. twelfth part of a foot, as a linear measure. —*v.i., v.t.* 2. move very slowly.

in·cho·ate (in kō it), *adj.* new and formless.

in′ci·dence, *n.* frequency of occurrence.

in′ci·dent, *n.* 1. something that happens. 2. minor fight, etc. —*adj.* 3. probably consequent.

in″ci·den′tal, *adj.* 1. happening in connection with something important. —*n.* 2. something incidental. 3. miscellaneous item.

in″ci·den′tal·ly, *adv.* 1. while we are on the subject. 2. in an incidental manner.

in·cin′er·ate″, *v.,* **-ated, -ating.** *v.t., v.i.* burn to ashes. —**in·cin′er·at″or,** *n.*

in·cip′i·ent, *adj.* beginning to develop. —**in·cip′i·ence,** *n.*

in·cise′, *v.t.,* **-cised, -cising.** cut into. —**in·ci′sion,** *n.*

in·cis′ive, *adj.* penetrating in perception.

in·cis′or, *n.* human front tooth.

in·cite′, *v.t.,* **-cited, -citing.** urge to act. —**in·cite′ment,** *n.*

in·cline, *v.,* **-clined, -clining,** *v.i.* (inklīn′) 1. slope or slant. 2. have a tendency or liking. —*v.t.* 3. cause to incline. —*n.* (in′klīn) 4. slope. —**in·cli·na′tion,** *n.*

in·close′, *v.t.,* **-closed, -closing.** enclose.

in·clude′, *v.t.,* **-cluded, -cluding.** have or consider among other things. —**in·clu′sion,** *n.*

in·clu′sive, *adj.* 1. including the limiting items mentioned. 2. considering everything.

in·cog′ni·to, *adj.* under an assumed name.

in′come″, *n.* money received.

in″com·mu″ni·ca′do, *adj.* without being allowed to communicate.

in·com′par·a·ble, *adj.* not to be compared to others, esp. as an equal. —**im·com′par·a·bly,** *adv.*

in·cor′po·rate″, *v.,* **-rated, -rating.** *v.t., v.i.* 1. form into a corporation. —*v.t.* 2. embody. —**in·cor″po·ra′tion,** *n.*

in·cor′ri·gi·ble, *adj.* incapable of correction.

in·crease, *v.,* **-creased, -creasing,** *n. v.t.* (in krēs′) 1. add to. —*v.i.* 2. become larger or more numerous. —*n.* (in′ krēs) 3. act, instance, or amount of increasing. —**in·creas′ing·ly,** *adv.*

in′cre·ment, *n.* increase.

in·crim′i·nate″, *v.t.,* **-nated, -nating.** 1. accuse of crime. 2. subject to such accusation.

in·crust′, *v.t.* cover thickly. —**in″crus·ta′tion,** *n.*

in′cu·bate″, *v.t.,* **-bated, -bating.** 1. hatch. 2. encourage the development of. —**in″cu·ba′tion,** *n.* —**in′cu·ba″tor,** *n.*

in′cu·bus, *n.* annoying burden.

in·cul′cate, *v.t.,* **-cated, -cating.** impress on the mind.

in·cul′pate, *v.t.,* **-pated, -pating.** incriminate.

in·cum′bent, *adj.* 1. obligatory. 2. in office. —*n.* 3. present office holder. —**in·cum′ben·cy,** *n.*

in·cur′, *v.t.,* **-curred, -curring.** bring on oneself.

in·cur′sion, *n.* invasion.

in·debt′ed, *adj.* owing a debt of money or gratitude. —**in·debt′ed·ness,** *n.*

in·deed′, *adv.* 1. truly. —*interj.* 2. (exclamation of surprise).

in″de·fat′i·ga·ble, *adj.* tireless.

in·def′i·nite·ly, *adj.* 1. in an indefinite way. 2. with no known termination.

in·del′i·ble, *adj.* impossible to erase.

in·dem'ni·fy'', *v.t.*, -fied, -fying. compensate for. —in·dem'ni·ty, *n.*

in·dent, *v.t.* 1. notch. 2. begin to the right of the normal margin. —in·den'tion, in''den·ta'tion, *n.*

in·den'ture, *n., v.t.*, -tured, -turing. *n.* 1. contract, esp. for work. —*v.t.* 2. bind with an indenture.

in''de·pen'dent, *adj.* free of or needing no outside control. —in''de·pen'dent·ly, *adv.* —in''de·pen'dence, *n.*

in'dex, *n., pl.* -dexes, -dices, *v.t. n.* 1. orderly list of subjects. 2. something that indicates. 3. forefinger. —*v.t.* 4. make an index for.

in'di·cate'', *v.t.*, -cated, -cating. 1. call attention to. 2. imply. —in''di·ca'tion, *n.* —in·dic'a·tive, *adj.* —in'di·ca''tor, *n.*

in·dict (in dīt'), *v.t.* charge formally with crime. —in·dict'ment, *n.*

in·dif'fer·ent, *adj.* 1. not caring. 2. mediocre. 3. neutral. —in·dif'fer·ence, *n.*

in·dig'en·ous, *adj.* native.

in'di·gent, *adj.* needy. —in'di·gence, *n.*

in·di·ges'tion, *n.* difficulty in digesting food; discomfort caused by this.

in·dig'nant, *adj.* righteously angry. —in·dig'nant·ly, *adv.* —in''dig·na'tion, *n.*

in·dig'ni·ty, *n., pl.* -ties. offense to dignity.

in'di·go'', *n.* deep blue dye.

in''dis·posed', *adj.* 1. disinclined. 2. slightly ill. —in·dis''po·si'tion, *n.*

in''di·vid'u·al, *adj.* 1. separate or distinct. 2. pertaining to one person or thing. —*n.* 3. single or unique person or thing. —in''di·vid'u·al·ly, *adv.* —in''di·vid''u·al'i·ty, *n.*

in''di·vid'u·al·ism, *n.* use of personal judgment alone. —in''di·vid'u·al·ist, *n.*

in·doc'tri·nate'', *v.t.*, -nated, -nating. instill doctrine into. —in·doc''tri·na'tion, *n.*

in'do·lent, *adj.* making little effort. —in'do·lence, *n.*

in·dom'i·ta·ble, *adj.* impossible to defeat or dishearten.

in'door'', *adj.* for use, etc. inside.

in'doors', *adv.* within a building.

in·du'bi·ta·ble, *adj.* impossible to doubt. —in·du'bi·ta·bly, *adv.*

in·duce', *v.t.*, -duced, -ducing. 1. persuade. 2. cause. 3. infer. —in·duce'ment, *n.*

in·duct', *v.t.* enter formally, as in a military organization. —in·duc·tee', *n.*

in·duc'tion, *n.* 1. act or instance of inducing or inducting. 2. reasoning from the particular to the general. —in·duc'tive, *adj.*

in·dulge', *v.*, -dulged, -dulging. satisfy.

in·dul'gence, *n.* 1. act or instance of indulging. 2. indulgent manner.

in·dul'gent, *adj.* leniently kind.

in'dus·try, *n., pl.* -tries. 1. manufacture and commerce. 2. type of manufacture or commerce. 3. diligent work. —in·dus'tri·al, *adj.* —in·dus'tri·al·ist, *n.* —in·dus'tri·al·ize'', *v.t.* —in·dus'tri·ous, *adj.*

in·e·bri·ate, *v.t.*, -ated, -ating, *n. v.t.* (inē'brē āt'') 1. make drunk. —*n.* (in ē' brēət) 2. drunkard. —in·e''bri·a'tion, *n.*

in·ef'fa·ble, *adj.* indescribable in words.

in''e·luc'ta·ble, *adj.* inescapable.

in·ept', *adj.* 1. unsuitable. 2. foolish or awkward. —in·ept'i·tude'', in·ept'ness, *n.*

in·ert', *adj.* 1. powerless to move. 2. without active properties. —in·er'tia, *n.* —in·er'tial, *adj.*

in·ev'i·ta·ble, *adj.* impossible to avoid. —in·ev'i·ta·bly, *adv.* —in·ev''i·ta·bil'i·ty, *n.*

in·ex'o·ra·ble, *adj.* 1. impossible to persuade. 2. impossible to halt or change. —in·ex'o·ra·bly, *adv.*

in·ex'pli·ca·ble, *adj.* impossible to explain.

in ex·tre'mis, at the point of death.

in'fa·mous, *adj.* of evil reputation.

in'fa·my, *n., pl.* -mies. infamous state or act.

in'fant, *n.* very young child. —in'fan·cy, *n.* —in'fan·tile'', *adj.*

in'fan·try, *n., pl.* -tries. corps of foot soldiers. —in'fan·try·man, *n.*

in·fat'u·ate'', *v.t.*, -ated, -ating. make foolish with love. —in·fat''u·a'tion, *n.*

in·fect', *v.t.* 1. afflict with germs or a virus. 2. influence with one's feelings. —in·fec'tion, *n.* —in·fec'tious, *adj.*

in·fer', *v.t.*, -ferred, -ferring. conclude from evidence. —in'fer·ence, *n.* —in''fer·en'tial, *adj.*

in·fe'ri·or, *adj.* 1. of lesser worth. 2. inadequate. 3. of lesser rank. —*n.* 4. inferior person. —in·fe''ri·or'i·ty, *n.*

in·fer'nal, *adj.* hellish.

in·fer'no, *n.* hell, esp. as a fiery place.

in·fest', *v.t.* penetrate harmfully in large numbers. —in''fes·ta'tion, *n.*

in'fi·del, *n.* unbeliever.

in'fight''ing, *n.* combat at close range.

in'fil·trate'', *v.t.*, -trated, -trating. penetrate in many places. —in''fil·tra'tion, *n.*

in'fi·nite, *adj.* without bounds or end. —in'fin·ite·ly, *adv.* —in·fin'i·tude'', *n.* —in·fin'i·ty, *n.*

in''fin·i·tes'i·mal, *adj.* extremely small.

in·fin'i·tive, *n.* form of a verb without person, number, or tense.

in·firm', *adj.* not in good health. —in·firm'i·ty, *n.*

in·fir'ma·ry, *n., pl.* -ries. place for treating the sick.

in·flame', *v.t.*, **-flamed, -flaming. 1.** cause to become red, sore, swollen, etc. **2.** rouse to anger, etc. —**in''flam'ma'tion**, *n.* —**in·flam'ma·to''ry**, *adj.*

in·flam'ma·ble, *adj.* **1.** readily burned. **2.** readily aroused to anger, etc.

in·flate', *v.*, **-flated, -flating.** *v.t.* **1.** cause inflation in or to. —*v.i.* **2.** be filled with air or gas. —**in·flat'a·ble**, *adv.*

in·fla'tion, *n.* **1.** filling with air or gas. **2.** fall in the value of money. —**in·fla'tion·ar''y**, *adj.*

in·flect', *v.t.* vary in tone, form, etc. —**in·flec'tion**, *n.* —**in·flec'tion·al**, *adj.*

in·flict', *v.t.* harm or punish someone with. —**in·flic'tion**, *n.*

in·flu·ence, *n.*, *v.t.*, **-enced, -encing.** *n.* **1.** ability to determine events or decisions. **2.** person or thing that influences. —*v.t.* **3.** use influence on.

in''flu·en'tial, *adj.* having much influence.

in''flu·en'za. *n.* contagious virus infection.

in'flux'', *n.* inward flow.

in·form', *v.t.* give knowledge to. —**in·form'ant, in·form'er**, *n.* —**in''for·ma'tion**, *n.* —**in·form'a·tive**, *adj.*

in·formed', *adj.* **1.** in possession of essential facts. **2.** learned; erudite.

in·frac'tion, *n.* violation, as of a law.

in''fra·red', *adj.* pertaining to invisible rays beyond the red end of the spectrum.

in·fringe', *v.*, **-fringed, -fringing.** *v.t.* **1.** violate. —*v.i.* **2.** encroach. —**in·fringe'ment**, *n.*

in·fu'ri·ate'', *v.t.*, **-ated, -ating.** make furious.

in·fuse', *v.t.*, **-fused, -fusing. 1.** instill. **2.** steep. —**in''fu'sion**, *n.*

in·gen'ious, *adj.* clever. —**in·gen'ious·ly**, *adv.* —**in''gen·u'i·ty**, *n.*

in·gen'u·ous, *adj.* **1.** naive. **2.** candid. —**in·gen'u·ous·ness**, *n.*

in·gest', *v.t.* eat. —**in·ges'tion**, *n.*

in'got, *n.* cast piece of metal.

in·grained', *adj.* deeply imbedded.

in'grate, *n.* ungrateful person.

in·gra'ti·ate'', *v.t.*, **-ated, -ating.** make favored by another. —**in·gra''ti·a'tion**, *n.*

in·gre'di·ent, *n.* component.

in'gress, *n.* entry.

in'grown'', *adj.* grown into the flesh.

in·hab'it, *v.t.* live in. —**in·hab'it·ant**, *n.*

in·hale', *v.t.*, *v.i.*, **-haled, -haling.** breathe in. —**in''ha·la'tion**, *n.*

in·here', *v.i.*, **-hered, -hering.** be naturally part of something. —**in·her'ent**, *adj.*

in·her'it, *v.t.* be an heir to. —**in·her'i·tance**, *n.*

in·hib'it, *v.t.* check; restrain. —**in''hi·bi'tion**, *n.*

in·hu'man, *adj.* emotionally cold; callous. —**in''hu·man'i·ty**, *n.*

in·im'i·cal, *adj.* hostile.

in·iq'ui·ty, *n.*, *pl.* **-ties.** wickedness or wicked act. —**in·iq'ui·tous**, *adj.*

in·i'tial, *adj.*, *n.*, *v.t.*, **-tialed, -tialing.** *adj.* **1.** beginning. —*n.* **2.** beginning letter of a word. —*v.t.* **3.** mark with initials. —**in·i'tial·ly**, *adv.*

in·i'ti·ate'', *v.t.*, **-ated, ating. 1.** begin. **2.** acquaint with basics. **3.** accept as a member with ceremony. —**in·i''ti·a'tion**, *n.*

in·i'ti·a·tive, *n.* **1.** readiness to initiate actions. **2.** personal decision to act.

in·ject', *v.t.* force beneath the skin. —**in·jec'tion**, *n.*

in·junc'tion, *n.* order, as from a court.

in·jure', *v.t.*, **-injured, -juring.** harm. —**in''ju'ri·ous**, *adj.* —**in'ju·ry**, *n.*

ink, *n.* **1.** pigmented liquid for printing, writing, or drawing. —*v.t.* **2.** apply ink to. —**ink'y**, *adj.*

ink'ling, *n.* vague perception.

in'land'', *adj.*, *adv.* **1.** away from the shore, etc. —*n.* **2.** inland region.

in'-law'', *n.* relative by marriage.

in'lay'', *v.t.*, **-laid, -laying.** *n.* *v.t.* **1.** set into another piece. —*n.* **2.** something inlaid.

in'let, *n.* small extension of a body of water.

in'mate'', *n.* person under confinement.

inn, *n.* small hotel or restaurant.

in'nate'', *adj.* present from birth. —**in·nate'ly**, *adv.*

in'ner, *adj.* farther inside. —**in'ner·most''**, *adj.*

in'ning, *adj.* turn at bat.

in'no·cent, *adj.* **1.** free of guilt. **2.** unsophisticated. —*n.* **3.** innocent person. —**in'no·cent·ly**, *adv.* —**in'no·cence**, *n.*

in·noc'u·ous, *adj.* harmless.

in''no·va'tion, *n.* new discovery or development. —**in'no·vat''or**, *n.* —**in'no·vat''ive**, *adj.*

in''nu·en'do, *n.*, *pl.* **-does, -dos.** sly implication.

in·nu'mer·a·ble, *adj.* too many to count.

in·oc'u·late'', *v.t.*, **-lated, -lating.** immunize with an injection. —**in·noc''u·la'tion**, *n.*

in·or'di·nate, *adj.* excessive. —**in·or'di·nate·ly**, *adv.*

in''put, *n.* **1.** something supplied. **2.** (computers) data entered into a computer.

in'quest'', *n.* coroner's investigation.

in·quire', *v.i.*, **-quired, -quiring. 1.** ask. **2.** investigate. —**in'quir·y**, *n.*

in·quis'i·tive, *adj.* desiring to know many things.

in'road'', *n.* encroachment.

in·scribe', *v.t.*, -scribed, -scribing. write or letter. —in·scrip'tion, *n.*

in·scru'ta·ble, *adj.* hard to understand. —in·scru'ta·bly, *adv.*

in'sect, *n.* six-legged invertebrate.

in·sec'ti·cide", *n.* insect-killing preparation.

in·sem'i·nate", *v.t.*, -nated, -nating. inject semen into. —in·sem"i·na'tion, *n.*

in·sen'sate, *adj.* insensitive.

in·sen'si·ble, *adj.* 1. unconscious. 2. impossible to sense. —in·sen"si·bil'i·ty, *n.*

in·sert', *v.t.* (in surt') 1. place into something. —*n.* (in'sort) 2. something inserted. —in·ser'tion, *n.*

in'side', *adv., prep.* 1. within. —*adj.* 2. inner. —*n.* 3. inner part. —in·sid'er, *n.*

in·sid'i·ous, *adj.* slyly dangerous.

in'sight", *n.* deep understanding.

in·sig'ni·a, *n., pl.* distinguishing badges, etc.

in·sin'u·ate", *v.t.*, -ated, -ating. 1. imply slyly. 2. introduce imperceptibly. —in·sin"u·a'tion, *n.*

in·sip'id, *adj.* flavorless; dull. —in"si·pid'i·ty, *n.*

in·sist', *v.t.* make repeated demands or assertions. —in·sis'tent, *adj.* —in·sis'tence, *n.*

in"so·far', *adv.* to such an extent.

in'so·lent, *adj.* disrespectful. —in'so·lence, *n.*

in·som'ni·a, *n.* inability to sleep. —in·som'ni·ac", *n.*

in·spect", *v.t.* examine carefully. —in·spec'tion, *n.* —in·spec'tor, *n.*

in·spire', *v.*, -spired, -spiring. *v.t., v.i.* 1. breathe in. —*v.t.* 2. stimulate to mental activity. 3. arouse in someone. —in"spi·ra'tor, *n.* —in"spi·ra'tion·al, *adj.*

in·stall', *v.t.* -stalled, -stalling. put in place. —in"stal·la'tion, *n.*

in·stall'ment, *n.* item in a series.

in'stance, *n., v.t.*, -stanced, -stancing. 1. example. 2. occasion. —*v.t.* 3. cite.

in'stant, *n.* 1. moment. —*adj.* 2. happening or ready quickly. 3. imminent. —in"stan·ta'ne·ous, *adj.* —in'stant·ly, *adv.*

in·stead', *adv.* in the place.

in'sti·gate", *v.t.*, -gated, -gating. urge, as to action. —in"sti·ga'tion, *n.* —in'sti·ga"tor.

in·still', *v.t.*, -stilled, -stilling. implant. Also, in·stil'.

in'stinct, *n.* inborn prompting or reaction. —in·stinc'tive, *adj.* —in·stinc'tu·al, *adj.*

in'sti·tute", *n., v.t.*, -tuted, -tuting. *n.* 1. professional organization or school. —*v.t.* 2. establish. 3. start.

in"sti·tu'tion, *n.* 1. act or instance of instituting. 2. institute. 3. established law or custom. —in"sti·tu'tion·al, *adj.*

in·struct', *v.t.*, 1. inform or advise. 2. command. —in·struc'tion, *n.* —in·struc'tive, *adj.* —in·struc'tor, *n.*

in'stru·ment, *n.* 1. tool, etc. 2. means. 3. measuring device. 4. musical device. 5. legal document.

in"stru·men'tal, *adj.* 1. pertaining to music by instruments. 2. useful. —in"stru·men'tal·ist, *n.* —in"stru·men·tal'i·ty, *n.*

in"su·lar, *adj.* 1. pertaining to islands. 2. narrow-minded; parochial.

in'su·late", *v.t.*, -lated, -lating. isolate, esp. from heat, sound, or electricity. —in"su·la'tion, *n.* —in·su·la"tor, *n.*

in·su·lin, *n.* hormone secreted by the pancreas.

in·sult', *v.t.* (in sult') 1. treat so as to hurt the feelings. —*n.* (in'sult) 2. epithet, etc. that insults. —in·sult'ing, *adj.*

in·su'per·a·ble, *adj.* impossible to overcome.

in"sup·port'a·ble, *adj.* 1. intolerable. 2. impossible to prove.

in·sure', *v.t.*, -sured, -suring. 1. guarantee against loss with money. 2. make sure. —in·sur'ance, *n.*

in·sur'gent, *n, adj.* revolutionary. —in·sur'gence, *n.*

in"sur·rec'tion, *n.* revolution.

in·tact', *adj.* undamaged.

in'take", *n.* 1. amount received, absorbed, etc. 2. opening for receiving air, etc.

in·tan'gi·ble, *adj.* 1. non-material. 2. non-monetary. 3. indefinable.

in·te·ger (in'tə jər), *n.* whole number.

in'te·gral, *adj.* 1. forming an essential part. 2. complete.

in'te·grate", *v.t.*, -grated, -grating. 1. make complete. 2. bring together into a whole. 3. end racial segregation in or among. —in"te·gra'tion, *n.*

in·teg'ri·ty, *n.* 1. intactness. 2. firmness of character, honesty, etc.

in·teg'u·ment, *n.* covering, e.g. skin.

in'tel·lect, *n.* ability to comprehend or reason. —in"tel·lec'tu·al, *adj., n.*

in·tel'li·gence, *n.* 1. ability to comprehend, reason, and think creatively. 2. news. —in·tel'li·gent, *adj.*

in·tel"li·gent'si·a, *n., pl.* intellectuals as a group.

in·tel'li·gi·ble, *adj.* able to be understood.

in·tend', *v.t.* have as a purpose.

in·tend'ed, *n.* fiancé or fiancée.

in·tense', *adj.* 1. very strong. 2. with much emotion. —in·ten'si·ty, *n.* —in·ten'si·fy, *v.t., v.i.*

in·ten'sive, *adj.* 1. thorough. 2. *Grammar.* giving emphasis.

in·tent', *adj.* 1. earnest. 2. firmly intending. —*n.* 3. purpose. —in·tent'ly, *adv.*

in·ten′tion, *n.* purpose. —**in·ten′tion·al,** *adj.*

in·ter′, *v.t.,* **-terred, -terring.** bury.

in″ter·cede′, *v.i.,* **-ceded, -ceding.** mediate. —**in″ter·ces′sion,** *n.*

in″ter·cept′, *v.t.* halt or attack along the way. —**in″ter·cep′tion,** *n.*

in·ter·change, *v.,* **-changed, -changing,** *n.* *v.i., v.t.* (in″tər chānj′), **1.** exchange. **2.** alternate. —*n.* (in′tər chănj″) **3.** access to an express highway. —**in″ter·change′a·ble,** *adj.*

in″ter·con·nect′, *v.i.* connect with one another. —**in″ter·con·nec′tion,** *n.*

in′ter·course′, *n.* **1.** communication. **2.** copulation.

in″ter·de·pen′dent, *adj.* dependent on one another. —**in″ter·de·pen′dence,** *n.*

in·ter·dict, *v.t.* (in″tər dikt′) **1.** prohibit. —*n.* (in′tər dikt″) **2.** prohibition. —**in″ter·dic′tion,** *n.*

in″ter·dis′ci·pli·nar″y, *adj.* involving varied disciplines.

in′ter·est, *n.* **1.** willing attention. **2.** share in a business. **3.** profit on a loan. —*v.t.* **4.** obtain willing attention from.

in″ter·fere′, *v.i.,* **-fered, -fering. 1.** meddle. **2.** intervene. —**in″ter·fer′ence,** *n.*

in′ter·im, *n.* intervening time.

in·te′ri·or, *n.* **1.** inside. **2.** room. —*adj.* **3.** inside. **4.** personal.

in″ter·ject′, *v.t.* insert as an interruption or addition.

in″ter·jec′tion, *n.* **1.** exclamation. **2.** act or instance of interjecting.

in′ter·lace″, *v.i.* be entwined or woven together.

in′ter·lard″, *v.t.* scatter throughout.

in′ter·lock″, *v.i.* be connected or act together.

in′ter·lop″er, *n.* person who interferes.

in′ter·lude″, *n.* episode, musical piece, etc. between major events.

in″ter·mar′ry, *v.i.,* **-ried, -rying. 1.** become associated my marriage. **2.** marry a close relation. —**in″ter·mar′riage,** *n.*

in″ter·me′di·ar″y, *adj., n., pl.* **-ies.** *adj.* **1.** coming between. —*n.* **2.** go-between.

in″ter·me′di·ate, *adj.* coming between.

in·ter′ment, *n.* burial.

in·ter′min·a·ble, *adj.* seemingly endless. —**in·ter′min·a·bly,** *adv.*

in″ter·min′gle, *v.i.,* **-gled, -gling.** be blended.

in″ter·mis′sion, *n.* pause, as between acts of a play.

in″ter·mit′tent, *adj.* occurring at intervals. —**in″ter·mit′tent·ly,** *adv.*

in·tern, *n.* (in′tərn) **1.** Also, **in′terne.** assistant resident doctor. —*v.t.* (intərn′) **2.** detain and confine. —**in·tern′ment,** *n.*

in·ter′nal, *adj.* **1.** interior. **2.** non-foreign. —**in·ter′nal·ly,** *adv.*

in″ter·na′tion·al, *adj.* **1.** among nations. **2.** regardless of nation.

in″ter·ne′cine, *adj.* deadly to both sides.

in′ter·nist, *n.* doctor using non-surgical treatment.

in′ter·play″, *n.* mutual influence.

in·ter′po·late″, *v.t.,* **-lated, -lating.** alter with new material. —**in·ter″po·la′tion,** *n.*

in′ter·pose″, *v.t.,* **-posed, -posing.** place between or among. —**in″ter·po·si′tion,** *n.*

in·ter′pret, *v.t.,* **1.** clarify. **2.** understand. **3.** translate. —**in·ter′pret·er,** *n.* —**in·ter″pre·ta′tion,** *n.* —**in·ter′pre·tive,** *adj.*

in′ter·ra′cial, *adj.* among races.

in″ter·re·late″, *v.t.,* **-lated, -lating.** relate one to the other. —**in″ter·re·la′tion,** *n.*

in·ter′ro·gate″, *v.t.,* **-gated, -gating.** question. —**in·ter″ro·ga′tion,** *n.* —**in·ter′ro·ga″tor,** *n.* —**inter·rog′a·tive,** *in″ter·rog′a·to·ry,** *adv.*

in″ter·rupt′, *v.t.,* **1.** halt with an action, remark etc. **2.** break the uniformity of. —**in″ter·rup′tion,** *n.*

in″ter·sect′, *v.t., v.i.* cross. —**in′ter·sec′tion,** *n.*

in′ter·sperse″, *v.t.,* **-spersed, -spersing. 1.** scatter. **2.** vary with scattered things.

in′ter·state″, *adj., adv.* from state to state.

in·ter′stice, *n.* gap.

in″ter·ur′ban, *adj.* from city to city.

in′ter·val, *n.* intervening period or space.

in″ter·vene′, *v.i.,* **-vened, -vening. 1.** come or occur between. **2.** mediate. —**in″ter·ven′tion,** *n.*

in′ter·view″, *n.* **1.** person-to-person meeting. —*v.t.* **2.** question at an interview. —**in′ter·view″er,** *n.* —**in″ter·view″ee′,** *n.*

in·tes′tate″, *adj.* without having made a will.

in·tes′tine, *n.* either of two organs for converting food. Also, **in·tes′tines.** —**in·tes′tin·al,** *adj.*

in·ti·mate, *adj., n., v.t.,* **-mated, -mating.** *adj.* (in′tə mət) **1.** emotionally close. **2.** personal. **3.** thorough. —*n.* **4.** intimate friend. —*v.t.* (in′tə māt′) **5.** hint. —**in′ti·mate·ly,** *adv.* —**in′ti·ma·cy,** *n.* —**in″ti·ma′tion,** *n.*

in·tim′i·date″, *v.t.,* **-dated, -dating.** command through fear. —**in·tim″i·da′tion,** *n.*

in′to, *prep.* **1.** to the interior or depths of. **2.** up against. **3.** to some material, number of parts, etc.

in·tone′, *v.t.,* **-toned, -toning. 1.** utter in a songlike tone. **2.** utter with a controlled or varied pitch. —in"to·na' tion, n.

in·to'to, as a whole.

in·tox'i·cate", v.t., -cated, -cating. make drunk. —in·tox"i·ca'tion, n. —in·tox'i·cant, n.

in·trac'ta·ble, adj. unruly.

in"tra·mu'ral, adj. within an institution.

in·tran'si·gent, adj. uncompromising. —in·tran'si·gence, n.

in"tra·ve'nous, adj. into a vein from outside the body.

in·trep'id, adj. fearless. —in"tre·pid'i· ty, n.

in"tri·cate, adj. complicated; complex. —in"tri·cate·ly, adv. —in"tri·ca·cy, n.

in·trigue', v., -trigued, -triguing. v.i. 1. plot in stealth. —v.t. 2. make curious. —n. 3. stealthy plot or plotting.

in·trin'sic, adj. essential; inherent. —in· trin'si·cal·ly, adv.

in"tro·duce', v.t., -duced, -ducing. 1. present for the first time. 2. bring into use. 3. insert. —in"tro·duc'tion, n. —in"tro·duc'to·ry, adj.

in"tro·spec'tion, n. self-examination. —in"tro·spec'tive, adj.

in"tro·vert", n. withdrawn person. —in" tro·ver'sion, n.

in·trude', v., -truded, -truding. v.i. 1. come as an interruption or surprise. —v.t. 2. force upon others. —in·trud' er, n. —in·tru'sion, n. —in·tru'sive, adj.

in"tu·i'tion, n. non-logical insight. —in· tu'i·tive, adj.

in·un'date', v.t., -dated, -dating. flood. —in"un·da'tion, n.

in·ure', v.t., -ured, -uring. harden; accustom.

in·vade', v.t., -vaded, -vading. enter with force. —in·vad'er, n. —in·va'sion, n.

in·val'id, n. (in'və lid) 1. sick person. —adj. (in val'id) 2. not valid. —in·val' i·date",! v.t.

in·val'u·a·ble, adj. valuable beyond reckoning.

in·vec'tive, n. verbal attack.

in·veigh', v.i. make a verbal attack.

in·vei'gle, v.t., -gled, -gling. trick into an action.

in·vent', v.t. discover, as a product or process. —in·ven'tion, n. —in·ven' tive, adj. —in·ven'tor, n.

in'ven·to"ry, n., pl. -ries, v.t., -ried, -rying. n. 1. precise list. 2. stock of goods. —v.t. 3. make an inventory of.

in·verse', adj. 1. opposite in kind. —n. 2. something inverse. —in·verse'ly, adv.

in·vert', v.t. 1. turn upside down. 2. reverse in order or position. —in·ver' sion, n.

in·ver'te·brate, adj. 1. having no backbone. —n. 2. invertebrate animal.

in·vest', v.t. 1. put into something in the hope of profit. 2. give authority or office to. —v.i. 3. invest money. —in· vest'or, n. —in·vest'ment, n. —in· vest'i·ture", n.

in·ves'ti·gate", v.t., -gated, -gating. examine or explore. —in·ves'ti·ga"tor, n. —in·ves"ti·ga'tion, n.

in·vet'er·ate, adj. habitual. —in·vet'er· a·cy, n.

in·vid'i·ous, adj. causing ill will.

in·vig'or·ate", v.t., -ated, -ating. make vigorous. —in·vig"or·a'tion, n.

in·vin'ci·ble, adj. impossible to conquer. —in·vinc"i·bil'i·ty, n.

in·vi'o·la·ble, adj. not to be violated. —in·vi"ol·a·bil'i·ty, n.

in·vi'o·late, adj. unviolated.

in·vite', v.t., -vited, -viting. 1. ask to be present. 2. give a pretext for. —in"vi· ta'tion, n.

in·vit'ing, adj. enticing.

in"vo·ca'tion, n. prayerlike speech.

in'voice, n. list of goods supplied.

in·voke', v.t., -voked, -voking. 1. call upon, as a god. 2. cite as a justification.

in"vo·lu'tion, n. intricacy. —in'vo·lut" ed, adj.

in·volve', v.t., -volved, -volving. 1. include as relevant. 2. affect or trouble. 3. occupy. 4. complicate. —in·volve' ment, n.

in'ward, adj. 1. inside, 2. toward the inside. 3. mental. —adv. 4. Also, in' wards, towards the inside. —in·ward' ly, adv.

i'o·dine", n. nonmetallic chemical element. —i'o·dize", v.t.

i'on, n. electrically charged atom or group of these.

i·o'ta, n. minute quantity.

ip'so fac'to, by the very fact.

IQ, intelligence quotient (measure of intelligence). Also I.Q.

ir-, prefix meaning "not" or "lack of." **irrational, irreconcilable, irredeemable, irregular, irrelevant, irreligious, irremediable, irreparable, irreplaceable, irresponsible, irreverent, irreversible, irrevocable.**

i·ras·ci·ble (i ras'ə bl), adj. easily angered.

ire, n. wrath. —i·rate', adj.

ir"i·des'cent, adj. with a play of rainbow-like colors. —ir"i·des'cence, n.

i'ris, n., pl. irises. n. 1. pigmented part surrounding the eye pupil. 2. plant with sword-shaped leaves.

irk, v.t. annoy. —irk'some, adj.

i'ron, n. 1. metallic element attracting magnets. 2. device made of iron. 3. irons,shackles. —v.t. 4. smooth with an iron.

Iron Curtain, barrier to travel, information, etc. around the communist countries.

i·ro·ny, *n., pl.* **-nies.** figure of speech conveying meaning through words of opposite meaning. —**i·ron'i·cal, i·ron'ic,** *adj.*

ir·ra'di·ate", *v.t.,* **-ated, ating.** expose to rays.

ir"re·gard'less, *adj., adv.* regardless.

ir"re·sist'i·ble, *adj.* **1.** impossible to resist. **2.** overwhelmingly tempting.

ir'ri·gate", *v.t.,* **-gated, -gating.** introduce water to, to raise crops. —**ir"ri·ga'tion,** *n.*

ir'ri·ta·ble, *adj.* readily irritated. —**ir'ri·ta·bly,** *adv.* —**ir"ri·ta·bil'i·ty,** *n.*

ir'ri·tate", *v.t.,* **-tated, -tating. 1.** annoy. **2.** make sore. —**ir"ri·ta'tion,** *n.* —**ir'ri·tant,** *adj., n.*

ir·rupt', *v.i.* **1.** burst forth; expand. —**ir·rup'tion,** *n.*

i'sin·glass", *n.* **1.** gelatin from fish bladders. **2.** mica.

Is'lam, *n.* religion of Muhammad.

is·land (ī'lənd) *n.* **1.** body of land surrounded by water. **2.** isolated platform, etc.

is·let (ī'lət), *n.* small island.

i'so·late", *v.t.,* **-lated, -lating.** keep apart. —**i"so·la'tion,** *n.*

i"so·la'tion·ist, *n.* believer in no alliances with other countries. —**i"so·la'tion·ism,** *n.*

i"so·met'ric, *adj.* **1.** with all dimensions represented to the same scale. **2.** pertaining to isometrics. —*n.* **3. isometrics,** type of muscular exercise.

i·sos'cel·es", *adj.* pertaining to triangles with two equal sides.

i'so·tope", *n.* form of an element coinciding in atomic number but not in atomic weight with another.

is'sue, *v.,* **-sued, -suing,** *v.t.* **1.** give out. **2.** publish. —*v.i.* **3.** emerge. —*n.* **4.** something that issues. **5.** periodical of one date. **6.** thing in dispute. **7.** offspring. **8.** result. —**is'su·ance,** *n.*

isth'mus, *n., pl.* **-muses.** narrow neck of connecting land between bodies of water.

it, *pron., pl.* **they 1.** thing referred to. **2.** (subject of various impersonal verbs).

i·tal'ic, *adj.* **1.** pertaining to letters printed thus: *Italics.* —*n.* **2. italics, italic letters.** —**i·tal'i·cize",** *v.t.*

itch, *v.i.* **1.** feel a mild irritation tempting one to scratch. **2.** desire restlessly. —*n.* **3.** act or instance of itching. —**itch'y,** *adj.*

i'tem, *n.* **1.** listed thing. **2.** piece of news. —**i'tem·ize",** *v.t.* —**i'tem·i·za'tion,** *n.*

it'er·ate", *v.t.,* **-ated, -ating.** repeat. —**it"er·a'tion,** *n.*

i·tin'er·ant, *adj.* **1.** traveling; migratory. —*n.* **2.** itinerant person.

i·tin'er·ar"y, *n., pl.* **-ies.** plan of travel.

its, *pron.* belonging or pertaining to it.

it's, *pron.* contraction of *it is.*

it·self', *pron.* **1.** (intensive or reflexive of *it).* **2.** its true self.

i'vo·ry, *n.* creamy-white substance of tusks.

i'vy, *n., pl.* **ivies.** climbing evergreen vine. —**i'vied,** *adj.*

J

J, j, *n.* tenth letter of the English alphabet.

jab, *v.,* **jabbed, jabbing.** *v.t., v.i. n.* poke

jab'ber, *n.* **1.** fast, incoherent talk. —*v.i.* **2.** talk in a jabber.

jack, *n.* **1.** lifting machine. **2.** playing card; knave. **3.** flag at a ship's stern. **4.** point of connection; place where something is plugged in. —*v.t.* **5.** to raise something with a jack.

jack'al, *n.* wild African and Asian dog.

jack'ass", *n.* **1.** male donkey. **2.** fool.

jack'et, *n.* **1.** short coat. **2.** covering.

jack'knife", *n., v.i.,* **-knifed, -knifing.** *n.* **1.** folding knife. **2.** type of swimmer's dive. —*v.i.* **3.** fold accidentally at a joint.

jack'pot", *n.* accumulated stakes that are won.

jack'rab"bit, *n.* large North American hare.

jade, *n., v.t.,* **jaded, jading.** *n.* **1.** ornamental stone, usually green. —*v.t.* **2.** satiate.

jag, *n.* **1.** sharp point. **2.** *Informal.* orgy.

jag'ged, *adj.* with a rough, sharp edge or surface.

jag'uar, *n.* large cat of Latin America and the U.S. Southwest.

jail, *n.* **1.** prison for short confinements. —*v.t.* **2.** put in jail. —**jail'er, jail'or,** *n.*

ja·lop'y, *n., pl.* **-ies.** old, ill-kept car.

jal'ou·sie, *n.* louvered blind.

jam, *v.,* **jammed, jamming,** *n. v.t., v.i.* **1.** crowd. **2.** stick tight. —*n.* **3.** act or instance of jamming. **4.** fruit boiled with sugar. **5.** *Informal.* adverse situation.

jamb, *n.* upright of a doorway or window.

jam"bo·ree', *n. Informal.* noisy celebration.

jam'packed', *adj.* crowded to capacity.

jan'gle, *v.* **-gled, -gling.** *v.i.* **1.** jingle harshly. —*v.t.* **2.** irritate, as the nerves.

jan′i·tor, *n.* person who takes care of a building.

Jan′u·ar″y, *n.* first month.

jar, *n., v.,* **jarred, jarring.** *n.* 1. cylindrical container. 2. jolt. —*v.t.* 3. jolt. —*v.i.* 4. clash. 5. have an irritating effect.

jar′gon, *n.* abstruse technical language.

jas′mine, *n.* fragrant-flowered plant.

jas′per, *n.* opaque, colored quartz.

jaun′dice, *n., v.t.,* **-diced, -dicing.** *n.* 1. disease characterized by yellowing due to bile in the blood. —*v.t.* 2. predispose against.

jaunt, *n.* 1. pleasure excursion. —*v.i.* 2. go on a jaunt.

jaun′ty, *adj.,* **-tier, -tiest.** cheerful. —**jaun′ti·ly**, *adv.*

jav′e·lin, *n.* throwing spear.

jaw, *n.* 1. bony framing member of the mouth. 2. gripping part of a vise, etc.

jay, *n.* 1. crowlike bird. 2. bluejay.

jay′walk″, *v.i.* cross a street heedlessly. —**jay′walk″er**, *n.*

jazz, *n.* syncopated, rhythmic modern music.

jeal′ous, *adj.* 1. feeling jealousy. 2. watchful.

jeans, *n., pl.* trousers of strong cloth.

jeep, *n.* rugged, military-style car.

jeer, *v.i.* make scornful utterances. —*n.* 2. such an utterance.

Je·ho′vah, *n.* God.

je·june′, *adj.* 1. unfulfilling. 2. childish.

jell, *v.i.* 1. harden, as gelatin. 2. come to fulfillment.

jel′ly, *n., pl.* **-lies**, *v.t.* **-lied, -lying.** *n.* 1. gelatinous food. —*v.t.* 2. make into jelly.

jeo′pard·ize″, *v.t.,* **-ized, -izing.** put in danger. —**jeo′pard·y**, *n.*

jer″e·mi′ad, *n.* tale of lamentation or anger.

jerk, *n.* 1. sharp pull. —*v.t.* 2. pull sharply. —*v.i.* 3. twitch. —**jerk′y**, *adj.*

jer′ry-built, *adj.* cheaply and flimsily built.

jer′sey, *n., pl.* **-sies.** closefitting knitted shirt.

jest, *n.* joke.

jet, *n., v.i.* **jetted, jetting.** *n.* 1. forced stream. 2. jet-propelled airplane. 3. coal-like mineral used in jewelry. —*v.i.* 4. emerge in a jet. 5. travel by jet.

jet propulsion, propulsion by the reactive thrust of a jet. —**jet′pro·pelled′**, *adj.*

jet′sam, *n.* material thrown overboard.

jet′ti·son, *v.t.* throw away or overboard.

jet′ty, *n., pl.* **-ties.** pier or wall into the water.

jew′el, *n.* precious stone. —**jew′el·er**, **jew′el·ler**, *n.* —**jew′el·ry**, *n.*

jib, *n.* triangular sail at the bow.

jibe, *v.i.,* **jibed, jibing**, *n.* gibe.

jif′fy, *n., pl.* **-fies.** *Informal.* short period.

jig, *n., v.i.,* **jigged, jigging.** *n.* 1. fast dance. 2. tool guide. —*v.i.* 3. dance a jig.

jig′ger, *n.* one-and-a-half ounce glass.

jig′gle, *v.,* **-gled, gling**, *n.* *v.i., v.t.* 1. move in rapid jerks. —*n.* 2. act or instance of jiggling.

jig′saw″, *n.* narrow-bladed saw.

jilt, *v.t.* reject.

jin′gle, *v.,* **-gled, -gling**, *n.* *v.i., v.t.* 1. ring lightly and rapidly. —*n.* 2. act or instance of jingling. 3. simple verse.

jinx, *n.* 1. bringer of ill-luck. —*v.t.* 2. bring ill-luck to.

jit′ters, *n. Informal.* nervousness. —**jit′ter·y**, *adj.*

job, *n., v.t.,* **jobbed, jobbing.** *n.* 1. task. 2. occupation. 3. duty —*v.t., v.i.* 4. buy in quantity for resale to dealers. —**job′less**, *adj.* —**job′ber**, *n.*

jock′ey, *n., pl.* **-eys**, *v.i.,* **-eyed, -eying.** *n.* 1. rider of race horses. —*v.i.* 2. maneuver for advantage.

jo·cose′, *adj.* playful. Also, **joc′und.** —**jo·cos′i·ty**, *n.*

joc′u·lar, *adj.* joking; playful.

jog, *v.,* **jogged, jogging**, *n.* *v.t.* 1. nudge. —*v.i.* 2. run steadily. —*n.* 3. act or instance of jogging. 4. abrupt change of direction.

join, *v.t.* 1. put together. 2. become a member of. —*v.i.* 3. come or act together.

join′er, *n.* 1. woodworker. 2. *Informal.* person who likes to join groups. —**join′er·y**, *n.*

joint, *n.* 1. connection. —*adj.* 2. shared. 3. sharing with others. —*v.t.* 4. assemble with joints. —**joint′ly**, *adv.*

joist, *n.* floor beam.

joke, *n., v.i.* **joked, joking.** *n.* 1. laugh-provoking story or remark. 2. playful act. —*v.i.* 3. make a joke.

jol′ly, *adj.* **-lier, -liest,** *v.t.,* **-lied, -lying.** *adj.* 1. full of high spirits. —*v.t.* 2. *Informal.* **a.** cajole. **b.** tease. —**jol′li·ly**, *adv.* —**jol′lity**, *n.*

jolt, *v.t.* 1. shake or bump. —*v.i.* 2. move bumpily. —*n.* 3. act or instance of jolting.

josh, *v.t.* banter.

jos′tle, *v.,* **-tled, -tling.** *v.t., v.i.* shove, as in a crowd.

jot, *n., v.t.,* **jotted, jotting.** *n.* 1. minimal amount. —*v.t.* 2. make a note of.

jounce, *v.i.,* **jounced, jouncing.** jolt and bounce. —**jounc′y**, *adj.*

jour′nal, *n.* 1. periodical. 2. diary. 3. section of an axle in a bearing.

jour′nal·ism, *n.* work for a periodical. —**jour′nal·ist**, *n.* —**jour″nal·is′tic**, *adj.*

jour′ney, *n., pl.* **-neys**, *v.i.,* **-neyed, -neying.** *n.* 1. long trip. —*v.i.* 2. go on a journey.

jour′ney·man, *n.* skilled worker.

jo'vi·al, *adj.* merry. —jo''vi·al'i·ty, *n.*

jowl, *n.* lower cheek.

joy, *n.* 1. intense happiness. 2. source of this. —joy'ful, joy'ous, *adj.*

joy''stick, *n.* (computers) grippable device for data manipulation, used mostly for graphics and games.

ju'bi·lant, *adj.* rejoicing. —ju''bi·la'tion, *n.*

ju'bi·lee'', *n.* 1. major anniversary. 2. time of rejoicing.

Ju'da·ism, *n.* Jewish religion. —Ju·da'ic, *adj.*

judge, *n., v.t.,* judged, judging. *n.* 1. presider over a trial, contest, etc. 2. qualified evaluator. —*v.t.* 3. evaluate. —judg'ment, judge'ment, *n.* —judge'ship'', *n.*

ju·di'cial, *adj.* 1. pertaining to judges or courts. 2. impartial.

ju·di'ci·ar''y, *adj., n., pl.* -ies. *adj.* 1. judicial. —*n.* 2. judges.

ju·di'cious, *adj.* with sound judgment. —ju·di'cious·ly, *adv.*

ju'do, *n.* Japanese system of wrestling.

jug, *n.* broad vessel with a narrow neck.

jug'ger·naut'', *n.* crushing force.

jug'gle, *v.* -gled, -gling. *v.t.* toss, balance with skill. —*v.i.* 2. perform such activities for a living. —jug'gler, *n.*

jug'u·lar, *adj.* 1. pertaining to the neck. —*n.* 2. neck vein.

juice, *n., v.t.,* juiced, juicing. *n.* 1. liquid from a fruit, etc. —*v.t.* 2. extract juice from. —juic'y, *adj.*

ju·jit'su, *n.* Japanese system of wrestling. Also, ju·jut'su.

juke'box'', *n.* coin-operated record player.

Ju'ly, *n.* seventh month.

jum'ble, *v.t.,* -bled, -bling. *n. v.t.* 1. mix in disorder. —*n.* 2. disorderly mixture.

jum'bo, *adj.* very large.

jump, *v.i.* 1. leave the ground with a muscular effort. 2. move abruptly. —*v.t.* 3. jump over. —*n.* 4. act or instance of jumping.

jump'er, *n.* sleeveless dress.

jum'py, *adj.,* -pier, -piest. very nervous.

junc'tion, *n.* place of joining.

junc'ture, *n.* 1. junction. 2. moment. 3. crisis.

June, *n.* sixth month.

jun'gle, *n.* densely grown tropical area.

jun'ior, *adj.* 1. being the son of a father with the same name. 2. lesser in rank, size, etc. —*n.* 3. junior person. 4. third-year student.

ju'ni·per, *n.* evergreen with berry-like cones.

junk, *n.* 1. rejected or worthless material. 2. Chinese sailing boat. —*v.t.* 3. scrap.

junk'et, *n.* 1. curdled milk dish. 2. excursion. —*v.i.* 3. go on a junket.

junk'ie, *n. Informal.* narcotics addict. Also, junk'y.

jun·ta (hŏŏn tə), *n.* military in power after a coup d'etat.

ju''ris·dic'tion, *n.* 1. administration of justice. 2. area of authority. —ju''ris·dic'tion·al, *adj.*

ju''ris·pru'dence, *n.* philosophy of law.

ju'rist, *n.* expert in law.

ju'ry, *n., pl.* -ries. group deciding the outcome of a trial, hearing, or contest. —ju'ry·man, ju'ror, *n.*

just, *adj.* 1. fair. 2. righteous. 3. accurate. —*adv.* 4. exactly. 5. only. 6. by a short margin. —just'ly, *adv.* —just'ness, *n.*

jus'tice, *n.* 1. fairness. 2. righteousness. 3. administration of law. 4. judge.

jus'ti·fy'', *v.t.,* -fied, -fying. give valid reasons for. —jus''ti·fi'a·ble, *adj.* —jus''ti·fi·ca'tion, *n.*

jut, *v.i.,* jutted, jutting. project

jute, *n.* coarse plant fiber.

ju'ven·ile, *adj.* 1. pertaining to children. 2. childish. —*n.* 3. child.

jux'ta·pose'', *v.t.,* -posed, -posing. place close or in contrast. —jux''ta·po·si'tion, *n.*

K

K, k, *n.* eleventh letter of the English alphabet.

kai'ser, *n.* Germanic emperor.

kale, *n.* type of cabbage. Also, kail.

ka·lei'do·scope'', *n.* device creating symmetrical patterns for viewing. —ka·lei''do·scop'ic, *adj.*

kan''ga·roo', *n.* leaping Australian marsupial.

ka·put', *adj.* destroyed or out of order.

kar'at, *n.* twenty-fourth part pure gold.

ka·ra'te, *n.* Japanese technique of fighting with hands and feet.

kar'ma, *n.* one's acts as a determinant of one's fate.

ka'ty·did'', *n.* shrill, green insect.

kay'ak, *n.* Eskimo canoe.

keel, *n.* central structural member of a ship.

keen, *adj.* 1. sharp. 2. eager. 3. shrewd.

keep, *v.,* kept, keeping, *n. v.t.* 1. retain. 2. look after. 3. protect or support. 4. be observant of. —*v.i.* 5. be preserved. 6. abstain. 7. remain or continue. —*n.* 8. support; custody.

keep'ing, 1. care; custody. 2. conformity.

keep'sake'', *n.* souvenir.

keg, *n.* small barrel.

ken, *n.* range of awareness or knowledge.

ken'nel, *n., v.t.,* **-neled, -neling.** *n.* doghouse. —*v.t.* 2. put in a kennel.

ker'chief, *n.* cloth for covering the head.

ker'nel, *n.* 1. seed. 2. inner nut.

ker'o·sene'', *n.* petroleum derivative.

ketch'up, *n.* sauce, often made with tomatoes.

ket'tle, *n.* pot for boiling water.

ket'tle-drum'', *n.* large, potlike drum.

key, *n., adj., v.t.,* **keyed, keying.** *n.* 1. metal instrument operating a lock. 2. device on a piano, etc. pressed in operating it. 3. thing that explains. 4. system of musical tones. —*adj.* 5. decisive. —*v.t.* 6. *Music.* put into a key. —**key'hole''**, *n.*

key''board', *n.* (computers) 1. device resembling a typewriter keyboard used for data input. —*v.* 2. to input data with a keyboard.

key'note'', *n.* 1. lowest note of a scale. 2. basic theme.

key'stone'', *n.* top stone of an arch.

kha'ki, *n., pl.* **-kis.** 1. dull yellowish brown. 2. **khakis,** clothing made of cloth this color.

kib'bitz, *v.t.* give unwanted advice.

kib·butz', *n., pl.* **-butzim.** Israeli collective settlement.

kick, *v.t., v.i.* 1. strike with the foot. —*v.i.* 2. recoil. 3. *Informal.* complain. —*n.* 4. act or instance of kicking. 5. *Informal.* **a.** grievance. **b.** thrill.

kick'back'', *n. Informal.* rebate, usually illicit.

kid, *n., v.,* **kidded, kidding.** *n.* 1. young goat. 2. *Informal.* child. —*v.t.* 3. *Informal.* tease. —*v.i.* 4. *Informal.* joke.

kid'nap'', *v.t.,* **-napped** or **-naped, -napping** or **-naping.** abduct and hold prisoner. —**kid'nap''er,** *n.*

kid'ney, *n.* 1. organ that forms urine. 2. sort or kind.

kill, *v.t.* 1. cause to die. 2. end abruptly. —*n.* 3. act or instance of killing. 4. game killed. —**kill'er,** *n.*

kiln (kil, kiln), *n.* furnace for processing materials.

ki'lo, *n., pl.* **-los.** 1. kilogram. 2. kilometer.

ki'lo·gram'', *n.* one thousand grams or 2.2046 pounds.

ki'lo·hertz'', *n.* one thousand hertz. Also, **ki'lo·cy''cle.**

ki'lo·me''ter, *n.* one thousand meters or 3,281 feet.

kil'o·watt'', *n.* one thousand watts.

kilt, *n.* knee-length Scottish skirt for men.

kil'ter, *n. Informal.* good condition.

ki·mo'no, *n., pl.* **-nos.** *n.* full-length Japanese dress.

kin, *n.* relatives.

kind, *n.* 1. sort. —*adj.* 2. benevolent; compassionate. —**kind'ness,** *n.*

kin'der·gar''ten, *n.* pre-elementary school.

kin'dle, *v.,* **-dled, -dling.** *v.t.* 1. set on fire. 2. arouse. —*v.i.* 3. be kindled. —**kind'ling,** *n.*

kind'ly, *adj.* 1. kind. —*adv.* 2. in a kind way. 3. graciously; favorably. —**kind'li·ness,** *n.*

kin'dred, *n., pl.* 1. relatives. —*adj.* 2. of the same kind.

ki·net'ic, *adj.* pertaining to motion.

kin'folk'', *n., pl.* relatives. Also, **kin'folks''.**

king, *n.* 1. male national ruler. 2. playing card. —**king'ly,** *adj.*

king'dom, *n.* 1. state ruled by a king. 2. major category.

king'fish''er, *n.* diving bird that eats fish.

king'-size'', *adj. Informal.* extra-large.

kink, *n.* short loop or coil. —**kink'y,** *adj.*

kin'ship'', *n.* family relationship.

ki'osk, *n.* small open shelter.

kip'per, *n.* salted, smoked herring.

kiss, *n.* 1. touching with the lips as a sign of affection, etc. —*v.t.* 2. give a kiss to. —*v.i.* 3. exchange kisses.

kitch'en, *n.* place for preparing meals.

kite, *n.* flying toy on a string.

kith and kin, friends and relatives.

kitsch, *n.* vulgar, affected art. —**kitsch'y,** *adj.*

kit'ten, *n.* young cat. —**kit'ten·ish,** *adj.*

kit'ty, *n., pl.* **-ties.** *n. Informal.* 1. cat. 2. accumulated stakes.

ki'wi, *n.* any flightless bird of genus Apteryx. *n.* fuzzy fruit of Asian climbing plant, the Chinese gooseberry.

klep''to·ma'ni·a, *n.* compulsion to steal. —**klep''to·ma'ni·ac,** *n.*

knack, *n.* talent.

knap'sack'', *n.* sack worn on the back.

knave, *n.* 1. *Archaic.* deceitful person. 2. playing card; jack. —**knav'ish,** *adj.* —**knav'er·y,** *n.*

knead, *v.t.* press and work with the fingers.

knee, *n.* joint of the leg.

kneel, *v.i.,* **knelt** or **kneeled, kneeling.** be upright on the knees.

knell, *n.* slow tolling of a bell.

knick'ers, *n., pl.* trousers ending at the knees. Also **knick'er·bock''ers.**

knick'knack'', *n.* small decorative object.

knife, *n., pl.* **knives,** *v.t.,* **knifed, knifing.** *n.* 1. small cutting tool. —*v.t.* 2. stab with a knife.

knight, *n.* 1. possessor of an honorable rank, formerly military. 2. chesspiece. —*v.t.* 3. declare to be a knight. —**knight'hood,** *n.* —**knight'ly,** *adj.*

knight'-er'rant, *n., pl.* **knights-errant.** knight seeking adventure.

knish (kə nish'), *n.* filled, baked dish of thin dough.

knit, *v.,* **knitted** or **knit, kitting.** *v.t.* 1. assemble from yarn with two needles. 2.

draw together in wrinkles, as the brows. —*v.i.* 3. join again after a fracture.

knob, *n.* rounded projection or handle. —**knob'by,** *adj.*

knock, *v.t.* 1. hit, as with the fist. 2. *Informal.* disparage. —*v.i.* 3. strike blows. —*n.* 4. act or instance of knocking. 5. adverse happening. —**knock'er,** *n.*

knock'out", *n.* victory in boxing, esp. by knocking an opponent unconscious.

knoll, *n.* small, round hill.

knot, *n., v.t.,* **knotted, knotting.** *n.* 1. fastening of intertwined cord. 2. small cluster. 3. hard lump in wood. 4. one nautical mile per hour. —*v.t.* 5. make into a knot. —**knot'ty,** *adj.*

know, *v.t.,* **knew, known, knowing.** 1. have full evidence. 2. be fully informed or skilled. 3. have as an acquaintance. 4. recognize. —**know'ing·ly,** *adv.*

know'-how", *n.* technical ability.

know'ing, *n.* 1. ability to know. —*adj.* 2. shrewd.

know'-it-all", *n.* pretender to omniscience.

know'ledge, *n.* 1. state of knowing. 2. what is known.

know'ledge·a·ble, *adj.* well-informed.

knuck'le, *n.* central finger joint.

Ko·ran', *n.* Muslim holy scriptures.

ko'sher, *adj. Judaism.* fit to eat under religious law.

kow'tow', *v.t.* show servility or deference.

ku'dos, *n. Informal.* praise; fame.

kum'quat", *n.* small, tart citrus fruit.

L

L, l, *n.* twelfth letter of the English alphabet.

la'bel, *n., v.t.,* **-beled, -beling.** *n.* 1. attached paper with information. —*v.t.* 2. designate with a label.

la'bi·al, *adj.* pertaining to lips.

la'bor, *n.* 1. hard work. 2. workers collectively. 3. process of giving birth. —*v.i.* 4. work hard. —**la'bor·er,** *n.*

lab'o·ra·to"ry, *n., pl.* **ries.** place for scientific research.

la·bo'ri·ous, *adj.* difficult; tedious.

lab'y·rinth", *n.* 1. maze. 2. intricate problem. —**lab"y·rin'thine,** *adj.*

lace, *n., v.t.,* **laced, lacing.** *n.* 1. binding string, as on a shoe. 2. openwork cloth. —*v.t.* 3. fasten or furnish with a lace. —**lace'work",** *n.*

lac'er·ate", *v.t.,* **-ated, -ating.** tear jaggedly. —**lac"er·a'tion,** *n.*

lach'ry·mose", *adj.* tearful.

lack, *n.* 1. absence or shortage. —*v.t.* 2. be without. —*v.i.* 3. be deficient.

lack"a·dai'si·cal, *adj.* without spirit or drive.

lack'lus"ter, *adj.* dull.

la·con'ic, *adj.* short-spoken; terse. —**la·con'i·cal·ly,** *adv.*

lac'quer, *n.* 1. transparent varnish-like coating. —*v.t.* 2. coat with lacquer.

la·crosse', *n.* game with netlike racquets.

la·cu'na, *n., pl.* **-nas, -nae.** gap.

lac'y, *adj.,* **-ier, -iest.** open and intricate.

lad, *n.* boy.

lad'der, *n.* steep set of steps.

la'den, *adj.* burdened; loaded.

lad'ing, *n.* freight.

la'dle, *n., v.t.,* **-dled, -dling.** *n.* 1. long-handled bowl for dipping. —*v.t.* 2. dip with a ladle.

la'dy, *n.,* **-dies.** 1. respectable woman. 2. title of certain British women. —**la'dy·like',** *adj.* —**la'dy·ship",** *n.*

la'dy·bug", *n.* small, spotted red beetle. Also, **la'dy·bird".**

lag, *v.i.,* **lagged, lagging,** *n. v.i.* 1. fall behind. —*n.* 2. act or instance of lagging. —**lag'gard,** *n., adj.*

la'ger, *n.* type of beer.

la·goon', *n.* enclosed body of water near a larger one.

laid"back", *adj.* relaxed; serene.

lair, *n.* den, as of an animal.

lais"sez faire', noninterference, esp. in economic activity.

la'i·ty, *n., pl.* **-ties.** laymen collectively.

lake, *n.* inland body of water.

la'ma, *n.* Tibetan Buddhist monk. —**la'ma·ser"y,** *n.*

lamb, *n.* young sheep.

lam·baste', *v.t.,* **-basted, -basting.** *Informal.* punish with blows or words.

lam'bent, *adj.* gently glowing. —**lam'ben·cy,** *n.*

lame, *adj., v.t.,* **lamed, laming.** *adj.* 1. unable to walk properly. 2. ineffectual. —*v.t.* 3. make lame. —**lame'ly,** *adv.*

la·ment', *v.t., v.i.* 1. mourn. —*n.* 2. speech, poem, or song of mourning. —**la"men·ta'tion,** *n.* —**lam·en'ta·ble,** *adj.*

lam'i·nate", *v.t.,* **-nated, -nating.** 1. build up in layers. 2. cover with a layer of material. —**lam"i·na'tion,** *n.*

lamp, *n.* device for emitting rays of light, etc. —**lamp'post",** *n.*

lamp'black'', *n.* pigment of fine soot.

lam·poon', *n.* **1.** satirical writing. —*v.t.* **2.** satirize in a lampoon.

la·nai', *n.* Hawaiian open-air living area.

lance, *n., v.t.*, **lanced, lancing.** *n.* **1.** spear carried by a horseman. —*v.t.* **2.** prick, as to discharge pus.

land, *n.* **1.** earth's surface above water. **2.** nation; country. **3.** real estate. —*v.t.* **4.** bring to shore or earth. **5.** secure; obtain. —*v.i.* **6.** come to shore or earth. **7.** fall.

land'ed, *adj.* land-owning.

land'fall'', *n.* **1.** land sighted from a ship. **2.** sighting of such land.

land'ing, *n.* **1.** act of coming to shore or earth. **2.** place to land. **3.** unstepped area on a stair.

land'locked'', *adj.* with little or no access to the sea.

land'lord'', *n.* **1.** man from whom one rents. **2.** innkeeper. Also, *fem.*, **land'la''dy.**

land'mark'', *n.* visible aid to finding one's way.

land'mass'', *n.* major land area.

land'scape'', *n., v.t.*, **-scaped, scaping** *n.* **1.** large visible area of land. —*v.t.* **2.** create a landscape from.

land'slide'', *n.* fall of earth down a slope.

lane, *n.* **1.** path or narrow road. **2.** path of highway travel.

lan'guage, *n.* system of communication.

lan'guid, *adj.* without energy. —**lan'guid·ly**, *adv.*

lan'guish, *v.i.* **1.** long wistfully. **2.** weaken.

lan'guor, *n.* lack of vitality. —**lan'guorous**, *adj.*

lank, *adj.* **1.** lean. **2.** long and straight, as hair.

lan'ky, *adj.*, **-ier, iest.** awkwardly tall and lean.

lan'o·lin, *n.* oil from wool used in ointments and cosmetics.

lan'tern, *n.* **1.** transparent lamp casing. **2.** cupola.

lap, *n., v.*, **lapped, lapping.** *n.* **1.** area between waist and knees when seated. **2.** overlap. **3.** once around a racetrack. —*v.t.* **4.** wrap. **5.** overlap. —*v.i.* **6.** drink by licking. **7.** splash gently. —**lap'dog''.**

la·pel', *n.* continuation of a coat collar folded back.

lap'i·dar''y, *n., pl.* **-ies,** *adj. n.* **1.** worker in gems. —*adj.* **2.** fine; meticulous.

lapse, *v.i.*, **lapsed, lapsing,** *n. v.i.* **1.** go passively. **2.** elapse. **3.** become void. —*n.* **4.** act or instance of lapsing. **5.** minor error.

lar'ce·ny, *n., pl.* **-nies.** theft. —**lar'cenous**, *adj.*

lard, *n.* rendered animal fat.

lard'er, *n.* place for storing food.

large, *adj., adv.*, **larger, largest,** *n. adj.* **1.** big. **2.** large-scale. —*adv.* **3.** in a large way. —*n.* **4. at large, unconfined.** —**large'ly**, *adv.*

lar·gess', *n.* **1.** generous gift. **2.** generosity. Also, **lar·gesse'.**

lar'go, *adj., adv. Music.* slow.

lar'i·at, *n.* tether or lasso.

lark, *n.* **1.** songbird. **2.** frolic. —*v.i.* **3.** frolic.

lar·va, *n., pl.* **-vae.** early form of an animal. —**lar'val**, *adj.*

lar''yn·gi'tis, *n.* inflammation of the larynx.

lar'ynx, *n., pl.* **-ynxes, -ynges.** container of the vocal cords.

las·civ'i·ous, *adj.* lustful.

la'ser, *n.* device for amplifying and concentrating light waves.

lash, *v.t.* **1.** tie. **2.** whip. —*v.i.* **3.** strike. —*n.* **4.** whip. **5.** blow from a whip. **6.** eyelash.

lass, *Dialect.* young woman.

las'si·tude'', *n.* lack of vigor.

las'so, *n., pl.* **-sos, -soes,** *v.t.*, **-soed, -soing.** *n.* **1.** rope for capturing cattle, etc. —*v.t.* **2.** capture with a lasso.

last, *adj., adv.* **1.** after all others. —*n.* **2.** last one. —*v.i.* **3.** remain. —*v.t.* **4.** be enough for. —**last'ly**, *adv.*

latch, *n.* **1.** device to hold a door, etc. shut. —*v.t.* **2.** fasten with a latch.

late, *adj., adv.*, **later** or (for adj.) **latter, latest,** or **last.** *adj., adv.* **1.** after the right time. **2.** near the end. **3.** in recent times. —*adj.* **4.** recently alive.

late'ly, *adv.* recently.

la'tent, *n.* unmanifested or undeveloped. —**la'ten·cy**, *n.*

la'ter·al, *adj.* pertaining to a side. —**la'ter·al·ly**, *adv.*

lath, *n., pl.* **laths. 1.** wood strip for holding plaster. **2.** any material for this.

lathe, *n.* machine for cutting a rotating object.

lath'er, *n.* **1.** foam. —*v.t.* **2.** cover with foam.

lat'i·tude'', *n.* **1.** north-south measurement. **2.** scope.

la·trine', *n.* military bathroom.

lat'ter, *adj.* **1.** more recently mentioned. **2.** more recent. —**lat'ter·ly**, *adv.*

lat'tice, *n.* screen of crisscrossed strips. —**lat'tice·work''**, *n.*

laud, *v.t.* praise. —**laud'a·ble**, *adj.* —**laud'a·to''ry**, *adj.*

lau'dan·um, *n.* opium-alcohol solution.

laugh, *n.* **1.** rhythmic sound indicating amusement, scorn, etc. —*v.i.* **2.** make such a sound. —**laugh'a·ble**, *adj.* —**laugh'ter**, *n.*

launch, *v.t.* **1.** send from land. **2.** put into effect, use, etc. —*n.* **3.** open boat.

launder
124

laun'der, *v.t.* wash, as clothes. —**laun'-der·er**, *fem.*, **laun'dress**, *n.*

laun'dry, *n., pl.* -**dries.** place for laundering. —**laun'dry·man**, *n.*

lau'rel, *n.* 1. shrub with glossy leaves. 2. laurels, honors.

la'va, *n.* molten volcanic rock.

lav'a·to''ry, *n., pl.* -**ries.** washing place.

lav'en·der, *n.* 1. pale purple. 2. European mint with pale purple flowers.

lav'ish, *adj.* 1. very ample. 2. generous. —*v.t.* 3. give generously. —**lav'ish·ly**, *adv.* —**lav'ish·ness**, *n.*

law, *n.* 1. rule established by government. 2. legal profession. 3. police. 4. rule of natural phenomena. —**law'·a·bid''ing**, *adj.* —**law'break''er**, *n. adj.* —**law'giv''er**, *n.* —**law'less**, *adj.* —**law'mak''er**, *n.* —**law'suit''**, *n.*

lawn, *n.* 1. expanse of grass. 2. sheer cotton or linen.

law'yer, *n.* professional legal adviser and representative.

lax, *adj.* negligent. —**lax'i·ty**, *n.*

lax'a·tive, *adj.* 1. easing constipation. —*n.* 2. laxative medicine.

lay, *v.t.,* **laid, laying,** *n., adj. v.t.* 1. set down gently. 2. set in place. 3. place, as emphasis or a claim. —*n.* 4. situation. 5. ballad. —*adj.* 6. not professional or clerical. —**lay'man**, *n.*

lay'er, *n.* level or thickness of material.

lay'off'', *n.* dismissal due to lack of work.

la'zy, *adj.,* -**zier, -ziest.** unwilling to work. —**la'zi·ly**, *adv.* —**la'zi·ness**, *n.*

leach, *v.t., v.i.,* dissolve with a filtering liquid.

lead (lēd for 1 to 6; led for 7), *v.,* **led, leading,** *n. v.t.* 1. direct or guide. 2. be ahead of. 3. conduct. —*v.i.* 4. tend or result. —*n.* 5. leading role or place. 6. guidance. 7. heavy metallic chemical element. —**lead·er** (lē'dər), *n.* —**lead'er·ship''**, *n.* —**lead·en** (led'n), *adj.*

leaf, *n., pl.* **leaves,** *v.i. n.* 1. flat thin termination of a plant stem. 2. thin sheet. —*v.i.* 3. turn over pages. —**leaf'y**, *adj.*

leaf'let, *n.* small printed sheet.

league, *n., v.,* **leaguing.** *n.* 1. alliance. 2. unit of about 3 miles. —*v.t., v.i.* 3. form into a league.

leak, *n.* 1. accidental release or admission. —*v.i.* 2. have or pass through a leak. —*v.t.* 3. pass through a leak. —**leak'age**, *n.* —**leak'y**, *adj.*

lean, *v.,* **leaned** or **leant, leaning,** *adj. v.t., v.i.* 1. stand against something supporting the upper end. —*v.i.* 2. bend; incline. 3. be predisposed. 4. rely. —*adj.* 5. with little fat.

leap, *v.,* **leaped** or **leapt, leaping,** *n.* jump.

leap year, year with 29 days in February.

learn, *v.,* **learned** or **learnt, learning.** *v.t.* 1. come to know or know how. —*v.i.* 2. get information. —**learn'er**, *n.* —**learn'ing**, *n.* —**learn'ed**, *adj.*

lease, *n., v.t.,* **leased, leasing.** *n.* 1. rental contract. —*v.t.* 2. rent by lease.

leash, *n.* tether, as for a dog.

least, *adj.* 1. smallest in size, importance, etc. —*adv.* 2. to the smallest extent.

leath'er, *n.* tanned hide.

leave, *v.,* **left, leaving.** *n. v.i.* 1. go away. —*v.t.* 2. go away from. 3. abandon. 4. have remain behind one. 5. bequeath. —*n.* 6. departure. 7. permission. —**leave'tak''ing**, *n.*

leav·en (lev'n), *n.* 1. substance making dough rise. —*v.t.* 2. cause to rise.

leav'ings, *n., pl.* leftovers.

lech'er, *n.* lustful person. —**lech'er·ous**, *adj.* —**lech'er·y**, *n.*

lec'ture, *n., v.,* -**tured, -turing.** *n.* 1. informative speech. —*v.t.* 2. give a lecture to. —*v.i.* 3. give a lecture.

ledge, *n.* narrow shelf or platform.

led'ger, *n.* accountant's book.

lee, *adj.* 1. away from the wind. —*n.* 2. lee side, etc. 3. lees, dregs.

leech, *n.* blood-sucking worm.

leek, *n.* onionlike vegetable.

leer, *n.* 1. sly, malicious or lustful look. —*v.i.* 2. give a leer.

lee'way'', *n.* 1. *Informal.* scope for action. 2. *Nautical.* leeward drift.

left, *n.* 1. west when facing north. 2. liberal or socialistic position. —*adv.* 3. toward the left. 4. at or in the left. —**left'-ist**, *n., adj.* —**left'-hand'**, *adj.*

left'o''ver, *n.* remnant for later use.

left wing, political left. —**left'-wing''**, *adj.* —**left'-wing'er**, *n.*

leg, *n.* 1. supporting and walking limb. 2. vertical support.

leg'a·cy, *n., pl.* -**cies.** something left to posterity.

le'gal, *adj.* 1. permitted by law. 2. pertaining to law. —**le'gal·ly**, *adv.* —**le·gal'i·ty**, *n.* —**le'gal·ize''**, *v.t.*

leg'ate, *n.* papal envoy.

leg''a·tee', *n.* recipient of a legacy.

le·ga'tion, *n.* office of a diplomat.

le·ga'to, *adj. Music.* smooth and even.

leg'end, *n.* 1. folk tale. 2. inscription. —**leg'end·ar''y**, *adj.*

leg''er·de·main', *n.* cunning of the hand.

leg'ging, *n.* outer leg covering.

leg'i·ble, *adj.* possible to read. —**leg''i·bil'i·ty**, *n.*

le'gion, *n.* large band, esp. of soldiers. —**le'gion·ar''y**, *adj., n.* —**le''gion·naire'**, *n.*

leg'is·late'', *v.,* -**lated, -lating.** *v.t.* 1. determine by law. —*v.i.* 2. enact laws. —**leg''is·la'tion**, *n.* —**leg'is·la''tive**, *adj.* —**leg'is·la''tor**, *n.*

leg'is·la''ture, *n.* lawmaking body.

le·git'i·mate, *adj.* 1. right; proper. 2. of

125 **lie**

married parents. —le·git′i·ma·cy, *n.*
—le·git′i·mize″, *v.t.*

leg′ume, *n.* vegetable with seed pods.
—le·gu′mi·nous, *adj.*

lei (lā), *n., pl.* leis. Hawaiian flower garland.

lei′sure, *n.* 1. time for rest or recreation.
2. at one's leisure, when convenient.

lei′sure·ly, *adj. adv.* without haste or hurry.

lem′on, *n.* yellow citrus fruit. —lem″on·ade′, *n.*

lend, *v.t.,* lent, lending. 1. give for later return. 2. impart.

length, *n.* 1. end-to-end extent. 2. piece measured by length. —length′en, *v.t., v.i.* —length′wise″, length′ways″, *adj., adv.* —length′y, *adj.*

le′ni·ent, *adj.* not strict or harsh. —le′ni·en·cy, le′ni·ence, *n.*

lens, *n., pl.* lenses. transparent object concentrating or dispersing rays of light.

Lent, *n.* Christian time of penance from Ash Wednesday to Easter. —Lent′en, *adj.*

len′til, *n.* small legume seed used as food.

le′o·nine, *adj.* lion-like.

leop′ard, *n.* spotted cat of the panther family.

lep′er, *n.* person with leprosy.

le′pre·chaun″, *n.* Irish fairy.

lep′ro·sy, *n.* deforming chronic disease.
—lep′rous, *adj.*

les′bi·an, *n.* 1. homosexual woman.
—*adj.* 2. pertaining to such women.
—les′bi·an·ism, *n.*

le·sion, *n.* bodily injury resulting in impairment of function.

less, *adj.* 1. smaller or fewer. —*adv.* 2. to a smaller extent. —*prep.* 3. minus.
—les′sen, *v.t., v.i.*

les·see′, *n.* tenant on a lease.

les′ser, *adj.* smaller; less important.

les′son, *n.* something learned at one time.

les′sor, *n.* landlord on a lease.

lest, *conj.* for fear that.

let, *v.t.,* let, letting, *n. v.t.* 1. allow. 2. rent. 3. allow to issue. —*n.* 4. obstacle.

let′down″, *n.* 1. disappointment. 2. slackening.

le′thal, *adj.* deadly.

leth′ar·gy, *n., pl.* -gies. sluggishness.
—le·thar′gic, *adj.*

let′ter, *n.* 1. alphabetic character. 2. message in an envelope. 3. literal meaning.
4. letters, literature. —*v.t.* 5. write letter by letter. —let′ter·ing, *n.*

let′tered, *adj.* educated.

let′tuce, *n.* green, leafy vegetable.

leu·ke′mi·a, *n.* blood disease.

lev′ee, *n.* embankment against rising water.

lev′el, *n., v.t.,* -eled, -eling. *n.* 1. point or plane between top and bottom. 2. device for finding horizontals or verticals. 3. point on a scale of values.
—*adj.* 4. flat. 5. horizontal. 6. even.
—*v.t.* 7. make level.

lev′el-head′ed, *adj.* of calm, sound judgment.

lev′er, *n.* pivoted raising device lifted at one end. —lev′er·age, *n.*

le·vi′a·than, *n.* sea monster.

lev′i·ta′tion, *n.* raising or rising without physical support.

lev′i·ty, *n.* mirth, often unseemly.

lev·y (lev′ē), *v.t.,* -ied, -ying, *n., pl.* -ies. *v.t.* 1. impose for payment. 2. enlist.
—*n.* 3. something levied.

lewd, *adj.* obscene. —lewd′ly, *adv.*
—lewd′ness, *n.*

lex′i·con, *n.* dictionary.

li″a·bil′i·ty, *n., pl.* -ties. 1. loss or payment of money. 2. state of being liable.
3. disadvantage.

li′a·ble, *adj.* 1. responsible. 2. subject to something. 3. likely.

li′ai·son″, *n.* 1. connection, as for communication. 2. love affair.

li′ar, *n.* teller of lies.

li·ba′tion, *n.* outpouring of liquid.

li′bel, *n., v.t.,* -beled, -beling. *n.* 1. defamation *n.* 1. defamation in writing or print. —*v.t.* 2. defame by this means.
—li′bel·ous, li′bel·lous, *adj.*

lib′er·al, *adj.* 1. generous. 2. not literal.
3. favoring more civil liberty. —*n.* 4. person favoring more civil liberty.
—lib″er·al′i·ty, *n.* —lib′er·al·ism, *n.*
—lib′er·al·ize″, *v.t.*

lib′er·ate″, *v.t.,* -ated, -ating. free.
—lib″er·a′tion, *n.* —lib′er·a″tor, *n.*

lib″er·tar′i·an, *n.* believer in personal liberties.

lib′er·tine″, *n.* licentious person.

lib′er·ty, *n., pl.* -ties. 1. freedom. 2. privilege. 3. liberties, impertinences.

li·bi′do, *n.* 1. sexual urge. 2. psychic energy.

li′brar″y, *n., pl.* -ies. 1. collection of books. 2. place for books. —li·brar′i·an, *n.*

li·bret′to, *n., pl.* -tos, -ti. text of an opera, etc. —li·bret′tist, *n.*

li′cense, *n., v.t.,* -censed, -censing. *n.* 1. privilege of doing. 2. abuse of liberty.
—*v.t.* 3. grant a license to. —li″cen·see′, *n.* —li·cen′tious, *adj.*

li·chen (lī′kən), *n.* mosslike growth.

lic′it, *adj.* permitted.

lick, *v.t.* 1. rub with the tongue. 2. *Informal.* a. defeat. b. beat. —*v.i.* 3. lap.
—*n.* 4. act or instance of licking.

lic′o·rice, *n.* European root used for flavoring.

lid, *n.* cover.

lie, *v.i.,* lay (for 1, 2) or lied (for 3), lain (for 1, 2), lying, *n. v.i.* 1. rest on something horizontal. 2. be situated. 3. make statements intended to deceive.
—*n.* 4. situation. 5. lying statement.

lief 126

lief, *adv. Archaic.* willingly.

lien, *n.* legal claim on property.

lieu, *n.* in lieu of, in place of.

lieu·ten'ant, *n.* commissioned military or naval officer below a captain or lieutenant commander. —lieu·ten'an·cy, *n.*

life, *n., pl.* lives. 1. period of existence. 2. living things collectively. 3. human experience. 4. way of living. 5. animation. 6. biography. —life'less, *adj.* —life'long", *adj.* —life'time", *n.*

life'boat", *n.* emergency boat.

life'guard", *n.* one employed to protect bathers, esp. from drowning, etc.

life'like", *adj.* resembling a living being.

life'-size", *adj.* as large as the living model. Also, life'-sized".

lift, *v.t.* 1. raise. —*v.i.* 2. attempt to raise something. 3. rise. —*n.* 4. act or instance of lifting. 5. hoist.

lig'a·ment, *n.* body connective tissue.

lig'a·ture, *n.* tie.

light, *n., adj., v.,* lighted or lit, lighting. *n.* 1. visible radiant energy. 2. lamp. 3. flame. 4. truth. 5. public awareness. —*adj.* 6. not dark or serious. 7. not heavy. 8. not serious. —*v.t.* 9. set fire to. 10. cause to give off light. 11. show in light. —*v.i.* 12. be lighted. 13. alight. 14. happen; venture. —light'en, *v.t., v.i.* —light'weight", *adj.*

light'er, *n.* 1. lighting device. 2. freight barge.

light'-head'ed, *adj.* dizzy.

light'-heart'ed, *adj.* cheerful.

light'house", *n.* tower with a navigational beacon.

light'ning, *n.* flash of electricity in the sky.

light'-year', *n.* distance light travels in a year, about 6 trillion miles.

lig'nite, *n.* soft brown coal.

like, *prep., adj., n., v.t.,* liked, liking *prep.* 1. similar or similarly to. 2. characteristic or suggestive of. 3. inclined to. —*adj.* 4. similar. —*n.* 5. similar person or thing. 6. preference. —*v.t.* 7. be pleased with. 8. wish. —like'a·ble, lik'a·ble, *adj.* —like'ness, *n.*

like'ly, *adj.,* -lier, -liest, *adv. adj.* 1. probable. 2. suitable. —*adv.* 3. probably.

lik'en, *v.t.* compare.

like'wise", *adv.* similarly, also.

li'lac, *n.* pale purple flower.

lilt, *n.* light, bouncy rhythm.

lil'y, *n., pl.* -ies. flower with trumpet-shaped blossoms.

li'ma bean, broad, pale green bean.

limb, *n.* 1. large tree branch. 2. arm or leg.

lim'ber, *adj.* 1. flexible. —*v.t.* 2. make limber. —*v.i.* 3. become limber.

lim'bo, *n.* 1. abode of the unbaptized, innocent dead. 2. oblivion.

lime, *n., v.t.,* limed, liming. *n.* 1. calcium oxide. 2. tart green citrus fruit. —*v.t.* 3. treat with lime. —lime'ade', *n.*

lime'light", *n.* state of much publicity.

lim'er·ick, *n.* amusing five-lined verse.

lime'stone", *n.* stone containing much calcium carbonate.

lim'it, *n.* 1. edge or boundary. 2. permissible extent. —*v.t.* 3. set a limit to. —lim"i·ta'tion, *n.* —lim'it·ed, *adj.* —lim'it·less, *adj.*

lim'ou·sine", *n.* long, chauffeured automobile.

limp, *v.i.* 1. walk lamely. —*n.* 2. lame gait. —*adj.* 3. not rigid or firm.

lim'pid, *adj.* perfectly clear. —lim·pid'i·ty, *n.*

lin'den, *n.* tree with heart-shaped leaves.

line, *n., v.,* lined, lining. *n.* 1. long, narrow mark. 2. row. 3. boundary. 4. course. 5. transit system. 6. rope, pipe, etc. 7. occupation. —*v.t.* 8. put a lining in. 9. mark with lines. —*v.i.* 10. assemble in a line.

lin'e·age, *n.* ancestry.

lin'e·al, *adj.* 1. pertaining to direct ancestry. 2. linear.

lin'e·a·ments, *n., pl.* features of the face.

lin'e·ar, *adj.* pertaining to lines or length.

lin'en, *n.* 1. cloth made of flax. 2. linens, bedsheets, etc.

lin'er, *n.* 1. ship or airplane on scheduled service. 2. something that lines.

line'up", *n.* arrangement or muster in a row.

lin'ger, *v.i.* remain; stay.

lin·ger·ie (lan"ʒə rā'), *n.* women's underwear.

lin'go, *n., pl.* -goes. *Informal.* strange language.

lin'guist, *n.* 1. speaker of many languages. 2. student of languages. —lin·guis'tics, *n.* —lin·guis'tic, *adj.*

lin'i·ment, *n.* soothing liquid for external use.

lin'ing, *n.* material applied to an interior.

link, *n.* 1. unit of a chain or series. 2. connection. —*v.t., v.i.* 3. connect. —link'age, *n.*

links, *n., pl.* golf course.

li·no'le·um, *n.* smooth sheeting for floors.

lin'seed", *n.* flax seed.

lint, *n.* fibrous waste.

lin'tel, *n.* beam over a doorway, etc.

li'on, *n.* 1. large catlike animal of Africa and southwest Asia. 2. celebrity. Also, *fem.,* li'on·ess.

li'on·ize", *v.t.,* -ized, -izing. treat as a celebrity.

lip, *n.* 1. feature at top and bottom of the mouth. 2. surface for pouring.

lip'stick", *n.* coloring for the lips.

liq'ue·fy", *v.*, **-fied, -fying.** *v.t., v.i.* change to liquid. —**liq"ue·fac'tion,** *n.*

li'queur, *n.* sweet strong alcoholic drink.

liq'uid, *n.* **1.** fluid incapable of indefinite expansion. —*adj.* **2.** in the form of a liquid. **3.** readily turned into cash. —**li·quid'i·ty,** *n.*

liq'ui·date", *v.t.*, **-dated, -dating. 1.** terminate, as a business. **2.** convert into cash. **3.** kill. —**liq"ui·da'tion,** *n.*

liq'uor, *n.* alcoholic liquid.

lisle (līl), *n.* fine cotton.

lisp, *n.* **1.** mispronunciation of *s* and *z.* —*v.i.* **2.** make such mispronunciations.

lis'some, *adj.* agile and supple.

list, *n.* **1.** series of related items. **2.** tilt, as of a ship. —*v.t.* **3.** put on a list. —*v.i.* **4.** tilt.

lis'ten, *v.i.* **1.** hear attentively. **2.** pay heed. —**lis'ten·er,** *n.*

list'less, *adj.* indifferent from fatigue, etc. —**list'less·ly,** *adv.* —**list'less·ness,** *n.*

lit'a·ny, *n., pl.* **-nies.** uttered prayer with responses.

li'ter, *n.* metric unit equal to 1.0567 liquid quarts or 0.908 dry quart. Also, **li'tre.**

lit'er·al, *adj.* according to the exact wording. —**lit'er·al·ly,** *adv.*

lit'er·ar"y, *adj.* pertaining to literature.

lit'er·ate, *adj.* **1.** able to read. **2.** well-read. —**lit'er·a·cy,** *n.*

lit"e·ra'ti, *n., pl.* well-read persons.

lit'er·a·ture, *n.* fiction, poetry, etc. of lasting value.

lithe, *adj.* supple.

lith'o·graph", *n.* print from a flat surface with special ink. —**lith"o·graph'ic,** *adj.* —**li·thog'ra·phy,** *n.* —**li·thog'ra·pher,** *n.*

lit'i·gate", *v.*, **-gated, -gating.** *v.t., v.i.* contest in a lawsuit. —**lit"i·ga'tion,** *n.* —**lit'i·gant,** **lit'i·ga"tor,** *n.*

lit'ter, *n.* **1.** trash. **2.** newly-born animals. **3.** animal bedding. **4.** frame for carrying a person. —*v.t.* **5.** scatter carelessly.

lit'tle, *adj.* **littler** or **less** or **lesser, littlest** or **least**, *adv.*, **less, least,** *n. adj.* **1.** small. **2.** petty. —*adv.* **3.** not much. —*n.* **4.** short while. **5.** small amount.

lit'ur·gy, *n., pl.* **-gies.** ritual of worship. —**li·tur'gi·cal,** *adj.*

liv'a·ble, *adj.* pleasant to inhabit. Also, **live'a·ble.**

live'li·hood", *n.* means of sustenance.

live (liv for 1-5; līv for 6-8). *v.i.* **1.** be alive. **2.** dwell. **3.** spend one's life. **4.** depend for existence. —*v.t.* **5.** experience or spend. —*adj.* **6.** alive. **7.** vital. **8.** electrically charged.

live'ly, *adj.*, **-lier, -liest,** *adv. adj.* **1.** full of vitality. —*adv.* **2.** in a lively way. —**live'li·ness,** *n.*

liv'en, *v.t.* **1.** make lively. —*v.i.* **2.** become lively.

liv'er, *n.* organ secreting bile.

liv'er·wurst", *n.* sausage made with ground liver.

live'stock", *n.* cattle, sheep, etc.

liv'id, *adj.* **1.** discolored, as flesh. **2.** enraged.

liv'ing, *adj.* **1.** alive. **2.** pertaining to being alive. —*n.* **3.** livelihood.

liz'ard, *n.* scaly, four-legged reptile.

lla'ma, *n.* South American beast of burden.

load, *n.* **1.** something carried. —*v.t.* **2.** put a load on or in. **3.** supply in large amounts. **4.** make ready for firing. —*v.i.* **5.** take on a load.

loaf, *n., pl.* **loaves,** *v.i., n.* **1.** regularly shaped piece of bread. —*v.i.* **2.** be idle. —**loaf'er,** *n.*

loam, *n.* rich soil. —**loam'y,** *adj.*

loan, *n.* **1.** act or instance of lending. **2.** something lent. —*v.t., v.i.* **3.** lend.

loath, *adj.* reluctant.

loathe, *v.t.*, **loathed, loathing.** dislike intensely. —**loath'some,** *adj.*

lob, *v.t.*, **lobbed, lobbing.** hurl with a high curve.

lob'by, *n., pl.* **-bies.** *v.i.*, **-bied, -bying.** *n.* **1.** entrance room. **2.** group seeking favorable legislation. —*v.i.* **3.** seek favorable legislation. —**lob'by·ist,** *n.*

lobe, *n.* rounded projection. —**lo'bar, lo'bate,** *adj.*

lob'ster, *n.* sea crustacean with pincers.

lo'cal, *adj.* **1.** pertaining or limited to a place. **2.** making most or all stops. —*n.* **3.** local train or bus. **4.** local branch of a labor union. —**lo'cal·ly,** *adv.*

lo·cale', *n.* scene of an event.

lo·cal'i·ty, *n., pl.* **-ties. 1.** location. **2.** district.

lo'cal·ize", *v.t.*, **-ized, -izing.** trace or confine to one place. —**lo"cal·i·za'tion,** *n.*

lo'cate, *v.t.*, **-cated, -cating.** establish the place of. —**lo·ca'tion,** *n.*

lock, *n.* **1.** device for securing doors, etc. **2.** canal chamber between levels. **3.** firing mechanism. **4.** curl of hair. —*v.t.* **5.** fasten with a lock. **6.** shut in or out. —*v.i.* **7.** be jammed. —**lock'smith",** *n.*

lock'er, *n.* compartment that can be locked.

lock'et, *n.* round case worn as a pendant to a necklace.

lock'jaw", *n.* form of tetanus.

lock'out", *n.* exclusion of workers from a workplace.

lo'co, *adj. Informal.* crazy.

lo"co·mo'tion, *n.* movement from place to place.

lo"co·mo'tive, *n.* **1.** railroad traction engine. —*adj.* **2.** pertaining to locomotion.

lo'cust, *n.* **1.** crop-eating insect. **2.** flowering tree.

lo·cu'tion, *n.* spoken expression.

lode, *n.* deposit of metallic ore.

lode'stone'', *n.* magnetic iron ore.

lodge, *n., v.,* **lodged, lodging.** *n.* **1.** forest house. **2.** fraternity chapter. —*v.t.* **3.** house. **4.** push into a fixed position. —*v.i.* **5.** become fixed. **6.** dwell.

lodg'ing, *n.* **1.** temporary home. **2. lodgings,** rented rooms.

loft, *n.* open upper floor.

loft'y, *adj.,* **-ier, -iest.** very high. —**loft'i·ly,** *adv.*

log, *n., v.t.,* **logged, logging.** *n.* **1.** cut tree trunk or limb. **2.** record of events. —*v.t.* **3.** take logs from. **4.** record in a log.

lo'gan·ber''ry, *n.* hybrid of blackberry and red raspberry.

log'a·rithm, *n. Math.* power of one number if multiplied to equal another. —**log''a·rith'mic,** *adj.*

loge, *n.* theater mezzanine.

log'ger·head'', *n.* **at loggerheads,** in sharp dispute.

log'ic, *n.* **1.** correct reasoning. **2.** predictable sequence. —**log'i·cal,** *adj.* —**log'i·cal·ly,** *adv.* —**lo·gi'cian,** *n.*

lo·gis'tics, *n.* science of military housing, supply, etc. —**lo·gis'tic, lo·gis'ti·cal,** *adj.*

lo''go, *n.* symbol or trademark of an enterprise.

lo'gy, *adj.,* **-gier, -giest.** sluggish.

loin, *n.* **1.** Also, **loins,** lower human back. **2.** front hindquarter as a cut of meat.

loi'ter, *n.* linger in one place. —**loi'ter·er,** *n.*

loll, *v.i.* **1.** remain idle. **2.** hang loosely.

lol'li·pop'', *n.* candy on a stick for sucking.

lone, *adj.* single; solitary.

lone'ly, *adj.,* **-lier, -liest. 1.** sad because alone. **2.** isolated. Also, **lone'some.** —**lone'li·ness,** *n.*

long, *adj., adv.,* **longer, longest,** *v.i. adj.* **1.** of great distance between ends. **2.** in length. **3.** occupying much time. —*adv.* **4.** for a long time. **5.** from start to finish. **6.** at a long time. —*v.i.* **7.** wish passionately. —**long'ing,** *n., adj.*

lon·gev'i·ty, *n.* long life.

long'hand'', *n.* ordinary handwriting.

lon'gi·tude'', *n.* east-west measurement.

lon''gi·tu'di·nal, *adj.* pertaining to length or longitude.

long'shore''man, *n.* loader and unloader of ships.

long'-stand'ing, *adj.* long-continued.

long'-suf'fer·ing, *adj.* patient.

long ton, ton of 2,240 pounds.

look, *v.i.* **1.** direct one's gaze. **2.** search. **3.** appear to be. —*v.t.* **4.** stare at. —*n.* **5.** act or instance of looking. **6.** appearance. —*interj.* **7.** pay heed!

look'out'', *n.* **1.** vigilance. **2.** spy or sentinel. **3.** *Informal.* personal problem.

loom, *n.* **1.** weaving frame. —*v.i.* **2.** appear indistinctly as huge.

loon, *n.* diving bird.

loon'y, *adj.,* **-ier, -iest.** *Informal.* crazy.

loop, *n.* **1.** closed curve of rope, etc. —*v.t.* **2.** make into a loop. —*v.i.* **3.** form a loop.

loop'hole'', *n.* **1.** slit for shooting. **2.** means of evasion.

loose, *adj.,* **looser, loosest,** *v.t.,* **loosed, loosing.** *adj.* **1.** not tight. **2.** not confined. **3.** not strict or precise. **4.** immoral. —*v.t.* **5.** make loose. —**loose'ly,** *adv.* —**loos'en,** *v.t., v.i.*

loot, *n.* **1.** things stolen. —*v.t.* **2.** steal the contents of.

lop, *v.t.,* **lopped, lopping.** chop

lop'sid''ed, *adj.* out of balance.

lo·qua'cious, *adj.* talkative. —**lo·quac'i·ty,** *n.*

lord, *n.* **1.** landed noble. **2. the Lord, a.** God. **b.** Christ. —**lord'ly,** *adj., adv.* —**lord'ship'',** *n.*

lore, *n.* traditional learning.

lose, *v.,* **lost, losing.** *v.t.* **1.** fail to keep. **2.** misplace. **3.** fail to win. —*v.i.* **4.** have a loss. —**los'er,** *n.* —**lost,** *adj.*

loss, *n.* **1.** act or instance of losing. **2.** something lost.

lot, *n.* **1.** chance. **2.** personal fate. **3.** area of ground. **4.** Also, **lots.** *Informal.* many or much.

lo'tion, *n.* skin preparation.

lot'ter·y, *n., pl.* **-ies.** choice by chance, esp. of a winner.

lo'tus, *n.* **1.** tropical waterlily. **2.** legendary plant causing forgetfulness.

loud, *adj.* **1.** with much noise. **2.** *Informal.* flashy. —*adv.* **3.** loudly. —**loud'ly,** *adv.* —**loud'ness,** *n.*

lounge, *v.i.,* **lounged, lounging.** *n. v.i.* **1.** be idle or relaxed. —*n.* **2.** couch. **3.** place for lounging.

louse, *n., pl.* **lice.** parasitic insect.

lous'y, *adj.,* **-ier, -iest.** *Informal.* bad.

lout, *n.* stupid, offensive person. —**lout'ish,** *adj.*

lou'ver, *n.* opening screened with inclined slats.

love, *n., v.t.,* **loved, loving.** *n.* **1.** powerful attraction to another. **2.** warm concern. **3.** loved person. —*v.t.* **4.** feel love for. —**lov'a·ble, love'a·ble,** *adj.* —**love'less,** *adj.* —**lov'er,** *n.* —**lov'ing,** *adj.* —**lov'ing·ly,** *adv.*

love'lorn'', *adj.* pining with love.

love'ly, *adj.,* **-lier, -liest.** beautiful.

low, *adj.* **1.** of less than average height. **2.** of less than average quantity, etc. **3.**

depressed. **4.** vulgar. **5.** meanly wicked.
—*adv.* **6.** in a low way. —*n.* **7.** something low. —*v.i.* **8.** moo.

low′brow″, *n., adj.* non-intellectual.

low·er, *adj.* (lō′ər) **1.** more low. —*v.t.* **2.** cause to be low or lower. —*v.i.* **3.** become low or lower. **4.** (loŏ′ər) frown.

low′ly, *adj., -lier, -liest.* humble.

loy′al, *adj.* faithful. —**loy′al·ly,** *adv.* —**loy′al·ty,** *n.*

loz′enge, *n.* cough drop, etc.

lu·au′, *n.* Hawaiian feast.

lub′ber *n.* clumsy person. —**lub′ber·ly,** *adj.*

lu′bri·cate″, *v.t.,* **-cated, -cating. 1.** make slippery. **2.** cause the wearing parts of to slide easily. —**lu″bri·ca′ tion,** *n.* —**lu′bri·cant,** *n.*

lu′cid, *adj.* **1.** clear, as to understand. **2.** mentally competent. —**lu′cid·ly,** *adv.* —**lu·cid′i·ty,** *n.*

luck, *n.* **1.** chance. **2.** favorable chance. —**luck′less,** *adj.*

luck′y, *adj.,* **-ier, -iest.** having or marked by good luck. —**luck′i·ly,** *adv.*

luc′ra·tive, *adj.* profitable.

lu′cre, *n.* riches.

lu′di·crous, *adj.* laughable.

lug, *v.t.,* **lugged, lugging,** *n. v.t.* **1.** haul with effort. —*n.* **2.** projection for lifting, etc.

lug′gage, *n.* baggage.

lu·gu′bri·ous, *adj.* foolishly mournful.

luke′warm″, *adj.* **1.** slightly warm. **2.** unenthusiastic.

lull, *v.t., v.i., n.* calm.

lull′a·by″, *n., pl.* **-bies.** soothing song for children.

lum·ba′go, *n.* pain in the lower back.

lum′bar, *adj.* pertaining to the loins.

lum′ber, *n.* **1.** building wood. —*v.i.* **2.** move ponderously. —**lum′ber·man,** *n.*

lum′ber·jack″, *n.* feller of trees.

lu′mi·nar″y, *n., pl.* **-ies. 1.** light source. **2.** brilliant person.

lu″mi·nes′cence, *n.* light without heat. —**lu″min·nes′cent,** *adj.*

lu′mi·nous, *adj.* light-giving. —**lu″mi·nos′i·ty,** *n.*

lump, *n.* **1.** shapeless mass. **2.** swelling. —*adj.* **3.** collective. —*v.t.* **4.** assemble or treat in a lump. **5.** tolerate despite oneself. —*v.i.* **6.** form in lumps. —**lump′y,** *adj.*

lu′nar, *adj.* pertaining to the moon.

lu′na·tic, *n.* **1.** insane person. —*adj.* **2.** insane. —**lu′na·cy,** *n.*

lunch, *n.* **1.** midday meal. —*v.i.* **2.** eat lunch.

lunch′eon, *n.* formal lunch.

lung, *n.* breathing organ.

lunge, *n., v.,* **lunged, lunging.** *n.* **1.** sudden move forward. —*v.t., v.i.* **2.** move with a lunge.

lurch, *n.* **1.** sudden sideways movement. **2. leave in the lurch,** desert in time of need. —*v.i.* **3.** make a lurch.

lure, *v.t.,* lured, luring, *n. v.t.* **1.** entice —*n.* **2.** enticement; bait.

lur′id, *adj.* **1.** glowing through haze. **2.** violently sensational.

lurk, *v.i.* be in hiding.

lus′cious, *adj.* appealing to the senses.

lush, *adj.* **1.** rich; abundant. —*n.* **2.** *Informal.* alcoholic.

lust, *n.* **1.** strong appetite. **2.** strong sexual appetite. —*v.i.* **3.** feel lust. —**lust′ful,** *adj.*

lus′ter, *n.* **1.** sheen. **2.** brightness. —**lus′ trous,** *adj.*

lust′y, *adj.,* **-ier, -iest.** vigorous. —**lust′i· ly,** *adv.*

lux·u′ri·ant, *adj.* lavishly growing. —**lux· u′ri·ance,** *n.*

lux·u′ri·ate″, *v.i.,* **-ated, -ating.** live luxuriously.

lux′u·ry, *n., pl.* **-ries. 1.** great comfort or pleasure. **2.** something superfluous. —**lux·u′ri·ous,** *adj.*

ly·ce′um, *n.* institute for lectures.

lye, *n.* strong alkaline substance.

ly′ing-in′, *n.* confinement in childbirth.

lymph, *n.* clear, watery body liquid. —**lym·phat′ic,** *adj.*

lynch, *v.t.* kill as a mob.

lynx, *n., pl.* **lynxes, lynx.** wildcat of the northern hemisphere.

lyr′ic, *adj.* **1.** pertaining to emotion expressed in poetry. —*n.* **2.** lyric poem. **3.** Usually **lyrics,** words to music. —**lyr′i·cal,** *adj.* —**lyr′i·cist,** *n.*

M

M, m, *n.* thirteenth letter of the English alphabet.

mach·i·na·tion (mak″ə nä′shən), *n.* plot, scheme.

ma·chine′, *n., v.t.,* **-chined, -chining.** *n.* **1.** device for doing work. **2.** political organization. —*v.t.* **3.** shape by machine. —**ma·chin′er·y,** *n.*

ma·chin′ist, *n.* worker with machine-operated tools.

ma·chis′mo, *n.* assertion of masculinity.

mack′er·el, *n., pl.* **-el, -els.** North Atlantic fish.

mackinaw 130

mack′i·naw″, *n.* heavy jacketlike coat.

mack′in·tosh″, *n.* rubberized cloth coat.

mac′ra·me″, *n.* lace or string tied in patterns.

mac″ro·bi·ot′ics, *n.* art of lengthening life. —**mac″ro·bi·ot′ic**, *adj.*

mac′ro·cosm, *n.* 1. universe. 2. complex of microcosms.

mad, *adj.*, **madder, maddest. 1.** insane. **2.** infatuated. **3.** angry. —**mad′ly**, *adv.* —**mad′ness**, *n.* —**mad′den**, *v.t.* —**mad′house″**, *n.* —**mad′man″**, **mad′wom″an**, *n.*

mad′am, *n.* 1. polite form of address to a woman. 2. woman running a brothel.

mad′ame, *n., pl.* **mesdames.** *French.* madam or Mrs.

mad′cap″, *adj.* 1. reckless. —*n.* 2. reckless person.

ma″de·moi·selle′, *n., pl.* **mesdemoiselles.** *French.* Miss.

Ma·don′na, *n.* Virgin Mary.

mad′ri·gal, *n.* unaccompanied part song.

mael′strom, *n.* whirlpool.

mag′a·zine, *n.* 1. periodical with covers. 2. storage chamber, esp. for ammunition.

ma·gen′ta, *n.* purplish red.

mag′got, *n.* wormlike larva. —**mag′got·y**, *adj.*

mag′ic, *n.* 1. use of supernatural methods. 2. illusions using sleight of hand. —*adj.* 3. existing or operated by magic. —**mag′i·cal**, *adj.* —**ma·gi′cian**, *n.*

mag″is·te′ri·al, *adj.* authoritative.

mag′is·trate, *n.* minor judge. —**mag′is·tra·cy**, *n.*

mag·nan′i·mous, *adj.* above pettiness. —**mag·nan′i·mous·ly**, *adv.* —**mag″na·nim′i·ty**, *n.*

mag′nate, *n.* man of wealth or power.

mag·ne′sium, *n.* light metallic element.

mag′net, *n.* object attracting ferrous metal. —**mag·net′ic**, *adj.* —**mag′net·ism**, *n.* —**mag′net·ize″**, *v.t.*

mag·ne′to, *n., pl.* **-toes.** generator with permanent magnets.

mag·nif′i·cent, *adj.* splendid in form, accomplishments, etc. —**mag·nif′i·cence**, *n.* —**mag·nif′i·cent·ly**, *adv.*

mag′ni·fy″, *v.t.*, **-fied, -fying.** increase the apparent or real size of. —**mag″ni·fi·ca′tion**, *n.* —**mag′ni·fi″er**, *n.*

mag′ni·tude″, *n.* size.

mag·no′li·a, *n.* flowering tree.

mag′pie″, *n.* black-and-white bird.

ma″ha·ra′jah, *n.* major Indian ruler. Also, **ma″ha·ra′ja**, *fem.*, **ma″ha·ra′ni, ma″ha·ra′nee.**

ma·hog′a·ny, *n.* reddish-brown tropical wood.

maid, *n.* 1. Also, **maid′ser″vant**, woman servant. 2. *Archaic.* young woman.

maid′en, *n.* 1. *Archaic.* young woman.

—*adj.* 2. very first. —**maid′en·hood″**, *n.* —**maid′en·ly**, *adj.*

maid′en·head″, *n.* hymen.

mail, *n.* 1. material shipped by post offices. 2. flexible armor. —*v.t.* 3. give to a post office for shipping. —**mail′box″**, *n.* —**mail′man″**, *n.*

ma″il·gram, *n.* message teletyped between post offices and finally delivered by mail.

maim, *v.t.* mutilate.

main, *adj.* 1. principal. —*n.* 2. major utility line. 3. *Archaic.* sea. —**main′ly**, *adv.* —**main′spring″**, *n.*

main″frame, *n., adj.* (computers) large-scale, high-speed computing system.

main′land″, *n.* continental land, as opposed to islands.

main′stay″, *n.* main support.

main′stream″, *n.* main way of thinking, acting, etc.

main·tain′, *v.t.* 1. keep in good order. 2. house, feed, etc. 3. assert persistently. —**main′ten·ance**, *n.*

maî·tre d'ho·tel, (me′trə dô tel′) *n.* headwaiter. Also, *Informal.*, **mai·tre d'** (mât′ər dē′).

maj′es·ty, *n., pl.* **-ies. 1. Majesty,** title of respect for a sovereign. 2. grandeur. —**ma·jes′tic**, *adj.*

ma′jor, *adj.* 1. greater. 2. *Music.* in a scale a half tone above the minor. —*v.i.* 3. *Education.* specialize. —*n.* 4. army officer. 5. specialty in school.

ma·jor′i·ty, *n., pl.* **-ties. 1.** greater number. 2. legal adulthood.

make, *v.t.*, **made, making. 1.** cause to be or occur. 2. force. 3. constitute. 4. earn. 5. interpret.

make′-be·lieve″, *n.* 1. pretense to oneself. —*adj.* 2. imaginary.

make′shift″, *adj.* improvised; temporary.

make′up″, *n.* 1. constitution; contents. 2. cosmetics, etc.

mal″ad·just′ed, *adj.* badly adjusted, esp. to life. —**mal″ad·just′ment**, *n.*

mal″a·droit′, *adj.* clumsy.

mal′a·dy, *n., pl.* **-dies.** illness.

ma·laise′, *n.* uneasiness.

mal′a·prop·ism, *n.* ludicrous misuse of a word.

ma·lar′i·a, *n.* mosquito-transmitted disease. —**ma·lar′i·al**, *adj.*

mal′con·tent″, *n.* person discontented, esp. with society.

male, *adj.* 1. of the sex that inseminates. —*n.* 2. male being.

mal′e·dic″tion, *n.* curse.

mal′e·fac″tor, *n.* doer of evil.

ma·lev′o·lent, *adj.* wishing harm. —**ma·lev′o·lence**, *n.*

mal·fea′sance, *n.* wrongdoing in office.

mal″for·ma′tion, *n.* bad formation, esp. of a body part. —**mal·formed′**, *adj.*

mal′ice, *n.* ill will. —**ma·li′cious**, *adj.*

ma·lign′, *adj*. 1. intending or doing harm. —*v.t.* 2. slander.

ma·lig′nant, *adj*. harmful or dangerous. —**ma·lig′nan·cy**, *n*.

ma·lin′ger, *v.i.* pretend sickness or weakness.

mall, *n*. 1. tree-lined walk or lawn. 2. shopping area.

mal′lard, *n*. wild duck.

mal′le·a·ble, *adj*. readily shaped by hammering. —**mal″le·a·bil′i·ty**, *n*.

mal′let, *n*. short, heavy hammer.

mal″nu·tri′tion, *n*. inadequate nutrition. —**mal·nour′shed**, *adj*.

mal·o′dor·ous, *adj*. bad-smelling.

mal·prac′tice, *n*. improper professional practice.

malt, *n*. soaked and dried grain.

mal·treat″, *v.t.* treat badly. —**mal·treat′ment**, *n*.

mam″bo, *n*. dance of Latin American origin.

mam′ma, *n*. mother. Also, **ma′ma**.

mam′mal, *n*. 1. animal giving milk. —*adj*. 2. being such an animal. —**mam·mal′i·an**, *adj*., *n*.

mam′ma·ry, *adj*. pertaining to breasts.

Mam′mon, *n*. riches or their pursuit, personified.

mam′moth, *adj*. 1. very large. —*n*. 2. extinct, long-tusked elephant.

man, *n*., *pl*. **men**, *v.t.*, **manned, manning.** 1. human being. 2. adult male human. 3. humanity. —*v.t.* 4. furnish with persons.

man′a·cles, *n*., *pl*. shackles.

man′age, *v*., **-aged, -aging.** *v.t.* 1. supervise. 2. control. —*v.i.* 4. contrive to succeed. —**man′age·a·ble**, *adj*. —**man′age·ment**, *n*. —**man′ag·er**, *n*. —**man″a·ge′ri·al**, *adj*.

ma·ña′na, *adv*. *Spanish*. tomorrow; some time later.

man′da·rin, *n*. imperial Chinese official.

man′date, *n*. command.

man′da·to″ry, *adj*. required.

man″di·ble, *n*. lower jaw bone.

man′do·lin, *n*. plucked musical instrument.

man′drel, *n*. support for work being shaped. Also, **man′dril**.

mane, *n*. long hair on an animal's neck.

ma·neu′ver, *n*. 1. military exercise. 2. controlled movement. —*v.t.*, *v.i.* 3. move under control.

man′ful, *adj*. courageous.

man′ga·nese″, *n*. grayish chemical element.

mange, *n*. animal skin disease. —**man′gy**, *adj*.

man′ger, *n*. feeding trough.

man′gle, *v.t.*, **-gled, -gling,** *n*. *v.t.* 1. crush out of shape. —*n*. 2. ironing machine.

man′go, *n*., *pl*. **-goes.** fruit-bearing tropical tree.

man′grove, *n*. tropical tree.

man′han″dle, *v.t.*, **-dled, -dling.** handle roughly.

man′hole″, *n*. small access hole.

man′hood″, *n*. 1. virility. 2. majority.

ma′ni·a, *n*. 1. violent insanity. 2. excitement.

ma′ni·ac″, *n*. violently insane person. —**ma·ni′a·cal**, *adj*.

man″ic, *adj*. displaying unstable, frenzied behavior.

man′i·cure, *n*. care of the hands. —**man′i·cur″ist**, *n*.

man′i·fest″, *v.t.* 1. make apparent. —*adj*. 2. obvious. —*n*. 3. list of cargo or passengers.

man″i·fes′to, *n*., *pl*. **-toes.** public declaration.

man′i·fold″, *adj*. in many forms.

man′i·kin, *n*. professional model. Also, **man′ne·quin.**

man·il″a, *n*. a strong, light brown paper.

ma·nip′u·late″, *v.t.*, **-lated, -lating.** handle cunningly. —**ma·nip′u·la″tor**, *n*.

man′kind′, *n*. humanity.

man′ly, *adj*. **-lier, -liest.** virile; brave. —**man′li·ness**, *n*.

man·na, *n*. miraculous food.

man′ner, *n*. 1. way of doing. 2. sort. 3. **manners,** personal conduct.

man′ner·ism, *n*. personal peculiarity.

man′ner·ly, *adj*. well-mannered.

man′nish, *adj*. man-like.

ma·noeu′vre, *n*., *v*., **-vred, -vring.** *n*., *v.t.*, *v.i.* maneuver.

man′-of-war′, *n*. warship.

man′or, *n*. large estate. —**ma·no′ri·al**, *adj*.

man′pow″er, *n*. available labor force.

man′sard, *n*. hip roof with two pitches.

manse, *n*. home of a clergyman.

man′sion, *n*. impressive house.

man′slaugh″ter, *n*. unintentional homicide.

man′tel, *n*. fireplace surround. Also, **man′tel·piece″.**

man·til′la, *n*. lace shawl.

man′tle, *n*., *v.t.*, **-tled, -tling.** cloak.

man′u·al, *adj*. 1. pertaining to or operated by hands. —*n*. 2. handbook. —**man′u·al·ly**, *adv*.

man″u·fac′ture, *v.t.*, **-tured, -turing,** *n*. *v.t.* 1. make industrially. —*n*. 2. act or instance of manufacturing. —**man″u·fac′tur·er**, *n*.

ma·nure′, *n*., *v.t.*, **-nured, -nuring.** *n*. 1. animal feces. —*v.t.* 2. spread with manure as fertilizer.

man′u·script, *n*. 1. unprinted writing. —*adj*. 2. written or typed.

man′y, *adj*., **more, most.** in a large number.

map, *n*., *v.t.*, **mapped, mapping.** *n*. 1.

measured representation of an area of land, etc. —*v.t.* **2.** measure for a map. **3.** plan.

ma'ple, *n.* broad-leafed deciduous tree.

mar, *v.t.,* **marred, marring.** make imperfect.

mar'a·thon'', *n.* **1.** foot race of 26 miles, 385 yards. **2.** endurance contest.

ma·raud'er, *n.* raider and plunderer.

mar'ble, *n.* **1.** hard, fine-grained limestone. **2.** colored glass ball. **3. marbles,** game played with such balls.

march, *v.i.* **1.** walk with measured steps to a cadence. —*v.t.* **2.** cause to march. —*n.* **3.** marching walk or journey. **4.** piece of music accompanying such a walk. **5. March,** third month.

mar'chion·ess, *n.* wife of a marquess, or woman equal to one in rank.

mare, *n.* female horse.

mar'ga·rine, butter-like vegetable oil compound.

mar'gin, *n.* **1.** border or border area. **2.** difference in amounts. —**mar'gin·al,** *adj.*

mar'i·gold'', *n.* orange-flowered plant.

ma''ri·jua'na, *n.* dried hemp leaves and blossoms, sometimes smoked. Also, **ma''ri·hua'na.**

ma·rim'ba, *n.* xylophone with tubelike resonators.

ma·ri'na, *n.* yacht landing.

ma''ri·nade', *n.* pickling solution.

mar'i·nate'', *v.t.,* **-nated, -nating.** steep in a marinade.

ma·rine', *adj.* **1.** pertaining to the sea. —*n.* **2.** soldier performing sea duty.

mar'i·ner, *n.* sailor.

mar''i·o·nette', *n.* puppet hung from strings.

mar'i·tal, *adj.* pertaining to marriage. —**mar'i·tal·ly,** *adv.*

mar'i·time'', *adj.* pertaining to shipping.

mar'jo·ram, *n.* fragrant herb.

mark, *n.* **1.** something visible on a surface. **2.** target. —*v.t.* **3.** make a mark on. **4.** indicate. **5.** note. **6.** review and grade. —**mark'er,** *n.* —**mark'ing,** *n.*

marked, *adj.* noticeable; emphatic. —**mark'ed·ly,** *adv.*

mark'et, *n.* **1.** place for selling. —*v.t.* **2.** offer for sale. —*v.i.* **3.** shop. —**mark'et·a·ble,** *adj.*

marks'man, *n.* shooter at targets. —**marks'man·ship'',** *n.*

mar'lin, *n., pl.* **-lins, -lin.** large deep-sea fish.

mar·ma·lade'', *n.* fruit preserve.

ma·roon', *v.t.* **1.** abandon on a deserted island. —*n.* **2.** dark brownish red.

mar·quee', *n.* open projecting shelter.

mar'quess, *n.* nobleman superior to an earl or count. Also, **mar'quis,** *fem.,* **mar·quise'.**

mar'row, *n.* inner bone tissue.

mar'ry, *v.,* **-ried, -rying.** *v.t.* **1.** take as spouse. **2.** unite as spouses. —*v.i.* **3.** be married. —**mar'riage,** *n.* —**mar'riage·a·ble,** *adj.*

marsh, *n.* swamp. —**marsh'y,** *adj.*

mar'shal, *n., v.t.,* **-shaled, -shaling.** *n.* **1.** sheriff-like U.S. officer. —*v.t.* **2.** put in order. **3.** guide; escort.

marsh'mal''low, *n.* sweet, spongy confection.

mar·su'pi·al, *n.* animal carrying its young in a pouch.

mart, *n.* salesplace.

mar'ten, *n.* soft-furred weasel-like animal.

mar'tial, *adj.* pertaining to war or the military.

mar'tin, *n.* bird of the swallow family.

mar''ti·net', *n.* rigid disciplinarian.

mar·ti'ni, *n.* cocktail of gin or vodka and dry vermouth.

mar'tyr, *n.* **1.** person who dies or suffers for beliefs. —*v.t.* **2.** kill as a martyr. —**mar'tyr·dom,** *n.*

mar'vel, *n., v.i.,* **-veled, -veling.** wonder. —**mar'vel·ous,** *adj.*

mas·ca'ra, *n.* cosmetic for eyelashes and eyebrows.

mas'cot, *n.* **1.** thing kept for luck. **2.** group pet.

mas'cu·line, *adv.* pertaining to or characteristic of males. —**mas''cu·lin'i·ty,** *n.*

mash, *v.t.* **1.** crush to pulp. —*n.* **2.** pulped and watered grain.

mask, *n.* **1.** face covering. **2.** concealment. —*v.t.* **3.** cover with a mask.

mas'och·ism, *n.* abnormal pleasure obtained from suffering pain. —**mas'och·ist,** *n.* —**mas''och·is'tic,** *adj.*

ma'son, *n.* **1.** builder with stones, bricks, etc. **2. Mason,** Freemason. —**Ma·son'ic,** *adj.* —**ma'son·ry,** *n.*

mas'quer·ade'', *n., v.i.,* **-aded, -ading.** *n.* **1.** ball of masked and costumed persons. **2.** something falsified. —*v.i.* **3.** appear falsely.

mass, *n.* **1.** large, shapeless quantity. **2.** *Physics.* matter as related to inertia. **3.** Often **Mass,** Eucharistic service. —*v.t., v.i.* **4.** gather in a mass.

mas'sa·cre, *n., v.t.,* **-cred, -cring.** *n.* **1.** killing of many. —*v.t.* **2.** kill in a massacre.

mas·sage (mə sahzh'), *n., v.t.,* **-saged, -saging.** *n.* **1.** manipulation of muscles, as to stimulate circulation. —*v.t.* **2.** give a massage to. —**mas·seur',** *fem.,* **mas·seuse',** *n.*

mas'sive, *adj.* in a large mass.

mast, *n.* tall spar used as a support.

mas'ter, *n.* **1.** person in control. **2.** accomplished craftsman. —*adj.* **3.** principal; controlling. —*v.t.* **4.** make submissive. **5.** become expert in. —**mas'ter·y,** *n.*

mas'ter·ful, *adj.* imposing one's will.

mas'ter·ly, *adj.* accomplished.

mas'ter·piece'', *n.* 1. greatest accomplishment. 2. proof of masterly skill. Also, **mas'ter·work''.**

master sergeant, army sergeant of high rank.

mas'ti·cate'', *v.t.,* **-cated, -cating.** chew.

mas'tiff, *n.* large, strong-jawed dog.

mas'to·don'', *n.* extinct elephant-like animal.

mas'tur·bate'', *v.i.,* **-bated, -bating.** manipulate one's genitals.

mat, *n., v.t.,* matted, matting, *adj. n.* 1. thick, flat, flexible object. 2. tangled mass. —*v.t.* 3. cover with mats. 4. make into a mat. —*adj.* 5. without gloss.

mat'a·dor'', *n.* bullfighter who kills.

match, *n.* 1. fire-making friction device. 2. equal or counterpart. 3. marriage. 4. game. —*v.t.* 5. compare. 6. equal. —*v.i.* 7. be a match or matches. —**match'mak''er,** *n.*

match'less, *adj.* incomparable.

mate, *n., v.,* mated, mating. *n.* 1. spouse. 2. companion. 3. co-worker. 4. one of a pair. 5. ship's officer. —*v.t., v.i.* 6. join as mates.

ma·te'ri·al, *n.* 1. that which an object is made of. —*adj.* 2. composed of material. 3. non-spiritual. 4. relevant.

ma·te'ri·al·ism, *n.* 1. doctrine that all is matter. 2. concern with wealth, goods, etc. —**ma·te'ri·al·ist,** *n., adj.* —**ma·te''ri·al·is'tic,** *adj.*

ma·te''ri·el', *n.* military supplies.

ma·ter'nal, *adj.* 1. pertaining to mothers. 2. mother-like. —**ma·ter'ni·ty,** *n.*

math''e·mat'ics, *n.* study of the relations of quantities or forms. Also, *Informal,* **math.** —**math''e·mat'i·cal,** *adj.* —**math''e·ma·ti'cian,** *n.*

mat''i·nee', *n.* afternoon performance.

mat'ins, *n.* morning prayer service.

ma'tri·arch'', *n.* woman acting as master or ruler. —**ma''tri·ar'chal,** *adj.* —**ma' tri·ar''chy,** *n.*

ma·tric'u·late'', *v.,* **-lated, -lating.** *v.i., v.t.* enroll as a student.

mat'ri·mo''ny, *n., pl.* **-nies.** marriage. —**mat''ri·mo'ni·al,** *adj.*

ma'trix, *n.* environment in which one comes to be.

ma'tron, *n.* 1. mature woman. 2. woman supervisor or guard. —**ma'tron·ly,** *adj.*

matte, *n.* not glossy; flat.

mat'ter, *n.* 1. solid, liquid, or gas. 2. affair. 3. importance. —*v.i.* 4. be important.

mat'tock, *n.* digging tool.

mat'tress, *n.* pad for a bed.

ma·ture', *adj., v.,* **-tured, -turing.** *adj.* 1. fully ripe or grown. 2. due for payment. —*v.t.* 3. make mature. —*v.i.* 4.

become mature. —**mat''u·ri'tion,** *n.* —**ma·tu'ri·ty,** *n.*

mat'zo, *n., pl.* **-zos, -zot, -zoth.** unleavened wafer.

maud'lin, *adj.* foolishly sentimental.

maul, *v.t.* handle or beat severely.

mau''so·le'um, *n., pl.* **-leums, -lea.** large and magnificent tomb.

mauve, *n.* light bluish purple.

mav'er·ick, *n.* nonconformist.

maw, *n.* mouth and throat.

mawk'ish, *adj.* weakly sentimental.

max'im, *n.* rule of conduct.

max'i·mum, *n., pl.* **-mums, -ma,** *adj. n.* 1. greatest amount. —*adj.* 2. Also, **max'i·mal,** greatest.

may, *v.t.* 1. am, are, or is permitted to. 2. will possibly. 3. can. —*n.* 4. **May,** fifth month.

may'be, *adv.* possibly.

may''day, *n.* distress call used by aircraft and ships.

may'hem'', *n.* criminal maiming.

may'on·naise'', *n.* salad dressing made with egg yolks.

may'or, *n.* chief city official. —**may'or· al·ty,** *n.*

maze, *n.* intricate system of corridors, lines, etc.

ma·zur'ka, *n.* fast Polish dance.

mead'ow, *n.* area of grassy land.

mea'ger, *adj.* scanty; inadequate. Also, **mea'gre.** —**mea'ger·ly,** *adv.* —**mea' ger·ness,** *n.*

meal, *n.* 1. food at one sitting. 2. coarsely ground grain. —**meal'y,** *adj.*

meal'y-mouthed'', *adj.* not frank.

mean, *v.t.,* meant, meaning, *adj., n. v.t.* 1. intend. 2. wish to say. 3. signify. —*adj.* 4. ill-tempered. 5. shabby. 6. average. —*n.* 7. part between extremes. 8. **means, a.** something serving a purpose. **b.** personal resources. —**mean'ly,** *adv.* —**mean'ness,** *n.*

me·an'der, *v.i.* wander aimlessly.

mean'ing, *n.* 1. intended message. —*adj.* 2. intended as expressive. —**mean'ing· ful,** *adj.* —**mean'ing·less,** *adj.*

mean'time'', *n.* 1. time in between. —*adv.* 2. during the meantime. 3. at the same time. Also, **mean'while''.**

mea'sles, *n.* virus disease producing a rash.

meas'ly, *adj.,* **-lier, liest.** *Informal.* contemptibly small.

meas'ure, *v.,* **-ured, -uring,** *n., v.t.* 1. find the size or amount of. —*v.i.* 2. amount to. —*n.* 3. measurement. 4. means of measuring. 5. course of action. —**meas'ur·a·ble,** *adj.* —**meas' ure·less,** *adj.* —**meas'ure·ment,** *n.*

meas'ured, *adj.* deliberate.

meat, *n.* 1. animal flesh. 2. edible part of a nut. 3. essential part. —**meat'y,** *adj.*

me·chan'ic, *n.* **1.** worker with machinery. **2. mechanics,** study of the action of forces.

me·chan'i·cal, *adj.* **1.** working by machinery. **2.** unthinkingly automatic.

mech'a·nism, *n.* piece of machinery.

mech'a·nize'', *v.t.,* -nized, -nizing. equip with machinery.

med'al, *n.* metal disk indicating distinction, religious affiliation, etc.

me·dal'lion, *n.* round design.

med'al·list, *n.* winner of a medal.

med'dle, *v.i.,* -dled, -dling. interfere mischievously. —med'dler, *n.* —med'dle·some, *adj.*

me'di·an, *n.* **1.** *Math.* central in a series of numbers. —*adj.* **2.** *Math.* pertaining to a median. **3.** middle.

me'di·ate'', *v.,* -ated, -ating. *v.i.* **1.** act as an intermediary. —*v.t.* **2.** resolve as an intermediary. —me'di·a''tor, *n.*

med'i·cal, *adj.* pertaining to medicine.

med'i·cate'', *v.t.,* -cated, -cating. **1.** treat with medicine. **2.** put medicine in. —med''i·ca'tion, *n.*

me·dic'i·nal, *adj.* serving as medicine.

med'i·cine, *n.* **1.** science of healing. **2.** healing substance.

me''di·e'val, *adj.* pertaining to the Middle Ages.

me''di·o'cre, *adj.* of indifferent value. —me''di·oc'ri·ty, *n.*

med'i·tate'', *v.i.,* -tated, -tating. think deeply. —med''i·ta'tion, *n.* —med''i·ta'tive, *adj.*

me'di·um, *n., pl.* -ums, -a, *adj. n.* **1.** something in the middle. **2.** means. **3.** *pl,* **media,** means of communication. **4.** *pl,* **mediums,** communicator with the dead. —*adj.* **5.** intermediate.

med'ley, *n., pl.* -leys. mixture of tunes.

meek, *adj.* mild; submissive. —meek'ly, *adv.* —meek'ness, *n.*

meer'schaum, *n.* white, claylike mineral.

meet, *v.,* met, meeting, *n., adj. v.t.* **1.** come into contact with. **2.** be introduced to. —*v.i.* **3.** be mutually met. —*n.* **4.** sports meeting. —*adj.* **5.** *Archaic.* suitable. —meet'ing, *n.*

meg'a·hertz'', *n., pl.* -hertz. one million hertz.

meg''a·lo·ma'ni·a, *n.* delusions of or appetite for grandeur.

meg''a·lop'o·lis, *n.* huge urban area.

meg'a·phone'', *n.* horn magnifying the voice.

meg'a·ton'', *n.* explosive force equal to one million tons of TNT.

mel''an·cho'li·a, *n.* pathological melancholy.

mel'an·chol''y, *n.* **1.** sadness. —*adj.* **2.** sad.

me'lee, *n.* confused combat.

mel·li'flu·ous, *n.* smooth and sweet-sounding. Also, mel·lif'flu·ent.

mel'low, *adj.* **1.** rich-flavored. **2.** gentle. —*v.t.* **3.** make mellow. —*v.i.* **4.** become mellow.

me·lo'di·ous, *adj.* tuneful.

mel'o·dra''ma, *n.* drama of suspense and extravagant emotion. —mel''o·dra·mat'ic, *adj.* —mel''o·dra·mat'ics, *n., pl.*

mel'o·dy, *n., pl.* -dies. tune. —me·lod'ic, *adj.*

mel'on, *n.* large, juicy fruit.

melt, *v.,* melted, melted or molten, melting. *v.t., v.i.* liquefy by applying heat.

mem'ber, *n.* **1.** person in an organization. **2.** component part. —mem'ber·ship'', *n.*

mem'brane, *n.* thin organic tissue.

me·men'to, *n., pl.* -tos, -toes. souvenir.

mem'oirs, *n., pl.* written personal recollections.

mem'o·ra·ble, *adj.* compelling remembrance. —mem'o·ra·bly, *adv.*

mem''o·ran'dum, *n., pl.* -dums, -da. note of something to be remembered. Also, *Informal,* mem'o.

me·mo'ri·al, *adj.* **1.** in remembrance. —*n.* **2.** something made or done in remembrance.

Memorial Day, legal holiday in May, in memory of dead servicemen.

mem'o·rize'', *v.t.,* -rized, -rizing. act so as to remember. —mem''o·ri·za'tion, *n.*

mem''o·ry, *n., pl.* -ries. **1.** ability to recall past experience. **2.** something remembered. **3.** thing of the past. **4.** (computers) electronic data storage through circuitry or a recording medium.

men'ace, *n., v.t.,* -aced, -acing. *n.* **1.** visible threat. —*v.t.* **2.** threaten. —men'ac·ing·ly, *adv.*

me·nag'er·ie, *n.* collection of captive wild animals.

mend, *v.t.* **1.** repair. —*v.i.* **2.** improve in condition. —*n.* **3.** mended place.

men·da'cious, *adj.* lying. —men·dac'i·ty, *n.*

men'di·cant, *adj.* **1.** begging. —*n.* **2.** mendicant person.

me'ni·al, *adj.* **1.** servile. —*n.* **2.** menial person.

men'o·pause'', *n.* permanent end of menstruation.

men·o'rah, *n. Judaism.* branched candlestick.

men'ses, *n., pl.* periodic discharge of blood from the uterus.

men'stru·ate'', *v.i.,* -ated, -ating. experience menses. —men'stru·al, *adj.* —men''stru·a'tion, *n.*

men''su·ra'tion, *n.* measurement.

men'tal, *adj.* pertaining to the mind. —men'tal·ly, *adv.*

men·tal'i·ty, *n., pl.* -ties. mental power.

men'thol, *n.* alcohol from oil of peppermint. —**men'tho·lat''ed,** *adj.*

men'tion, *n.* 1. brief allusion. —*v.t.* 2. make a mention of.

men'tor, *n.* teacher or advisor.

men'u, *n.* list of dishes offered.

me·ow', *n.* sound of a cat.

mer'can·tile, *adj.* pertaining to trade.

mer'ce·nar''y, *adj., n., pl.* **-ies.** *adj.* 1. devoted to money-making. 2. done for pay. —*n.* 3. hired soldier.

mer'cer·ize'', *v.t.,* **-ized, -izing.** impart gloss and strength to, chemically.

mer·chan·dise, *n., v.t.,* **-dised, -dising.** *n.* (mər'chən dīs'') 1. goods for sale. —*v.t.* (mər'chən dīz'') 2. Also, **mer'chan·dize'',** promote the sale of.

mer'chant, *n.* seller of goods.

merchant marine, commercial ships of a country.

mer·cu'ri·al, *adj.* quick to change, esp. in emotion.

mer'cu·ry, *n.* heavy metallic chemical element.

mer'cy, *n., pl.* **-cies.** 1. kindness toward the helpless. 2. lucky thing. —**mer'ci·ful,** *adj.* —**mer'ci·less,** *adj.*

mere, *adj.* no more than. —**mere'ly,** *adv.*

mer''e·tri'cious, *adj.* showy and specious.

merge, *v.* **merged, merging.** *v.t., v.i.* combine

merg'er, *n.* unification of business organizations.

me·rid'i·an, *n.* north-south line.

me·ringue', *n.* stiff-beaten egg white.

mer'it, *n.* 1. worth. 2. **merits,** aspects right or wrong. —*v.t.* 3. deserve. —**mer''i·to'ri·ous,** *adj.*

mer'maid'', *n.* legendary sea creature, half-woman, half-fish. Also, *masc.,* **mer'man''.**

mer'ry, *adj.,* **-rier, -riest.** cheerful. —**mer'ri·ly,** *adv.* —**mer'ri·ment,** *n.*

mer'ry-go-round'', *n.* rotating structure giving a pleasure ride.

mer'ry·mak''ing, *n.* festivity. —**mer'ry·mak''er,** *n.*

me'sa, *n.* high, steep-sided plateau.

mesh, *n.* 1. open space in a net. 2. net-like material. 3. engagement of gears. —*v.t., v.i.* 4. entangle. —*v.i.* 5. become engaged.

mes'mer·ize'', *v.t.,* **-ized, -izing.** hypnotize. —**mes'mer·ism,** *n.* —**mes'mer·ist,** *n.*

mes·quite (mes kēt), *n.* southwestern U.S. tree.

mess, *n.* 1. disorder or disorderly scene. 2. difficult situation. 3. military meal. —*v.t.* 4. make untidy. 5. do badly. —*v.i.* 6. eat mess. —**mes'sy,** *adj.* —**mes'si·ly,** *adv.* —**mes'si·ness,** *n.*

mes'sage, *n.* 1. communication. 2. idea, etc. to communicate.

mes'sen·ger, *n.* carrier of messages.

Mes·si'ah, *n.* deliverer of mankind.

mes·ti·zo (mes tē'zō) *n., pl.* **-zos, -zoes.** Hispano-Indian.

me·tab'o·lism, *n.* breakdown of an organism's nourishment into protoplasm, energy, and waste. —**met''a·bol'ic,** *adj.*

met'al, *n.* iron, gold, brass, etc. —**me·tal'lic,** *adj.*

met'al·lur''gy, *n.* separation and refining of metals. —**met''al·lur'gi·cal,** *adj.* —**met'al·lur''gist,** *n.*

met''a·mor'pho·sis, *n.* transformation. —**met''a·mor'phic,** *adj.* —**met''a·mor'phose,** *v.t., v.i.*

met'a·phor'', *n.* use of an analogous idea. —**met''a·phor'i·cal,** *adj.*

met''a·phys'ics, *n.* study of the nature of being and reality. —**met''a·phys'i·cal,** *adj.* —**met''a·phy·si'cian,** *n.*

met''em·psy·cho'sis, *n., pl.* **-ses.** transfer of souls from body to body.

me'te·or, *n.* meteoroid in the earth's atmosphere.

me''te·or'ic, *adj.* temporarily brilliant.

me'te·or·ite'', *n.* meteoroid surviving a fall to earth.

me'te·or·oid'', *n.* solid body traveling through outer space.

me''te·or·ol'o·gy, *n.* study of climate and weather. —**me''te·or·o·log'i·cal,** *adj.* —**me''te·or·ol'o·gist,** *n.*

me'ter, *n.* 1. unit of 100 centimeters or 39.37 inches. 2. rhythmic pattern. 3. measuring device for fluids, etc. —*v.t.* 4. measure with a meter.

meth'od, *n.* process or system of doing.

me·thod'i·cal, *adj.* orderly; deliberate. —**me·thod'i·cal·ly,** *adv.*

meth''od·ol'o·gy, *n., pl.* **-gies.** system of methods.

me·tic'u·lous, *adj.* attentive to details.

met'ric, *adj.* 1. pertaining to the metric system. 2. metrical. —**met'ri·cal·ly,** *adv.*

met'ri·cal, *adj.* 1. pertaining to poetic meter. 2. pertaining to measurement.

met'ri·cize'', *v.t.,* **-cized, -cizing.** express in the metric system.

metric system, decimal system of measurement based on the meter, gram, and liter.

met'ro·nome'', *n.* time-beating machine.

me·trop'o·lis, *n.* 1. principal or major city. 2. city and surrounding built-up area. —**met''ro·pol'i·tan,** *adj.*

met'tle, *n.* spirit; courage. —**met'tle·some,** *adj.*

mez'za·nine'', *n.* balcony-like floor.

mez'zo·so·pra'no, *n., pl.* **-nos, -ni.** singer with a range between soprano and contralto.

mi·as'ma, *n.* marsh vapor.

mi′ca, *n.* crystallized transparent laminated mineral.

mi′crobe, *n.* microorganism, esp. harmful.

mi′cro·chip, *n.* small wafer of silicon, etc., containing electronic circuits.

mic″ro·com·pu′ter, *n.* a complete computing system of compact size, sometimes portable.

mi′cro·cosm, *n.* little world.

mi′cro·fiche″, *n.* card of microfilm images.

mi′cro·film″, *n.* **1.** film with images at greatly reduced size. —*v.t.* **2.** record on microfilm.

mi·crom′e·ter, *n.* instrument for fine measurements.

mi″cro·or′gan·ism, *n.* organism visible only through a microscope.

mi′cro·phone″, *n.* instrument transforming sound into electrical impulses.

mi′cro·scope″, *n.* instrument for very high magnification. —**mi″cro·scop′ic,** *adj.*

mic″ro·wave, *n.* electromagnetic radiation of extremely high frequency.

mid′air′, *n.* area away from the ground.

mid′day″, *n.* noon.

mid′dle, *n.* **1.** place with ends equally far away. —*adj.* **2.** intermediate.

mid′dle-aged′, *adj.* neither young nor old.

mid′dle·man″, *n.* intermediary between producer and consumer.

mid′dling, *adj.* **1.** intermediate. —*adv.* **2.** *Informal.* moderately.

mid′land, *n.* middle region.

mid′night″, *n.* twelve o'clock at night.

mid′point″, *n.* center point.

mid′riff, *n.* middle part of the torso.

mid′ship″man, *n.* naval cadet.

midst, *n.* middle part.

mid′way″, *n.* **1.** thoroughfare of sideshows. —*adj., adv.* **2.** halfway.

mid′wife″, *n.* deliverer of babies.— **mid′wife″ry,** *n.*

mid′year″, *n.* middle of the year.

mien, *n.* manner; bearing.

miff, *v.t.* offend.

might, *n.* **1.** strength. —*v.* **2.** (past tense of *may*). **3.** will possibly. —**might′y,** *adj.* —**might′i·ly,** *adv.*

mi′graine, *n.* intense headache.

mi′grate, *v.i.,* **-grated, -grating.** move in a group. —**mi·gra′tion,** *n.* —**mi′grant,** *adj., n.* —**mi′gra·to″ry,** *adj.*

mild, *adj.* not severe or harsh. —**mild′ly,** *adv.* —**mild′ness,** *n.*

mil′dew″, *n.* fungus of damp cloth, etc.

mile, *n.* unit equal to 5,280 feet on land, 6,076 feet on water.

mile′age, *n.* **1.** rate per mile. **2.** number of miles per unit.

mi·lieu′, *n.* social or working environment.

mil′i·tant, *adj.* **1.** fighting for a cause. —*n.* **2.** militant person. —**mil′i·tan·cy,** *n.*

mil′i·tar·ism, *n.* emphasis on military affairs. —**mil′i·tar·ist,** *n.* —**mil″i·ta·ris′tic,** *adj.*

mil′i·tar·ize″, *v.t.,* **-ized, -izing.** invest or equip with military force.

mil′i·tar″y, *adj.* **1.** pertaining to armed forces. —*n.* **2. the military,** armed forces.

mil′i·tate″, *v.i.,* **-tated, -tating.** be an influence.

mi·li′tia, *n.* emergency citizen army. —**mi·li′tia·man,** *n.*

milk, *n.* **1.** white fluid secreted by female mammals for nourishing their young. —*v.t.* **2.** get milk from. —**milk′maid″,** *n.* —**milk′man″,** *n.* —**milk′y,** *adj.*

milk′shake″, *n.* shaken drink of milk, ice cream, and flavoring.

mill, *n.* **1.** place for processing or manufacturing; factory. **2.** tenth of a cent. —*v.t.* **3.** process in a mill. —*v.i.* **4.** move about confusedly. —**mill′er,** *n.*

mil·len′i·um, *n., pl.* **-ums, -a. 1.** period of a thousand years. **2.** time of perfection.

mil′li·gram″, *n.* thousandth of a gram.

mil′li·me″ter, *n.* thousandth of a meter.

mil′li·ner, *n.* dealer in women's hats. —**mil′lin·er·y,** *n.*

mil′lion, *n.* a thousand thousand. —**mil′lionth,** *adj.*

mil″lion·aire′, *n.* owner of at least a million dollars.

mill′stone″, *n.* stone for grinding flour.

mime, *n., v.t.,* **mimed, miming.** *n.* **1.** acting without words. —*v.t.* **2.** imitate in mime. —**mi·met′ic,** *adj.*

mim′ic, *n., v.t.,* **-icked, -icking.** *n.* **1.** person who imitates mannerisms of others. —*v.t.* **2.** imitate as a mimic. —**mim′ic·ry,** *n.*

mi·mo′sa, *n.* flowering plant of warm regions.

min″a·ret′, *Islam.* tower for summoning to prayer.

mince, *v.,* **minced, mincing.** *v.t.* **1.** chop finely. **2.** mitigate the meaning of. —*v.i.* **3.** be affectedly dainty. —**minc′ing,** *adj.*

mince′meat″, *n.* finely chopped fruit, etc.

mind, *n.* **1.** that which thinks. **2.** personality. **3.** sanity. —*v.t.* **4.** heed. **5.** be troubled or annoyed by.

mind′ful, *adj.* heedful.

mind′less, *adj.* **1.** heedless. **2.** stupid.

mine, *pron., n., v.,* **mined, mining.** *pron.* **1.** my own. —*n.* **2.** excavation for coal or minerals. **3.** buried or floated bomb.

—*v.t.* **4.** dig from a mine. **5.** put mines in. —*v.i.* **6.** work a mine. —**min′er**, *n.*

min′er·al, *n.* **1.** something neither vegetable nor animal. **2.** inorganic earth material.

min″er·al′o·gy, *n.* study of minerals. —**min″er·al·og′i·cal**, *adj.* —**min″er·al′o·gist**, *n.*

min′gle, *v.*, **-gled, -gling.** *v.t.*, *v.i.* mix together.

min′i·a·ture″, *n.* **1.** small copy. **2.** small painting. —*adj.* **3.** smaller than standard. —**min′i·a·tur·ize″**, *v.t.*

mi″ni·com·pu′ter, *n.* a computing system that is larger than a microcomputer but smaller than a mainframe computer.

min′im, *n.* **1.** *Pharmacy.* liquid measure equalling a drop. **2.** *Music.* half note.

min′i·mize″, *v.t.*, **-mized, -mizing. 1.** reduce to a minimum. **2.** treat as of minimum importance.

min′i·mum, *n.*, *pl.* **-mums, -ma,** *adj.*, *n.* **1.** least amount. —*adj.* **2.** Also, **min′i·mal,** least.

min′ion, *n.* minor official.

min′is·ter, *n.* **1.** clergyman. **2.** diplomat. **3.** cabinet member. —*v.i.* **4.** give help. —**min″is·te′ri·al**, *adj.* —**min″is·tra′tion**, *n.* —**min′is·trant**, *n.*, *adj.*

min′is·try, *n.*, *pl.* **-tries. 1.** profession of a minister. **2.** government department. **3.** act of ministering.

mink, *n.* weasel-like mammal.

min′now, *n.* tiny fresh-water fish.

mi′nor, *adj.* **1.** lesser in size or importance. **2.** *Music.* in a scale a half tone below the major. —*n.* **3.** person not of age.

mi·nor′i·ty, *n.*, *pl.* **-ities. 1.** lesser part. **2.** social group too small to have control. **3.** state of being a minor.

min′strel, *n.* **1.** medieval strolling singer. **2.** blackface singer.

mint, *n.* **1.** place for coining money. **2.** plant with aromatic leaves. —*adj.* **3.** absolutely fresh. —*v.t.* **4.** coin.

min′u·end″, *n. Math.* number subtracted from.

min″u·et, *n.* slow dance.

mi′nus, *prep.* **1.** from which is subtracted. **2.** without.

mi·nus′cule, *adj.* tiny.

min·ute, *n.* (min′ət) **1.** one sixtieth of an hour. **2.** one sixtieth of a degree of arc. **3.** minutes, record of a meeting. —*adj.* (mī nyōōt′) **4.** tiny. **5.** precise.

min′ute·man″, *n.* volunteer soldier of the American Revolution.

mi·nu′ti·ae, *n.*, *pl.* minor details.

mir′a·cle, *n.* supernatural event. —**mi·rac′u·lous**, *adj.*

mi·rage′, *n.* optical illusion caused by the atmosphere.

mire, *n.*, *v.t.*, **mired, miring.** *n.* **1.** sticky mud. —*v.t.* **2.** stick fast, as with mud. —**mir′y**, *adj.*

mir′ror, *n.* **1.** reflecting object. —*v.t.* **2.** reflect.

mirth, *n.* gaiety. —**mirth′ful**, *adj.* —**mirth′less**, *adj.*

mis- prefix meaning "wrong" or "wrongly." **misapply, misbehave, miscalculate, misconceive, misconduct, misconstrue, miscount, misdeed, misdirect, misdoing, misgovern, misguide, mishandle, misinform, misinterpret, misjudge, mismanage, mismatch, misprint, mispronounce, misquote, misread, misrule, misshapen, misspell, misspend, misstate, mistime, mistreat, misunderstand.**

mis″ad·ven′ture, *n.* bad luck.

mis′an·thrope″, *n.* hater of mankind. Also **mis·an′thro·pist.** —**mis″an·throp′ic**, *adj.* —**mis·an′thro·py**, *n.*

mis·ap″pre·hend′, *v.t.* understand wrongly. —**mis·ap″pre·hen′sion**, *n.*

mis″ap·pro′pri·ate″, *v.t.*, **-ated, -ating.** take and use wrongly.

mis″be·got′ten, *adj.* begotten wrongly; illegitimate.

mis·car′ry, *v.i.*, **-ried, -rying. 1.** give birth to a fetus that cannot live. **2.** go wrong. —**mis·car′riage**, *n.*

mis·ce″ge·na′tion, *n.* interbreeding of races.

mis″cel·la′ne·ous, *adj.* various. —**mis′cel·la·ny**, *n.*

mis·chance′, *n.* bad luck.

mis′chief, *n.* **1.** damage. **2.** malice. **3.** gentle malice. —**mis′chie·vous**, *adj.*

mis″con·struc′tion, *n.* wrong interpretation.

mis′cre·ant, *n.* villain.

mis″de·mea′nor, *n.* offence less serious than a felony.

mi′ser, *n.* morbid saver of money. —**mi′ser·ly**, *adj.*

mis′er·a·ble, *adj.* **1.** very unhappy. **2.** causing misery. **3.** contemptibly meager or poor. —**mis′er·a·bly**, *adv.*

mis′er·y, *n.*, *pl.* **-ies. 1.** suffering. **2.** source of suffering.

mis·fire′, *v.i.*, **-fired, -firing. 1.** fail to fire. **2.** fail to be effective.

mis′fit′, *n.*, *v.i.*, **-fitted, -fitting.** *n.* **1.** person unhappy in society. —*v.t.*, *v.i.* **2.** fit badly.

mis·for′tune, *n.* **1.** bad luck. **2.** piece of bad luck.

mis·giv′ing, *n.* apprehension; doubt.

mis′hap, *n.* unfortunate incident.

mis·lay′, *v.t.*, **-laid, -laying.** put somewhere later forgotten.

mis·lead′, *v.t.*, **-led, -leading. 1.** advise or urge wrongly. **2.** deceive.

mis·no′mer, *n.* wrong name.

mi·sog′y·ny, *n*. hatred of women. **—mi·sog′y·nist**, *n*.

mis·place′, *v.t.*, **-placed, -placing**. 1. mislay. 2. put in a wrong place.

mis·pri′sion, *n*. deviation from duty.

mis″rep·re·sent′, *v.t.* give a wrong idea of. **—mis″rep·re·sen·ta′tion**, *n*.

miss, *v.t., n., pl.* **misses**. *v.t.* 1. fail to hit, seize, meet, etc. 2. be lonely without. **—n**. 3. act or instance of missing. 4. **Miss**, title for an unmarried woman.

mis′sal, *n*. book of prayers for Mass.

mis′sile, *n*. something thrown or shot to hit a target.

mis′sing, *adj.* lost or absent.

mis′sion, *n*. 1. commanded or requested journey. 2. group of missionaries. 3. group sent to a place. 4. duty or purpose.

mis′sion·ar″y, *n., pl.* **-ies**. person sent to make religious conversions.

mis′sive, *n*. written message.

mis·step′, *n*. 1. wrong step. 2. wrong act.

mist, *n*. 1. thin fog. **—v.t.** 2. fog. **—v.i.** 3. become misty. **—mist′y**, *adj.*

mis·take′, *n., v.t.*, **-took, -taken, -taking**. *n*. 1. wrong act or opinion. **—v.t.** 2. understand wrongly. **—mis·tak′a·ble**, *adj.*

mis′tle·toe″, *n*. parasitic evergreen.

mis′tress, *n*. 1. female master. 2. unmarried female sexual partner.

mis·tri′al, *n*. trial invalidated for technical reasons.

mis·trust′, *v.t.* 1. have no trust in. **—n.** 2. lack of trust. **—mis·trust′ful**, *adj.*

mis·use′, *v.t.*, **-used, -using**, *n., v.t.* (mis yōōz′) 1. use wrongly. 2. mistreat. **—n.** (mis yōōs′) 3. wrong use or treatment.

mite, *n*. 1. tiny arachnid. 2. tiny sum of money.

mi′ter, *n*. 1. bishop's headpiece. 2. diagonal joint. **—v.t.** 3. join in a miter.

mit′i·gate″, *v.*, **-gated, -gating**. *v.t., v.i.* lessen in severity. **—mit″i·ga′tion**, *n*.

mitt, *n*. padded glove.

mit′ten, *n*. glove with only the thumb separate.

mix, *v.*, **mixed, mixing**, *n., v.t.* 1. assemble and make uniform. 2. have together. **—v.i.** 3. be on social terms. **—n.** 4. mixture. **—mix′ture**, *n*.

mixed, *adj.* 1. blended. 2. imperfect or impure.

mix′up″, *n*. confusion.

mne·mon′ic, *adj.* helping memory.

moan, *n*. 1. low, sad sound. **—v.i.** 2. make such a sound.

moat, *n*. defensive, water-filled ditch.

mob, *n., v.t.*, **mobbed, mobbing**. *n*. 1. disorderly or hostile crowd. **—v.t.** 2. attack in a mob.

mo′bile, *adj.* movable. **—mo·bil′i·ty**, *n*.

mo′bi·lize″, *v.*, **-lized, -lizing**. *v.t., v.i.* make ready for war.

moc′ca·sin, *n*. soft heelless slipper.

mo′cha, *n*. 1. type of coffee. **—adj.** 2. coffee-flavored.

mock, *n*. 1. ridicule. 2. imitate; mimic. **—adj.** 3. imitation. **—mock′er·y**, *n*.

mock′ing·bird″, *n*. bird imitating calls of other birds.

mock′up″, *n*. full-scale model.

mode, *n*. 1. manner of doing. 2. fashion. **—mod′ish**, *adj.*

mod′el, *n*. 1. small-scale three-dimensional copy. 2. something to imitate. 3. poser for pictures. **—adj.** 4. exemplary. **—v.t.** 5. copy in three dimensions. 6. mold as in making a model. 7. make as a copy.

mo″dem, *n*. (computers) device for linking computers via telephone lines.

mod·er·ate, *adj., n., v.*, **-ated, -ating**. *adj.* (mod′ər ət) 1. avoiding extremes. **—n.** 2. moderate person. **—v.t.** (mod′ ər āt) 3. make moderate. 4. preside over. **—v.i.** 5. become moderate. **—mod′er·ate·ly**, *adv.* **—mod′er·a″tor**, *n*.

mod′ern, *adj.* 1. pertaining to the present. 2. reflecting advance taste, thought, technology, etc. **—n.** 3. modern person. **—mo·dern′i·ty**, *n*. **—mod′ern·ize″**, *v.t., v.i.*

mod′ern·ism, *n*. advocacy of something deemed modern.

mod″ern·is′tic, *adj.* self-consciously modern in style.

mod′est, *adj.* 1. disliking praise, publicity, etc. 2. avoiding self-exposure. 3. not outstanding. **—mod′est·ly**, *adv.* **—mod·es′ty**, *n*.

mod′i·cum, *n*. small amount.

mod′i·fy″, *v.*, **-fied, -fying**. *v.t., v.i.* 1. alter in nature. **—v.t.** 2. limit slightly. **—mod″i·fi·ca′tion**, *n*. **—mod′i·fi″er**, *n*.

mod′u·late″, *v.t.*, **-lated, -lating**. vary or adjust. **—mod″u·la′tion**, *n*.

mod′ule, *n*. 1. unit of measurement. 2. part scaled to the dimensions of such a unit.

mo′hair, *n*. fabric of Angora goat hair.

Mo·ham′med·an, *n., adj.* Muslim. **—Mo·ham′med·an·ism**, *n*.

moist, *adj.* slightly wet. **—moist′en**, *v.t., v.i.* **—mois′ture**, *n*.

mo′lar, *n*. grinding tooth.

mo·las′ses, *n*. syrup from sugar refining.

mold, *n*. 1. device for forming a casting. 2. model. 3. destructive fungus. **—v.t.** 4. model. 5. cast in a mold. **—v.i.** 6. become moldy. **—mold′y**, *adj.*

mold′er, *v.i.* crumble to dust.

mold′ing, *n*. shaped strip or band.

mole, *n*. 1. spot on the skin. 2. burrowing animal. 3. breakwater. **—mole′hill″**, *n*. **—mole′skin″**, *n*.

mol′e·cule″, *n*. smallest characteristic

particle of an element or compound. —mo·lec′u·lar, *adj.*

mo·lest′, *v.t.* trouble or interfere with. —mo″les·ta′tion, *n.*

mol′li·fy″, *v.t.*, -fied, -fying. 1. appease. 2. mitigate.

mol′lusk, *n.* soft-bodied invertebrate, often in a shell. Also, mol′lusc.

molt, *v.i.* shed hair, feathers, etc. for replacement.

mol′ten, *adj.* melted.

mo′ment, *n.* 1. very brief period. 2. present time. 3. importance. —mo′men·tar″y, *adj.* —mo″men·tar′i·ly, *adv.*

mo·men′tous, *adj.* of great importance.

mo·men′tum, *n.*, *pl.* -tums, -ta. force of a moving object.

mom′my, *n.*, *pl.* -mies. mother: child's word.

mon′arch, *n.* king, queen, etc. —mon′arch·y, *n.* —mo·nar′chi·cal, *adj.*

mon′arch·ist, *n.* person in favor of a monarchy. —mon′ar·chism″, *n.*

mon′as·ter″y, *n.*, *pl.* -ies. *n.* home of monks or nuns.

mo·nas′tic, *adj.* pertaining to monks and nuns. Also, mo·nas′ti·cal, *adj.*

mon·au′ral, *adj.* reproducing sound on one channel.

Mon′day, *n.* second day.

mon′ey, *n.*, *pl.* -eys, -ies. paper or metal accepted everywhere in payment of debts. —mon′eyed, *adj.* —mon′e·tar″y, *adj.*

mon′grel, *adj.* 1. of mixed breed. —*n.* 2. mongrel animal.

mon′i·tor, *n.* 1. device for checking or supervising. —*v.t.* 2. check or supervise.

monk, *n.* member of a religious order.

mon′key, *n.*, *pl.* -keys. 1. primate other than a human or lemur. 2. small, long-tailed primate.

mon′o·chrome″, *n.* color with shading varied but not hue.

mon′o·cle, *n.* corrective lens for one eye.

mo·nog′a·my, *n.* marriage to one spouse at a time. —mo·nog′a·mous, *n.*

mon′o·graph″, *n.* scholarly work on one subject.

mon′o·lith″, *n.* object made from one stone. —mon″o·lith′ic, *adj.*

mon′o·logue″, *n.* uninterrupted speech of one person. Also, mon′o·log″. —mon′o·log″ist, *n.*

mon″o·ma′ni·a, *n.* obsession with one thing. —mon″o·ma′ni·ac″, *n.*

mo·nop′o·ly, *n.*, *pl.* -lies. exclusive use, control, or possession. —mo·nop′o·list, *n.* —mo·nop″o·lis′tic, *adj.* —mo·nop′o·lize″, *v.t.*

mon′o·rail″, *n.* one-rail railway.

mon′o·syl″la·ble, *n.* one-syllable word. —mon″o·syl·lab′ic, *adj.*

mon″o·the′ism, *n.* belief in one god. —mon″o·the·ist, *n.* —mon″o·the·is′tic, *adj.*

mon′o·tone″, *n.* sound with unvarying pitch.

mo·not′o·nous, *adj.* tediously unvaried. —mo·not′o·ny, *n.*

mon·sieur′ (mə syur′), *n.*, *pl.* messieurs. *French.* 1. gentleman. 2. Monsieur. **a.** Sir. **b.** Mister.

Mon·si·gnor (mon sēn′yər), *n.*, *pl.* -gnors, -gnori. high-ranking Roman Catholic priest.

mon·soon′, *n.* season of wind and rain in south Asia.

mon′ster, *n.* 1. frightening legendary creature. 2. grotesque or disgusting person. —mon′strous, *adj.* —mon·stros′i·ty, *n.*

mon·tage (mahn tahzh′), *n.* composite photograph, etc.

month, *n.* one of the twelve divisions of the year. —month′ly, *adj.*, *adv.*, *n.*

mon′u·ment, *n.* 1. something built or put up in remembrance. 2. formal, impressive construction. —mon′u·men′tal, *adj.*

moo, *n.*, *v.i.*, mooed, mooing. *n.* 1. sound of a cow. —*v.i.* 2. make this sound.

mooch, *Informal. v.i.* 1. beg; cadge. —*v.t.* 2. obtain by begging.

mood, *n.* state of mind.

mood′y, *adj.*, -ier, -iest. 1. gloomy. 2. changing mood quickly. —mood′i·ly, *adv.* —mood′i·ness, *n.*

moon, *n.* 1. satellite of the earth. 2. lighted portion of this satellite as seen from the earth. —*v.i.* 3. be abstracted or sentimental. —moon′beam″, *n.* —moon′light″, *n.* —moon′lit″, *adj.* —moon′scape″, *n.*

moon′light″ing, *n.* holding of a second job.

moon′shine″, *n.* 1. illicit whiskey. 2. moonlight. —moon′shin″er, *n.*

moon′shot″, *n.* start of a trip to the moon.

moon′struck″, *adj.* 1. crazy. 2. dreamy.

moon′walk″, *n.* walk on the moon.

moor, *v.t.* tie or anchor.

moor′ings, *n.*, *pl.* 1. tackle for mooring. 2. place to moor.

moose, *n.*, *pl.* moose. large animal of the deer family.

moot, *adj.* 1. hypothetical. 2. open to question.

mop, *n.*, *v.t.*, mopped, mopping. *n.* 1. long-handled device for washing or dusting. —*v.t.* 2. clean with a mop.

mope, *v.i.*, moped, moping. brood. —mop′ey, mop′y, *adj.*

mo·raine′, *n.* mass of rock, etc. left by a glacier.

mor′al, *adj.* 1. pertaining to morality. 2.

in accord with morality. **3.** pertaining to morale. —*n.* **4.** lesson of an experience. **5. morals,** moral principles. —**mor'al·ist,** *n.* —**mo·ral'i·ty,** *n.*

mo·rale', *n.* confidence in oneself, a situation, etc.

mor''al·is'tic, *adj.* **1.** pertaining to morals. **2.** overconcerned with morals.

mor'al·ize'', *v.i.,* **-ized, -izing.** discuss morality.

mo·rass', *n.* swamp.

mor''a·to'ri·um, *n., pl.* **-ums, -a.** authorized delay.

mor'bid, *adj.* **1.** pertaining to disease. **2.** mentally unhealthy. —**mor·bid'i·ty,** *n.* —**mor'bid·ly,** *adv.*

mor'dant, *adj.* biting. —**mor'dan·cy,** *n.*

more, *adj.* **1.** greater in number, amount, etc. **2.** additional. —*adv.* **3.** additionally. —*n.* **4.** greater number, amount, etc. **5.** something additional.

more·o'ver, *adv.* besides.

mo'res, *n., pl.* prevailing social customs.

morgue, *n.* place for keeping the unidentified dead.

mor'i·bund, *adj.* about to die.

morn'ing, *n.* early part of the day.

morning glory, vine with trumpet-shaped flowers.

mo·roc'co, *n.* goat leather.

mo'ron, *n.* feeble-minded person. —**mo·ron'ic,** *adj.*

mo·rose', *adj.* downhearted or surly. —**mo·rose'ly,** *adv.* —**mo·rose'ness,** *n.*

mor'phine, *n.* analgesic opiate.

morse, *n.* code of dots and dashes. Also, **Morse.**

mor'sel, *n.* small portion of food.

mor'tal, *adj.* **1.** having eventually to die. **2.** human. **3.** fatal. **4.** threatening the soul. —*n.* **5.** human being. —**mor'tal·ly,** *adv.* —**mor·tal'i·ty,** *n.*

mor'tar, *n.* **1.** adhesive for masonry. **2.** bowl for grinding. **3.** short cannon.

mor'tar·board'', *n.* academic cap.

mort'gage, *n., v.t.,* **-gaged, -gaging.** *n.* **1.** pledge or property as security for a loan. —*v.t.* **2.** pledge in this way. —**mort''ga·gee',** *n.* —**mort'ga·gor,** *n.*

mor·ti'cian, *n.* undertaker.

mor'ti·fy'', *v.t.,* **-fied, -fying. 1.** humiliate. **2.** suppress with austerities. —**mor''ti·fi·ca'tion,** *n.*

mor'tise, *n., v.t.* **-tised, -tising.** *n.* **1.** socket forming part of a joint. —*v.t.* **2.** join with a mortise.

mor'tu·ar''y, *adj., n., pl.* **-ies.** *adj.* **1.** pertaining to death or funerals. —*n.* **2.** place for receiving the dead.

mo·sa'ic, *n.* picture of inlaid pieces.

mo'sey, *v.i. Informal.* amble.

Mos'lem, *n.* Muslim.

mosque, *n.* Muslim house of prayer.

mos·qui'to, *n., pl.* **-toes, -tos.** small blood-sucking insect.

moss, *n.* green, velvety plant. —**mos'sy,** *adj.*

most, *adj.* **1.** greatest in number, amount, etc. **2.** in the majority. —*adv.* **3.** to the greatest extent. —*n.* **4.** greatest number, extent, etc.

most'ly, *adv.* in most cases.

mo·tel', *n.* hotel for motorists.

moth, *n., pl.* **moths.** nocturnal flying insect.

moth'ball'', *n.* ball of moth repellent.

moth'er, *n.* **1.** female parent. —*v.t.* **2.** act as a mother to. —**moth'er·hood'',** *n.* —**moth'er·less,** *adj.* —**moth'er·ly,** *adj.*

moth'er-in-law'', *n., pl.* **mothers-in-law.** mother of a spouse.

moth'er-of-pearl', *n.* inner shell of the pearl oyster.

mo·tif', *n.* basic theme or subject.

mo'tion, *n.* **1.** movement. **2.** formal proposal. —*v.i.* **3.** gesture. —*v.t.* **4.** direct with a gesture. —**mo'tion·less,** *n.*

motion picture, series of photographs projected at high speed.

mo'ti·vate'', *v.t.,* **-vated, -vating.** give desire or incentive. —**mo''ti·va'tion,** *n.*

mo'tive, *n.* **1.** desire for action. **2.** motif. —*adj.* **3.** pertaining to motion.

mot'ley, *adj.* of many colors or kinds.

mo'tor, *n.* **1.** machine providing motive force. —*adj.* **2.** causing motion. —**mo'tor·bike'',** *n.* —**mo'tor·boat'',** *n.* —**mo'tor·car'',** *n.* —**mo'tor·ize'',** *v.t.*

mo'tor·cade'', *n.* procession of automobiles.

mo'tor·cy''cle, *n.* two-wheeled motorized vehicle.

mo'tor·ist, *n.* automobile driver.

mo'tor·man, *n.* driver of a streetcar.

mot'tle, *v.t.,* **-tled, -tling.** mark with spots, etc.

mot'to, *n., pl.* **-toes, -tos.** formal statement of aims or ideals.

mould, *n., v.t.* mold.

mound, *n., v.t.* heap.

mount, *v.t.* **1.** climb onto or up. **2.** set in place. —*v.i.* **3.** climb. —*n.* **4.** steed. **5.** setting or support. —**mount'ing,** *n.*

moun'tain, *n.* very high feature of the earth. —**moun'tain·ous,** *adj.*

moun''tain·eer', *n.* **1.** mountain dweller. **2.** mountain climber. —**moun''tain·eer'ing,** *n.*

moun'te·bank'', *n.* charlatan.

mourn, *v.t., v.i.* lament. —**mourn'ful,** *adj.* —**mourn'ing,** *n.*

mouse, *n., pl.* **mice. 1.** small, timid rodent. **2.** (computers) compact device for convenient data manipulation on a monitor.

mous·tache', *n.* mustache.

mous'y, *adj.,* **-ier, -iest.** mouse-like, esp. in timidity.

mouth, *n.* **1.** orifice for eating and

breathing. 2. opening of a river, etc.
—**mouth'ful**, *n.*

mouth'piece", *n.* 1. part of a horn, etc. blown through. 2. spokesman or apologist.

move, *v.*, **moved**, **moving**, *n.* *v.t.* 1. change the place of. 2. inspire or motivate. 3. propose formally. —*v.i.* 4. change place. 5. change residence or workplace. 6. become in motion. —*n.* 7. act or instance of moving. 8. purposeful action. —**mov'a·ble**, **move'a·ble**, *adj.*

move'ment, *n.* 1. motion. 2. action in a cause. 3. assembly of clockwork. 4. division of a musical composition.

mov'ie, *n.* motion picture. Also, **moving picture.**

mow, *v.t.*, **mowed**, **mowed** or **mown**, **mowing**. 1. cut down, as grass. 2. cut down the plants on.

Mr. (mis'tər), title for a man. Also, **Mis'ter.**

Mrs. (mis'iz), title for a married woman.

Ms. (miz, em'es'), *n.* title for a woman disregarding marital status.

much, *adj.*, *adv.*, *n.* *adj.* 1. in great quantity. —*adv.* 2. to a great extent. 3. about. —*n.* 4. something considerable. 5. a great amount.

mu'ci·lage, *n.* liquid glue.

muck, *n.* sticky filth. —**muck'y**, *adj.*

muck'rak"ing, *n.* searching for scandalous information. —**muck'rak"er**, *n.*

mu'cous, *adj.* 1. having mucus. 2. slimy.

mu'cus, *n.* slimy body secretion, esp. from the nose.

mud, *n.* sticky earth. —**mud'dy**, *adj.*, *v.t.*

mud'dle, *v.t.*, **-dled**, **-dling**, *n.* *v.t.* 1. bungle or confuse. —*n.* 2. act or instance of muddling. —**mud'dle·head'ed**, *adj.*

mud'sling"ing, *n.* defamation, esp. of a political opponent. —**mud'sling"er**, *n.*

mu·ez'zin, *n.* Muslim caller to prayer.

muff, *n.* 1. cylinder made esp. of fur for keeping the hands warm. —*v.t.* 2. bungle.

muf'fin, *n.* small round bread or cake.

muf'fle, *v.t.*, **-fled**, **-fling**. 1. wrap closely. 2. deaden, as sound.

muf'fler, *n.* 1. heavy scarf. 2. sound deadener.

muf'ti, *n.* dress other than a uniform.

mug, *n.*, *v.t.*, **mugged**, **mugging**, *n.* 1. cylindrical cup. —*v.t.* 2. attack from behind, esp. in order to rob.

mug'gy, *adj.*, **-gier**, **-giest**. hot and humid.

Mu·ham'ma·dan, *n.*, *adj.* Muslim.

mu·lat'to, *n.*, *pl.* **-toes**. person of mixed white and colored blood.

mul'ber"ry, *n.*, *pl.* **-ries**. tree with purplish-red fruit.

mulch, *n.* plant matter spread to keep the ground from freezing.

mulct, *v.t.* 1. fine. 2. obtain by fraud.

mule, *n.* 1. offspring of a donkey and a mare. 2. heelless slipper. —**mu·le·teer'**, *n.*

mul'ish, *adj.* stubborn.

mull, *v.t.* 1. warm and spice, as wine. —*v.i.* 2. *Informal*. ponder.

mul"ti·far'i·ous, *adj.* with many components.

mul"ti·mil'lion·aire', *n.* one who has many millions of dollars.

mul'ti·ple, *adj.* 1. in a large number. —*n.* 2. number evenly divisible by another.

mul"ti·pli·cand', *n. Math.* number to be multiplied.

mul"ti·plic'i·ty, *n.* large number or variety.

mul'ti·ply", *v.*, **-plied**, **-plying**. *v.t.* 1. repeat a specified number of times for a final sum. —*v.i.* 2. increase in size or number. —**mul'ti·pli"er**, *n.* —**mul"ti·pli·ca'tion**, *n.*

mul'ti·stage", *adj.* in many stages.

mul'ti·tude", *n.* large number. —**mul"ti·tu'di·nous**, *adj.*

mum, *adj.* unspeaking.

mum'ble, *v.i.*, **-bled**, **-bling**, *n.* *v.i.* 1. say something quietly and indistinctly. —*n.* 2. mumbling speech or remark.

mum'bo jum'bo, pretentious or meaningless ceremony.

mum'mer, *n.* wearer of a mask or costume. —**mum'mer·y**, *n.*

mum'my, *n.*, *pl.* **-mies**. preserved dead body. —**mum'mi·fy"**, *v.t.*, *v.i.*

mumps, *n.* communicable disease.

munch, *v.t.*, *v.i.* chew crunchingly.

mun·dane', *adj.* 1. wordly. 2. common-place.

mu·nic'i·pal, *adj.* pertaining to city government.

mu·nic"i·pal'i·ty, *n.*, *pl.* **-ties**. incorporated community.

mu·nif'i·cent, *adj.* lavish; generous. —**mu·nif'i·cence**, *n.*

mu·ni'tions, *n.*, *pl.* military supplies, esp. guns and ammunition.

mu'ral, *n.* wall painting. —**mu'ral·ist**, *n.*

mur'der, *n.* 1. willful unlawful killing. —*v.t.* 2. commit murder against. —**mur'der·er**, *fem.*, **mur'der·ess**, *n.* —**mur'der·ous**, *adj.*

murk, *n.* gloom; darkness. —**murk'y**, *adj.*

mur'mur, *n.* 1. low, indistinct speech or sound. —*v.i.* 2. make a murmur.

mus"ca·tel', *n.* sweet wine.

mus'cle, *n.* body tissue which contracts to cause movement. —**mus'cu·lar**, *adj.* —**mus'cu·la·ture**, *n.*

muse, *v.i.* **1.** be meditative. —*n.* **2. Muse,** goddess presiding over an art.

mu·se′um, *n.* public institution for displaying things of interest.

mush, *n.* **1.** porridge of boiled meal. **2.** *Informal.* foolish sentiment. —**mush′y,** *adj.*

mush′room″, *n.* **1.** edible fungus. —*v.i.* **2.** grow rapidly.

mu′sic, *n.* art of composing series of tones, etc. —**mu·si′cian,** *n.* —**mu″si·col′o·gy,** *n.*

mu′si·cal, *adj.* **1.** pertaining to music. **2.** sweet-sounding. —*n.* **3.** Also, **musical comedy,** play with frequent musical numbers.

mu″si·cale′, *n.* party with music.

musk, *n.* animal secretion used in perfumes. —**musk′y,** *adj.*

mus′ket, *n.* antique smooth-bored gun. —**mus″ket·eer′,** *n.*

musk′mel″on, *n.* type of sweet melon.

Mus′lim, *n.* **1.** follower of the teachings of Muhammad. —*adj.* **2.** pertaining to Islam or the Muslims.

mus′lin, *n.* cotton cloth.

muss, *n.* **1.** disorderly state. —*v.t.* **2.** put in a muss. —**mus′sy,** *adj.*

mus′sel, *n.* type of bivalve.

must, *v.* **1.** have or has to. **2.** am, is, or are very probably being or doing as stated.

mus·tache′, *n.* hair on the upper lip.

mus′tang, *n.* wild horse of the Southwest.

mus′tard, *n.* condiment made from ground yellow seeds.

mus′ter, *v.t.* **1.** summon; rally. **2.** enlist or discharge from military service. —*n.* **3.** gathering, as for inspection.

mus′ty, *adj.,* **-ier, -iest.** moldy in smell or taste.

mu′ta·ble, *adj.* changeable. —**mu″ta·bil′i·ty,** *n.*

mu·ta′tion, *n.* **1.** living thing with characteristics not inherited; sport. **2.** change. —**mu′tate,** *v.i., v.t.* —**mu′tant,** *adj., n.*

mute, *adj., n., v.t.,* **muted, muting.** *adj.* **1.** unable to speak. **2.** not speaking. —*n.* **3.** mute person. —*v.t.* **4.** soften the effect of. —**mute′ly,** *adv.* —**mute′ness,** *n.*

mu′ti·late″, *v.t.,* **-lated, -lating.** injure severely and conspicuously. —**mu″ti·la′tion,** *n.*

mu′ti·ny, *n., pl.* **-nies,** *v.i.,* **-nied, -nying.** revolt against superiors. —**mu″ti·neer′,** *n.* —**mu′ti·nous,** *adj.*

mut′ter, *v.i.* **1.** speak in a low, indistinct voice. —*n.* **2.** muttering voice.

mut′ton, *n.* sheep meat.

mu′tu·al, *adj.* affecting one another. —**mu′tu·al·ly,** *adv.*

muz′zle, *n., v.t.,* **-zled, -zling.** *n.* **1.** nose and jaws of an animal. **2.** device to prevent biting. **3.** end of a gun facing the target. —*v.t.* **4.** put a muzzle on. **5.** keep from talking.

my, *pron.* pertaining or belonging to me.

my·o′pi·a, *n.* nearsightedness. —**my·op′ic,** *adj.*

myr′i·ad, *adj.* **1.** very many. —*n.* **2.** great number.

myr′mi·don, *n.* follower.

myrrh, *n.* fragrant resin.

myr′tle, *n.* flowering evergreen shrub.

my·self′, *pron., pl.* **ourselves. 1.** (intensive and reflexive of *me*). **2.** my true self.

mys′ter·y, *n., pl.* **-ies. 1.** something not readily explained. **2.** secrecy. **3.** story based on the solution of a criminal case. —**mys·te′ri·ous,** *adj.*

mys′tic, *adj.* **1.** pertaining to secret rites and teachings. **2.** Also, **mys′ti·cal,** of spiritual significance. —*n.* **3.** person having deep spiritual experiences. —**mys′ti·cism,** *n.*

mys′ti·fy″, *v.t.,* **-fied, -fying.** puzzle. —**mys″ti·fi·ca′tion,** *n.*

mys·tique′, *n.* air of mysticism surrounding a person, profession, etc.

myth, *n.* **1.** religious legend. **2.** false belief. —**myth′i·cal,** *adj.* —**my·thol′o·gy,** *n.* —**myth″o·log′i·cal,** *adj.* —**my·thol′o·gist,** *n.*

N

N, n, *n.* fourteenth letter of the English alphabet.

nab, *v.t.,* **nabbed, nabbing.** *Informal.* seize

na′dir, *n.* lowest point.

nag, *v.t.,* **nagged, nagging,** *n. v.t.* **1.** pester. —*n.* **2.** poor horse.

nail, *n.* **1.** pointed, driven fastening. **2.** horny growth on fingers or toes. —*v.t.* **3.** fasten with nails.

na·ive (nah ēv′), *adj.* simple; unsophisticated. —**na·ive·té′,** *n.*

na′ked, *adj.* **1.** unclothed; unconcealed. **2.** unassisted by lenses.

nam′by-pam′by, *adj.* insipid; characterless.

name, *n., v.t.,* **named, naming.** *n.* **1.** word or words by which a person or thing is recognized. **2.** reputation. **3.** insulting epithet. —*v.t.* **4.** give a name to. **5.** appoint. —**name′less,** *adj.*

name'ly, *adv.* that is to say.

name'sake", *n.* person or thing having the same name as another.

nap, *n., v.i.,* **napped, napping.** *n.* **1.** brief sleep. **2.** fuzzy surface. —*v.i.* **3.** have a brief sleep.

nape, *n.* back of the neck.

naph'tha, *n.* inflammable fluid.

nap'kin, *n.* cloth covering the lap at meals.

nar·cis·sism, *n.* love of oneself. —**nar'cis·sist,** *n.* —**nar"cis·sis'tic,** *adj.*

nar·cis'sus, *n.* flowering bulb plant.

nar·co'sis, *n.* unconsciousness from a narcotic.

nar·cot'ic, *n.* **1.** pain-relieving drug, often addictive. —*adj.* **2.** pertaining to narcotics.

nar'rate, *v.t.,* **-rated, -rating.** tell the story of. —**nar'ra·tor,** *n.*

nar'ra·tive, *adj.* **1.** story-telling. —*n.* **2.** story; account.

nar'row, *n.* **1.** not wide. **2.** not ample **3.** illiberal. —*v.t.* **4.** make narrow. —*v.i.* **5.** become narrow.

nar'row-mind'ed, *adj.* lacking a broad, liberal outlook.

nar'whal, *n.* small, tusked whale.

nar'y, *adj. Dialect.* not any.

na'sal, *adj.* spoken through the nose.

nas'cent, *adj.* coming into being.

nas·tur'tium, *n.* pungent-smelling flower.

nas'ty, *adj.,* **-tier, -tiest. 1.** revolting as from filth. **2.** unpleasant.

na'tal, *adj.* pertaining to birth.

na'tion, *n.* **1.** group with common ancestral and traditional associations. **2.** politically independent state. —**na'tion·al,** *adj.* —**na'tion·wide",** *adj., adv.*

na'tion·al·ism, *n.* assertion of the rights, cultural values, etc. of a nation. —**na'tion·al·ist,** *n., adj.* —**na"tion·al·is'tic,** *adj.*

na'tion·al·ize", *v.t.,* **-ized, -izing.** put under government ownership. —**na"tion·al·i·za'tion,** *n.*

na'tive, *adj.* **1.** born in or characteristic of a certain place. **2.** inborn. —*n.* **3.** native person.

na·tiv'i·ty, *n., pl.* **-ties. 1.** birth. **2.** the **Nativity,** birth of Jesus.

nat'ty, *adj.,* **-tier, -tiest.** neat and stylish.

nat'u·ral, *adj.* **1.** pertaining to nature. **2.** inborn. **3.** unaffected; easy. **4.** to be expected. **5.** *Music.* not sharped or flatted.

nat'u·ral·ist, *n.* student of nature.

nat'u·ral·ize", *v.t.,* **-ized, -izing.** admit to citizenship.

nat'u·ral·ly, *adv.* **1.** by nature. **2.** of course. **3.** in a natural way.

na'ture, *n.* **1.** everything not man-made. **2.** essential quality or composition.

naught, *n.* **1.** nothing. **2.** zero.

naugh'ty, *adj.,* **-tier, -tiest.** ill-behaved. —**naugh'ti·ly,** *adv.*

nau'se·a, *n.* sickness at the stomach. —**nau'se·ate",** *v.t.* —**nau'se·ous,** *adj.*

nau'ti·cal, *adj.* pertaining to ships and navigation.

nau'ti·lus, *n.* mollusk with a spiral shell.

na'val, *adj.* **1.** pertaining to navies. **2.** pertaining to ships.

na'vel, *n.* mark where the umbilical cord was attached.

nav'i·ga·ble, *adj.* able to be sailed over.

nav'i·gate", *v.,* **-gated, -gating.** *v.t.* **1.** cross or pass through in a ship or aircraft. **2.** determine the position and course of. —*v.i.* **3.** direct a ship or aircraft. —**nav'i·ga"tor,** *n.*

na'vy, *n., pl.* **-ies.** seagoing fighting force.

nay, *n.* vote of no.

neap tide, lowest of high tides.

near, *adj.* **1.** short in distance. **2.** closely related. —*adv.* **3.** at a short distance. —*prep.* **4.** close to. —*v.t.* **5.** approach.

near'by', *adj., adv.* near.

near'ly, *adv.* almost.

near'sight'ed, *adj.* seeing distant objects poorly.

neat, *adj.* **1.** free of dirt and clutter. **2.** finely done.

neb'u·la, *n., pl.* **-lae, -las.** cloudlike cluster of stars, etc. —**neb'u·lar,** *adj.*

neb'u·lous, *adj.* vague.

nec'es·sar"y, *adj.* **1.** not to be dispensed with. **2.** inevitable. —**nec"es·sar'i·ly,** *adv.*

ne·ces'si·tate", *v.t.,* **-tated, -tating.** require.

ne·ces'si·tous, *adj.* needy.

ne·ces'si·ty, *n., pl.* **-ties. 1.** state of needing. **2.** something needed.

neck, *n.* **1.** part of the body which supports the head. **2.** narrow feature. —**neck'wear",** *n.*

neck'er·chief, *n.* broad covering for the neck.

neck'lace, *n.* ornamental chain, string of beads, etc. worn around the neck.

neck'tie", *n.* decorative band of cloth tied around the neck.

ne·crol'o·gy, *n., pl.* **-gies.** list of the dead.

nec'ro·man"cy, *n.* **1.** divination by communication with the dead. **2.** sorcery. —**nec'ro·man"cer,** *n.*

nec'tar, *n.* **1.** drink of the classical gods. **2.** sweetish liquid of flowers.

nec"tar·ine', *n.* small, smooth peach.

nee, *adj.* born as: said of the maiden name of a married woman. Also, **née.**

need, *v.t.* **1.** be obliged to have or do. —*n.* **2.** state of needing. **3.** thing needed. **4.** poverty or trouble. —**need'ful,** *adj.* —**need'less,** *adj.*

nee′dle, *n., v.t.,* **-dled, -dling.** *n.* **1.** sharp object used for passing thread through cloth. **2.** any of various sharp or pointed objects. —*v.t.* **3.** *Informal.* goad; annoy. —**nee′dle·work″,** *n.*

nee′dle·point″, *n.* **1.** embroidery on canvas. **2.** lace made on a paper pattern.

needs, *adv.* of necessity.

need′y, *adj.,* **-ier, -iest.** in need. —**need′i·ness,** *n.*

ne′er′-do-well″, *n.* shiftless person.

ne·far′i·ous, *adj.* wicked.

ne·gate′, *v.t.,* **-gated, -gating. 1.** deny. **2.** render ineffective.

neg′a·tive, *adj.* **1.** saying or meaning no. **2.** opposite to positive. **3.** less than zero. —*n.* **4.** negative statement or attitude. **5.** photographic film, etc. that reverses light and shade. —**neg′a·tive·ly,** *adv.*

neg·lect′, *v.t.* **1.** deny proper care to. **2.** disregard. —*n.* **3.** state of being neglected. **4.** state of neglecting. —**neg′lect′ful,** *adj.*

neg·li·gee (neg″lə zhā′), *n.* loosely fitting woman's gown.

neg′li·gent, *adj.* neglecting responsibilities. —**neg′li·gence,** *n.*

neg′li·gi·ble, *adj.* too unimportant to matter.

ne·go′ti·a·ble, *adj.* transferable.

ne·go′ti·ate″, *v.,* **-ated, -ating.** *v.i.* **1.** bargain. —*v.t.* **2.** establish by bargaining. **3.** succeed in passing through or across. —**ne·go′ti·a″tor,** *n.*

Ne′gro, *n., pl.* **-groes.** dark-skinned person of African origin. —**Neg′roid,** *adj.*

neigh, *n.* **1.** sound of a horse. —*v.i.* **2.** emit such a sound.

neigh′bor, *n.* **1.** person living near by. **2.** fellow human. —*v.i.* **3.** be situated near by. —**neigh′bor·ing,** *adj.* —**neigh′bor·ly,** *adj.*

neigh′bor·hood″, *n.* **1.** area within a town. **2.** approximate area or range.

neither, *adj., pron., conj.* not either.

nem′e·sis, *n., pl.* **-ses. 1.** just fate or vengeance. **2.** bringer of this.

Ne″o·lith′ic, *adj.* pertaining to the later Stone Age.

ne·ol′o·gism, *n.* newly invented word or expression.

ne′on, *n.* rare gaseous element used in lighting tubes.

ne′ophyte″, *n.* beginner.

neph′ew, *n.* son of a brother, sister, brother-in-law, or sister-in-law.

nep′o·tism, *n.* favoritism toward relatives in giving employment.

nerve, *n.* **1.** fiber carrying signals through the body. **2.** courage. **3.** insolent boldness. **4. nerves,** nervousness.

nerve′less, *adj.* **1.** without strength. **2.** not nervous.

nerve′-rack″ing, *adj.* emotionally upsetting. Also, **nerve′wrack″ing.**

nerv′ous, *adj.* **1.** full of apprehension or restlessness. **2.** pertaining to nerves.

nerv′y, *adj.,* **-ier, -iest.** *Informal.* impudent.

nest, *n.* **1.** place for bearing and sheltering young. —*v.i.* **2.** settle in a nest.

n′est-ce pas? (nes pah′), *French.* isn't it so?

nes′tle, *v.i.,* **-tled, -tling.** settle down.

net, *n., adj., v.t.,* **netted, netting.** *n.* **1.** open cloth for capturing or supporting. **2.** amount after deductions. —*adj.* **3.** after deductions. —*v.t.* **4.** capture, as in a net.

neth′er, *adj.* lower. —**neth′er·most″,** *adj.*

net′tle, *n., v.t.,* **-tled, -tling.** *n.* **1.** prickly weed. —*v.t.* **2.** irritate; annoy.

net′work″, *n.* **1.** net-like arrangement. **2.** system of isolated entities working in coordination.

neu′ral, *adj.* pertaining to nerves.

neu·ral′gia, *n.* pain along a nerve.

neu″ras·the′ni·a, *n.* neurosis with lassitude, anxiety, etc. —**neu″ras·the′nic,** *adj., n.*

neu·ri′tis, *n.* inflammation of a nerve.

neu·rol′o·gy, *n.* study of nerves. —**neu″ro·log′i·cal,** *adj.* —**neu·rol′o·gist,** *n.*

neu·ro′sis, *n., pl.* **-ses.** compulsive mental disorder. —**neu·rot′ic,** *adj., n.*

neu′ter, *adj.* **1.** without sex. **2.** without gender. —*v.t.* **3.** remove the sex organs of.

neu′tral, *adj.* **1.** taking no sides. **2.** having no pronounced character. —*n.* **3.** neutral person or country. —**neu′tral·ism,** *n.* —**neu·tral′i·ty,** *n.* —**neu′tra·lize,** *v.t.*

neu′tron, *n.* uncharged atomic particle.

nev′er, *adv.* at no time.

nev″er·more′, *adv.* never again.

never-never land, purely imaginary place.

nev″er·the·less′, *adv.* despite this.

new, *adj.* **1.** never existing before. **2.** unfamiliar. **3.** fresh. **4.** additional. —**new′born″,** *adj.* —**new′com″er,** *n.*

new′el, *n.* support for a winding stair.

news, *n., sing.* **1.** information of public interest, esp. as published. **2.** recent information. —**news′boy″,** *n.* —**news′deal″er,** *n.* —**news′let″ter,** *n.* —**news′man″,** *n.* —**news′pa″per,** *n.* —**news′stand″,** *n.* —**news′wor″thy,** *adj.*

news′cast″, *n.* broadcast of news.

newt, *n.* amphibious salamander.

next, *adj.* **1.** directly alongside another. —*adv.* **2.** directly afterward.

next′-door′, *adj.* in the next building.

nib, *n.* **1.** bird's beak. **2.** pen point.

nib′ble, *v.,* **-bled, -bling,** *n. v.t., v.i.* **1.** eat with small bites. —*n.* **2.** small bite.

nice, *adj.*, **nicer, nicest. 1.** agreeable. **2.** delicate; subtle.

ni'ce·ty, *n., pl.* **-ties. 1.** precision. **2.** fine detail or distinction.

niche, *n.* recessed area in a wall, as for a statue.

nick, *n.* **1.** small notch. —*v.t.* **2.** cut with such a notch.

nick'el, *n.* **1.** white metallic element. **2.** five-cent piece.

nick"el·o'de·on, *n.* coin-operated automatic piano.

nick'name", *n, v.t.,* **-named, -naming.** *n.* **1.** informal name. —*v.t.* **2.** give a nickname to.

nic'o·tine", *n.* poisonous extract from tobacco leaves.

niece, *n.* daughter of a brother, sister, brother-in-law, or sister-in-law.

nif'ty, *adj.,* **-tier, -tiest.** *Informal.* smart; handsome.

nig'gard·ly, *adj.* stingy.

nigh, *adj., adv. Archaic.* near.

night, *n.* period when the sun is absent. —**night'clothes"**, *n., pl.* —**night' dress"**, *n.* —**night'fall"**, *n.* —**night' gown"**, *n.* —**night'ly**, *adv., adj.* —**night'time"**, *n.* —**night'wear"**, *n.*

night'cap", *n.* **1.** cap for sleeping in. **2.** *Informal.* drink just before bed.

night'mare", *n.* bad dream. —**night' mar"ish,** *adj.*

night'shade", *n.* plant related to potatoes, tomatoes, etc.

ni'hil·ism, *n.* rejection of all social institutions. —**ni'hil·ist**, *n.* —**ni"hil·is'tic,** *adj.*

nim'ble, *adj.,* **-bler, -blest.** quick and deft.

nim'bus, *n., pl.* **-bi, -buses.** halo.

nin'com·poop", *n.* fool.

nine, *n.* eight plus one. —**ninth**, *adj.*

nine·teen', *n.* ten plus nine. —**nine' teenth'**, *adj.*

nine'ty, *adj., n.* nine times ten. —**nine'ti· eth**, *adj.*

nip, *v.t.,* **nipped, nipping,** *n. v.t.* **1.** bite or pinch lightly. **2.** freeze injuriously. —*n.* **3.** act or instance of nipping. **4.** sharp chill. **5.** tiny drink. —**nip'per**, *n.* —**nip'pers**, *n.*

nip'ple, *n.* **1.** small projection from the breast from which milk is sucked. **2.** anything resembling this.

nir·va'na, *Buddhism.* loss of self in ultimate bliss.

nit'-pick"ing, *n.* quibbling. —**nit'-pick" er**, *n.*

ni'tro·gen, *n.* gaseous element. —**ni· trog'e·nous,** *adj.*

ni'tro·glyc'er·in, *n.* explosive oil used in dynamite.

nit'ty-grit'ty, *n. Informal.* fundamentals.

nit'wit", *n.* stupid person.

nix, *adv. Informal.* no.

no, *adv., adj., n., pl.* **noes.** *adv.* **1.** it is not so. **2.** I will not. **3.** do not. **4.** not at all. —*adj.* **5.** not any. —*n.* **6.** vote of no.

no'ble, *adj.,* **-bler, -blest.** *adj.* **1.** of high and titled rank. **2.** having or revealing a fine character. **3.** of high quality. —*n.* **4.** person of noble rank. —**no'bly,** *adv.* —**no·bil'i·ty**, *n.* —**no'ble·man,** *n.*

no'bod·y, *pron., n., pl.* **-ies.** *pron.* **1.** no person. —*n.* **2.** unimportant person.

noc·tur'nal, *adj.* pertaining to night.

noc'turne, *n.* musical composition to be heard at night.

nod, *v.i.,* **nodded, nodding,** *n. v.i.* **1.** give a quick forward motion of the head. —*n.* **2.** act or instance of nodding.

node, *n.* **1.** swelling. **2.** focal point. —**nod'al,** *adj.*

nog'gin, *n.* small cup.

noise, *n.* loud sound. —**noise'less**, *adj.* —**nois'y,** *adj.* —**nois'i·ly,** *adv.*

noi'some, *adj.* smelly.

no'mad, *n.* wanderer. —**no·mad'ic,** *adj.*

nom de plume, author's assumed name.

no'men·cla"ture, *n.* system of names.

nom'in·al, *adj.* **1.** in name only. **2.** trifling in amount.

nom'i·nate", *v.t.,* **-nated, -nating. 1.** appoint. **2.** propose for election. —**nom" i·nee',** *n.*

nom'i·na·tive, *n. Grammar.* case of a verb subject.

non-, prefix meaning "not." **nonalcoholic, nonassignable, nonattendance, nonbeliever, nonbreakable, nonburnable, noncombatant, noncombustible, noncommunicable, noncompetitive, noncompliance, nonconducting, nonconductor, nonconforming, nonconformist, nonconformity, nondeductible, nonessential, nonexclusive, nonexempt, nonexistence, nonexistent, nonfactual, nonfiction, nonflammable, nonhazardous, nonhereditary, nonhuman, noninclusive, noninterference, nonintervention, nonintoxicating, nonirritating, nonliterary, nonmilitary, nonobjective, nonobligatory, nonobservance, nonpartisan, nonpayment, nonperishable, nonpolitical, nonproductive, nonprofessional, nonracial, nonreciprocal, nonreligious, nonresident, nonresidential, nonresistant, nonreturnable, nonscientific, nonseasonal, nonsectarian, nonsmoker, nonspiritual, nonstandard, nonstop, nonstructural, nonsupport, nontaxable, nontoxic, nontransferable, nonuser, nonviolent, nonvoter, nonvoting.**

non'age, *n.* minority; non-adulthood.

non"a·ge·nar'i·an, *n.* person in his or her nineties.

nonce, *n.* time being.

non''cha·lant', *adj.* casual in manner. —**non''cha·lance',** *n.*

non''com·mis'sioned officer, military or naval officer with no commission, e.g. a sergeant or petty officer.

non''com·mit'tal, *adj.* not committing oneself.

non' com'pos men'tis, of unsound mind.

non''de·script', *adj.* not to be described precisely.

none, *pron.* 1. not one or any. —*n.* 2. not any amount. —*adv.* 3. by no means.

non·en'ti·ty, *n., pl.* -ties. very unimportant person or·thing.

none''the·less', *adv.* nevertheless.

non'plus', *v.t.,* -plused, -plusing. baffle into inaction.

non·prof'it, *adj.* not established for profit.

non'sense, *n.* meaningless talk or action. —**non·sen'si·cal,** *adj.*

non·se'qui·tur, illogical continuation of something previously said.

noo'dle, *n.* strip of dough.

nook, *n.* semi-enclosed place.

noon, *n.* twelve o'clock in the daytime.

no one, nobody.

noose, *n.* loop made with a knot.

nor, *conj.* and not; and yet not.

norm, *n.* something generally expected.

nor'mal, *adj.* 1. conforming to a norm. 2. average. —**nor·mal'i·ty,** *n.* —**nor'mal·ize'',** *v.t.*

norm'a·tive, *adj.* establishing a norm.

north, *n.* 1. direction of the north pole. 2. region lying northward. —*adv.* 3. toward or in the north. —**north'ern,** *adj.* —**north'ern·er,** *n.* —**north'er·ly,** *adj.* —**north'ward,** *adj., adv.* —**north'wards,** *adv.*

north''east', *n.* 1. direction halfway between north and east. 2. region lying northeastward. —*adj., adv.* 3. toward or in the northeast. —**north''east'ern,** *adj.* —**north''east·ern·er,** *n.*

north''west', *n.* 1. direction halfway between north and west. 2. region lying northwestward. —*adj.* 3. toward or in the northwest. —**north''west'ern,** *adj.* —**north''west'ern·er,** *n.*

nose, *n., v.,* nosed, nosing. *n.* 1. part of the head with nostrils. 2. noselike features. —*v.t.* 3. nuzzle. —*v.i.* 4. sniff. 5. advance. —**nose'bleed'',** *n.*

nose dive, headlong plunge. —**nose'dive'',** *v.i.*

nose'gay'', *n.* small bouquet.

nos·tal'gia, *n.* sentiment over the bygone or remote. —**nos·tal'gic,** *adj.*

nos'tril, *n.* one of the openings in the nose for breathing.

nos'trum, proprietary medicine.

nos'y, *adj.,* -ier, -iest. *Informal.* inquisitive. Also, **nos'ey.**

not, *adv.* in no way.

no'ta·ble, *adj.* remarkable.

no'ta·ry, *n., pl.* -ries. official who certifies documents. Also, **notary public.** —**no'ta·rize'',** *v.t.*

no·ta'tion, *n.* 1. symbol or system of symbols. 2. brief note.

notch, *n.* 1. shallow knife cut. —*v.t.* 2. make such cuts in.

note, *n., v.t.,* noted, noting. *n.* 1. short message. 2. reminder of something. 3. sound. 4. notice. 5. distinction. 6. feeling; air. —*v.t.* 7. observe. 8. make a note of. —**note'book'',** *n.* —**note'wor''thy,** *adj.*

not'ed, *adj.* well-known.

noth'ing, *n.* 1. not any thing. 2. something non-existent. 3. something insignificant. —*adv.* 4. in no way. —**noth'ing·ness,** *n.*

no'tice, *v.t.,* -ticed, -ticing, *n., v.t.* 1. be aware of. —*n.* 2. awareness. 3. announcement or warning. —**no'tice·a·ble,** *adj.*

no'ti·fy'', *v.t.,* -fied, -fying. give notice to.

no'tion, *n.* 1. idea, 2. vague opinion. 3. whim. 4. **notions,** minor but useful merchandise. —**no'tion·al,** *adj.*

no·to'ri·ous, *adj.* unfavorably well-known. —**no''to·ri'e·ty,** *n.*

not''with·stand'ing, *adv.* 1. nevertheless. —*prep.* 2. in spite of. —*conj.* 3. although.

noun, *n.* name of a person, place, or thing.

nour'ish, *v.t.* feed. —**nour'ish·ment,** *n.*

nou'veau riche, *Fr.* person recently acquiring large sums of money.

nov'el, *adj.* 1. new; unprecedented. —*n.* 2. long written story. —**nov'el·ty,** *n.* —**nov''el·ette',** *n.* —**nov'el·ist,** *n.*

No·vem'ber, *n.* eleventh month.

nov'ice, *n.* 1. monk or nun in a religious house who has not yet taken the vow. 2. beginner. —**no·vi'ti·ate,** *n.*

now, *adj.* 1. at present. 2. at some past or future moment. 3. as matters are. —*conj.* 4. inasmuch. —*n.* 5. present moment.

now'a·days'', *adv.* at present.

no'where'', *adv.* not in any place.

nox'ious, *adj.* harmful.

noz'zle, *n.* pouring end of a pipe, etc.

nth, *adj.* concluding an unspecified number or amount.

nu'ance, *n.* slight variation in meaning, etc.

nu'bile, *adj.* mature enough to take a husband.

nu'cle·ar, *adj.* 1. forming a nucleus. 2. pertaining to atomic nuclei.

nu'cle·us, *n., pl.* -clei, -cleuses. 1. core.

2. center of growth or development. **3.** center of an atom.

nude, *adj.* **1.** naked. —*n.* **2.** state of nakedness. —**nu′di·ty,** *n.*

nudge, *v.t.,* nudged, nudging, *n. v.t.* **1.** jab with the elbow. **2.** hint to sharply. —*n.* **3.** act or instance of nudging.

nud′ism, *n.* practice of nudity. —**nud′ist,** *n., adj.*

nu′ga·to″ry, *adj.* **1.** worthless. **2.** invalid.

nug′get, *n.* lump of natural gold.

nui′sance, *n.* source of annoyance.

null, *adj.* **null and void,** invalid; without force.

nul′li·fy″, *v.t.,* -fied, -fying. invalidate.

numb, *adj.* **1.** without feeling. —*v.t.* **2.** make numb.

num′ber, *n.* **1.** expression of quantity or order. **2.** quantity or order. **3.** item on a program of entertainment. —*v.t.* **4.** establish the number of. **5.** include in a group. —**num′ber·less,** *adj.*

numb′skull″, *n. Informal.* stupid person. Also, **num′skull″.**

nu′mer·al, *n.* symbol for a number.

nu′mer·a″tor, *n.* expression of the number of parts in a fraction.

nu·mer′i·cal, *adj.* pertaining to or expressed in numbers.

nu″mer·ol′o·gy, *n.* study of occult meanings in numbers.

nu′mer·ous, *adj.* in large numbers.

nu″mis·mat′ics, *n.* study of money and medals. —**nu·mis′ma·tist,** *n.*

nun, *n.* female member of a religious order. —**nun′ner·y,** *n.*

nup′tial, *adj.* **1.** pertaining to marriage. —*n.* **2.** nuptials, wedding.

nurse, *n., v.t.,* nursed, nursing. *n.* **1.** attendant of the sick. **2.** attendant of children. —*v.t.* **3.** suckle. **4.** tend in illness. **5.** conserve or foster.

nurse′maid″, *n.* children's nurse.

nurs′er·y, *n., pl.* -ies. **1.** day room for children. **2.** place for the care of children. **3.** place for raising plants. —**nurs′er·y·man,** *n.*

nur′ture, *v.t.,* -tured, -turing, *n. v.t.* **1.** nourish. **2.** raise, as a child. —*n.* **3.** food. **4.** upbringing.

nut, *n.* **1.** dry seed in a woody husk. **2.** threaded block used with a bolt. **3.** *Informal.* insane person. —*adj.* **4.** nuts, *Informal.* crazy. —*interj.* **5.** nuts, bah! —**nut′crack″er,** *n.* —**nut′meat″,** *n.* —**nut′shell″,** *n.* —**nut′ty,** *adj.*

nut′meg″, *n.* East Indian spice.

nu′tri·ent, *adj.* **1.** nourishing. —*n.* **2.** Also, **nu′tri·ment,** nourishment.

nu·tri′tion, *n.* **1.** assimilation of food. **2.** food. —**nu·tri′tion·al,** *adj.* —**nu′tri·tive,** *adj.* —**nu·tri′tious,** *adj.*

nuz′zle, *v.,* -zled, -zling. *v.t., v.i.* rub with the nose.

ny′lon, *n.* synthetic material.

nymph, *n.* classical nature goddess.

nym″pho·ma·ni·a, *n.* uncontrollable sexual desire in women. —**nym″pho·ma′ni·ac″,** *n., adj.*

O

O, o, *n.* fifteenth letter of the English alphabet.

oaf, *n.* clumsy person. —**oaf′ish,** *adj.*

oak, *n.* acorn-bearing hardwood tree. —**oak′en,** *adj.*

oar, *n.* bladed lever for rowing. —**oars′man,** *n.* —**oar′lock″,** *n.*

o·a′sis, *n., pl.* -ses. place in the desert with water.

oat, *n.* cereal grass. —**oat′meal″,** *n.*

oath, *n., pl.* oaths. **1.** vow in the name of a god. **2.** blasphemous remark.

ob·du′rate, *adj.* stubborn. —**ob′du·ra·cy,** *n.*

o·bei′sance, *n.* bow.

ob′e·lisk, *n.* tapered monument.

o·bese′, *adj.* very fat. —**o·bes′i·ty,** *n.*

o·bey′, *v.i.* **1.** do as told. —*v.t.* **2.** perform as told. **3.** perform the orders of. —**o·be′di·ent,** *adj.* —**o·be′di·ence,** *n.*

ob′fus·cate″, *v.t.,* -cated, -cating. obscure or confuse.

o·bit′u·ar″y, *n., pl.* -ies. death notice.

ob·ject, *n.* (ob′jekt) **1.** something tangible. **2.** something acted toward or aimed for. **3.** matter for consideration. —*v.i.* (ob jekt′) **4.** protest. —**ob·jec′tion,** *n.* —**ob·jec′tion·a·ble,** *adj.* —**ob·jec′tion·a·bly,** *adv.* —**ob·jec′tor,** *n.*

ob·jec′tive, *adj.* **1.** in the world outside the mind. **2.** concerned with reality, rather than thought or emotion. —**ob″jec·tiv′i·ty,** *n.*

ob′jur·gate″, *v.t.,* -gated, -gating. rebuke. —**ob·jur′ga·to″ry,** *adj.*

ob′li·gate″, *v.t.,* -gated, -gating. bind with a duty. —**ob·lig′a·to″ry,** *adj.*

o·blige′, *v.t.,* -bliged, -bliging. **1.** force. **2.** put in one's debt.

o·blig′ing, *adj.* ready to do favors. —**o·blig′ing·ly,** *adv.*

ob·lique′, *adj.* **1.** slanting. **2.** indirect. —**ob·liq′ui·ty,** **ob·lique′ness,** *n.*

ob·lit′er·ate″, *v.t.,* -ated, -ating. efface.

ob·liv′i·on, *n.* **1.** forgetfulness. **2.** unremembered past. —**ob·liv′i·ous,** *adj.*

ob′long, *adj.* **1.** longer than broad. —*n.* **2.** oblong figure, esp. a rectangle.

ob′lo·quy, *n., pl.* -quies. **1.** censure. **2.** infamy.

ob·nox'ious, *adj.* offensive.

o'boe, *n.* low-pitched musical reed instrument. —o'bo·ist, *n.*

ob·scene', *adj.* offensive to decency. —ob·scen'i·ty, *n.*

ob·scure', *adj., v.t.,* -scured, -scuring. *adj.* 1. indefinite. 2. dark. 3. little-known. —*v.t.* 4. make obscure. —ob·scur'i·ty, *n.* —ob"scu·ra'tion, *n.*

ob'se·quies, *n., pl.* funeral ceremonies.

ob·se'qui·ous, *adj.* fawningly servile.

ob·serv'a·to"ry, *n., pl.* -ries. place for observing heavenly bodies.

ob·serve', *v.t.,* -served, -serving. 1. study with the eye. 2. notice. 3. remark. 4. obey or respect. —ob·serv'ance, *n.* —ob·serv'ant, *adj.* —ob"ser·va'tion, *n.* —ob·serv'er, *n.*

ob·sess', *v.t.* preoccupy constantly. —ob·ses'sive, *adj.* —ob·ses'sion, *n.*

ob"so·les'cent, *adj.* going out of date. —ob"so·les'cence, *n.* —obso·lesce', *v.i.*

ob"so·lete', *adj.* out of date.

ob'sta·cle, *n.* something hindering advance.

ob·stet'rics, *n.* branch of medicine for pregnancy and childbirth. —ob·stet'ric, ob·stet'ri·cal, *adj.* —ob"ste·tri'cian, *n.*

ob'sti·nate, *adj.* stubborn. —ob'sti·na·cy, *n.*

ob·strep'er·ous, *adj.* rowdy.

ob·struct', *v.t.* 1. hinder; thwart. 2. block. —ob·struc'tion, *n.* —ob·struc'tion·ism, *n.* —ob·struc'tion·ist, *n., adj.* —ob·struc'tive, *adj.*

ob·tain', *v.t.* 1. get. —*v.i.* 2. be in effect. —ob·tain'ment, *n.*

ob·trude', *v.,* -truded, -truding. *v.t.* 1. force on others. —*v.i.* 2. obtrude oneself. —ob·tru'sion, *n.* —ob·tru'sive, *adj.*

ob·tuse', *adj.* 1. blunt, as an angle. 2. slow to understand.

ob·verse', *adj.* 1. toward an observer. 2. being a counterpart. —*n.* 3. counterpart.

ob'vi·ate", *v.t.,* -ated, -ating. avoid by alternatives.

ob'vi·ous, *adj.* perceived or understood without effort.

oc·ca'sion, *n.* 1. specific time or event. 2. opportunity. 3. reason; pretext. —*v.t.* 4. bring about.

oc·ca'sion·al, *adj.* occurring now and then.

Oc'ci·dent, *n.* Europe and the Americas. —Oc"ci·den'tal, *adj.*

oc·cult', *adj.* 1. hidden from ordinary persons. 2. mystical. —oc·cult'ism, *n.*

oc"cu·pa'tion, *n.* 1. type of work. 2. act or instance of occupying.

oc'cu·py", *v.t.,* -pied, -pying. 1. be in. 2. be engaged in or concerned with. 3.

take possession of, as by capture. —oc'cu·pan·cy, *n.* —oc'cu·pant, *n.*

oc·cur', *v.i.,* -curred, -curring. 1. happen. 2. come to mind. —oc·cur'rence, *n.*

o'cean, *n.* vast body of salt water. —o·ce·an'ic, *adj.*

o"cean·og'ra·phy, *n.* study of the ocean.

o'ce·lot", *n.* American wildcat.

o'cher, *n.* yellow or reddish-brown clay used as pigment. Also, o'chre.

o'clock', *adv.* by the clock.

oc'ta·gon, *n.* eight-sided plane figure. —oc·tag'o·nal, *adj.*

oc"ta·he'dron, *n.* eight-sided solid.

oc'tave, *n.* 1. *Music.* group including eight full tones. 2. *Poetry.* unit of eight lines.

oc·tet', *n.* group of eight musicians. Also, oc·tette'.

Oc·to'ber, *n.* tenth month.

oc"to·ge·nar'i·an, *n.* person in his or her eighties.

oc'to·pus, *n., pl.* -puses, -pi. soft mollusk with eight arms.

oc'u·lar, *adj.* pertaining to the eyes.

oc'u·list, *n.* ophthalmologist.

odd, *adj.* 1. not evenly divisible by two. 2. peculiar. 3. occasional. 4. remaining. —*n.* 5. odds, factors for or against. —odd'i·ty, *n.*

odds and ends, miscellaneous things.

ode, *n.* poem of praise.

o'di·ous, *adj.* hateful.

o'di·um, *n.* hatred or disgrace.

o'dor, *n.* smell. —o'dor·ous, *adj.* —o'dor·less, *adj.*

o"dor·if'er·ous, *adj.* giving off an odor.

of, *prep.* 1. coming from or produced by. 2. belonging to. 3. owning. 4. regarding. 5. specified as.

off, *prep.* 1. away or up from. 2. with sustenance from. —*adv.* 3. away or up. 4. so as not to work or be in effect. —*adj.* 5. not working or in effect. 6. on one's way. 7. not right.

of'fal, *n.* garbage.

off'-col'or, *adj.* risqué.

of·fend', *v.i.* 1. commit an offense. —*v.t.* 2. annoy or wound. 3. displease.

of·fense', *n.* 1. unlawful act. 2. resentment or hurt. 3. cause of this. 4. attack. Also, of·fence'.

of·fen'sive, *adj.* 1. tending to offend. 2. attacking. —*n.* 3. attacker's status.

of'fer, *v.t.* 1. present, as for acceptance or consideration. 2. shown signs of. —*v.i.* 3. present itself. —*n.* 4. act or instance of offering. —of'fer·ing, *n.*

off'hand', *adv.* 1. unprepared. —*adj.* 2. Also, off'hand'ed, casual.

of'fice, *n.* 1. position of authority. 2. Often offices, endeavor for another. 3.

place for commercial or government work.

of'fi·cer, *n.* **1.** holder of a position of authority. **2.** policeman.

of·fi'cial, *adj.* **1.** pertaining to or coming from supreme authority. —*n.* **2.** person in public office. —**of·fi'cial·dom,** *n.*

of·fi'ci·ate'', *v.i.,* **-ated, -ating.** perform official or ceremonial duties.

of·fi'cious, *adj.* giving unwanted help or orders.

of'fing, *n.* distance.

off'-lim'its, *adj. Military.* not to be entered.

off''-line'', *n.* not connected to a network or system.

off''-road'', *adj.* designed to be used in rough terrain, as an *off-road vehicle.*

off'set'', *v.t.,* **-set, -setting.** compensate for.

off'shoot'', *n.* thing derived from a major source.

off'shore', *adj., adv.* away from the shore.

off'spring'', *n., pl.* **-spring. -springs.** young of a human or animal.

off'-white', *n.* white tinted with grey or yellow.

of'ten, *adv.* many times.

o'gre, *n.* man-eating giant. Also, *fem.* **o'gress.** —**o'gre·ish,** *adj.*

oh, *n.* (exclamation of surprise, etc.).

ohm, *n. Electricity.* unit of resistance.

o·ho', *n.* (exclamation of surprise or triumph).

oil, *n.* **1.** any of various combustible liquids. **2.** paint with an oil vehicle. —*v.t.* **3.** lubricate with oil. —**oil'y,** *adj.* —**oil'i·ness,** *n.*

oil'cloth'', *n.* cloth treated to be waterproof.

oint'ment, *n.* fatty salve.

O.K., *interj., adj., adv., v.t.,* **O.K.'d, O.K.'ing.** *interj., adj., adv.* **1.** all right. —*v.t.* **2.** approve.

o'kra, *n.* plant with edible pods.

old, *adj.,* **older** or **elder, oldest** or **eldest. 1.** long in existence. **2.** experienced. **3.** longer in existence than another. **4.** former.

old'-fash'ioned, *adj.* **1.** obsolete. **2.** favoring older manners, etc. —*n.* **3.** whiskey cocktail.

old maid, mature, virginal woman.

old school, conservatives collectively. —**old'-school',** *adj.*

old'-tim'er, *n. Informal.* **1.** old man. **2.** long-time incumbent.

Old World, Europe, Asia, and Africa. —**Old'-World', old'-World',** *adj.*

o''le·o·mar'ga·rine, *n.* margarine. Also, **o''le·o·mar'ga·rin.**

ol·fac'to·ry, *adj.* pertaining to smell.

ol'i·garch''y, *n., pl.* **-ies.** government by a few. —**ol'i·garch'ic,** *adj.* —**oli·garch,** *n.*

ol'ive, *n.* fruit of a Mediterranean tree.

om·buds'man, *n., pl.* **-men.** investigator of citizen's complaints.

om'e·let, *n.* fried pancake of beaten eggs. Also, **om'e·lette.**

o'men, *n.* sign of the future.

om'i·nous, *adj.* threatening.

o·mit', *v.t.,* **-mitted, -mitting. 1.** leave out. **2.** forget; neglect. —**o·mis'sion,** *n.*

om'ni·bus, *n.* **1.** bus. **2.** complete anthology.

om·nip'o·tent, *adj.* all-powerful. —**om·nip'o·tence,** *n.*

om''ni·pres'ent, *adj.* present everywhere at once. —**om''ni·pres'ence,** *n.*

om·nis'cient, *adj.* knowing everything. —**om·nis'cience,** *n.*

om·niv'o·rous, *adj.* consuming anything.

on, *prep.* **1.** supported by. **2.** down against. **3.** regarding. **4.** with the help or sustenance of. **5.** at the time of. **6.** engaged in. **7.** being part of. —*adv.* **8.** onto oneself or something else. **9.** further; forward. **10.** into operation. —*adj.* **11.** in operation or effect.

once, *adv.* **1.** one time. **2.** formerly. **3.** at any time. —*conj.* **4.** when.

on'com''ing, *adj.* approaching.

one, *n.* **1.** lowest whole cardinal number. **2.** person. —*adj.* **3.** being one in number. **4.** identical. **5.** united. —*pron.* **6.** one person or thing.

on'er·ous, *adj.* burdensome.

one·self', *pron.* **1.** person's own self. **2.** person's true self. Also, **one's self.**

one'-sid'ed, *adj.* **1.** involving only one side. **2.** with all advantages on one side. **3.** prejudiced.

on'go''ing, *adj.* in progress.

on'ion, *n.* edible bulb of the lily family.

on''-line'', *n.* connected to a network or system.

on'look''er, *n.* spectator.

on'ly, *adj.* **1.** single; sole. —*adv.* **2.** solely. **3.** at last, however. **4.** as lately as.

on·o·mat·o·poe''ia (ahn''ə mat''ə pē'ə), *n.* coining of a word imitating a sound.

on'set'', *n.* attack.

on'slaught'', *n.* vigorous attack.

on'to, *prep.* into a position on.

o'nus, *n.* **1.** burden. **2.** blame.

on'ward, *adv.* **1.** Also, **on'wards, forward.** —*adj.* **2.** forward.

on'yx, *n.* striped agate.

oo'dles, *n., pl. Informal.* vast amounts.

ooze, *v.* **oozed, oozing,** *n. v.i.* **1.** flow slowly. —*v.t.* **2.** emit slowly. —*n.* **3.** slime. —**ooz'y,** *adj.*

o'pal, *n.* gem of multicolored silica. —o''pal·es'cent, *adj.*

o·paque', *adj.* 1. passing no light. 2. obscure. —o·paque'ness, o·pac'i·ty, *n.*

o'pen, *adj.* 1. able to be entered, seen through, etc. 2. with the inside revealed. 3. available or accessible. 4. candid. —*v.t.* 5. make open. —*v.i.* 6. become open. —*v.t.*, *v.i.* 7. start. —*n.* 8. open or unconcealed place or state.

o'pen-air', *adj.* outdoor.

o'pen-end'ed, *adj.* unrestricted.

o'pen-hand'ed, *adj.* generous.

o'pen·ing, *n.* 1. perforation. 2. beginning. 3. opportunity.

op'er·a, *n.* musical drama. —op''er·at'ic, *adj.*

op'er·a·ble, *adj.* 1. treatable by surgery. 2. able to be operated.

op'er·ate'', *v.*, -ated, -ating. *v.t.* 1. cause to function. 2. control; manage. —*v.i.* 3. function; act. 4. perform surgery. —op''er·a'tion, *n.* —op''er·a'tion·al, *adj.* —op''er·a''tor *n.*

op'er·a·tive, *adj.* 1. pertaining to operations. 2. able to operate. —*n.* 3. detective.

op'er·a''tor, *n.* 1. person who operates something, as telephone equipment. 2. *Informal.* person living on his wits.

op''er·et'ta, *n.* light opera.

ophth''al·mol'o·gy, *n.* branch of medicine concerning the eye. —opth''al·mo·log'i·cal, *adj.* —opth''al·mol·o·gist, *n.*

o'pi·ate, *n.* opium-based drug.

o·pin'ion, *n.* 1. personal belief. 2. personal evaluation.

o·pin'ion·at''ed, *adj.* stubborn in one's opinions.

o'pi·um, *n.* drug derived from poppies.

o·pos'sum, *n.* small tree-dwelling marsupial,

op·po'nent, *n.* adversary.

op''por·tune', *adj.* occuring when useful.

op''por·tun'ism, *n.* unprincipled advantage-taking.

op''por·tun'i·ty, *n.*, *pl.* -ties. favorable occasion.

op·pose', *v.t.*, -posed, -posing. 1. resist; fight. 2. be in contrast with. —op''po·si'tion, *n.*

op'po·site, *adj.* 1. in the other direction from somewhere between. 2. totally different in nature. —*n.* 3. something opposite.

op·press', *v.t.* 1. bully or exploit. 2. worry or make uncomfortable. —op·pres'sion. —op·pres'sor, *n.* —op·pres'sive, *adj.*

op·pro'bri·um, *n.* scorn; shame. —op·pro'bri·ous, *adj.*

opt, *v.i.* make a choice.

op'tic, *adj.* pertaining to sight.

op'ti·cal, *adj.* 1. visual. 2. pertaining to optics.

op·ti'cian, *n.* dealer in aids to eyesight.

op'tics, *n.* study of light and vision.

op'ti·mism, *n.* readiness to see or predict the best. —op'ti·mist, *n.* —op''ti·mis'tic, *adj.*

op'ti·mum, *adj.* 1. best, esp. in amount, etc. —*n.* 2. optimum amount, etc.

op'tion, *n.* 1. choice. 2. right to buy or not buy something. —op'tion·al, *adj.*

op·tom'e·try, *n.* profession of testing and prescribing for eye conditions. —op·tom'e·trist, *n.*

op'u·lent, *adj.* 1. rich. 2. lavish. —op'u·lence, *n.*

o'pus, *n.*, *pl.* -pera, -puses. work of an artist, musician, etc., esp. when numbered.

or, *conj.* 1. (indicating alternatives). 2. (indicating synonyms).

or'a·cle, *n.* 1. medium for consulting a god. 2. great authority. —o·rac'u·lar, *adj.*

o'ral, *adj.* 1. pertaining to the mouth. 2. spoken.

or'ange, *n.* 1. mixture of red and yellow. 2. fruit of this color. —or'ange·ade', *n.*

o·rang'u·tan'', *n.* manlike ape of Indonesia. Also, o·rang'u·tang''.

o·ra'tion, *n.* formal speech. —o·rate', *v.i.* —o'ra·tor, *n.*

or''a·to'ri·o'', *n.*, *pl.* -os. play sung but not acted.

or'a·to''ry, *n.*, *pl.* -ies. 1. public speaking. 2. small chapel. —or''a·tor'i·cal, *adj.*

orb, *n.* heavenly body.

or'bit, *n.* 1. path of a heavenly body. —*v.i.* 2. be in orbit. —or'bit·al, *adj.*

or'chard, *n.* grove of fruit trees.

or'ches·tra, *n.* 1. large, varied musical group. 2. main floor in an auditorium. —or·ches'tral, *adj.*

or'ches·trate'', *v.t.*, -trated, -trating. arrange for orchestra.

or'chid, *n.* tropical flowering plant.

or·dain', *v.t.* 1. decree; establish. 2. grant the office of clergyman to. —or·dain'ment, or''di·na'tion, *n.*

or·deal', *n.* severe trial.

or'der, *n.* 1. proper or meaningful condition. 2. command. 3. request to purchase. 4. group of monks, etc. —*v.t.* 5. make an order for. 6. put in order.

or'der·ly, *adj.*, *n.*, *pl.* -lies. *adj.* 1. in order. 2. quiet in behavior. —*n.* 3. attendant.

or'di·nal, *adj.* 1. pertaining to a meaningful series. —*n.* 2. ordinal number.

or'di·nance, *n.* law.

or'di·nar''y, *adj.* 1. usual, customary. —*n.* 2. customary experience.

ord'nance, *n.* military weapons.

ore, *n.* metal-bearing mineral.

o·reg'a·no, *n.* fragrant-leafed plant.

or'gan, *n.* **1.** body part performing a specific function. **2.** keyboard wind or electronic instrument. **3.** institutional periodical. —**or'gan·ist,** *n.*

or·gan'ic, *adj.* **1.** pertaining to or suggesting organisms. **2.** pertaining to bodily organs. **3.** containing carbon.

or'gan·ism, *n.* living thing.

or'gan·ize", *v.,* **-ized, -izing.** *v.t., v.i.* **1.** join in a coordinated group. —*v.t.* **2.** coordinate the functioning of. **3.** arrange for. **4.** cause to join a group. —**or"gan·i·za'tion,** *n.* —**or"gan·i·za' tion·al,** *adj.*

or'gasm, *n.* climax of a sex act.

or·gy (or'jē), *n., pl.* **-gies.** wild revelry.

o'ri·ent, *v.i.* **1.** establish one's location or course. —*v.t.* **2.** establish the location or course of. **3.** initiate in fundamentals. **4.** face in a certain direction. —*n.* **4. the Orient,** Asia. —**o"ri·en·ta'tion,** *n.* —**O"ri·en'tal,** *adj., n.*

or'i·fice, *n.* opening.

or'i·gin, *n.* **1.** commencement. **2.** source.

o·rig'i·nal, *adj.* **1.** earliest. **2.** copied to make others. **3.** never before seen. **4.** creative. —*n.* **5.** original thing. —**o· rig"i·nal'i·ty,** *n.* —**o·rig'i·nate",** *v.t., v.i.* —**o·rig'i·na"tor,** *n.*

o'ri·ole", *n.* black and orange bird.

or·na·ment, *n.* (or'nə ment) **1.** decoration. —*v.t.* (or'nə ment") **2.** decorate. —**or"na·men'tal,** *adj.* —**or"na·men· ta'tion,** *n.*

or·nate', *adj.* greatly ornamented.

or'ner·y, *adj. Dialect.* mean or stubborn. —**or'ner·i·ness,** *n.*

or"ni·thol'o·gy, *n.* study of birds. —**or" ni·thol'o·gist,** *n.* —**or"ni·tho·log'i· cal,** *adj.*

o'ro·tund", *adj.* with resonant, often pompous, speech.

or'phan, *n.* **1.** child of dead parents. —*v.t.* **2.** kill the parents of.

or'phan·age, *n.* home for orphans.

or"tho·don'tics, *n.* branch of dentistry that corrects irregular teeth. —**or"tho· don'tist,** *n.*

or'tho·dox", *adj.* **1.** conforming to standard doctrine. **2. Orthodox,** pertaining to an east European or Near Eastern church. —**or'tho·dox"y,** *n.*

or·thog'ra·phy, *n., pl.* **-phies.** spelling. —**or"tho·graph'ic,** *adj.*

or"tho·pe'dics, *n.* surgery of bones and joints. —**or"tho·pe'dic,** *adj.* —**or" tho·pe'dist,** *n.*

os'cil·late", *v.* **-lated, -lating.** *v.t., v.i.* swing back and forth.

os'cu·late", *v.,* **-lated, -lating.** *v.i., v.t.* kiss.

os·mo'sis, *n.* passage of fluids through membranes. —**os·mot'ic,** *adj.*

os'se·ous, *adj.* bony.

os'si·fy", *v.,* **-fied, -fying.** *v.t., v.i.* **1.** turn to bone. **2.** turn inadaptable, as a custom.

os·ten'si·ble, *adj.* seeming.

os"ten·ta'tion, *n.* great and deliberate display. —**os"ten·ta'tious,** *adj.*

os"te·op'a·thy, *n.* school of medicine emphasizing bones and muscles. —**os" te·o·path'ic,** *adj.* —**os'te·o·path",** *n.*

os'tra·cize", *v.t.,* **-cized, -cizing.** expel; exclude. —**os'tra·cism,** *n.*

os'trich, *n.* running bird of Africa and the Near East.

oth'er, *adj.* **1.** not yet mentioned. **2.** additional; remaining. —*pron.* **3.** other one. —*adv.* **4.** otherwise.

oth'er·wise", *adv.* **1.** in a different way. **2.** in other respects. **3.** under other conditions.

o'ti·ose", *adj.* idle; useless.

ot'ter, *n.* furred swimming mammal.

ot'to·man, *n.* upholstered footstool.

ouch, *interj.* (exclamation of pain).

ought, *aux. v.* **1.** am, is, or are obligated. **2.** will very probably.

oui, *adv. French.* yes.

ounce, *n.* **1.** sixteenth of an avoirdupois pound or twelfth of a troy pound. **2.** thirty-second of a liquid quart.

our, *adj.* pertaining to us.

ours, *pron.* our own.

our·selves', *pron.* **1.** (intensive or reflexive of *we*). **2.** our true selves.

oust, *v.t.* expel.

oust'er, *n.* act or instance of ousting.

out, *adv.* **1.** away from inside. **2.** away from existence, action, etc. **3.** away from a group. **4.** away from consciousness. —*adj.* **5.** away from one's usual place. **6.** out of existence, action, etc. **7.** inaccurate. **8.** unconscious. **9. out of,** with no supply of. —*n.* **10.** *Informal.* means of evasion.

out'-and-out', *adj.* utter.

out'board", *adj., adv.* outside the hull of a boat.

out'break", *n.* sudden manifestation.

out'build"ing, *n.* separate, subsidiary building.

out'burst", *n.* vigorous outbreak.

out'cast", *adj.* **1.** rejected by all. —*n.* **2.** outcast person.

out'come", *n.* result.

out'crop", *n.* rock rising above the soil.

out'cry", *n., pl.* **-cries.** strong protest.

out'dat"ed, *adj.* obsolete.

out'dis'tance, *v.t.,* **-tanced, -tancing.** get ahead of in a race or pursuit.

out'do', *v.t.,* **-did, -done, -doing.** act more effectively than.

out'door", *adj.* pertaining to the outdoors.

out'doors', *adv.* **1.** away from the insides of buildings. —*n.* **2.** nature.

out'er, *adj.* further out. —**out'er·most"**, *adj.*

out'fit", *n., v.t.,* **-fitted, -fitting.** *n.* **1.** equipment. **2.** ensemble of clothes. —*v.t.* **3.** supply with an outfit.

out"fox', *v.t.* outwit.

out"go'ing, *adj.* **1.** departing. **2.** affable.

out"grow", *v.t.,* **-grew, -grown, -growing.** become too large or mature for.

out"growth", *n.* **1.** something that grows out. **2.** development; consequence.

out"guess', *v.t.* guess better than.

out'ing, *n.* pleasure trip.

out"land'ish, *adj.* strange.

out"last", *v.t.* last longer than.

out'law", *n.* **1.** criminal. —*v.t.* **2.** forbid by law.

out'lay", *n.* expenditure.

out'let", *n.* **1.** means of emergence. **2.** sales market.

out'line", *n., v.t.,* **-lined, -lining.** *n.* **1.** outer edge; silhouette. **2.** summary of essentials. —*v.t.* **3.** make an outline of.

out"live', *v.t.,* **-lived, -living.** live longer than.

out"look", *n.* **1.** view. **2.** viewing place. **3.** prospect.

out"ly"ing, *adj.* situated at a distance.

out·mod'ed, *adj.* no longer in use.

out"num'ber, *v.t.* be more than.

out'-of-date', *adj.* obsolete.

out'-of-the-way', *adj.* not often encountered.

out'pa"tient, *n.* non-resident hospital patient.

out'post", *n.* remote fort, settlement, etc.

out"put, *n.* **1.** production. **2.** (computers) data sent from a computer after processing.

out'rage, *n., v.t.,* **-raged, -raging.** *n.* **1.** indignation. **2.** act causing indignation. —*v.t.* **3.** make indignant. —**out·ra'geous,** *adj.*

out'rig"ger, *n.* **1.** floating spar giving a narrow boat stability. **2.** boat with such a spar.

out'right", *adj.* **1.** pure and unambiguous. —*adv.* **2.** entirely. **3.** candidly.

out'set", *n.* beginning.

out'side', *n.* **1.** exterior. —*adj.* **2.** pertaining to an exterior. **3.** extreme. **4.** remotely possible. —*adv.* **5.** to the exterior. —*prep.* **6.** away from the interior of.

out"sid'er, *n.* non-member.

out"size', *adj.* over normal size.

out'skirts", *n., pl.* border areas.

out"smart', *v.t.* be more cunning than.

out"spo'ken, *adj.* frank.

out'spread', *adj.* extended.

out"stand'ing, *adj.* **1.** prominent. **2.** unpaid.

out"stretch', *v.t.* extend.

out"strip', *v.t.,* **-stripped, -stripping.** **1.** go faster than. **2.** surpass.

out'ward, *adj.* **1.** outer; exterior. —*adv.* **2.** Also, **out'wards,** towards the outside.

out"weigh', *v.t.* **1.** matter more than. **2.** be heavier than.

out"wit', *v.t.,* **-witted, -witting.** outsmart.

o'val, *n.* **1.** closed curve with a longer and a shorter axis. —*adj.* **2.** shaped like such a curve.

o'va·ry, *n., pl.* **-ries.** female reproductive gland. —**o·var'i·an,** *adj.*

o·va'tion, *n.* act of enthusiastic applause.

ov'en, *n.* heating chamber.

o'ver, *prep.* **1.** above or on. **2.** to or on the far side of. **3.** superior to. **4.** more than. **5.** concerning. —*adv.* **6.** above. **7.** across. **8.** more. **9.** again. **10.** upside down. **11.** to a new attitude or belief. **12.** to completion. —*adj.* **13.** upper. **14.** finished.

o'ver-, prefix indicating "to excess." **overabundant, overactive, overanxious, overburden, overcautious, overcharge, overconfident, overcrowd, overdo, overdose, overeat, overemphasize, overestimate, overexert, overexpose, overheat, overindulge, overload, overmuch, overpopulate, overprice, overproduce, overreact, overripe, oversexed, overspend, overstock, overstrict, oversupply, overwork.**

o'ver·all", *adj., adv.* **1.** end-to-end. —*adj.* **2.** total. —*n.* **3.** overalls, protective covering for other clothes.

o"ver·awe', *v.t.,* **-awed, -awing.** subdue with awe.

o"ver·bear'ing, *adj.* domineering.

o"ver·board", *adv.* into the water from a vessel.

o"ver·cast", *adj.* cloudy, as the sky.

o"ver·coat", *n.* heavy outer coat.

o"ver·come', *v.t.,* **-came, -come, -coming.** get the better of.

o"ver·dose', *v.* to ingest, with harmful effect, too much of a drug.

o"ver·draw', *v.t.,* **-draw, -drawn, -drawing.** draw on in excess of one's balance. —**o"ver·draft",** *n.*

o"ver·due', *adj.* past the time when due.

o"ver·es'ti·mate", *v.t.,* **-mated, -mating.** esteem too highly or as too much. —**o"ver·es'ti·mate, o"ver·es"ti·ma'tion,** *n.*

o·ver·flow', *v.t.* (o"vər flō') **1.** spill over the rim of. —*v.i.* **2.** be filled beyond capacity. —*n.* (o'vər flō") **3.** act or instance of overflowing. **4.** amount that overflows.

o"ver·grow', *v.t.* **-grew, -grown, -growing.** cover with growth.

o'ver·hand', *adv., adj.* with the hand raised.

o'ver·haul', *v.t.* **1.** inspect thoroughly. **2.** repair. —*n.* **3.** act or instance of overhauling.

o'ver·head'', *adj.*, *adv.* **1.** above one's head. —*n.* **2.** continuing business costs.

o''ver·hear', *v.t.*, **-heard, -hearing.** hear without being spoken to.

o''ver·joyed', *adj.* filled with joy.

o'ver·land'', *adj.*, *adv.* across the land.

o·ver·lap, *v.*, **-lapped, -lapping,** *n.* *v.t.* (ō''vər lap') **1.** extend within the edge of. —*v.i.* **2.** extend within each other's edges. —*n.* (ō'vər lap'') **3.** act or instance of overlapping.

o''ver·lay', *v.t.*, **-laid, -laying.** cover or lay over.

o'ver·look', *v.t.* **1.** omit by mistake. **2.** look out over.

o'ver·ly, *adv.* excessively.

o·ver·night, *adv.* (ō''vər nīt') **1.** during the night. —*adj.* (ō'vər nīt') **2.** from beginning to end of one night. **3.** for one night.

o'ver·pass'', *n.* roadway passing over another, etc.

o''ver·pow'er, *v.t.* reduce to helplessness.

o''ver·rate', *v.t.*, **-rated, -rating.** rate too highly.

o''ver·reach', *v.t.* reach beyond.

o''ver·ride', *v.t.*, **-rode, -ridden, -riding.** prevail against or nullify.

o''ver·rule', *v.t.*, **-ruled, -ruling.** nullify with superior authority.

o''ver·run', *v.t.*, **-ran, -run, -running. 1.** overflow. **2.** infest.

o''ver·seas', *adv.*, *adj.* **1.** beyond the sea. —*adj.* Also, **o'ver·sea''. 2.** foreign.

o''ver·see', *v.t.*, **-saw, -seen, -seeing.** supervise.

o'ver·shoe'', *n.* waterproof shoe covering.

o'ver·sight'', *n.* mistaken omission.

o''ver·sim'pli·fy'', *v.t.*, **-fied, -fying.** distort by simplification.

o'ver·size'', *adj.* **1.** too large. **2.** larger than usual. Also, **o'ver·sized''.**

o''ver·sleep', *v.i.* **-slept, -sleeping.** sleep too long.

o''ver·state', *v.t.*, **-stated, -stating.** exaggerate.

o''ver·step', *v.t.*, **-stepped, -stepping.** exceed.

o''ver·stuff', *v.t.* **1.** upholster with stuffing all over. **2.** stuff to excess.

o·vert', *adj.* **1.** unhidden. **2.** open and deliberate.

o''ver·take', *v.t.*, **-took, -taken, -taking.** catch up with.

o''ver-the-coun''ter, *adj.* (drugs) available without a prescription.

o·ver·throw, *v.t.*, **-threw, -thrown, -throwing,** *n.* *v.t.* (ō''vər thrō') **1.** cause to fall over. **2.** banish from power. —*n.* (ō'vər thrō'') **3.** act or instance of overthrowing.

o'ver·time'', *adj.*, *adv.* **1.** beyond regular hours. —*n.* **2.** time beyond regular hours. **3.** overtime pay.

o'ver·tone'', *n.* **1.** tone modifying a pure tone. **2.** subtle implication.

o'ver·ture'', *n.* **1.** musical composition beginning an opera, etc. **2.** friendly advance.

o''ver·turn', *v.t.*, *v.i.* upset.

o''ver·ween'ing, *adj.* arrogant.

o'ver·weight'', *adj.* too heavy.

o'ver·whelm', *v.t.* render powerless.

o'ver·wrought'', *adj.* very nervous.

o'void, *adj.* egg-shaped.

o'vum, *n.*, *pl.* **-va.** female germ cell.

owe, *v.t.*, **owed, owing. 1.** be obligated to give or pay. **2.** be obligated to. **3.** have someone to thank for.

owl, *n.* nocturnal bird of prey.

own, *v.t.* **1.** be the rightful possessor of. —*v.t.*, *v.i.* **2.** admit or confess. —*adj.* **3.** personally or individually possessed. —**own'er·ship,** *n.*

ox, *n.*, *pl.* **oxen.** castrated bull.

ox'ide, *n.* compound containing oxygen.

ox'y·gen, *n.* gaseous element needed for breathing and burning.

ox·y·mor'on, *n.* figure of speech in which two ideas of opposite meaning are combined to form an expressive phrase.

oys'ter, *n.* edible mollusk.

o'zone, *n.* a form of oxygen created by electric spark.

P

P, p, *n.* sixteenth letter of the English alphabet.

pab'u·lum. *n.* soft food, esp. for babies.

pace, *n.*, *v.*, **paced, pacing.** *n.* **1.** rate of movement, esp. in walking or running. **2.** linear measure roughly equivalent to a footstep. **3.** an individual step. —*v.t.* **4.** establish the pace for, esp. in a race. **5.** measure by pacing off. —*v.i.* **6.** take slow, measured steps.

pace''mak·er, *n.* artificial device to regulate the heartbeat.

pach·y·derm (pak'i·derm), *n.* thick-skinned mammal, e.g., an elephant.

pa·cif'ic, *adj.* **1.** peaceful; calm. **2.** peace-making; conciliatory.

pac'i·fism, *n.* opposition to violence and war. —**pac'i·fist**, *n.* —**pac'i·fis'tic,** *adj.*

pac'i·fy', *v.t.*, **-fied, -fying. 1.** quiet or calm. **2.** appease. —**pac'i·fi·ca'tion,** *n.* —**pac'i·fi''er,** *n.*

pack, *n*. **1.** bundle or package. **2.** group of people, animals, or things. **3.** complete set of. —*v.t*. **4.** make into a bundle. **5.** fill, as with things for a journey. **6.** cram. **7.** carry, as a gun.

pack'age, *n*., *v.t*., **-aged, -aging**. *n*. **1.** bundle; parcel. **2.** container. —*v.t*. **3.** enclose or wrap in a package.

pack'et, *n*. **1.** small package or bundle. **2.** passenger boat on a regular schedule.

pact, *n*. agreement; treaty.

pad, *n*., *v.t*., **padded, padding**. *n*. **1.** soft cushion **2.** tablet of writing paper. **3.** cushioned part of an animal foot. —*v.t*. **4.** furnish with pads. **5.** lengthen or falsify with extraneous matter.

pad'dle, *n*., *v*., **-dled, -dling**. *n*. **1.** oarlike implement, esp. for a canoe. **2.** ping pong racket. —*v.t*. **3.** move with paddles. **4.** spank. —*v.i*. **5.** move in water using the hands.

pad'dock, *n*. enclosed area for horses.

pad'lock, *n*. **1.** portable lock with a shackle. —*v.t*. **2.** fasten with a padlock.

pae·an (pē'ən), *n*. song of praise, joy, or thanksgiving.

pa'gan, *n*. **1.** heathen. —*adj*. **2.** heathen: barbaric. —**pa'gan·ism**, *n*.

page, *n*., *v.t*. **paged, paging**. *n*. **1.** single side of a leaf, as in a book. **2.** young servant. —*v.t*. **3.** number the pages of. **4.** hail by naming loudly.

pag'eant, *n*. elaborate spectacle. —**pag'eant·ry**, *n*.

pag''er, *n*. electronic device for remote alerting and communication with a person.

pa·go'da, *n*. tall Oriental building, usually in a Buddhist temple.

pail, *n*. bucket.

pain, *n*. **1.** physical or mental suffering. **2.** effort; struggle. **3.** punishment. —*v.t*. **4.** hurt; distress. —**pain'ful**, *adj*. —**pain'less**, *adj*.

pains'tak''ing, *adj*. careful.

paint, *n*. **1.** pigmented liquid used to coat surfaces. —*v.i*. **2.** engage in the art of painting. —*v.t*. **3.** cover with paint. —**paint'er**, *n*. —**paint'ing**, *n*.

pair, *n*., *pl*. **pairs, pair**, *v*. *n*. **1.** set of two, esp. when matching. —*v.t*. **2.** arrange in pairs. —*v.i*. **3.** **pair off**, separate in couples.

pais'ley, *n*. soft fabric with colorful, intricate design.

pa·ja'mas, *n*., *pl*. loose, two-piece sleeping clothes.

pal, *n*. *Informal*. friend or acquaintance.

pal'ace, *n*. official residence of a sovereign, etc. —**pa·la'tial**, *adj*.

pal'at·a·ble, *adj*. tasty.

pal'ate, *n*. roof of the mouth. —**pal'a·tal**, *adj*.

pa·lav'er, *n*. long parley.

pale, *adj*., **paler, palest**, *v*. **paled, paling**. *n*. *adj*. **1.** lacking intensity of color; whitish. **2.** lacking vividness. —*v.i*. **3.** become pale. —*n*. **4.** stake. **5.** limits, bounds. **6.** enclosed area.

pa''le·o·lith'ic, *adj*. pertaining to the Old Stone Age.

pal'ette, *n*. board on which a painter spreads colors.

pal'id, *adj*. pale, drawn. —**pal'lor**, *n*.

pal'ing, *n*. board or picket.

pal'i·sade', *n*. **1.** high fence of palings. **2.** line of high cliffs.

pall (pol), *n*. **1.** cloth draped over a coffin. —*v.i*. **2.** become tiresome or distasteful.

pall'bear''er, *n*. person who attends or carries the coffin at a funeral.

pal'let, *n*. **1.** straw mattress. **2.** platform used to support freight.

pal'li·ate'', *v.t*. **1.** ease without curing. **2.** mitigate with excuses. —**pal'li·a''tive**, *adj*.

palm, *n*. **1.** soft inner surface of the hand. **2.** tall unbranched tropical tree or shrub topped with large leaves. —*v.t*. **3.** conceal in the hand.

palm'is·try, *n*. fortune-telling from the lines on a person's palm.

pal·o·mi·no (pal''ō mē'nō), *n*., *pl*. **-nos**. *n*. light tan horse.

pal'pa·ble, *adj*. **1.** tangible. **2.** obvious, clear. —**pal'pa·bly**, *adv*.

pal'pi·tate'', *v.i*., **-tated, -tating**. pulsate with unnatural rapidity. —**pal''pi·ta'tion**, *n*.

pal·sy (pahl'zē), *n*., *pl*. **-sies**, *v.t*., **-sied, -sying**. *n*. **1.** paralysis. **2.** condition characterized by tremors. —*v.t*. **3.** paralyze.

pal'try, *adj*., **-trier, -triest**. *adj*. trifling, trivial.

pam'per, *v.t*. treat with excessive indulgence; coddle.

pam·phlet, *n*. unbound booklet with a paper cover.

pan, *n*., *v*. **panned, panning**. *n*. **1.** broad, shallow metal container. —*v.t*. **2.** separate from sand by washing. **3.** *Informal*. criticize severely, in a review.

pan·a·ce·a (pan''a sē'a), *n*. cure-all.

pan'cake'', *n*. flat batter cake fried on both sides.

pan'cre·as, *n*. gland that secretes digestive fluid. —**pan''cre·at'ic**, *adj*.

pan'da, *n*. bear-like, black and white Asiatic mammal.

pan''de·mo'ni·um, *n*. wild uproar, chaos.

pan'der, *n*. **1.** pimp. —*v.i*. **2.** cater to another's passions or weaknesses. —**pan'der·er**, *n*.

pane, *n*. sheet of glass, esp. for doors and windows.

pan·e·gyr·ic (pan''ə jir'ik), *n*. eulogy.

pan'el, *n*. **1.** list of persons called for a special task, e.g. jury duty. **2.** wood filling for a wall or door. **3.** mounting for controls or instruments. —**pan'el·ing.** *n.* —**pan'el·ist,** *n.*

pang, *n.* sudden feeling of distress or guilt.

pan'han''dle, *v.i.* -**dled, -dling.** *Informal.* beg for money on the street. —**pan'han''dler,** *n.*

pan'ic, *n.* **1.** sudden, overpowering fear. —*v.i.* **2.** be affected by panic. —**pan'ick·y,** *adj.* —**pan'ic-strick''en,** *adj.*

pan'o·ply, *n., pl.* -**plies.** *n.* **1.** impressive array. **2.** suit of armor.

pan''o·ram'a, *n.* **1.** wide view of a large area. **2.** continuously changing scene or unfolding of events. —**pan''o·ram'ic,** *adj.*

pan'sy, *n.* colorful outdoor flower related to the violet.

pant, *v.i.* **1.** breathe hard and quickly, as after exercise. **2.** long or yearn for.

pan'the''ism, *n.* doctrine that equates God with nature and natural forces.

pan'ther, *n.* large wild cat, e.g. leopard, cougar, puma.

pan'to·mime'', *n., v.t.,* -**mimed, miming.** *n.* **1.** expression through movement and gesture only. **2.** drama using movement and no speech. —*v.t.* **3.** express in pantomime; mime.

pan'try, *n., pl.* -**tries.** small supply room or closet off a kitchen.

pants, *n., pl.* trousers.

pap, *n.* soft food for babies or the infirm.

pa'pa, *n.* father.

pa'pa·cy, *n.* office of the pope. —**pa'pal,** *adj.*

pa·pa·ya (pa pah'yə), *n.* tropical tree with yellow-black edible fruit.

pa'per, *n.* **1.** fibrous compound made in sheets to receive writing, etc. **2.** scholarly essay. **3.** newspaper. **4.** papers, documents. —*v.t.* **5.** decorate with wallpaper.

pa'per·back'', *n.* inexpensive book with paper cover.

pa·pier-ma·che (pa''per mə shā'), *n.* molding material made of wet paper pulp and glue.

pa·pil'la, *n., pl.* -**pillae** (pə pil'lē), *n.* small protuberance concerned with the senses, e.g. taste buds.

pa'pist, *n. Disparaging.* Roman Catholic. —**pa'pism,** *n.* —**pa·pis'ti·cai, pa·pis'tic,** *adj.*

pa·poose', *n.* North American Indian baby.

pap·ri'ka, *n.* red spice made from sweet peppers.

pa·py·rus, *n.* plant from the Nile from which the Egyptians prepared paperlike material.

par, *n.* **1.** equality in level or value. **2.** accepted standard; average.

par'a·ble, *n.* story conveying a moral.

par'a·chute'', *n., v.,* -**chuted, -chuting,** *n.* **1.** umbrellalike device used for descents from aircraft. —*v.i.* **2.** jump with a parachute. —*v.t.* **3.** send by parachute.

pa·rade', *n., v.,* -**raded, -rading.** *n.* **1.** ostentatious display. **2.** ceremonial procession or march. —*v.t.* **3.** display ostentatiously. —*v.i.* **4.** march in a parade.

par·a·digm (par'a dîm), *n.* ideal; model.

par'a·dise'', *n.* **1.** heaven. **2.** Garden of Eden.

par'a·dox'', *n.* true statement that seems to contradict itself. —**par''a·dox'i·cal,** *adj.*

par'af·fin, *n.* waxy substance used in candles and to seal jars.

par'a·gon'', *n.* model of perfection.

par'a·graph'', *n.* **1.** subdivision of a writing that contains one or more sentences. —*v.t.* **2.** divide into paragraphs.

par'a·keet'', *n.* any of numerous slender, small parrots.

par'al·lax'', *n.* apparent displacement of an object seen from different positions.

par'al·lel'', *adj., n., v.t.* -**leled, -leling.** *adj.* **1.** lying or moving in the same direction but equidistant at all points. **2.** essentially similar or comparable. —*n.* **3.** anything parallel. **4.** counterpart. **5.** similarity. —*v.t.* **6.** compare. **7.** be parallel to.

par''al·lel'o·gram'', *n.* quadrilateral with parallel opposite sides.

pa·ral'y·sis, *n., pl.* -**ses,** loss of voluntary muscular control. —**par''a·lyt'ic,** *n., adj.* —**par'a·lyze'',** *v.t.*

par'a·mount'', *adj.* superior; predominant.

par'a·mour'', *n.* extra-marital lover.

par''a·noi'a, *n.* mental disorder characterized by delusions. —**par'a·noid'',** *n., adj.* —**par''a·noi'ac,** *n., adj.*

par'a·pet, *n.* protecting wall or railing.

par''a·pher·nal'ia, *n., pl.,* **1.** personal belongings. **2.** equipment.

par'a·phrase'', *v.t.,* -**phrased, -phrasing,** *n. v.t.* **1.** restate in other words. —*n.* **2.** restatement in different words.

par·a·ple·gi·a (par''a plē'gēa), *n.* paralysis of the lower half of the body. —**par''a·pleg'ic,** *n.*

par'a·site'', *n.* **1.** organism which lives in or on another. **2.** person who depends on or exploits another. —**par''a·sit'ic,** *adj.*

par'a·sol'', *n.* sun umbrella.

par'a·troops'', *n., pl.* soldiers who parachute from planes. —**par'a·trooper,** *n.*

par'boil'', *v.t.* boil partly.

par'cel, *n., v.t.,* -**celed, -celing.** *n.* **1.** wrapped package, esp. for mailing. **2.** lot, esp. for sale. **3.** tract of land. —*v.t.* **4.** divide.

parch, *v.t.* **1.** dry by heat. —*v.i.* **2.** suffer from heat or thirst.

parch′ment, *n.* skin of sheep or goat prepared for writing on.

par′don, *n.* **1.** official release from penalty or punishment. **2.** indulgence, forgiveness. —*v.t.* **3.** grant pardon to. —**par′don·a·ble,** *adj.*

pare, *v.t.* **pared, paring. 1.** trim off the outside part or skin of. **2.** reduce.

par′′e·gor′ic, *n.* soothing medicine, esp. to control diarrhea.

par′ent, *n.* mother or father. —**pa·ren′tal,** *adj.* —**par′ent·hood′′.** *n.*

par′ent·age, *n.* descent, origin or lineage.

pa·ren′the·sis, *n., pl.* **-ses, 1.** punctuation marks, (or), used to enclose parenthetic material. **2.** matter interpolated in writing to modify or explain the idea. —**par′′en·thet′ic, par′′en·thet′i·cal,** *adj.*

par·fait′ (pahr fā′) *n.* frozen, layered dessert.

pa·ri·ah (pa rī′ah), *n.* outcast.

par′i·mu′tu·el, *n.* system of betting in which winners share the winnings and the management takes a percentage.

par′ish, *n.* **1.** ecclesiastical district under one pastor. **2.** local church community. —**pa·rish′ion·er,** *n.*

par′i·ty, *n.* equality; equivalence.

park, *n.* **1.** land set aside as a recreation area or game preserve. **2.** site for athletic events. —*v.t., v.i.* **3.** halt for an extended period.

par′ka, *n.* hooded, cold-weather coat.

park′way′′, *n.* highway with landscaped median strip.

par′lance, *n.* manner of speaking; idiom.

par′lay, *n.* **1.** bet of previous winnings along with the original sum betted. —*v.t.* **2.** bet as a parlay.

par′ley, *n., pl.* **-leys,** *v.i.,* **-leyed, -leying.** *n.* **1.** informal conference, esp. to settle differences. —*v.i.* **2.** hold a parley.

par′lia·ment, *n.* national legislative body. —**par′′lia·men·tar′i·an,** *n.* —**par′′lia·men′ta·ry,** *adj.*

par′lor, *n.* room for entertaining.

pa·ro·chi·al (pa ro′kē al), *adj.* **1.** pertaining to a parish. **2.** narrow or limited in scope. —**pa·ro′chi·al·ism,** *n.*

par′o·dy, *n., pl.* **-dies,** *v.t.,* **-died, -dying.** *n.* **1.** satiric or humorous imitation. —*v.t.* **2.** ridicule, travesty. —**par′o·dist,** *n.* —**pa·rod′ic,** *adj.*

pa·role′, *n., v.t.,* **-roled, -roling.** *n.* **1.** conditional early release from prison. —*v.t.* **2.** put on parole.

par·ox·ysm (par′ok siz′′im), *n.* sudden, sharp attack; convulsion, fit.

par·quet (par ka′), *n.* floor with an inlaid design, esp. in wood.

par′ri·cide, *n.* killing of a parent or close relative.

par′rot, *n.* **1.** hook-billed tropical bird capable of talking. —*v.t.* **2.** repeat or imitate unthinkingly.

par′ry, *v.t.,* **-ried, rying,** *n., pl.* **-ries.** —*v.t.* **1.** evade, avoid. —*n.* **2.** act or instance of parrying.

par′si·mo′′ny, *n.* extreme frugality or cheapness. —**par′′si·mo′ni·ous,** *adj.*

pars′ley, *n.* garden herb used as garnish or seasoning.

pars′nip, *n.* plant with long, white edible root.

par′son, *n.* clergyman, esp. Protestant.

par′son·age, *n.* house for a parson.

part, *n.* **1.** portion or division. **2.** spare or replacement piece for a machine. **3.** function, duty, job. **4.** role in drama, etc. —*v.t.* **5.** divide. —*v.i.* **6.** dissolve a relationship.

par·take′, *v.i.,* **-took -taken, -taking.** *v.i.* **1.** participate. **2.** receive or take a portion.

par·tial (par′shal), *adj.* **1.** favoring one over another; biased. **2.** especially fond. **3.** affecting a part only. —**par·tial′i·ty,** *n.* —**par′tial·ly,** *adv.*

par·tic′i·pate′′, *v.i.,* **-pated, -pating.** take part; share. —**par·tic′i·pant,** *n.* —**par·tic′′i·pa′tion,** *n.*

par′ti·ci·ple, *n.* adjective based on a verb. —**par′′ti·cip′i·al,** *adj.*

par′ti·cle, *n.* **1.** very small piece or amount. **2.** small, functional word, e.g. a preposition, etc.

par·tic′u·lar, *adj.* **1.** pertaining to a specific person or thing. **2.** distinctive, special. **3.** attentive to details; fastidious. —*n.* **4.** detail. —**par·tic′u·lar·ly,** *adv.*

part′ing, *n.* **1.** separation, division. **2.** departure. —*adj.* **3.** done, etc. in farewell.

par′ti·san, *n.* **1.** person who takes a side in a controversy. **2.** guerrilla.

par·ti′tion, *n.* **1.** division into parts. **2.** divider. —*v.t.* **3.** divide into parts.

part′ly, *adv.* in some measure; not fully.

part′ner, *n.* **1.** associate, colleague. **2.** spouse. **3.** joint owner. —**part′ner·ship′′,** *n.*

par′tridge, *n.* any of various game birds.

par′ty, *n., pl.* **-ties.** *n.* **1.** social gathering. **2.** group of people with common political interests and opinions. **3.** person or group concerned in a specific action; participant. **4.** group engaged in a special task.

pass, *v.t.* **1.** go past. **2.** hand over; serve. **3.** spend, as time. **4.** approve or ratify. **5.** succeed at, as a test. —*v.i.* **6.** go past. **7.** come to an end. **8.** go from place to place. **9.** be approved or ratified. —*n.* **10.** situation. **11.** paper granting admission, leave, etc. **12.** route, as between mountains. **13.** motion of the hands.

pass′a·ble, *adj.* **1.** able to be passed or

crossed. **2.** good enough; tolerable. —**pass′ab·ly**, *adv.*

pas′sage, *n.* **1.** right or freedom to pass. **2.** means of passing. **3.** transportation, esp. ship passage. **4.** act or instance of passing. **5.** enactment. —**pas′sage·way″**, *n.*

pass′book″, *n.* bankbook, esp. for a savings account.

pas′sen·ger, *n.* traveler, esp. on a vehicle.

pas·sé (pa sā′), *adj.* out of date; old fashioned.

pas′sing, *adj.* **1.** transitory; fleeting. —*n.* **2.** act of a person who passes, esp. in death.

pas′sion, *n.* **1.** strong feeling or emotion. **2.** love, esp. sexual desire. **3.** anger, rage. **4.** the Passion, sufferings of Christ. —**pas′sion·ate**, **pas′sion·less**, *adj.* —**pas′sion·ate·ly**, *adv.*

pas′sive, *n.* **1.** inactive; not in action. **2.** acted upon. **3.** submissive, meek; patient. —**pas·siv′i·ty**, **pas′sive·ness**, *n.* —**pas′sive·ly**, *adv.*

Pass′o″ver, *n.* Jewish holiday celebrating the Hebrews′ liberation from slavery in Egypt.

pass′port″, *n.* official document carried by a foreign traveler.

past, *adj.* **1.** gone by or elapsed. **2.** pertaining to an earlier time or age. **3.** *Grammar.* pertaining to a verb tense expressing time gone by. —*n.* **4.** time gone by. **5.** past tense. **6.** secret past life. —*prep. adv.* **7.** beyond.

pas′ta, *n.* food, Italian in origin, prepared from flour and egg dough.

paste, *n., v.t.,* **pasted, pasting**, *n.* **1.** soft mixture, esp. for sticking things together. **2.** shiny glass used in imitation gems. —*v.t.* **3.** fasten with paste. —**pas′ty**, *adj.*

paste′board″, *n.* board made of sheets of paper pasted together.

pas·tel′, *n.* **1.** light or pale color. **2.** drawing or painting in pastel.

pas′tern, *n.* part of horse′s foot between the fetlock and the hoof joint.

pas′teur·ize″, *v.t.,* **-ized, -izing.** heat to destroy harmful bacteria. —**pas′teur·i·za′tion**, *n.*

pas·tiche (pas tēsh′), *n.* artistic composition composed of selections or motifs from other works.

pas′time″, *n.* diversion; hobby.

pas′tor, *n.* clergyman serving a local parish or church.

pas′to·ral, *adj.* **1.** pertaining to shepherds or the rural life. **2.** pertaining to a golden age. **3.** pertaining to pastors.

pas′try, *n.* sweet baked goods.

pas′ture, *n., v.t.,* **-tured, -turing**, *n.* **1.** grassy land used for grazing animals. —*v.t.* **2.** feed by allowing to graze.

pat, *n., adj., v.i.,* **patted, patting**. *n.* **1.** light stroke with the flat of the hand. **2.** flat piece of butter, etc.—*adj.* **3.** glib. **4.** perfectly learned.—*v.i.* **5.** place the flat of the hand on lightly.

patch, *n.* **1.** piece used to cover or repair a worn spot. **2.** a small area distinct from that around it. —*v.t.* **3.** mend or cover with a patch. **5.** repair hastily. —**patch′work″**, *n., adj.* —**patch′y**, *adj.*

pate, *n.* head, esp. the crown.

pa·tel′la, *n., pl.* **-tellae.** kneecap.

pat′en, *n.* plate, esp. one used in the Eucharist.

pat′ent, *n.* **1.** certificate of exclusive rights to an invention. —*v.t.* **2.** secure a patent on. —*adj.* **3.** something protected by a patent. **4.** evident; obvious.

pa·ter′nal, *adj.* **1.** fatherly. **2.** related through or derived from a father.

pa·ter′nal·ism, *n.* benevolent or fatherly administration. —**pa·ter″nal·is′tic**, *adj.*

pa·ter′ni·ty, *n.* fatherhood.

path, *n.* **1.** narrow road. **2.** course of action. —**path′way″**, *n.*

pa·thet′ic, *adj.* **1.** evoking pity. **2.** miserably inadequate. —**pa·thet′i·cal·ly**, *adv.*

pa·thol′o·gy, *n.* **1.** study of the nature of disease. **2.** characteristics of a disease. —**path″o·log′i·cal**, *adj.* —**pa·thol′o·gist**, *n.*

pa′thos, *n.* element evoking pity or compassion.

pa′tient, *n.* **1.** person under the care of a doctor. —*adj.* **2.** enduring without complaint. —**pa′tience**, *n.* —**pa′tient·ly**, *adv.*

pa·ti′na, *n.* green film formed on copper and bronze.

pa′ti·o″, *n., pl.* **patios**, open courtyard

pa′tri·arch″, *n.* **1.** father or founder, e.g. of a tribe or institution. **2.** venerable old man; father. **3.** ecclesiastical dignitary. —**pa′tri·ar″chal**, *adj.* —**pa′tri·ar″chy**, *n.*

pa·tri′cian, *adj.* **1.** aristocratic; of high birth. —*n.* **2.** aristocrat.

pat′ri·mo″ny, *n.* inherited estate.

pa′tri·ot, *n.* person who loves and supports his country. —**pa″tri·ot′ic**, *adj.* —**pa′tri·ot″ism**, *n.*

pa·trol′, *n., v.t.,* **-trolled, -trolling**. *n.* **1.** guard making a round. —*v.t.* **2.** guard with a patrol. **3.** pass along regularly. —**pa·trol′man**, *n.*

pa′tron, *n.* **1.** influential or wealthy supporter. **2.** customer or client.

pa′tron·age, *n.* **1.** support by a patron. **2.** support of a business by customers. **3.** personal control of appointments to government jobs.

pa′tron·ize″, *v.t.,* **-ized, -izing. 1.** be a customer of. **2.** treat with condescension.

patter

pat'ter, *v.i.* **1.** make a succession of light tapping sounds. **2.** talk glibly or nonsensically. **3.** walk quickly and lightly. —*n.* **4.** glib, rapid speech. **5.** quick pattering sound.

pat'tern, *n.* **1.** decorative design. **2.** ideal model. **3.** model for making or copying. —*v.t.* **4.** make after a pattern.

pat'ty, *n., pl.* **-ties. 1.** little pie. **2.** flat, round cake of chopped food, e.g. hamburger.

pau'ci·ty, *n.* scarcity.

paunch, *n.* belly, esp. when large. —**paunch'y,** *adj.*

pau'per, *n.* poor person.

pause, *n.* **1.** temporary stop. —*v.i.* **2.** stop temporarily.

pave, *v.t.,* **paved, paving.** cover with hard material, as a road. —**pave'ment,** *n.*

pa·vil'ion, *n.* **1.** light, open structure for entertainment or shelter. **2.** large tent.

paw, *n.* **1.** animal foot with nails or claws. —*v.t., v.i.* **2.** scrape or strike with or as with paws.

pawn, *v.t.* **1.** pledge or stake. **2.** deposit as security for a loan. *n.* **3.** state of being pawned. **4.** chess piece of the lowest value.

pawn'bro''ker, *n.* person who lends money on pledged goods.

pay, *v.,* **paid, paying.** *n. v.t.* **1.** give money to in return for goods or services. **2.** satisfy, as a debt. —*v.i.* **3.** give money in exchange. **4.** yield a profit. **5.** undergo punishment. —*n.* **6.** wages or salary. **7.** paid employment. **8.** profit. —**pay·ee',** *n.* —**pay'er,** *n.* —**pay'ment,** *n.*

pay'a·ble, *adj.* **1.** to be paid. **2.** able to be paid.

pay'-off, *n.* **1.** final payment. **2.** final consequence.

pea, *n.* round, edible vegetable seed.

peace, *n.* **1.** calm and quiet. **2.** state of accord. **3.** freedom from troubling emotions or thoughts. —**peace'a·ble,** *adj.* —**peace'ful,** *adj.* —**peace'time'',** *n.*

peach, *n.* sweet juicy fruit.

pea'cock'', *n.* male peafowl with long, brilliant tail feathers.

pea'fowl'', *n.* large, domesticated Asiatic pheasant.

pea'hen'', *n.* female peafowl.

peak, *n.* **1.** pointed top. **2.** top of a mountain or hill.

peaked, *adj.* **1.** pointed. **2.** (pē'kid) pale, sickly.

peal, *n.* **1.** loud, prolonged ringing of bells. **2.** set of tuned bells. **3.** any loud, prolonged series of sounds. —*v.i.* **4.** sound in a peal.

pea'nut'', *n.* pod or edible seed of an annual herb.

pear, *n.* fleshy fruit related to the apple.

pearl, *n.* hard, lustrous gem formed within the shell of an oyster. —**pearl'y,** *adj.*

peas'ant, *n.* poor farm worker.

peat, *n.* highly organic soil dried for use as fuel.

peb'ble, *n.* small stone. —**peb'bly,** *adj.*

pe·can (pē kahn'), *n.* smooth-shelled nut from the hickory tree.

pec''ca·dil'lo, *n., pl.* **-loes, -los,** slight or minor offense.

pec'ca·ry, *n.* small pig-like animal.

peck, *v.t., v.i.* **1.** jab repeatedly with a beak. —*v.t.* **2.** dig with such jabs. —*n.* **3.** dry measure of eight quarts.

pec'tin, *n.* plant substance used to thicken jellies, etc.

pec'u·late'', *v.t.,* **-lated, -lating,** embezzle. —**pec''u·la'tion,** *n.*

pe·cu'liar, *adj.* **1.** strange, odd. **2.** unique. **3.** distinctive, characteristic. —**pe·cu''li·ar'i·ty,** *n.* —**pe·cul'iar·ly,** *adv.*

pe·cu'ni·ar''y, *adj.* pertaining to money; monetary.

ped'a·gogue'', *n.* teacher; scholar. Also, **ped'a·gog'', —ped'a·go''gy,** *n.* —**ped''a·gog'ic, ped''a·gog'i·cal,** *adj.*

ped'al, *n.* **1.** lever worked by the foot. —*v.t., v.i.* **2.** move by means of pedals.

ped'ant, *n.* **1.** person who makes a display of his learning. **2.** unimaginative adherent to the letter of a doctrine. —**pe·dan'tic,** *adj.* —**ped'an·try,** *n.*

ped'dle, *v.t., v.i.,* **-dled, -dling.** sell on the street or road. —**ped'dler,** *n.*

ped'es·tal, *n.* base for a statue, etc.

pe·des'tri·an, *n.* **1.** walker. —*adj.* **2.** prosaic; commonplace.

pe''di·at'rics, *n.* study of care and diseases of children. —**pe'di·a·tri''cian,** *n.* —**pe''di·at'ric,** *adj.*

ped'i·gree'', *n.* **1.** certificate of ancestry. **2.** ancestry, esp. when distinguished. —**ped'i·greed'',** *adj.*

ped'i·ment, *n.* decorative triangular gable.

peek, *v.i.* **1.** glance furtively. —*n.* **2.** brief or furtive glance.

peel, *v.t.* **1.** strip or remove. —*n.* **2.** skin of fruit or vegetable. —**peel'ing,** *n.*

peen, *n.* wedge or ball-shaped end of a hammer.

peep, *v.i.* **1.** peek. **2.** utter a faint, shrill cry. —*n.* **3.** quick look or glance. **4.** faint sound.

peer, *v.i.* **1.** look intently or searchingly. —*n.* **2.** equal in rank or abilities. **3.** nobleman. —**peer'age,** *n.*

peer'less, *adj.* without equal, supreme.

peeve, *n., v.t.,* **peeved, peeving,** *v.t.* **1.** annoy, irritate. —*n.* **2.** source of annoyance. **3.** complaint. —**peev'ish,** *adj.*

peg, *n., v.t.,* **pegged, pegging.** *n.* **1.** small hook, pin or fastener, esp. one fitting into a hole. —*v.t.* **2.** fasten with pegs.

pe·jo'ra·tive, *adj.* disparaging, negative.

pe·koe (pē'kō), *n.* black Oriental tea.

pelf, *n.* money; riches.

pel'i·can, *n.* large bird with a pouched lower bill.

pel·la'gra, *n.* chronic disease caused by inadequate diet.

pel'let, *n.* small ball.

pell'-mell', *adv.* in a disorderly or hasty manner.

pel·lu·cid (pe lōō'sid), *adj.* clear or limpid; transparent.

pelt, *n.* **1.** animal hide, esp. with fur. —*v.t.* **2.** attack with blows or missiles. —*v.i.* **3.** beat relentlessly, as rain.

pel'vis, *n.* basinlike bone in the lower part of the trunk. —**pel'vic**, *adj.*

pen, *n., v.t.,* penned, penning. *n.* **1.** instrument for writing with ink. **2.** small enclosure for animals or storage. —*v.t.* **3.** write. **4.** enclose.

pe'nal, *adj.* pertaining to punishment. —**pe'nal·ize''**, *v.t.*

pen'al·ty, *n., pl.* -ties. **1.** punishment. **2.** disadvantage, hardship.

pen'ance, *n.* **1.** self-imposed punishment for sin. **2.** sacrament of confession of sin.

pen'chant, *n.* strong inclination; liking.

pen'cil, *n.* **1.** cylindrical implement containing graphite for writing, etc. —*v.t.* **2.** paint, draw or write.

pend'ant, *n.* **1.** hanging ornament, e.g. an earring. **2.** duplicate or balancing feature.

pend'ent, *adj.* hanging; overhanging.

pend'ing, *adj.* **1.** undecided; imminent. —*prep.* **2.** while awaiting; until.

pen'du·lum, *n.* freely swinging suspended weight.

pen'e·trate'', *v.t.* -trated, -trating. **1.** enter. **2.** permeate. **3.** understand. **4.** affect deeply. —**pen'e·tra·ble**, *adj.* —**pen''e·tra'tion**, *n.*

pen'guin, *n.* short-legged, flightless aquatic bird.

pen''i·cil'lin, *n.* antibiotic produced by certain molds.

pen·in'su·la, *n.* land body surrounded by water on three sides.

pe'nis, *n.* male organ of copulation and urination.

pen'i·tent, *adj.* **1.** feeling repentance. —*n.* **2.** repentant person. —**pen'i·tence**, *n.* —**pen''i·ten'tial**, *adj.*

pen''i·ten'tia·ry, *n.* prison.

pen'knife'', *n.* small pocketknife; jackknife.

pen'man, *n., pl.* -men. person skilled in using a pen. —**pen'man·ship''**, *n.*

pen'nant, *n.* **1.** small flag for signaling. **2.** flag of championship.

pen'ny, *n., pl.* -nies. smallest denomination of currency. —**pen'ni·less**, *adj.*

pe·nol'o·gy, *n.* study of criminal punish-

ment. —**pe·nol'o·gist**, *n.* —**pe''no·log'i·cal**, *adj.*

pen'sion, *n.* **1.** fixed, periodic payment to a retiree. —*v.t.* **2.** give a pension to. —**pen'sion·er**, *n.*

pen'sive, *adj.* sadly or dreamily thoughtful;quiet.

pent, *adj.* confined; shut up.

pen'ta·gon'', *n.* polygon of five sides.

pen·tam'e·ter, *n.* verse line of five metrical feet

Pen·ta·teuch (pen'ta tōōk''), *n.* first five books of the Old Testament.

pent'house'', *n.* habitable structure on the roof of a building.

pent'-up', *adj.* confined, as emotions.

pen·ul'ti·mate, *adj.* next to the last.

pe·num'bra, *n.* partial shadow. —**pe·num'bral**, *adj.*

pe·nu'ri·ous, *adj.* **1.** miserly; stingy. **2.** impoverished. —**pen'u·ry**, *n.*

pe'on, *n.* unskilled worker, esp. one in bondage. —**pe'on·age**, *n.*

pe'o·ny, *n., pl.* -nies, perennial garden plant with large colorful flowers.

peo'ple, *n., v.t.,* -pled, -pling. *n.* **1.** humanity generally. **2.** random group of persons. **3.** peoples, national, cultural, or racial group. *v.t.* **4.** populate.

pep, *Informal. n.* **1.** energy, vigor. —*v.t.* **2.** pep up, make lively; energize. —**pep'py**, *adj. adj.*

pep'per, *n.* **1.** pungent condiment from an East Indian plant. **2.** hot or mild fruit used as a condiment vegetable. —*v.t.* **3.** season with pepper. **4.** pelt with missiles. **5.** sprinkle as with pepper. —**pep'per·y**, *adj.*

pep'per·mint'', *n.* aromatic herb used as a flavoring.

pep'sin, *n.* stomach enzyme which digests proteins.

pep'tic, *adj.* pertaining to digestion; digestive.

per, *prep.* through; by means of; according to.

per·am'bu·late'', *v.i.,* -ated, -ating, walk about; stroll. —**per·am''bu·la'tion**, *n.*

per·cale', *n.* smooth, closely woven cotton.

per·ceive', *v.t.* **1.** become aware of. **2.** apprehend or understand. —**per·ceiv'a·ble, per·cep'ti·ble**, *adj.* —**per·cep'tion**, *n.*

per·cent', *n.* part in a hundred.

per·cent'age, *n.* **1.** proportion per hundred. **2.** allowance, commission, or rate of interest.

per·cep'tive, *adj.* **1.** pertaining to perception. **2.** understanding; discerning.

perch, *n.* **1.** roost for birds. **2.** high spot. **3.** freshwater food fish. —*v.t., v.i.* **4.** set or rest as on a perch.

per·chance', *adv.* perhaps.

per·co·late'', *v.t., v.i.* -lated, -lating. filter. —per''co·la'tion, *n.*

per·cus'sion, *n.* 1. hard, sharp impact. 2. musical instruments plucked or struck. —per·cus'sive, *adj.*

per·di·em (par dē'əm), by the day.

per·di'tion, *n.* damnation.

per''e·gri·na'tion, *n.* travel from one place to another. —per'e·gri·nate'', *v.i.*

per·emp'to·ry, *adj.* 1. giving no opportunity to refuse or deny. 2. imperative. —per·emp'to·ri·ly, *adv.*

pe·ren'ni·al, *adj.* 1. enduring. 2. lasting more than two years. —*n.* 3. plant growing every year. —per·en·ni·al·ly, *adv.*

per·fect, *adj.* (pər'fəkt) 1. flawless and complete. 2. unmodified. 3. *Grammar.* denoting completed action. —*v.t.* (pərfekt') 4. make perfect. —per'fect·ly, *adj.* —per·fec'tion, *n.*

per·fec'tion·ist, *n.* person who demands perfection.

per'fi·dy, *n., pl.* -dies, treachery; faithlessness. —per·fid'i·ous, *adj.*

per'fo·rate'', *v.t.,* -rated, -rating. pierce through.

per·force', *adv.* necessarily.

per·form', *v.t.* 1. carry out; execute. 2. enact, play, etc. for an audience. —*v.i.* 3. appear in a play, concert, etc. —per·form'ance, *n.* —per·form'er, *n.*

per·fume, *n., v.t.,* -fumed, -fuming, *n.* (pər'fyōōm) 1. sweet odor; fragrance. 2. sweet-smelling liquid for scenting. —*v.t.* (pər fyōōm') 3. scent.

per·func'to·ry, *adj.* routine and unenthusiastic. —per·func'to·ri·ly, *adv.* —per·func'tori·ness, *n.*

per·haps', *adv.* maybe, possibly.

per·i·gee (per'i jē''), *n.* nearest point of an orbit to the earth.

per''i·he'li·on, *n.* nearest point of an orbit to the sun.

per'il, *n.* 1. danger. 2. source of danger. —per'il·ous, *adj.*

pe·rim'e·ter, *n.* outer boundary.

pe''ri·od, *n.* 1. division or extent of time. 2. end; stop. 3. punctuation point at the end of a declarative sentence.

pe''ri·od'ic, *adj.* intermittently or regularly recurring.

pe''ri·od'i·cal, *adj.* 1. periodic. 2. publication appearing at regular intervals. —pe''ri·od'i·cal·ly, *adv.*

pe·riph'er·y, *n., pl.* -eries, 1. boundary of a rounded figure. 2. outer limits; border. —pe·riph'er·al, *adj.*

per'i·scope, *n.* optical instrument for viewing around an obstruction with prisms or mirrors.

per'ish, *v.i.* 1. die, esp. from privation or violence. 2. decay. —per'ish·a·ble, *adj.*

per·i·to·ni·tis (per''i to ni'tis), *n.* inflammation of the abdominal lining.

per'i·win''kle, *n.* 1. edible snail. 2. trailing evergreen plant.

per'jure, *v.t.,* -jured, -juring. make guilty of perjury. —per'jur·er, *n.* —per'jured, *adj.*

per'ju·ry, *n., pl.* -ries. 1. lying under oath. 2. lie so uttered. —per·ju'ri·ous, *adj.*

perk, *v.i.* 1. become lively or vigorous. —*v.t.* 2. raise jauntily, as the head. —perk'y, *adj.*

per'ma·nent, *adj.* existing always. —per'ma·nence, per'ma·nen·cy, *n.* —per'ma·nent·ly, *adj.*

per'me·ate'', *v.* -ated, -ating, *v.t.* 1. penetrate. 2. be diffused through. —*v.i.* 3. become diffused. —per''me·a'tion, *n.* —per'me·a·ble, *adj.*

per·mis'sive, *adj.* 1. granting permission. 2. indulgent; lenient.

per·mit *v.t.,* -mitted, -mitting, *n. v.t.* (pərmit') 1. allow. 2. tolerate. 3. give opportunity for. —*n.* (pər'mit) 4. written permission; license. —per·mis'sion, *n.* —per·mis'si·ble, *adj.*

per''mu·ta'tion, *n.* change, alteration.

per·ni'cious, *adj.* injurious, hurtful.

per''o·ra'tion, *n.* concluding part of a speech.

per·ox'ide, *n.* 1. oxide containing a large amount of oxygen. —*v.t.* 2. bleach with a peroxide, esp. the hair.

per''pen·dic'u·lar, *adj.* 1. vertical. 2. meeting another line at a right angle. —*n.* 3. perpendicular plane or line.

per'pe·trate'', *v.t.,* -trated, -trating, commit; be guilty of. —per''pe·tra'tion, *n.* —per'pe·tra''tor, *n.*

per·pet'u·al, *adj.* 1. permanent. 2. unceasing; constant. —per·pet'u·al·ly, *adv.* —per·pet'u·ate'' *v.t.* —per·pet''u·a'tion, *n.*

per''pe·tu'i·ty, *n.* endless duration.

per·plex', *v.t.* bewilder. —per·plex'i·ty, *n.*

per'quis·ite, *n.* benefit added to regular salary.

per se (pər sā'), by, of, or in itself.

per'se·cute, *v.t.,* -cuted, -cuting, continually harass or oppress. —per''se·cu'tion, *n.* —per'se·cu·tor, *n.*

per''se·vere', *v.t.,* -vered, -vering, persist in spite of obstacles. —per''se·ver'ance, *n.*

per·sim'mon, *n.* astringent, edible North American fruit.

per·sist', *v.i.* 1. continue resolutely. 2. last; endure. —per·sist'ence, *n.* —per·sist'ent, *adj.* —per·sist'ent·ly, *adv.*

per'son, *n.* 1. human being; individual. 2. personality. 3. one's body.

per'son·a·ble, *adj.* 1. pleasing in appearance. 2. sociable.

per'son·age, *n.* person of distinction or note.

per'son·al, *adj.* 1. pertaining to one individual. 2. pertaining to the body and its care, clothing, etc. —**per'son·al·ly**, *adv.* —**per'son·al·ize''**, *v.t.*

per''son·al'i·ty, *n., pl.* -**ties**. 1. distinctive personal character. 2. personally disparaging remark. 3. notable person.

per·so·na non gra·ta (per sō'nə non grat'ə), unwelcome or unacceptable person.

per·son'i·fy, *v.t.,* -**fied**, -**fying**. 1. attribute personal character to. 2. embody; typify. —**per·son''i·fi·ca'tion**, *n.*

per''son·nel', *n.* employees of an organization.

per·spec'tive, *n.* 1. technique of three-dimensional representation. 2. extended view. 3. basis for interpretation.

per''spi·ca'cious, *adj.* acutely perceptive; discerning. —**per''spi·cac'i·ty**, *n.*

per·spire', *v.i.* sweat. —**per''spi·ra'tion**, *n.*

per·suade', *v.t.,* -**suaded**, -**suading**. 1. prevail on by argument. 2. induce belief in; convince. —**per·sua'sive**, *adj.*

per·sua'sion, *n.* 1. process or act of persuading. 2. conviction or belief, opinion.

pert, *adj.* 1. bold; saucy, impudent. 2. lively, sprightly.

per·tain', *v.i.* have reference to; relate.

per''ti·na'cious, *adj.* holding firmly to an opinion or purpose. —**perti·nac'i·ty**, *n.*

per'ti·nent, *adj.* relevant; applicable. —**per'ti·nence, per'ti·nen·cy**, *n.*

per·turb', *v.t.* greatly disturb in mind; upset. —**pertur·ba'tion**, *n.*

pe·ruse', *v.t.* read or survey, esp. with thoroughness. —**pe·ru'sal**, *n.*

per·vade', *v.t.,* -**vaded**, -**vading**. extend or spread throughout; permeate. —**per·va'sive**, *adj.*

per·verse', *adj.* 1. abnormal; corrupt. 2. stubbornly contrary; obstinate. —**per·verse'ly**, *adv.* —**per·ver'si·ty**, *n.*

per·vert', *n.* 1. perverted person, esp. sexually. —*v.t.* 2. deviate from the proper or right course of action. 3. misapply; misconstrue; distort. —**per·ver'sion**, *n.*

pe'so, *n.* monetary unit of Mexico, etc.

pes'si·mism'', *n.* disposition toward the least favorable interpretation or expectation. —**pes'si·mist**, *n.* —**pessi·mis'tic**, *adj.*

pest, *n.* troublesome person or thing; nuisance.

pes'ter, *v.t.* annoy.

pes'ti·cide'', *n.* insecticide.

pes'ti·lence, *n.* deadly epidemic or disease; plague. —**pes'ti·lent**, *adj.*

pes'tle, *n.* implement for grinding or crushing (with a mortar).

pet, *n., adj., v.t.,* **petted**, **petting**. *n.* 1. tamed animal kept for pleasure. 2. darling; favorite. —*v.t.* 3. indulge; pamper. 4. stroke or fondle affectionately. —*adj.* 5. treated lovingly.

pet'al, *n.* colored leaf of a flower.

pe·tite (pə tēt'), *adj.* small or tiny: used in reference to women.

pe·ti'tion, *n.* 1. request or entreaty, esp. when written. —*v.t.* 2. present a petition; ask for. —**pe·ti'tion·er**, *n.*

pet'rel, *n.* small sea bird.

pet'ri·fy'', *v.,* -**fied**, -**fying**. *v.t.* 1. turn into stone; stiffen. 2. paralyze or stupefy with horror, wonder, etc. —*v.i.* 3. become petrified.

pet''ro·chem'i·cal, *n.* chemical derived from petroleum.

pe·tro·le'um, *n.* natural oily liquid found underground.

pe·trol'o·gy, *n.* study of rocks.

pet'ti·coat'', *n.* skirt worn under a dress.

pet'tish, *adj.* peevish; petulant.

pet'ty, *adj.,* -**tier**, -**tiest**. 1. of little importance; trivial. 2. narrow-minded; mean. —**pet'ti·ness**, *n.*

pet'u·lant, *adj.* marked by impatient irritation; irritable, peevish.

pe·tu'nia, *n.* annual garden plant with bright funnelshaped flowers.

pew, *n.* enclosed church bench.

pe'wee, *n.* any of various small birds.

pew'ter, *n.* alloy composed primarily of tin.

pey·o·te, (pā ō'tē), *n.* hallucinogenic drug derived from the mescal cactus.

pha'lanx, *n., pl.* **planxes**, **phalanges**, 1. body or group in formation, e.g. troops. 2. any of the bones of the fingers or toes of mammals.

phal'lus, *n., pl.* **phalli**, 1. penis. 2. symbolic representation of the phallus. —**phal'lic**, *adj.*

phan'tasm, *n.* apparition; illusion.

phan·tas''ma·go'ria, *n.* succession of imagined things.

phan'tom, *n.* insubstantial image; dreamlike apparition.

Phar·aoh, (fa'rō), *n.* ancient Egyptian ruler.

phar'i·see'', *n.* self-righteous person.

phar''ma·ceu'ti·cal, *adj.* of or pertaining to pharmacy. Also, **phar''ma·ceu'tic**.

phar''ma·col'o·gy, *n.* study of drugs, esp. for medical use. —**phar''ma·col'o·gist**, *n.*

phar'ma·cy, *n., pl.* -**cies**. 1. practice of preparing medicines. 2. drug store. —**phar'ma·cist**, *n.*

phar'ynx, *n., pl.* **pharynges**, **pharynxes**. cavity that connects mouth and nasal passages with the esophagus. —**pha·ryn'ge·al**, *adj.*

phase, *n.* **1.** stage of a process. **2.** aspect. —*v.t.* **3.** introduce or withdraw in stages.

pheas'ant, *n.* large, long-tailed, brightly colored game bird.

phe''no·bar'bi·tol, *n.* white powder used as sedative and hypnotic.

phe·nom'e·nal, *n.* **1.** amazing. **2.** pertaining to phenomena.

phe·nom'e·non, *n., pl.* **-na, -nons. 1.** apparent occurrence, circumstance, or fact. **2.** extraordinary person or thing.

phi'al, *n.* vial.

phi·lan'der, *v.i.* (of a man) make love with no serious intentions, —**phi·lan'der·er,** *n.*

phi·lan'thro·py, *n., pl.* **-pies. 1.** love of mankind. **2.** charitable act, work, or organization. —**phil''an·throp'ic, phil''an·throp'i·cal,** *adj.* —**phi·lan'thro·pist,** *n.*

phi·lat'e·ly, *n.* collection and study of postage stamps. —**phi·lat'e·list,** *n.*

phil'har·mon'ic, *adj.* music-loving.

phi·lis'tine, *n.* person indifferent to cultural matters.

phi·lol'o·gy, *n.* linguistics. —**phi·lol'o·gist,** *n.*

phi·los'o·pher, *n.* **1.** reflective thinker; **2.** scholar trained in philosophy. **3.** person who meets difficulties calmly.

phi·los'o·phy, *n., pl.* **-phies. 1.** study of the fundamental truths of life and the universe. **2.** system of philosophical concepts. —**phil''o·soph'i·cal, phil''o·soph'ic,** *adj.* —**phi·los'o·phize'',** *v.i.*

phlegm, (flem) *n.* thick mucus secreted in the nose and throat.

phleg·ma'tic, *adj.* stolid, impassive; apathetic.

phlox, *n.* garden plant with colorful flowers.

pho'bi·a, *n.* persistent and irrational morbid fear.

phoe·be (fē'bē), *n.* small eastern American bird.

phoe·nix (phē'nicks), *n.* mythical bird said to rise from its own ashes.

phone, *n., v.t.,* **phoned, phoning. 1.** telephone. —*v.t.* **2.** make a phone call to.

pho·net'ics, *n.* study of speech sounds. —**pho·net'ic,** *adj.*

pho'no·graph'', *n.* machine for playing records.

pho'ny, *n., adj.,* **-nier, -niest,** *Informal. n.* **1.** fake person or thing.—*adj.* **2.** fake; counterfeit.

phos'phate, *n.* chemical salt often used in fertilizers.

phos''pho·res'cence, *n.* luminescence without sensible heat. —**phos''pho·res'cent,** *adj.*

phos'pho·rus, *n.* solid nonmetallic element found in bones, nerves, etc. —**phos·phor'ic, phos'pho·rous,** *adj.*

pho'to, *n., pl.* **-tos,** photograph.

pho''to·e·lec'tric, *adj.* pertaining to electric effects resulting from light.

pho'to·en·grav''ing, *n.* process of producing an etched printing plate from a photograph or drawing. —**pho'to·en·grave'',** *v.t.*

pho''to·gen'ic, *adj.* suitable for being photographed.

pho'to·graph'', *n.* **1.** picture taken by photography. —*v.i.* **2.** take a photograph. —**pho·tog'ra·pher,** *n.*

pho·tog'ra·phy, *n.* process of producing images on treated surfaces by the action of light. —**pho''to·graph'ic,** *adj.*

pho''to·sen'si·tive, *adj.* sensitive or sensitized to light.

pho''to·syn'the·sis, *n.* process by which chlorophyll-containing plants exposed to sunlight produce carbohydrates.

phrase, *n., v.t.,* **phrased, phrasing,** *n.* **1.** sequence of words conveying a thought. **2.** brief expression or remark. **3.** unit of musical composition. —*v.t.* **4.** express in a certain way.

phra''se·ol'o·gy, *n.* **1.** manner of speaking. **2.** collective expressions or phrases.

phre·net'ic, *adj.* delirious.

phre·nol'o·gy, *n.* study that infers personal characteristics from the shape of the skull. —**phre·nol'o·gist,** *n.*

phy'lum, *n., pl.* **-la.** major division of plant and animal classes.

phys'ic, *n.* medicine, esp. a purgative.

phys'i·cal, *adj.* **1.** pertaining to the body. **2.** pertaining to matter or the material world. **3.** pertaining to physics. —*n.* **4.** medical examination. —**phys'i·cal·ly,** *adv.*

phy·si'cian, *n.* medical doctor.

phys'ics, *n.* science dealing with motion, matter, energy, and force. —**phys'i·cist,** *n.*

phys''i·og'no·my, *n., pl.* **-mies.** facial appearance.

phys''i·og'ra·phy, *n.* science of the earth's surface.

phys''i·ol'o·gy, *n.* science of the functioning of living matter and beings. —**phys''i·o·log'i·cal,** *adj.* —**phys''i·ol'o·gist,** *n.*

phys''i·o·ther'a·py, *n.* treatment of disease by physical means, e.g. exercise, massage, etc.

phy·sique (fə zēk'), *n.* physical constitution of the body; build.

pi, (pī), *n.* Greek letter π, symbol for the value 3.1416, ratio of circumference to diameter.

pi''a·nis'si·mo, *adj* or *adv. Music.* very soft.

pi·an'o, *n., pl.* **-anos,** *adj., adv. n.* **1.** Also, **pi·an''o·for'te,** percussive, musical keyboard instrument with steel strings struck by hammers. —*adj.* **2.** soft. —*adv.* **3.** softly. —**pi·an'ist,** *n.*

pi·az′za, *n.* veranda or porch.

pi′ca, *n.* measure of printing type equal to about a sixth of an inch.

pic″a·yune′, *adj.* insignificant; trivial; petty.

pic′ca·lil′li, *n.* spicy vegetable relish.

pic′co·lo″, *n., pl.* **-los,** small shrill flute.

pick, *v.t.* 1. choose or select. 2. gather, e.g. flowers. 3. separate or pull apart. 4. pierce with a pointed instrument. 5. provoke, e.g. pick a fight. —*n.* 6. choice; selection. 7. Also, **pick′ax,** **pick′axe,** sharp tool for breaking rock. —**pick′er,** *n.*

pick′er·el, *n.* small pike.

pick′et, *n.* 1. protestor stationed by a striking labor union. 2. body or group of soldiers on lookout. 3. pointed fence with pickets. —*v.i.* 4. serve as a picket.

pick′ings, *n.* 1. gleanings. 2. rewards; spoils.

pick′le, *n., v.t.,* **-led, -ling,** *n.* 1. cucumber cured in spiced vinegar. 2. any food preserved in a pickling solution. 3. *Informal.* difficult predicament; bind. —*v.t.* 4. preserve in brine or vinegar.

pick′pock″et, *n.* thief who steals from pockets.

pick′up, *n.* 1. acceleration; energy. 2. revival of action. 3. small open-body truck for hauling.

pick′y, *adj.* fussy, finicky.

pic′nic, *n., v.i.,* **-nicked, -nicking,** *n.* 1. outing with an outdoor meal. —*v.t.* go on a picnic. —**pic′nick·er,** *n.*

pic′ture, *n., v.t.,* **-tured, -turing,** *n.* 1. painting, drawing, photograph, etc. 2. motion picture. —*v.t.* 3. represent in a picture. 4. conceive; visualize. —**pic·tor′i·al,** *adj.*

pic″tur·esque′, *adj.* 1. charming; quaint. 2. striking; vivid.

pie, *n.* baked dish of pastry crust and filling, e.g. meat, fruit, etc.

pie′bald″, *adj.* marked by patches of different colors.

piece, *n., v.t.,* **pieced, piecing,** *n.* 1. part or single portion. 2. artistic creation. 3. firearm. —*v.t.* 4. join or repair from pieces.

piece′meal″, *adv.* 1. piece by piece. 2. into fragments.

pied (pid), *adj.* many-colored; variegated.

pier, *n.* 1. massive support. 2. structure loading and unloading vessels.

pierce, *v.t.,* **pierced, piercing,** 1. penetrate into or through. 2. make a hole into.

pi′e·ty, *n.* religious dutifulness; devoutness.

pig, *n.* 1. swine, esp. young. 2. oblong metal casting.

pi′geon, *n.* short-legged, stout-bodied bird.

pi′geon·hole″, *n., v.t.,* **-holed, -holing,** *n.* 1. small compartment, e.g. in a desk. —*v.t.* 2. place in a pigeonhole; classify.

pig′ment, *n.* coloring matter. —**pig″men·ta′tion,** *n.*

pig′tail, *n.* tight braid of back hair.

pike, *n.* 1. large, slender freshwater fish. 2. long wooden spear. 3. highway.

pik′er, *n. Informal.* person who does things in a small or cheap way.

pi·laf (pēʹlaf″), *n.* seasoned rice dish.

pi·las′ter, *n.* column that projects slightly from a wall.

pile, *n., v.t.,* **piled, piling.** *n.* 1. heap. 2. support driven into the ground. 3. short standing fibers, as in a rug. 4. nuclear reactor. 5. **piles,** hemorrhoids —*v.t.* 6. put in a pile. —*v.t., v.i.* 7. accumulate.

pil′fer, *v.i., v.t.* steal.

pil′grim, *n.* traveler in foreign lands, esp. to a holy place. —**pil′grim·age,** *n.*

pill, *n.* medicine in tablet or capsule form.

pil′lage, *v.t.,* **-laged, -laging.** loot; plunder.

pil′lar, *n.* masonry column.

pill′box″, *n.* 1. low shelter against gunfire. 2. small container for pills.

pil′lory, *n., pl.* **-ries.** wooden frame with head and arm holes for public punishment.

pil′low, *n.* cushion filled with feathers, etc. for support, esp. of the head. —**pil′low·case″,** *n.*

pi′lot, *n.* 1. person who guides a ship or airplane. —*v.t.* 2. steer; guide. —*adj.* 3. experimental.

pi·men′to, *n., pl.* **-tos.** 1. dried fruit of a tropical tree; allspice. 2. pimiento.

pi·mien′to, *n., pl.* **-tos.** sweet, red, garden pepper.

pimp, *n.* person who finds clients for a prostitute.

pim′ple, *n.* small, inflamed swelling on the skin. —**pim′ply,** *adj.*

pin, *n., v.t.,* **pinned, pinning,** *n.* 1. slender, pointed fastener. 2. piece of jewelry fastened to a garment. 3. wooden target piece in bowling. —*v.t.* 4. fasten with a pin. 5. hold tight, bind.

pin′a·fore″, *n.* sleeveless dress or apron, esp. for a child.

pince·nez (pansʹnā″), *n.* eyeglasses held on the nose by a pinching spring.

pin′cers, *n.* gripping tool with two handles.

pinch, *v.t.* 1. squeeze, e.g. with the thumb and forefinger. 2. economize. 3. steal. 4. arrest. —*n.* 5. act or instance of pinching. 6. tiny amount.

pinch′hit″, *v.i.,* **-hit, -hitting,** substitute for someone else. —**pinch″hit′ter,** *n.*

pine, *n., v.i.,* **pined, pining,** *v.i.* 1. yearn, esp. painfully. 2. gradually fail in health from grief. —*n.* 3. cone-bearing evergreen tree with needle-like leaves.

pine′ap″ple, *n.* tropical plant with a juicy, edible fruit.

pin′feath″er, *n.* feather just beginning to develop.

pin·ion (pin′yən), *n.* **1.** end of a bird's wing. **2.** small gear wheel. —*v.t.* **3.** restrain; bind.

pink, *n.* **1.** light red. **2.** colorful, showy garden flower. **3.** highest condition of health. —*adj.* **4.** of the color pink.

pin′na·cle, *n.* highest part or position.

pi·noch·le, (pē′nuk il″), *n.* game played with forty-eight cards.

pint, *n.* **1.** unit of liquid measure equal to 16 fluid ounces or half a quart. **2.** unit of dry measure equal to half a quart.

pin′to, *n., pl.* **-tos.** horse with white and brown patches.

pin′up″, *n.* picture of a beautiful man or woman, esp. unclothed.

pin′wheel″, *n.* toy with a wheel that spins on the end of a stick.

pi″o·neer′, *n.* **1.** early settler or adventurer. **2.** first person to do something. —*v.i.* **3.** prepare a way for others.

pi′ous, *adj.* **1.** devout. **2.** sacred. —**pi′ous·ly,** *adv.* —**pi′ous·ness,** *n.*

pipe, *n., v.t.,* **piped, piping. 1.** tube for carrying gas, water, etc. **2.** tube with a bowl at one end for smoking tobacco. **3.** tube used in a musical instrument. —*v.t.* **4.** carry by pipe. —**pi′per,** *n.* —**pipe′line″,** *n.*

pip′ing, *n.* **1.** pipes; plumbing. **2.** music of pipes. **3.** material to trim edges.

pip′pin, *n.* kind of yellowish apple.

pi·quant (pē′kənt), *adj.* **1.** pleasantly sharp; pungent. **2.** provocative; charming. —**pi′quan·cy,** *n.*

pique, *n., v.t.,* **piqued, piquing. 1.** irritation; resentment. —*v.t.* **2.** arouse resentment in, esp. by wounding pride. **3.** provoke or incite.

pi′ra·cy, *n., pl.* **-cies. 1.** robbery at sea or in the air. **2.** unauthorized use of copyrighted or patented material. —**pi′rate,** *n., v.t.*

pir″ou·ette′, *v.i.,* **-etted, -etting.** *n. v.i.* **1.** whirl about on one foot or on the toes, esp. in ballet. —*n.* **2.** such a movement.

pis·ca·to·ri·al (pis″kə to′bi al), *adj.* pertaining to fishing.

pis·ta′chi·o″, *n., pl.* **-os.** nut with an edible greenish seed.

pis′til, *n.* seed-bearing organ in a flower.

pis′tol, *n.* small hand-carried firearm.

pis′ton, *n.* reciprocating disk moved by the pressure of steam, combustion gas, etc. in a cylinder.

pit *n., v.t.,* **pitted, pitting. 1.** hole in the ground. **2.** cavity or hollow in the body. **3.** front part of the main floor in a theater. **4.** stone or seed of a fruit.

—*v.t.* **5.** set against another. **6.** remove the pit from.

pitch, *v.t.* **1.** set up, as a tent. **2.** throw or toss. **3.** set at a certain level or point. —*v.i.* **4.** fall or plunge. —*n.* **5.** height. **6.** slope. **7.** musical tone. **8.** sticky substance from coal tar or pine bark. **9.** act or instance of pitching.

pitch′blende″, *n.* mineral that is the principal source of radium and uranium.

pitch′er, *n.* **1.** spouted container for liquids. **2.** one who pitches.

pitch′fork″, *n.* large, sharp-pointed fork for pitching hay.

pit′e·ous, *adj.* pitiful; pathetic.

pit′fall″, *n.* snare; hidden difficulty.

pith, *n.* **1.** loose spongy tissue. **2.** essence; gist. —**pith′y,** *adj.*

pit′i·a·ble, *adj.* **1.** deserving pity. **2.** contemptible. —**pit′i·a·bly,** *adv.*

pit′i·ful, *adj.* deserving pity. **2.** feeling pity. —**pit′i·ful·ly,** *adv.* —**pit′i·ful·ness,** *n.*

pit′tance, *n.* small portion or amount.

pi·tu′i·tar″y, *n.* pertaining to a gland at the base of the brain.

pity, *n., pl.* **pities,** *v.t.,* **pitied, pitying,** *n.* **1.** sympathy for wretchedness. **2.** cause for regret. —*v.t.* **3.** feel pity for. —**pit′i·less,** *adj.* —**pit′i·less·ly,** *adv.*

piv′ot, *n.* **1.** point or object for turning. —*v.i.* **2.** turn around a point.

pix′y, *n., pl.* **pixies.** fairy; mischievous sprite. Also, **pix′ie.**

piz′za, *n.* flat pie covered with a spiced mixture of tomato sauce, cheese, etc.

plac′ard, *n.* posted public notice.

pla′cate, *v.t.,* **-cated, -cating.** appease; pacify. —**pla′ca·ble,** *adj.* —**pla·ca′tion,** *n.*

place, *n., v.t.,* **placed, placing. 1.** particular point in space. **2.** function. **3.** social position. **4.** stead; lieu. —*v.t.* **5.** put in a place. **6.** identify; recognize. —**place′ment,** *n.*

pla·cen′ta, *n.* uterine organ which nourishes the fetus.

plac′er, *n.* gravel containing gold particles.

plac′id, *adj.* serene; peaceful. —**plac′id·ly,** *adv.* —**pla·cid′i·ty,** *n.*

plack′et, *n.* slit in a garment.

pla′gia·rize″, *v.t.,* **-rized, -rizing.** appropriate wrongfully, as another's writings. —**pla′gia·rism″,** *n.* —**pla′gia·rist,** *n.*

plague, *n., v.t.,* **plagued, plaguing. 1.** pestilence. **2.** affliction, vexation; irritation. —*v.t.* **3.** trouble; annoy.

plaid, *n.* **1.** woolen garment with a pattern of multi-colored crossbars. —*adj.* **2.** such a pattern.

plain, *adj.* **1.** evident; obvious. **2.** candid. **3.** unpretentious. **4.** simple, uncomplicated. **5.** homely. —*n.* **6.** flat, open area or space of ground. —**plain'ly,** *adv.*

plain'tiff, *n.* complaining party in a civil case.

plain'tive, *adj.* melancholy, sad.

plait, *n., v.t.* 1. braid. 2. pleat.

plan, *n., v.t.,* **planned, planning.** *n.* 1. drawing or diagram. 2. intended scheme or method. —*v.t.* 3. make a plan of. —**plan'ner,** *n.*

plane, *n., adj., v.,* **planed, planing,** *n.* 1. flat surface. 2. level, e.g. of experience, attainment, etc. 3. airplane. 4. bladed tool for smoothing wood. —*adj.* 5. flat, level. —*v.t.* 6. smooth or shape with a plane. —*v.i.* 7. glide.

plan'et, *n.* solid celestial body that revolves around the sun. —**plan'e·tar''y,** *n.*

plan''e·tar'i·um, *n.* optical device which projects images of celestial bodies on a dome.

plank, *n.* long slab of lumber.

plant, *n.* 1. any of the vegetable group of organisms. 2. buildings and equipment of a business. —*v.t.* 3. put in the ground to grow. 4. put plants in. —**plant'er,** *n.*

plan·ta'tion, *n.* estate esp. for farming, etc.

plaque, *n.* decorative or commemorative tablet.

plas'ma, *n.* liquid element of blood or lymph.

plas'ter, *n.* 1. composition applied to walls, etc. 2. medicinal dressing. —*v.t.* 3. treat or cover with plaster.

plas'tic, *n.* 1. molded synthetic material.—*adj.* 2. capable of being molded. 3. characterized or produced by molding. —**plas·tic'i·ty,** *n.*

plate, *n., v.t.,* **plated, plating.** *n.* 1. thin, flat piece of material. 2. shallow dish from which food is served and eaten. 3. silver or gold ware. 4. denture. —*v.t.* 5. coat with metal.

pla·teau', *n.* large, raised plain.

plat'form, *n.* 1. raised floor area. 2. declaration of political principles.

plat'i·num, *n.* valuable, silver-white metallic element.

plat'i·tude'', *n.* trite, pompous, or self-righteous remark. —**plat''i·tu'di·nous,** *adj.*

pla·ton'ic, *adj.* 1. spiritual; idealistic. 2. pertaining to close, non-sexual love.

pla·toon', *n.* small military unit.

plat'ter, *n.* large, shallow serving dish.

plat'y·pus, *n.* small Australian aquatic mammal.

plau'dit, *n.* burst of applause.

plau'si·ble, *adj.* seemingly true or believable. —**plau''si·bil'i·ty,** *n.* **plau'si·bly,** *adv.*

play, *n.* 1. dramatic composition. 2. recre-

ational activity. 3. fun; pleasure. 4. maneuver, as in sports. 5. free motion. —*v.t.* 6. participate in a play or game. 7. perform on a musical instrument. —*v.i.* 8. amuse onself. 9. move freely. —**play'er,** *n.* —**play'ful,** *adj.*

play'pen, *n.* portable enclosed play area for a baby.

play'thing, *n.* toy.

play'wright, *n.* writer of plays.

pla'za, *n.* 1. public square. 2. shopping center.

plea, *n.* 1. appeal. 2. acknowledgment of denial of guilt.

plead, *v.,* **pleaded** or **plead, pleading,** *v.i.* 1. appeal earnestly. 2. make allegations in court. 3. argue a case in court. —*v.t.* 4. allege in excuse or justification.

pleas'ant, *adj.* agreeable; pleasing. —**pleas'ant·ly,** *adv.*

pleas'an·try, *n., pl.* **-tries,** humorous or agreeable remark.

please, *v.,* **pleased, pleasing,** *v.t.* 1. give satisfaction or pleasure to. —*v.i.* 2. give pleasure. —*interj.* 3. will you kindly? —**pleas'ing·ly,** *adv.*

pleas'ure, *n.* 1. enjoyment. 3. will or desire. —**pleas'ur·a·ble,** *adj.*

pleat, *n.* 1. double fold in cloth. —*v.t.* 2. fold in pleats.

ple·be'ian (ple bē'ən), *adj.* 1. of or pertaining to the common people. 2. common; vulgar. —*n.* 3. plebeian person.

pleb''i·scite'', *n.* direct vote by the people.

plec'trum, *n.* pick for a guitar, etc.

pledge, *n., v.,* **pledged, pledging,** *n.* 1. solemn promise or oath. 2. property given in security for a loan. —*v.t.* 3. bind or vow by a pledge. 4. stake.

ple'na·ry, *adj.* full; complete.

plen''i·po·ten'ti·ar''y, *n., pl.* **-aries,** diplomat having full authority.

plen'i·tude'', *n.* fullness.

plen'ty, *n.* abundant supply. —**plen'te·ous, plen'ti·ful,** *adj.*

pleth'o·ra, *n.* profuseness.

pleu'ri·sy, *n.* inflammation of chest and lung membranes.

plex'us, *n.* 1. network of nerves or blood vessels. 2. intricate network of component parts.

pli'a·ble, *adj.* 1. flexible or easily bent. 2. easily influenced; adaptable. —**pli''a·bil'i·ty,** *n.*

pli'ant, *adj.* pliable. —**pli'an·cy,** *n.*

pli'ers, *n., pl.* small pincers for grabbing, bending, etc.

plight, *n.* 1. predicament. —*v.t.* 2. promise in marriage.

plod, *v.i.,* **plodded, plodding,** 1. walk slowly or heavily. 2. work laboriously; drudge. —**plod'der,** *n.*

plot, *v.,* **plotted, plotting,** *n.* 1. secret scheme. 2. outline of a novel, etc. 3. piece of land. —*v.t.* 4. plan secretly. 5.

mark on a map, esp. position or course. —*v.i.* **6.** make secret plans; conspire. —**plot′ter,** *n.*

plov′er, *n.* shore bird related to the sandpiper.

plow, *n.* **1.** implement for dividing soil. **2.** scraping implement for removing snow. —*v.t.* **3.** turn or furrow with or as with a plow. —*v.i.* **4.** move slowly or forcefully. Also, **plough.** —**plow′man,** *n.*

plow′share″, *n.* blade of a plow.

ploy, *n.* trick intended to trap or embarrass; tactic.

pluck, *v.t.* **1.** pull things from. **2.** pull suddenly or forcefully. —*n.* **3.** courage.

plug, *n., v.,* **plugged, plugging.** *n.* **1.** object for stopping a hole. **2.** device on an electrical cord which makes the connection in the socket. **3.** *Informal.* endorsement or advertisement. —*v.t.* **4.** stop or close with a plug; insert.

plum, *n.* sweet, juicy fruit.

plum′age, *n.* feathers of a bird; finery, esp. in dress.

plumb, *n.* **1.** heavy weight on a measuring line. —*adv.* **2.** vertically. **3.** fully. —*adj.* **4.** vertical. —*v.t.* **5.** measure the depth of.

plumb′ing, *n.* system of water pipes. —**plumb′er,** *n.*

plume, *n.* **1.** feather, esp. a large, conspicuous one. **2.** ornamental tuft.

plum′met, *n.* **1.** plumb on a line. —*v.i.* **2.** plunge.

plump, *adj.* **1.** fat; chubby. —*v.i.* **2.** drop or fall heavily. **3.** favor something strongly.

plun′der, *v.t.* **1.** rob or pillage. —*n.* **2.** act or instance of plundering. **3.** loot; spoils.

plunge, *v.,* **plunged, plunging** *n., v.t.* **1.** thrust, as into liquid. **2.** thrust into a condition or predicament. —*v.i.* **3.** rush; dash. **4.** pitch forward. —*n.* **5.** dive or fall.

plu′ral, *adj.* denoting more than one.

plu·ral′i·ty, *n.* **1.** majority. **2.** number of votes for a leading candidate over the number for a rival.

plus, *prep.* **1.** increased by. —*n.* **2.** mathematical sign for addition or for a positive number. **3.** something additional. —*adj.* **4.** pertaining to addition. **5.** positive.

plush, *n.* **1.** long-piled fabric. —*adj.* **2.** fancy. —**plush′y,** *adj.*

plu·toc′ra·cy, *n., pl.* **-cies, 1.** rule by or power of the wealthy. **2.** controlling wealthy group. —**plu′to·crat″,** *n.*

plu·to′ni·um, *n.* radioactive element.

ply, *v.,* **plied, plying,** *n., pl.* **plies.** *v.t.* **1.** work at or with. **2.** attempt to persuade. —*v.t., v.i.* **3.** travel regularly. —*n.* **4.** thickness or layer.

ply′wood, *n.* sheeting of thin plies of wood glued together.

pneu·mat·ic (noo mat′ik), *adj.* pertaining to, or using air or wind.

pneu·mo·nia (noo mō′nyə), *n.* inflamed lung disease.

poach, *v.i.* **1.** trespass to hunt or fish illegally. —*v.t.* **2.** cook in hot but not boiling water. —**poach′er,** *n.*

pock, *n.* mark on the skin; scar, esp. from smallpox.

pock′et, *n.* **1.** pouch in a garment. **2.** cavity. **3.** isolated group or area. —*v.t.* **4.** put in one's pocket. **6.** take possession of.

pock′et·book″, *n.* purse; handbag.

pod, *n.* vegetable seed covering.

po·di′a·try, *n.* medical treatment of the foot. —**po·di′a·trist,** *n.*

po′di·um, *n.* small platform.

po′em, *n.* composition in verse.

po′et·ry, *n.* rhythmical, verse composition. —**po′et,** *fem.,* **po′et·ess,** *n.* —**po·et′ic, po·et′i·cal,** *adj.*

po′grom, *n.* organized massacre.

poign·ant (poin′yənt), *adj.* deeply moving. —**poign′an·cy,** *n.*

poin·set′ti·a, *n.* tropical plant with scarlet flowers.

point, *n.* **1.** sharp end. **2.** dot. **3.** specific time or position. **4.** individual detail or idea. **5.** reason or meaning. —*v.i.* **6.** indicate a direction. —*v.t.* **7.** direct or turn. —**point′less,** *adj.*

point′-blank′, *adj.* **1.** direct; plain. —*adv.* **2.** directly.

point′er, *n.* **1.** something that points or indicates. **2.** breed of hunting dog.

poise, *n., v.,* **poised, poising.** *n.* **1.** balance; composure. —*v.i.* **2.** be balanced. **3.** hover, e.g. a bird in the air. —*v.t.* **4.** balance.

poi′son, *n.* **1.** substance that kills or harms. —*v.t.* **2.** administer poison to. **3.** corrupt. —**poi′son·ous,** *adj.*

poke, *v.,* **poked, poking** *n., v.i., v.t., n.* thrust.

pok′er, *n.* **1.** metal rod for poking fires. **2.** card game.

po′lar, *adj.* pertaining to a pole of the earth, a magnet, etc.

pole, *n.* **1.** long, slender, round object. **2.** end of an axis. **3.** terminal of a battery. **4.** areas where magnetism is concentrated.

pole′cat″, *n.* skunk.

po·lem′ics, *n.* art of argument. —**po·lem′ic,** *adj.*

po·lice′, *n., v.t.,* **-liced, -licing.** *n.* **1.** governmental organization for enforcing the law. —*v.t.* **2.** control or regulate. —**po·lice′man,** *fem.,* **po·lice′wom″an,** *n.*

pol′i·cy, *n., pl.* **-cies, 1.** course of principle action. **2.** insurance contract.

pol"i·o·my"e·li'tis *n.* infantile spinal paralysis. Also, po'li·o.

pol'ish, *v.t.* 1. make smooth and glossy. 2. refine in behavior. 3. bring to a perfected state. —*n.* 4. polishing material. 5. gloss. 6. refinement.

po·lit'bu"ro, *n.* primary governing body of a Communist country.

po·lite', *adj.* 1. marked by good manners. 2. cultivated. —po·lite'ly, *adv.* —po·lite'ness, *n.*

pol'i·tic, *adj.* 1. expedient. 2. political.

pol'i·tics, *n.* 1. theory and conduct of government. 2. political affairs and methods. —po·lit'i·cal, *adj.* —pol'i·ti'cian, *n.*

pol'ka, *n.* lively dance.

poll, *n.* 1. casting of votes. 2. total of votes. 3. place of voting. 4. solicitation of opinion. —*v.t.* 5. receive votes. 6. question regarding opinions.

pol'len, *n.* spores of a seed plant. —pol'li·nate", *v.t.* —pol"li·na'tion, *n.*

pol·lute', *v.t.*, -luted, -luting. make impure; contaminate. —pol·lu'tion, *n.*

po'lo, *n.* ball game played on horseback.

pol"o·naise', *n.* slow dance from Poland.

po·lo'ni·um, *n.* radioactive metallic element.

pol'ter·geist", *n.* mischievous ghost or spirit.

pol·troon', *n.* coward.

pol'y·an"dry, *n.* marriage to more than one husband at a time.

po·lyg'a·my, *n.* marriage to more than one spouse at a time. —po·lyg'a·mist, *n.* —po·lyg'a·mous, *adj.*

pol'y·glot", *adj.* 1. knowing a number of languages. 2. made up of several languages.

pol'y·gon", *n.* closed plane figures with three or more sides. —po·lyg'o·nal, *adj.*

pol"y·graph, *n.* a lie detector.

pol"y·he'dron, *n., pl.* -drons, -dra, closed solid figure.

pol'y·mer, *n.* chemical compound of large molecules formed by smaller but similar molecules.

pol'yp, *n.* 1. projecting growth from a mucous membrane surface. 2. small aquatic organism.

po·ly'pho·ny, *n.* musical composition with independent melodic lines. —pol"y·phon'ic, *adj.*

pol"y·syl·lab'ic, *adj.* having many syllables.

pol'y·the"ism, *n.* belief in more than one god. —pol'y·the"ist, *n.* —pol"y·the'is·tic, *adj.*

pome'gran"ate, *n.* tropical, red fruit with edible seeds.

pom·mel (pum'əl), *n., v.t.*, -eled, -eling. *n.* 1. knob, e.g. on a sword hilt. —*v.t.* 2. beat or strike repeatedly.

pomp, *n.* stately display.

pom'pa·dour", *n.* hair style with hair brushed high over the forehead.

pom'pon, *n.* ornamental ball or tuft.

pomp'ous, *adj.* 1. pretentiously self-important; ostentatious. 2. excessively dignified. —pom·pos'i·ty, *n.* —pomp'ous·ly, *adv.*

pon'cho, *n., pl.* -chos, *n.* blanket-like cloak with an opening for the head.

pond, *n.* small body of water.

pon'der, *v.i., v.t.* consider deeply.

pon'der·ous, *adj.* 1. heavy. 2. lacking grace.

pone, *n.* oval-shaped cornmeal biscuit.

pon'iard, *n.* dagger.

pon'tiff, *n.* bishop or head priest, esp. a pope. —pon·tif'i·cal, *adj.*

pon·tif'i·cate, *v.i.*, -cated, -cating. speak dogmatically.

pon·toon', *n.* flat-bottomed boat used esp. in construction.

po'ny, *n., pl.* -nies. young horse.

poo'dle, *n.* curly-haircd breed of dog.

pool, *n.* 1. small, still body of fresh water. 2. group of available workers, automobiles, etc. 3. game similar to billiards. —*v.t.* 4. put into a common fund or effort.

poop, *n.* upper deck at the stern of a ship.

poor, *adj.* 1. having little money. 2. lacking. 3. inferior. —*n.* 4. poor people. —poor'ly, *adv.*

pop, *v.*, popped, popping, *n., v.i., v.t.* 1. burst with a quick, explosive sound. —*v.i.* 2. bulge, as the eyes. —*n.* 3. sound of popping. 4. carbonated soft drink.

pop'corn", *n.* Indian corn whose kernels open into a soft, starchy mass when heated.

pope, *n. Often cap.* head of the Roman Catholic Church.

pop'lar, *n.* any of various quick-growing trees.

pop'lin, *n.* ribbed, plain-woven fabric.

pop'o"ver, *n.* very light biscuit.

pop'py, *n., pl.* -pies, herb with a showy flower, one type of which yields opium.

pop'u·lace, *n.* people; general public.

pop'u·lar, *adj.* 1. pertaining to the general public. 2. widely liked or approved. —pop'u·lar·ly, *adv.* —pop"u·lar'i·ty, *n.* —pop'u·lar·ize, *v.t.*

pop'u·late", *v.t.*, -lated, -lating. 1. inhabit. 2. furnish with inhabitants.

pop"u·la'tion, *n.* 1. number of people. 2. body of inhabitants.

pop'u·lous, *adj.* having many people.

por'ce·lain, *n.* shiny ceramic ware.

porch, *n.* open, often roofed, appendage to a building; veranda.

por·cine (por' sīn), *adj*. of or suggesting swine.

por·cu·pine'', *n*. rodent covered with stiff, sharp quills.

pore, *v.i.*, pored, poring, *n.*, *v.i.* 1. meditate or read attentively. —*n*. 2. minute opening in the skin.

por'gy, *n*. salt-water food fish.

pork, *n*. flesh of swine used as food.

por·nog'ra·phy, *n*. erotic writing or art intended for sexual excitement. —**por''no·graph'ic**, *adj*.

po'rous, *adj*. permeable to liquids and air.

por'poise, *n*. any of several aquatic mammals including the common dolphin.

por'ridge, *n*. cereal boiled in milk or water.

por'rin·ger, *n*. low dish, often with a handle.

port, *n*. 1. loading and unloading place for ships and aircraft. 2. when facing the bow, the left side of a ship. 3. a sweet, red wine. 4. (computers) point at which peripheral components can be connected.

port'a·ble, *adj*. easily carried; small. —**port''a·bil'i·ty**, *n*.

por'tage, *n*. carrying of goods and boats overland.

por'tal, *n*. gate or door.

por·tend', *v.t.* 1. indicate in advance. 2. indicate; signify.

por'tent, *n*. 1. omen. 2. ominous significance. —**por·ten'tous**, *adj*.

por'ter, *n*. 1. doorman. 2. baggage carrier.

por'ter·house'', *n*. choice cut of beefsteak with a large tenderloin.

port'fo'li·o'', *n*. 1. portable case for documents. 2. office and duties of a government minister. 3. securities and stocks held by an investor.

port'hole'', *n*. window, esp. round, in the side of a plane or ship.

por'ti·co'', *n.*, *pl.* -coes or -cos. roof supported by a colonnade; porch.

por'tion, *n*. 1. part or share. 2. personal fate. —*v.t.* 3. divide into portions.

port'ly, *adj*. fat; chubby.

por'trait, *n*. picture or description of a person. —**por'trai·ture**, *n*.

por·tray', *v.t.* 1. depict or represent in a portrait. 2. represent dramatically. —**por·tray'al**, *n*.

por·tu·lac'a, *n*. tropical herb with showy flowers.

pose, *v.*, posed, posing, *n.*, *v.i.* 1. hold a position. 2. assume a character or attitude. —*v.t.* 3. propound or state. —*n*. 4. fixed position. 5. assumed character. —**po'ser**, *n*.

po·si'tion, *n*. 1. location. 2. posture. 3. opinion on an issue. 4. job. —*v.t.* 5. place.

pos'i·tive, *adj*. 1. affirmative. 2. certain. 3. with light and shade as in the original. 4. numerically greater than zero. 5. electrical charge with more protons than electrons. 6. showing the presence of something tested for. —*n*. 7. something positive. —**pos'i·tive·ly**, *adv*. —**pos'i·tive·ness**, *n*.

pos'se, *n*. group of persons assisting a law enforcement officer.

pos·sess', *v.t.* 1. have or own. 2. dominate. —**pos·ses'sive**, *adj*. —**pos·ses'sion**, *n*. —**pos·ses'sor**, *n*.

pos'si·ble, *adj*. capable of existing or happening. —**pos'sibly**, *adv*. —**pos''si·bil'i·ty**, *n*.

pos'sum, *n*. opossum.

post, *n*. 1. upright column or pole. 2. appointed job, station or task. 3. permanent military station. —*v.t.* 4. put up, as a public announcement. 5. assign to a place. 6. enter in a ledger. 7. mail.

post'age, *n*. 1. charge for mailing. 2. stamps, etc. for mailing.

post'al, *adj*. pertaining to mail.

post'card, *n*. message card mailed without an envelope.

post'er, *n*. public advertisement.

pos·te'ri·or, *adj*. 1. situated behind. 2. later in time. —*n*. 3. buttocks, rump.

pos'ter''i·ty, *n*. 1. descendants. 2. succeeding or future generations.

pos'tern, *n*. 1. back door or gate. 2. private entrance.

post'haste', *adv*. as quickly as possible.

post'hu·mous, *adj*. 1. published after the death of the author. 2. born after the death of the father. —**post'hu·mous·ly** *adv*.

post'man, *n*. mailman.

post'mark'', *n*. 1. postal mark indicating a time and place of reception by a post office. —*v.t.* 2. put a postmark on.

post'mas''ter, *n*. manager of a post office.

post·mor'tem, *adj*. 1. following death. —*n*. 2. examination of a corpse.

post'of''fice, *n*. government agency that handles mail.

post·op'er·a·tive, *adj*. following a surgical operation.

post'paid', *adj.*, *adv*. with postage prepaid.

post·pone', *v.t.*, -poned, -poning, delay, as action. —**post·pone'ment**, *n*.

post'script'', *n*. note added to a finished letter.

pos·tu·late, *v.t.*, -lated, -lating, *n.*, *v.t.* (pos'tyŏŏ lāt) 1. assume as true. —*n*. (pos'tyŏŏ lət) 2. postulated proposition.

pos'ture, *n.*, *v.*, -tured, -turing, *n*. 1. position of the body. 2. attitude on a given subject. —*v.i.* 3. affect an attitude. —*v.t.* 4. place in a specific position.

post'war', *adj.* after a war.

po'sy, *n.*, *pl.* **-sies**, small bouquet.

pot, *n.*, *v.t.*, **potted, potting.** *n.* 1. deep, round container. —*v.t.* 2. put or plant in a pot.

po'ta·ble, *adj.* drinkable.

pot'ash'', *n.* potassium carbonate, esp. from wood ashes.

po·tas'si·um, *n.* silver, metallic, chemical element used in glass, fertilizer, etc.

po·ta'tion, *n.* drink, esp. alcoholic.

po·ta'to, *n.*, *pl.* **-toes.** edible tuber of a common vegetable plant.

po'tent, *adj.* 1. powerful. 2. sexually capable. —**po'tence, po'ten·cy,** *n.*

po'ten·tate'', *n.* sovereign; ruler.

po·ten'tial, *adj.* 1. possible; capable of being realized. —*n.* 2. possible ability. —**po·ten''ti·al'i·ty,** *n.* —**po·ten'tial·ly,** *adv.*

po'tion, *n.* drink, esp. a medicinal one.

pot·pour·ri (pŏ'' pə rē'), *n.* miscellaneous collection.

pot'ter, *n.* maker of earthenware.

pot'ter·y, *n.* 1. dishes, pots, mugs, etc. made of baked clay. 2. place where earthenware is made.

pouch, *n.* 1. sack or bag. 2. baglike part of a marsupial.

poul'try, *n.* domestic fowl, e.g. chicken.

pounce, *v.i.*, **pounced, pouncing.** swoop down suddenly.

pound, *n.* 1. unit of avoirdupois weight equal to 16 ounces or troy weight equal to 12 ounces. 2. British monetary unit. 3. enclosure for stray dogs, etc. —*v.t.* 4. strike forcefully and repeatedly. 5. crush or compact by pounding. —*v.i.* 6. throb or beat violently, as the heart.

pound'cake'', *n.* rich, sweet cake.

pour, *v.t.* 1. cause to flow. —*v.i.* 2. rain heavily. —*n.* 3. act or instance of pouring.

pout, *v.i.* 1. look sullen; act hurt. —*n.* 2. sullen mood, look or behavior.

pov'er·ty, *n.* 1. lack of money. 2. deficiency.

pow'der, *n.* 1. dry substance of very fine particles. —*v.t.* 2. reduce to powder. 3. apply powder to. —**pow'der·y,** *adj.*

pow'er, *n.* 1. ability to act. 2. personal ability. 3. authority. 4. influential person, nation, etc. 5. physical force. 6. magnifying capacity of a lens. —**pow'er·ful,** *adj.* —**pow'er·ful·ly,** *adv.* —**pow'er·less,** *adj.*

pow'wow'', *n.* American Indian conference.

pox, *n.* any disease marked by skin pustules.

prac'ti·ca·ble, *adj.* feasible.

prac'ti·cal, *adj.* 1. pertaining to practice. 2. useful. 3. aware of realities. 4. virtual. —**prac''ti·cal'i·ty,** *n.* —**prac'ti·cal·ly,** *adv.*

prac'tice, *n.*, *v.*, **-ticed, -ticing.** *n.* 1. custom. 2. actual performance. 3. repeated exercise. 4. professional activity. —*v.i.*, *v.t.* 5. Also, **prac'tise,** perform habitually or repeatedly. —**prac'ticed,** *adj.*

prac'ti·tion·er, *n.* person who practices a profession.

prag·ma'tic, *adj.* concerned with practical values and consequences. —**prag'ma·tist,** *n.* —**prag'ma·tism,** *n.*

prai'rie, *n.* flat, treeless, rolling grassland.

praise, *n.*, *v.t.*, **praised, praising,** *n.* 1. expressed approval. 2. homage. —*v.t.* 3. express approval of. 4. worship. —**praise'wor''thy,** *adj.*

prance, *v.i.*, **pranced, prancing.** 1. spring on the hind legs. 2. swagger.

prank, *n.* mischievous trick. —**prank'ster,** *n.*

prate, *v.*, **prated, prating,** *v.i.*, *v.t.* talk excessively and foolishly.

prat'tle, *v.i.*, **-tled, -tling,** *n.*, *v.i.* 1. chatter childishly or foolishly. —*n.* 2. chatter. —**prat'tler,** *n.*

prawn, *n.* large, edible, shrimplike shellfish.

pray, *v.i.* 1. petition or worship a divinity. —*v.t.* 2. implore. 3. ask earnestly for.

prayer, *n.* 1. act of addressing a divinity. 2. earnest request. —**prayer'ful,** *adj.*

preach, *v.t.* 1. advocate. —*v.i.* 2. give a sermon. —**preach'er,** *n.*

pre'am''ble, *n.* introductory section.

pre·car'i·ous, *adj.* risky. —**pre·car'i·ous·ly,** *adv.*

pre·cau'tion, *n.* caution beforehand. —**pre·cau'tion·ar''y,** *adj.*

pre·cede', *v.*, **-ceded, -ceding,** *v.i.*, *v.t.* go before. —**pre·ced'ence,** *n.*

prec'e·dent, *n.* past occurrence or principle used as an example or justification.

pre'cept, *n.* principle or rule of conduct.

pre·cep'tor, *n.* teacher or tutor.

pre'cinct, *n.* administrative district.

pre'cious, *adj.* 1. valuable. 2. cherished. 3. overly refined. —**pre'cious·ly,** *adv.*

prec'i·pice, *n.* steep cliff.

pre·cip'i·tate'', *v.t.*, **-tated, -tating,** *adj.*, *n.*, *v.t.* 1. throw down violently. 2. hasten in occurring. 3. separate from a solution. 4. condense. —*adj.* 5. hasty; rash; headlong. —*n.* 6. condensed moisture. —**pre·cip''i·ta'tion,** *n.*

pre·cip'i·tous, *adj.* 1. steep. 2. precipitate.

pré·cis (prā sē), *n.* concise summary.

pre·cise', *adj.* 1. specific. 2. scrupulous; strict. —**pre·ci'sion, pre·cise'ness,** *n.* —**pre·cise'ly,** *adv.*

pre·clude', *v.t.*, **-cluded, -cluding.** exclude the possibility of. —**pre·clu'sion,** *n.* —**pre·clu'sive,** *adj.*

pre·co'cious, *adj.* advanced in development, esp. of the mind. —**pre·coc'i·ty,** *n.*

pre''con·ceive, *v.t.* form an idea or opinion of in advance. —**pre''con·cep'tion**, *n.*

pre·cur'sor, *n.* 1. forerunner. 2. harbinger.

pred''e·ces'sor, *n.* person or thing that precedes another.

pre·des''ti·na'tion, *n.* determination in advance of actions and consequences; fate. —**pre·des'tine**, *v.t.*

pre·dic'a·ment, *n.* difficult or dangerous situation.

pred·i·cate, *v.t.*, **-cated, -cating**, *n., v.t.* (pred'ə kāt'') 1. declare; assume. 2. base on an assumption. —*n.* (pred'ək ət) 3. *Grammar.* part of a sentence or clause expressing what is said of its subject. —**pred''i·ca'tion**, *n.*

pre·dict', *v.t.*, tell in advance. —**pre·dic' tion**, *n.* —**pre·dict'a·ble**, *adj.*

pre''di·lec'tion, *n.* preference; inclination.

pre·dom'i·nate'', *v.*, **-nated, -nating**, *v.i.* 1. be stronger or more numerous. —*v.t.* 2. master. —**pre·dom'i·nance**, *n.* —**pre·dom'i·nant**, *adj.* —**pre·dom' i·nant·ly**, *adv.*

pre·em'i·nent, *adj.* outstanding; superior. —**pre·em'i·nent·ly**, *adv.* —**pre· em'i·nence**, *n.*

pre''empt', *v.t.* 1. acquire before others do. 2. settle on to establish the right of purchase.

preen, *v.t.* 1. trim with the beak, as a bird. —*v.i.* 2. fuss over one's appearance.

pre·fab'ri·cate'', *v.t.*, **-cated, -cating**, assemble from large, previously finished, components.

pre'face, *n., v.t.*, **-aced, -acing**, *n.* 1. introductory text. —*v.t.* 2. serve as a preface to. —**pref'a·to''ry**, *adj.*

pre'fect, *n.* magistrate; high official.

pre·fer', *v.t.*, **-ferred, -ferring**. 1. like better or favor more than others. 2. present, as an accusation. —**pref'er·a·ble**, *adj.* —**pref'er·a·bly**, *adv.* —**pref'er· ence**, *n.* —**pref''er·en'tial**, *adj.*

pre·fer'ment, *n.* promotion; advancement.

pre'fix, *n.* 1. qualifying beginning of a word. —*v.t.* 2. put before.

preg'nant, *adj.* 1. being with child. 2. significant; meaningful. —**preg'nan·cy**, *n.*

pre·hen'sile, *adj.* able to grasp.

pre''his·tor'ic, *adj.* pertaining to the time before recorded history.

prej'u·dice, *n., v.t.*, **-diced, -dicing**. *n.* 1. opinion without adequate basis. 2. disadvantage or injury. —*v.t.* 3. influence or affect with prejudice. —**prej'' u·di'cial**, *adj.*

prel'ate, *n.* high church official.

pre·lim'i·nar''y, *adj., n., pl.* **-naries**, *adj.* 1.—

introductory. —*n.* 2. introductory feature.

prel'ude, *n.* preliminary to a larger work.

pre'ma·ture'', *adj.* 1. born or happening too early. 2. overly hasty. —**pre''ma· ture'ly**, *adv.* —**pre''ma·tur'i·ty**, *n.*

pre·med'i''tate'', *v., v.t.*, **-tated, -tating**. *v.i., v.t.* plan or consider beforehand. —**pre''med·i·ta'tion**, *n.*

pre·mier' (pre mir'), *n.* 1. chief officer, esp. a prime minister. —*adj.* 2. first in rank.

pre·miere' (pre mir'), *n.* first public performance.

prem'ise, *n.* 1. basis of an argument or conclusion. 2. **premises**, building and grounds; property.

pre'mi·um, *n.* 1. prize. 2. high evaluation. 3. bonus. 4. cost of an insurance policy.

pre''mo·ni'tion, *n.* foreboding; presentiment. —**pre·mon'i·to'ry**, *adv.*

pre·na'tal, *adj.* prior to birth.

pre·oc'cu·pied'', *adj.* completely engrossed. —**pre·oc'cu·py''**, *v.t.* —**pre· oc''cu·pa'tion**, *n.*

pre·pare', *v.*, **-pared, paring**, *v.t.* 1. put in readiness. 2. manufacture. —*v.i.* 3. get or put oneself in readiness. —**prep''a·ra'tion**, *n.* —**pre·par'a·to''ry**, *adj.* —**pre·par'ed·ness**, *n.*

pre·pon'der·ant, *adj.* superior in numbers, strength, etc. —**pre·pon'der· ance**, *n.*

prep''o·si'tion, *n.* word or words placed before a noun or adjective to form a modifying phrase. —**prep''o·si'tion·al**, *adj.*

pre''pos·sess'ing, *adj.* impressing favorably.

pre''pos·ter·ous, *adj.* absurd.

pre·req'ui·site, *n.* something required beforehand; condition.

pre·rog'a·tive, *n.* special power, right, or privilege.

pres'age, *v.t.*, **-aged, -aging**, 1. foreshadow. 2. predict.

pres''by·te'ri·an, *adj.* 1. of or pertaining to the principle of church government by a presbytery. 2. pertaining to a Protestant church with this form of government. —*n.* 3. member of a Presbyterian church.

pres'by·ter''y, *n., pl.* **-teries**, group of church elders and ministers.

pre·sci·ence (pre'shē əns, presh'əns), *n.* foreknowledge; foresight. —**pre'sci· ent**, *adj.*

pre·scribe', *v.t.*, **-scribed, -scribing**, order for use, or adoption. —**pre·scrip' tion**, *n.* —**pre·scrip'tive**, *adj.*

pres'ence, *n.* 1. state of being present. 2. vicinity or view. 3. figure or bearing of a person.

pres·ent, *adj.* (prez'ənt) 1. being or hap-

pening now. **2.** being in a specific
place. **3.** *Grammar.* denoting state or
action now taking place. —*n.* **4.** present time. **5.** present tense. **6.** gift. —*v.t.*
(pri zent′) **7.** give, bring, or offer. **8.**
furnish or allow. **9.** introduce or make
public. —**pres″en·ta′tion,** *n.*

pre·sent′a·ble, *adj.* suitable in appearance, manners, etc. —**pre·sent′ab·ly,**
adv.

pre·sen′ti·ment, *n.* premonition.

pres′ent·ly, *adv.* **1.** soon. **2.** at present;
now.

pre·serve′, *v.t.,* **-served, -serving,** *n., v.t.*
1. keep safe. **2.** keep in good condition.
3. prepare for storage, as food. —*n.* **4.**
preserves, preserved fruit. **5.** sanctuary
for game animals. —**pres″er·va′tion,**
n. —**pre·serv′a·tive,** *n., adj.*

pre·side′, *v.i.,* **-sided, -siding.** act as
chairman; be at the head of.

pres′i·dent, *n.* **1.** chief officer of a corporation. **2.** highest elected official.
—**pres′i·den·cy,** *n.* —**pres″i·den′tial,**
adj.

pre·sid′i·um, *n.* major administrative
committee of a communist state.

press, *v.t.* **1.** act against with weight or
force. **2.** urge forcefully. **3.** oppress. **4.**
iron, as clothing. —*v.i.* **5.** move or
push forcefully. —*n.* **6.** journalism. **7.**
machine for printing. **8.** urgency.

press′ing, *adj.* urgent.

pres′sure, *n.* **1.** exertion of force. **2.** compulsion toward a certain action or decision. **3.** urgency.

pres″ti·dig″i·ta′tion, *n.* sleight of hand.
—**pres″ti·dig′i·ta″tor,** *n.*

pres·tige (pres tēzh′) *n.* respected standing or reputation. —**pres·tig′ious,** *adj.*

pres′to, *adv.* quickly.

pre·sume′, *v.,* **-sumed, -suming,** *v.t.* **1.**
take for granted. —*v.i.* **2.** act with unwarranted boldness. —**pre·sum′a·ble,**
adj. —**pre·sum′a·bly,** *adv.*

pre·sump′tion, *n.* **1.** assumption. **2.** unwarranted boldness. —**pre·sump′tive,**
adj. —**pre·sump′tu·ous,** *adj.*

pre″sup·pose′, *v.t.,* **-posed, -posing. 1.**
suppose beforehand. **2.** require beforehand as a condition.

pre·tend′, *v.t.* **1.** imagine as a fantasy. **2.**
profess or appear falsely. —*v.i.* **3.**
make believe. **4.** make a claim. —**pre·
ten′der,** *n.* —**pre·tense′,** *n.*

pre·ten′sion, *n.* **1.** ostentation; self-importance. **2.** act or instance of alleging
or pretending. —**pre·ten′tious,** *adj.*
—**pre·ten′tious·ly,** *adv.*

pre″ter·nat′u·ral, *adj.* **1.** supernatural.
2. abnormal or exceptional.

pre′text, *n.* ostensible or false reason; excuse.

pret′ty, *adj.,* **-tier, -tiest,** *adv. adj.* **1.**
pleasingly attractive. —*adv.* **2.** moderately. —**pret′ti·fy″,** *v.t.* —**pret′ti·ly,**
adv. —**pret′ti·ness,** *n.*

pret′zel, *n.* brittle, salted cracker, usually
twisted.

pre·vail′, *v.i.* **1.** be widespread. **2.** prove
superior in force, etc. **3.** succeed in persuasion. —**prev′a·lent,** *adj.* —**prev′a·
lence,** *n.*

pre·var′i·cate″, *v.i.,* **-cated, -cating,**
speak falsely; lie. —**pre·var″i·ca′tion,**
n.

pre·vent′, *v.t.* stop; hinder. —**pre·vent′
a·ble, pre·vent′i·ble.** *adj.* —**pre·ven′
tion,** *n.* —**pre·ven′tive, pre·vent′a·
tive,** *adj.*

pre′view″, *n.* **1.** advance showing, as of a
motion picture. —*v.t.* **2.** show or view
in advance.

pre′vi·ous, *adj.* happening or going earlier. —**pre′vi·ous·ly,** *adv.*

prey, *n.* **1.** animal hunted for food. **2.** victim. —*v.i.* **3.** search for prey. **4.** have
an oppressive effect.

price, *n., v.t.* **-priced, pricing,** *n.* **1.**
amount for which something is sold. **2.**
value. —*v.t.* **3.** set a price on. **4.** check
or ask the price of.

price′less, *adj.* invaluable; beyond any
price.

prick, *n.* **1.** puncture or cut from a thorn,
needle, etc. —*v.t.* **2.** pierce or stab
lightly.

prick′ly, *adj.* sharp; scratchy.

pride, *n., v.t.,* **prided, priding.** *n.* **1.** high
opinion of one's worth. **2.** self-respect.
3. person or object one is proud of.
—*v.t.* **4.** give pride to.

priest, *n.* **1.** clergyman; person authorized
to perform religious ceremonies. **2.**
Also, *fem.,* **priest′ess,** one who performs religious rites. —**priest′hood,** *n.*
—**priest′ly,** *adj.*

prig, *n.* self-righteous person. —**prig′gish,**
adj.

prim, *adj.* rigidly proper. —**prim′ly,** *adv.*

pri″ma·don′na, *n.* **1.** principal female
opera singer. **2.** *Informal.* temperamental or vain person.

pri′mal, *adj.* **1.** primitive; original. **2.**
most important; basic.

pri′ma″ry, *adj., n., pl.* **-ries.** *adj.* **1.** first
in rank or importance. **2.** first in time.
—*n.* **3.** preliminary election. —**pri·
mar′i·ly,** *adv.*

pri′mate, *n.* **1.** any of the order of mammals that includes man. **2.** high church
official.

prime, *adj., n., v.t.,* **primed, priming,**
adj. **1.** first in rank, value, etc. **2.** original. —*n.* **3.** best part or period. —*v.t.*
4. prepare.

prim·er, *n.* (prim′ər) **1.** elementary or basic book. **2.** (prī′mər) material for preparing a surface.

pri·me′val, *adj.* pertaining to the earliest
ages.

prim′i·tive, *adj.* **1.** earliest. **2.** simple;
crude. —*n.* **3.** naive work of art.

—**prim′i·tive·ly,** *adv.* —**prim′i·tive·
ness,** *n.*

primp, *v.t., v.i.* dress or adorn oneself
fastidiously.

prim′rose″, *n.* colorful perennial garden
flower.

prince, *n.* **1.** son of royalty. **2.** ruler.
Also, *fem.,* **prin′cess.**

prince′ly, *adj.* lavish.

prin′ci·pal, *adj.* **1.** most important. —*n.*
2. leader. **3.** head of a school. **4.** capital
sum. —**prin′ci·pal·ly,** *adv.*

prin″ci·pal′i·ty, *n., pl.* -ties. state governed by a prince.

prin′ci·ple, *n.* **1.** rule of action, conduct,
or belief. **2.** adherence to rules of conduct. **3.** scientific law.

print, *v.t.* **1.** reproduce from inked type.
2. produce a photographic positive
from. —*v.i.* **3.** draw letters or characters. —*n.* **4.** state of being printed. **5.**
printed lettering. **6.** printed picture.
—**print′er,** *n.*

print″er, *n.* **1.** one who prints. **2.** (computers) device for transcribing data to
paper.

print″out, *n.,v.* (computers) data tran-
scribed onto paper.

pri′or, *adj.* **1.** earlier. —*adv.* **2.** previously. —*n.* **3.** Also, *fem.,* **pri′or·ess,** head
of a religious house. —**pri′o·ry,** *n.*

pri·or′i·ty, *n., pl.* -ties. **1.** state of being
earlier in time. **2.** precedence in order,
privilege, etc.

prism, *n.* three-sided glass object that
breaks light into its spectrum. —**pris·
ma′tic,** *adj.*

pris′on, *n.* jail; building for confining
criminals. —**pris′on·er,** *n.*

pris′tine, *adj.* unspoiled; pure.

pri′vate, *adj.* **1.** belonging to a specific
person or group. **2.** confidential. —*n.*
3. lowest soldier. —**pri′vate·ly,** *adv.*
—**pri′va·cy,** *n.*

pri″va·teer′, *n.* private ship commissioned for warfare.

pri·va′tion, *n.* **1.** deprivation. **2.** lack;
want; need.

priv′i·lege, *n.* special advantage. —**priv′
i·leged,** *adj.*

priv′y, *adj., n., pl.* privies. *adj.* **1.** admitted to a secret. **2.** private; personal.
—*n.* **3.** outhouse; outdoor toilet.

prize, *n., v.t.,* prized, prizing. *n.* **1.** reward for victory. **2.** something desirable. —*v.t.* **3.** value or esteem highly.

pro, *n., pl.* pros, *adv., adj. n.* **1.** *Informal.* professional. —*adv.,* *adj.* **2.** in favor.

prob′a·ble, *adj.* **1.** likely to happen, etc.
2. giving ground for belief. —**prob′a·
bly,** *adv.* —**prob″a·bil′i·ty,** *n.*

pro′bate, *n., adj., v.t.,* -bated, -bating. *n.*
1. certification of a will. —*adj.* **2.** of or
pertaining to probate. —*v.t.* **3.** establish the validity of.

pro·ba′tion, *n.* act or instance of testing.
—**pro·ba′tion·ar″y,** *adj.*

probe, *v.t.,* probed, probing, *n., v.t.* **1.**
search into thoroughly. —*n.* **2.** surgical
instrument for examining wounds, etc.

pro′bi·ty, *n.* honesty; uprightness.

prob′lem, *n.* question or situation involving difficulty. —**prob″lem·at′i·cal,**
adj.

pro·bos′cis (prō bos′is), *n., pl.* -ces. flexible snout, e.g. an elephant's trunk.

pro·ceed′, *v.i.* **1.** go onward. **2.** continue
an action. **3.** issue forth. —*n.* **4.** pro-
ceeds, revenue from selling. —**pro·ce′
dure,** *n.* —**pro·ce′du·ral,** *adj.*

pro·ceed′ing, *n.* **1.** action or conduct. **2.**
proceedings, **a.** records of a meeting,
etc. **b.** legal action.

pro′cess, *n.* **1.** series of actions ending in
a result. **2.** continuous action. **3.** legal
summons. —*v.t.* **4.** treat or prepare by
a specific process.

pro·ces′sion, *n.* parade.

pro·ces′sion·al, *n.* **1.** hymn for a procession. **2.** hymnbook.

pro-choice, *adj.* supporting legalized
abortion.

pro·claim′, *v.t.* **1.** announce publicly. **2.**
reveal conspicuously. —**proc″la·ma′
tion,** *n.*

pro·cliv′i·ty, *n., pl.* -ties. natural tendency or inclination.

pro·cras′ti·nate″, *v.,* -nated, -nating.
v.i., v.t. put off to another time.
—**pro·cras″ti·na′tion,** *n.* —**pro·cras′
ti·na″tor,** *n.*

pro·cure′, *v.t.,* -cured, -curing. **1.** obtain.
2. bring about. —**pro·cure′ment,** *n.*

prod, *v.t.,* prodded, prodding, *n., v.t.* **1.**
poke; jab. **2.** goad; incite. —*n.* **3.**
poke. **4.** pointed instrument.

prod′i·gal, *adj.* **1.** recklessly extravagant.
2. lavish. —**prod″i·gal′i·ty,** *n.*

pro·di′gious, *adj.* **1.** wonderful. **2.** huge.
—**pro·di′gious·ly,** *adv.*

prod′i·gy, *n., pl.* -gies. very talented person.

pro·duce, *v.,* -duced, -ducing, *v.t.* (prə′
dyōōs) **1.** bring into existence. **2.** give
birth to or bear. **3.** exhibit. —*n.* (prō′
dōōs) **4.** product. **5.** fresh fruit and
vegetables. —**pro·duc′er,** *n.* —**pro·
duc′tion,** *n.* —**pro·duc′tive,** *adj.*
—**pro″duc·tiv′i·ty,** —**pro·duc′tive·
ness,** *adj.* —**pro″duc·tiv′i·ty,** —**pro·
duc′tive·ness,** *n.*

pro-family, *adj.* antiabortion; pro-life.

pro·fane′, *adj., v.t.,* -faned, -faning, *adj.*
1. secular. **2.** impure; foul. **3.** irreverent; disrespectful. —*v.t.* **4.** treat with
irreverence.

pro·fan′i·ty, *n.* **1.** sacrilege. **2.** cursing.

pro·fess′, *v.t.* **1.** claim of oneself. **2.** affirm allegiance to or faith in.

pro·fes′sion, *n.* **1.** learned occupation. **2.**
act or instance of professing.

pro·fes′sion·al, *adj.* **1.** pursuing a profession. **2.** pertaining to a profession. **3.** meeting the standards of a profession. —*n.* **4.** professional person. —**pro·fes'sion·al·ly**, *adv.* —**pro·fes'sion·al"ism**, *n.*

pro·fes'sor, *n.* college teacher of the highest rank. —**pro"fes·sor'i·al**, *adj.*

prof'fer, *v.t., n.*, offer.

pro·fi'cient, *adj.* skillful; learned. —**pro·fic'ient·ly**, *adv.* —**pro·fi'cien·cy**, *n.*

pro'file, *n.* **1.** side view. **2.** succinct sketch of a person. —*v.t.* **3.** do a biographical profile of.

prof'it, *n.* **1.** gain from a business deal. **2.** net gain from business. **3.** benefit. —*v.i.* **4.** gain a profit. **5.** take advantage. —**prof'it·a·ble**, *adj.* —**prof'it·a·bly**, *adv.*

prof"it·eer', *n.* **1.** person who takes an unreasonably large profit. —*v.i.* **2.** act as a profiteer.

prof'li·gate, *adj.* **1.** licentious. **2.** extravagant. —*n.* **3.** profligate person. —**prof'li·ga·cy**, *n.*

pro·found', *adj.* **1.** characterized by deep thought. **2.** deeply felt. **3.** deep. —**pro·found'ly**, *adv.* —**pro·fun'di·ty**, *n.*

pro·fuse', *adj.* **1.** plentiful. **2.** lavish. —**pro·fuse'ly**, *adv.* —**pro·fus'ion**, **pro·fuse'ness**, *n.*

pro·gen'i·tor, *n.* forefather; precursor.

prog'e·ny, *n., pl.* **-nies.** children; descendants.

prog·no'sis, *n., pl.* **-noses**, forecast of the course of a disease.

prog·nos'ti·cate", *v.*, **-cated, -cating**, *v.t.* **1.** predict; presage. —*v.i.* **2.** prophesy. —**prog·nos"ti·ca'tion**, *n.*

pro"gram, *n.* **1.** plan, method. **2.** list of subjects or events. **3.** (computers) a set of instructions to perform specific operations to data. —*v.* **4.** create a computer program. —**pro"gram·ming**, *n.*

prog·ress, *n.* (prog'res) **1.** advancement. **2.** improvement. —*v.i.* (pro·gres') **3.** advance. **4.** improve. —**pro·gres'sion**, *n.* —**pro·gres'sive**, *adj.* —**pro·gres'sive·ly**, *adv.*

pro·hib'it, *v.t.* **1.** forbid. **2.** prevent. —**pro·hib'i·tive**, *adj.* —**pro"hi·bi'tion**, *n.* —**pro"hi·bi'tion·ist**, *n.*

proj·ect, *n.* (proj'ekt) **1.** plan; scheme. —*v.t.* (prō·jekt') **2.** plan or intend. **3.** throw or impel forward. **4.** cast on a surface, as an image. —*v.i.* **5.** protrude. —**pro·jec'tion**, *n.* —**pro·jec'tor**, *n.*

pro·jec'tile, *n.* missile from a gun.

pro"le·tar'i·at, *n.* working class. —**pro"le·tar'i·an**, *n., adj.*

pro·lif'er·ate", *v.*, **-ated, ating.** *v.i., v.t.* **1.** grow rapidly by multiplication. **2.** spread rapidly. —**pro·lif"er·a'tion**, *n.*

pro·lif'ic, *adj.* productive.

pro'logue, *n.* introduction to a play, novel, etc. Also, **pro'log.**

pro·long', *v.t.* lengthen, esp. in duration.

prom"e·nade', *n., v.*, **-naded, -nading**. *n.* **1.** leisurely walk. **2.** place for strolling. —*v.i.* **3.** take a promenade. —*v.t.* **4.** promenade on or through.

prom'i·nent, *adj.* **1.** conspicuous. **2.** distinguished. —**prom'i·nence**, *n.* —**prom'i·nent·ly**, *adv.*

pro·mis'cu·ous, *adj.* indiscriminate. —**prom"is·cu'i·ty**, *n.* —**pro·mis'cu·ous·ly**, *adv.*

prom'ise, *n., v.t.*, **-ised, -ising.** *n.* **1.** assurance to do or not to do something. **2.** indication of future improvement or success. —*v.t.* **3.** make a promise. —*v.i.* **4.** give grounds for hope. —**prom'is·ing**, *adj.*

prom'is·so"ry, *adj.* containing a promise.

prom'on·to"ry, *n., pl.* **-ries**, high land mass jutting into the sea.

pro·mote', *v.t.* **1.** advance in rank or position. **2.** further the growth or progress of. —**pro·mo'ter**, *n.* —**pro·mo'tion**, *n.*

prompt, *adj.* **1.** ready to act. **2.** quick or punctual. —*v.t.* **3.** induce to action. —**prompt'ly**, *adv.*

pro·mul'gate, *v.t.*, **-gated, -gating.** proclaim publicly. —**pro"mul·ga'tion**, *n.*

prone, *adj.* **1.** inclined; liable. **2.** lying face downward.

prong, *n.* pointed projection.

pro'noun', *n.* word used as a substitute for a noun.

pro·nounce', *v.*, **-nounced, -nouncing.** *v.t.* **1.** utter; deliver. **2.** declare to be. —*v.i.* **3.** articulate words or phrases. —**pro·nounce'ment**, *n.*

pro·nounced', *adj.* strongly marked or apparent.

pro·nun"ci·a'tion, *n.* act or manner of speaking.

proof, *n.* **1.** evidence demonstrating a fact. **2.** standardized strength for liquor. **3.** preliminary printing, for inspection. —*adj.* **4.** impervious; invulnerable.

proof'read", *v.t.*, **-read, -reading.** read to check for errors. —**proof'read"er**, *n.*

prop, *n., v.t.*, **propped, propping**, *n.* **1.** rigid support. **2.** emotional support. **3.** any object used in a stage play. —*v.t.* **4.** support; strengthen.

prop"a·gan'da, *n.* assertions, etc. intended to help or oppose a cause. —**prop'a·gan'dist**, *n.* —**prop"a·gan·dis'tic**, *adj.* —**prop"a·gan'dize**, *v.t., v.i.*

prop'a·gate", *v.*, **-gated, -gating.** *v.t., v.i.* **1.** reproduce; breed. —*v.t.* **2.** transmit, as ideas. —**prop"a·ga'tion**, *n.*

pro·pel′ler, *n.* screwlike propelling device.

pro·pen′si·ty, *n.* inclination; tendency.

prop′er, *adj.* 1. suitable. 2. correct. 3. *Grammar.* indicating a specific person, place, or thing. —**prop′er·ly**, *adv.*

prop′er·ty, *n., pl.* -ties. 1. possessions. 2. attribute.

proph·e·sy (prof′ə sī), *v.,* -sied, -sying. *v.t.* 1. foretell; predict. —*v.i.* 2. speak by divine inspiration. —**proph′e·cy**, *n.*

proph′et, *n.* 1. utterer of divine revelations. 2. person who prophesies the future. Also, *fem.,* **proph′et·ess.** —**pro·phet′ic**, *adj.* —**pro·phet′i·cal·ly**, *adv.*

pro″phy·lax′is, *n.* prevention of or protection from disease. —**pro″phy·lac′tic**, *adj.*

pro·pin′qui·ty, *n.* kinship; nearness.

pro·pi′ti·ate″, *v.t.,* -ated, -ating. make favorable; appease.

pro·pi′tious, *adj.* favorable; auspicious. —**pro·pi′tious·ly**, *adv.*

pro·po′nent, *n.* advocate; backer.

pro·por′tion, *n.* 1. quantitative relation. 2. due relationship. 3. **proportions,** dimensions. —*v.t.* 4. put in due proportion. —**pro·por′tion·al, pro·por′tion·ate**, *adj.*

pro·pose′, *v.,* -posed, -posing, *v.t.* 1. suggest or offer. 2. intend. —*v.i.* 3. suggest marriage. —**prop″o·si′tion**, *n.* —**pro·pos′al**, *n.*

pro·pound′, *v.t.* offer for consideration.

pro·pri′e·tor, *n.* manager or owner. —**pro·pri′e·tor·ship″**, *n.* —**pro·pri′e·tar″y**, *adj.*

pro·pri′e·ty, *n., pl.* -ties. 1. respectability. 2. suitability.

pro·pul′sion, *n.* propelling force.

pro·rate′, *v.,* -rated, -rating. *v.i., v.t.* distribute or divide proportionately.

pro·sa′ic, *adj.* commonplace; dull.

prose, *n.* ordinary language of speech and writing.

pros′e·cute″, *v.t.,* -cuted, -cuting. 1. begin legal proceedings against. 2. continue to completion. —**pros″e·cu′tion**, *n.* —**pros″e·cu′tor**, *n.*

pros′e·lyte″, *n.* convert.

pros′pect, *n.* 1. likelihood, esp. of success. 2. view. 3. potential customer or buyer. —*v.i.* 4. search or explore, e.g. for gold. —**pros·pec′tive**, *adj.* —**pros′pec·tor**, *n.*

pro·spec′tus, *n.* description of a new venture, esp. for prospective buyers.

pros′per, *v.i.* be successful. —**pros·per′i·ty**, *n.* —**pros′per·ous**, *adj.* —**pros′per·ous·ly**, *adv.*

pros′tate, *n.* gland at the base of the male bladder.

pros′ti·tute″, *n., v.t.,* -tuted, -tuting. *n.* 1. person who engages in sexual intercourse for pay. —*v.t.* 2. misuse, as talent. —**pros″ti·tu′tion**, *n.*

pros′trate, *v.t.,* -trated, -trating, *adj. v.t.* 1. lay flat. 2. exhaust of strength. —*adj.* 3. lying. 4. without strength. —**pros·tra′tion**, *n.*

pros′y, *adj.,* **prosier, prosiest.** dull; uninteresting.

pro·tect′, *v.t.* defend or preserve. —**pro·tec′tion**, *n.* —**pro·tec′tive**, *adj.* —**pro·tec′tive·ly**, *adv.* —**pro·tec′tor**, *n.*

pro·tec′tor·ate, *n.* protection and partial control of one state by another.

pro·té·gé (prō′tə zhā″), *n.* person under patronage. Also, *fem.,* **pro′té·gée″.**

pro′te·in, *n.* nitrogenous compound essential for life processes present in living matter.

pro′test, *n.* 1. objection. —*v.i., v.t.* 2. make an objection. —*v.t.* 3. declare solemnly. —**prot″es·ta′tion**, *n.* —**pro·tes′ter**, *n.*

Prot′es·tant, *n.* western Christian not belonging to the Roman Catholic Church. —**Prot′es·tant·ism″**, *n.*

pro′to·col, *n.* code of etiquette, esp. diplomatic.

pro′ton, *n.* elementary atomic particle carrying a positive charge.

pro′to·plasm″, *n.* basic protein substance of living matter.

pro′to·type″, *n.* model; first specimen.

pro·tract′, *v.t.* lengthen; prolong. —**pro·trac′tion**, *n.*

pro·trac′tor, *n.* instrument for measuring angles.

pro·trude′, *v.i.,* -truded, truding. project. —**pro·tru′sion**, *n.* —**pro·tru′sive**, *adj.*

pro·tu′ber·ant, *adj.* bulging out. —**pro·tu′ber·ance**, *n.*

proud, *adj.* 1. having self-respect. 2. feeling honored. 3. arrogant. 4. glorious. —**proud′ly**, *adv.*

prove, *v.,* proved, proving, *v.t.* 1. establish the truth of. 2. test. —*v.i.* 3. turn out. —**prov′a·ble**, *adj.*

prov′en·der, *n.* food.

prov′erb, *n.* wise popular saying. —**pro·ver′bi·al**, *adj.*

pro·vide′, *v.,* -vided, -viding. *v.t.* 1. supply; equip. 2. yield. —*v.i.* 3. prepare beforehand. —**pro·vi′der**, *n.*

pro·vi′ded, *conj.* if; on condition that.

prov′i·dence, *n.* 1. divine care or guidance. 2. economy. —**prov′i·den″tial**, *adj.* —**prov′i·dent**, *adj.*

prov′ince, *n.* 1. administrative district. 2. personal area of operations or expertise.

pro·vin′cial, *adj.* 1. of a province. 2. narrow-mindedly local.

pro·vi′sion, *n.* 1. stipulation. 2. act or instance of providing. 3. prearrangement. 4. **provisions,** food supply; goods. —*v.t.* 5. supply with provisions.

pro·vi'sion·al, *adj.* temporary; conditional.

pro·vi'so, *n., pl.* **-sos, -soes.** stipulation.

pro·voke', *v.t.,* **-voked, -voking. 1.** exasperate. **2.** call into being or effect. **—prov''o·ca'tion,** *n.* **—pro·voc'a·tive,** *adj.* **—pro·voc'a·tive·ly,** *adv.*

pro·vost (prō'vōst) *n.* high official, esp. of a university.

prow, *n.* bow of a ship or airplane.

prow'ess, *n.* **1.** bravery; strength, esp. military. **2.** extraordinary ability.

prowl, *v.i.* roam about or search stealthily. **—prowl'er,** *n.*

prox·im'i·ty, *n.* nearness.

prox'y, *n., pl.* **proxies. 1.** agent. **2.** authority to act or vote for another.

prude, *n.* extremely modest person. **—prud'ish,** *adj.*

pru'dence, *n.* **1.** caution. **2.** practical wisdom. **—pru'dent,** *adj.*

prune, *v.t.,* **pruned, pruning,** *n., v.t.* **1.** cut off; trim. **—n. 2.** dried plum.

pru'ri·ent, *adj.* having lewd thoughts. **—pru'ri·ence,** *n.*

pry, *v.,* **pried, prying,** *n., v.i.* **1.** inquire unjustifiably into another's affairs. **—v.t. 2.** move by leverage. **—n. 3.** act or instance of prying. **4.** lever.

psalm (sahm), *n.* sacred song or poem.

pseu·do (sōō'dō), *adj.* false; spurious.

pseu'do·nym, *n.* assumed name.

psy·che (sī'kē), *n.* human self or soul.

psy·che·del·ic (sī''kə del'ik), *adj.* **1.** pertaining to intense hallucinatory effects. **—n. 2.** hallucination-producing drug.

psy·chi'a·try, *n.* science of healing mental disorders. **—psy·chi'a·trist,** *n.* **—psy''chi·at'ric,** *adj.*

psy'chic, *n., adj. n.* **1.** medium or clairvoyant. **—adj.** Also, **psy'chi·cal. 2.** pertaining to the psyche. **3.** supernatural.

psy''cho·a·nal'y·sis, *n.* detailed study and treatment of neuroses. **—psy''cho·an'a·lyst,** *n.* **—psy''cho·an'a·lyze,** *v.t.* **—psy''cho·an''a·lyt'ic,** *adj.*

psy·chol'o·gy, *n.* **1.** study of the mind and behavior. **2.** mental and behavioral constitution. **—psy''cho·log'i·cal,** *adj.* **—psy·chol'o·gist,** *n.*

psy''cho·neu·ro'sis, *n., pl.* **-ses,** *n.* emotional disorder or disease. **—psy''cho·neu·rot'ic,** *adj.*

psy'cho·path'', *n.* mentally ill person. **—psy''cho·path'ic,** *adj.* **—psy·chop'a·thy,** *n.*

psy·cho'sis, *n., pl.* **-ses,** mental disease marked by loss of contact with reality. **—psy·chot'ic,** *n., adj.*

psy''cho·so·mat'ic, *adj.* pertaining to physical effects caused by mental states.

psy''cho·ther'a·py, *n.* treatment of mental and emotional disorders. **—psy''cho·ther'a·pist,** *n.*

pto·maine (tō'mān), *n.* substance produced by bacteria in decaying matter.

pub, *n. British.* bar; tavern.

pu·ber·ty (pyōō'bər tē), *n.* sexual maturity.

pub'lic, *adj.* **1.** of or for all people. **2.** known by or knowable to all. **—n. 3.** people generally. **—pub'lic·ly,** *adv.*

pub''li·ca'tion, *n.* **1.** act or instance of publishing. **2.** published work.

pub·lic'i·ty, *n.* **1.** public attention or notice. **2.** material claiming public attention.

pub'li·cize', *v.t.,* **-cized, -cizing,** bring to public attention or notice.

pub'lish, *v.t.* **1.** print or issue for distribution. **2.** announce publicly. **—pub'lish·er,** *n.*

puck'er, *v.t., v.i., n.* curl; wrinkle.

pud'ding, *n.* soft, sweet dessert.

pud'dle, *n.* small pool of water.

pudg'y, *adj.,* **pudgier, pudgiest.** *adj.* short and fat; chubby. **—pudg'i·ness,** *n.*

pueb·lo (pweb'lō), *n.* **1.** adobe Indian village of U.S. Southwest. **2. Pueblo,** Southwestern U.S. Indian people.

pu·er·ile (pōō'ər il), *adj.* silly; childish. **—pu''er·il'i·ty,** *n.*

pu·er·per·al (pōō ur'pər əl), *adj.* pertaining to childbirth.

puff, *n.* **1.** short quick gust, e.g. of wind. **2.** anything soft and light. **3.** light piece of pastry. **—v.i. 4.** blow or breathe in puffs. **5.** become inflated or swollen. **—v.t. 6.** blow or puff on.

puf'fin, *n.* sea bird.

pug, *n.* small short-haired dog.

pu'gil·ism'', *n.* boxing. **—pu'gil·ist,** *n.*

pug·na'cious, *adj.* fond of fighting; belligerent. **—pug·nac'i·ty,** *n.*

puke, *v.,* **puked, puking.** *v.i., v.t.* vomit.

pul'chri·tude'', *n.* beauty.

pull, *v.t.* **1.** move toward or after one. **2.** strain by pulling. **3.** select from a group. **—v.i. 4.** attempt to move toward one. **5.** move oneself. **—n. 6.** act or instance of pulling. **7.** something to pull on. **8.** *Informal.* influence.

pul'let, *n.* young hen.

pul'ley, *n., pl.* **-leys.** wheel with a rim grooved for a rope.

pul'mo·nar''y, *adj.* of the lungs.

pulp, *n.* **1.** soft, fleshy material. **—v.t. 2.** crush or grind to pulp. **—v.i. 3.** become pulp. **—pulp'y,** *adj.*

pul'pit, *n.* raised platform or lectern used by a clergyman.

pul'sate, *v.i.,* **-sated, -sating.** throb; quiver. **—pul·sa'tion,** *n.*

pulse, *n.* **1.** regular throb of the arteries

produced by the heart. —*v.i.* **2.** throb regularly.

pul'ver·ize'', *v.*, **-ized, -izing.** *v.t.* **1.** reduce to powder or dust. **2.** completely crush. —*v.i.* **3.** become reduced to dust. —**pul''ver·i·za'tion,** *n.*

pu'ma, *n.* cougar.

pum'ice, *n.* porous volcanic glass.

pum'mel, *v.t.* beat; thrash.

pump, *n.* **1.** device for applying force to liquids and gases. **2.** low shoe. —*v.t.* **3.** move with a pump. **4.** inflate. **5.** attempt to wheedle information from.

pum''per·nick'el, *n.* hard rye bread.

pump'kin, *n.* large orange fruit that grows on a vine.

pun, *n., v.i.,* **punned, punning,** *n.* **1.** play with similar-sounding words with different meanings. —*v.i.* **2.** make a pun.

punch, *n.* **1.** quick blow, esp. with the fist. **2.** piercing or sinking implement. **3.** sweet mixed beverage. —*v.t.* **4.** hit. **5.** perforate. —**punch'er,** *n.*

punc·til'i·ous, *adj.* adhering to correct procedure.

punc'tu·al, *adj.* on time; prompt. —**punc''tu·al'i·ty,** *n.* —**punc'tu·al·ly,** *adv.*

punc'tu·ate'', *v.t.,* **-ated, -ating. 1.** mark with commas, periods, etc. **2.** mark or interrupt periodically. **3.** give emphasis to. —**punc''tu·a'tion,** *n.*

punc'ture, *v.t.,* **-tured, -turing,** *n. v.t.* **1.** pierce with a pointed object. —*n.* **2.** act or instance of puncturing.

pun'dit, *n.* expert.

pun'gent, *adj.* **1.** sharp of taste. **2.** biting. —**pun'gen·cy,** *n.* —**pun'gent·ly,** *adv.*

pun'ish, *v.t.* **1.** subject to a penalty or revenge. **2.** inflict a penalty for. —**pun'ish·a·ble,** *adj.* —**pun'ish·ment,** *n.*

pu'ni·tive, *adj.* punishing.

punt, *n.* **1.** flat-bottomed shallow boat. **2.** kick in football. —*v.i.* **3.** kick in mid-air.

pu'ny, *adj.,* **-nier, -niest.** small; slight; weak.

pup, *n.* young dog. Also, **pup'py.**

pu'pa, *n., pl.* **-pae, -pas.** insect halfway between larva and adult.

pu'pil, *n.* **1.** student. **2.** dark opening in the iris of the eye.

pup'pet, *n.* **1.** small figure moved by hand or by wires. **2.** supposedly autonomous party obeying another. —**pup''pe·teer',** *n.*

pur'chase, *v.t.,* **-chased, -chasing,** *n.* **1.** buy. —*n.* **2.** act or instance of purchasing. **3.** thing purchased. **4.** leverage. —**pur'chas·er,** *n.*

pure, *adj.,* **purer, purest. 1.** unmixed or unpolluted. **2.** absolute. **3.** abstract. —**pure'ly,** *adv.*

pu·ree' (pyŏŏ rā'), *n.* cooked and sieved food.

pur'ga·to''ry, *n., pl.* **-ries, 1.** temporary punishment. **2.** place for purification from sin after death.

purge, *v.t.,* **purged, purging,** **1.** cleanse; purify. **2.** rid; remove. **3.** eliminate or kill for political reasons. —*n.* **4.** act or instance or purging. —**pur·ga'tion,** *n.* —**pur'ga·tive,** *adj., n.*

pu'ri·fy, *v.,* **-fied, -fying.** *v.t.* **1.** make pure. **2.** free from sin or guilt. —*v.i.* **3.** become pure. —**pu''ri·fi·ca'tion,** *n.*

pu'ri·tan, *n.* **1.** member of a strict religious group. **2.** adherent to an unusually strict moral code. —**puri·tan'i·cal,** *adj.*

pu'ri·ty, *n.* quality or condition of being pure.

purl, *v.t., v.i.* knit with an inverted stitch.

pur·lieu (pər'lōō), *n.* bordering or outlying district.

pur·loin', *v.t.* steal.

pur'ple, *n.* **1.** bluish-red color. —*adj.* **2.** of the color purple.

pur·port, *v.t.* (pər''port') **1.** claim or profess. **2.** express; imply. —*n.* **3.** (pər'port) significance.

pur'pose, *n., v.t.,* **-posed, -posing,** *n.* **1.** intention; object. —*v.t.* **2.** intend. —**pur'pose·ful,** *adj.* —**pur'pose·less,** *adj.*

pur'pose·ly, *adv.* intentionally.

purr, *n.* **1.** soft continuous sound made by a cat. —*v.i.* **2.** make this sound.

purse, *n., v.t.,* **pursed, pursing,** *n.* **1.** small bag for money. **2.** sum of money offered as a prize. —*v.t.* **3.** pucker.

purs'er, *n.* financial officer of a ship.

pur·su'ant, *adv.* according.

pur·sue', *v.t.,* **-sued, -suing. 1.** chase. **2.** proceed with. —**pur·su'ance,** *n.* —**pur·su'er,** *n.*

pur·suit', *n.* **1.** act or instance of pursuing. **2.** occupation; calling.

pu·ru·lent (pyŏŏr'ə lənt), *adj.* containing pus. —**pu·ru'lence,** *n.*

pur·vey, *v.t.* furnish; supply. —**pur·vey'ance,** *n.* —**pur·vey'or,** *n.*

pus, *n.* yellowish fluid found in sores.

push, *v.t.* **1.** press against to move. **2.** urge; press. —*v.i.* **3.** move with force. —*n.* **4.** act or instance of pushing. —**push'er,** *n.*

push'y, *adj.,* **-ier, -iest.** aggressive.

pu'sil·lan''i·mous, *adj.* cowardly.

puss'y, *n., pl.* **-sies.** cat. Also, **puss.**

puss'y·foot, *v.i.* act stealthily.

pussy willow, *n.* small American willow tree.

pus'tule, *n.* pus-filled pimple.

put, *v.,* **put, putting.** *v.t.* **1.** carry to a specified place. **2.** cause to be in a specified condition. **3.** present for consideration. **4.** hurl overhand. **5. put off,** postpone. **6. put out, a.** extinguish. **b.** trouble. —*v.i.* **7. put up with,** tolerate.

pu'ta·tive, *adj.* reputed; supposed.

pu′tre·fy″, v., -fied, -fying. v.i., v.t. decay; rot. —**pu″tre·fac′tion**, n.

pu′trid, adj. 1. rotten; decayed. 2. corrupt; vile.

putt, v.t. Golf. 1. hit gently. —n. 2. act or instance of putting.

put′ter, v.i. 1. be active without effect. —n. 2. golf club for putting.

put′ty, n., v.t., -tied, -tying. n. 1. cement of linseed oil and whiting. —v.t. 2. secure with putty.

puz′zle, n., v., -zled, -zling. n. 1. device or problem posing difficulties. —v.t. 2. mystify; perplex. —v.i. 3. attempt to study or figure out a problem.

pyg′my, n., pl. -mies. dwarf.

py′lon, n. thin tower.

py″or·rhe′a, n. disease of the gums.

pyr′a·mid, n. 1. structure or form with triangular sides. —v.t. 2. increase gradually. —**py·ram′i·dal**, adj.

pyre, n. heap of material for burning a corpse.

py′rite, n. yellow sulfur and iron.

py″ro·ma′ni·a, n. mania for starting fires. —**py″ro·ma′ni·ac″**, n.

py″ro·tech′nics, n. 1. fireworks 2. display of virtuosity. —**pyro·tech′nic**, adj.

py′thon, n. large constricting snake.

Q

Q, q, n. seventeenth letter of the English alphabet.

quack, n. 1. fraudulent doctor. 2. sound of a duck. —v.i. 3. utter a quack. —**quack′er·y**, n.

quad′ran″gle, n. 1. closed figure with four angles. 2. enclosed four-sided yard. —**quad·ran′gu·lar**, adj.

quad′rant, n. 1. arc of 90°. 2. instrument for measuring altitudes.

quad″ri·lat′er·al, adj. 1. four-sided. —n. 2. plane figure with four sides.

quad·ra·phon′ic, adj. of a sound system using four independent speakers.

qua·droon′, n. a person of one-quarter black ancestry.

quad′ru·ped″, n. animal with four feet.

quad′ru·ple, adj., v., -pled, -pling. adj. 1. fourfold. 2. having four parts. —v.t., v.i. 3. multiply by four.

quad′ru·plet, n. one of four children born together.

quad·ru′pli·cate, n. any of four copies.

quaff (kwof), v.t. drink with gusto.

quag′mire″, n. boggy area.

qua·hog (quo′hog), n. edible American clam.

quail, n., pl. quails, quail, v.i., n. 1. game bird. —v.i. 2. lose heart or courage.

quaint, adj. pleasingly odd or old-fashioned. —**quaint′ness**, n. —**quaint′ly**, adv.

quake, v.i., quaked, quaking, n. v.i. 1. tremble or shake. —n. 2. earthquake.

Quak′er, n. member of the Society of Friends.

qual′i·fy″, v., -fied, -fying. v.t. 1. make eligible or capable. 2. modify. —v.i. 3. be qualified. —**qual″i·fi·ca′tion**, n. —**qual′i·fied″**, adj.

qual′i·ty, n., pl. -ties. 1. essential characteristic. 2. degree of merit. 3. excellence. —**qual′i·ta″tive**, adj.

qualm (kwahm), n. 1. misgiving. 2. sick feeling.

quan′da·ry, n., pl. -ries. perplexed state.

quan′ti·ty, n., pl. -ties. 1. amount or number. 2. large or considerable amount. —**quan′ti·ta″tive**, adj.

quar′an·tine″, n., v.t., -tined, -tining. n. 1. isolation of suspected disease bearers. —v.t. 2. put in quarantine.

quar′rel, n. 1. angry argument; fight. —v.i. 2. have a quarrel. —**quar′rel·some**, adj.

quar′ry, n., pl. -ries, v.t., -ried, -rying. 1. place from which stone is extracted. 2. object of pursuit; prey. —v.t. 3. get or take from a quarry.

quart, n. unit of measure equal to one fourth of a gallon.

quar′ter, n. 1. fourth part. 2. coin with the value of 25 cents. 3. quarters, lodgings. 4. mercy. —v.t. 5. divide into quarters. 6. lodge. —adj. 7. being a quarter.

quar′ter·back″, n. position in football.

quar′ter·ly, adj., n., pl. -lies. adj. 1. occurring every three months. —n. 2. periodical published four times a year.

quar′ter·mas″ter, n. 1. army officer who oversees supplies, etc. 2. petty officer in charge of a ship's signals, steering, etc.

quar·tet′, n. 1. group of four, esp. musicians. 2. composition for four instruments. Also, **quar·tette′**.

quar′to, n. book printed on sheets folded into quarters.

quartz, n. common shiny crystalline mineral.

quash, v.t. 1. put down completely. 2. invalidate.

qua·si (kwah′sī), adj. 1. resembling. —adv. 2. seemingly.

quat′rain, n. four-line verse unit.

qua′ver, v.i. 1. tremble. 2. speak or sing tremulously. —n. 3. quavering tone.

quay (kē), n. pier; wharf.

quea′sy, adj., -sier, -siest. 1. nauseous. 2. uneasy.

queen, n. 1. female sovereign. 2. spouse of a king. 3. fertile female of bees.

queer, *adj.* peculiar. **—queer'ly,** *adv.*
—**queer'ness,** *n.*

quell, *v.t.* 1. subdue. 2. pacify.

quench, *v.t.* 1. slake, as thirst. 2. extinguish. 3. cool by immersion.

quer'u·lous, *adj.* peevish.

que'ry, *n., pl.* **-ries,** *v.t.,* **-ried, -rying.** *n.*
1. question; inquiry. —*v.t.* 2. inquire
regarding.

quest, *n., v.i.* search.

ques'tion, *n.* 1. interrogative sentence. 2.
problem or issue. —*v.t.* 3. ask questions of. 4. challenge; doubt. —**ques'-tion·a·ble,** *adj.* —**ques'tion·er,** *n.*

ques"tion·naire', *n.* set or list of questions.

queue (kyōō), *n., v.,* **queued, queuing.** *n.*
1. line of waiting persons. 2. braid of
hair at the back of the head. —*v.t., v.i.*
3. form in a line.

quib'ble, *v.i.,* **-bled, -bling,** *n. v.i.* 1.
speak evasively. 2. cavil; carp. —*n.* 3.
act or instance of quibbling.

quiche (kēsh), *n.* French tart filled with
egg, cheese, etc.

quick, *adj.* 1. prompt. 2. intelligent. 3.
speedy. —*n.* 4. living persons. 5. vital
part. —**quick'ly,** *adv.* —**quick'ness,** *n.*

quick'en, *v.t.* 1. hasten. —*v.i.* 2. become
alive or sensitive.

quick'sand", *n.* watery, soft mass of
sand that yields under weight.

quick'sil"ver, *n.* mercury.

quid, *n.* cut of something chewable, esp.
tobacco.

qui·es·cent (kwē·es'ənt), *adj.* inactive.
—**qui·es'cence,** *n.*

qui'et, *adj.* 1. at rest. 2. silent. 3. restrained. —*v.t.* 4. make quiet. —*v.i.* 5.
become quiet. —*n.* 6. silence; tranquillity. —**qui'et·ly,** *adv.* —**qui'et·ness,** *n.*
—**qui'e·tude",** *n.*

qui·e·tus (kwī ēt'əs), *n.* 1. final settlement. 2. death.

quill, *n.* 1. large stiff feather. 2. bristle or
spine.

quilt, *n.* lined and padded bedspread.

quince, *n.* hard yellowish fruit.

qui'nine, *n.* bitter saltlike substance used
medically.

quin·tes'sence, *n.* 1. purest essence. 2.
completely typical example. —**quin"-tes·sen'tial,** *adj.*

quin·tet', *n.* 1. group of five, esp. musicians. 2. composition for five instruments. Also **quin·tette'.**

quin·tu'ple, *adj., v.,* **-pled, -pling.** *adj.* 1.
fivefold. 2. having five parts. —*v.t.,
v.i.* 3. multiply by five.

quin'tu·plet, *n.* 1. one of five children
born together. 2. group of five.

quip, *n., v.i.,* **quipped, quipping.** *n.* 1.
sarcastic or clever remark. —*v.i.* 2.
make a quip.

quire, *n.* set of 24 sheets of paper.

quirk, *n.* peculiarity.

quis'ling, *n.* traitor.

quit, *v.,* **quitted, quitting.** *v.t., v.i.* 1. discontinue. —*v.t.* 2. leave. 3. abandon.
—**quit'ter,** *n.*

quite, *adv.* 1. completely. 2. positively.

quits, *adj.* on equal terms.

quit'tance, *n.* 1. recompense. 2. discharge
from obligation or debt.

quiv'er, *v.t., v.i.* 1. tremble; shake. —*n.*
2. case for arrows.

quix·ot'ic, *adj.* foolishly idealistic.

quiz, *v.t.,* **quizzed, quizzing,** *n., v.t.* 1.
give a brief test to. 2. question closely.
—*n.* 3. test or questioning.

quiz'zi·cal, *adj.* 1. comically odd. 2.
questioning. 3. chaffing. —**quiz'zi·cal·ly,** *adv.*

quoit, *n.* flat ring used in throwing games.

quon'dam, *adj.* former.

quo'rum, *n.* sufficient number of attending members.

quo'ta, *n.* assigned share or number.

quo·ta'tion, *n.* 1. word-for-word citation. 2. specified price.

quo·ta'tion marks, *n.* pair of punctuation marks, " ", used to mark the beginning and end of a direct quotation.

quote, *v.t.,* **quoted, quoting,** *n. v.t.* 1. repeat verbatim. 2. cite as evidence. 3.
state, as a price. —*n.* 4. quotation.
—**quot'a·ble,** *adj.*

quoth, *v.t. Archaic.* said.

quo'tient, *n. Math.* number of times one
number contains another.

R

R, r, *n.* eighteenth letter of the English alphabet.

rab'bet, *n., v.t.,* **-beted, -beting.** *n.* 1.
L-shaped notch on an edge of timber,
etc. —*v.t.* 2. cut a rabbet on. 3. join
with rabbets.

rab'bi, *n., pl.* **-bis.** Jewish preacher.
—**rab·bin'ic, rab·bin'i·cal,** *adj.*

rab'bit, *n.* small long-eared mammal.

rab'ble, *n.* mob.

rab'id, *adj.* 1. irrationally extreme. 2.
having rabies.

ra'bies, *n.* infectious disease transmitted
by animal bites.

rac·coon', *n.* small nocturnal mammal.

race, *n., v.,* **raced, racing.** *n.* 1. contest of
speed. 2. group of persons with a common origin. —*v.i.* 3. participate in a
race. 4. move quickly. —*v.t.* 5. cause
to move quickly.

ra'cial, *adj.* concerning race (2), or the

differences between races. —**rac′ism,** *n.*

rack, *n.* **1.** framework for storage. **2.** bar-like gear engaging a pinion. —*v.t.* **3.** torture. **4.** strain.

rack′et, *n.* **1.** noise; commotion. **2.** dishonest or illegal activity. **3.** cross-stringed light bat, used esp. in tennis.

rack″e·teer′, *n.* gangster.

rac·on·teur (rak″on·tər′) *n.* story-teller.

rac′y, *adj.,* **-ier, -iest. 1.** lively. **2.** risqué.

ra′dar, *n.* device using radio waves to locate objects.

ra′di·al, *adj.* pertaining to rays or a radius.

ra′di·ant, *adj.* **1.** bright; shiny. **2.** emitting light. —**ra′di·ance,** *n.*

ra′di·ate″, *v.,* **-ated, -ating.** *v.i.* **1.** move or spread like rays from a center. —*v.t.* **2.** emit, as rays.

ra′di·a″tor, *n.* convection heater.

rad′i·cal, *adj.* **1.** fundamental. **2.** favoring drastic or extreme change. —*n.* **3.** person with radical ideas. —**rad′i·cal·ism″,** *n.*

ra′di·o″, *n.* **1.** wireless transmission of sound by electromagnetic waves. **2.** device for receiving radio transmissions.

ra″di·o·ac′tive, *adj.* emitting nuclear radiation.

rad′ish, *n.* edible root of a garden plant.

ra′di·um, *n.* radioactive metallic element.

ra′di·us, *n., pl.* **-dii, -diuses. 1.** straight line to an arc from its center. **2.** forearm bone.

raf′fle, *n., v.t.,* **-fled, -fling.** *n.* **1.** lottery for which chances are sold. —*v.t.* **2.** dispose of by raffle.

raft, *n.* floating platform.

raf′ter, *n.* roof beam.

rag, *n.* torn or waste piece of cloth. —**rag′ged,** *adj.*

rag′a·muf″fin, *n.* scruffy child.

rage, *n., v.i.,* **raged, raging.** *n.* **1.** violent anger. **2.** popular vogue. —*v.i.* **3.** be violently angry. **4.** proceed or prevail with violence.

rag′lan, *n.* loose overcoat with shoulders continuing from the sleeves.

ra·gout (ra goo′), *n.* stew.

rag′time″, *n.* syncopated American popular music.

rag′weed″, *n.* weed whose pollen causes hay fever.

raid, *n.* **1.** sudden attack. —*v.t.* **2.** attack suddenly.

rail, *n.* **1.** horizontal bar or beam. **2.** guide for a wheel of a railroad car. **3.** railroad. **4.** wading bird. —*v.i.* **5.** complain bitterly.

rail′ing, *n.* barrier of uprights and rails.

rail′ler·y, *n.* banter; ridicule.

rail′road″, *n.* **1.** road of rails on which trains run. —*v.t.* **2.** transport by rail-road. **3.** *Informal.* convict wrongly an innocent person.

rain, *n.* **1.** condensed water falling in drops from the clouds. **2.** rainstorm. —*v.i.* **3.** fall as rain. —*v.t.* **4.** give abundantly; shower. —**rain′y,** *adj.* —**rain′fall″,** *n.*

rain′bow″, *n.* colored arc of sunlight refracted through raindrops.

rain′coat″, *n.* water-repellent overcoat.

raise, *v.t.,* **raised, raising,** *n., v.t.* **1.** lift. **2.** set upright. **3.** solicit and collect. **4.** grow. **5.** bring up. **6.** call to attention. —*n.* **7.** increase in salary.

rai′sin, *n.* sweet dried grape.

ra′jah, *n.* oriental prince or king. Also **ra′ja.**

rake, *n., v.t.,* **raked, raking.** *n.* **1.** pronged implement for collecting leaves, etc. **2.** libertine. **3.** slope. —*v.t.* **4.** smooth, collect, etc. with a rake.

rak′ish, *adj.* jaunty.

ral′ly, *v.,* **-lied, -lying,** *n., pl.* **-lies.** *v.t., v.i.* **1.** gather. —*v.t.* **2.** reorganize. **3.** tease. —*v.i.* **4.** recover strength. —*n.* **5.** gathering. **6.** recovery of strength.

ram, *n., v.t.,* **rammed, ramming.** *n.* **1.** male sheep. **2.** device for battering, crushing, etc. —*v.t.* **3.** run into forcibly.

ram′ble, *v.i.,* **-bled, -bling,** *n.* *v.i.* **1.** wander leisurely. **2.** talk discursively. —*n.* **3.** leisurely stroll.

ram′i·fy″, *v.,* **-fied, -fying.** *v.t., v.i.* branch out.

ramp, *n.* sloping road or walk.

ram′page, *n., v.i.,* **-paged, -paging.** *n.* **1.** violent behavior. —*v.i.* **2.** rush about furiously.

ramp′ant, *adj.* **1.** unchecked; raging. **2.** standing on the hind legs.

ram′part, *n.* mound of earth erected as a defense; parapet.

ram′shack″le, *adj.* shaky; rickety.

ranch, *n.* large stock farm.

ran·cid (ran′sid), *adj.* stale; spoiled. —**ran·cid′i·ty,** *n.*

ran′cor, *n.* resentment. —**ran′cor·ous,** *adj.*

ran′dom, *adj.* without pattern or aim.

range, *n., v.* **ranged, ranging.** *n.* **1.** extent. **2.** row. **3.** mountain chain. **4.** grazing area. **5.** distance of gunfire, reach, etc. **6.** shooting ground. **7.** stove. —*v.t.* **8.** put in a row. **9.** pass over. —*v.i.* **10.** have a range.

rang′er, *n.* warden or trooper policing a rural area.

rank, *n.* **1.** group, class, or standing. **2.** high position. **3.** row. **4. ranks,** ordinary troops. —*v.t.* **5.** arrange in formation. —*v.i.* **6.** have a specified standing. —*adj.* **7.** excessively grown. **8.** offensively strong in taste or smell. **9.** utter.

ran′kle, *v.* **-kled, -kling.** *v.t.* **1.** cause

long-lasting resentment in. —v.i. 2. cause long-lasting resentment.

ran'sack, v.t. 1. search thoroughly. 2. plunder; pillage.

ran'som, n. 1. price demanded for return of a prisoner. —v.t. 2. redeem for money.

rant, v.i. 1. speak violently or wildly. —n. 2. violent or extravagant speech.

rap, v.t., rapped, rapping, n., v.t. 1. strike sharply. —n. 2. quick, sharp blow. 3. *Informal.* blame; responsibility.

ra·pa'cious, adj. predatory.

rape, n., v.t., raped, raping. n. 1. forced sexual violation of a woman. —v.t. 2. commit rape on. 3. seize and carry off by force. —**ra'pist,** n.

rap'id, adj. 1. speedy. —n. 2. rapids, fast-moving sections of a river. —**ra·pid'i·ty,** n.

ra·pi·er (rā'pē ər), n. small narrow sword.

rap·ine (rap'in), n. plunder.

rapt, adj. engrossed.

rap'ture, n. ecstatic or beatific joy. —**rap'tur·ous,** adj.

rare, adj. rarer, rarest. 1. unusual. 2. thin. 3. not completely cooked. —**rar'i·ty,** n.

rar'e·fy", v., -fied, -fying. v.t., v.i. thin. —**rar"e·fac'tion,** n.

ras'cal, n. unscrupulous person. —**ras·cal'i·ty,** n.

rash, adj. 1. unreasonably hasty. —n. 2. skin irritation.

rash'er, n. thin slice of ham or bacon.

rasp, v.t. 1. scrape or grate. 2. talk with a grating sound. —n. 3. rasping sound. 4. coarse file.

rasp'ber"ry, n., pl. -ries. juicy small red or black fruit.

rat, n. long-tailed rodent larger than a mouse.

ratch'et, n. gear controlled by a pawl.

rate, n., v., rated, rating. n. 1. fixed relation between variables. —v.t. 2. establish a rate for. 3. judge to be as specified. —v.i. 4. have a specified value.

rath'er, adv. 1. to a certain extent. 2. on the contrary. 3. in preference.

rat'i·fy", v.t., -fied, -fying. approve formally.

ra'tion, n. 1. limited allotment. —v.t. 2. put on a ration.

ra'tion·al, adj. 1. reasonable. 2. sane. —**ra"tion·al'i·ty,** n.

ra·tion·ale, n. rational basis.

ra'tion·al·ize", v.t., -ized, -izing. 1. attempt to justify with reasons. 2. make methodical. —**ra"tion·al·i·za'tion,** n.

ra·tio, (rā'shō) n. relation of quantities.

rat·tan', n. hollow stem of a climbing palm.

rat'tle, v., -tled, -tling, n., v.i. 1. make successive short sharp noises. 2. chatter. —v.t. 3. confuse; disconcert. —n. 4. rattling sounds. 5. child's toy that rattles.

rat'tle·snake', n. poisonous American snake.

rau·cous, adj. harsh; hoarse.

rav'age, n., v.t., v.i., -aged, -aging. ruin; pillage.

rave, v.i., raved, raving, n., v.i. 1. talk wildly. —n. 2. *Informal,* unequivocally favorable review.

rav'el, v.t. 1. disengage the threads of. 2. solve; make clear. —v.i. 3. fray. 4. become tangled.

ra'ven, n. large glossy black bird.

rav'en·ous, adj. exceedingly hungry.

ra·vine', n. narrow valley.

rav'ish, v.t. 1. transport or fill with joy. 2. rape.

raw, adj. 1. in a natural state; naked. 2. uncooked. 3. untrained; young.

raw'hide", n. untanned hide.

ray, n. 1. narrow beam of light. 2. glimpse. 3. radiating line. 4. flat ocean fish.

ray'on, n. synthetic silk-like fabric.

raze, v.t., razed, razing. demolish.

ra'zor, n. sharp instrument for shaving.

re (rē), prep. in the affair of.

re-, prefix meaning "again." reaccustom, reacquaint, reacquire, readapt, reaffirm, realign, reappear, reapply, reappoint, reappraisal, rearrange, reassemble, reassert, reassess, reassign, rebind, rebutton, recheck, recommence, reconnect, reconquer, recopy, rededicate, redefine, redevelop, rediscover, redo, reelect, reemerge, reemphasize, reerect, reestablish, reevaluate, reexperience, refill, reformulate, refurnish, regrow, reheat, reignite, reinsert, reinterpret, rekindle, remarry, rename, renumber, reoccur, reorient, replant, replay, reread, resell, resupply, retake, retell, retest, retrain, retransmit, retype, reusable, reuse, reunion, reunite, reverify, rewarm, rewin, rework, rewrap.

reach, v.t. 1. arrive at. 2. extend. 3. be able to touch. 4. communicate with. —v.i. 5. extend the hand. —n. 6. act, instance, or extent of reaching.

re·act', v.i. 1. act in response. 2. interact.

re·ac'tion, n. 1. action in response. 2. extreme political conservatism. —**re·ac'tion·ar"y,** adj., n.

read'ing, n. interpretation of a play or musical composition.

read'y, adj., v.t., readied, readying, n. adj. 1. prepared. 2. willing. 3. imminent. —v.t. 4. make ready. —n. 5. state of readiness. —**read'i·ly,** adv. —**read'i·ness,** n.

re'al, adj. 1. not false; genuine. 2. not imaginary or ideal. —**re·al'i·ty,** n. —**re'al·ly,** adv.

real estate, *n.* property, esp. land with buildings. Also, **re′al·ty.**

re′al·ism, *n.* 1. close imitation of reality. 2. acceptance of actual conditions. —**re′al·ist**, *n.* —**re″al·is′tic**, *adj.*

re′al·ize″, *v.t.* 1. understand completely. 2. bring into actuality. 3. obtain as a profit. —**re″al·i·za′tion**, *n.*

realm (relm), *n.* 1. special field of expertise. 2. kingdom.

re′al·tor, *n.* agent selling real estate.

ream, *n.* 1. twenty quires of paper. —*v.t.* 2. make or enlarge by a rotary tool.

reap, *v.t.* 1. harvest. 2. get as a reward. —**reap′er**, *n.*

rear, *n.* 1. back part. 2. backside. —*adj.* 3. pertaining to the rear. —*v.t.* 4. raise; erect. 5. bring up to maturity. —*v.i.* 6. rise on the rear legs.

rea′son, *n.* 1. cause or justification. 2. objectivity; logic. 3. sanity. —*v.i.* 4. think or argue logically. —*v.t.* 5. infer or conclude. —**rea′son·a·ble**, *adj.* —**rea′son·a·bly**, *adv.*

re″as·sure′, *v.t.,* **-sured, -suring.** restore the confidence of. —**re″as·sur′ance**, *n.*

re′bate, *v.t.,* **-bated, -bating,** *n., v.t.* 1. refund after payment. —*n.* 2. amount rebated.

re·bel′, *v.i.,* **-belled, -belling,** *n., v.i.* (rēbel′) 1. arise against authority. —*n.* (reb′əl) 2. person who rebels. —**re·bel′lion**, *n.* —**re·bel′lious**, *adj.*

re·bound′, *v.i.* (rē bownd′) 1. bounce back after impact. —*n.* (rē′bownd) 2. act or instance of rebounding.

re·buff′, *n.* 1. blunt rejection or refusal. —*v.t.* 2. reject curtly.

re·buke′, *v.t.,* **-buked, -buking,** *n.* reprimand.

re′bus, *n.* combination of pictures whose names combine to form a word.

re·but′, *v.t.,* **-butted, -butting.** refute. —**re·but′tal**, *n.*

re·cal·ci·trant (rē kal′sə trənt), *adj.* stubborn; refractory. —**re·cal′ci·trance,** *n.*

re·call′, *v.t.* 1. remember. 2. withdraw. 3. call or summon back. —*n.* 4. act or instance of recalling. 5. memory.

re·cant′, *v.t., v.i.* retract; renounce. —**re″can·ta′tion**, *n.*

re·ca·pit·u·late, *v.* **-lated, -lating.** *v.t., v.i.* restate briefly; sum up. —**re″ca·pit″u·la′tion**, *n.*

re·cede′, *v.i.,* **-ceded, -ceding.** 1. move back. 2. diminish.

re·ceipt′, *n.* 1. act or instance of receiving. 2. document acknowledging payment or delivery. 3. **receipts,** income.

re·ceive′, *v.t.,* **-ceived, -ceiving.** 1. take when offered or sent. 2. sustain; experience. 3. welcome. —**re·ceiv′a·ble,** *adj.*

re·ceiv′er, *n.* 1. person or thing that receives. 2. apparatus receiving radio signals. 3. administrator of property in litigation. —**re·ceiv′er·ship,** *n.*

re′cent, *adj.* not long past. —**re′cen·cy,** *n.*

re·cep′ta·cle, *n.* container.

re·cep′tion, *n.* 1. act or instance of receiving. 2. formal social function. 3. quality of radio signals, etc. as received.

re·cep′tive, *adj.* 1. ready to consider new ideas. 2. amenable.

re·cess′, *n.* 1. pause in work. 2. hollowed-out space. 3. **recesses,** inner areas. —*v.i.* 4. pause in work.

re·ces′sion, *n.* 1. withdrawal. 2. economic decline.

re·ces′sion·al, *n.* hymn sung during the withdrawal of clergy.

rec′i·pe″, *n.* method or formula, esp. in cooking.

re·cip′i·ent, *n.* receiver.

re·cip′ro·cal, *adj.* 1. mutual. —*n.* 2. counterpart.

re·cip′ro·cate″, *v.,* **-cated, -cating.** *v.t., v.i.* 1. give, receive, etc. in return. 2. move back and forth. —**rec″i·proc′i·ty,** *n.*

re·ci′tal, *n.* 1. account or narration. 2. performance of music.

re·cite′, *v.t.,* **-cited, -citing.** 1. repeat from memory. 2. narrate; read aloud. —**rec″i·ta′tion**, *n.*

reck′less, *adj.* foolhardy, careless.

reck′on, *v.t.* 1. calculate. 2. esteem. 3. *Dialect.* believe; suppose. —*v.i.* 4. deal; cope.

reck′on·ing, *n.* 1. computation. 2. settling of accounts. 3. accounting.

re·claim′, *v.t.* 1. make usable. 2. make reusable. 3. redeem from vice, etc. —**re″cla·ma′tion**, *n.*

re·cline′, *v.,* **-clined, -clining.** *v.i., v.t.* lie or lay back.

rec′luse, *n.* person who lives in seclusion. —**re·clu′sive**, *adj.*

re·cog′ni·zance, *n.* formal pledge of action.

rec′og·nize″, *v.t.,* **-nized, -nizing.** 1. identify from memory. 2. be aware of. 3. acknowledge formally. —**rec″og·ni′tion,** *n.*

re·coil′, *v.i.* 1. draw or shrink back. 2. spring back. —*n.* 3. act or instance of recoiling.

re″col·lect′, *v.t., v.i.* remember. —**rec″ol·lec′tion,** *n.*

rec″om·mend′, *v.t.* 1. speak favorably of. 2. advise. —**rec″om·men·da′tion,** *n.*

rec·om·pense″, *v.t.,* **-pensed, -pensing,** *n. v.t.* 1. reward or compensate. —*n.* 2. reward or compensation.

rec·on·cile″, *v.t.,* **-ciled, -ciling.** 1. return to harmony. 2. make compatible. 3. settle amicably. 4. make acquiescent. —**rec″on·cil′a·ble,** *adj.* —**rec″on·cil″i·a′tion**, *n.*

re"con·noi'ter, *v.t.*, *v.i.* search or scout. —**re·con'nais·sance**, *n.*

re·cord, *v.t.* (rē kord') **1.** make a written account of. **2.** put in reproducible form. —*n.* (rek'ərd) **3.** written account. **4.** disk for sound reproduction. **5.** best performance. —*adj.* **6.** being the best to date.

re·count, *v.t.* (re kownt') **1.** narrate. **2.** count again. —*n.* **3.** (rē'kownt). second count.

re·coup (ri kōōp'), *v.t.* recover; make up.

re'course, *n.* **1.** appeal for help. **2.** possible source of help.

re·cov'er, *v.t.* **1.** get back. **2.** salvage. —*v.i.* **3.** regain health. **4.** regain composure. —**re·cov'er·a·ble**, *adj.* —**re·cov'er·y**, *n.*

rec"re·a'tion, *n.* refreshing occupation. —**rec"re·a'tion·al**, *adj.*

re·crim'i·nate", *v.i.*, **-nated, -nating.** make an accusation in return.

re·cruit', *n.* **1.** newly enlisted person. —*v.t.* **2.** enlist. —**re·cruit'ment**, *n.*

rec'tan·gle, *n.* parallelogram with four right angles. —**rec·tan'gu·lar**, *adj.*

rec'ti·fy", *v.t.*, **-fied, -fying.** correct. —**rec"ti·fi'a·ble**, *adj.* —**rec"ti·fi·ca' tion**, *n.*

rec"ti·lin'e·ar, *adj.* **1.** forming a straight line. **2.** bounded by straight lines.

rec'ti·tude", *n.* moral uprightness.

rec'tor, *n.* **1.** clergyman in charge of a parish. **2.** head of certain universities and colleges.

rec'to·ry, *n.* parsonage.

rec'tum, *n.* terminal part of the large intestine. —**rec'tal**, *adj.*

re·cum'bent, *adj.* lying down. —**re·cum' ben·cy**, *n.*

re·cu'per·ate", *v.i.*, **-ated, -ating,** regain health. —**re·cu'per·a·tive**, *adj.*

re·cur', *v.i.*, **-curred, -curring. 1.** occur again or repeatedly. **2.** return to one's thoughts. —**re·cur'rence**, *n.* —**re·cur' rent**, *adj.* —**re·cur'rent·ly**, *adv.*

re·cy'cle, *v.t.* convert into reusable material.

red, *n.*, *adj.*, **redder, reddest.** *n.* **1.** color of blood. **2.** **Red**, *Informal.* Communist. —*adj.* **3.** of or pertaining to red. —**red'den**, *v.t.*, *v.i.*

re·deem', *v.t.* **1.** recover. **2.** pay off. **3.** exchange for premiums. **4.** deliver from sin. **5.** fulfill, as a promise. —**re·demp' tion**, *n.*

Re·deem'er, *n.* Jesus Christ.

red'-let'ter, *adj.* memorable.

red'o·lent, *adj.* **1.** odorous. **2.** suggestive. —**red'o·lence**, *n.*

re·doubt'a·ble, *adj.* formidable.

re·dound', *v.i.* occur as a consequence.

re·dress', *v.t.* (rē dres') **1.** right, as a wrong. —*n.* (rē'dres) **2.** act or instance of redressing.

red tape, bureaucratic procedures.

re·duce', *v.*, **-duced, -ducing.** *v.t.* **1.** lessen. **2.** alter. **3.** lower in rank, etc. **4.** subdue. —*v.i.* **5.** act so as to lose weight. —**re·duc'i·ble**, *adj.* —**re·duc' tion**, *n.*

re·dun'dant, *adj.* **1.** excess; surplus. **2.** repetitive. —**re·dun'dance, re·dun' dan·cy**, *n.*

red'wood", *n.* huge California evergreen tree.

reed, *n.* **1.** tall marsh grass. **2.** vibrating part of the mouthpiece on certain wind instruments. —**reed'y**, *adj.*

reef, *n.* **1.** ridge near the surface of a body of water. **2.** part of a sail. —*v.t.* **3.** shorten, as a sail.

reef'er, *n.* **1.** short jacket or coat. **2.** *Informal.* marijuana cigarette.

reek, *v.i.* **1.** smell strongly. —*n.* **2.** strong or foul smell.

reel, *n.* **1.** revolving drum for winding. **2.** lively dance. —*v.t.* **3.** wind on a reel. —*v.i.* **4.** stagger or sway. **5.** whirl.

re·fec'to·ry, *n.* dining hall.

re·fer', *v.*, **referred, referring.** *v.i.* **1.** allude. **2.** look for information. —*v.t.* **3.** direct for help or information. **4.** submit for arbitration. —**ref'er·a·ble**, *adj.* —**re·fer'ral**, *n.*

ref·er·ee', *n.* **1.** arbiter. *v.t.*, *v.i.* **2.** arbitrate.

ref'er·ence, *n.* **1.** act or instance of referring. **2.** something referred to. **3.** recommendation. **4.** person giving a recommendation.

ref"er·en'dum, *n.* submission of a proposed law for citizen approval.

re·fine', *v.t.*, **-fined, -fining. 1.** free from impurities. **2.** make cultured. —**re· fine'ment**, *n.*

re·fin'er·y, *n.*, *pl.* **-eries.** factory for refining, esp. petroleum.

re·flect', *v.t.* **1.** return, as images, light, etc. **2.** period of rule. Also, **ré·gime'.** carefully. —**re·flec'tion**, *n.* —**re·flec' tive**, *adj.* —**re·flec'tor**, *n.*

re'flex, *adj.* **1.** denoting involuntary reaction. —*n.* **2.** involuntary reaction.

re·flex'ive, *adj.* **1.** having the same subject and object as a verb. **2.** used as the object of a reflexive verb, as a pronoun.

re·form', *n.* **1.** correction of wrongs. —*v.t.* **2.** correct the wrongs of. —*v.i.* **3.** correct one's wrongdoing. —**ref"or· ma'tion**, *n.*

re·form'a·to"ry, *n.*, *pl.* **-ries.** penal institution for minors.

re·frac'tion, *n.* bending of light or heat rays in passing from one medium to another. —**re·fract'**, *v.t.* —**re·frac' tive**, *adj.* —**re·frac'tor**, *n.*

re·frain', *v.i.* **1.** hold back; forbear. —*n.* **2.** recurring passage in a song or poem.

re·fresh', *v.t.* **1.** revive after stress. **2.**

quicken; stimulate. —re·fresh'ment, *n.*

re·frig'er·ate'', *v.t.,* -ated, -ating. keep or make cold. —re·frig'er·ant, *n.* —re·frig'er·a''tor, *n.*

ref'uge, *n.* shelter from danger.

ref''u·gee', *n.* seeker of refuge.

re·fund, *v.t.* (re fund') 1. repay. —*n.* 2. (rē'fund). repayment.

re·fur'bish, *v.t.* renovate.

re·fuse, *v.t.,* -fused, -fusing, *n. v.t.* (rē fyōōz') 1. decline. 2. decline to accept. 3. deny, as a request. —*n.* (ref'yōōz). 4. rubbish. —re·fus'al, *n.*

re·fute', *v.t.,* -futed, -futing. prove wrong or false. —ref'u·ta·ble, *adj.* —ref''u·ta'tion, *n.*

re·gain', *v.t.* 1. get again. 2. return to again.

re'gal, *adj.* royal.

re·gale', *v.t.,* -galed, -galing. entertain lavishly.

re·ga'li·a, *n. pl.* royal or official insignia.

re·gard', *v.t.* 1. look on. 2. consider. 3. concern; relate to. 4. hold in respect. —*n.* 5. look; gaze. 6. relation. 7. affection and respect. 8. particular point. 9. regards, good wishes.

re·gard'less, *adj.* 1. careless. —*adv.* 2. anyway.

re·gat'ta, *n.* boat race.

re·gen'er·ate'', *v.t., adj.,* -ated, -ating. *v.t.* 1. produce anew. 2. reform. 3. *Biol.* regrow. —*adj.* 4. renewed; reformed. —re·gen'er·a·tive, *adj.*

re'gent, *n.* 1. appointed substitute for a monarch. 2. member of a governing board. —re'gen·cy, *n.*

re·gime', *n.* 1. system of government, etc. 2. period of rule. Also, ré·gime'.

reg'i·men, *n.* 1. government; rule. 2. *Medicine.* system of diet, etc.

reg·i·ment, *n.* (rej'ə mənt) 1. army unit of two or more battalions. —*v.t.* (rej'ə ment'') 2. subject to strict discipline. —reg''i·men'tal, *adj.* —reg''i·men'ta·tion, *n.*

re'gion, *n.* part of the earth's surface. —re'gion·al, *adj.*

re'gion·al·ism, *n.* 1. sponsorship of or adherence to regional culture. 2. regional peculiarity.

reg'is·ter, *n.* 1. written record, list, etc. 2. cash register. 3. device for regulating the passage of air. 4. *Music.* range. —*v.t., v.i.* 5. enroll. —*v.t.* 6. show, as on the face. —*v.i.* 7. make an impression. —reg'is·trant, *n.* —reg''is·tra'tion, *n.* —reg'is·try, *n.*

reg'is·trar'', *n.* official record keeper.

re·gress', *v.i.* 1. go back. 2. revert. —*n.* 3. going back. —re·gres'sion, *n.* —re·gres'sive, *adj.*

re·gret', *v.t.,* -gretted, -gretting, *n. v.t.* 1. feel sorry about. —*n.* 2. sorrow or re-

morse. —re·gret'ful, *adj.* —re·gret'ta·ble, *adj.*

reg·u·lar, *adj.* 1. customary. 2. consistent. 3. symmetrical. 4. permanent, as an army. 5. *Informal.* a. complete. b. likeable. —*n.* 6. someone regularly seen. 7. regular soldier. —reg''u·lar'i·ty, *n.* —reg'u·lar·ize'', *v.t.*

reg'u·late'', *v.t.,* -lated, -lating. 1. control by rule. 2. make regular. —reg'u·la''tor, *n.* —reg'u·la·to''ry, *adj.* —reg'u·la''tive, *adj.*

re·gur'gi·tate'', *v.,* -tated, -tating. *v.i., v.t.* belch or vomit.

re''ha·bil'i·tate'', *v.t.,* -tated, -tating. restore to a former good condition. —re''ha·bil'i·ta''tive, *adj.*

re·hash', *v.t.* 1. work over again. —*n.* 2. rehashing.

re·hearse', *v.,* -hearsed, -hearsing. *v.t., v.i.* practice for a performance. —re·hears'al, *n.*

reign (rān), *n.* 1. royal power. 2. period of rule. —*v.i.* 3. rule as a monarch. 4. prevail.

re''im·burse', *v.t.,* -bursed, -bursing. pay back. —re''im·burse'ment, *n.*

rein (rān), strap for controlling a horse.

re''in·car·na'tion, *n.* rebirth in a new body.

rein'deer'', *n., pl.* -deer. large northern deer.

re''in·force', *v.t.,* -forced, -forcing. strengthen. —re''in·force'ment, *n.*

re''in·state', *v.t.,* -stated, -stating. restore to a former state. —re''in·state'ment, *n.*

re·it'er·ate'', *v.t.,* -ated, -ating. say or do again. —re·it'er·a''tive, *adj.*

re·ject, *v.t.* (ri'jekt') 1. refuse to accept. 2. discard. —*n.* (rē jekt) 3. rejected person or thing. —re·jec'tion, *n.*

re·joice', *v.,* -joiced, -joicing. *v.t.* 1. gladden. —*v.i.* 2. feel joy. —re·joic'ing, *n.*

re·join', *v.t., v.i.* 1. join again. 2. answer.

re·join'der, *n.* 1. reply. 2. *Law.* defendant's response.

re·ju've·nate'', *v.t.,* -nated, -nating. make young again.

re·lapse', *v.i.,* -lapsed, -lapsing, *n. v.i.* 1. fall into a former state. —*n.* 2. act or instance of relapsing.

re·late', *v.,* -lated, -lating. *v.t.* 1. tell; narrate. 2. connect; associate. —*v.i.* 3. have a relation.

re·la'tion, *n.* 1. narrative. 2. connection; association. 3. connection by blood or marriage. —re·la'tion·ship'', *n.*

rel'a·tive, *adj.* 1. comparative. 2. related to each other. —*n.* 3. person related by blood or marriage.

rel''a·tiv'i·ty, *n.* 1. interdependence. 2. *Physics.* theory of the relative character of position, motion, etc. and the interdependence of time and space.

re·lax', *v.t.*, *v.i.* rest, as from work or tension. —**re''lax·a'tion**, *n.*

re·lay *n.* (rē'lā) **1.** relief crew or team. **2.** race in which team members run individual portions. —*v.t.* (rē' lā; also ri lā') **3.** send by relay or relays. **4.** lay again.

re·lease', *v.t.*, -leased, -leasing, *n.* *v.t.* **1.** free. **2.** let go of. **3.** license for publication. —*n.* **4.** act or instance of releasing. **5.** communication, etc. **6.** *Law.* surrender, as of a claim.

rel'e·gate'', *v.t.*, -gated, -gating. **1.** consign to a lesser place or position. **2.** refer for decision.

re·lent', *v.i.* become less severe, cruel, etc. —**re·lent'less**, *adj.*

rel'e·vant, *adj.* relating to the matter at hand. —**rel'e·vance, rel'e·van·cy**, *n.*

re·li'a·ble, *adj.* dependable. —**re·li''a·bil'i·ty**, *n.*

re·li'ance, *n.* **1.** trust; confidence. **2.** something relied on. —**re·li'ant**, *adj.*

rel'ic, *n.* **1.** survival from the past. **2.** souvenir.

re·lief', *n.* **1.** release from pain, discomfort, etc. **2.** means of such relief. **3.** sculptured surface. **4.** projection from a background.

re·lieve', *v.t.*, -lieved, -lieving. **1.** ease, as from pain or discomfort. **2.** vary. **3.** release from duty.

re·li'gion, *n.* **1.** belief in a divine being or beings. **2.** specific form of belief and practice. —**re·li'gious**, *adj.*

re·lin'quish, *v.t.* **1.** give up. **2.** renounce, as a right. —**re·lin'quish·ment**, *n.*

rel'ish, *n.* **1.** zest. **2.** condiment. **3.** appetizing flavor. —*v.t.* **4.** take pleasure in.

re·live', *v.t.*, -lived, -living. experience again in the imagination.

re·lo'cate, *v.*, -cated, -cating. *v.t.*, *v.i.* settle in a new location.

re·luc'tant, *adj.* unwilling. —**re·luc'tance**, *n.*

re·ly', *v.i.*, -lied, -lying. depend; trust.

re·main', *v.i.* **1.** stay behind. **2.** endure; persist. **3.** continue as before. —*n.* **4. remains**, **a.** remainder. **b.** corpse. —**re·main'der**, *n.*

re·mand', *v.t.* send back or consign again.

re·mark', *v.t.*, *v.i.*, *n.* **1.** comment. —*v.t.*, *n.* **2.** notice.

re·mark'a·ble, *adj.* worthy of notice or comment.

rem'e·dy, *n.*, *v.t.*, -died, -dying. *n.* **1.** medicine or treatment. **2.** something that corrects wrong. —*v.t.* **3.** cure; correct. —**re·me'di·al**, *adj.*

re·mem'ber, *v.t.* **1.** recall to mind. **2.** not forget. **3.** carry greetings from. —**re·mem'brance**, *n.*

re·mind', *v.t.* cause to remember. —**re·mind'er**, *n.*

rem''i·nisce', *v.i.*, -nisced, -niscing. discuss or think of the past. —**rem''i·nis'cence**, *n.* —**rem''i·nis'cent**, *adj.*

re·miss', *adj.* careless; slack.

re·mis'sion, *n.* **1.** forgiveness. **2.** diminution, as of disease.

re·mit', *v.t.*, -mitted, -mitting. **1.** forgive. **2.** refrain from imposing. **3.** relax; abate. **4.** send in payment. —**re·mit'tance**, *n.*

rem'nant, *n.* something left over.

re·mod'el, *v.t.*, -eled, -eling. make over; rebuild.

re·mon'strate, *v.*, -strated, -strating. *v.t.*, *v.i.* protest; object. —**re·mon'strance**, *n.*

re·morse', *n.* mental anguish from guilt. —**re·morse'ful**, *adj.* —**re·morse'less**, *adj.*

re·mote', *adj.*, -moter, -motest. **1.** distant. **2.** slight.

re·move', *v.*, -moved, -moving, *n.* *v.t.* **1.** move from a place. **2.** dismiss, as from office. —*v.i.* **3.** change residence. —*n.* **4.** interval; step. —**re·mov'a·ble**, *adj.* —**re·mov'al**, *n.*

re·mu'ner·ate', *v.t.*, -ated, -ating. pay; recompense. —**re·mu'ner·a''tive**, *adj.*

ren'ais·sance'', *n.* **1.** rebirth. **2. Renaissance**, revival of classical learning in Europe.

re'nal, *adj.* pertaining to the kidneys.

re·nas'cence, *n.* rebirth; revival.

rend', *v.*, rent, rending. *v.t.*, *v.i.* split apart by force.

ren'der, *v.t.* **1.** give in return. **2.** submit. **3.** state, as a decision. **4.** furnish. **5.** express or interpret. **6.** translate.

ren·dez·vous (rän'dā voo''), *n.*, *pl.* -vous. **1.** meeting place. **2.** appointment to meet.

ren·di'tion, *n.* rendering; performance.

ren'e·gade'', *n.* deserter of a cause.

re·nege', *v.i.*, -neged, -neging. *Informal.* go back on one's word.

re·new', *v.t.* **1.** make new. **2.** revive. —**re·new'al**, *n.*

re·nounce', *v.t.*, -nounced, -nouncing. give up formally. —**re·nun''ci·a'tion, re·nounce'ment**, *n.*

ren'o·vate'', *v.t.* -vated, -vating. make as if new.

re·nown', *n.* great reputation. —**re·nowned'**, *adj.*

rent, *n.* **1.** Also **rent'al**, payment for temporary use. **2.** tear; rip. —*v.t.* **3.** use by paying. **4.** grant temporarily for payment.

re·pair', *v.t.* **1.** return to good condition. **2.** set right. —*v.i.* **3.** go. —*n.* **4.** act or instance of repairing. **5.** good condition. —**rep'a·ra·ble, re·pair'a·ble**, *adj.*

rep''a·ra'tion, *n.* **1.** amends for injury. **2. reparations**, compensation for war damage.

rep"ar·tee', *n.* clever, quick-witted talk.

re·past', *n.* meal.

re·pa'tri·ate", *v., -ated, -ating. v.t., v.i.* return to one's country.

re·pay', *v.t., -paid, -paying.* pay back. —**re·pay'ment**, *n.*

re·peal', *v.t.* 1. revoke. —*n.* 2. revocation.

re·peat', *v.t., v.i.* 1. say or do again. —*n.* 2. act or instance of repeating. —**rep"e·ti'tion**, *n.* —**rep"e·ti'tious**, *adj.*

re·pel', *v.t., -pelled, -pelling.* 1. drive back. 2. disgust. —**re·pel'lent**, *adj., n.*

re·pent', *v.t., v.i.* regret as wrong or mistaken. —**re·pent'ance**, *n.* —**re·pent'ant**, *adj.*

re"per·cus'sion, *n.* 1. indirect result. 2. reverberation. —**re"per·cus'sive**, *adj.*

rep'er·toire", *n.* stock of songs, plays, etc. performed. Also **rep'er·to"ry**, *n.*

re·place', *v.t., -placed, -placing.* 1. put back in place. 2. substitute for. —**re·place'a·ble**, *adj.* —**re·place'ment**, *n.*

re·plen'ish, *v.t.* make full again. --**re·plen'ish·ment**, *n.*

re·plete', *adj.* plentifully filled. —**re·ple'tion**, *n.*

rep'li·ca, *n.* copy.

re·ply', *v., -plied, -plying, n., pl. -plies. v.t., v.i., n.* answer.

re·port', *n.* 1. statement. 2. rumor. 3. explosive noise. —*v.t.* 4. give an account of. 5. inform against. —*v.i.* 6. make a report. 7. present oneself.

re·pose', *v.t., -posed, -posing, n. v.t.* 1. rest or sleep. 2. place. 3. depend. —*n.* 4. rest or sleep. 5. tranquillity.

re·pos'i·tor"y, *n., pl. -tories.* place of storage.

rep"re·hend', *v.t.* rebuke. —**rep"re·hen'si·ble**, *adj.* —**rep"re·hen'sion**, *n.*

rep"re·sent', *v.t.* 1. exemplify. 2. portray. 3. act or speak for. —**rep"re·sen·ta'tion**, *n.*

rep"re·sen'ta·tive, *adj.* 1. serving as an example. 2. acting or speaking for others. —*n.* 3. person who represents. 4. elected legislator.

re·press', *v.t.* restrain; check. —**re·pres'sive**, *adj.* —**re·pres'sion**, *n.*

re·prieve', *v.t., -prieved, -prieving, n. v.t.* 1. relieve temporarily. —*n.* 2. temporary delay; respite.

rep'ri·mand", *n.* 1. severe or formal rebuke. —*v.t.* 2. rebuke; censure.

re·pris'al, *n.* retaliation.

re·proach', *v.t.* 1. scold for a fault; blame. —*n.* 2. discredit. —**re·proach'ful**, *adj.*

rep'ro·bate', *n., adj., v.t., -bated, -bating. n.* 1. depraved person. —*adj.* 2. depraved. —*v.t.* 3. condemn.

re"pro·duce', *v.t., -duced, -ducing.* 1. copy; duplicate. 2. produce by propagation. —**re"pro·duc'tion**, *n.* —**re"pro·duc'tive**, *adj.*

re·proof', *n.* rebuke; censure.

re·prove', *v.t., -proved, -proving.* rebuke; censure. —**re·prov'al**, *n.*

rep'tile, *n.* cold-blooded vertebrate. —**rep·til'i·an**, *adj.*

re·pub'lic, *n.* state governed by elected legislators.

re·pub'li·can, *adj.* 1. pertaining to or favoring a republic. —*n.* 2. **Republican**, member of the Republican party. 3. partisan of a republican form of government. —**re·pub'li·can·ism**, *n.*

re·pu'di·ate", *v.t., -ated, -ating.* disown; disavow.

re·pug'nant, *adj.* distasteful. —**re·pug'nance**, *n.*

re·pulse', *v.t., -pulsed, -pulsing, n. v.t.* 1. drive back, as an attack. 2. reject; rebuff. —*n.* 3. act or instance of repulsing. —**re·pul'sion**, *n.*

re·pul'sive, *adj.* disgusting.

rep'u·ta·ble, *adj.* of good reputation.

rep"u·ta'tion, *n.* 1. estimation of a person or thing. 2. fame.

re·pute', *n., v.t., -puted, -puting. n.* 1. reputation. —*v.t.* 2. consider or regard.

re·quest', *v.t.* 1. ask for. —*n.* 2. act or instance of requesting. 3. something requested.

re'qui·em, *n.* service for the dead.

re·quire', *v.t., -quired, -quiring.* 1. need. 2. demand. —**re·quire'ment**, *n.*

req'ui·site, *n.* 1. something necessary. —*adj.* 2. required; necessary.

req"ui·si'tion, *n.* 1. act or instance of requiring. 2. formal order for goods, etc. —*v.t.* 3. take by authority.

re·quite', *v.t., -quited, -quiting.* repay; return. —**re·quit'al**, *n.*

re·scind', *v.t.* revoke; annul.

res'cue, *v.t., -cued, -cuing, n. v.t.* 1. free or save. —*n.* 2. act or instance of rescuing.

re·search', *n.* 1. careful investigation. —*v.t.* 2. do research on or in.

re·sem'ble, *v.t., -bled, -bling.* be like or similar to. —**re·sem'blance**, *n.*

re·sent', *v.t.* feel indignant at. —**re·sent'ful**, *adj.* —**re·sent'ment**, *n.*

res"er·va'tion, *n.* 1. act or instance of reserving. 2. advance request for accommodation. 3. public land for Indians.

re·serve', *v.t., -served, -serving, n. v.t.* 1. keep back; set aside. —*n.* 2. something reserved. 3. reticence, as about feelings. 4. inactive troops subject to call. 5. reserved district.

re·serv'ist, *n.* member of a military reserve.

res'er·voir", *n.* storage place for water.

re·side', *v.i., -sided, -siding.* 1. dwell. 2. be present.

res'i·dence, *n.* 1. dwelling place. 2. act or

instance of residing. —res'i·dent, n., adj. —res"i·den'tial, adj.

res'i·due', n. remainder. —re·sid'u·al, adj.

re·sign', v.i. 1. give up a job or duty. —v.t. 2. give up. 3. yield or submit.

res"ig·na'tion, n. 1. act or instance of resigning. 2. submission, as to the inevitable.

re·signed', adj. reluctantly submissive.

re·sil'i·ent, adj. elastic; buoyant. —re·sil'i·ence, n.

res'in, n. substance exuded by certain plants. —res'in·ous, adj.

re·sist', v.t., v.i. withstand; oppose. —re·sist'ance, n.

res'o·lute", adj. firm in purpose; determined.

res"o·lu'tion, n. 1. formal expression of opinion. 2. decision. 3. firmness of purpose.

re·solve', v., -solved, -solving, n. v.t., v.i. 1. decide; determine. —v.t. 2. analyze. 3. solve. 4. dispel, as fear. —n. 5. determination.

res'o·nant, adj. 1. resounding. 2. vibrant; sonorous. —res'o·nance, n. —res'o·nate", v.t., v.i. —res'o·na"tor, n.

re·sort', v.i. 1. have recourse. —n. 2. public place, as for recreation. 3. recourse.

re·sound', v.i. reverberate; ring out. —re·sound'ing, adj.

re·source', n. 1. source of help or support. 2. resources, money; means.

re·source'ful, adj. clever; able.

re·spect', n. 1. esteem; honor. 2. consideration. 3. detail. 4. deference; regard. —v.t. 5. show consideration for. 6. hold in honor. —re·spect'a·ble, adj. —re·spect'ful, adj.

re·spect'ing, prep. concerning.

re·spec'tive, adj. relating to each of several.

res'pi·ra"tor, n. apparatus for artificial breathing.

re·spire', v., -spired, -spiring. v.t., v.i. breathe. —res"pi·ra'tion, n. —re·spir'a·to"ry, adj.

res'pite, n. temporary relief.

re·splend'ent, adj. shining brightly. —re·splend'ence, n.

re·spond', v.i. 1. answer. 2. react.

re·spond'ent, n. Law. defendant.

re·sponse', n. reply. —re·spon'sive, adj.

re·spon"si·bil'i·ty, n., pl. -ties. 1. state of being responsible. 2. obligation.

re·spon'si·ble, adj. 1. accountable. 2. reliable. 3. distinguishing between right and wrong. —re·spon'si·bly, adv.

rest, n. 1. sleep; repose. 2. inactivity after work. 3. support; base. 4. Music. silent interval. —v.i. 5. be at rest. 6. lay. 7.

lie. —v.t. 8. cause to rest. 9. base. —rest'ful, adj. —rest'less, adj.

res'tau·rant, n. public eating place.

res"tau·ra·teur', n. proprietor of a restaurant.

res"ti·tu'tion, n. 1. return of something taken away. 2. reparation.

res'tive, adj. 1. balky; stubborn. 2. restless.

re·store', v.t., -stored, -storing. 1. return to a former state. 2. give back. —res'to·ra'tion, n. —re·stor'a·tive, adj.

re·strain', v.t. 1. hold back; check. 2. confine.

re·straint', n. 1. control of emotions, etc. 2. confinement. 3. something that restrains.

re·strict', v.t. limit; confine. —re·stric'tion, n. —re·stric'tive, adj. —re·strict'ed, adj.

re·sult', n. 1. consequence; outcome. —v.i. 2. follow as a consequence. —re·sult'ant, adj., n.

re·sume', v.t., -sumed, -suming. 1. continue. 2. take again. —re·sump'tion, n.

ré·su·mé', n. summary, as of work experience.

re·sur'gent, adj. tending to rise again. —re·sur'gence, n.

res"ur·rect', v.t. raise from the dead. —res"ur·rec'tion, n.

re·sus'ci·tate", v., -tated, -tating. v.t., v.i. revive from unconsciousness. —re·sus"ci·ta'tion, n. —re·sus'ci·ta"tor, n.

re'tail, n. 1. sale of consumer goods. —v.t., v.i. 2. sell at retail.

re·tain', v.t. 1. keep; hold. 2. hire by a retainer.

re·tain'er, n. 1. fee for continuing services. 2. servant.

re·tal'i·ate', v.i., -ated, -ating. give like for like, esp. in revenge. —re·tal'i·a·to"ry, adj.

re·tard', v.t. hinder; slow. —re·tar·da'tion, n. —re·tard'ant, n.

re·tard'ed, adj. limited or slow in mental development.

retch (rech), v.i. try to vomit.

re·ten'tion, n. 1. act or instance of retaining. 2. power of remembering. —re·ten'tive, adj.

ret'i·cent, adj. disposed to silence; taciturn. —ret'i·cence, n.

ret'i·na, n. coating of the posterior interior of the eyeball.

ret'i·nue", n. group of attendants.

re·tire', v., -tired, -tiring. v.i., v.t. 1. withdraw. 2. withdraw from working life. —v.i. 3. go to bed. —v.t. 4. pay off, as bonds. —re·tir'ee', n. —re·tire'ment, n.

re·tir'ing, adj. shy; reserved.

re·tort', v.t., v.i. 1. answer smartly or wittily. —n. 2. quick, witty answer.

re·touch', v.t. touch up or improve, as a photograph.

re·tract', v.t., v.i. withdraw. —**re·tract'a·ble**, adj. —**re·trac'tion**, n.

re·treat', n. 1. withdrawal, as from danger. 2. secluded place. —v.i. 3. withdraw.

re·trench', v.t., v.i. cut down as an economy. —**re·trench'ment**, n.

ret"ri·bu'tion, n. retaliation; punishment. —**re·trib'u·tive**, adj.

re·trieve', v.t., -trieved, -trieving. 1. regain. 2. recover. 3. make good, as a mistake. —**re·triev'al**, n.

ret"ro·ac'tive, adj. valid for some past period.

ret"ro·grade", adj., v.i., -graded, -grading. adj. 1. directed backward; reversed. —v.i. 2. go backward. 3. degenerate. —**ret"ro·gres'sion**, n. —**ret"ro·gres'sive**, adj.

ret"ro·spect", n. look to the past. —**ret"ro·spec'tive**, adj. —**ret"ro·spec'tion**, n.

re·turn', v.i. 1. go back. 2. reply. —v.t. 3. put back. 4. repay. 5. elect or re-elect. 6. yield, as a profit. —n. 7. act or instance of returning. 8. recurrence. 8. repayment; yield. 9. report; response. —**re·turn'a·ble**, adj.

rev, v.t., revved, revving, n. Informal. v.t. 1. increase the speed of, as a motor. —n. 2. revolution, as of a machine.

re·vamp', v.t. redo; revise.

re·veal', v.t. 1. disclose. 2. manifest.

rev·eil·le (rev'ə lē), n. Military. signal for awakening.

rev'el, v.i., -eled, -eling, n. v.i. 1. take great delight. 2. make merry. —n. 3. merrymaking. —**rev'el·ry**, n.

rev"e·la'tion, n. 1. act or instance of revealing. 2. **Revelation**, last book of the New Testament.

re·venge', n., v.t., -venged, -venging. n. 1. retaliation. 2. vindictiveness. —v.t. 3. take revenge for. —**re·venge'ful**, adj.

rev'e·nue", n. income, as from taxes.

re·ver'ber·ate", v., -ated, -ating. v.t., v.i. reecho; resound.

re·vere', v.t., -vered, -vering. regard with deep respect, love, etc.

rev'er·ence, n., v.t., -enced, -encing. n. 1. deep respect. —v.t. 2. revere; honor. —**rev'er·ent**, **rev"er·en'tial**, adj.

rev'er·end, adj. 1. worthy of reverence. 2. **Reverend**, title of respect for a clergyman.

rev'er·ie, n., pl. -ies. daydreaming; deep musings. Also **rev'er·y**.

re·verse', adj., n., v., -versed, -versing. adj. 1. turned backward. 2. making an opposite motion. —n. 3. opposite; contrary. 4. misfortune. —v.t. 5. turn back or in an opposite direction. 6. ex-

change; transpose. —v.i. 7. move in an opposite direction. —**re·vers'i·ble**, adj.

re·vert', v.i. return as to a former way or state, etc. —**re·ver'sion**, n.

re·view', n. 1. reexamination. 2. general survey or report. 3. critical writing. —v.t. 4. reexamine. 5. look back on. 6. write a review of. 7. inspect formally.

re·vile', v.t., -viled, -viling. speak abusively. —**re·vile'ment**, n.

re·vise', v.t., -vised, -vising. amend. —**re·vi'sion**, n.

re·viv'al, n. 1. return to life, use, etc. 2. emotional religious meeting. —**re·viv'al·ist**, n.

re·vive', v., -vived, -viving. v.i., v.t. return to consciousness or effectiveness.

re·voke', v.t., -voked, -voking. repeal or nullify. —**rev'o·ca·ble**, adj. —**rev"o·ca'tion**, n.

re·volt', n. 1. uprising; rebellion. —v.i. 2. rebel. —v.t. 3. disgust.

rev"o·lu'tion, n. 1. war against one's government. 2. complete change 3. rotation. —**rev"o·lu'tion·ar"y**, adj., n. —**rev"o·lu'tion·ist**, n.

rev"o·lu'tion·ize", v.t., -ized, -izing. change completely or radically.

re·volve', v., -volved, -volving. v.t. 1. cause to rotate. —v.i. 2. rotate.

re·volv'er, n. pistol with a revolving magazine.

re·vue', n. light musical show.

re·vul'sion, n. 1. violent change of feeling. 2. disgust.

re·ward', n. 1. grateful gift or payment. —v.t. 2. give a reward to.

rhap'so·dy, n., pl. -dies. free, irregular musical composition. —**rhap·sod'ic**, adj.

rhe'o·stat", n. device for varying an electric current.

rhe'sus, n. monkey of India.

rhet'o·ric, n. 1. art of using language effectively. 2. exaggerated speech. —**rhe·tor'i·cal**, adj.

rheu'ma·tism", n. painful condition of the muscles and joints. —**rheu·mat'ic**, adj.

rhine'stone", n. imitation diamond.

rhi·noc'er·os, n. massive, thick-skinned mammal with a horned snout.

rho"do·den'dron, n. evergreen shrub with pink, white, or purple flowers.

rhom'bus, n., pl. -buses, -bi. equilateral parallelogram with oblique angles.

rhu'barb, n. edible plant with long, thick stalks.

rhyme, n., v. **rhymed, rhyming**. n. 1. similarity of sound at verse ends. 2. poetry with such similarity. —v.i., v.t. 3. compose in rhyme.

rhythm, n. regular recurrence of stress, as in poetry or music. —**rhyth'mic**, adj.

rib, *n.*, *v.t.*, **ribbed, ribbing.** *n.* **1.** one of the curved bones around the chest cavity. **2.** rib-like structure. —*v.t.* **3.** reinforce with ribs. **4.** *Informal.* tease.

rib'ald, *adj.* indecent or vulgar in language. —**rib'ald·ry,** *n.*

rib'bon, *n.* narrow strip of fabric.

ri'bo·fla''vin, *n.* component of the vitamin B complex found in milk, eggs, meat, etc.

rice, *n.* edible cereal of warm climates.

rich, *adj.* **1.** having much wealth. **2.** abundant; abounding. **3.** full of desirable qualities or resources. **4.** appetizing but hard to digest. **5.** mellow. —*n.* **6. the rich,** people of wealth. **7. riches,** wealth. —**rich'ly,** *adv.* —**rich'ness,** *n.*

rick, *n.* stack of hay, straw, etc.

rick'ets, *n.* nutritional deficiency disease of childhood characterized by bone deformities.

rick'et·y, *adj.* shaky; feeble.

rick'shaw, *n.* carriage pulled by a man. Also **rick'sha.**

ric·o·chet (rik'ə sha''), *n.*, *v.i.*, **-cheted, -cheting.** *n.* **1.** rebound of an object from a hard surface. —*v.i.* **2.** rebound.

rid, *v.t.*, **rid** or **ridded, ridding.** free; clear. —**rid'dance,** *n.*

rid'dle, *n.*, *v.*, **-dled, -dling.** *n.* **1.** puzzle; enigma. **2.** coarse sieve. —*v.t.* **3.** pierce with holes. **4.** sift through a riddle. **5.** permeate.

ride, *v.*, **rode, ridden, riding,** *n.*, *v.t.* **1.** be carried on or within. **2.** be carried over or through. —*v.i.* **3.** be carried. **4.** depend (on). **5.** be at anchor. —*n.* **6.** act or instance of riding.

rid'er, *n.* **1.** person who rides. **2.** addition to a document.

ridge, *n.*, *v.*, **ridged, ridging.** *n.* **1.** narrow, raised edge. **2.** sharp crest or elevation of land. —*v.t.*, *v.i.* **3.** form into a ridge.

rid'i·cule'', *n.*, *v.t.*, **-culed, -culing.** *n.* **1.** derision. —*v.t.* **2.** make fun of; mock. —**ri·dic'u·lous,** *adj.*

rife, *adj.* **1.** widespread. **2.** abundant.

riff'raff'', *n.*, *pl.* worthless people.

ri'fle, *n.*, *v.t.*, **-fled, -fling.** *n.* **1.** shoulder gun with a rifled barrel. —*v.t.* **2.** ransack and rob. **3.** cut spiral grooves in, as a gun barrel. —**ri'fle·man,** *n.*

rift, *n.*, *v.t.*, *v.i.* split.

rig, *v.t.*, **rigged, rigging,** *n.*, *v.t.* **1.** equip, as for sailing. **2.** manipulate. —*n.* **3.** arrangement of the sails, etc. on a ship. **4.** equipment. **5.** tractor-trailer.

rig'a·ma·role'', *n.* complicated, often meaningless, procedure or talk. Also, **rig'ma·role''.**

rig'ging, *n.* ropes and other tackle for a ship, crane, etc.

right, *adj.* **1.** good; virtuous. **2.** correct. **3.** suitable. **4.** opposite to left. **5.** straight. —*n.* **6.** what is right, just, etc. **7.** lawful power or privilege. **8.** *Politics.* conservative. —*adv.* **9.** properly. —*v.t.* **10.** correct; put in order. **11.** set upright.

right angle, 90-degree angle.

right'eous, *adj.* **1.** virtuous; blameless. **2.** just; worthy.

right'ful, *adj.* just; legitimate.

right'ist, *n.*, *adj.* conservative in politics.

right-wing, *adj.* politically conservative.

rig'id, *adj.* **1.** stiff; unyielding. **2.** strict. —**rig'id·ness, ri·gid'i·ty,** *n.*

rig'or, *n.* **1.** strictness. **2.** hardship. —**rig'or·ous,** *adj.*

ri'gor mor'tis, stiffening of the muscles after death.

rile, *v.t.*, **riled, riling.** *Informal.* anger; irritate.

rill, *n.* small stream.

rim, *n.*, *v.t.*, **rimmed, rimming.** *n.* **1.** edge; border; margin. —*v.t.* **2.** furnish with a rim.

rime, *n.*, *v.*, **rimed, riming.** *n.* **1.** rhyme. **2.** hoarfrost —*v.t.*, *v.i.* **3.** form a rhyme.

rind, *n.* hard outer coating, as of cheese or fruit.

ring, *n.*, *v.*, **rang, rung, ringing.** *n.* **1.** sound of a bell. **2.** finger band. **3.** circular object or area. **4.** group of conspirators. **5.** telephone call. —*v.t.* **6.** sound, as a bell. **7.** call by telephone. **8.** encircle. —*v.i.* **9.** resound. **10.** sound clearly. **11.** seem to be true or false.

ring'er, *n.* **1.** person who rings bells. **2.** *Informal.* **a.** fraudulent substitute. **b.** identical-seeming person or thing.

ring'lead'er, *n.* person who leads others in mischief.

ring'let, *n.* **1.** little ring. **2.** curl of hair.

ring'worm'', *n.* contagious fungous skin disease.

rink, *n.* area for skating.

rinse, *v.t.*, **rinsed, rinsing,** *n.* *v.t.* **1.** wash lightly, as to remove soap. —*n.* **2.** act or instance of rinsing. **3.** solution for rinsing.

ri'ot, *n.* **1.** act of mob violence. —*v.i.* **2.** take part in a riot. —**ri'ot·ous,** *adj.*

rip, *v.t.*, *v.i.*, **ripped, ripping,** *n.* tear.

ripe, *adj.*, **riper, ripest.** fully aged or developed. —**rip'en,** *v.i.*, *v.t.*

rip'ple, *v.*, **-pled, -ling,** *n.* *v.i.*, *v.t.* **1.** form in little waves. —*n.* **2.** little wave.

rip'-roar'ing, *adj.* *Informal.* lively and boisterous.

rip'saw'', *n.* saw for cutting wood along the grain.

rise, *v.i.*, **rose, risen, rising,** *n.* *v.i.* **1.** get up. **2.** rebel. **3.** ascend. **4.** begin. **5.** increase in amount, degree, etc. **6.** originate. —*n.* **7.** act or instance of rising. **8.** small hill. **9.** increase. **10.** advance in rank, power, etc.

ris''i·bil'i·ty, *n.*, *pl.* **-ties.** ability to laugh.

ris'i·ble, *adj.* causing laughter; ridiculous.

risk, *n.* 1. chance of defeat, injury, loss, etc. —*v.t.* 2. expose to risk. 3. incur the risk of. —**risk'y,** *adj.*

ris·qué', *adj.* suggestive of indency.

rite, *n.* ceremonial act.

rit'u·al, *n.* 1. set form for rites. —*adj.* 2. according to a ritual. —**rit'u·al·ism'',** *n.* —**rit'u·al·ist,** *n.* —**rit''u·al·is'tic,** *adj.*

ri'val, *n., adj., v.t.,* **-valed, -valing.** *n.* 1. competitor. 2. equal. —*adj.* 3. competing. —*v.t.* 4. compete with. 5. equal. —**ri'val·ry,** *n.*

rive (rīv), *v.t., v.i.,* **rived, rived** or **riven, riving.** 1. tear apart. 2. split.

riv'er, *n.* large natural stream of water.

riv'et, *n.* 1. metal bolt forged tight after insertion. —*v.t.* 2. fasten with rivets.

riv'u·let, *n.* small brook.

roach, *n.* cockroach.

road, *n.* way for travel. —**road'side'',** *n., adj.* —**road'way'',** *n.*

roam, *v.i.* wander.

roan, *n.* horse with white or gray spots.

roar, *v.i.* 1. emit a bellow. —*n.* 2. act or instance of roaring.

roast, *v.t.* 1. cook with dry heat. —*n.* 2. roasted piece of meat.

rob, *v.t.,* **robbed, robbing.** take from without right. —**rob'ber·y,** *n.*

robe, *n., v.t.,* **robed, robing.** *n.* 1. long, loose piece of clothing. —*v.t.* 2. clothe in a robe.

rob'in, *n.* bird with a red breast.

ro'bot, *n.* man-like machine.

ro·bust', *adj.* vigorous.

rock, *n.* 1. piece of stone. —*v.i., v.t.* 2. swing back and forth. —**rock'y,** *adj.*

rock'er, *n.* curved base for rocking objects.

rock'et, *n.* object propelled by reactive thrust. —**rock'et·ry,** *n.*

rock' n' roll, *n., adj.* a form of popular music originating in the U.S. and characterized by a distinct beat. Also, **rock.**

rod, *n.* 1. round, slender object. 2. five-and-a-half linear yards.

ro'dent, *n.* gnawing mammal.

ro'de·o'', *n., pl.* **-os.** cowboy show.

roe, *n.* fish eggs.

rogue, *n.* rascal. —**ro'guish,** *adj.* —**ro'guer·y,** *n.*

roil, *v.t.* soil. —**roil'y,** *adj.*

rois'ter, *v.i.* carouse.

role, *n.* character assumed. Also, **rôle.**

roll, *v.i.* 1. move like a ball, or as if on wheels. 2. revolve; turn over and over. 3. move like waves; billow. —*v.t.* 4. cause to roll. 5. move on wheels. 6. shape into a round or cylindrical form. 7. smooth or flatten with a cylinder, as metal. —*n.* 8. act or instance of rolling. 9. a cylinder, as of paper, wire, etc. 10. list of names. 11. small loaf of bread.

rol'lick·ing, *adj.* jolly; boisterous.

ro·maine', *n.* type of lettuce.

ro·man' à clef'', *n.* novel that disguises real people and events.

ro·mance', *n.* 1. love affair. 2. fanciful story. 3. realm of fantasy. —**ro·man' tic,** *adj.* —**ro·man'ti·cal·ly,** *adv.*

Roman numerals, I for 1, V for 5, X for 10, L for 50, C for 100, D for 500, M for 1,000.

ro·man'ti·cism, *n.* romantic artistic movement. —**ro·man'ti·cist,** *n., adj.*

romp, *v.i.* 1. play boisterously. —*n.* 2. act or instance of romping.

romp'ers, *n., pl.* loose overall for a child.

roof, *n., pl.* **roofs,** *v.t., n.* 1. covering for a building. —*v.t.* 2. furnish with a roof. —**roof'ing,** *n.* —**roof'less,** *adj.* —**roof'top'',** *n.*

rook, *n.* 1. castle-like chesspiece. —*v.t.* 2. *Informal.* cheat.

rook'ie, *n. Informal.* raw recruit.

room, *n.* 1. space. 2. fully enclosed space in a building. —*v.i.* 3. lodge. —**room' ful'',** *n.* —**room'mate'',** *n.* —**room'y,** *adj.*

roost, *n., v.i.* perch.

roost'er, *n.* male chicken.

root, *n.* 1. buried part of a plant. 2. similar part of a tooth, hair, etc. 3. basic cause. —*v.t.* 4. plant. 5. dig. —*v.i.* 6. grow roots. 7. cheer.

rope, *n., v.t.,* **roped, roping.** *n.* 1. length composed of strands used for pulling or binding. —*v.t.* 2. tie with rope.

ro'sa·ry, *n., pl.* **-ries.** 1. chain of beads used by Roman Catholics to count prayers said. 2. series of prayers.

rose, *n.* pink or yellow scented flower. —**rose'bud'',** *n.* —**rose'bush'',** *n.*

ro·sé', *n.* pink light wine.

ro'se·ate, *adj.* 1. rose-colored. 2. brightly promising.

rose'mar''y, *n.* leaves of an evergreen shrub, used in cooking.

ro·sette', *n.* round ornament.

rose'wood'', *n.* reddish wood used in cabinetmaking.

ros'in, *n.* solid substance remaining after distilling turpentine, used esp. for treating bows of violins, etc.

ros'ter, *n.* list.

ros'trum, *n., pl.* **-trums, -tra.** speaker's platform.

ros'y, *adj.* **-ier, -iest.** 1. pink. 2. optimistic; promising. —**ros'i·ly,** *adv.*

rot, *v.,* **rotted, rotting,** *n., v.t., v.i.,* decay. —**rot'ten,** *adj.*

ro'ta·ry, *adj.* rotating as a whole or in part.

ro'tate'', *v.,* **-tated, -tating.** *v.t., v.i.* 1. turn around a point. —*v.t.* 2. assign regular turns to. —**ro'ta·to''ry,** *adj.*

rote, *n.* memorization.

ro'tor, *n.* rotating part of a machine.

ro·tund', *adj.* plump. **—ro·tun'di·ty,** *n.*

ro·tun'da, *n.* round hall.

rou·é', *n.* dissipated man.

rouge, *n.* red cosmetic or polishing powder.

rough, *adj.* 1. unfinished. 2. violent. 3. *Informal.* troublesome. **—rough'en,** *v.t., v.i.*

rough'age, *n.* coarse food.

rough'house'', *n. Informal.* violent amusement or fight.

rough'neck'', *n. Informal.* boisterous or violent person.

rou·lette', *n.* gambling wheel.

round, *adj.* 1. curved, or with a curved exterior. 2. approximate. **—n.** 3. repeated series. 4. single shot. **—adv.,** *prep.* 5. around. **—v.t.** 6. make round. 7. go around.

round'a·bout'', *adj.* indirect.

round'ly, *adv.* 1. in a round way. 2. thoroughly.

round'up'', *n.* 1. gathering of cattle. 2. summary.

rouse, *v.,* **roused, rousing.** *v.t., v.i.* 1. awaken. **—v.t.** 2. excite.

rout, *v.t.* 1. put to flight. 2. gouge. **—n.** 3. disorderly flight.

route, *n., v.t.,* **routed, routing.** *n.* 1. course of travel. **—v.t.** 2. assign a route to.

rou·tine', *n.* 1. standard course of action. **—adj.** 2. ordinary; customary.

rove, *v.i.,* **roved, roving.** wander.

row, *v.,* **rowed, rowing,** *n. v.t., v.i.* (rō) 1. move with oars. **—n.** 2. group in a line. 3. (row) fight; quarrel. **—row'boat'',** *n.*

row'dy, *adj.,* **-dier, -diest,** *n., pl.* **-dies.** *adj.* 1. boisterous or violent. **—n.** 2. rowdy person.

roy'al, *adj.* 1. pertaining to kings or queens. **—n.** 2. sail above a top gallant. **—roy'al·ist,** *n.*

roy'al·ty, *n., pl.* **-ties.** 1. kings and queens. 2. fee to an author, patentee, etc.

R.S.V.P., Abbr. for (*French*) *répondez s'il vous plaît:* please send an answer.

rub, *v.,* **rubbed, rubbing,** *n. v.t.* 1. apply friction to. 2. apply with friction. **—v.i.** 3. apply friction. **—n.** 4. act or instance of rubbing. 5. source of difficulty.

rub'ber, *n.* 1. resilient substance. 2. decisive game. **—rub'ber·ize'',** *v.t.* **—rub'ber·y,** *adj.*

rub'bish, 1. cast-off material. 2. worthless speech, etc.

rub'ble, *n.* broken stone or masonry.

rub'i·cund, *adj.* ruddy.

rub'ric, *n.* note to a text.

ru'by, *n., pl.* **-bies.** deep red precious stone.

ruck'us, *n. Informal.* disturbance.

rud'der, *n.* steering device.

rud'dy, *adj.,* **-dier, -diest.** reddish. **—rud'di·ness,** *n.*

rude, *adj.* **ruder, rudest.** 1. offensive in manner. 2. rough; rugged.

ru'di·ment, *n.* basic principle, etc. **—ru''di·men'ta·ry,** *adj.*

rue, *v.t.,* **rued, ruing,** *n., v.t.* 1. feel remorse or regret for. **—n.** 2. remorse or regret. **—rue'ful,** *adj.*

ruf'fi·an, *n.* hoodlum.

ruf'fle, *v.t.,* **-fled, fling.** 1. disturb the surface of. 2. disturb the calm of.

rug, *n.* floor cloth.

rug'ged, *adj.* 1. rough in surface or outline. 2. harsh.

ruin, *n.* 1. Also, **ruins,** remains of something destroyed or injured. 2. downfall. 3. source of one's downfall. **—v.t.** 4. bring to ruin. **—ru''in·a'tion,** *n.* **—ru'in·ous,** *adj.*

rule, *n., v.,* **ruled, ruling.** *n.* 1. principle or law. 2. government; dominion. 3. measuring stick. **—v.t., v.i.** 4. govern. **—v.t.** 5. make a formal authoritative decision. **—rul'ing,** *n., adj.*

rul'er, *n.* 1. sovereign. 2. measuring stick.

rum, *n.* alcoholic liquor made from sugar.

rum'ba, *n.* Cuban dance.

rum'ble, *v.i.,* **-bled, -bling,** *n., v.i.* 1. dull continuous noise. **—n.** 2. act or instance of rumbling.

ru'mi·nate'', *v.i.,* **-nated, -nating.** 1. chew the cud. 2. muse; meditate. **—ru'mi·nant,** *adj., n.*

rum'mage, *v.,* **-maged, -maging.** *v.t., v.i.* search thoroughly.

ru'mor, *n.* 1. unconfirmed popular report. **—v.t.** 2. tell in a rumor.

rump, *n.* hindquarters.

rum'ple, *v.t.,* **-pled, -pling.** muss.

rum'pus, *n.* disorderly or noisy activity.

run, *v.,* **ran, run, running,** *n., v.i.* 1. move quickly on the feet. 2. be in motion; operate. 3. flow. **—v.t.** 4. operate or manage. 5. drive. **—n.** 6. act or instance of running. 7. route or journey. 8. series. 9. brook.

run'a·round'', *n. Informal.* evasive treatment.

run'a·way'', *n., adj.* fugitive.

run'-down'', *adj.* 1. without energy. 2. out of repair. 3. (of a clock, etc.) needing to be wound up.

run'down'', *n.* summary.

rung, *n.* rodlike crosspiece.

run'let, *n.* small stream. Also, **run'nel.**

run'ner, *n.* 1. person who runs. 2. long foot or slide, as on a sled, etc. 3. long rug.

run'ner-up'', *n., pl.* **-ners-up.** second-best racer or performer.

run'ning, *n.* 1. competitive condition.

—*adj.* 2. operating. 3. (of measurement) linear. 4. continuous.

run'-of-the-mill', *adj.* not special.

runt, *n.* stunted creature. —**runt'y,** *adj.*

run'way'', *n.* strip, pavement, etc. for running, esp. by airplanes landing or taking-off.

rup'ture, *n., v.,* **-tured, -turing.** *n.* 1. hernia. 2. break. —*v.t.* 3. cause a rupture. —*v.i.* 4. undergo a rupture.

rur'al, *adj.* pertaining to the country.

ruse, *n.* trick.

rush, *v.t., v.i., n.* 1. hurry. —*v.t.* 2. charge; attack with speed. —*n.* 3. hurry. 4. grasslike marsh plant.

rus'set, *n.* reddish brown.

rust, *n.* 1. coating of oxydized iron or steel. 2. plant fungus disease. —*v.i.* 3. have rust. —*v.t.* 4. cause to rust. —**rust'y,** *adj.*

rus'tic, *adj.* 1. rural. —*n.* 2. rural person.

rus'tle, *v.,* **-tled, -tling,** *n., v.i.* 1. make a soft, whispering sound. —*v.t.* 2. steal, as cattle. —*n.* 3. rustling sound.

rut, *n., v.t.,* **rutted, rutting.** *n.* 1. worn track. 2. fixed routine. —*v.t.* 3. make ruts in. —**rut'ty,** *adj.*

ru''ta·ba'ga, *n.* type of turnip.

ruth'less, *adj.* without compunction or compassion.

rye, *n.* 1. edible grain. 2. whiskey distilled from this.

S

S, s, *n.* nineteenth letter of the English alphabet.

Sab'bath, *n.* day of worship and rest.

sa'ber, *n.* single-edged curved sword. Also, **sa'bre.**

sa'ble, *n.* weasel-like mammal with dark-brown fur.

sab'o·tage'', *n., v.t.* **-taged, -taging.** *n.* 1. intentional damage to equipment. —*v.t.* 2. damage intentionally. —**sab' o·teur''.**

sac, *n.* baglike part of the body.

sac·cha·rin (sak'kə rin), *n.* sugar substitute.

sac·cha·rine, *adj.* 1. too sweet, as in manner. —*n.* 2. saccharin.

sac·er·do·tal (sas''ər dō'təl, sak''ər dō' təl), *adj.* pertaining to or suggesting priests.

sa·chet (sa chā'), *n.* bag of scented powder.

sack, *n.* 1. bag, esp. a large, strong one. 2. plunder. —*v.t.* 3. put into a sack or sacks. 4. plunder.

sack'cloth, *n.* coarse cloth worn by penitents.

sac'ra·ment, *n.* 1. ceremony or act regarded as sacred. 2. **Sacrament,** Eucharist. —**sac''ra·men'tal,** *adj.*

sa'cred, *adj.* 1. holy. 2. safe from attack, ridicule, etc. 3. binding, as a promise. —**sa'cred·ly,** *adv.* —**sa'cred·ness,** *n.*

sac'ri·fice, *n., v.,* **-ficed, -ficing.** *n.* 1. offer of something valuable to a deity. 2. intentional loss of one thing to gain another. —*v.t.* 3. offer or lose in a sacrifice. —*v.i.* 4. make a sacrifice. —**sac'' ri·fi'cial,** *adj.*

sac'ri·lege, *n.* violation or mockery of something sacred. —**sac''ri·le'gious,** *adj.*

sac'ris·tan, *n.* person in charge of a sacristy.

sac'ris·ty, *n., pl.* **-ties.** place for keeping the sacred vessels, etc. of a church.

sac'ro·sanct, *adj.* sacred.

sad, *adj.,* **sadder, saddest.** low in spirits; melancholy. —**sad'ly,** *adv.* —**sad'ness,** *n.* —**sad'den,** *v.t., v.i.*

sad'dle, *n., v.t.,* **-dled, -dling.** *n.* 1. seat for the rider of a horse, bicycle, etc. —*v.t.* 2. put a saddle on. 3. impose a burden on. —**sad'dle·bag,** *n.*

sad'ism, *n.* practice of cruelty for pleasure. —**sad'ist,** *n.* —**sa·dis'tic,** *adj.*

sa·fa·ri (sə fah'rē), *n.* journey, esp. in central Africa, for hunting or exploration.

safe, *adj.,* **safer, safest,** *n., adj.* 1. free from danger or risk. —*n.* 2. container protecting against theft, fire, etc. —**safe'ly,** *adv.* —**safe'ty,** *n.*

safe'guard, *v.t.* 1. protect from danger. —*n.* 2. something protective.

sag, *v.i.,* **sagged, sagging,** *n., v.i.* 1. bend or hang downwards where not supported; droop. —*n.* 2. distortion caused by sagging.

sa'ga, *n.* Nordic heroic legend.

sa·ga'ci·ty, *n.* wisdom. —**sa·ga'cious,** *adj.* —**sa·ga'cious·ly,** *adv.*

sage, *n., adj.,* **sager, sagest.** *n.* 1. wise and learned person. 2. seasoning herb. —*adj.* 3. wise. —**sage'ly,** *adv.* —**sage' ness,** *n.*

sa·hib (sah'ēb), *n.* respectful term for a European, used in the Indian subcontinent.

said, *adj.* previously mentioned.

sail, *n.* 1. area of cloth used to drive a ship or boat by the force of moving air. 2. excursion in a ship or boat so driven. —*v.i.* 3. make such an excursion or excursions. 4. depart in a ship.

sail'boat'', *n.* boat moved by sails.

sail'fish, *n.* large fish with sail-like back fin.

sail'or, *n.* 1. member of a ship's crew. 2. enlisted man in a navy.

saint, *n.* 1. person officially venerated by a church. 2. person leading a religious or upright life. —**saint'hood,** *n.* —**saint'ly,** *adj.*

sake, *n.* **1.** (sāk) benefit. **2.** purpose. **3.** (sak'ē) Japanese rice wine.

sal′a·ble, *adj.* able to be sold. Also, **sale′a·ble.**

sa·la·cious, *adj.* obscene; lewd.

sal′ad, *n.* dish mainly of raw vegetables or fruits.

sal′a·man″der, *n.* small, tailed amphibian.

sa·la′mi, *n.* spiced sausage.

sal′a·ry, *n., pl.* **-ries.** regular payment for a permanent employee. **—sal′a·ried,** *adj.*

sale, *n.* **1.** act or occasion of selling. **2.** demand for something sold. **3.** offer of goods at reduced prices. **—sales′clerk″,** *n.* **—sale′room″, sales′room″,** *n.*

sales′man, *n.* man who sells merchandise, etc. Also, *fem.,* **sales′wom″an, sales′la″dy, sales′girl″.**

sa′lient, *adj.* **1.** outstanding. **2.** projecting. **—n.** **3.** area that projects. **—sa′li·ent·ly,** *adv.* **—sa′li·ence,** *n.*

sa·line (sā′līn), *adj.* salty. **—sa·lin′i·ty,** *n.*

sa·li′va, *n.* fluid secreted in mouth by glands to aid digestion. **—sa′li·va″ry,** *adj.*

sal′low, *adj.* with a sickly, yellowish complexion.

sal′ly, *n., pl.* **-lies,** *v.i.,* **-lied, -lying.** *n.* **1.** counterattack from a fortified position. **2.** witticism. **—v.i.** **3.** emerge briskly.

sal′mon, *n.* edible fish with pink flesh.

sa·lon′, *n.* **1.** room for conversation. **2.** art gallery.

sa·loon′, *n.* **1.** place where liquor is served and drunk. **2.** public room, esp. on a ship.

salt, *n.* **1.** sodium chloride. **2.** *Chemistry.* compound derived from an acid. **3.** wit; piquancy. **—v.t.** **4.** treat with salt. **—salt′y,** *adj.* **—salt′shak″er,** *n.*

salt·ine′, *n.* salted cracker.

salt″pe′ter, *n.* potassium nitrate. Also, **salt″pe′tre.**

sa·lu′bri·ous, *adj.* promoting health. **—sa·lu′bri·ous·ly,** *adv.*

sal′u·tar″y, *adj.* beneficial.

sal″u·ta′tion, *n.* **1.** greeting. **2.** opening phrase of a letter, naming the addressee.

sa·lute′, *n., v.* **-luted, -luting.** *n.* **1.** act expressing respect or attention in military etiquette. **2.** greeting. **3.** firing of cannons, etc. as a sign of welcome. **—v.t.** **4.** recognize with a salute. **—v.i.** **5.** perform a salute.

sal′vage, *v.t.,* **-vaged, -vaging,** *n., v.t.* **1.** rescue from loss, as a ship. **2.** gather for reuse, as discarded material. **—n.** **3.** salvaged material.

sal·va′tion, *n.* act of saving or state of being saved, as from damnation or destruction.

salve (sav), *n., v.t.,* **salved, salving.** *n.* **1.**

soothing or healing ointment. **—v.t.** **2.** cover with salve.

sal′vo, *n., pl.* **salvos, salvoes.** discharge of many guns, etc. in rapid succession.

same, *adj.* **1.** identical. **2.** without change. **3.** previously mentioned. **—n.** **4.** same thing or person. **—same′ness,** *n.*

sam′o·var, *n.* metal tea urn.

sam′pan, *n.* sculled Chinese or Japanese boat.

sam′ple, *n., adj., v.t.,* **-pled, -pling.** *n.* **1.** something representing more or others of its kind. **—adj.** **2.** serving as a sample. **—v.t.** **3.** take a sample of.

sam′pler, *n.* piece of needlework demonstrating skill.

san″a·to′ri·um, *n.* sanitarium.

sanc′ti·fy, *v.t.,* **-fied, -fying.** **1.** make sacred. **2.** free of sin. **—sanc″ti·fi·ca′tion,** *n.*

sanc′ti·mo″ny, *n.* showy or false piety. **—sanc″ti·mo′ni·ous,** *adj.*

sanc′tion, *n.* **1.** permission or support. **2.** non-belligerent measure against a nation by other nations. **—v.t.** **3.** authorize.

sanc′ti·ty, *n.* holiness or sacredness.

sanc′tu·ar″y, *n., pl.* **-aries.** **1.** consecrated place. **2.** place of refuge.

sanc′tum, *n.* consecrated place.

sand, *n.* **1.** fine pieces of rock. **2.** sands, sandy area. **—v.t.** **3.** rub with sandpaper. **—sand′er,** *n.* **—sand′storm″,** *n.*

san′dal, *n.* open shoe secured by straps.

san′dal·wood, *n.* aromatic Asiatic wood.

sand′bar″, *n.* low island of sand.

sand′pa″per, *n.* **1.** sand-coated paper for smoothing or reducing surfaces. **—v.t.** **2.** rub with sandpaper.

sand′pip″er, *n.* small shore bird.

sand′stone, *n.* stone made of sand naturally cemented together.

sand′wich, *n.* **1.** bread, roll, etc. in two slices with meat, etc. between them. **—v.t.** **2.** insert.

sand′y, *adj.,* **-ier, -iest.** **1.** abounding in sand. **2.** colored like sand.

sane, *adj.,* **saner, sanest.** mentally sound. **—sane′ly,** *adv.*

sang-froid (säh″frwah′), *n.* control of one's emotions.

san′gui·nar″y, *adj.* **1.** bloody. **2.** bloodthirsty.

san′guine, *adj.* optimistic.

san″i·tar′i·um, *n.* place for the recovery of health.

san″i·tar″y, *adj.* **1.** free of harmful bacteria, etc. **2.** pertaining to health.

san″i·ta′tion, *n.* provisions against disease.

san′i·ty, *n.* mental soundness.

sap, *n., v.t.,* **sapped, sapping.** *n.* **1.** juice of a tree, etc. **2.** *Informal.* fool. **—v.t.** **3.** weaken.

sa′pi·ent, *adj.* wise; knowing. —**sa′pi·ence,** *n.*

sap′ling, *n.* young tree.

sap′phire, *n.* blue gemstone.

sap′suck″er, *n.* variety of woodpecker.

sar′casm, *n.* **1.** making of agreeably worded but harshly intended remarks. **2.** such a remark. —**sar·cas′tic,** *adj.* —**sar·cas′ti·cal·ly,** *adv.*

sar·coph′a·gus, *n., pl.* **-gi.** stone coffin.

sar·dine′, *n.* trade name for a small canned ocean fish.

sar·don′ic, *adj.* bitterly sarcastic. —**sar·don′i·cal·ly,** *adv.*

sar·sa·pa·ril·la (sas″pə ril′ə, sahrs″ pəril′ə), *n.* tropical vine with fragrant roots.

sar·to′ri·al, *adj.* pertaining to tailors or tailoring.

sash, *n.* **1.** cloth band worn over the upper part of the body or around the waist. **2.** frame for window glass.

sas′sa·fras, *n.* American tree with aromatic bark at the roots.

Sa′tan, *n.* the Devil. —**sa·tan′ic,** *adj.*

satch′el, *n.* small cloth suitcase or bag.

sate, *v.t.,* **sated, sating.** satisfy fully or to excess, as an appetite.

sa·teen′, *n.* satinlike cotton fabric.

sat′el·lite, *n.* **1.** heavenly body moving around a planet. **2.** organization, etc. dominated or controlled by another.

sa·ti·ate (sā′shē āt), *v.t.,* **-ated, -ating.** glut. —**sa″ti·a′tion, sa·ti′e·ty,** *n.*

sat′in, *n.* glossy fabric or silk or a silk substitute. —**sa′tin·y,** *adj.*

sat′ire, *n.* **1.** sarcasm or ridicule in the exposure of wrongful actions or attitudes. **2.** story, etc. using these means. —**sa·tir′i·cal, sa·tir′ic,** *adj.* —**sa·tir′i·cal·ly,** *adv.* —**sa′tir·ist,** *n.*

sat′ir·ize, *v.t.,* **-ized, -izing.** portray satirically.

sat′is·fy, *v.t.,* **fied, fying. 1.** fulfill the wishes or needs of. **2.** convince. **3.** pay, as a debt. —**sat″is·fac′tion,** *n.* —**sat″is·fac′to·ry,** *adj.*

sat′u·rate, *v.t.,* **-rated, -rating.** cause complete absorption by. —**sat″u·ra′tion,** *n.*

Sat′ur·day, *n.* seventh day of the week.

Sat′urn, *n.* second-largest planet in the solar system.

sat·ur·nine (sat′ər nīn″), *adj.* gloomy.

sa′tyr, *n.* **1.** classical forest deity. **2.** lecherous man.

sauce, *n.* **1.** liquid for flavoring or cooking. **2.** semiliquid stewed fruit.

sauce′pan″, *n.* small, handled cooking pot.

sau′cer, *n.* small dish.

sau′cy, *adj.,* **-cier, -ciest.** impudent. —**sau′ci·ness,** *n.* —**sau′ci·ly,** *adv.*

sauer′kraut″, *n.* chopped fermented cabbage.

sau′na, *n.* Finnish hot-air bath.

saun′ter, *v.i., n.* stroll.

sau′sage, *n.* minced and seasoned meat, often in a casing.

sau·té (sō tā′), *v.t.,* **-téed, téeing.** fry quickly in a little fat.

sau·terne (sō tərn′), *n.* sweet white wine.

sav′age, *adj.* **1.** uncivilized. **2.** fierce or harsh. —*n.* **3.** uncivilized person. —**sav′age·ly,** *adv.* —**sav′age·ry,** *n.*

sa·vant (sa vahnt′), *n.* learned person.

save, *v.t.,* **saved, saving,** *prep., conj., v.t.* **1.** keep from harm. **2.** keep for future use. **3.** keep from being wasted. **4.** keep from sin or its consequences. —*prep., conj.* **5.** except.

sav′ing, *adj.* **1.** redeeming. **2.** thrifty. —*n.* **3.** economy. **4. savings,** money saved. —*prep.* **5.** with the exception of.

sav′ior, 1. rescuer. **2. the Savior,** Christ. Also, **sav′iour.**

sa·voir-faire (sav″wahr fār′), *n.* skill in human relations.

sa′vor, *n., v.t.* taste or smell. Also, **sa′vour.**

sa′vor·y, *adj.* pleasant-tasting or smelling.

saw, *n., v.t.,* **sawed, sawing. n. 1.** cutting tool with a row of teeth. **2.** saying or proverb. —*v.t.* **3.** cut with a saw. —**saw′mill″,** *n.* —**saw′yer,** *n.*

sax′o·phone, *n.* keyed metal reed instrument. —**sax′o·phon′ist,** *n.*

say, *v.t.,* **said, saying,** *n., v.t.* **1.** speak. **2.** declare to be true. —*n.* **3.** chance to speak.

say′ing, *n.* proverb.

scab, *n., v.i.,* **scabbed, scabbing. n. 1.** crust over a healing wound or sore. **2.** worker who replaces a striking worker. —*v.i.* **3.** form a scab. —**scab′by,** *adj.*

scab′bard, *n.* sword sheath.

sca′bies, *n.* itching skin disease.

scaf′fold, *n.* **1.** Also, **scaf′fold·ing,** temporary platform. **2.** platform for execution of condemned persons.

scal′a·wag″, *n.* scoundrel.

scald, *v.t.* **1.** burn with hot fluid. **2.** heat almost to boiling. —*n.* **3.** burn made by hot fluid.

scale, *n., v.t.,* **scaled, scaling. n. 1.** platelike portion of the covering of a fish, snake, etc. **2.** flake or layer of material. **3.** Also, **scales,** weighing device. **4.** range of musical tones. **5.** system of relations, as of actual size to represented size or of different degrees of a thing. —*v.t.* **6.** remove scales from. **7.** climb. **8.** determine the relative size of. —**scal′y,** *adj.*

scal′lion, *n.* any of several varieties of small onion.

scal·lop (skol′ləp), *n.* **1.** bivalve mollusk.

2. any of the curves forming part of a decorative border. —*v.t.* 3. decorate with scallops.

scalp, *n.* 1. hair and skin covering the top of the head. —*v.t.* 2. take a scalp from, esp. as a trophy.

scal'pel, *n.* surgical knife.

scam, *n.* con game; deception practiced to defraud.

scamp, *n.* rascal; imp.

scam'per, *v.i.* 1. run quickly. —*n.* 2. fast run.

scan, *v.t.,* **scanned, scanning.** 1. examine in detail. 2. examine quickly. 3. analyze the rhythmic pattern of.

scan'dal, *n.* 1. malicious gossip. 2. disgraceful occurrence or situation. —**scan'dal·ous,** *adj.*

scan'dal·ize, *v.t.,* **-ized, -izing.** shock with a scandal.

scant, *adj.* scarcely sufficient. Also, **scant'y.** —**scant'i·ly,** *adv.* —**scant'i·ness,** *n.*

scape'goat, *n.* person blamed for the misdeeds of others.

scape'grace, *n.* rascal.

scap'u·la, *n., pl.* **-lae, -las.** shoulder blade. —**scap'u·lar,** *adj.*

scar, *v.t.,* **scarred, scarring.** *n.* 1. mark left by a cut. —*v.t.* 2. cut so as to make a scar.

scar'ab, *n.* carved image of a beetle.

scarce, *adj.,* **scarcer, scarcest.** not plentiful or common. —**scarc'i·ty, scarce'ness,** *n.*

scarce'ly, *adv.* 1. only just; barely. 2. hardly.

scare, *n., v.t.,* **scared, scaring,** *v.t.* 1. frighten. —*v.i.* 2. become frightened. —*n.* 3. frightening occurrence.

scare'crow'', *n.* device to frighten birds from a planted field.

scarf, *n., pl.* **scarfs, scarves.** length of cloth for warming the neck and chest.

scar'i·fy, *v.t.,* **-fied, -fying.** scratch.

scar'let, *adj., n.* bright red.

scarlet fever, contagious disease marked by fever and a scarlet rash.

scat, *v.i.,* **scatted, scatting.** *Informal.* run away.

scath'ing, *adj.* bitterly harsh, as something said or written. —**scath'ing·ly,** *adv.*

scat'ter, *v.t.* 1. throw in all directions. —*v.i.* 2. move away rapidly in all directions.

scav'enge, *v.,* **-enged, -enging.** *v.t.* 1. clean out. —*v.i.* 2. search for refuse that can be eaten or reused. —**scav'en·ger,** *n.*

sce·nar'i·o, *n.* story outline, esp. in motion pictures.

scene, *n.* 1. what is seen from a certain place. 2. location of an action. 3. sub-

division of a dramatic act. 4. emotional display in public. —**scen'ic,** *adj.*

scen'er·y, *n.* 1. pleasant outdoor scene. 2. painted canvases, etc. representing the scene of a dramatic action.

scent, *n.* 1. distinctive smell. 2. trail left by something with such a smell. 3. perfume. 4. sense of smell. —*v.t.* 5. smell. 6. perfume.

scep·ter (sep'tər), *n.* short staff symbolizing royal power. Also, **scep'tre.**

scep'tic, *n.* skeptic.

sched'ule, *n., v.t.,* **-uled, -uling.** *n.* 1. list of the times of planned actions or events. 2. any orderly list. —*v.t.* 3. put on a schedule.

scheme, *n., v.i.,* **schemed, scheming.** *n.* 1. plan or design. 2. plot; intrigue. —*v.i.* 3. plot to do or attain something. —**schem'er,** *n.*

sche·miel', *n. Yiddish.* a person who is a habitual failure.

schism (siz'əm), *n.* division, as between factions in an organization. —**schis·mat'ic,** *adj., n.*

schist (shist), *n.* layered crystalline rock.

schiz·o·phre·ni·a (skit''zə frē'nē ə), *n.* mental disorder. —**schiz''o·phre'nic, schiz'oid,** *adj.*

schlock, *Yiddish. n.* 1. inferior goods or materials. —*adj.* 2. inferior in material or workmanship.

schmaltz, *n. Informal.* sentimental art.

schol'ar, *n.* 1. person who studies to acquire knowledge. 2. school pupil.

schol'ar·ly, *adj.* pertaining to or in the manner of scholars.

schol'ar·ship, *n.* 1. activities and accomplishments of scholars. 2. grant of money to make school attendance possible.

scho·las'tic, *adj.* pertaining to education.

school, *n.* 1. place or institution for education or training. 2. educational activity. 3. group with a common set of beliefs or practices. 4. group of fish, etc. —*v.t.* 5. educate or train. —**school'book,** *n.* —**school'boy,** *n.* —**school'girl,** *n.* —**school'mate,** *n.* —**school'house,** *n.* —**school'room,** *n.* —**school'teacher,** *n.*

schoon'er, *n.* fore-and-aft rigged sailing vessel with two or more masts, including a foremast.

schwa (shwah), *n.* unstressed vowel sound, e.g. the *o* in *factor,* represented by the symbol ə.

sci·at·i·ca (sî at'ik ə), *n.* neuralgia of the hip and thigh. —**sci·at'ic,** *adj.*

sci'ence, *n.* 1. systematic acquisition of knowledge, esp. knowledge that can be measured precisely. 2. precise method or skill. —**sci''en·tif'ic,** *adj.* —**sci''en·tif'i·cal·ly,** *adv.* —**sci'en·tist,** *n.*

scin·til·la (sin til'lə), *n.* glimmering; trace.

scin·til·late (sin'təl lāt), v.i. **-lated, -lating.** sparkle. —**scin''til·la'tion,** n.

sci·on (sī'ən), n. 1. descendant. 2. plant shoot or bud, esp. for grafting.

scis'sors, n. instrument for cutting by means of two moving blades.

scle·ro'sis, n. hardening of body tissue. —**scle·rot'ic,** adj.

scoff, n., v.i., jeer. —**scof'fer,** n.

scold, v.t. 1. reproach at length. —n. 2. person who scolds.

sconce, n. wall bracket for lights.

scone, n. flat biscuit.

scoop, n. 1. device for digging deeply. 2. act or instance of scooping. 3. amount held by a scoop. 4. Informal. prior publication of news. —v.t. 5. remove or empty with a scoop. 6. Informal. get the better of by publishing news first.

scoot, v.i. go quickly.

scoot'er, n. small, low-built two-wheeled vehicle.

scope, n. range of responsibility or possibility for action.

scorch, v.t. 1. burn on the surface. —n. 2. surface burn.

score, n., v., **scored, scoring.** n. 1. total, as of points in a game. 2. Informal. **know the score,** know the actual situation. 3. long, shallow cut. 4. group of twenty. 5. musical arrangement. —v.t. 6. add, as points in a game. 7. mark with a long, shallow cut. —v.i. 8. gain points, as in a game.

scorn, n. 1. contempt. 2. derision. —v.t. 3. treat with scorn. —**scorn'ful,** adj. —**scorn'ful·ly,** adv.

scor'pi·on, n. poisonous, long-tailed eight-legged animal.

Scotch, n. malted-barley whisky made in Scotland.

scotch, v.t. make ineffective.

scoun'drel, n. rascal.

scour, v.t. 1. clean with a steady rubbing action. 2. go over repeatedly, as during a search.

scourge (skərj), n., v.t., **scourged, scourging.** n. 1. whip. 2. major affliction. —v.t. 3. beat with a whip. 4. punish or harass severely.

scout, n. 1. person sent to explore or search. —v.t. 2. reject as absurd. —v.i. 3. act as a scout.

scow, n. flat-bottomed barge or boat.

scowl, v.t. 1. frown angrily. —n. 2. angry frown.

scrab'ble, v.i., **-bled, -bling.** 1. scratch or scrape with the hands. 2. struggle without dignity.

scrag'gly, adj., **-glier, -gliest.** ragged.

scraggy, adj., **-gier, -giest.** scrawny.

scram'ble, v., **-bled, -bling,** n., v.t. 1. mix up; confuse. —v.i. 2. move in short, rapid steps. —n. 3. scrambling motion or gait. 4. undignified struggle, as for something of value.

scrap, n., adj., v.t., **scrapped, scrapping.** n. 1. small piece. 2. refuse material, esp. when reclaimable. 3. Informal. fight. —adj. 4. in the form of scrap. —v.t. 5. make into scrap. 6. discard. —**scrap'heap,** n.

scrap'book, n. album for printed and written material, etc.

scrape, v., **scraped, scraping,** n., v.t. 1. rub against roughly. 2. remove by rough rubbing. 3. get by tedious labor. —v.i. 4. rub roughly against something. —n. 5. act of scraping. 6. area scraped. 7. dangerous situation. —**scrap'er,** n.

scrap'ple, n. fried dish of meal and meat scraps.

scratch, v.t. 1. make a long, shallow cut in. 2. cross out; eliminate. —n. 3. long, shallow cut. 4. **from scratch,** from the beginning. 5. **up to scratch,** up to standard.

scratch'y, adj., **-ier, -iest.** suggesting scratching, esp. in sound.

scrawl, v.t., v.i. 1. write with a bad hand. —n. 2. writing in a bad hand.

scrawn'y, adj., **-nier, -niest.** disagreeably thin.

scream, n. 1. loud, high-pitched cry. —v.i. 2. utter such a cry.

screech, n. 1. harsh screamlike sound. —v.i. 2. utter such sounds.

screen, n. 1. flat object or surface for division, protection, or concealment. 2. surface on which motion pictures, television programs, etc. are projected. 3. **the screen,** motion-picture industry. —v.t. 4. enclose or protect with or as if with a screen. 5. sift through a screen. 6. investigate for suitability.

screw, n. 1. simple machine for fastening, moving, etc., in the form of an inclined plane wound around an axis. 2. propeller. —v.t. 3. fasten with screws. 4. turn as one does a screw. —**screw'driv''er,** n.

scrib'ble, v., **-bled, -bling,** n., v.t., v.i. 1. write hastily and carelessly. —n. 2. hasty or careless writing.

scribe, n. Archaic. writer or clerk.

scrim'mage, n., v.i. **-maged, -maging.** n. 1. play in football. —v.i. 2. take part in a scrimmage.

scrimp, v.i. save; economize.

scrip, n. certificate used in place of money.

script, n. 1. handwriting. 2. manuscript, esp. of a play, etc.

Scrip'ture, n. 1. portion or portions of the Bible. 2. **the Scriptures,** the Bible. —**scrip'tur·al,** adj.

scrof'u·la, n. tuberculosis of the lymph glands.

scroll, n. 1. roll of paper, etc. bearing writing or print. 2. spiral ornamental motif. —v. 3. (computers) to move the display on a monitor so that other data can be read.

scro'tum, *n.* baglike skin enclosure for testicles.

scrounge, *v.,* **scrounged, scrounging.** *v.t.* **1.** *Informal.* beg or steal in a minor way. —*v.i.* **2.** *Informal.* look for something desired.

scrub, *v.t.,* **scrubbed, scrubbing,** *n., adj., v.t.* **1.** wash with a vigorous rubbing action. **2.** *Informal.* eliminate; cross off. —*n.* **3.** stunted trees or shrubbery. —*adj.* **4.** inferior.

scruff, *n.* nape of the neck.

scru'ple, *n.* prompting of the conscience.

scru'pu·lous, *adj.* **1.** conscientious. **2.** careful. —**scru'pu·lous·ly** *adv.*

scru'ti·nize, *v.t.,* **-nized, -nizing.** examine carefully. —**scru'ti·ny,** *n.*

scud, *v.i.,* **scudded, scudding.** move rapidly.

scuff, *v.t.* **1.** wear by rubbing or scraping. —*v.t., v.i.* **2.** shuffle, as the feet.

scuf'fle, *v.i.,* **-fled, -fling,** *n., v.i.* **1.** fight confusedly at close quarters. —*n.* **2.** confused fight at close quarters.

scull, *n.* **1.** oar used at a boat's stern. **2.** racing rowboat. —*v.t., v.i.* **3.** move with a scull.

scul'ler·y, *n.* room for cleaning dishes, kitchen utensils, etc.

sculp'ture, *n.* **1.** art of composing in three dimensions. **2.** example of this art. —**sculp'tur·al,** *adj.* —**sculp'tor,** *n., fem.,* **sculp'tress.**

scum, *n.* **1.** film on a liquid surface. **2.** rabble. —**scum'my,** *adj.*

scup'per, *n.* drainage opening in a deck or flat roof.

scurf, *n.* flecks of dead skin.

scur'ril·ous, *adj.* grossly insulting. —**scur'ril·ous·ly,** *adv.* —**scur·ril'i·ty, scur'ril·lous·ness,** *n.*

scur'ry, *v.i.,* **-ried, -rying,** *n., pl.* **-ries.** *v.i.* **1.** move hastily. —*n.* **2.** hasty movement.

scur'vy, *n.* disease due to vitamin deficiency.

scut'tle, *n., v.,* **-tled, -tling.** *n.* **1.** hatchlike opening in a deck or roof. **2.** coal bucket. —*v.t.* **3.** sink intentionally. —*v.i.* **4.** scurry.

scythe, *n.* mowing instrument with curved blade and long handle.

sea, *n.* **1.** part of an ocean, esp. one partly bounded by land. **2. the sea,** the oceans. **3.** large inland body of water. **4.** relative turbulence of ocean water at a given time. —**sea'board", sea'coast",** *n.*

sea'far"ing, *n.* activity of one who travels on or works at sea. —**sea'far"er,** *n.*

sea'go"ing, *adj.* pertaining to or suitable for travel on the sea.

sea horse, semitropical fish with head of horselike form.

seal, *n.* **1.** device for giving official character or preventing tampering with a document, locked space, etc. **2.** stamp used to shape such a device. **3.** device to prevent passage of air, etc. **4.** four-flippered sea mammal. —*v.t.* **5.** put seal on. **6.** enclose with a seal.

sea'lion, large seal.

seam, *n.* **1.** line of junction. **2.** mineral stratum. —*v.t.* **3.** join at or with a seam. —**seam'less,** *adj.*

sea'man, *n., pl.* **-men.** sailor. —**sea'man·ship",** *n.*

seam'stress, *n.* sewing woman.

seam'y, *adj.,* **seamier, seamiest. 1.** having seams. **2.** less attractive; sordid.

sé·ance (sā'ahns), *n.* meeting for communication with the dead.

sea'plane, *n.* airplane able to land on water.

sea'port", *n.* port fronting on an ocean.

sear, *v.t.* **1.** burn the surface of. **2.** wither.

search, *n.* **1.** methodical attempt to find something. —*v.t.* **2.** examine in making a search. —*v.i.* **3.** hunt. —**search'er,** *n.*

search'ing, *adj.* deep and perceptive, as an investigation.

search'light, *n.* directed light for distinguishing objects in the dark.

sea'shell", *n.* shell of a saltwater mollusk.

sea'shore", *n.* shore of an ocean. Also, **sea'side".**

sea'sick", *adj.* sick from the motion of a ship. —**sea'sick"ness,** *n.*

sea'son, *n.* **1.** quarter of the year beginning at a solstice or equinox. **2.** appropriate time. —*v.t.* **3.** flavor with salt, spices, herbs, etc. **4.** prepare for use by aging or exposure to weather. —**sea'son·al,** *adj.*

sea'son·a·ble, *adj.* coming at the appropriate time.

sea'son·ing, *n.* flavoring of salt, spices, herbs, etc.

seat, *n.* **1.** place for sitting. **2.** place of governmental activities, residence, etc. **3.** location. **4.** place in a legislature, etc. —*v.t.* **5.** put onto a seat. **6.** install in a seat.

sea'way", *n.* **1.** inland waterway to the sea. **2.** area of open sea.

sea'weed", *n.* ocean plant.

sea'wor"thy, *adj.* suitable for navigation at sea.

se·ba·ceous (si bā'shəs), *adj.* fatty.

se·cede', *v.i.,* **-ceded, -ceding.** withdraw from a political state, etc. —**se·ces'sion,** *n.*

se·clude', *v.t.,* **-cluded, -cluding.** isolate, esp. from society or activity. —**se·clu'sion,** *n.*

sec'ond, *adj.* **1.** next after the first. —*n.* **2.** sixtieth of a minute. **3.** person serving as an assistant or witness. **4. seconds,** goods rejected for ordinary sale.

—*v.t.* **5.** approve. —*adv.* **6.** as a second point. —**sec'ond·ly**, *adv.*

sec'ond·ar·y, *adv.* **1.** forming a second stage or phase. **2.** of a second level of importance. —**sec'on·dar'i·ly**, *adv.*

sec'ond-hand', *adj.* **1.** belonging or offered to a new owner. **2.** not original.

se'cret, *n.* **1.** something not to be known by everyone. **2.** hidden cause or reason. —*adj.* **3.** hidden or not to be known by everyone. —**se'cret·ly**, *adv.* —**se'cre·cy**, *n.*

sec"re·tar"i·at, *n.* group of administrative officials.

sec're·tar"y, *n., pl.* **-taries. 1.** assistant to a businessman, official, etc. **2.** head of a government department. **3.** writing desk. —**sec"re·tar'i·al**, *adj.*

se·crete', *v.t.*, **-creted, -creting. 1.** produce and release substances, as a gland. **2.** hide. —**se·cre'tion**, *n.* —**se·cre'to·ry**, *adj.*

se'cre·tive, *adj.* **1.** reluctant to reveal information. **2.** pertaining to secretion. —**se'cre·tive·ly**, *adv.* —**se'cre·tive·ness**, *n.*

sect, *n.* religious group.

sec·tar'i·an, *adj.* **1.** pertaining to separate sects. —*n.* **2.** member of a sect.

sec'tion, *n.* **1.** separate part. **2.** act or instance of dividing. **3.** view of a thing as if divided. —*v.t.* **4.** divide. —**sec'tion·al**, *adj.*

sec'tor, *n.* **1.** *Geometry.* plane figure formed of a segment of a circle and two of its radii. **2.** area, esp. of military operation.

sec'u·lar, *adj.* not religious. —**sec'u·lar·ize**, *v.t.*

se·cure', *adj., v.t.*, **-cured, -curing.** *adj.* **1.** safe or certain. **2.** firmly in place. —*v.t.* **3.** make secure. **4.** obtain. —**se·cure'ly**, *adv.*

se·cur'i·ty, *n., pl.* **-ties. 1.** state of being secure. **2.** protection or precaution. **3.** pledge on a loan, etc. **4. securities,** bonds, stocks, etc.

se·dan', *n.* closed automobile with front and rear seats.

se·date', *n.* quiet in manner.

sed'a·tive, *n.* **1.** medicine to relieve pain or nervousness. —*adj.* **2.** relieving pain or nervousness. —**se·da'tion**, *n.*

sed'en·tar"y, *adj.* not physically active.

Se·der (sā'dər'), *n.* Jewish home ceremony at Passover.

sed'i·ment, *n.* matter falling to the bottom of a body of liquid.

se·di'tion, *n.* incitement to rebellion. —**se·di'tious**, *adj.*

se·duce', *v.t.*, **-duced, -ducing. 1.** tempt or induce to commit a wrong. **2.** induce to perform a sexual act. —**se·duc'er**, *fem.*, **se·duc'tress**, *n.* —**se·duc'tion**, *n.*

se·duc'tive, *adj.* tempting; attractive.

sed'u·lous, *adj.* diligent.

see, *v.*, **saw, seen, seeing**, *n., v.t.* **1.** sense with the eyes. **2.** realize or understand. **3.** make sure. **4.** escort. —*v.i.* **5.** have use of the eyes. **6.** find out or understand. **7.** attend, as to a task. **8.** bishopric.

seed, *n., pl.* **seeds, seed**, *v.t., n.* **1.** thing from which a plant grows. **2.** offspring. —*v.t.* **3.** sow seed in. **4.** remove seeds from. —**seed'less**, *adj.*

seed'ling, *n.* new growth from a seed.

seed'y, *adj.* **seedier, seediest. 1.** having seeds. **2.** shabby.

see'ing, *conj.* in view of the fact.

seek, *v.t.*, **sought, seeking. 1.** look for. **2.** intend and attempt. —**seek'er**, *n.*

seem, *v.t., v.i.* give the effect of being or acting in some specified way.

seem'ing, *adj.* apparent. —**seem'ing·ly**, *adv.*

seem'ly, *adj.*, **-lier, -liest.** proper in appearance or effect. —**seem'li·ness**, *n.*

seep, *v.i.* ooze. —**seep'age**, *n.*

seer, *n.* person who professes to foresee the future. Also, *fem.*, **seer'ess**.

seer'suck"er, *n.* crinkled striped fabric.

see'saw", *n.* recreation of swinging up and down on a balanced plank.

seethe, *v.*, **seethed, seething.** *v.t., v.i.* boil.

seg'ment, *n.* **1.** portion. —*v.t.* **2.** divide into portions. —**seg"men·tal**, *adj.* —**seg"men·ta'tion**, *n.*

seg're·gate, *v.t.*, **-gated, -gating.** keep apart from others. —**seg"re·ga'tion**, *n.*

seine (sān), *n.* **1.** weighted fishing net. —*v.t., v.i.* **2.** fish with such a net.

seis·mic (sīz'mik), *adj.* pertaining to or affected by earth tremors.

seis'mo·graph, *n.* device for measuring earth tremors.

seize, *v.t.*, **seized, seizing. 1.** take by authority or force. **2.** grasp, as an idea.

seiz'ure, *n.* **1.** taking by authority or force. **2.** attack of illness.

sel'dom, *adv.* rarely.

se·lect', *v.t.* **1.** choose. —*adj.* **2.** selected; choice. —**se·lec'tion**, *n.*

se·lec'tive, *adj.* **1.** pertaining to selection. **2.** careful in selecting.

se·lect'man, *n.* New England town officer.

self, *n.* **1.** one's own person. **2.** one's own well-being. —*adj.* **3.** of the same kind.

self"-as·sur'ance, *n.* self-confidence. —**self"-as·sured'**, *adj.*

self'-cen'tered, *adj.* seeing all things in reference to one's self or self-interest.

self'-con·ceit', *n.* excessively good opinion of oneself.

self"-con'fi·dence, *n.* confidence in one's own ability, rightness, etc. —**self"-con'fi·dent**, *adj.*

self″·con′scious, *adj.* excessively aware of the impression one may be making.

self′-con·tained′, *adj.* **1.** complete in itself. **2.** reserved in manner.

self″-con·trol′, *n.* ability to restrain one's impulses or expressions of emotion.

self′-de·ni′al, *n.* readiness to forgo gratifications to further a cause, help another, etc. —**self″-de·ny′ing,** *adj.*

self′-es·teem′, *n.* good opinion of one's self.

self′-ev′ident, *adj.* evident without further proof or explanation.

self′-ex·plan′a·to″ry, *adj.* needing no explanation; obvious.

self″-im·port′ant, *adj.* seeming to have an excessive idea of one's own importance.

self″-in′ter·est, *n.* concern for one's own well-being.

self′ish, *adj.* acting for or thinking of one's own well-being alone. —**self′ish·ly,** *adv.* —**self′ish·ness,** *n.*

self′less, *n.* self-sacrificing.

self′-made′, *n.* prosperous, famous, or powerful through one's own efforts.

self″-pos·ses′sion, *n.* self-control. —**self″-pos·sessed′,** *adj.*

self′-re·li′ance, *n.* reliance on one's own resources. —**self″-re·li′ant,** *adj.*

self′-re·spect′, *n.* respect for one's own dignity, rights, etc. —**self′-re·spect′ing,** *adj.*

self″-right′eous, *adj.* conceitedly sure of one's righteousness.

self′same″, *adj.* identical.

self″-sat′is·fied, *adj.* satisfied with one's own personality, accomplishments, etc. —**self′-sat″is·fac′tion,** *n.*

self-seek′ing, *adj.* motivated by self-interest.

self′-styled′, *adj.* thus named by the one so named.

self″-suf·fi′cient, *adj.* able to depend on one's own resources. —**self″-suf·fi′cien·cy,** *n.*

sell, *v.t.,* **sold, selling. 1.** exchange for money. **2.** offer for sale. —*v.i.* **3.** attract the buying public. —**sel′ler,** *n.*

selt′zer, *n.* carbonated water.

sel′vage, *n.* woven edge on a length of cloth. Also, **sel′vedge.**

se·man′tics, *n.* study of word meanings. —**se·man′tic,** *adj.*

sem′a·phore″, *n.* signal using different positions of arms or flags.

sem′blance, *n.* **1.** seeming state. **2.** resemblance.

se′men, *n.* fluid containing sperm.

se·mes′ter, *n.* unit consisting of half a school year.

se′mi·cir″cle, *n.* half a circle. —**se″mi·cir′cu·lar,** *adj.*

sem′i·col″on, *n.* punctuation mark of the form; that is used to divide clauses of a sentence.

sem″i·con·duc′tor, *n.* a material used to modify electrical current, used in solid-state circuitry.

sem′i·nar″, *n.* academic class with a format of discussion or research.

sem′i·nar″y, *n., pl.* **-naries. 1.** school for divinity students. **2.** school for young women. —**sem′i·nar′i·an,** *n.*

sem″i·pre′cious, *adj.* not considered precious, as certain decorative stones used as gems.

sen′ate, *n.* **1.** senior legislative body. **2.** **the senate,** upper legislative house in the United States or Canada. —**sen′a·tor,** *n.* —**sen″a·tor′i·al,** *adj.*

send, *v.,* **sent, sending.** *v.t.* **1.** cause to go. —*v.i.* **2.** send for, cause to come. —**send′er,** *n.*

se·nile (sē′nīl), *adj.* decrepit, esp. mentally, in old age. —**se·nil′i·ty,** *n.*

sen′ior, *adj.* **1.** older. **2.** higher in authority. **3.** having more years of employment or service. **4.** in the last year of school. —*n.* **5.** senior person. —**sen·ior′i·ty,** *n.*

se·ñor (senyor′), *n., pl.* **-nores.** *Spanish.* Mr. or Sir.

se·ño·ra (se nyor′ah), *n., pl.* **-noras.** *Spanish.* Mrs. or Madam.

se·ño·ri·ta (se″nyō rē′tah), *n., pl.* **-ritas.** *Spanish.* Miss.

sen·sa′tion, *n.* **1.** use of the senses. **2.** experience obtained through the senses. **3.** intuition or feeling. **4.** something causing excited public interest.

sen·sa′tion·al, *adj.* causing or intended to cause excited public interest. —**sen·sa′tion·al·ly,** *adv.* —**sen·sa′tion·al·ism,** *n.*

sense, *n., v.t.,* **sensed, sensing.** *n.* **1.** sight, hearing, touch, taste, or smell. **2.** impression obtained through one of these. **3.** intuition regarding a situation. **4.** Often, **senses,** reason. **5.** meaning. —*v.t.* **6.** perceive by or as if by one of the senses.

sense′less, *adj.* **1.** unreasonable. **2.** unconscious.

sen″si·bil′i·ty, *n., pl.* **-ties. 1.** ability to sense or be aware of things. **2.** Often, **sensibilities,** emotional sensitivity.

sen′si·ble, *n.* **1.** reasonable. **2.** perceptible through the senses. **3.** aware. —**sen′si·bly,** *adv.*

sen′si·tive, *n.* **1.** able to sense or register obects, data, etc. in small amounts. **2.** easily disturbed. —**sen″si·tiv′i·ty,** *n.*

sen′si·tize, *v.t.,* **-tized, -tizing.** make sensitive.

sen′so·ry, *adj.* pertaining to the senses.

sen′su·al, *adj.* **1.** given to the pleasures of the senses. **2.** pertaining to such pleasure. —**sen′su·al·ism,** *n.* —**sen′su·al·ist,** *n.*

sen'su·ous, *n.* **1.** pertaining to the senses. **2.** pleasing to the senses or emotions. —**sen'su·ous·ly,** *adv.* —**sen'su·ous·ness,** *n.*

sen'tence, *n., v.t.,* **-tenced, -tencing.** *n.* **1.** unit of prose writing expressing one thought. **2.** legal decision, esp. regarding a punishment. **3.** punishment, esp. a term of imprisonment. —*v.t.* **4.** determine the punishment of.

sen''ten'tious, *adj.* tiresomely opinionated or voluble on matters of right and wrong.

sen'tient (sen'shənt), *adj.* having feeling or perception. —**sen'tience,** *n.*

sen'ti·ment, *n.* **1.** personal feeling. **2.** statement of such feeling. **3.** opinion.

sen''ti·men'tal, *adj.* characterized by love, pity, etc., esp. to an unreasonable extent. —**sen''ti·men''tal'i·ty,** *n.* —**sen''ti·men'tal·ism,** *n.* —**sen''ti·men'tal·ist,** *n.*

sen'ti·nel, *n.* guard.

sen'try, *n., pl.* **-tries.** soldier on guard duty.

sep·a·rate, *v.,* **-rated, -rating,** *adj. v.t., v.i.* (sep'ə rāt) **1.** part. —*adj.* (sep'ə rət) **2.** unconnected; individual. —**sep'a·rate·ly,** *adv.* —**sep''a·ra'tion,** *n.* —**sep'a·ra·ble,** *adj.* —**sep'a·ra'tor,** *n.*

se'pi·a, *n.* dark brown.

sep'sis, *n.* infection of the blood. —**sep'tic,** *adj.*

Sep·tem'ber, *n.* ninth month.

sep'tic, *adj.* **1.** pertaining to putrefaction. **2.** pertaining to sepsis.

sep·tu·a·ge·nar·i·an (sep''cho͞o ə jə ner'ēən), *n.* person in his or her seventies.

sep·ul·cher (sep'əl kər), *n.* tomb. Also, **sep'ul·chre.**

se·pul'chral, *adj.* **1.** lugubrious or gloomy. **2.** pertaining to sepulchers.

se'quel, *n.* **1.** event that follows. **2.** story continuing the subject of a previous one.

se'quence, *n.* **1.** succession or series. **2.** consequence. **3.** episode in a motion picture or television program.

se·ques'ter, *v.t.* **1.** set apart. **2.** seize or impound. —**se''ques·tra'tion,** *n.*

se'quin, *n.* small glittering disk sewn to a costume.

ser'aph, *n., pl.* **-aphs, -aphim.** angel of the highest order. —**se·raph'ic,** *adj.*

sere, *adj.* withered.

ser'e·nade'', *n., v.t.,* **-naded, -nading.** *n.* **1.** musical composition for outdoor evening performance. —*v.t.* **2.** perform a serenade for.

se·rene', *adj.* **1.** calm. **2.** fair, as the weather. —**se·ren'i·ty,** *n.* —**se·rene'ly,** *adv.*

serf, *n.* person in bondage to a landlord. —**serf'dom,** *n.*

serge, *n.* twilled fabric.

ser'geant, *n.* highest noncommissioned army officer.

se'ri·al, *adj.* **1.** forming part of a series. —*n.* **2.** story appearing in installments. —**se'ri·al·ly,** *adv.*

se'ries, *n., pl.* **-ries.** group of things coming one after the other.

se'ri·ous, *adj.* **1.** solemn. **2.** earnest, sincere. **3.** important. —**se'ri·ous·ly,** *adv.* —**se'ri·ous·ness,** *n.*

ser'mon, *n.* speech to a religious congregation.

ser'pent, *n.* any large snake.

ser·pen·tine (sər'pən tēn), *adj.* winding in snakelike loops.

ser'rat·ed, *adj.* resembling sawteeth in outline. —**ser·ra'tion,** *n.*

se'rum, *n.* liquid part of the blood, sometimes used in inoculation.

serv'ant, *n.* person hired to work in a household.

serve, *v.,* **served, serving.** *v.t.* **1.** act in the service of. **2.** be of use to. **3.** present for consumption, as food or drink. **4.** undergo, as a prison sentence. —*v.i.* **5.** act in the service of a person, organization, or cause. **6.** suffice.

serv'ice, *n., v.t.,* **-viced, -vicing.** *n.* **1.** activity in behalf of a person, organization, or cause. **2.** employment as a domestic worker. **3.** military organization or the military. **4.** favor. **5.** session of public worship. **6.** set of matched dishes, eating implements, etc. —*v.t.* **7.** supply, maintain, or repair.

serv'ice·a·ble, *adj.* useful.

serv'ice·man'', *n.* **1.** member of an armed force. **2.** person who maintains, repairs, or fuels machinery.

ser·vile (sər'vil), *adj.* slavelike; obsequious. —**ser·vil'i·ty,** *n.*

ser'vi·tude, *n.* bondage.

ses'a·me, *n.* East Indian plant yielding oil and edible seeds.

ses''qui·cen·ten'ni·al, *n.* **1.** one hundred fiftieth anniversary. —*adj.* **2.** pertaining to such an anniversary.

ses'sion, *n.* **1.** occasion of the gathering of members of a group. **2. in session,** formally convened.

set, *v.,* **set, setting,** *n., adj. v.t.* **1.** place or put. **2.** put in proper or specified order or condition. **3.** place before others, as an example, problem, etc. —*v.i.* **4.** become fixed or firm. **5.** go below the horizon, as a star or planet. **6. set out** or **off,** begin to travel. —*n.* **7.** apparatus. **8.** complete group or collection. **9.** television or radio receiver. **10.** arrangement of theatrical scenery. —*adj.* **11.** firm or fixed. **12.** determined. **13.** prearranged.

set'back'', *n.* temporary defeat or hindrance.

set·tee', *n.* sofa or bench with a back.

set'ter, *n.* hunting dog.

set'ting, *n.* **1.** locale of a story. **2.** environment. **3.** music of a song.

set'tle, *v.*, **-tled, -tling.** *v.t.* **1.** resolve, as a dispute. **2.** free from disturbance. **3.** pay, as a debt. **4.** set in a position of rest. **5.** colonize. —*v.i.* **6.** fall gently into a position of rest. **7.** reach an agreement or compromise. **8.** take up residence. —**set'tler**, *n.* —**set'tle·ment**, *n.*

sev'en, *n., adj.* one more than six.

sev''en·teen', *n., adj.* seven more than ten. —**sev''en·teenth'**, *adj.*

sev'en''ty, *n., adj.* seven times ten. —**sev'en·ti''eth**, *adj.*

sev'er, *v.t.* cut off or separate. —**sev'er·ance**, *n.*

sev'er·al, *adj.* **1.** a few. **2.** individual. **3.** respective. —**sev'er·al·ly**, *adv.*

se·vere', *adj.* **1.** sternly demanding. **2.** harsh or violent. **3.** seriously bad. **4.** austerely simple. —**se·vere'ly**, *adv.* —**se·ver'i·ty**, *n.*

sew, *v.t.*, **sewed, sewed** or **sewn, sewing.** join with thread. —**sew'er**, *n.*

sew'age, *n.* waste material in sewers. Also, **sew'er·age.**

sew'er, *n.* covered channel for waste.

sex, *n.* **1.** individual nature as determined by the reproductive system. **2.** either of two divisions of a species as so determined. **3.** activities, thoughts, etc. as influenced by the reproductive system. —**sex'u·al**, *adj.* —**sex'u·al·ly**, *adv.*

sex''is·m, *n.* discrimination on the basis of sex.

sex'tant, *n.* navigational instrument using the elevation of the sun.

sex·tet', *n.* **1.** group of six, esp. musicians. **2.** musical composition for six instruments. Also, **sex·tette'.**

sex'ton, *n.* caretaker of a church.

sex'tu·ple, *adj.* occurring six times.

shab'by, *adj.*, **-bier, -biest. 1.** worn and untidy-looking. **2.** mean. —**shab'bi·ness**, *n.* —**shab'bi·ly**, *adv.*

shack, *n.* shanty.

shack'le, *n., v.t.*, **-led, -ling.** *n.* **1.** Usually, **shackles**, chains for binding prisoners. **2.** binding part of a padlock. —*v.t.* **3.** bind with or as with shackles.

shad, *n., pl.* **shads, shad.** herringlike fish spawning in rivers.

shade, *n., v.t.*, **shaded, shading.** *n.* **1.** area sheltered from direct light. **2.** device for cutting off direct light. **3.** variety of color or tone. **4.** slight degree. **5.** soul of a dead person. —*v.t.* **6.** shelter from direct light. **7.** vary, as a color or tone.

shad'ow, *n.* **1.** darkness of a shaded area. **2.** slight remnant or trace. —*v.t.* **3.** shade. **4.** follow secretly. —**shad'ow·y**, *adj.*

shad'y, *adj.* **1.** in the shade. **2.** *Informal.* to be suspected.

shaft, *n.* **1.** long, cylindrical object for support, rotation, etc. **2.** beam of light. **3.** narrow vertical space.

shag, *n.* long, rough hair, fur, or nap. —**shag'gy**, *adj.*

shah, *n.* ruler of Persia.

shake, *v.*, **shook, shaken, shaking**, *n. v.t.* **1.** cause to move rapidly back and forth. **2.** upset emotionally. —*v.i.* **3.** move rapidly back and forth. —*n.* **4.** act or instance of shaking. **5.** wood shingle.

shak'er, *n.* **1.** device for sprinkling seasoning. **2. Shaker**, member of an American celibate religious sect.

shak'y, *adj.*, **-kier, -kiest. 1.** unstable. **2.** tending to shake. **3.** of doubtful validity. —**shak'i·ly**, *adv.* —**shak'i·ness**, *n.*

shale, *n.* layered rock of hardened clay.

shall, *v.* am, is, or are going to.

shal'lot, *n.* onionlike plant used in cooking.

shal'low, *adj.* **1.** not deep. **2.** without depth of thought or feeling.

sham, *adj., n., v.*, **shammed, shamming.** *adj.* **1.** false; imitation. —*n.* **2.** something false or imitative. —*v.t.* **3.** pretend; feign.

sham'ble, *v.i.*, **-bled, -bling**, *n. v.i.* **1.** walk draggingly or awkwardly. —*n.* **2. shambles**, **a.** scene of disorder. **b.** slaughterhouse. **3.** shambling gait.

shame, *n., v.t.*, **shamed, shaming**. *n.* **1.** painful sense of guilt or inadequacy. **2.** disgrace. **3.** deplorable situation. —*v.t.* **4.** put to shame. —**shame'ful**, *adj.* —**shame'less**, *adj.*

shame'faced, *adj.* showing embarrassment. —**shame'fac'ed·ly**, *adv.*

sham·poo', *v.t.*, **-pooed, -pooing**, *n. v.t.* **1.** wash with soap, as the hair or a carpet. —*n.* **2.** soap, etc. used for shampooing.

sham'rock, *n.* cloverlike plant with a triple leaf: symbol of Ireland.

shang'hai, *v.t.*, **-haied, -haiing.** abduct for work on a ship.

shank, *n.* **1.** lower leg above the ankle. **2.** shaft of a hand tool between the handle and working end.

shan'tung, *n.* textured silk.

shan'ty, *n., pl.* **-ties.** roughly built wooden house.

shape, *n., v.t.*, **shaped, shaping**. *n.* **1.** form. **2.** *Informal.* condition. —*v.t.* **3.** give form to. —**shape'less**, *adj.*

shape'ly, *adj.* handsome in form. —**shape'li·ness**, *n.*

share, *n., v.t.* **shared, sharing**. *n.* **1.** rightful or predetermined portion. —*v.t.* **2.** divide into such portions. **3.** use or experience together.

shark, *n.* **1.** large predatory fish. **2.** person who preys on others.

sharp, *adj.* 1. having or as if having a cutting point or edge. 2. clearly defined. 3. shrewd. 4. alert. 5. abrupt. 6. *Music.* raised in pitch. —*adv.* 7. punctually. —*n.* 8. a semitone higher than a stated tone. —**sharp'en·er,** *n.* —**sharp'ly,** *adv.* —**sharp'ness,** *n.* —**sharp'en,** *v.t.*

sharp'er, *n.* swindler.

sharp'shoot''er, *n.* good marksman.

shat'ter, *v.t., v.i.* break in small pieces.

shave, *v.,* **shaved, shaved** or **shaven, shaving,** *n. v.t.* 1. cut the hair off with a razor. 2. remove with a razor. 3. cut in thin layers with a tool. —*n.* 4. act or instance of being shaved.

shav'ing, *n.* thin layer of material shaved from a larger piece.

shawl, *n.* cloth covering head and shoulders.

she, *pron.* woman or female previously mentioned.

sheaf, *n., pl.* **sheaves.** bundle.

shear, *v.t.,* **sheared, sheared** or **shorn, shearing,** *n. v.t.* 1. divide as with the motion of one blade across another. —*n.* 2. device for shearing.

shears, *n., pl.* large scissors.

sheath, *n., pl.* **sheaths.** closely fittingcase or cover.

sheathe, *v.t.,* **sheathed, sheathing.** put into a sheath.

shed, *v.t.,* **shed, shedding,** *n. v.t.* leave or cast off. 2. pour forth, as light. —*n.* 3. rough shelter.

sheen, *n.* dull reflection.

sheep, *n., pl.* **sheep.** mammal yielding fleece and mutton.

sheep'ish, *adj.* bashful or embarrassed.

sheer, *adj.* 1. absolute; utter. 2. very steep or perpendicular. 3. transparent, as a fabric. —*v.i.* 4. swerve.

sheet, *n.* 1. broad, thin piece of material. 2. cloth used to cover a mattress or a sleeper. 3. rope for controlling the position of a sail.

sheik, *n.* Arab chief.

shek'el, *n.* ancient Hebrew coin.

shelf, *n., pl.* **shelves.** 1. horizontal ledge or slab for supporting objects. 2. ledge, as of rock.

shell, *n.* 1. hard outer covering. 2. shotgun cartridge. 3. explosive artillery missile. 4. racing rowboat. —*v.t.* 5. separate from its shell. 6. bombard with shells.

shel·lac', *n.* 1. varnish containing a certain resin. 2. the resin itself. —*v.t.* 3. varnish with shellac.

shell'fish'', *n.* any aquatic animal with a shell.

shel'ter, *n.* 1. something serving as a protection, as against the weather. —*v.t.* 2. protect. —*v.i.* 3. take shelter.

shelve, *v.,* **shelved, shelving.** 1. put on a shelf. 2. postpone action or decision on. 3. provide with shelves. —*v.i.* 4. slope.

shep'herd, *n.* 1. Also, *fem.,* **shep'herd·ess,** person who leads and guards sheep. —*v.t.* 2. escort with close vigilance.

sher'bet, *n.* frozen dessert of water, gelatin, flavoring, and sometimes milk.

sher'iff, *n.* county police officer.

sher'ry, *n., pl.* **-ries.** Spanish fortified wine.

shield, *n.* 1. piece of armor worn on the arm. 2. any defensive device. —*v.t.* 3. protect or hide.

shift, *v.t., v.i.* 1. move from place to place. 2. change, as one's place. 3. change, as the gears of a motor vehicle. —*n.* 4. act or instance of shifting. 5. lever for changing gears in a motor vehicle. 6. daily period of labor.

shift'less, *n.* lazy or feeble.

shift'y, *adj.,* **shiftier, shiftiest.** tricky; unreliable. —**shift'i·ly,** *adv.* —**shift'i·ness,** *n.*

shil'ling, *n.* former British coin, one-twentieth of a pound.

shil'ly-shal'ly, *v.i.,* **-lied, -lying.** hesitate or quarrel over trifles. or quarrel over trifles.

shim, *n.* thin piece for raising an object or filling a gap.

shim'mer, *v.i.* 1. glow or appear in a flickering, unsteady way. —*n.* 2. effect given in so doing. —**shim'mer·y,** *adj.*

shin, *n.* front of the shank of the leg.

shine, *v.,* **shone** or, for *v.t.,* **shined, shining,** *n. v.i.* 1. emit or reflect strong light. 2. gain distinction. —*v.t.* 3. polish to a high gloss. —*n.* 4. shining light. —**shin'y,** *adj.*

shin'gle, *n.* 1. thin plate of wood or other material used in courses as a roof covering or siding. 2. **shingles.** virus disease with blisters as a symptom. —*v.t.* 3. cover with shingles.

shin'ny, *n.* street hockey.

ship, *n., v.,* **shipped, shipping.** *n.* 1. large ocean-going vessel. 2. sailing vessel square-rigged on all of at least three masts. —*v.t.* 3. send by a freight carrier. —*v.i.* 4. engage to work on a voyage. —**ship'mate'',** *n.* —**ship'ment,** *n.* —**ship'per,** *n.*

ship'ping, *n.* vessels, esp. merchant ships.

ship'shape'', *adj., adv.* in good order.

ship'wreck'', *n.* destruction of a ship from running aground.

ship'yard'', *n.* place for building or repairing ships.

shire, *n.* British county.

shirk, *v.t.* 1. evade, as an obligation. —*n.* 2. person who shirks something. —**shirk'er,** *n.*

shirr, *v.t.* gather on parallel strands for decorative effect, as curtain material.

shirt, *n.* a long- or short-sleeved upper garment usually having a front opening, collar and cuffs, worn esp. by men.

shiv'er, *v.i.* 1. tremble. —*v.t.* 2. smash to pieces. —*n.* 3. trembling movement. 4. broken fragment. —**shiv'er·y,** *adj.*

shoal, *n.* 1. area of shallow water. 2. large number of fish.

shoat, *n.* young pig.

shock, *n.* 1. violent impact. 2. violent emotional disturbance. 3. bodily disturbance caused by loss of blood circulation, a current of electricity passing through the body, etc. 4. stack of sheaves of grain. 5. tangled mass, as of hair. —*v.t.* 6. disturb with a shock. —**shock'ing,** *adj.*

shod'dy, *adj.* poor in quality. —**shod'di·ness,** *n.*

shoe, *n., v.t.,* **shod, shoeing.** *n.* 1. protective covering for the foot. 2. something suggesting this. —*v.t.* 3. provide with shoes. —**shoe'lace'', shoe'string'',** *n.* —**shoe'mak''er,** *n.*

shoe'horn'', *n.* device to assist slipping the foot into a shoe.

shoot, *v.t.* 1. send a missile from. 2. hit with a missile. 3. emit rapidly, as a missile. —*v.i.* 4. use a gun, bow, etc. 5. grow or sprout. —*n.* 6. sporting event with shooting. 7. young plant growth. —**shoot'er,** *n.*

shop, *n., v.i.,* **shopped, shopping.** *n.* 1. store, esp. a small specialized one. 2. industrial workroom. —*v.i.* 3. look for or make purchases. —**shop'per,** *n.* —**shop'keep''er,** *n.*

shop'lift''er, *n.* person who steals from shops.

shore, *n., v.t.,* **shored, shoring.** *n.* 1. land bordering a body of water. 2. seacoast. 3. prop. —*v.t.* 4. prop.

short, *n.* 1. not tall or long. 2. abrupt in manner. 3. scanty, as a supply. 4. below the required amount. 5. flaky, as pastry. —*adv.* 6. abruptly. —*n.* 7. short circuit. 8. **shorts,** short-legged pants or underpants. —*v.t.* 9. create a short circuit in. —**short'ly,** *adv.* —**short'ness,** *n.* —**short'en,** *v.t.*

short'age, *n.* short supply.

short circuit, deviation of current in an electrical circuit rendering it useless.

short'com''ing, *n.* fault or inadequacy.

short'cut'', *n.* shorter way than the usual.

short'en·ing, *n.* greasy substance for making pastry short.

short'hand'', *n.* system of writing for fast note-taking.

short-lived (short'līvd''), *adj.* not living or existing long.

short'-sight''ed, *adj.* without foresight.

shot, *n., pl.* **shots** or (for 3) **shot.** 1. discharge of a missile. 2. range of a gun, bow, etc. 3. *Often pl.* missiles, esp.

shotgun pellets or cannonballs. 4. iron ball for hurling in athletic contests. 5. marksman.

shot'gun, *n.* gun firing shells filled with metal pellets.

should, *v.* 1. ought to. 2. were to. 3. past tense of *shall.*

shoul'der, *n.* 1. part of the human body between the upper arms and neck. 2. corresponding area in animals. 3. unpaved strip alongside a road. —*v.t.* 4. push with the shoulder. 5. take up and carry.

shout, *n.* 1. very loud call or voice. —*v.i.* 2. give such a call. —*v.t.* 3. utter in such a voice.

shove, *v.,* **shoved, shoving,** *n., v.t., v.i.* 1. push vigorously. —*n.* 2. vigorous push.

shov'el, *n.* 1. hand tool or machine for scooping up material. —*v.t.* 2. raise or move with a shovel. 3. clear with a shovel.

show, *v.,* **showed, shown** or **showed, showing,** *n., v.t.* 1. display. 2. guide. 3. prove or demonstrate. —*v.i.* 4. be visible or apparent. —*n.* 5. entertainment. 6. exhibit. 7. ostentation. —**show'boat'',** *n.* —**show'case'',** *n.* —**show'man,** *n.* —**show'piece,** *n.* —**show'room,** *n.*

show'down'', *n.* 1. confrontation, as between enemies. 2. climactic event.

show'er, *n.* 1. brief rainstorm. 2. bath in which water is sprayed from above. 3. large number of small objects dropped or hurled. —*v.t.* 4. bestow liberally. —*v.i.* 5. rain briefly.

show'off'', *n.* vain, ostentatious person.

show'y, *adj.,* **-ier, -iest.** attracting attention, esp. through gaudiness.

shrap'nel, *n.* small fragments hurled by the bursting of an artillery shell.

shred, *n., v.t.,* **shredded, shredding.** *n.* 1. torn strip. 2. bit, as of doubt or evidence. —*v.t.* 3. tear into shreds.

shrew, *n.* 1. small mouselike mammal. 2. quarrelsome woman. —**shrew'ish,** *adj.*

shrewd, *adj.* clever in dealing with or understanding others. —**shrewd'ly,** *adv.* —**shrewd'ness,** *n.*

shriek, *n.* 1. loud, shrill cry. —*v.i.* 2. utter such a cry.

shrike, *n.* bird of prey.

shrill, *adj.* high-pitched. —**shrill'ly,** *adv.* —**shrill'ness,** *n.*

shrimp, *n.* small, long-tailed shellfish.

shrine, *n.* sacred place.

shrink, *v.,* **shrank** or **shrunk, shrunk** or **shrunken, shrinking** *v.i.* 1. become smaller. 2. draw back, as in fear. —*v.t.* 3. cause to shrink. —**shrink'age,** *n.*

shrivel, *v.i.* shrink and become wrinkled.

shroud, *n.* 1. wrapping for a corpse. 2. line steadying a ship's mast. —*v.t.* 3. wrap or conceal.

shrub, *n.* small, treelike plant. —**shrub′ber·y,** *n.*

shrug, *n., v.,* shrugged, shrugging. *n.* 1. movement of raising both shoulders. —*v.i.* 2. make such a movement. —*v.t.* 3. move in shrugging.

shuck, *n., v.t.* husk or shell.

shud′der, *v.i.* 1. tremble violently and briefly. —*n.* 2. act or instance of shuddering.

shuf′fle, *v.i.,* -fled, -fling, *n., v.i.* 1. walk with feet scraping the ground. 2. mix, as playing cards. —*n.* 3. shuffling gait.

shuf′fle·board′, *n.* game played by shoving wooden disks along a marked surface.

shun, *v.t.,* shunned, shunning. avoid.

shunt, *v.t.* 1. divert. 2. move, as cars in a railroad yard.

shut, *v.,* shut, shutting, *adj., v.t.* 1. close. 2. keep in or out. —*v.i.* 3. be closed. —*n.* 4. closed.

shut′ter, *n.* 1. cover for a window opening. 2. device for timed exposure of film in a camera.

shut′tle, *v.i.,* -tled, -tling, *n., v.i.* 1. go short distances back and forth. —*n.* 2. device on a loom for moving warp thread back and forth. 3. public transit vehicle that runs between two closely spaced terminals.

shy, *adj.,* shier, shiest, *v.,* shied, shying, *n., pl.* shies. *adj.* 1. timid in the presence of others. 2. lacking by a specified number. —*v.t.* 3. toss, esp. with a sideways motion. —*v.i.* 4. start with surprise, as a horse. —*n.* 5. act or instance of shying. —**shy′ly,** *adv.* —**shy′ness,** *n.*

sib′ling, *n.* brother or sister.

sic, *v.t.,* sicked, sicking, *adv. v.t.* 1. urge to an attack. —*adv.* 2. *Latin.* thus; (it is written).

sick, *adj.,* 1. not in health. 2. suffering nausea. 3. disgusted or upset. 4. *Informal.* mentally warped. —*n.* 5. sick people. —**sick′ness,** *n.* —**sick′en,** *v.t., v.i.*

sick′le, *n.* crescent-shaped tool for mowing.

sick′ly, *adj.,* -lier, -liest. not healthy or robust.

side, *n., adj., v.i.,* sided, siding. *n.* 1. area of someone or something to the right or left of the face or front. 2. direction or location to the right or left. 3. any direction or location from a central point. 4. line or surface defining a form. 5. aspect. 6. person or group in a dispute or conflict. 7. opinion or cause of such a person or group.—*adj.* 8. pertaining to a side direction or location. 9. of secondary importance.—*v.i.* 10. ally oneself.

side′board′, *n.* article of furniture for dishes, silver, and napkins.

side′burns′, *n., pl.* whiskers down the sides of the face.

side′line′, *n.* secondary source of income.

side′long′, *adj., adv.* to the side.

si·de′re·al, *adj.* pertaining to stars.

side′show′, *n.* minor entertainment at a circus.

side′step′, *v.t.,* stepped, stepping. evade by or as if by stepping sideways.

side′swipe′, *v.t.,* swiped, swiping. brush the side of in passing.

side′track′, *v.t.* divert or distract from accomplishing a purpose.

side′walk′, *n.* walk beside a roadway.

side′ways′, *adv., adj.* 1. with a side foremost. 2. to or from one side. Also, **side′wise′.**

sid′ing, *n.* short track for trains halted beside a through track.

sidle, *v.i.,* -dled, -dling. move sideways.

SIDS, sudden infant death syndrome, unexplained death of baby while asleep.

siege, *n.* prolonged attack on a fortified place.

sienna, *n.* reddish- or yellowish-brown.

si·es′ta, *n.* brief daytime nap.

sieve, *n., v.t.,* sieved, sieving. *n.* 1. strainer of wire mesh. —*v.t.* 2. run through or separate with a sieve.

sift, *v.t.* separate with a sieve. —**sift′er,** *n.*

sigh, *v.i.* 1. release pent-up breath in reaction to grief, annoyance, etc. —*n.* 2. such a release of breath.

sight, *n.* 1. sense perceived by the eyes. 2. something seen. 3. something remarkable to see. 4. range of distances one's eyes can see clearly. 5. aiming device for shooting or bombing. —*v.t.* 6. discover with the eye. 7. aim with a sight. —**sight′less,** *adj.*

sight′ly, *adj.,* -lier, -liest. pleasing to see.

sign, *n.* 1. indication. 2. written, printed, or hand-given symbol. 3. display surface containing such symbols or writing. —*v.t.* 4. put a signature on. —**sign′er,** *n.*

sig′nal, *n., adj., v.t.,* -naled, -naling. *n.* 1. device presenting a message in symbols. 2. message so presented. —*adj.* 3. acting as a signal. 4. marked. —*v.t.* 5. indicate through a signal. 6. communicate through a signal. —**sig′nal·er,** *n.* —**sig′nal·man,** *n.* —**sig′nal·ly,** *adv.*

sig′nal·ize″, *v.t.,* -ized, -izing. call attention to or make noteworthy.

sig′na·to″ry, *n., pl.* -ries. signer, esp. of a document.

sig′na·ture, *n.* 1. one's name in one's handwriting. 2. *Music.* sign indicating key and tempo.

sig′net, *n.* letter seal, often mounted on a ring.

sig·nif′i·cance, *n.* 1. meaning. 2. importance. —**sig·nif′i·cant,** *adj.*

sig′ni·fy″, *v.t.,* -fied, -fying. 1. mean. 2. indicate. —**sig″ni·fi·ca′tion,** *n.*

si′lence, *n., v.t.,* -lenced, -lencing. *n.* 1.

silhouette

absence of noise, conversation, or sound. 2. absence of information or communication. —*v.t.* 3. make silent. 4. put out of action, as enemy guns. —si'lent, *adj.* —si'lent·ly, *adv.*,

sil·hou·ette (sil″ŏŏ et′), *n.*, *v.t.*, -etted, -etting *n.* 1. outline figure, usually filled in with black. —*v.t.* 2. cause to appear in outline against a lighter background.

sil'i·ca, *n.* hard, glassy substance appearing as sand, quartz, etc.

sil'i·con, *n.* nonmetallic element appearing in various compounds.

silk, *n.* cloth made of fiber spun by silkworms.

silk'en, *adj.* 1. made of silk. 2. suggesting silk in smoothness. Also, silk'y.

silk'worm″, *n.* moth caterpillar whose cocoons provide silk fiber.

sill, *n.* horizontal structural member, esp. below a wall or opening.

sil'ly, *adj.*, -lier, -liest. 1. foolish or stupid. 2. unreasonable. —sil'li·ness, *n.*

si'lo, *n.* airtight place for storing fodder.

silt, *n.* 1. fine earth, etc. deposited by running water. —*v.t.* 2. fill or clog with silt.

sil'ver, *n.* 1. white noble metallic element. 2. coins, utensils, etc. customarily made of silver. 3. lustrous whitish gray. —*adj.* 4. made of or colored silver. 5. pertaining to a twenty-fifth wedding anniversary. 6. eloquent, as the tongue. —sil'ver·y, *adj.* —sil'ver·smith″, *n.*

sil'ver·ware″, *n.* tableware traditionally made of silver.

sim'i·an, *adj.* 1. pertaining to or suggesting apes and monkeys. —*n.* 2. ape or monkey.

sim'i·lar, *adj.* of the same sort. —sim'i·lar·ly, *adv.* —sim″i·lar'i·ty, *n.*

sim'i·le″, *n.* expression comparing one thing to another.

si·mil'i·tude″, *n.* likeness.

sim'mer, *v.t.*, *v.i.* almost boil.

si″mul·ta'ne·ous, *adj.* at the very same time. —si″mul·ta'ne·ous·ly, *adv.*

si'mo·ny, *n.* profiting financially from religion.

sim'per, *v.i.* 1. smile foolishly or affectedly. —*n.* 2. foolish or affected smile.

sim'ple, *adj.*, -pler, -plest. 1. of the most basic kind. 2. readily understood or mastered. 3. low in intelligence. —sim'ply, *adv.* —sim·plic'i·ty, *n.*

sim'ple-mind'ed, *adj.* foolish; low in intelligence.

sim'ple·ton, *n.* foolish or naive person.

sim'pli·fy, *v.t.*, -fied, -fying. make easier to understand or master. —sim″pli·fi·ca'tion, *n.*

sim·plis'tic, *adj.* unrealistically oversimplified.

sim'u·late, *v.t.*, -lated, -lating. 1. pretend feign. 2. imitate closely. —sim″u·la'tion, *n.*

sin, *n.*, *v.i.*, sinned, sinning. *n.* 1. violation of religious law. —*v.i.* 2. commit such a violation. —sin'ful, *adj.* —sin'ful·ly, *adv.* —sin'ful·ness, *n.*

since, *conj.* 1. during the time after. 2. because or inasmuch as. —*adv.* 3. from that time on. 4. at some time afterwards.

sin·cere', *adj.*, -cerer, -cerest. genuine; honest and unaffected. —sin·cere'ly, *adv.* —sin·cer'i·ty, *n.*

si·ne·cure (si'ne kyŏŏr″), *n.* salaried job requiring no serious work.

sin'ew, *n.* 1. tendon. 2. muscular strength. —sin'ew·y, *adj.*

sing, *v.*, sang or sung, sung, singing. *v.i.* 1. make musical sounds with the voice. —*v.t.* 2. render by singing. —sing'er, *n.*

singe, *v.t.*, singed, singeing. burn on the surface.

sin'gle, *adj.*, *v.t.*, -gled, -gling, *n. adj.* 1. alone or unique. 2. unmarried. —*v.t.* 3. single out, select. —*n.* 4. something single. —sin'gly, *adv.*

sing'song″, *adj.* monotonously rhythmical.

sin'gu·lar, *adj.* 1. peculiar or extraordinary. 2. unique. 3. *Grammar.* pertaining to one person or thing. —*n.* 4. *Grammar.* singular number of a word. —sin'gu·lar·ly, *adv.* —sin″gu·lar'i·ty, *n.*

sin'is·ter, *adj.* evilly threatening.

sink, *v.*, sank or sunk, sunk or sunken, sinking *n. v.i.* 1. descend beneath a surface. 2. pass into a depressed state. —*v.t.* 3. cause to descend or penetrate beneath a surface. —*n.* 4. basin with a drain. —sink'er, *n.*

sin'ner, *n.* person who sins.

sin'u·ous, *adj.* meandering; serpentine.

si'nus, *n.* cavity, esp. one in the skull opening into the nasal passages.

sip, *v.*, sipped, sipping, *n. v.t.* 1. drink in tiny amounts. —*n.* 2. act or instance of sipping. 3. amount sipped at a time.

si'phon, *n.* 1. curved tube for sucking liquids automatically from place to place. —*v.t.* 2. pass through a siphon.

sir, *n.* 1. formal term used in addressing a man. 2. title given a British knight or baronet.

sire, *n.*, *v.t.*, sired, siring. *n.* 1. male parent, esp. of an animal. 2. formal term used in addressing a king. —*v.t.* 3. beget.

si'ren, *n.* 1. mythical sea nymph luring sailors with singing to shipwreck. 2. horn with a wavering tone used on emergency vehicles.

sir'loin, *n.* cut of beef at the loin end by the rump.

sir'up, *n.* syrup.

si'sal, *n.* plant fiber used for ropes, etc.

sis'sy, *n. Informal.* timid or unmanly male.

sis'ter, *n.* 1. daughter of one's own parents. 2. nun. —**sis'ter·ly**, *adj.*

sis'ter·hood", *n.* 1. organization of nuns. 2. condition of being a sister.

sis'ter-in-law", *n., pl.* **sisters-in-law.** 1. sister of a spouse. 2. wife of a brother.

sit, *v.*, **sat, sitting.** *v.i.* 1. rest on the behind. 2. be located. 3. pose, as for a portrait. 4. be in session, as a court. —*v.t.* 5. seat. —**sit'ter**, *n.*

site, *n.* location, as of a building.

sit'ting, *n.* session.

sit'u·ate", *v.t.*, **-ated, -ating.** place or locate.

sit"u·a'tion, *n.* 1. location. 2. condition or predicament. 3. job.

six, *n., adj.* one more than five. —**sixth**, *adj.*

six"teen', *n., adj.* six more than ten. —**six·teenth'**, *adj.*

six'ty, *n., adj.* six times ten. —**six'ti·eth**, *adj.*

siz'a·ble, *adj.* fairly large. Also, **size'a·ble.**

size, *n., v.t.*, **sized, sizing.** *n.* 1. area, volume, number, etc. by which something is measured or graded. 2. Also, **siz'ing** pasty substance used to coat or fill cloth, paper, etc. —*v.t.* 3. **size up,** measure or appraise intuitively. 4. treat with sizing.

siz'zle, *v.i.*, **-zled, -zling**, *n.* *v.i.* 1. hiss or crackle, as from being fried. —*n.* 2. hissing or crackling, as from being fried.

skate, *n., v.i.*, **skated, skating.** *n.* 1. piece of footwear for gliding across ice. 2. roller skate. 3. flat-bodied fish of the ray family. —*v.i.* 4. go on skates. —**skat'er**, *n.*

skein (skān), *n.* coil of yarn or thread.

skel'e·ton, *n.* 1. bone structure of an animal. 2. structural frame. —**skel'e·tal**, *adj.*

skep'tic, *n.* doubter. —**skep'ti·cal**, *adj.* —**skep'ti·cal·ly**, *adv.* —**skep'ti·cism"**, *n.*

sketch, *n.* 1. rough drawing. 2. brief outline. —*v.t.* 3. make a sketch of.

sketch'y, *adj.* vague or without detail. —**sketch'i·ly**, *adv.*

skew, *v.t., v.i.* 1. slant. —*adj.* 2. aslant.

skew'er, *n.* 1. needle for holding pieces of meat together. —*v.t.* 2. pierce with or as if with a skewer.

ski, *n., pl.* **skis,** *v.i.*, **skied, skiing.** *n.* 1. long flat runner for gliding or walking on snow. —*v.i.* 2. glide on skis. —**ski'er,** *n.*

skid, *v.*, **skidded, skidding**, *n.* *v.i., v.t.* 1. lide, by accident or intention. —*n.* 2. object or surface on which objects are skidded. 3. skidding motion.

skiff, *n.* rowboat.

skill, *n.* practised ability. —**skilled**, *adj.* —**skill'ful**, *adj.* —**skill'ful·ly**, *adv.*

skil'let, *n.* frying pan.

skim, *v.*, **skimmed, skimming.** *v.t.* 1. remove from a liquid surface. —*v.i.* 2. move lightly across a surface.

skimp, *v.i.* economize; scrimp.

skimp'y, *adj.*, **skimpier, skimpiest.** scant.

skin, *n., v.t.*, **skinned, skinning.** *n.* 1. outer covering of an animal body. —*v.t.* 2. remove skin or hide from. —**skin'ner**, *n.* —**skin'less**, *adj.*

skin'flint", *n.* miserly person.

skin'ny, *adj.* thin of body.

skip, *v.*, **skipped, skipping**, *n.*, *v.i.* 1. jump lightly. —*v.t.* 2. omit. —*n.* 3. light jump

skip'per, *n.* ship or boat captain.

skir'mish, *n.* 1. brief, minor battle. —*v.i.* 2. have a skirmish.

skirt, *n.* 1. open-bottomed garment fastened around the waist. 2. Often, **skirts**, portion of a coat, dress, etc. that falls below the waist. —*v.t.* 3. pass around the border of. 4. evade, as subject of controversy.

skit, *n.* brief comic play.

skit'tish, *adj.* readily excited or frightened.

skul"dug'ger·y, *n.* treacherous intrigue.

skulk, *v.i.* lurk.

skull, *n.* bony shell of a head.

skunk, *n.* small mammal defending itself with foul-smelling liquid.

sky, *n., pl.* **skies.** 1. part of the atmosphere visible from the earth. 2. condition of this at a certain place and time.

sky'light", *n.* window in the surface of a roof or ceiling.

sky'line", *n.* silhouette against the horizon.

sky'rock"et, *n.* 1. firework rising high before exploding. —*v.i.* 2. rise rapidly.

sky'scrap"er, *n.* very tall building, esp. one for offices.

slab, *n.* flat, fairly thick piece of material.

slack, *adj.* 1. loose. 2. inactive. 3. lazy or indifferent. —*n.* 4. slack part. 5. period of inactivity. —*v.t., v.i.* 6. slacken. —**slack'ly**, *adv.* —**slack'ness**, *n.*

slack'en, *v.t., v.i.* 1. make or become slack. 2. lessen in intensity or vigor.

slacks, *n., pl.* loosely fitting trousers.

slag, *n.* molten waste from smelting.

slake, *v.t.*, **slaked, slaking.** 1. quench with a drink. 2. pour water on, as quicklime.

slam, *v.t.*, **slammed, slamming**, *n., v.t.* 1. push violently and noisily into place. —*n.* 2. act of pushing thus.

slan'der, *n.* 1. maliciously untrue statement or statements about someone.

—*v.t.* **2.** utter such statements about.
—**slan′der·ous,** *adj.*

slang, *n.* highly informal speech. —**slang′y,** *adj.*

slant, *v.t., v.i.* **1.** move or head diagonally. —*n.* **2.** diagonal movement or heading. **3.** attitude or opinion.

slap, *v.t.,* **slapped, slapping,** *n., v.t.* **1.** hit with a flat object, esp. the hand. **2.** put together, etc. in haste. —*n.* **3.** act or instance of slapping.

slash, *v.t.* **1.** cut deeply with a long, sweeping motion. —*n.* **2.** long, deep cut.

slat, *n.* thin board.

slate, *n., v.t.,* **slated, slating.** *n.* **1.** stone that can be cleaved into thin pieces. **2.** list of candidates. —*v.t.* **3.** cover with slate. **4.** intend for nomination, promotion, dismissal, etc.

slat′tern, *n.* slovenly woman.

slaugh′ter, *n.* **1.** mass killing; massacre. **2.** killing of animals for meat. —*v.t.* **3.** submit to slaughter. —**slaugh′ter·house″,** *n.*

slave, *n., v.i.,* **slaved, slaving.** *n.* **1.** person treated as the property of another. —*v.i.* **2.** drudge. —**slav′ery,** *n.*

slav·er (slăhv′ər), *v.i.* drool.

slav′ish, *adj.* in the manner of a slave, esp. in lacking originality or initiative.

slaw, *n.* coleslaw.

slay, *v.t.,* **slew, slain, slaying.** skill. —**slay′er,** *n.*

slea′zy, *adj.,* **-zier, -ziest.** shoddy.

sled, *n., v.i.,* **sledded, sledding.** *n.* **1.** vehicle for gliding across snow or ice. —*v.i.* **2.** travel by sled.

sledge, *n., v.t.,* **sledged, sledging.** *n.* **1.** sledlike vehicle. **2.** Also, **sledge′hammer,** heavy hammer. —*v.t.* **3.** transport by sledge.

sleek, *adj.* **1.** smooth or glossy. —*v.t.* **2.** make smooth. —**sleek′ly,** *adv.* —**sleek′ness,** *n.*

sleep, *n., v.i.,* **slept, sleeping.** *n.* **1.** periodic state of unconscious rest. —*v.i.* **2.** be in such a state. —**sleep′y,** *adj.* —**sleep′less,** *adj.*

sleep′er, *n.* **1.** sleeping person. **2.** sill-like timber. **3.** railroad car with berths.

sleet, *n.* rain frozen in fine particles.

sleeve, *n.* part of a shirt or coat covering an arm.

sleigh, *n.* horse-drawn light sled.

sleight of hand (slīt), rapid, secret hand movements for creating illusions.

slen′der, *adj.* **1.** attractively thin. **2.** meager, as means of livelihood. —**slen′der·ness,** *n.*

sleuth, *n. Informal.* detective.

slice, *n., v.t.,* **sliced, slicing.** *n.* **1.** thin piece cut from a larger one. —*v.t.* **2.** cut as a slice. **3.** cut slices from. —**slic′er,** *n.*

slick, *adj.* **1.** smooth or slippery. **2.** cunning. —*n.* **3.** area of floating oil. —*v.t.* **4.** make smooth.

slick′er, *n.* raincoat with a slick outer surface.

slide, *v.,* **slid, sliding,** *n. v.t., v.i.* **1.** move with surface contact between the object moving and something else. —*n.* **2.** act or instance of sliding. **3.** object or surface used in sliding. **4.** fall of earth, rock, etc. down a slope. **5.** transparent plate used with a microscope, magic lantern, etc.

slight, *adj.* **1.** unimportantly little. **2.** slender. —*v.t., n.* **3.** snub. —**slight′ly,** *adv.* —**slight′ness,** *n.* —**slight′ing·ly,** *adv.*

sli′ly, *adv.* slyly.

slim, *adj.,* **slimmer, slimmest.** **1.** slender. **2.** small in amount or size. —**slim′ness,** *n.*

slime, *n.* semi-liquid, sticky matter.

slim′y, *adj.,* **slimier, slimiest.** **1.** of the nature of slime. **2.** disgustingly wheedling.

sling, *n., v.t.,* **slung, slinging.** *n.* **1.** flexible device for hurling missiles. **2.** suspended cloth support. —*v.t.* **3.** hurl or shy. **4.** put in a sling.

slink, *v.i.,* **slunk, slinking.** walk furtively

slip, *v.,* **slipped, slipping.** *v.t., v.i.* **1.** slide smoothly. **2.** escape. —*v.i.* **3.** loose grip or footing. **4.** make a mistake. —*n.* **5.** act or instance of slipping. **6.** underskirt. **7.** space between piers for a ship.

slip′per, *n.* soft, unlaced shoe for household wear.

slip′per·y, *adj.,* **-ier, -iest.** **1.** allowing slipping. **2.** cunning and unreliable.

slip′shod″, *adj.* careless.

slit, *n., v.t.,* **slitted, slitting.** *n.* **1.** long, deep opening. —*v.t.* **2.** cut with slits.

slith′er, *v.i.* slide with a side-to-side motion.

sliv′er, *n., v.t.* splinter.

slob, *n. Informal.* uncouth or clumsy person.

slob′ber, *v.i., n.* drool.

slog, *v.i.,* **slogged, slogging.** advance heavily or with difficulty; plod.

slo′gan, *n.* motto.

sloop, *n.* one-masted sailing vessel.

slop, *v.,* **slopped, slopping,** *n., v.t., v.i.* **1.** spill or toss carelessly, as a liquid. —*n.* **2.** something slopped. **3.** swill.

slope, *n., v.,* **sloped, sloping.** *n.* **1.** angled rise or descent. —*v.t.* **2.** cause to rise or descend in a slope. —*v.i.* **3.** form a slope.

slop′py, *adj.* **1.** untidy. **2.** carelessly done. —**slop′pi·ly,** *adv.* —**slop′pi·ness,** *n.*

slosh, *v.t.* splash or slop.

slot, *n.* narrow opening.

sloth (sloth, slōth), *n.* **1.** South American aboreal mammal. **2.** laziness. —**sloth′ful,** *adj.*

slouch, *v.i.* **1.** have a drooping posture. —*n.* **2.** drooping posture. **3.** incompetent or lazy person. —**slouch′y,** *adj.*

slough, *n.* **1.** (slōō or slō) muddy or marshy area. **2.** (sluf) dead, cast-off skin. —*v.t.* **3.** cast off. —*v.i.* **4.** be cast off, as dead skin.

slov·en (sluv′ən), *n.* untidy or careless person. —**slov′en·ly,** *adj.*

slow, *adj.* **1.** moving or acting without speed. **2.** not learning or understanding readily. **3.** behind the correct or appointed time. **4.** lacking in activity or vigor. —*adv.* **5.** slowly. —*v.t.* **6.** cause to move or act slowly. —*v.i.* **7.** move or act slowly. —**slow′ly,** *adv.* —**slow′ness,** *n.*

sludge, *n.* semi-liquid sediment.

slue, *v.,* **slued, sluing.** *v.t., v.i.* turn or swerve.

slug, *v.t.,* **slugged, slugging,** *n., v.t.* **1.** hit, esp. with the fists. —*n.* **2.** crawling mollusk leaving a slimy trail. **3.** bullet. **4.** false coin.

slug′gard, *n.* lazy person.

slug′gish, *adj.* abnormally slow or lacking in vigor. —**slug′gish·ly,** *adv.* —**slug′gish·ness,** *n.*

sluice, *n.* **1.** artificial channel controlled by a gate. **2.** Also, **sluice gate,** gate controlling this channel.

slum, *n.* squalid home or residential area.

slum′ber, *v.i.* **1.** sleep deeply. —*n.* **2.** deep sleep.

slump, *v.i.* **1.** drop or sag heavily. —*n.* **2.** act or instance of slumping.

slur, *v.t.,* **slurred, slurring,** *n., v.t.* **1.** say indistinctly. **2.** disparage. —*n.* **3.** indistinct speech. **4.** disparaging remark.

slush, *n.* melting snow. —**slush′y,** *adj.*

slut, *n.* immoral or slatternly woman.

sly, *adj.,* **slyer** or **slier, slyest** or **sliest. 1.** cunning; tricky. **2.** gently mischievous. —**sly′ly, sli′ly,** *adv.* —**sly′ness,** *n.*

smack, *v.t.* **1.** separate noisily, as the lips. **2.** slap. —*v.i.* **3.** have a taste or suggestion. —*n.* **4.** act or instance of smacking. **5.** taste or suggestion. **6.** fishing boat.

small, *adj.* **1.** little. **2.** of no great importance, value, etc. **3.** petty or mean. —*adv.* **4.** into small pieces. —*n.* **5.** narrow part, esp. of the back. —**small′ness,** *n.*

small′pox″, *n.* contagious disease with fever and pustules as symptoms.

smart, *adj.* **1.** severe, as a blow. **2.** intelligent or clever. **3.** briskly efficient. **4.** in style. —*n.* **5.** sharp, stinging pain. —*v.i.* **6.** feel such a pain. —**smart′ly,** *adv.* —**smart′ness,** *n.* —**smart′en,** *v.t.*

smash, *v.t.* **1.** break into fragments. —*n.* **2.** act or instance of smashing. **3.** serious automobile accident.

smat′ter·ing, *n.* slight knowledge.

smear, *v.t.* **1.** rub with greasy clinging material. **2.** slander. —*n.* **3.** smeared area. **4.** slander.

smell, *n.* **1.** sense perceived by the nose and olfactory organs. **2.** odor. —*v.t.* **3.** sense with the nose and olfactory organs. —*v.i.* **4.** have an odor.

smelt, *n., pl.* **smelts, smelt,** *v.t., n.* **1.** small northern salt-water fish. —*v.t.* **2.** melt or fuse to as to extract metal. **3.** extract from ore by melting or fusing. —**smelt′er,** *n.*

smile, *v.i.,* **smiled, smiling,** *n., v.i.* **1.** assume a look of pleasure, etc., by upturning the corners of the mouth. **2.** look favorably. —*n.* **3.** smiling appearance.

smirch, *v.t.* **1.** stain or soil. —*n.* **2.** stain.

smirk, *v.i.* **1.** have an affected or self-satisfied smile. —*n.* **2.** such a smile.

smite, *v.t.,* **smote, smitten** or **smitting.** *Archaic.* **1.** hit; strike. **2.** overcome with charm.

smith, *n.* metalworker.

smith′y, *n., pl.* **smithies.** blacksmith's shop.

smock, *n.* loose garment covering the whole body.

smog, *n.* fog with smoke.

smoke, *n., v.,* **smoked, smoking.** *n.* **1.** unconsumed material emitted by a fire. —*v.i.* **2.** inhale and exhale smoke from smoldering tobacco, etc. —*v.t.* **3.** burn in order to inhale and exhale the smoke. **4.** treat with smoke. —**smok′y,** *adj.* —**smoke′stack″,** *n.*

smok′er, *n.* **1.** person who smokes. **2.** railroad car or compartment where smoking is permitted.

smol′der, *v.i.* **1.** burn flamelessly. **2.** exist partly suppressed. Also, **smoul′der.**

smooth, *adj.* **1.** without unevenness. **2.** without difficulty. **3.** without harsh or disturbing qualities. **4.** ingratiating. —*v.t.* **5.** make smooth. —**smooth′ly,** *adv.* —**smooth′ness,** *n.*

smoth′er, *v.t.* **1.** suffocate. **2.** cover completely.

smudge, *n., v.t.,* **smudged, smudging.** *n.* **1.** spot of smoke, dirt, ink, etc. —*v.t.* **2.** stain or treat with smoke, dirt, ink, etc.

smug, *adj.* excessively self-satisfied. —**smug′ly,** *adv.* —**smug′ness,** *n.*

smug′gle, *v.t.,* **-gled, -gling.** bring in or out secretly in violation of laws or regulations. —**smug′gler,** *n.*

smut, *n.* **1.** soot or smudge. **2.** obscenity. **3.** fungous plant disease. —**smut′ty,** *adj.*

snack, *n.* small meal.

snag, *n., v.,* **snagged, snagging.** *n.* **1.** projection that catches or tears. **2.** obstacle. —*v.t.* **3.** catch or damage, as with a snag.

snail, *n.* crawling mollusk with a shell.

snake, *n., v.i.* **snaked, snaking.** *n.* **1.** scaly reptile without limbs. —*v.i.* **2.** move or lie sinuously.

snap, *v.,* **snapped, snapping,** *n., adj. v.i.* **1.** make a sharp clicking sound. **2.** go into or out of a close-fitting socket. **3.** break abruptly. **4.** bite. **5.** speak crossly and abruptly. —*v.t.* **6.** cause to snap. **7.** photograph. —*n.* **8.** act or instance of snapping. **9.** fastener that snaps shut. —*adj.* **10.** hasty, as a judgement.

snap'drag''on, *n.* plant with flowers in spikes.

snap'pish, *adj.* short-tempered.

snap'py, *adj.* quick.

snap'shot'', *n.* uncomposed photograph from a small, hand-held camera.

snare, *n., v.t.* **snared, snaring.** trap.

snarl, *v.i.* **1.** growl. —*v.t.* **2.** tangle.

snatch, *v.t.* **1.** grab. —*v.i.* **2.** reach suddenly or eagerly. —*n.* **3.** act or instance of snatching. **4.** fragment.

sneak, *v.i.* **1.** go furtively. —*v.t.* **2.** bring in or out furtively. —*n.* **3.** furtive, dishonest person. —**sneak'y,** *adj.*

sneak'er, *n.* low, soft-soled shoe.

sneer, *v.i.* **1.** express contempt. —*n.* **2.** expression of contempt.

sneeze, *v.i.,* **sneezed, sneezing,** *n., v.i.* **1.** expel breath explosively and involuntarily. —*n.* **2.** act or instance of sneezing.

snick'er, *n.* **1.** contemptuous, high-pitched laugh. —*v.i.* **2.** give such a laugh. Also, **snig'ger.**

snide, *adj.* malicious, as a remark.

sniff, *v.i.* **1.** inhale quickly through the nose. **2.** exhale loudly through the nose. —*n.* **3.** act or instance of sniffing.

snif'fer, *v.i.* **1.** inhale through the nose. —*n.* **2. sniffles,** *Informal.* mild cold symptoms.

snip, *v.t.,* **snipped, snipping,** *n., v.t.* **1.** cut as with scissors. —*n.* **2.** snipped-off fragment. **3. snips,** shears.

snipe, *n., v.i.,* **sniped, sniping.** *n.* **1.** wading bird. —*v.i.* **2.** shoot from a hidden position. —**snip'er,** *n.*

snip'pet, *n.* small piece, as of information.

sniv'el, *v.i.* plead, complain, etc. in a whining tone.

snob, *n.* person with ostentatious likes and dislikes based on pretentious standards of excellence. —**snob'bish,** *adj.* —**snob'ber·y,** *n.*

snood, *n.* net covering the back of a woman's hair.

snoop, *Informal. v.i.* **1.** seek information furtively. —*n.* **2.** Also, **snoop'er,** person who snoops.

snooze, *v.i.,* **snoozed, snoozing,** *n.* nap.

snore, *v.i.,* **snored, snoring,** *n., v.i.* **1.** breathe noisily while sleeping. —*n.* **2.** sound of such breathing.

snor'kel, *n.* ventilating tube for a submarine, etc. under water.

snort, *n.* **1.** loud exhalation through the nose. —*v.i.* **2.** give such an exhalation.

snot, *n. Informal.* mucus from the nose.

snout, *n.* protruding front of an animal head.

snow, *n.* **1.** precipitation frozen in crystalline flakes. —*v.i.* **2.** precipitate snow. —**snow'drift'',** *n.* —**snow'fall'',** *n.* —**snow'flake'',** *n.* —**snow'storm'',** *n.* —**snow'y,** *adj.*

snow'ball'', *n.* **1.** ball of compacted snow. —*v.i.* **2.** increase with gathering speed.

snow'shoe'', *n.* webbed flat frame for supporting the foot on snow.

snub, *v.t.,* **snubbed, snubbing,** *n., adj., v.t.* **1.** refuse attention or respect to. —*n.* **2.** act or instance of snubbing. —*adj.* **3.** short and upturned, as a nose.

snuff, *v.t.* **1.** trim, as a burned wick. **2.** extinguish or eliminate. —*n.* **3.** powdered tobacco.

snuf'fle, *v.i.,* **-fled, -fling.** sniffle.

snug, *adj.,* **snugger, snuggest. 1.** cozy. **2.** neat. **3.** tight in fit. —**snug'ly,** *adv.*

snug'gle, *v.i.* **-gled, -gling.** cuddle or nestle.

so, *adv.* **1.** as stated or indicated. **2.** to such an extent. **3.** *Informal.* very; very much. **4.** in this way. —*conj.* **5.** therefore. **6.** in order that. —*adj.* **7.** true.

soak, *v.t.* **1.** put into a cover with a liquid. **2.** absorb. —*v.i.* **3.** become absorbed. —*n.* **4.** act or instance of soaking.

soap, *n.* **1.** substance used in washing. —*v.t.* **2.** cover with soap. —**soap'y,** *adj.*

soar, *v.i.* **1.** rise into the air. **2.** glide or hover in the air.

sob, *v.i.,* **sobbed, sobbing,** *n., v.i.* **1.** weep convulsively. —*n.* **2.** sound of sobbing.

so'ber, *adj.* **1.** not drunk. **2.** serious or quiet. —*v.t.* **3.** make sober. **4.** cause grave feelings in. —**so'ber·ly,** *adv.* —**so''bri'e·ty, so'ber·ness,** *n.*

so-called, *adj.* called thus; used esp. when so named without justification.

soc'cer, *n.* a variety of football played without using the hands and arms.

so'cia·ble, *adj.* friendly; gregarious. —**so''cia·bly,** *adv.* —**so''cia·bil'i·ty,** *n.*

so'cial, *adj.* **1.** pertaining to society. **2.** sociable. —**so'cial·ly,** *adv.*

so'cial·ism, *n.* theory advocating public ownership of means of production, with work and products shared. —**so'cial·ist,** *n.* —**so''cial·is'tic,** *adj.* —**so'cial·ize'',** *v.t.*

so'cial·ite'', *n.* person in fashionable society.

so·ci'e·ty, *n., pl.* **-ties. 1.** group sharing a common culture, location, etc. **2.** human beings, in their relations with one another. **3.** world of the upper class. **4.** organization, esp. a professional or public-service one.

so″ci·ol′o·gy, *n.* study of society. **—so″ci·o·log′i·cal,** *adj.* **—so″ci·ol′o·gist,** *n.*

sock, *n.* **1.** short stocking. **—v.t. 2.** *Informal.* hit.

sock′et, *n.* a hollow part in which something is inserted and held.

sod, *n.* earth with growing grass.

so′da, *n.* **1.** drink with soda water. **2.** mixture of soda water, ice cream, and flavoring. **3.** chemical containing sodium.

so·dal′i·ty, *n.,* *pl.* **-ties.** Catholic religious or charitable society.

soda water, water charged with carbon dioxide.

sod′den, *n.* **1.** stupefied. **2.** soggy.

so′di·um, *n.* alkaline chemical element.

sod·o·my (sod′ə mē), *n.* abnormal sexual intercourse. **—sod′o·mite,** *n.*

so′fa, *n.* wide, upholstered seat with a back and arms.

soft, *adj.* **1.** yielding readily to pressure. **2.** gentle. **3.** quiet. **4.** weak. **5.** non-alcoholic. **6.** permitting lathering, as water. **—soft′ly,** *adv.* **—soft′ness,** *n.* **—soft′en,** *v.t., v.i.*

soft′ball″, *n.* baseball-like game using a softer ball.

soft″ware, *n.* (computers) programming enabling a system to function.

sog′gy, *adj.* moist and heavy with absorbed liquid.

soil, *v.t.* **1.** dirty. **—n. 2.** earth. **3.** sewage.

so′journ, *v.i.* **1.** stay briefly. **—n. 2.** brief stay.

sol′ace (sol′əs), *n.* comfort in unhappiness.

so′lar, *adj.* pertaining to the sun.

sol·der (sod′ər), *n.* **1.** alloy with low melting point for joining or patching metal. **—v.t. 2.** treat with solder.

sol′dier, *n.* **1.** member of an army. **—v.i. 2.** live as a soldier. **—sol′dier·ly,** *adj.* **—sol′dier·y,** *n.*

sole, *n.,* *v.t.,* **soled, soling,** *adj. n.* **1.** salt-water flatfish. **2.** wearing surface on the bottom of a shoe. **—v.t. 3.** fit with soles. **—adj. 4.** single; only. **—sole′ly,** *adv.*

sol′emn, *adj.* **1.** serious; earnest. **2.** formal. **3.** sacred. **—sol′emn·ly,** *adv.* **—so·lem′ni·ty,** *n.*

sol′em·nize, *v.t.,* **-nized, -nizing.** observe or put into effect with a ceremony. **—sol″em·ni·za′tion,** *n.*

so·lic′i·tor, *n.* **1.** person who solicits. **2.** English lawyer other than a barrister.

so·lic·it (sə lis′ət), *v.t.* **1.** request. **2.** canvass for. **—so·li″ci·ta′tion,** *n.*

so·lic′i·tous, *adj.* showing friendly concern. **—so·lic′i·tous·ly,** *adv.* **—so·lic′i·tude″,** *n.*

sol′id, *adj.* **1.** pertaining to or existing in three dimensions. **2.** firm; substantial. **3.** not hollow. **4.** dense. **5.** reliable. **6.** entire. **—n. 7.** three-dimensional object. **8.** non-fluid material. **—sol′id·ly,** *adv,* **—so·lid′i·ty,** *n.* **—so·lid′i·fy″,** *v.t., v.i.*

sol″i·dar′i·ty, *n.* unity of purpose, resolve, etc.

sol″id-state′, *adj.* designating electronic circuitry that uses solid semiconductors, as transistors, to control current.

so·lil′o·quy, *n., pl.* **-quies.** speech made to or as if to oneself. **—so·lil′o·quize,** *v.i.*

sol′i·taire″, *n.* **1.** card game for one. **2.** single gemstone in a setting.

sol′i·tar″y, *adj.* **1.** single. **2.** alone. **3.** isolated.

sol′i·tude, *n.* state of being alone or isolated.

so′lo, *n.* performance by one person, esp. in music or aviation. **—so′lo·ist,** *n.*

sol′stice, *n.* point when the sun is furthest from the equator; beginning of summer or winter.

sol′u·ble, *adj.* able to be dissolved. **—sol″u·bil′i·ty,** *n.*

so·lu′tion, *n.* **1.** means of solving a problem. **2.** dispersal of one material in another. **3.** material, usually a liquid, that results from this.

solve, *v.t.,* **solved, solving.** explain or find means to overcome, as a problem. **—solv′a·ble,** *adj.*

sol′vent, *n.* **1.** material that dissolves another. **—adj. 2.** able to dissolve something. **3.** able to meet one's debts. **—sol′ven·cy,** *n.*

som′ber, *adj.* gloomy. Also, **som′bre.** **—som′ber·ly,** *adv.*

som·bre·ro (som brā′rō), *n.* broad-brimmed hat worn in Hispanic countries.

some, *adj.* **1.** indefinite amount or number of. **2.** certain unknown or unspecified. **—pron. 3.** unknown or unspecified number.

some′body″, *pron.* unspecified person. Also, **some′one″.**

some′how″, *adv.* in some way. Also, **some′way″.**

som′er·sault″, *n.* **1.** overturn forward or backward of a crouched person. **—v.i. 2.** execute a somersault.

some′thing, *n.* thing not specified.

some′time″, *adv.* **1.** at an indefinite time. **—adj. 2.** *Archaic.* former.

some′times″, *adv.* now and then.

some′what″, *adv.* to some extent.

some′where″, *adv.* at or to an unspecified place.

som·nam′bu·lism, *n.* sleepwalking. **—som·nam′bu·list,** *n.*

som′no·lent, *adj.* drowsy. **—som′no·lence,** *n.*

son, *n.* male offspring.

so·na′ta, *n.* instrumental musical composition.

song, *n.* vocal musical composition.

son′ic, *adj.* pertaining to sound.

son′-in-law, *n., pl.* **sons-in-law.** husband of one's daughter.

son′net, *n.* poem with one eight-line and one six-line part.

so·no′rous, *adj.* deep or rich in sound. —**so·nor′ous·ly,** *adv.* —**so·nor′i·ty,** *n.*

soon, *adv.* after a short time.

soot, *n.* black particles in smoke. —**soot′y,** *adj.*

soothe, *v.t.,* **soothed, soothing. 1.** free of agitation or annoyance. **2.** relieve, as pain.

sooth′say″er, *n.* person who claims to know the future.

sop, *n.* **1.** morsel dipped in liquid. **2.** something that appeases. —*v.t., v.i.* **3.** soak. —*v.t.* **4.** absorb.

so·phis·ti·cate, *v.t.* **1.** (sō fis′tə kāt″) make sophisticated. —*n.* **2.** (sō fis′tə kət) sophisticated person.

so·phis′ti·cat″ed, *adj.* **1.** acquainted with the ways of society. **2.** technologically advanced. —**so·phis″ti·ca′tion,** *n.*

soph′is·try, *n.* specious, unsound reasoning. —**soph′ist,** *n.*

soph′o·more″, *n.* second-year secondary or college student.

soph′o·mor′ic, *adj.* intellectually immature.

so″po·rif′ic, *adj.* **1.** sleep-inducing. —*n.* **2.** soporific drug.

so·pran′o, *n.* singer in the highest vocal range.

sor′cer·er, *n.* magician. Also, *fem.,* **sor′cer·ess.** —**sor′cer·y,** *n.*

sor′did, *adj.* **1.** disgustingly mean or ignoble. **2.** filthy.

sore, *adj.,* **sorer, sorest,** *n., adj.* **1.** aching or tender. **2.** grieving. **3.** causing trouble or annoyance. **4.** *Informal.* angry. —*n.* **5.** sore place on the body. —**sore′ly,** *adv.* —**sore′ness,** *n.*

sor·ghum (sor′gəm), *n.* cereal grass made into syrup, etc.

so·ror′i·ty, *n., pl.* **-ties.** women's organization, esp. in a college.

sor′rel, *n.* **1.** reddish-brown. **2.** horse of this colour. **3.** plant with sour-tasting leaves.

sor′row, *n.* **1.** great unhappiness or regret. —*v.i.* **2.** feel sorrow. —**sor′row·ful,** *adj.* —**sor′row·ful·ly,** *adv.*

sor′ry, *adj.* **1.** feeling regret. **2.** feeling pity. **3.** miserable.

sort, *n.* **1.** type; classification. **2.** quality. —*v.t.* **3.** arrange by type.

sor′tie, *n.* **1.** swift counterattack, as from a besieged place. **2.** aerial combat mission.

SOS, call for help.

so′-so′, *adj.* **1.** not especially good or bad. —*adv.* **2.** not especially well or badly.

sot, *n.* drunkard.

souf·flé, *n.* light, puffy baked dish.

sough (sow, suf), *v.i.* rustle or sigh, as the wind.

soul, *n.* **1.** non-material aspect of a person. **2.** emotional or moral aspect of the personality. **3.** feeling or sensitivity. **4.** essence. **5.** human being. —**soul′ful,** *adj.* —**soul′less,** *adj.*

sound, *n.* **1.** air vibrations perceptible in part to the ear. **2.** tone or noise that is heard. **3.** inlet or channel of sea water. —*v.t.* **4.** cause to make a sound. **5.** measure the depth of. **6.** determine the attitude or opinion of. —*v.i.* **7.** make a sound. **8.** seem. **9.** sound like, imply. —*adj.* **10.** healthy. **11.** reasonable. **12.** reliable. —**sound′less,** *adj.* —**sound′proof″,** *adj.* —**sound′ly,** *adv.* —**sound′ness,** *n.*

soup, *n.* savoury, mainly liquid food.

sour, *adj.* **1.** acid-tasting. **2.** fermented beyond the normal state. **3.** ill-tempered. —*v.i.* **4.** become sour. —**sour′ly,** *adv.* —**sour′ness,** *n.*

source, *n.* origin.

souse, *v.t.,* **soused, sousing,** *n., v.t.* **1.** immerse or steep. **2.** pickle. —*n.* **3.** pickled food. **4.** act or instance of sousing.

south, *n.* **1.** direction of the South Pole. **2.** region located in this direction. —*adj., adv.* **3.** to or toward the south. **4.** from the south, as a wind. —**south′ward,** *adv., adj.* —**south′ern,** *adj.* —**south′ern·er,** *n.* —**south′er·ly,** *adj., adv.*

south″east′, *n.* direction halfway between south and east. —**south″east′,** *adj., adv.*

south″west′, *n.* direction halfway between south and west. —**south″west′,** *adj., adv.*

sou·ve·nir (sōō′və nēr), *n.* thing to remember a place, event, etc. by.

sov·er·eign (sov′rən), *n.* **1.** monarch. **2.** former British gold coin. —*adj.* **3.** having supreme political power. **4.** politically independent. —**sov′er·eign·ty,** *n.*

so′vi·et, *adj.* **1. Soviet,** pertaining to the Soviet Union. —*n.* **2.** Russian governmental council.

sow, *v.t.* **1.** (sō) plant, as seed. —*n.* **2.** (sow) female hog. —**sow′er,** *n.*

soy′bean″, *n.* plant grown for its seeds.

spa, *n.* resort with mineral springs.

space, *n., v.t.,* **spaced, spacing.** *n.* **1.** limitless three-dimensional expanse. **2.** specific area within this. **3.** outer space. **4.** distance. —*v.t.* **5.** separate, esp. as regular intervals.

space'craft'', *n*. vehicle for exploration of outer space.

space'flight'', *n*. flight through outer space.

space'ship'', *n*. vehicle for travel in outer space.

space'walk'', *n*. personal movement away from a spacecraft in outer space.

spa'cious, *adj*. amply extensive.

spade, *n*., *v.t.*, **spaded, spading**. *n*. **1.** shovel with long shaftlike handle. **2. spades**, black suit of playing cards. —*v.t.* **3.** dig with a spade.

spa·ghet'ti, *n*. stringy pasta, usually served with a sauce.

span, *n*., *v.t.*, **spanned, spanning**. *n*. **1.** something between two supports. **2.** distance between the thumb and little finger, when extended. **3.** duration. **4.** pair of harnessed animals. —*v.t.* **5.** cross.

span'gle, *n*., *v.t.*, **-gled, -gling**. *n*. **1.** glittering decoration. —*v.t.* **2.** decorate with spangles.

span'iel, *n*. short-legged, long-eared dog.

spank, *v.t.* slap on the behind.

spank'ing, *adj*. brisk.

spar, *v.i.*, **sparred, sparring**, *n*., *v.i.* **1.** box with the fists. —*n*. **2.** pole. **3.** crystalline rock.

spare, *v.t.*, **spared, sparing**, *adj.*, **sparer, sparest**. *v.t.* **1.** use or spend with restraint. **2.** prevent from occurring, being known, etc., as something unpleasant. **3.** treat leniently. **4.** give without inconvenience. —*adj.* **5.** in reserve; extra. **6.** gaunt; lean.

spare'rib'', *n*. pork rib cut at the thin end.

spark, *n*. **1.** glowing, burning piece of matter from a fire. **2.** electric flash. **3.** trace, as of life.

spar'kle, *v.i.*, **-kled, -kling**, *n.*, *v.i.* **1.** emit or reflect small flashes of light. **2.** effervesce, as wine. **3.** glitter, as eyes. —*n.* **4.** act or instance of sparkling.

spar'row, *n*. bird of the finch family.

sparse, *adj.*, **sparser, sparsest**. **1.** scattered. **2.** scanty. —**sparse'ly**, *adv*. —**sparse'ness, spars'i·ty**, *n*.

Spar'tan, *adj*. austere; disciplined.

spasm, *n*. sudden and involuntary contraction of the muscles.

spas·mod'ic, *adj*. **1.** in spasms. **2.** at unpredictable intervals. —**spas·mod'i·cal·ly**, *adv*.

spas'tic, *adj*. characterized by spasms.

spat, *n*. *Informal*. quarrel about a small matter.

spa'tial, *adj*. pertaining to space.

spatter, *v.t.* splash, esp. in small amounts over a wide area.

spat·u·la (spach'ə lə), *n*. broad-bladed device for handling foods, etc.

spawn, *n*. **1.** eggs of some animals, esp. fish and mollusks. —*v.t.* **2.** originate in abundance. —*v.i.* **3.** lay spawn.

speak, *v.*, **spoke, spoken, speaking**. *v.i.* **1.** communicate with the voice. **2.** give a speech or lecture. —*v.t.* **3.** present by means of the voice. **4.** use in speaking, as a language.

speak'er, *n*. **1.** person who speaks. **2.** president of a legislature. **3.** loudspeaker.

spear, *n*. **1.** long-handled, pointed weapon for hurling or thrusting. —*v.t.* **2.** wound with a spear. —**spear'head**, *n*.

spear'mint'', *n*. fragrant mint used as flavoring.

spe'cial, *adj*. **1.** distinct from all others. **2.** remarkable. —**spe'cial·ly**, *adv*.

spe'cial·ize, *v.i.*, **-ized, -izing**. study, work, or trade in a special area. —**spe'cial·ist**, *n*.

spe'cial·ty, *n.*, *pl*. **-ties**. area of specialization.

spe·cie (spē'shē), *n*. coins.

spe'cies, *n*. group of fundamentally identical plants or animals.

spe·cif'ic, *adj*. **1.** detailed. **2.** exact. **3.** characteristic.

spe'ci·fy'', *v.t.*, **-fied, -fying**. state or demand specifically.

spec'i·men, *n*. typical example.

spe'cious, *adj*. falsely seeming good or valid. —**spe'cious·ly**, *adv*. —**spe'cious·ness**, *n*.

speck, *n*. **1.** small particle or spot. —*v.t.* **2.** mark with specks.

speck'le, *n.*, *v.t.*, **-led, -ling**. *n*. **1.** small spot. —*v.t.* **2.** mark with speckles.

spec'ta·cle, *n*. **1.** marvelous event or sight. **2.** grandiose public entertainment. **3. spectacles**, eyeglasses.

spec·tac'u·lar, *adj*. marvelous or grandiose in appearance, etc.

spec'ta·tor, *n*. person who sees an event or view.

spec'ter, *n*. ghost; apparition. Also, **spec'tre**. —**spec'tral**, *adj*.

spec'tro·scope, *n*. instrument for producing and analyzing spectra. —**spec''tro·scop'ic**, *adj*.

spec'trum, *n.*, *pl*. **-tra, -trums**. group of color bands produced when light is dispersed by a prism.

spec'u·late, *v.i.*, **-lated, -lating**. **1.** think contemplatively. **2.** undertake a business risk in the hope of large profits. —**spec''u·la'tion**, *n*. —**spec'u·la·tive**, *adj*. —**spec''u·la'tor**, *n*.

speech, *n*. **1.** ability to speak. **2.** way of speaking. **3.** something spoken. **4.** talk to an audience. —**speech'less**, *adj*.

speed, *n.*, *v.*, **sped** or **speeded, speeding**. *n*. **1.** swiftness of motion or action. **2.** rate of motion or action. —*v.t.* **3.** increase the speed of. —*v.i.* **4.** move swiftly. **5.** drive with excessive speed. —**speed'y**, *adj*. —**speed'i·ly**, *adv*. —**speed'er**, *n*.

speed·om'e·ter, *n.* speed-registering device.

spell, *v.,* **spelled** or **spelt, spelling,** *n., v.t.*
1. name the letters of. 2. comprise the letters of. 3. take over from, as in a shared task. —*v.i.* 4. name the letters forming ordinary words. —*n.* 5. enchantment. 6. period of time.

spell'bound", *adj.* entranced.

spend, *v.t.,* **spent, spending.** 1. pay. 2. pass, as a period of time. 3. use up or exhaust. —**spend'er,** *n.*

spend'thrift", *n.* spender to excess.

spent, *adj.* 1. exhausted. 2. used up or worn out.

sperm, *n.* male germ cell carried by semen. —**sper·mat'ic,** *adj.*

spew, *v.t., v.i.* vomit or pour with force.

sphere, *n.* 1. round solid with all radii equal; ball. 2. area of influence, activity, knowledge, etc. —**spher'i·cal,** *adj.*

spher'oid, *n.* approximately spherical solid.

sphinx, *n. Classical mythology.* creature with a human head and the body of a lion.

spice, *n., v.t.,* **spiced, spicing.** *n.* 1. aromatic plant substance for seasoning, preservation, etc. —*v.t.* 2. season or treat with spice. —**spic'y,** *adj.*

spi'der, *n.* eight-legged predatory animal that captures insects in a web. —**spi'der·y,** *adj.*

spig'ot, *n.* faucet.

spike, *n., v.t.,* **spiked, spiking.** *n.* 1. large hammer-driven fastener. 2. pointed feature. 3. long stalk bearing grains or blossoms. —*v.t.* 4. fasten with spikes. 5. frustrate; thwart.

spill, *v.,* **spilled** or **spilt, spilling.** *v.t.* 1. lose, as from the tipping of a container. 2. shed, as blood. —*v.i.* 3. be lost, as over the rim of a container.

spill'way", *n.* channel letting excess water escape.

spin, *v.,* **spun, spinning,** *n., v.t.* 1. make from twisted yarn. 2. make into yarn or thread. 3. make from secretions, as a spider web. —*v.t., v.i.* 4. whirl. —*n.* 5. whirling motion. 6. *Informal.* brief ride. —**spin'ner,** *n.*

spin'ach, *n.* plant with dark-green edible leaves.

spin'dle, *n.* 1. rod used in spinning thread. 2. any slender round rod.

spin'dling, *adj.* lanky. Also, **spin'dly.**

spin'drift", *n.* spray from wave crests.

spine, *n.* 1. Also called **spinal column.** backbone; vertebrae. 2. thorn. —**spin'al,** *adj.* —**spin'y,** *adj.*

spine'less, *adj.* without courage.

spin'et, *n.* small upright piano.

spin'ster, *n.* unmarried woman past the normal marriageable age.

spi'ral, *n.* 1. flat curve with steadily increasing radius. —*adj.* 2. formed along such a curve. —*v.i.* 3. move in such a curve. —**spi'ral·ly,** *adj.*

spire, *n.* tall pyramidal structure forming the roof of a tower.

spir'it, *n.* 1. spiritual part of a person; soul. 2. ghost. 3. mood, sentiment, or intent. 4. vigor or courage. 5. **spirits, a.** state of mind. **b.** distilled alcoholic liquor. 6. Holy Ghost. —*v.t.* 7. smuggle. —**spir'it·ed,** *adj.* —**spir'it·less,** *adj.*

spir'it·u·al, *adj.* 1. pertaining to religion. 2. pertaining to the soul. 3. concerned with matters of the soul. —*n.* 4. Negro religious song. —**spir'it·u·al·ly,** *adv.* —**spir"it·u·al'i·ty,** *n.*

spir'it·u·al·ism", *n.* belief that the living and the dead can communicate. —**spir'it·u·al·ist,** *n.* —**spir"it·u·al·is'tic,** *adj.*

spir'it·u·ous, *adj.* alcoholic and distilled.

spit, *v.,* **spat, spit,** or (for 2) **spitted, spitting,** *n., v.t.* 1. eject from the mouth. 2. skewer. —*v.i.* 3. eject saliva from the mouth. —*n.* 4. saliva. 5. long skewer. 6. small peninsula.

spite, *n., v.t.,* **spited, spiting.** *n.* 1. small-minded hostility or vengefulness. 2. **in spite of,** notwithstanding. —*v.t.* 3. offend or hurt out of spite. —**spite'ful,** *adj.* —**spite'ful·ly,** *adv.* —**spite'ful·ness,** *n.*

spit'tle, *n.* saliva.

spit·toon', *n.* receptacle for spit.

splash, *v.t.* 1. cause to fly in various directions, as a liquid. —*v.i.* 2. fly in various directions, as a liquid. —*n.* 3. act, instance, or sound of splashing.

splat'ter, *v.i.* be splashed.

splay, *v.t., v.i.* 1. spread apart. —*adj.* 2. spreading apart.

spleen, *n.* 1. organ for modifying the blood structure. 2. anger or irritation. —**sple·net'ic,** *adj.*

splen'did, *adj.* 1. magnificent. 2. excellent. —**splen'did·ly,** *adv.* —**splen'dor,** *n.*

splice, *v.t.,* **spliced, splicing,** *n., v.t.* 1. join into a single piece. —*n.* 2. joint created by splicing.

splint, *n.* 1. temporary reinforcement for a broken bone. 2. thin slip of wood forming part of a basket.

splin'ter, *n.* 1. sharp, broken fragment. —*v.t., v.i.* 2. break into splinters.

split, *v.,* **split, splitting,** *n., adj., v.t., v.i.* 1. break or pull in two. —*v.t.* 2. share or divide. —*n.* 3. act or instance of splitting. —*adj.* 4. having been split.

splotch, *n., v.t.* spot or stain. —**splotch'y,** *adj.*

splurge, *v.i.,* **splurged, splurging,** *n., v.i.* 1. spend money lavishly and showily. —*n.* 2. act or instance of splurging.

splut'ter, *v.i.* 1. babble, as with confusion or rage. —*n.* 2. spluttering speech.

spoil, v., **spoiled** or **spoilt**, **spoiling**, n., v.t. 1. ruin. 2. damage the character of with indulgence. —v.i. 3. become unfit to eat, drink, or use. —n. 4. **spoils**, loot. —**spoil'er**, n. —**spoil'age**, n.

spoke, n. shaft between the hub and rim of a wheel.

spokes'man, n. person who speaks for a group.

spo''li·a'tion, n. looting.

sponge, n., v., **sponged**, **sponging**. n. 1. marine animal. 2. skeleton of this animal or an imitation in plastic, used to absorb water. —v.t. 3. wipe with a sponge. —v.i. 4. Informal. live at the expense of others. —**spong'y**, adj.

sponger, n. Informal. one who lives at the expense of others.

spon'sor, n. 1. person who undertakes responsibility for another. 2. godparent. 3. advertiser who buys television or radio time. —v.t. 4. act as sponsor for.

spon·ta'ne·ous, adj. 1. occurring without an external cause. 2. lively and natural in manner. —**spon·ta'ne·ous·ly**, adv. —**spon''ta·ne'i·ty**, **spon·ta'ne·ousness**, n.

spook, n. Informal. ghost. —**spook'y**, adj.

spool, n. small drum on which thread, film, recording tape, etc. is wound.

spoon, n. 1. utensil for handling or stirring liquids or food. —v.t. 2. handle or serve with a spoon.

spoor (spŏor), n. trail of animal scent.

spo·rad'ic, adj. occasional. —**spo·rad'i·cal·ly**, adv.

spore, n. seedlike body from which fungi, mosses, etc. grow.

sport, n. 1. recreation involving bodily activity. 2. amusement. 3. plant or animal of abnormal form. —v.i. 4. play vigorously. —**sports'man**, n. —**sports'manship''**, n. —**sports'man·ly**, adj.

spor'tive, adj. playful. —**spor'tive·ly**, adv. —**spor'tive·ness**, n.

spot, n., v.t., **spotted**, **spotting**, adj. n. 1. round mark. 2. place. —v.t. 3. mark with spots. 4. notice. —adj., 5. immediate. 6. random, as a survey. —**spot'less**, adj. —**spot'ty**, adj. —**spot'ter**, n.

spouse, n. husband or wife.

spout, n. 1. channel for discharging liquids, grain, etc. —v.t. 2. emit with force. 3. recite enthusiastically.

sprain, v.t. 1. injure by wrenching muscles or ligaments. —n. 2. injury so produced.

sprat, n. small fish of the herring family.

sprawl, v.i. 1. stretch out in an ungraceful way. —n. 2. act or instance of sprawling.

spray, n. 1. liquid driven in fine particles. 2. device for shooting such liquid. 3. small branch with flowers or leaves. —v.t. 4. drive as a spray. 5. apply spray to. —**spray'er**, n.

spread, v., **spread**, **spreading**, n., v.t., v.i. 1. extend. 2. scatter or disperse. —v.t. 3. cover or apply thinly. —n. 4. extent, 5. distribution. 6. cloth for covering a bed. 7. soft food eaten with breadstuffs. —**spread'er**, n.

spree, n. occasion of uninhibited activity.

sprig, n. twig or spray.

spright'ly, adj., **-lier**, **-liest**. lively. —**spright'li·ness**, n.

spring, n., v., **sprang** or **sprung**, **sprung**, **springing**, adj. n. 1. season between winter and summer, beginning at the vernal equinox. 2. stream emerging from the earth. 3. resilient elastic device, e.g. a wire coil. 4. jump. —v.i. 5. jump. 6. arise or emerge. —v.t. 7. cause to act suddenly. 8. disclose suddenly. —**spring'time**, n. —**spring'y**, adj.

sprin'kle, v., **-kled**, **-kling**, n. v.t. 1. scatter thinly. —v.i. 2. rain lightly. —n. 3. act or instance of sprinkling. 4. something sprinkled. —**sprink'ler**, n.

sprint, n. 1. short run. —v.i. 2. make a short run. —**sprint'er**, n.

sprite, n. elf or fairy.

sprock'et, n. gear tooth engaging with a chain.

sprout, v.i. 1. begin to grow or send forth shoots. —n. 2. shoot that has sprouted.

spruce, n., adj., **sprucer**, **spruciest**, v.t., n. 1. coniferous evergreen. —adj. 2. tidy; neat. —v.t. 3. make tidy.

spry, adj., **sprier** or **spryer**, **spriest** or **spryest**. active; lively. —**spry'ly**, adv. —**spry'ness**, n.

spud, n. 1. type of spade. 2. Informal. potato.

spume, n. foam.

spunk, n. Informal. courage. —**spunk'y**, adj.

spur, n., v.t., **spurred**, **spurring**. n. 1. sharp device for urging on a horse. 2. short extension. —v.t. 3. urge on.

spur·i·ous (spyŏŏr'ē əs), adj. false; fraudulent. —**spur'i·ous·ly**, adv. —**spur'i·ous·ness**, n.

spurn, v.t. reject with scorn.

spurt, v.t., v.i. 1. shoot forth, as a liquid. —v.i. 2. have a sudden, short increase of energy or activity. —n. 3. act or instance of spurting.

sput'nik, n. man-made satellite, esp. one from the U.S.S.R.

sput'ter, v.t. 1. eject in drops or particles. —v.i. 2. splutter. —n. 3. act, instance, or sound of sputtering.

spu·tum (spyŏŏ'təm), n. saliva, etc. ejected from the mouth.

spy, n., pl. **spies**, v. **spied**, **spying**. n. 1. person who attempts to obtain secret information. —v.t. 2. notice, esp. at a distance. —v.i. 3. act as a spy.

squab, *n.* young pigeon.

squab′ble, *n., v.i.,* **-bled, -bling.** quarrel over trifles.

squad, *n.* small group, as of soldiers.

squad′ron, *n.* military unit of airplanes, ships, or cavalry.

squal′id, *adj.* **1.** dirty or nasty. **2.** in miserable condition. —**squal′id·ly,** *adv.* —**squal′id·ness,** *n.* —**squal′or,** *n.*

squall, *n.* **1.** strong, brief storm or gust of wind. —*v.i.* **2.** weep loudly. —**squal′ly,** *adj.*

squan′der, *v.t.* spend or use up wastefully.

square, *n., adj.,* **squarer, squarest,** *v.t.,* **squared, squaring.** *n.* **1.** right-angled figure with four equal sides. **2.** paved public area. **3.** tool for laying out or checking angled lines. **4.** *Math.* product of a number multiplied by itself. —*adj.* **5.** formed like a square. **6.** of an area equal to linear measure squared. **7.** honest or substantial. —*adv.* **8.** fairly; straightforwardly. —*v.t.* **9.** make square. **10.** *Math.* multiply by itself. —*v.i.* **11.** be consistent. —**square′ly,** *adv.*

square′-rigged′, *adj.* with sails rigged athwart the vessel. —**square′-rig′ger,** *n.*

squash, *v.t.* **1.** crush. —*n.* **2.** game played with rackets. **3.** gourdlike fruit.

squat, *v.i.,* **squatted** or **squat, squatting,** *n., adj., v.i.* **1.** crouch with the legs doubled under the body. **2.** settle without authority. —*n.* **3.** squatting position. —*adj.* **4.** Also, **squat′ty,** short and broad of figure. —**squat′ter,** *n.*

squaw, *n.* American Indian woman.

squawk, *n.* **1.** loud, harsh cry. —*v.i.* **2.** utter a squawk.

squeak, *n.* **1.** shrill noise. —*v.i.* **2.** make squeaks. —**squeak′y,** *adj.*

squeal, *n.* **1.** shrill cry. —*v.i.* **2.** make squeals.

squeam′ish, *adj.* **1.** easily disgusted. **2.** prudish. —**squeam′ish·ly,** *adv.* —**squeam′ish·ness,** *n.*

squee′gee, *n.* flat-bladed cleaner for plate glass.

squeeze, *v.t.,* **squeezed, squeezing,** *n., v.t.* **1.** press from both sides. **2.** cram. —*n.* **3.** act or instance of squeezing. **4.** hug.

squelch, *v.t.* **1.** silence with a crushing remark. —*n.* **2.** crushing remark.

squid, *n.* ten-armed sea mollusk.

squint, *v.i.* **1.** see through partly-closed eyes. **2.** be crosseyed. —*n.* **3.** act or instance of squinting.

squire, *n., v.t.,* **squired, squiring.** *n.* **1.** country gentleman. **2.** gentleman escorting a lady. —*v.t.* **3.** escort.

squirm, *v.i., n.* wriggle.

squir′rel, *n.* bushy-tailed rodent living in trees.

squirt, *v.t., v.i.* **1.** shoot, as a liquid. —*n.* **2.** jet of liquid. **3.** device for squirting.

stab, *v.t.,* **stabbed, stabbing,** *n., v.t.* **1.** wound with a knife, etc. —*n.* **2.** wound or thrust from such a weapon.

sta·bil·ize, *v.t.,* **-lized, -lizing.** cause to be or remain stable. —**sta′bi·liz″er,** *n.* —**sta″bi·li·za″tion,** *n.*

sta′ble, *n., v.t.,* **-bled, -bling,** *adj. n.* **1.** Also, **stables,** accommodation for animals, esp. horses. —*v.t.* **2.** put into a stable, as a horse. —*adj.* **3.** resistant to displacement or change. —**sta·bil′i·ty,** *n.*

stac·ca·to (stə kah′tō), *adj. Music.* separated by brief silences.

stack, *n.* **1.** orderly pile. **2.** Often, **stacks,** storage space for library books. **3.** chimney or funnel. —*v.t.* **4.** gather into stacks.

sta′di·um, *n., pl.* **-diums, -dia.** outdoor arena for spectator sports.

staff, *n., pl.* **staves** or **staffs** (for 1), **staffs** (for 1, 3), *v.t., n.* **1.** stick carried in the hand. **2.** group of employees, esp. in administrative jobs. **3.** *Music.* group of five horizontal lines used in musical notation. —*v.t.* **4.** provide or work as a staff for.

stag, *n.* **1.** adult male deer. —*adj.* **2.** for men only.

stage, *n., v.t.,* **staged, staging.** *n.* **1.** distinct phase of a process, journey, etc. **2.** performers′ platform. **3.** theatrical profession. —*v.t.* **4.** present on a stage. **5.** divide into phases.

stage′coach″, *n.* horse-drawn coach for long-distance travel.

stag′ger, *v.i.* **1.** walk or stand unsteadily. —*v.t.* **2.** cause to stagger or falter. **3.** schedule over a range of times. —*n.* **4.** staggering gait.

stag′ing, *n.* scaffolding.

stag′nant, *adj.* **1.** not flowing, as a body of water. **2.** undesirably inactive. —**stag′nate,** *v.i.* —**stag″na′tion,** *n.*

staid, *adj.* sober and quiet; sedate. —**staid′ly,** *adv.* —**staid′ness,** *n.*

stain, *n.* **1.** discoloration. **2.** dye applied to wood or other materials. —*v.t.* **3.** discolor. **4.** apply dye to.

stair, *n.* tall flight of steps. Also, **stairs, stair′way″.** —**stair′well″,** *n.*

stair′case″, *n.* interior stair.

stake, *n., v.t.,* **staked, staking.** *n.* **1.** upright post. **2.** something wagered. **3.** **stakes,** something to be gained through risk. **4. at stake,** in danger of loss. —*v.t.* **5.** mark or secure with a stake. **6.** wager.

sta·lac′tite, *n.* icicle-like deposit of lime on a cave roof.

sta·lag′mite, *n.* conical deposit of lime on a cave floor.

stale, *adj.,* **staler, stalest,** *v.i., adj.* **1.** no

longer fresh. —*v.i.* **2.** become stale.
—**stale′ness,** *n.*

stale′mate″, *n.* **1.** *Chess.* situation making a move impossible. **2.** deadlock. —*v.t.* **3.** halt through a stalemate.

stalk, *v.t.* **1.** pursue stealthily. —*v.i.* **2.** walk proudly or deliberately. —*n.* **3.** plant stem.

stall, *n.* **1.** compartment. **2.** stop because of malfunctioning. **3.** *Informal.* pretext for delay. —*v.t.* **4.** put or keep in a stall. **5.** *Informal.* delay or keep waiting. —*v.i.* **6.** stop because of malfunctioning.

stal′lion, *n.* ungelded male horse.

stal′wart, *adj.* **1.** reliable through bravery, vigor, or faithfulness. —*n.* **2.** stalwart person.

stam′i·na, *n.* enduring vigor.

stam′mer, *v.i.* **1.** speak with involuntary repetitions or pauses. —*n.* **2.** stammering way of speaking.

stamp, *v.t.* **1.** step on forcefully. **2.** form or print with a stamp. **3.** affix a stamp to. —*n.* **4.** act or instance of stamping. **5.** descending device for printing, embossing, cutting, etc. **6.** adhesive paper proving payment of postage, etc. **7.** type of personal character.

stam″pede′, *n.*, *v.*, **-peded, -peding.** *n.* **1.** mass flight, as of frightened cattle. —*v.i.* **2.** flee in a stampede. —*v.t.* **3.** cause to stampede.

stance, *n.* **1.** position of a standing person. **2.** attitude or policy.

stanch, *adj.* **1.** (stonch) stalwart. —*v.t.* **2.** (stanch) stop from escaping, as blood. **3.** stop from bleeding. —**stanch′ly,** *adv.* —**stanch′ness,** *n.*

stan′chion, *n.* structural post.

stand, *v.*, **stood, standing,** *n.*, *v.i.* **1.** be or become upright on the feet. **2.** be located, as a tall object. **3.** halt or refrain from moving. **4.** take a position, as in a controversy. **5.** have toleration. —*v.t.* **6.** cause to be upright. **7.** endure or tolerate. —*n.* **8.** small platform or table. **9.** small sales booth. **10.** position, as in a controversy. **11.** halt, **12.** area of trees.

stand′ard, *n.* **1.** basis for evaluation or measurement. **2.** upright support. **3.** military or personal flag. —*adj.* **4.** of the normal or typical sort.

stand′ard·ize, *v.*, **-ized, -izing.** *v.t.*, *v.i.* conform to a standard. —**stan″dard·i·za′tion,** *n.*

stand′-by, *n.*, *pl.* **-bys,** *adj.*, *n.* **1.** possible substitute. —*adj.* **2.** for emergency use.

stand′ing, *n.* **1.** status. **2.** duration. —*adj.* **3.** upright. **4.** permanent. **5.** fixed in place. **6.** stagnant.

stand′point″, *n.* viewpoint.

stan′za, *n.* set of verses.

sta′ple, *n.*, *v.t.*, **-pled, -pling,** *adj.*, *n.* **1.** fastener of bent wire or bar stock. **2.** main or standard commodity. **3.** textile fiber. —*v.t.* **4.** fasten with staples. —*adj.* **5.** main or standard. —**sta′pler,** *n.*

star, *n.*, *adj.*, *v.*, **starred, starring.** *n.* **1.** heavenly body of incandescent gas. **2.** figure with radiating points. **3.** prominent or leading performer or player. —*v.t.* **4.** have in a leading role. **5.** mark with a star. —*v.i.* **6.** have a leading role. —**star′ry,** *adj.*

star′board″, *Nautical.* *n.* **1.** right-hand side, facing forward. —*adj.* **2.** located on this side. —*adv.* **3.** toward this side.

starch, *n.* **1.** tasteless vegetable substance found in potatoes, flour, etc. and used for stiffening. —*v.t.* **2.** treat with starch. —**starch′y,** *adj.*

stare, *v.i.*, **stared, staring,** *n.*, *v.i.* **1.** gaze with fixed, open eyes. —*n.* **2.** act or instance of staring.

star′fish″, *n.* star-shaped sea animal.

stark, *adj.* **1.** outright. **2.** bleak. **3.** stiff. —*adv.* **4.** utterly.

star′ling, *n.* small bird of European origin.

start, *v.t.*, *v.i.* **1.** begin. —*v.t.* **2.** knock loose. —*v.i.* **3.** jump with surprise. **4.** move or arise suddenly. —*n.* **5.** beginning. **6.** sudden movement from surprise. **7.** lead in a race or pursuit. —**start′er,** *n.*

star′tle, *v.t.*, **-tled, -tling.** disturb with sudden surprise.

starve, *v.*, **starved, starving.** *v.t.* **1.** skill or trouble with hunger. —*v.i.* **2.** die or be troubled from hunger. —**star″va′tion,** *n.*

state, *n.*, *adj.*, *v.t.*, **stated, stating.** *n.* **1.** condition. **2.** politically autonomous or semi-autonomous region. **3.** civil government. **4.** pomp. —*adj.* **5.** formally conducted. —*v.t.* **7.** declare. —**state′hood″,** *n.*

state′house″, *n.* U.S. state capitol.

state′ly, *adj.*, **-lier, -liest.** dignified. —**state′li·ness,** *n.*

state′ment, *n.* **1.** declaration. **2.** financial account or bill.

state-of-the-art, *adj.* of or pertaining to the highest level of technological achievement to date.

state′room″, *n.* private cabin on a ship.

states′man, *n.* person wise in government. —**states′man·ship,** *n.*

stat′ic, *adj.* **1.** not moving. —*n.* **2.** unmoving electrical charges. **3.** radio interference caused by such charges.

sta′tion, *n.* **1.** building where a train, bus, etc. stops or originates. **2.** place for sending broadcasts. **3.** place of duty. **4.** place where one stops. **5.** position, as in society. —*v.t.* **5.** assign to a place.

sta′tion·ar″y, *adj.* **1.** not in motion. **2.** not moving to another place.

sta'tion·er, *n.* seller of paper and writing materials. —**sta'tion·er''y**, *n.*

sta·tis'tics, *n.* collection and analysis of numerical data. —**sta·tis'ti·cal**, *adj.* —**sta·tis'ti·cal·ly**, *adv.* —**sta''tis·ti'cian**, *n.*

stat'u·ar''y, *n.* statues collectively.

stat'ue, *n.* three-dimensional sculpture of a human or animal.

stat'u·esque', *adj.* like a statue, esp. in posture.

stat''u·ette', *n.* small statue.

stat'ure, *n.* 1. tallness. 2. eminence or achievement.

status quo, *Latin.* present condition.

sta·tus (stā'təs, sta'təs), *n.* 1. position, as in society. 2. state or condition.

stat'ute, *n.* law; ordinance. —**stat'u·to''ry**, *adj.*

staunch, *n., adj.* stanch.

stave, *n., v.t.,* **staved** or (for 3) **stove**, **staving.** *n.* 1. curved board forming part of a barrel side. 2. *Music.* staff. —*v.t.* 3. break in or crush. 4. repel.

stay, *v.,* **stayed, staying,** *n., v.i.* 1. remain or continue. —*v.t.* 2. halt or delay. 3. support or prop. —*n.* 4. temporary residence. 5. halt or delay. 6. support or prop. 7. fore-and-aft line supporting a mast.

stead, *n.* 1. **in one's stead,** in place of one. 2. **in good stead,** advantageously.

stead'fast'', *adj.* 1. unchanging. 2. loyal or determined. —**stead'fast''ly**, *adv.* —**stead'fast''ness**, *n.*

stead'y, *adj.,* **steadier, steadiest,** *v.,* **steadied, steadying.** *adj.* 1. firm; unwavering. 2. regular; unvarying. 3. reliable. —*v.t., v.i.* 4. make or become steady. —**stead'i·ly**, *adv.*

steak, *n.* slice of meat or fish for broiling or frying.

steal, *v.,* **stole, stolen, stealing.** *v.t.* 1. take without right. —*v.i.* 2. move silently.

stealth, *n.* secret activity. —**stealth'y**, *adj.* —**stealth'i·ly**, *adv.*

steam, *n.* 1. gaseous or vaporized water. —*v.t.* 2. treat with steam. —*v.i.* 3. turn into or give off steam. —*adj.* 4. working by steam. 5. carrying steam. —**steam'y**, *adj.* —**steam'boat''**, *n.* —**steam'ship''**, *n.*

steam'er, *n.* 1. vehicle operated by steam, esp. a ship or automobile. 2. device for treating with steam.

steed, *n.* riding horse.

steel, *n.* 1. iron alloyed with carbon. —*adj.* 2. made of or resembling steel. —*v.t.* 3. make resolute or courageous. —**steel'y**, *adj.*

steel'yard'', *n.* scale with a weighted arm.

steep, *adj.* 1. far from horizontal. —*v.t.* 2. soak. 3. absorb. —**steep'ly**, *adv.* —**steep'ness**, *n.*

steep'le, *n.* 1. tall tower with a spire. 2. spire.

steep'le·chase'', *n.* horse race over obstacles.

steer, *v.t.* 1. direct or guide. —*n.* 2. castrated bull.

steer'age, *n.* cheap, cabinless passenger accommodations on a ship.

stein, *n.* beer mug, esp. one of earthenware.

stel'lar, *adj.* pertaining to or suggesting stars.

stem, *n., v.,* **stemmed, stemming.** *n.* 1. support of a plant, leaf, or fruit. 2. single support, as of a glass. 3. uninflected part of a word. 4. extreme forepart of a ship's bow. —*v.t.* 5. take the stem from. 6. check, as liquid. 7. make headway against. —*v.i.* 8. be derived or originate.

stench, *n.* stink.

sten'cil, *n., v.t.,* **-ciled, -ciling.** *n.* 1. pierced sheet allowing paint or ink to mark an underlying surface. —*v.t.* 2. paint or ink with a stencil.

ste·nog'ra·phy, *n.* shorthand writing. —**sten''o·graph'ic**, *adj.* —**ste·nog'ra·pher**, *n.*

sten·to'ri·an, *adj.* very loud of voice.

step, *n., v.i.,* **stepped, stepping.** *n.* 1. movement of the walking foot. 2. gait. 3. raised surface on which one walks upwards. 4. stage of a process. —*v.i.* 5. walk. 6. press down with the foot.

step-, by the remarriage of a parent: a prefix.

step'lad''der, *n.* ladder with steps.

steppe, *n.* plain, esp. in southeast Europe or Asia.

ster'e·o, *n.* device for playing recorded or broadcast music in stereophonic sound.

ster''e·o·phon'ic, *adj.* pertaining to realistic sound reproduction through two or more loudspeakers.

ster'e·o·scope'', *n.* viewer using twin pictures and two eyepieces for a realistic effect.

ster'e·o·type'', *n., v.t.,* **-typed, typing.** *n.* 1. process for casting printing plates. 2. unimaginative or oversimplified conception. —*v.t.* 3. reproduce by the stereotype process. 4. conceive as a stereotype.

ster'ile, *adj.* 1. free of microbes. 2. barren. 3. uncreative or unimaginative. —**ster·il'i·ty**, *n.*

ster'i·lize'', *v.t.,* **-lized, -lizing.** make sterile. —**ster'i·liz''er**, *n.* —**ster''i·li·za'tion**, *n.*

ster'ling, *adj.* 1. composed of 92.5° silver. 2. in British money. 3. fine; noble.

stern, *adj.* 1. grimly strict. —*n.* 2. after end of a ship. —**stern'ly**, *adv.* —**stern'ness**, *n.*

ster'num, *n.* breastbone.

steth'o·scope", *n.* instrument for listening to body sounds.

ste've·dore", *n.* handler of ship's cargoes.

stew, *n.* 1. dish of simmered food. —*v.t.* 2. simmer to cook.

stew'ard, *n.* 1. business manager, esp. on an estate. 2. person in charge of food, supplies, and services. 3. attendant. Also, *fem.*, **stew'ard·ess**.

stick, *v.*, **stuck, sticking**, *n.*, *v.t.* 1. pierce. 2. thrust. 3. cause to adhere. —*v.i.* 4. fail to move properly. 5. adhere. 6. project. 7. remain. —*n.* 8. length of wood. 9. short length. 10. lever. 11. walking cane.

stick'er, *n.* 1. person or thing that sticks. 2. adhesive label.

stick'ler, *n.* person who insists on something.

stick'y, *adj.*, **stickier, stickiest**. 1. adhesive. 2. *Informal.* a. muggy. b. troublesome or difficult.

stiff, *adj.* 1. unbending. 2. not moving easily. 3. formal or distant in manner. —**stiff'ly**, *adv.* —**stiff'ness**, *n.* —**stif'fen**, *v.t.*, *v.i.*

sti'fle, *v.*, **-fled, -fling**. *v.t.* 1. smother. 2. suppress. —*v.i.* 3. suffer from lack of air.

stig'ma, *n.*, *pl.* **stigmata, stigmas**. mark or indication of disrepute. —**stig'ma·tize"**, *v.t.*

stile, *n.* 1. steps over a fence. 2. upright framing member.

sti·let'to, *n.* Italian dagger.

still, *adj.* 1. motionless or silent. 2. tranquil. 3. not sparkling, as wine. —*adv.* 4. up to an indicated time. 5. even more or even less. —*adv.*, *conj.* 6. nevertheless. —*v.t.*, *v.i.* 7. make or become still. —*n.* 8. distillation apparatus. —**still'ness**, *n.*

still'born", *adj.* 1. born dead. 2. abortive.

stilt, *n.* pole serving as an extention of the legs.

stilt'ed, *adj.* affectedly dignified.

stim'u·late, *v.t.*, **-lated, -lating**. 1. cause to be active or more active. 2. inspire. —**stim"u·la'tion**, *n.* —**stim'u·la·tive**, *adj.* —**stim'u·lant**, *n.*

stim'u·lus, *n.*, *pl.* **-li**. something stimulating.

sting, *v.t.*, **stung, -ing**. *n.*, *v.t.* 1. inflict a small, painful wound or blow. 2. annoy or goad severely. —*n.* 3. wound from stinging. 4. sharp part for stinging. 5. undercover operation run by a law enforcement agency to catch suspected criminals.

stin'gy, *adj.* characteristic of or suggesting miserliness. —**stin'gi·ly**, *adv.* —**stin'gi·ness**, *n.*

stink, **stank** or **stunk, stunk, stinking**, *n.*, *v.i.* 1. have a bad smell. —*n.* 2. bad smell.

stint, *v.t.* 1. limit. 2. limit oneself. —*n.* 3. limitation. 4. task or work period.

sti'pend, *n.* regular payment.

stip'ple, *v.t.*, **-pled, -pling**, *n.*, *v.t.* 1. paint in small dots. —*n.* 2. texture of small dots.

stip'u·late, *v.t.*, **-lated, -lating**. require as a condition. —**stip"u·la'tion**, *n.*

stir, *v.t.*, **stirred, stirring**, *n.*, *v.t.* 1. mix by moving. 2. move. 3. rouse. —*n.* 4. public excitement or commotion.

stir'ring, *adj.* 1. exciting. 2. active.

stir'rup, *n.* foothold hanging from a saddle.

stitch, *n.* 1. single repeated operation in sewing, knitting, etc. 2. sharp pain. —*v.t.* 3. sew.

stock, *n.* 1. goods, materials, etc. on hand. 2. cattle. 3. any of various parts of guns, implements, etc. 4. ancestry. 5. soup or stew base. 6. dividend-bearing shares. —*adj.* 7. standard; uniform. —*v.t.* 8. keep for sale or use. 9. supply with stock. 10. supply with live fish, as a pond. —**stock'brok"er**, *n.* —**stock'hold"er**, *n.* —**stock'pile"**, *n.* —**stock'yard"**, *n.*

stock·ade', *n.*, *v.t.*, **-aded, -ading**. *n.* 1. barrier of upright stakes. —*v.t.* 2. put a stockade around.

stock'ing, *n.* clothing for the foot and lower parts of the leg.

stock'y, *adj.* broad and short of figure.

stodg'y, *adj.*, **stodgier, stodgiest**. heavy and boring. —**stodg'i·ly**, *adv.* —**stodg'i·ness**, *n.*

sto'ic, *n.* 1. person who maintains indifference to pain or sorrow. —*adj.* 2. Also, **sto'i·cal**, characteristic of a stoic. —**sto'i·cal·ly**, *adv.* —**sto'i·cism**, *n.*

stoke, *v.t.*, **stoked, stoking**. keep burning by adding fuel. —**stok'er**, *n.*

stole, *n.* scarflike garment worn behind the neck and over the shoulders.

stol'id, *adj.* showing no liveliness. —**stol'id·ly**, *adv.* —**sto·lid'i·ty**, *n.*

stom'ach, *n.* 1. organ of digestion. 2. tolerance. —*v.t.* 3. take into the stomach. 4. tolerate. —**sto·mach'ic**, *adj.* —**stom'ach·ache"**, *n.*

stone, *n.*, *pl.* **stones**, *adj.*, *v.t.*, **stoned, stoning**. *n.* 1. hard mineral substance. 2. small piece of this. 3. gem. 4. pit of a fruit. 5. hard object formed in a digestive organ. —*adj.* 6. made of stone. —*v.t.* 7. attack with stones. 8. pit, as a fruit. —**ston'y**, *adj.*

stooge, *n.* *Informal.* 1. comedian's assistant. 2. underling or henchman.

stool, *n.* armless, backless seat.

stoop, *v.i.* 1. bend forward. 2. demean oneself. —*n.* 3. bent posture. 4. small porch.

stop, *v.,* **stopped, stopping,** *n., v.t.* **1.** prevent from starting or going on. **2.** clog or plug. —*v.i.* **3.** act or move no further or not at all. **4.** stay briefly. —*n.* **5.** act, instance or place of stopping. **6.** device for controlling tone in a musical instrument. —**stop′page,** *n.*

stop′gap′, *n., adj.* makeshift.

stop′ov·er, *n.* brief pause during a journey.

stop′per, *n.* **1.** plug, as for a bottle. —*v.t.* **2.** close with a stopper. Also, **stop′ple.**

stop′watch″, *n.* watch for measuring elapsed time.

stor′age, *n.* **1.** act or instance of storing. **2.** condition of being stored.

store, *n., v.t.,* **stored, storing.** *n.* **1.** place for the sale of goods. **2.** place of storage. **3. stores,** supplies. **4. in store,** waiting in the future. —*v.t.* **5.** accumulate and save. **6.** put away for future use. —**store′front,** *n.* —**store′house″,** *n.* —**store′keeper″,** *n.* —**store′room,″** *n.*

stork, *n.* long-billed, long-legged wading bird.

storm, *n.* **1.** high wind, often with rain, snow, etc. **2.** sudden attack. —*v.t.* **3.** attack suddenly and violently. —*v.i.* **4.** blow as a storm. **5.** rage. —**storm′y,** *adj.* —**storm′i·ly,** *adv.*

stor′y, *n., pl.* **-ries. 1.** account of events, often fictitious. **2.** newspaper report. **3.** *Informal.* lie. **4.** level in a building.

stoup (stoop), *n.* basin for holy water.

stout, *adj.* **1.** sturdy. **2.** courageous; resolute. **3.** heavy-set. —*n.* **4.** dark, sweet, beerlike drink. —**stout′ly,** *adv.* —**stout′ness,** *n.*

stove, *n.* device for heating or cooking.

stow, *v.t.* **1.** put in storage, as on a ship. —*v.i.* **2. stow away,** hide on a ship for a free passage. —**stow′age,** *n.* —**stow′a·way″,** *n.*

strad′dle, *v.t.,* **-dled, -dling,** *n., v.t.* **1.** stand over or mount with a leg on each side. —*n.* **2.** straddling posture.

strafe, *v.t.,* **strafed, strafing.** fire down upon from an aircraft.

strag′gle, *v.i.,* **-gled, -gling.** stray or fall behind. —**strag′gler,** *n.*

straight, *adj.* **1.** from point to point in the shortest way; direct. **2.** unmodified or undiluted. **3.** in good order or condition. **4.** honest or unevasive. —*adv.* **5.** directly. **6.** without modification. **7.** honestly; without evasion. **8.** so as to be clearly understood. —**straight′ness,** *n.* —**straight′en,** *v.t., v.i.*

straight′a·way″, *n.* **1.** straight part of a racetrack, etc. —*adv.* **2.** Also, **straight′way″,** at once.

straight″for′ward, *adj.* unevasive; honest.

strain, *v.t.* **1.** tax the strength of. **2.** injure or distort through force. **3.** run

through a filter or sieve. —*n.* **4.** major effort or burden. **5.** injury from straining. **6.** trying experience. **7.** melody. **8.** chain of ancestors or descendants. **9.** heredity. —**strain′er,** *n.*

strait, *n.* **1.** narrow natural waterway. **2. straits,** difficulties.

strait′en, *v.t.* make narrow or meager.

strand, *n.* **1.** length of fiber for twisting into rope. **2.** length of hair. **3.** river or ocean shore. —*v.t.* **4.** run aground. **5.** put in a helpless position.

strange, *adj.,* **stranger, strangest. 1.** strikingly unfamiliar; odd. **2.** not known to one. —**strange′ly,** *adv.* —**strange′ness,** *n.*

stran′ger, *n.* unfamiliar person.

stran′gle, *v.,* **-gled, -gling.** *v.t.* **1.** kill by choking. —*v.i.* **2.** choke. —**stran′gler,** *n.* —**stran″gu·la′tion,** *n.*

strap, *n., v.t.,* **strapped, strapping.** *n.* **1.** band for fastening. —*v.t.* **2.** fasten with a strap.

stra·ta·gem (stra′tə jəm), *n.* plot; trick.

stra·teg′ic, *adj.* **1.** pertaining to strategy. **2.** important in a strategy.

strat′e·gy, *n., pl.* **-gies. 1.** art of planning military operations. **2.** stratagem or series of stratagems. —**strat′e·gist,** *n.*

strat′i·fy, *v.,* **-fied, -fying.** *v.t., v.i.* form in layers. —**strat″i·fi·ca′tion,** *n.*

strat′o·sphere″, *n.* atmospheric zone 6 to 15 miles above the earth. —**strat″o·spher′ic,** *adj.*

stra′tum, *n., pl.* **strata, stratums.** layers, as of rock.

straw, *n.* **1.** stalk of threshed grain. **2.** quantity of such stalks. **3.** tube for sucking liquids.

straw′ber″ry, *n., pl.* **-ries.** red fruit of a vinelike plant.

stray, *v.i.* **1.** wander aimlessly. **2.** wander away. —*adj.* **3.** passing or occurring by chance. —*n.* **4.** animal that strays.

streak, *n.* **1.** long mark. **2.** trait of character. **3.** brief period, as of luck. —*v.t.* **4.** mark with streaks. —*v.i.* **5.** move swiftly. **6.** run naked through a public place. —**ing,** *n.*

stream, *n.* **1.** body of running water. **2.** steady flow. —*v.i.* **3.** flow quickly and steadily. **4.** run with moisture.

stream′er, *n.* long, narrow flag or piece of bunting.

stream′line″, *v.t.* **1.** make with a form minimizing air or water resistance. **2.** purge of unnecessary elements.

street, *n.* road in an urban area.

street′car″, *n.* rail car for transportation along streets.

strength, *n.* **1.** power of the muscles. **2.** resistance to force. **3.** ability of the mind. **4.** purity.

strength′en, *v.t., v.i.* make or become stronger.

stren'u·ous, *adj.* 1. involving great effort. 2. vigorous.

stress, *n.* 1. emphasis. 2. difficulties. 3. force causing a strain. —*v.t.* 4. put a stress on.

stretch, *v.t., v.i.* 1. extend or spread. 2. strain, as a muscle. 3. pull taut. —*n.* 4. act or instance of stretching. 5. unbroken extent.

stretch'er, *n.* 1. device for carrying a sick person lying down. 2. device for stretching.

strew, *v.t.,* **strewed, strewed** or **strewn, strewing.** scatter.

stri'at·ed, *adj.* with closely-spaced grooves or furrows. —**stri·a'tion,** *n.*

strict, *adj.* 1. demanding exact conformity. 2. conforming exactly. —**strict'ly,** *adv.* —**strict'ness,** *n.*

stric'ture, *n.* adverse criticism.

stride, *v.i.,* **strode, stridden, striding,** *n., v.i.* 1. walk with long steps. —*n.* 2. long step. 3. distance covered by such a step.

stri'dent, *adj.* loud and harsh.

strife, *n.* conflict.

strike, *v.,* **struck, struck** or **stricken, striking,** *n., v.t.* 1. hit. 2. make an impression on. 3. afflict. 4. discover, as a mineral. 5. ignite, as a match. —*v.i.* 6. stop work to enforce demands. —*n.* 7. act or instance of striking. 8. *Baseball.* failure to bat. 9. *Bowling.* perfect score with the first bowl. —**strik'er,** *n.*

strik'ing, *adj.* remarkable.

string, *n., v.t.,* **strung, stringing.** *n.* 1. thin cord. 2. cord on a musical instrument. 3. **strings,** musical instruments using such cords. 4. series or row. —*v.t.,* 5. furnish with strings. 6. hang from a cord. 7. set in a series or row. —**stringed,** *adj.* —**string'y,** *adj.*

string bean, bean with edible pods.

strin'gent, *adj.* very strict. —**strin'gent·ly,** *adv.* —**strin'gen·cy,** *n.*

strip, *n., v.t.,* **stripped, stripping.** *n.* 1. long narrow piece. —*v.t.* 2. remove the clothing or covering from. 3. remove from an underlying surface. 4. steal or confiscate the possessions of.

stripe, *n.* 1. long, broad mark. 2. sort or kind. —*v.t.* 3. mark with stripes.

strip'ling, *n.* boy.

strive, *v.i.,* **strove, striven, striving.** try hard; strain.

stroke, *v.t.,* **stroked, stroking,** *n., v.t.* 1. rub or graze gently. —*n.* 2. act or instance of stroking. 3. blow. 4. single movement that is repeated. 5. sudden attack of illness, esp. apoplexy. 6. sudden occasion, as of luck. 7. line made by a pen or pencil. 8. way of swimming.

stroll, *v.i.* 1. walk idly. 2. wander. —**strol'ler,** *n.*

strong, *adj.* having strength. —**strong'ly,** *adv.*

strong'hold'', *n.* place secure against attack.

strop, *n., v.t.,* **stropped, stropping.** *n.* 1. leather strap for sharpening. —*v.t.* 2. sharpen with a strop.

struc'ture, *n.* 1. part of a building giving strength. 2. something built. 3. basic form, as of a composition. —**struc'tur·al,** *adj.* —**struc'tur·al·ly,** *adv.*

strug'gle, *v.i.,* **-gled, -gling,** *n., v.i.* 1. strive. 2. fight. —*n.* 3. strenuous effort. 4. fight.

strum, *v.t.* **strummed, strumming.** play lightly or carelessly, as a piano or plucked string instrument.

strut, *v.i.,* **strutted, strutting,** *n., v.i.* 1. walk affectedly. —*n.* 2. act or instance of strutting. 3. postlike brace.

strych·nine (strik'nin), *n.* poisonous alkaloid.

stub, *n., v.t.,* **stubbed, stubbing.** *n.* 1. short remnant. 2. stump. —*v.t.* 3. ram against something, esp. a toe.

stub'ble, *n.* 1. plant stalks mown short. 2. short growth of beard.

stub'born, *adj.* refusing to obey, give up, etc. —**stub'born·ly,** *adv.* —**stub'born·ness,** *n.*

stuc'co, *n., pl.* **-coes, -cos,** *v.t.,* **-coed, -coing.** *n.* 1. coarse exterior plaster. 2. fine interior plaster. —*v.t.* 3. cover with stucco.

stud, *n., v.t.,* **studded, studding.** *n.* 1. projecting feature. 2. upright wall-framing member. 3. buttonlike fastener. 4. collection of horses. 5. male animal, esp. a horse, for breeding. —*v.t.* 6. furnish or sprinkle with or as if with studs.

stu'dent, *n.* person who studies.

stud'ied, *adj.* intentional.

stu'di·o, *n.* 1. artist's workplace. 2. room for television or radio performers. 3. place for television or radio performers. 4. place for making motion pictures.

stu'di·ous, *adj.* studying diligently. —**stu'di·ous·ly,** *adv.*

study, *n., pl.* **studies,** *v.t.,* **studied, studying.** *n.* 1. methodical acquisition of skill or knowledge. 2. subject of such activity. 3. room for reading or writing. 4. deep thought. —*v.t.* 5. make a subject of study.

stuff, *n.* 1. material. 2. assorted or worthless objects or materials. —*v.t.* 3. fill under pressure.

stuf'fing, *n.* material stuffed into a hollow object.

stuff'y, *adj.,* **stuffier, stuffiest.** 1. dull and formal. 2. lacking fresh air.

stul'ti·fy, *v.t.,* **-fied, -fying.** cause to seem foolish.

stum′ble, *v.i.,* **-bled, -bling.** trip and begin to fall.

stump, *n.* **1.** remnant of something cut off. —*v.t.* **2.** baffle. —*v.i.* **3.** walk ponderously. **4.** travel on a political campaign.

stun, *v.t.,* **stunned, stunning. 1.** shalt with amazement. **2.** knock unconscious.

stunt, *n.* **1.** act displaying skill. —*v.t.* **2.** hinder in growing.

stu′pe·fy, *v.t.,* **-fied, -fying. 1.** put in a stupor. **2.** amaze. —**stu″pe·fac′tion,** *n.*

stu·pen′dous, *adj.* astounding.

stu′pid, *adj.* **1.** low in intelligence. **2.** pointless. —**stu′pid·ly,** *adv.* —**stu·pid′i·ty,** *n.*

stu′por, *n.* unconscious or semi-conscious state.

stur′dy, *n.* **1.** strong. **2.** vigorous. —**stur′di·ly,** *adv.* —**stur′di·ness,** *n.*

stur′geon, *n.* large fish whose roe is caviar.

stut′ter, *v.i., n.* stammer.

sty, *n., pl.* **sties. 1.** pig shelter. **2.** swollen inflammation of the eyelid.

style, *n., v.t.,* **styled, styling.** *n.* **1.** manner of artistic composition, writing, living, etc. **2.** kind or variety. **3.** elegance. **4.** formal name. —*v.t.* **5.** apply a style to. —**sty′lis′tic,** *adj.*

styl′ish, *adj.* in style; elegant.

styl′ist, *n.* artist as a possessor of a style.

sty′lus, *n.* **1.** pointed writing instrument. **2.** phonograph needle.

sty′mie, *v.t.,* **-mied, -mying.** hinder.

styp′tic, *adj.* stopping the flow of blood.

sua·sion (swa′zhən), *n.* persuasion. —**sua′sive,** *adj.*

suave (swahv), *adj.* smoothly polite. —**suave′ly,** *adv.* —**suav′i·ty, suave′ness,** *n.*

sub′com·mit″ee, *n.* committee reporting to a committee.

sub·con′scious, *n.* **1.** part of the mind beyond consciousness. —*adj.* **2.** pertaining to this part of the mind. —**sub·con′scious·ly,** *adv.*

sub·con′ti·nent, *n.* large land mass within a continent.

sub′di·vide″, *v.t.,* **-vided, -viding.** divide still further. —**sub′di·vi″sion,** *n.*

sub·due′, *v.t.,* **-dued, -duing. 1.** overcome. **2.** lower in intensity.

sub·ject, *n.* (sub′jekt) **1.** thing thought, written, etc. about. **2.** person or thing acted upon. **3.** person ruled by a government. **4.** *Grammar.* person or thing about which a sentence tells. —*adj.* **5.** being a subject. **6.** exposed to a specified treatment. —*v.t.* (sub jekt′) **7.** submit to a specified treatment. —**sub·jec′tion,** *n.*

sub·jec′tive, *adj.* existing or originating in one person's mind. —**sub·jec′tive·ly,** *adv.* —**sub″jec·tiv′i·ty,** *n.*

sub·join′, *v.t.* add at the end.

sub′ju·gate″, *v.t.,* **-gated, -gating.** conquer. —**sub″ju·ga′tion,** *n.*

sub·junc′tive, *Grammar. adj.* **1.** pertaining to a verbal mode of possibility, etc. —*n.* **2.** subjunctive mode.

sub·lease, *n., v.t.,* **-leased, -leasing.** *n.* (sub′lēs) **1.** lease from a tenant. —*v.t.* (sub lēs′) **2.** rent with such a lease.

sub·let′, *v.t.,* **-letted, -letting.** sublease.

sub·li·mate, *v.t.,* **-mated, -mating,** *n., v.t.* (sub lə māt′) **1.** divert into a more acceptable form. **2.** sublime. —*n.* (sub′lə mət) **3.** product of subliming. —**sub″li·ma′tion,** *n.*

sub·lime′, *adj., n., v.t.,* **-limed, -liming.** *adj.* **1.** noble and exalted. —*n.* **2.** realm of sublime things. —*v.t.* **3.** vaporize, then solidify. —**sub·lime′ly,** *adv.* —**sub·lim′i·ty,** *n.*

sub·ma·rine, *n.* (sub′mə rēn), **1.** underwater vessel. —*adj.* (sub mə rēn′) **2.** undersea. **3.** pertaining to submarines.

sub·merge′, *v.,* **-merged, -merging.** *v.t., v.i.* sink into a liquid. —**sub·mer′gence,** *n.*

sub·merse′, *v.t.,* **-mersed, -mersing.** submerge. —**sub·mer′sion,** *n.* —**sub·mers′i·ble,** *adj.*

sub·mit′, *v.,* **-mitted, -mitting.** *v.t.* **1.** offer, as in surrender. **2.** offer for consideration. **3.** subject to a specified treatment. —*v.i.* **4.** surrender or yield oneself. —**sub·mis′sion,** *n.* —**sub·mis′sive,** *adj.*

sub·or·di·nate, *v.t.,* **-ated, -ating,** *adj., n., v.t.* (sub ôr′də nāt″) **1.** subject to the will of another. —*adj.* (sub ôr′də nət) **2.** lower in rank or importance. —*n.* **3.** someone or something subordinate. —**sub·or″di·na′tion,** *n.*

sub·orn′, *v.t.* induce to commit a wrong.

sub·poe·na (sə pē′nə), *n., v.t.,* **-naed, -naeing.** *n.* **1.** summons to court. —*v.t.* **2.** serve with such a summons.

sub·scribe′, *v.,* **-scribed, -scribing.** *v.i.* **1.** pay for continued supply of a periodical, service, etc. **2.** promise to contribute money. **3.** agree. —*v.t.* **4.** sign. —**sub·scrib′er,** *n.* —**sub·scrip′tion,** *n.*

sub′se·quent, *adj.* occurring after. —**sub′se·quent·ly,** *adv.*

sub·ser′vi·ent, *adj.* **1.** servile. **2.** subordinate. —**sub·ser′vi·ence,** *n.* —**sub·ser′vi·ent·ly,** *adv.*

sub·side′, *v.i.,* **-sided, -siding. 1.** settle or sink. **2.** die down. —**sub·sid′ence,** *n.*

sub·sid′i·ar″y, *adj., n., pl.* **-ries.** *adj.* **1.** subordinate or auxiliary. —*n.* **2.** subsidiary entity.

sub′si·dy, *n., pl.* **-dies.** monetary aid, esp. from a government. —**sub′si·dize″,** *v.t.*

sub·sist′, *v.i.* **1.** exist. **2.** maintain one's existence. —**sub·sist′ence,** *n.*

sub′stance, *n.* **1.** material. **2.** essential part or aspect. **3.** basic meaning.

sub·stan'tial, *adj.* 1. solid. 2. considerable in amount. 3. material. 4. essential. 5. important in the community. —**sub·stan'tial·ly,** *adv.*

sub·stan'ti·ate, *v.t.,* **-ated, -ating.** show to be true. —**sub·stan''ti·a'tion,** *n.*

sub'stan·tive, *n.* 1. noun or word used as a noun. —*adj.* 2. pertaining to essences. 3. serving as a substantive.

sub'sti·tute, *v.,* **-tuted, -tuting** *n., v.t., v.i.* 1. put or act in another's place. —*n.* 2. person or thing that substitutes. —**sub''sti·tu'tion,** *n.*

sub'ter·fuge'', *n.* evasive trick or trickery.

sub''ter·ra'ne·an, *adj.* underground.

sub·tle (sut'əl), *adj.* 1. highly sensitive. 2. scarcely perceived. 3. cunning. —**sub'tly,** *adv.* —**sub'tle·ty,** *n.*

sub·tract', *v.t.* remove, as one quantity from another. —**sub·trac'tion,** *n.*

sub·trop'i·cal, *adj.* close to the tropics.

sub'urb, *n.* community adjoining or dependent on a city. —**sub·ur'ban,** *adj.*

sub·vert', *v.t.* undermine or corrupt. —**sub·ver'sion,** *n.* —**sub·ver'sive,** *adj., n.*

sub'way'', *n.* 1. underground railroad. 2. pedestrian underpass.

suc·ceed', *v.i.* 1. obtain good results. 2. attain success. —*v.t.* 3. follow in an office, inheritance, etc.

suc·cess', *n.* 1. favorable outcome of an attempt. 2. commonly sought goals. 3. person or thing that attains success. —**suc·cess'ful,** *adj.*

suc·ces'sion, *n.* 1. sequential order of things. 2. act of succeeding another. —**suc·ces'sive,** *adj.* —**suc·ces'sive·ly,** *adv.* —**suc·ces'sor,** *n.*

suc·cinct (suk sinkt'), *adj.* restricted to essential information. —**suc·cinct'ly,** *adv.* —**suc·cinct'ness,** *n.*

suc'cor, *n., v.t.* help in need.

suc'co·tash, *n.* cooked corn and lima beans.

suc'cu·lent, *adj.* juicy. —**suc'cu·lence,** *n.*

suc·cumb', *v.i.* 1. yield. 2. die.

such, *adj.* 1. of the kind mentioned. 2. so much of. —*adv.* 3. so greatly. —*pron.* 4. the kind mentioned. 5. such a person or thing.

suck, *v.t.* 1. draw by suction. 2. absorb by capillarity. 3. lick and absorb.

suck'er, *n.* 1. person or thing that sucks. 2. fresh-water fish. 3. lollipop. 4. *Informal.* person easily cheated.

suck'le, *v.t.,* **-led, -ling.** feed at the breast.

suck'ling, *n.* unweaned child or animal.

suc'tion, *n.* forcing of a fluid into a vacuum by atmospheric pressure.

sud'den, *adj.* quick and unexpected. —**sud'den·ly,** *adv.* —**sud'den·ness,** *n.*

suds, *n., pl.* 1. fine soap bubbles. 2. soapy water.

sue, *v.,* **sued, suing.** *v.t.,* 1. claim damages from in court. —*v.i.* 2. make an appeal.

suede (swād), *n.* soft leather with a nap.

su'et, *n.* hard animal fat.

suf'fer, *v.t.* 1. undergo. 2. permit or tolerate. —**suf'fer·er,** *n.*

suf'fer·ance, *n.* 1. tacit permission. 2. endurance.

suf·fice', *v.i.,* **-ficing, -ficing.** be enough.

suf·fi'cient, *adj.* enough. —**suf·fi'cient·ly,** *adv.* —**suf·fi'cien·cy,** *n.*

suf'fix, *n. Grammar.* ending added to a word to give a new meaning.

suf'fo·cate, *v.,* **-cated, -cating.** *v.t., v.i.* cut off or be without air for breathing. —**suf''fo·ca'tion,** *n.*

suf'frage, *n.* right to vote.

suf·fuse', *v.t.* spread light, color, etc. over.

sug'ar, *n.* 1. sweet carbohydrate. —*v.t.* 2. add sugar to. —**sug'ar·y,** *adj.*

sug·gest', *v.t.* 1. offer as advice. 2. propose. 3. imply. —**sug·ges'tion,** *n.*

sug·ges'tive, *adj.* full of implication, esp. of impropriety.

su'i·cide'', *n.* 1. willful killing of oneself. 2. person who kills himself willfully. —**su''i·cid'al,** *adj.*

suit, *n.* 1. complete set of clothes. 2. lawsuit. 3. appeal. 4. playing cards with a common symbol. —*v.t.* 5. satisfy; please. 6. adapt. 7. clothe.

suit'a·ble, *adj.* right; appropriate. —**suit'a·bly,** *adv.*

suit'case'', *n.* travel case for clothes, etc.

suite (swēt), *n.* 1. apartment of connected rooms. 2. set of musical compositions.

suit'or, *n.* wooer.

sul'fate, *n.* salt of sulfuric acid.

sul·fur'ic, *adj.* pertaining to or containing sulfur. Also, **sul'fur·ous.**

sulk, *v.i.* 1. be angry and aloof. —*n.* 2. fit of sulking. —**sulk'y,** *adj.*

sul'len, *adj.* 1. quietly resentful. 2. gloomy. —**sul'len·ly,** *adv.* —**sul'len·ness,** *n.*

sul'ly, *v.t.,* **-lied, -lying.** 1. disgrace. 2. soil or pollute.

sul'phur, *n.* sulfur.

sul'tan, *n.* Muslim ruler.

sul'try, *adj.,* **-trier, -triest.** 1. hot and humid. 2. sexually inviting. —**sul'tri·ness,** *n.*

sum, *n., v.t.,* **summed, summing.** *n.* 1. number obtained by addition. 2. **in sum,** as a summary. —*v.t.* 3. add up. 4. summarize.

su·mac (shōō'mak), *n.* small tree. Also, **su'mach.**

sum'ma·rize, *v.t.,* **-rized, -rizing.** present in a summary.

sum'ma·ry, *n., pl.* **-ries,** *adj., n.* 1. presentation of essential information only. —*adj.* 2. without formalities or preliminaries. —**sum·ma'ri·ly,** *adv.*

sum·ma′tion, *n*. concluding summary.

sum′mer, *n*. **1**. season between spring and autumn, beginning at the summer solstice. —*v.i.* **2**. spend the summer. —**sum′mer·y**, *adj*.

sum′mit, *n*. highest point.

sum′mon, *v.t.* order or ask to come.

sum′mons, *n*. **1**. order to appear in court. **2**. order or request to come.

sump, *n*. pit for collecting ground water.

sump′tu·ous, *adj*. costly and luxurious. —**sump′tu·ous·ly**, *adv*. —**sump′tu·ous·ness**, *n*.

sun, *n., v.t.*, **sunned, sunning**. *n*. **1**. star of the solar system. **2**. rays from this star. —*v.t.* **3**. expose to the sun. —**sun′ny**, *adj*. —**sun′beam′′**, *n*. —**sun′light′′**, *n*. —**sun′lit′′**, *adj*.

sun′bathe′′, *v.i.*, **-bathed, -bathing**. lie down to receive solar rays. —**sun′bath**, *n*.

sun′burn′′, *n., v.t.*, **-burned, -burning**. burn from or with the rays of the sun.

sun′dae, *n*. ice cream topped with flavored syrup.

Sun′day, *n*. first day of the week.

sun′di′′al, *n*. instrument telling time by the shadow of a pointer.

sun′down′′, *n*. time of sunset.

sun·dry (sun′drē), *adj*. various.

sun′flow′′er, *n*. tall plant with large, yellow-petaled blossoms.

sun′glas′′ses, *n., pl*. spectacles tinted to weaken the sun's rays.

sun′lamp′′, *n*. ultraviolet lamp.

sun′rise′′, *n*. rise of the sun above the horizon.

sun′set′′, *n*. descent of the sun below the horizon.

sun′shine, *n*. rays of the sun.

sun′stroke′′, *n*. collapse from overexposure to the sun.

sun′tan′′, *n*. darkening of the skin resulting from sunbathing.

sup, *v.i.*, **supped, supping**. have supper

su·perb′, *adj*. admirably excellent. —**su·perb′ly**, *adv*.

su·per·cil·i·ous (soo′′pər sil′e əs), *adj*. proudly contemptuous. —**su′′per·cil′i·ous·ly**, *adv*. —**su′′per·cil′i·ous·ness**, *n*.

su′′per·fi′cial, *adj*. **1**. on the surface only. **2**. lacking depth of thought or feeling. —**su′′per·fi′cial·ly**, *adv*. —**su′′per·fi·ci·al′i·ty**, *n*.

su·per′flu·ous, *adj*. **1**. more than is useful. **2**. redundant; useless. —**su·per′flu·ous·ly**, *adv*. —**su′′per·flu′i·ty**, *n*.

su′′per·hu′man, *adj*. beyond ordinary human limitations.

su′′per·im·pose′, *v.t.*, **-posed, -posing**. place over something else.

su′per·in·tend′′, *v.t.* supervise. —**su′′per·in·ten′dence**, *n*. —**su′′per·in·ten′dent**, *n., adj*. —**su′′per·in·ten′den·cy**, *n*.

su·pe′ri·or, *adj*. **1**. better. **2**. excellent. **3**. proud; haughty. **4**. higher in position. —*n*. **5**. superior person. **6**. head of a religious community. —**su·pe′′ri·or′i·ty**, *n*.

su·per′la·tive, *adj*. **1**. of the highest excellence. **2**. *Grammar*. denoting the extreme in a comparison. —*n*. **3**. something superlative. —**su·per′la·tive·ly**, *adv*.

su′′per·nat′u·ral, *adj*. **1**. outside the laws of nature. —*n*. **2**. realm of things outside such laws. —**su′′per·nat′u·ral·ly**, *adv*.

su′′per·nu′mer·ar·y, *adj., n., pl*. **-ries**. *adj*. **1**. extra; nonessential. —*n*. **2**. something supernumerary. **3**. non-speaking actor.

su′per·scribe′′, *v.t.*, **-scribed, -scribing**. write over. —**su′′per·scrip′tion**, *n*.

su′′per·sede′, *v.t.*, **-seded, -seding**. replace, esp. in importance or function.

su′′per·son′ic, *adj*. pertaining to speeds faster than that of sound.

su′′per·sti′tion, *n*. unconfirmed belief, esp. in the supernatural. —**su′′per·sti′tious**, *adj*. —**su′′per·sti′tious·ly**, *adv*.

su′per·struc′ture, *n*. upper structure.

su′′per·vene′, *v.i.*, **-vened, -vening**. **1**. arrive or occur in addition. **2**. occur afterward. —**super·ven′tion**, *n*.

su′per·vise′′, *v.t.*, **-vised, -vising**. direct and inspect. —**su′per·vis′′or**, *n*. —**su′′per·vi′so·ry**, *adj*. —**su′′per·vi′sion**, *n*.

su′pine, *adj*. **1**. lying on the back. **2**. wrongly passive. —**su′pine·ly**, *adv*.

sup′per, *n*. late dinner.

sup·plant′, *v.t.* replace, as in favor or function.

sup′ple, *adj.*, **-pler, -plest**. flexible. —**sup′ple·ly**, *adv*. —**sup′ple·ness**, *n*.

sup·ple·ment, *n*. (sup′plə mənt) **1**. desirable addition. —*v.t.* (sup′pləment′′) **2**. give a supplement to. —**sup′′ple·men′tal, sup′′ple·men′ta·ry**, *adj*.

sup′pli·cate′′, *v.t.*, **-cated, -cating**. implore. —**sup′′pli·ca′tion**, *n*. —**sup′′pli·ant, sup′pli·cant**, *n*.

sup·ply′, *v.t.*, **-plied, -plying**, *n., pl*. **-plies**. *v.t.* **1**. provide, as goods. **2**. fill, as a need. —*n*. **3**. act or instance of supplying. **4**. something supplied. **5**. stock, as of goods. —**sup·pli′er**, *n*.

sup·port′, *v.t.* **1**. hold up. **2**. provide a livelihood for. **3**. endure. **4**. be loyal to. **5**. confirm. —*n*. **6**. someone or something that supports.

sup·pose′, *v.t.*, **-posed, -posing**. **1**. assume as true. **2**. expect to act as stated. —**sup·pos′ed·ly**, *adv*. —**suppo·si′tion**, *n*.

sup·press′, *v.t.* **1**. force into inaction. **2**. kept from being known or apparent. —**sup·pres′sion**, *n*.

sup·pu·rate (sup'yə rāt), *v.i.*, **-rated, -rating.** form pus. —**sup''pu·ra'tion,** *n.*

su·preme', *adj.* highest or greatest. —**su·preme'ly,** *adv.* —**su·prem'a·cy,** *n.*

sur·charge, *n., v.t.,* **-charged, -charging.** *n.* (sər'chahrj) 1. added or excessive charge. —*v.t.* (sər chahrj') 2. impose a surcharge on.

sure (shŏŏr), *adj.*, **surer, surest.** 1. convinced; positive. 2. reliant. 3. reliable. 4. unerring. 5. *Informal.* yes indeed. —**sure'ly,** *adv.*

sure·ty (shŏŏr'i tē, shŏŏr'tē), *n., pl.* **-ties.** 1. certainty. 2. security against risk. 3. guarantor.

surf, *n.* waves breaking against land, shoals, etc.

sur'face, *n., adj., v.,* **-faced, -facing.** *n.* 1. outer area. 2. upper area of a body of water. 3. outer appearance. —*adj.* 4. apparent; specious. —*v.t.* 5. finish or dress the surface of. —*v.i.* 6. come to the surface, as of a body of water.

sur·feit (sər'fit), *n.* 1. excess, as of eating or drinking. 2. revulsion from such excess. —*v.t.* 3. cause to feel such revulsion.

surge, *v.i.* **surged, surging,** *n., v.i.* 1. move in a sudden swell. 2. gather volume or force suddenly. —*n.* 3. act or instance of surging.

sur'geon, *n.* practitioner of surgery.

sur'ger·y, *n., pl.* **-ries** *n.* 1. treatment of illness by physical rather than chemical means. 2. place where such treatment is given. —**sur'gi·cal,** *adj.* —**sur'gi·cal·ly,** *adv.*

sur'ly, *adj.*, **-lier, -liest.** sullenly ill-tempered. —**sur'li·ness,** *n.*

sur·mise', *v.t.,* **-mised, -mising,** *n.* guess.

sur·mount', *v.t.* 1. get or be on top of. 2. overcome, as an obstacle. —**sur·mount'a·ble,** *adj.*

sur'name'', *n.* last name; family name.

sur·pass', *v.t.* 1. be superior to. 2. exceed.

sur·plice (sər'plis), *n.* loose-fitting robe.

sur'plus, *adj.* 1. beyond the needed amount. —*n.* 2. surplus amount.

sur·prise', *n., v.t.,* **-prised, -prising.** *n.* 1. emotion on encountering the unexpected. 2. unexpected occurrence. —*v.t.* 3. fill with surprise. 4. attack, etc. when not expected.

sur·ren'der, *v.t.* 1. give up. —*v.i.* 2. yield to superior force. —*n.* 3. act or instance of surrendering.

sur''rep·ti'tious, *adj.* stealthy. —**sur''rep·ti'tious·ly,** *adv.*

sur'ro·gate'', *n.* 1. substitute. 2. judge for legacies and estates.

sur·round', *v.t.* enclose or be close to on all sides.—**surrounding,** *adj.*

sur·round'ings, *n., pl.* things all around; environment.

sur·tax'', *n.* tax added to a tax.

sur·veil'lance, *n.* close observation.

sur·vey, *v.t., n., pl.* **-veys.** *v.t.* (sər vā') 1. measure or evaluate precisely. 2. view. —*n.* (sər'vā) 3. act or instance of surveying. 4. general summary. —**sur'vey'** or, *n.*

sur·vive', *v.,* **-vived, -viving.** *v.i.* 1. remain alive. —*v.t.* 2. outlive. —**sur·viv'** or, *n.* —**sur·viv'al,** *n.*

sus·cep·ti·ble (sus sep'tə bəl), *adj.* easily affected. —**sus·cep''ti·bil'i·ty,** *n.*

sus·pect, *v.t.* (səs pekt') 1. regard without trust. 2. guess. —*n.* (sus'pekt) 3. suspected person. —*adj.* 4. to be regarded without trust.

sus·pend', *v.t.* 1. hang. 2. postpone. 3. dismiss or expel temporarily.

sus·pen'ders, *n., pl.* straps for holding up the trousers.

sus·pense', *n.* anxiety due to uncertainty.

sus·pen'sion, *n.* 1. act or instance of suspending. 2. postponement. 3. distribution of particles throughout a fluid.

sus·pi'cion, *n.* 1. feeling of one who suspects. 2. state of being suspected. 3. trace.

sus·pi'cious, *adj.* 1. having suspicions. 2. arousing suspicion. —**sus·pi'cious·ly,** *adv.*

sus·tain', *v.t.* 1. maintain; continue. 2. support. 3. endure. 4. suffer. —**sus·tain'er,** *n.*

sus'te·nance, *n.* 1. means of existence. 2. act or instance of sustaining.

su·ture (sōō'chər), *n., v.t.,* **-tured, -turing.** *n.* 1. line of junction. 2. means by which a wound is sewn. —*v.t.* 3. join with a suture.

svelte, *adj.* slender.

swab, *n., v.t.,* **swabbed, swabbing.** *n.* 1. absorbent wiping device. —*v.t.* 2. wipe with a swab.

swag'ger, *v.i.* 1. walk arrogantly. —*n.* 2. swaggering gait.

swale, *n.* 1. low, marshy area. 2. valley-like area between slopes.

swal'low, *v.t.* 1. take down the throat. 2. suppress, as an emotion. 3. *Informal.* accept foolishly as true. —*n.* 4. small, forked-tailed bird. 5. act or instance of swallowing.

swamp, *n.* 1. area of wet land and water vegetation. —*v.t.* 2. drench. 3. overload, as with work. —**swamp'y,** *adj.*

swan, *n.* large, long-necked water bird.

swap, *v.t.,* **swapped, swapping,** *n. Informal.* exchange.

swarm, *n.* 1. large, unorganized group. —*v.i.* 2. move in a swarm.

swarth'y, *adj.*, **-ier, -iest.** rather dark-skinned. —**swarth'i·ness,** *n.*

swash'buck''ling, *adj.* showily brave or belligerent.

swas'ti·ka, *n.* cross with end pieces forming right angles: in one form the Nazi symbol.

swat, *v.t.*, **swatted, swatting**, *n. Informal*, *v.t.* **1.** hit sharply. —*n.* **2.** act or instance of swatting. —**swat′ter**, *n.*

swath (swoth), *n.* mown pathlike area.

sway, *v.i.* **1.** move unsteadily from side to side. —*v.t.* **2.** influence through argument. —*n.* **3.** act or instance of swaying. **4.** domination.

swear, *v.*, **swore, sworn, swearing**. *v.t.* **1.** affirm with an oath. **2.** bind with an oath. —*v.i.* **3.** utter profanity.

sweat, *v.i.*, **sweat** or **sweated, sweating**, *n.*, *v.i.* **1.** pass moisture through the pores. **2.** accumulate surface moisture. —*n.* **3.** sweated body moisture. **4.** sweating condition. —**sweat′y**, *adj.*

sweat′er, *n.* knitted garment covering the area from waist to neck.

sweep, *v.*, **swept, sweeping**. *v.t.* **1.** free of loose dirt, etc., esp. with brushing motions. **2.** free of enemies or rivals. —*v.i.* **3.** move swiftly and continuously. —*n.* **4.** act or instance of sweeping. **5.** scope.

sweep′stakes″, *n.* race for a prize given by the competitors.

sweet, *adj.* **1.** somewhat sugarlike in taste. **2.** agreeable, esp. to the senses. **3.** gentle. —*n.* **4.** piece of candy, etc. —**sweet′ly**, *adv.* —**sweet′ness**, *n.* —**sweet′en**, *v.t.*, *v.i.*

sweet′heart″, *n.* loved one.

sweet′pea, *n.* fragrant, flowering climbing plant.

sweet potato, trailing plant with sweet, edible, orange root.

swell, *v.*, **swelled, swelled** or **swollen, swelling**, *n.*, *adj.*, *v.t.*, *v.i.* **1.** expand beyond natural size from pressure. —*n.* **2.** act or instance of swelling. **3.** large rounded ocean wave or waves. —*adj.* **4.** *Informal.* excellent.

swel′ter, *v.i.* suffer from heat.

swerve, *v.*, **swerved, swerving**, *n.*, *v.t.*, *v.i.* **1.** turn suddenly aside. —*n.* **2.** act or instance of swerving.

swift, *adj.* **1.** quick or prompt. **2.** fast. —*n.* **3.** fast, swallowlike bird. —**swift′ly**, *adv.* —**swift′ness**, *n.*

swig, *n.*, *v.t.*, **swigged, swigging**. *Informal.* *n.* **1.** swallow. —*v.t.* **2.** drink in swallows.

swill, *v.t.* **1.** drink greedily. —*n.* **2.** liquified garbage used as pig food.

swim, *v.i.*, **swam, swum, swimming**, *n.*, *v.i.* **1.** move through water by actions of the body. **2.** be drenched or immersed. **3.** be confused or dizzy. —*n.* **4.** occasion of swimming. —**swim′mer**, *n.*

swin′dle, *v.t.*, **-dled, -dling**, *n.*, *v.t.* **1.** cheat. **2.** fraud. —**swin′dler**, *n.*

swine, *n.*, *pl.* **swine**. pig or hog.

swing, *v.*, **swung, swinging**, *n.*, *v.t.*, *v.i.* **1.** move back and forth through part of a circle. **2.** move one way in a circular path. —*n.* **3.** suspended seat for swinging. **4.** swinging blow. **5.** act, example, or magnitude of swinging.

swipe, *v.t.*, **swiped, swiping**, *n. Informal.* *v.t.* **1.** steal. **2.** hit with a swinging blow. —*n.* **3.** act or instance of swiping.

swirl, *v.t.*, *v.i.*, *n.* whirl.

swish, *v.t.*, *v.i.* **1.** whirl through the air with a sound. —*n.* **2.** sound of such whirling.

switch, *n.* **1.** change. **2.** device for controlling electric current. **3.** device for directing train movements. **4.** rodlike whip. —*v.t.* **5.** change or exchange. **6.** control or direct with a switch. **7.** beat with a switch. —**switch′board″**, *n.*

swiv′el, *n.* **1.** rotating support. —*v.t.*, *v.i.* **2.** turn on or as if on a swivel.

swoon, *n.*, *v.i.* faint.

swoop, *v.i.* **1.** descend speedily, as a bird of prey. —*n.* **2.** act or instance of swooping.

sword (sōrd), *n.* long, sharp-pointed or -bladed weapon. —**sword′play″**, *n.* —**swords′man**, *n.*

sword′fish″, *n.* large salt-water fish with swordlike upper jawbone.

syb′a·rite″, *n.* lover of luxury. —**syb″a·rit′ic**, *adj.*

syc′a·more″, *n. U.S.* plane tree.

syc·o·phant (sĭk′ə fənt), *n.* flatterer and parasite. —**syc′o·phan·cy**, *n.*

syl′la·ble, *n.* individual sound that is part of a spoken word. —**syl·lab′ic**, *adj.*

syl′la·bus, *n.*, *pl.* **-buses, -bi**. academic course outline.

sylph, *n.* graceful, slender woman.

syl′van, *adj.* **1.** pertaining to forests. **2.** forested.

sym′bol, *n.* **1.** something representing another thing. **2.** sign representing instructions or orders. —**sym·bol′ic, sym·bol′i·cal**, *adj.* —**sym·bol′i·cal·ly**, *adv.* —**sym′bol·ize″**, *v.t.*

sym′bol·ism, *n.* group of symbols.

sym′me·try, *n.*, *pl.* **-tries**. **1.** mirror-image uniformity on opposite sides. **2.** harmony of arrangement. —**sym·met′ric, sym·met′ri·cal**, *adj.* —**sym·met′ri·cal·ly**, *adv.*

sym′pa·thize″, *v.i.*, **-thized, -thizing**. **1.** be in sympathy. **2.** express sympathy. —**sym″pa·thiz′er**, *n.*

sym′pa·thy, *n.*, *pl.* **-thies**. **1.** oneness of feeling or opinion. **2.** regret for another's unhappiness. **3.** loyalty. —**sym″pa·thet′ic**, *adj.* —**sym″pa·thet′i·cal·ly**, *adv.*

sym′pho·ny, *n.*, *pl.* **-nies**. major orchestral composition. —**sym·phon′ic**, *adj.*

sym·po′si·um, *n.*, *pl.* **-siums, -sia**. **1.** formal discussion by experts. **2.** collection of papers on a topic.

symp'tom, *n.* characteristic indication, esp. of an illness. —**symp"to·mat'ic**, *adj.*

syn'a·gogue", *n.* congregation or house of Jewish worship.

syn'chro·nize", *v.t.*, **-nized**, **-nizing**. 1. cause to occur at the same time or rate of speed. 2. cause to register the same time. —**syn"chro·ni·za'tion**, *n.* —**syn'chro·nous**, *adj.*

syn'co·pate", *v.t.*, **-pated**, **-pating**. *Music.* stress the normally unaccented beat. —**syn"co·pa'tion**, *n.*

syn·di·cate, *n.*, *v.t.*, **-cated**, **-cating**. *n.* (sin'də kit) 1. organization of independent organizations for a major effort. 2. organization selling material to newspapers. —*v.t.* (sin'di kāt") 3. sell as a syndicate to newspapers. —**syn"di·ca'tion**, *n.*

syn'drome", *n.* group of symptoms of a given illness.

syn"fuel, *n.* synthetic fuel.

syn·od (sin'əd), *n.* ecclesiastical council.

syn'o·nym, *n.* different word of similar meaning. —**syn·on'y·mous**, *adj.* —**syn·on'y·mous"ly**, *adv.*

syn·op'sis, *n.*, *pl.* **-ses**. summary; brief outline.

syn'tax, *n.* arrangement of words, as in a sentence.

syn'the·sis, *n.*, *pl.* **-ses**. combination of different parts.

syn'the·size", *v.t.*, **-sized**, **-sizing**. make into or as a synthesis.

syn·thet'ic, *adj.* 1. imitating a natural material, esp. in composition. 2. pertaining to synthesis. —**syn·thet'i·cal·ly**, *adv.*

syph'i·lis, *n.* a venereal disease. —**syph"i·lit'ic**, *adj.*, *n.*

syr·inge', *n.* plunger-operated device for drawing up and ejecting fluids.

sy'rup, *n.* heavy, sweet liquid, esp. one of sugar and water. —**syr'up·y**, *adj.*

sys'tem, *n.* 1. order or method. 2. coordinated arrangement of working elements. —**sys"tem·at'ic**, *adj.* —**sys"tem·at'i·cal·ly**, *adv.*

sys'tem·a·tize", *v.t.*, **-tized**, **-tizing**. arrange according to a system.

sys·to·le (sis'tə lē), *n.* rhythmic contraction of the heart. —**sys·tol'ic**, *adj.*

T

T, t, . twentieth letter of the English alphabet.

tab, *n.* 1. extension for pulling. 2. bill of charges.

tab'by, *n.*, *pl.* **-bies**. house cat.

tab'er·nac"le, *n.* place of worship.

ta'ble, *n.*, *v.t.*, **-bled**, **-bling**. *n.* 1. piece of furniture with a broad horizontal surface. 2. orderly arrangement of data. —*v.t.* 3. postpone, as legislation. —**ta'ble·cloth"**, *n.* —**ta'ble·ware"**, *n.*

tab'leau, *n.*, *pl.* **-leaux**. picture: scene

ta·ble d'hôte (tah"bəl dōt'), *n.* fixed-price meal.

ta'ble·land", *n.* plateau.

ta'ble·spoon", *n.* spoon of one half a fluid ounce. —**ta'ble·spoon"ful**, *n.*

tab'let, *n.* 1. slab for writing or lettering. 2. pill. 3. pad of paper.

tab'loid, *n.* small-format newspaper.

ta·boo', *n.*, *pl.* **-boos**, *adj.*, *v.t.*, **-booed**, **-booing**. *n.* 1. prohibition, as by society. —*adj.* 2. prohibited. —*v.t.* 3. prohibit. Also, **ta·bu'**.

tab'u·lar, *adj.* in table form.

tab'u·late", *v.t.*, **-lated**, **-lating**. arrange in a table. —**tab"u·la'tion**, *n.* —**tab'u·la"tor**, *n.*

tac'it, *adj.* understood though not stated. —**tac'it·ly**, *adv.*

tac'i·turn", *adj.* choosing to speak little. —**tac"i·turn'i·ty**, *n.*

tack, *n.* 1. short, pointed fastener. 2. change of course. —*v.t.* 3. fasten with tacks. 4. cause to change course. —*v.i.* 5. change course.

tack'le, *n.*, *v.t.*, **-led**, **-ling**. *n.* 1. equipment. 2. system of ropes and pulleys. 3. felling, as in football, by grasping the legs. —*v.t.* 4. undertake. 5. fell with a tackle.

tack'y, *adj.*, **-ier**, **-iest**. 1. sticky. 2. *Informal.* of poor quality.

ta'co, *n.* folded and filled fried tortilla.

tact, *n.* sense of how not to offend —**tact'ful**, *adj.* —**tact'less**, *adj.*

tac'tics, *n.* 1. science of maneuvering armed forces. 2. connivance; artifice. —**tac'ti·cal**, *adj.* —**tac·ti'cian**, *n.*

tac'tile, *adj.* pertaining to touch. —**tac·til'i·ty**, *n.*

tad'pole", *n.* larva of a frog or toad.

taf'fe·ta, *n.* stiff silky fabric.

taf'fy, *n.* chewy candy.

tag, *n.*, *v.*, **tagged**, **tagging**. *n.* 1. label attached with a cord. 2. chasing game. —*v.t.* 3. apply a tag to. —*v.i.* 4. follow closely.

tail, *n.* 1. distinct hindmost extremity of an animal. 2. feature similar in shape or location, as on a vehicle. —**tail'gate"**, *n.* —**tail'light"**, *n.* —**tail'less"**, *adj.*

tail'or, *n.* 1. maker of clothes. —*v.t.* 2. make as a tailor does.

tail'spin", *n.* winding plunge of an airplane.

taint, *v.t.* 1. pollute or poison. —*n.* 2. trace of pollution.

take, *v.*, **took**, **taken**, **taking**. *v.t.* 1. carry.

takeoff

2. escort. 3. accept. 4. seize. 5. make use of. 6. select. 7. require. 8. react to. 9. assume. 10. engage in. —*v.i.* 11. be effective.

take′off″, *n.* beginning of a flight.

take′o″ver, *n.* assumption of control.

tak′ing, *adj.* 1. attractive. —*n.* 2. takings, profits.

talc, *n.* soft mineral. Also, **tal′cum.**

tale, *n.* 1. narrative. 2. piece of gossip. 3. lie. —**tale′bear″er,** *n.*

tal′ent, *n.* 1. personal ability. 2. person or persons of talent. —**tal′ent·ed,** *adj.*

tales′man, *n.* person called for jury duty.

tal′is·man, *n.* object warding off evil.

talk, *v.i.* 1. speak words. 2. confer. 3. gossip. —*v.t.* 4. persuade. —*n.* 5. conversation. 6. speech 7. gossip or rumor.

talk′a·tive, *adj.* loving to talk.

talk′ing-to″, *n. Informal.* scolding.

tall, *adj.* 1. very high. 2. of a specified height.

tal′low, *n.* solid animal fat.

tal′ly, *n., pl.* **-lies,** *v.,* **-lied, -lying.** *n.* 1. sum. 2. account; score. —*v.t.* 3. add up. —*v.i.* 4. correspond.

Tal′mud, *n.* compilation of Hebrew law. —**Tal·mud′ic,** *adj.*

tal′on, *n.* bird claw.

ta·ma′le, *n.* Mexican dish of meat, red peppers, and corn meal in corn husks.

tam′bou·rine″, *n.* shallow drumlike instrument.

tame, *adj.,* **tamer, tamest,** *v.t.,* **tamed, taming.** *adj.* 1. obedient to a master. 2. without spirit. —*v.t.* 3. make tame. —**tame′ly,** *adv.* —**tame′ness,** *n.* —**tam′a·ble, tame′a·ble,** *adj.* —**tam′er,** *n.*

tamp, *v.t.* pack or drive with gentle blows.

tam′per, *v.i.* interfere wrongly.

tan, *n., adj.,* **tanner, tannest,** *v.t.,* **tanned, tanning. n.** 1. yellow-brown. 2. suntan. —*adj.* 3. yellow-brown. —*v.t.* 4. convert into leather.

tan′a·ger, *n.* small, colorful American songbird.

tan′dem, *adv., adj.* with one behind the other.

tang, *n.* penetrating flavor. —**tang′y,** *adj.*

tan′gent, *n.* line touching a curve. —**tan·gen·tial,** *adj.* —**tan′gen·cy,** *n.*

tan″ger·ine′, *n.* type of orange.

tan′gi·ble, *adj.* 1. able to be touched. 2. able to be defined. —**tan″gi·bil′i·ty,** *n.*

tan′gle, *v.,* **-gled, -gling,** *n., v.t.* 1. intertwine in a disorderly way. —*n.* 2. tangled state.

tan′go, *n., pl.* **-gos.** South American dance.

tank, *n.* 1. container for fluids. 2. armored fighting vehicle. —**tank′ful,** *n.*

tank′ard, *n.* tall mug with a side handle.

tank′er, *n.* ship carrying liquids in bulk.

tan′ner, *n.* maker of leather. —**tan′ner·y,** *n.*

tan′ta·lize″, *v.t.,* **-lized, -lizing.** torment with gratification witheld. —**tan″tal·i·za′tion,** *n.*

tan′ta·mount″, *adj.* equivalent.

tan′trum, *n.* outburst of rage.

tap, *v.,* **tapped, tapping,** *n., v.t., v.i.* 1. strike lightly. —*v.t.* 2. draw off or upon. —*n.* 3. light blow. 4. valve or plug.

tap dance, dance with light taps of the foot. —**tap′-dance″,** *v.i.*

tape, *n., v.t.,* **taped, taping.** *n.* 1. thin, flat, long strip. —*v.t.* 2. bind with tape. 3. record on tape.

ta′per, *n.* 1. convergence of sides or edges. —*v.t., v.i.* 2. decrease steadily in thickness.

tap′es·try, *n., pl.* **-tries.** *n.* woven decorative panel.

tape′worm″, *n.* flat parasitic worm.

tap″i·o′ca, *n.* starchy substance from cassava roots.

tap′root″, *n.* single, deep-going root.

taps, *n. Military.* bugle call signifying retirement for the night and also played after military funerals.

tar, *n., v.t.,* **tarred, tarring.** *n.* 1. thick black liquid distilled from wood, coal, etc. —*v.t.* 2. coat with tar.

ta·ran′tu·la, *n.* large, hairy spider.

tar′dy, *adj.,* **-dier, -diest.** behind the expected time. —**tar′di·ly,** *adv.* —**tar′di·ness,** *n.*

tare, *n.* container weight.

tar′get, *n.* something aimed at.

tar′iff, *n.* 1. tax on imports or exports. 2. price or charge.

tar′nish, *v.t.* 1. spoil the luster of. —*v.i.* 2. become tarnished. —*n.* 3. tarnished state.

ta·rot (ta′rō), *n.* set of fortune-telling cards.

tar·pau′lin, *n.* waterproof cloth cover.

tar′pon, *n.* large west Atlantic game fish.

tar′ra·gon, *n.* seasoning of fragrant leaves.

tar·ry, *v.i.,* **-ried, -rying,** *adj. v.i.* (tar′ē) 1. linger. —*adj.* (tahr′ē) 2. covered with or suggesting tar.

tart, *adj.* 1. acid, as to the taste. —*n.* 2. small pie.

tar′tan, *n.* cloth pattern of crisscrossed bands of color.

tar′tar, *n.* 1. potassium salt used as a condiment. 2. deposit on the teeth. —**tar·tar′ic,** *adj.*

task, *n.* 1. something to be done. —*v.t.* 2. burden.

task′mas″ter, *n.* person who exacts work of others.

tas′sel, *n.* ornamental gathering of hanging threads.

taste, *v.,* **tasted, tasting,** *n., v.t.* 1. sense

with the tongue. 2. experience. —*v.i.* 3. have a specific flavor. —*n.* 4. sense operating through the tongue. 5. flavor. 6. sense of what is appropriate or seemly. 7. liking. —**tast′er**, *n.* —**taste′less**, *adj.*

taste′ful, *adj.* in good taste.

tast′y, *adj.*, **-ier**, **-iest**. good-tasting. —**tast′i·ness**, *n.*

tat′ter, *n.* 1. ragged fragment. —*v.t.* 2. reduce to tatters. —**tat′tered**, *adj.*

tat′tle, *v.i.*, **-tled**, **-tling**. gossip.

tat′tle·tale′′, *n.* betrayer of secrets.

tat·too′, *v.t.*, **-tooed**, **-tooing**, *n.*, *pl.* **-toos**. *v.t.* 1. mark with pigments under the skin. —*n.* 2. tattooed design. 3. military drum or bugle signal.

taunt, *v.t.* 1. mock. —*n.* 2. mocking remark.

taut, *adj.* tight or tense. —**taut′ly**, *adv.* —**taut′ness**, *n.*

tau·tol′o·gy, *n.*, *pl.* **-gies**. use of redundant words. —**tau′′to·log′i·cal**, *adj.*

tav′ern, *n.* public drinking place.

taw′dry, *adj.*, **-drier**, **-driest**. cheap and showy. —**taw′dri·ly**, *adv.* —**taw′dri·ness**, *n.*

taw′ny, *adj.*, **-nier**, **-niest**. tan.

tax, *n.* 1. money exacted by a government. 2. demand on resources. —*v.t.* 3. exact a tax on or from. 4. accuse. —**tax′a·ble**, *adj.* —**tax·a′tion**, *n.* —**tax′pay′′er**, *n.*

tax′i, *n.*, *pl.* **-is**, *v.i.*, **-ied**, **-iing** or **-ying**. *n.* 1. Also, **tax′i·cab′′**, hired vehicle with metered charges. —*v.i.* 2. travel by taxi. 3. move without flying, as an airplane.

tax′i·der′′my, *n.* art of simulating animals using their skins. —**tax′′i·der′mist**, *n.*

tea, *n.* 1. drink made from the dried leaves of a shrub grown in Asia. 2. drink made from other leaves and flowers. 3. meal, etc. at which tea is served. —**tea′cup′′**, *n.* —**tea′ket′′tle**, *n.* —**tea′pot′′**, *n.*

teach, *v.*, **taught**, **teaching**. *v.t.* 1. inform on a subject. 2. inform students regarding. —*v.i.* 3. be a teacher. —**teach′a·ble**, *adj.* —**teach′er**, *n.*

teak, *n.* brown East Indian hardwood.

teal, *n.*, *pl.* **teals**, **teal**. freshwater duck.

team, *n.* 1. group of animals or persons acting together. —*v.i.* 2. join or act in a team. —**team′mate′′**, *n.* —**team′work′′**, *n.*

tear, *v.*, **tore**, **torn**, **tearing**, *n.*, *v.t.* (ter) 1. pull apart by force. 2. make by piercing or rending. 3. lacerate or harass. —*v.i.* 4. be torn. 5. hurry. —*n.* 6. torn place. 7. (tēr) liquid from the weeping eye. —**tear′drop′′**, *n.* —**tear′ful**, *adj.*

tease, *v.t.*, **teased**, **teasing**. 1. bother with gentle malice. 2. comb.

tea′spoon′′, *n.* spoon holding one and a third fluid drams. —**tea′spoon·ful′′**, *n.*

teat, *n.* nipple.

tech′ni·cal, *n.* 1. pertaining to technology. 2. pertaining to technique. 3. pertaining to specific details. —**tech′ni·cal·ly**, *adv.* —**tech′′ni·cal′i·ty**, *n.* —**tech·ni′cian**, *n.*

tech·nique′, *n.* 1. working method. 2. proficiency. Also, **tech′nic**.

tech·noc′ra·cy, *n.* government by technical experts.

tech·nol′o·gy, *n.*, *pl.* **-gies**. application of science, esp. to industry. —**tech′′no·log′i·cal**, *adj.*

te′di·um, *n.* wearisome or boring quality or state. —**te′di·ous**, *adj.*

tee, *n.* stand for a golf ball being driven.

teem, *v.i.* swarm.

teen′-age′′, *adj.* pertaining to the teens as an age. Also **teen′age′′**. —**teen′ag′′er**, *n.*

teens, *n.*, *pl.* 1. years of life between 13 and 19. 2. numbers in a series between 10 and 19.

tee′ny, *adj.*, **-nier**, **-niest**. *Informal.* tiny.

teethe, *v.i.*, **teethed**, **teething**. grow teeth.

tee·to′tal·er, *n.* total abstainer from alcohol. Also, **tee·to′tal·ler**.

tel′e·cast′′, *v.t.*, **-cast** or **-casted**, **-casting**, *n.* broadcast via television. —**tel′e·cast′′er**, *n.*

tel′e·graph′′, *n.* 1. apparatus sending messages in code by electrical impulses. —*v.t.* 2. reach by telegraph. 3. send by telegraph. —**tel′′e·graph′ic**, *adj.* —**te·leg′ra·phy**, *n.* —**te·leg′ra·pher**, *n.* —**tel′e·gram′′**, *n.*

te·lep′a·thy, *n.* extra-sensory communication. —**tel′′e·path′ic**, *adj.* —**te·lep′a·thist**, *n.*

tel′e·phone′′, *n.*, *v.t.*, **-phoned**, **-phoning**. *n.* 1. device for transmitting personal spoken messages. —*v.t.* 2. reach by telephone. 3. transmit by telephone. —**tel′′e·phon′ic**, *adj.*

tel′e·scope′′, *n.*, *v.*, **-scoped**, **scoping**. *n.* 1. device for magnifying distant images. —*v.t.*, *v.i.* 2. slide lengthwise into one another. —**tel′′e·scop′ic**, *adj.*

tel′′e·type·writ′′er, *n.* telegraphic apparatus sending and receiving typed messages.

tel′e·vise′′, *v.t.*, **-vised**, **-vising**. transmit by television.

tel′e·vi′′sion, *n.* 1. method of transmitting images by radio waves and electrical impulses. 2. industry using this method. 3. television receiving set.

tell, *v.*, **told**, **telling**. *v.t.* 1. inform. 2. recount. 3. order. 4. distinguish; recognize. —*v.i.* 5. give a narrative. 6. have an effect. —**tel′ling**, *adj.* —**tel′ling·ly**, *adv.*

tel′ler, *n.* 1. narrator. 2. bank clerk.

tell′tale′′, *adj.* secret-revealing.

te·mer'i·ty, *n.* audacity.

tem'per, *n.* 1. mood. 2. anger. 3. control of one's anger. 4. hardness and flexibility, as of steel. —*v.t.* 5. moderate. 6. give toughness to.

tem'per·a, *n.* paint with egg, glue, etc.

tem'per·a·ment, *n.* natural mental disposition. —tem''per·a·men'tal, *adj.*

tem'per·ance, *n.* moderation, esp. in drinking.

tem'per·ate, *adj.* 1. moderate. 2. **Temperate**, situated between a tropic and the Arctic or Antarctic Circle.

tem'per·a·ture, *n.* 1. relative heat. 2. condition of excessive body heat.

tem'pered, *adj.* 1. modified. 2. having a specified temperament.

tem'pest, *n.* violent storm. —tem·pes'tu·ous, *adj.*

tem'plate, *n.* pattern for forming.

tem'ple, *n.* 1. place of worship. 2. area to either side of the brow.

tem'po, *n., pl.* -pos, -pi. rate of speed, as for music.

tem'po·ral, *adj.* 1. worldly, not spiritual. 2. pertaining to time.

tem'po·rar''y, *adj.* for a limited time. —tem''po·rar'i·ly, *adv.*

tem'po·rize'', *v.i.,* -rized, -rizing. evade argument or time requirements. —tem''po·ri·za'tion, *n.*

tempt, *v.t.* create an appetite or inclination in. —temp·ta'tion, *n.* —tempt'er, *fem.,* tempt'ress, *n.*

ten, *n.* nine plus one.

ten'a·ble, *adj.* defensible, as an argument. —ten''a·bil'i·ty, *n.* —ten'a·bly, *adv.*

te·na'cious, *adj.* 1. holding firmly. 2. stubborn. —te·na'cious·ly, *adv.* —te·nac'i·ty, *n.*

ten'ant, *n.* renter of building space or land. —ten'an·cy, *n.*

tend, *v.i.* 1. have a tendency. —*v.t.* 2. manage or care for.

ten'den·cy, *n., pl.* -cies. mild predominance of a certain result, preference, etc.

ten·den'tious, *adj.* expressed with a bias. —ten·den'tious·ly, *adv.*

ten'der, *adj.* 1. soft. 2. warmly affectionate. 3. feeling pain readily. —*n.* 4. person who tends. 5. railroad car for fuel. 6. something offered in payment. —*v.t.* 7. offer. —ten'der·ly, *adv.* —ten'der·ness, *n.* —ten'der·heart'ed, *adj.* —ten'der·ize'', *v.t.*

ten'der·foot'', *n., pl.* -foots, -feet. newcomer to out-of-door pursuits.

ten'der·loin'', *n.* 1. tenderest cut of beef or pork loin. 2. graft-ridden city neighborhood.

ten'don, *n.* muscle attachment.

ten'dril, *n.* attachment on a climbing plant.

ten'e·ment, *n.* 1. shabby apartment building. 2. apartment in such a building.

ten'et, *n.* doctrine accepted as truth.

tennis, *n.* game played with rackets and a ball.

ten'on, *n.* end of a rail, etc., held in the mortise of another such piece.

ten'or, *n.* 1. highest male singing voice. 2. gist.

ten'pins'', *n.* bowling game.

tense, *adj.,* tenser, tensest, *v.,* tensed, tensing, *n., adj.* 1. taut. 2. nervous; strained. —*v.t.* 3. make tense. —*v.i.* 4. become tense. —*n.* 5. *Grammar.* expression of past, present, future, etc. —tense'ly, *adv.* —ten'sion, tense'ness, ten'si·ty, *n.*

ten'sile, *adj.* capable of being stretched.

tent, *n.* 1. fabric shelter spread over poles. —*v.i.* 2. lodge in a tent.

ten'ta·cle, *n.* grasping or feeling attachment of an invertebrate.

ten'ta·tive, *adj.* made or done as a trial. —ten'ta·tive·ly, *adv.*

ten'ter·hook'', *n.* on tenterhooks, in suspense.

tenth, *adj.* 1. following nine others. —*n.* 2. one of ten equal parts.

ten'u·ous, *adj.* 1. thin. 2. insubstantial. —ten'u·ous·ly, *adv.* —ten·u'i·ty, ten'u·ous·ness, *n.*

ten'ure, *n.* 1. right to continuing employment. 2. occupation, as of public office.

te'pee, *n.* conical tent of American Indians.

tep'id, *adj.* lukewarm. —te·pid'ity, tep'id·ness, *n.* —tep'id·ly, *adv.*

te·qui'la, *n.* Mexican distilled liquor.

term, *n.* 1. word with a specific meaning. 2. period of activity. 3. terms, a. requirements of an agreement. b. basis of a relationship.

ter''min·al, *n.* 1. station at the end of a railroad, etc. 2. electrical connecting point. 3. (computers) work station for data processing. —*adj.* 4. coming at the end. 5. causing death. —ter''min·al·ly', *adv.*

ter'mi·nate'', *v.,* -nated, -nating. *v.t., v.i.* finish. —ter'mi·na·ble, *adj.* —ter''mi·na'tion, *n.*

ter''mi·nol'o·gy, *n., pl.* -gies. employment of terms.

ter'mi·nus, *n., pl.* -ni, -nuses. 1. end or limit. 2. station at the end of a railroad, etc.

ter'mite, *n.* wood-eating insect.

tern, *n.* gull-like bird.

ter'race, *n., v.t.,* -raced, -racing. *n.* 1. raised outdoor platform. —*v.t.* 2. form in terraces.

ter'ra cot'ta, earthenware material used in building and decoration.

ter·ra fir'ma, dry land.

ter·rain', *n.* land with its natural features.

ter'ra·pin, *n.* type of turtle.

ter·rar'i·um, *n., pl.* -iums, -ia. glass box for growing small plants and animals.

ter·res'tri·al, *adj.* pertaining to the earth.

ter'ri·ble, *adj.* 1. bad; poor. 2. awesome.

ter'ri·bly, *adv.* 1. in a terrible manner. 2. *Informal.* extremely.

ter'ri·er, *n.* small hunting dog.

ter·rif'ic, *adj.* 1. awesome in force. 2. *Informal.* very good.

ter'ri·fy, *v.t.,* -fied, -fying. fill with terror.

ter'ri·to'ry, *n., pl.* -ries. 1. region without full political status. 2. distinct area of land. —ter''ri·to'ri·al, *adj.*

ter'ror, *n.* 1. great fear. 2. cause of such fear.

ter'ror·ism, *n.* use of terror to enforce demands. —ter'ror·ist, *n., adj.* —ter''ror·is'tic, *adj.*

ter'ror·ize'', *v.t.,* -ized, -izing. intimidate with terror. —ter''ror·i·za'tion, *n.*

terse, *adj.,* terser, tersest. short-spoken; concise. —terse'ly, *adv.* —terse'ness, *n.*

ter'ti·ar''y, *adj.* third in order.

test, *n.* 1. act or event that reveals qualities, accomplishments, illnesses, etc. —*v.t.* 2. subject to a test. —*v.i.* 3. perform a test. —test'er, *n.*

tes'ta·ment, *n.* 1. *Law.* will. 2. part of the Bible. —tes''ta·men'ta·ry, *adj.*

tes'ta·tor, *n.* maker of a will.

tes'ti·cle, *n.* male sex gland.

tes'ti·fy'', *v.,* -fied, -fying. *v.t., v.i.* bear witness.

tes''ti·mo'ni·al, *adj.* 1. expressing gratitude. —*n.* 2. recommendation.

tes'ti·mo''ny, *n., pl.* -nies. declaration.

tes'ty, *adj.,* -tier, -tiest. irritable. —tes'ti·ly, *adv.* —tes'ti·ness, *n.*

tet'a·nus, *n.* acute spasmodic disease.

tête-a-tête (tet'ə tet'), *n.* intimate conversation.

teth'er, *n.* 1. long tying rope. —*v.t.* 2. fasten with a tether.

tet''ra·he'dron, *n., pl.* -drons, -dra. four-sided solid.

text, *n.* 1. written matter. 2. textbook. —tex'tu·al, *adj.*

text'book'', *n.* school book.

tex'tile, *n.* cloth.

tex'ture, *n.* surface quality. —tex'tur·al, *adj.*

than, *conj.* (introduces a basis of comparison).

thank, *v.t.* express gratitude to. —thank'ful, *adj.* —thank'ful·ly, *adv.* —thank'less, *adj.* —thank'less·ly, *adv.*

thanks, *n.* 1. gratitude. —*interj.* 2. I thank you.

thanks'giv''ing, *n.* 1. expression of

thanks to God. 2. **Thanksgiving**, U.S. holiday.

that, *pron., adj., pl.* those, *conj., pron., adj.* 1. the one. 2. the other. —*pron.* 3. which. —*conj.* 4. (used to introduce noun and adverbial clauses). —*adv.* 5. to such an extent.

thatch, *n.* 1. roof surface of straw, reeds, etc. —*v.t.* 2. cover with such a surface.

thaw, *v.i.* 1. warm above freezing. —*n.* 2. state of thawing.

the, *def. article.* (refers to a particular person, thing, or type).

the'a·ter, *n.* 1. place for plays, etc. 2. theatrical profession. Also, the'a·tre. —the·at'ri·cal, *adj.* —the·at'ri·cal·ly, *adv.*

theft, *n.* stealing.

their, *adj.* pertaining to them.

theirs, *pron.* something pertaining to them.

them, *pron.* (objective of they).

theme, *n.* 1. subject. 2. basic melody. —the·mat'ic, *adj.*

them·selves', *pron.* 1. (intensive and reflexive of they). 2. their true selves.

then, *adv.* 1. at that time. 2. and after. 3. in that case. —*n.* 4. that time.

thence, *adv.* from there or then.

thence''forth', *adv.* from then on. Also, thence''for'ward.

the·oc'ra·cy, *n., pl.* -cies. rule by priests. —the''o·crat'ic, *adj.*

the·ol'o·gy, *n., pl.* -gies. study of religious doctrine. —the''o·log'i·cal, *adj.* —the''o·lo'gian, *n.*

the'o·rem, *n.* something to be proved.

the'o·ry, *n., pl.* -ies. 1. statement of a possible truth. 2. untried assumption. —the''o·ret'i·cal, *adj.* —the''o·ret'i·cal·ly, *adv.* —the'o·rize,'' *v.i.* —the'orist, *n.*

the·os'o·phy, *n.* mystical religion. —the''o·soph'ic, *adj.* —the·os'o·phist, *n.*

ther''a·peu'tic, *adj.* aiding health. —ther''a·peu'tics, *n.*

ther'a·py, *n., pl.* -pies. healing process. —ther'a·pist, *n.*

there, *adv.* 1. at or to that place. 2. in that respect. 3. (used to introduce expressions of existence or nonexistence).

there·af'ter, *adv.* from then on.

there'by, *adv.* in connection with that.

there'fore'', *adj.* for this reason.

there·in', *adv.* in that.

there·of', *adv.* of that.

there·on', *adv.* 1. on that. 2. just afterward.

there·to', *adv.* to that place.

there'up·on', *adv.* 1. just afterward. 2. in consequence.

ther'mal, *adj.* pertaining to heat.

ther·mom'e·ter, *n.* heat-measuring device.

ther″mo·nu′cle·ar, *adj.* pertaining to atomic fusion at high heat.

ther′mos, *n.* heat-insulated bottle.

ther′mo·stat″, *n.* heating control.

the·sau′rus, *n., pl.* -ri, -ruses. *n.* book of synonyms and antonyms.

the′sis, *n. pl.* -ses. 1. belief to be defended. 2. research paper.

thes′pi·an, *n.* 1. actor or actress. —*adj.* 2. pertaining to the theater.

they, *n.* (plural of *he, she,* or *it.*)

thick, *n.* 1. deep from front to back. 2. dense. —thick′ly, *adv.* —thick′ness, *n.* —thick′en, *v.t., v.i.*

thick′et, *n.* thick clump of shrubbery.

thick′set′, *adj.* stout.

thick′-skinned′, *adj.* coarse; insensitive.

thief, *n., pl.* thieves. person who steals. —thiev′er·y, *n.* —thiev′ish, *adj.*

thigh, *n.* upper leg. —thigh′bone″, *n.*

thim′ble, *n.* fingertip protector.

thin, *adj.*, thinner, thinnest, *v.t.*, thinned, thinning. *adj.* 1. shallow from front to back. 2. not dense; meager. —*v.t.* 3. make thin. —thin′ly, *adv.* —thin′ness, *n.* —thin′ner, *n.*

thing, *n.* inanimate entity.

think, *v.*, thought, thinking. *v.t.* 1. have in the mind. 2. believe. —*v.i.* 3. employ the mind. —think′er, *n.*

thin′-skinned′, *adj.* sensitive to insult.

third, *adj.* 1. being number three. —*n.* 2. one of three equal parts.

thirst, *n.* desire to absorb liquids. —thirst′y, *adj.* —thirst′i·ly, *adv.*

thir·teen′, *adj., n.* ten plus three. —thir′teenth″, *adj.*

thir′ty, *adj., n.* three times ten. —thir′ti·eth, *adj., n.*

this, *pron., adj., pl.* these, *adv., pron., adj.* 1. (designating something near at hand). —*adv.* 2. to this extent.

this′tle, *n.* prickly plant.

thith′er, *adv.* to that place.

thong, *n.* small flexible strap.

tho′rax, *n., pl.* -raxes, -races. center of the body. —tho·rac′ic, *adj.*

thorn, *n.* spike of a plant stalk. —thorn′y, *adj.*

thor′ough, *adj.* complete in every detail. —thor′ough·ly, *adv.* —thor′ough·ness, *n.*

thor′ough·bred″, *adj.* pedigreed.

thor′ough·fare″, *n.* way through.

thor′ough·go′ing, *adj.* thorough.

thou, *pron. Archaic.* you.

though, *conj.* 1. despite the fact that. —*adv.* 2. however.

thought, *n.* 1. thinking process. 2. something thought. 3. something to consider. —thought′ful, *adj.* —thought′ful·ly, *adv.* —thought′ful·ness, *n.* —thought′less, *adj.* —thought′less·ly, *adv.* —thought′less·ness, *n.*

thou′sand, *adj., n.* ten times one hundred. —thou′sandth, *adj., n.*

thrash, *v.t.* beat vigorously.

thread, *n.* 1. length of spun fiber. 2. ridge on a screw. —*v.t.* 3. put a thread through.

thread′bare″, *adj.* worn thin.

threat, *n.* warning of revenge or danger.

threat′en, *v.t.* make or constitute a threat against.

three, *n.* two plus one.

thresh, *v.t.* separate from husks. —thresher, *n.*

thresh′old, *n.* doorway pavement.

thrice, *adv.* three times.

thrift, *n.* saving of money, etc.

thrift′y, *adj.*, -ier, -iest. characterized by thrift. —thrift′i·ly, *adv.*

thrill, *v.t.* 1. excite emotionally. —*v.i.* 2. be excited emotionally. —*n.* 3. act or instance of thrilling.

thrive, *v.i.*, thrived or throve, thrived or thriven, thriving. be prosperous or healthy.

throat, *n.* interior of the neck.

throb, *v.i.*, throbbed, throbbing, *n., v.i.* 1. beat, as the heart or pulse, with more than usual force. —*n.* 2. act or instance of throbbing.

throe, *n.* pang.

throm·bo′sis, *n.* clotting of blood.

throne, *n.* chair of state.

throng, *n., v.i.* crowd.

throt′tle, *n., v.t.*, -tled, -tling. *n.* 1. valve. —*v.t.* 2. squeeze and choke.

through, *prep.* 1. from end to end of. 2. by means of. —*adv.* 3. from end to end. —*adj.* 4. from end to end. 5. finished.

through·out′, *prep.* 1. in every part of. —*adv.* 2. in every part.

throw, *v.t.*, threw, thrown, *n., v.t.* 1. propel unsupported. 2. send forcefully. —*n.* 3. act or instance of throwing. 4. distance of throwing. —throw′er, *n.*

throw′back″, *n.* reversion.

thru, *prep., adv., adj.* through.

thrush, *n.* songbird.

thrust, *v.*, thrust, thrusting, *n., v.t., v.i., n.* push.

thud, *v.i.*, thudded, thudding, *n.* boom with a dull sound.

thug, *n.* hoodlum.

thumb, *n.* 1. innermost hand digit. —*v.t.* 2. move with the thumb.

thumb′tack″, *n.* broad-headed tack.

thump, *n.* 1. heavy blow. 2. sound produced by such a blow.

thun′der, *n.* 1. sound following lightning. —*v.t.* 2. say loudly or vehemently. —thun′der·ous, *adj.* —thun′der·bolt″, *n.* —thun′der·clap″, *n.* —thun′der·cloud″, *n.* —thun′der·show″er, *n.* —thun′der·storm″, *n.*

thun′der·struck″, *adj.* stupefied with

amazement. Also, **thun'der·strick"en.**

Thurs'day, *n.* fifth day of the week.

thus, *adv.* **1.** in this way. **2.** to this extent. **3.** therefore.

thwart, *v.t.* obstruct.

thy, *adj. Archaic.* your.

thyme (tīm), *n.* plant used for seasoning.

thy'roid gland, ductless gland regulating growth.

thy·self', *pron. Archaic.* yourself.

ti·ar'a, *n.* woman's decorative coronet.

tic, *n.* repeated muscular spasm.

tick, *n.* **1.** sound of a mechanical clock. **2.** bloodsucking insect. **3.** mattress cloth. —*v.i.* **4.** make a ticking sound. —**tick'er,** *n.*

tick'et, *n.* **1.** paper giving admission. **2.** list of candidates.

tick'le, *v.,* **-led, -ling.** *v.t.* **1.** cause to twitch by light stroking. **2.** amuse. —*v.i.* **3.** cause tickling.

tick'lish, *adj.* **1.** susceptible to tickling. **2.** needing caution.

tid'bit", *n.* small morsel.

tide, *n.* periodic fluctuation of sea level. —**tid'al,** *adj.* —**tide'wa"ter,** *n., adj.*

ti'dings, *n., pl.* news.

ti'dy, *adj.,* **-dier, -diest,** *v.t.,* **-died, -dying.** *adj.* **1.** orderly. —*v.t.* **2.** make orderly. —**ti'di·ness,** *n.* —**ti'di·ly,** *adv.*

tie, *v.t.,* **tied, tying,** *n., v.t.* **1.** fasten with ropes, etc. **2.** equal in scoring. —*n.* **3.** something that ties. **4.** something that prevents spreading. **5.** equal score. **6.** necktie.

tier, *n.* horizontal row.

tie'-up", *n.* stoppage.

tiff, *n.* slight quarrel.

ti'ger, *n.* large catlike African and south Asian animal. Also, *fem.,* **ti'gress.**

tight, *adj.* **1.** preventing movement. **2.** fully stretched. —*adv.* **3.** securely. —*n.* **4. tights,** tight-fitting trousers. —**tight'ly,** *adv.* —**tight'ness,** *n.* —**tight'en,** *v.t., v.i.* —**tight'-fit'ting,** *adj.*

tight'-fist'ed, *adj.* stingy.

tight'rope", *n.* taut rope for balancing acrobats.

tile, *n., v.t.,* **tiled, tiling.** *n.* **1.** thin piece of material, originally baked earth. —*v.t.* **2.** furnish with tiles. —**til'ing,** *n.*

till, *prep., conj.* **1.** until. —*v.t.* **2.** prepare for growing crops. —*n.* **3.** money drawer. —**till'age,** *n.*

til'ler, *n.* steering lever.

tilt, *v.t., v.i.* **1.** slant from an upright position. —*n.* **2.** act or instance of tilting.

tim'ber, *n.* **1.** cut wood. **2.** trees collectively. —**tim'bered,** *adj.*

tim·bre (tam'bər), *n.* distinctive quality of sound.

time, *n., v.t.,* **timed, timing.** *n.* **1.** past, present, and future. **2.** Often, **times,** period of occurrence. **3.** instance. —*prep.* **4. times,** multiplied by. —*v.t.*

5. determine the time or duration of. —**tim'er,** *n.*

time'-hon'ored, *adj.* honored after long duration.

time'less, *adj.* eternal.

time'ly, *adj.,* **-lier, -liest.** coming at the right time. —**time'li·ness,** *n.*

time'piece", *n.* clock or watch.

time'serv"er, *n.* exploiter of popular trends. —**time'serv"ing,** *n., adj.*

time'ta"ble, *n.* schedule of times.

time'worn", *adj.* worn or hackneyed by long use.

tim'id, *adj.* lacking self-confidence. —**tim'id·ly,** *adv.* —**ti·mid'i·ty,** *n.*

tim'ing, *n.* performance with regard to time.

tim'or·ous, *adj.* fearful. —**tim'or·ous·ly,** *adv.*

tim'o·thy, *n.* grass used for hay.

tim'pa·ni, *n., pl.* kettledrums. —**tim'pa·nist,** *n.*

tin, *n., v.t.,* **tinned, tinning.** *n.* **1.** white metallic element. —*v.t.* **2.** plate with tin. —**tin'foil",** *n.* —**tin'smith",** *n.*

tinc'ture, *n.* **1.** tinge. **2.** medicine in alcohol.

tin'der, *n.* dry flammable material. —**tin'der·box".**

tine, *n.* fork prong.

tinge, *n., v.t.,* **tinged, tingeing** or **tinging.** *n.* **1.** slight color or trace. —*v.t.* **2.** give a tinge to.

tin'gle, *v.i.,* **-gled, -gling.** feel a slight prickle.

tin'ker, *v.i.* work inexpertly.

tin'kle, *v.i.,* **-kled, -kling,** *n., v.i.* **1.** ring lightly. —*n.* **2.** light ringing sound.

tin'sel, *n.* metal foil.

tint, *n.* **1.** light color or shade. —*v.t.* **2.** give a tint to.

ti'ny, *adj.,* **-nier, -niest.** very small.

tip, *n., v.,* **tipped, tipping.** *n.* **1.** outermost point. **2.** reward for a service. —*v.t., v.i.* **3.** overturn. —*v.t.* **4.** give a tip to. —**tip'per,** *n.*

tip'sy, *adj.,* **-sier, -siest.** intoxicated. —**tip'si·ly,** *adv.*

tip'toe", *v.i.,* **-toed, -toing.** walk on the balls of the feet.

tip'top", *adj.* **1.** highest. **2.** best.

ti'rade, *n.* vehement speech.

tire, *v.,* **tired, tiring,** *n., v.t.* **1.** make tired. —*v.i.* **2.** become tired. —*n.* **3.** wearing surface of a wheel.

tired, *adj.* without strength because of exertion. —**tired'ly,** *adv.*

tire'less, *adj.* without becoming tired. —**tire'less·ly,** *adv.*

tire'some, *adj.* annoying; tedious. —**tire'some·ly,** *adv.* —**tire'some·ness,** *n.*

tis'sue, *n.* **1.** thin cloth or paper. **2.** organic matter.

ti'tan, *n.* giant. —**ti·tan'ic,** *adj.*

tit′il·late″, *v.t.*, **-lated**, **-lating**. excite pleasantly. —**tit″il·la′tion**, *n.*

ti′tle, *n.*, *v.t.*, **-tled**, **-tling**. *n.* **1**. formal name. **2.** right of ownership. —*v.t.* **3.** give a title to. —**ti′tled**, *adj.*

tit′ter, *v.i.*, *n.* giggle.

tit′tle, *n.* minute amount.

tit′u·lar, *adj.* **1.** having a title. **2.** in name only. —**tit′u·lar·ly**, *adv.*

tiz′zy, *n.*, *pl.* **-zies**. *Informal.* excited state.

to, *prep.* **1.** as far as. **2.** in the direction of. **3.** until; before. **4.** being supported or held by. **5.** along with. **6.** in comparison or equivalence with.

toad, *n.* froglike animal.

toad′stool″, *n.* poisonous mushroom.

toast, *n.* **1.** browned sliced bread. **2.** drink in honor of someone. —*v.t.* **3.** brown with heat. **4.** drink in honor of. —**toas′ter**, *n.* —**toast′mas″ter**, *n.*

to·bac′co, *n.*, *pl.* **-cos**. leaves prepared for smoking, chewing, etc. —**to·bac′co·nist**, *n.*

to·bog′gan, *n.* **1.** long, flat sled. —*v.i.* **2.** coast on such a sled.

to·day′, *adv.* **1.** on the present day. —*n.* **2.** present day. **3.** modern times.

tod′dle, *n.*, *v.i.*, **-dled**, **-dling**. *n.* **1.** unsteady walk. —*v.i.* **2.** walk in a toddle.

tod′dy, *n.*, *pl.* **-dies**. hot alcoholic drink.

toe, *n.* foot digit. —**toed**, *adj.* —**toe′nail″**, *n.*

to·geth′er, *adv.* one with another.

toil, *n.*, *v.i.* labor. —**toil′er**, *n.* —**toil′some**, *adj.*

toi′let, *n.* **1.** dress and grooming. **2.** place or fixture for excretion.

toil′et·ry, *n.*, *pl.* **-ries**. aid to grooming.

toils, *n.*, *pl.* snare.

to′ken, *n.* **1.** souvenir. **2.** indication. **3.** metal disk used in payment. —*adj.* **4.** intended as a gesture.

tol′er·ance, *n.* **1.** patience or understanding. **2.** permissible deviation. **3.** resistance to poison, etc. —**tol′er·ant**, *adj.*

tol′er·ate″, *v.t.*, **-ated**, **-ating**. **1.** be patient with. **2.** endure. —**tol″er·a′tion**, *n.* —**tol′er·a·ble**, *adj.* —**tol′er·a·bly**, *adv.*

toll, *n.* **1.** tariff. —*v.t.*, *v.i.* **2.** ring solemnly. —**toll′gate″**, *n.*

tom, *adj.* male.

tom′a·hawk″, *n.* American Indian ax.

to·ma′to, *n.*, *pl.* **-toes**. juicy red or yellow vegetable.

tomb, *n.* burial place. —**tomb′stone,″** *n.*

tom′boy″, *n.* boyish girl.

to·mor′row, *n.*, *adv.* day after this.

tom′-tom″, *n.* hand drum.

ton, *n.* U.S. unit of 2,000 pounds.

tone, *n.* **1.** sound of a certain pitch. **2.** shade of color. **3.** air or appearance. —**ton′al**, *adj.* —**to·nal′i·ty**, *n.* —**tone′deaf″**, *adj.*

tongs, *n.*, *pl.* pincers.

tongue, *n.* **1.** flexible licking and tasting organ in the mouth. **2.** language. **3.** projection.

tongue′-lash″ing, *n.* severe scolding.

tongue′-tied″, *adj.* rendered speechless.

ton′ic, *n.* **1.** invigorating medicine. **2.** *Music.* keynote.

to·night′, *n.*, *adv.* this night.

ton′nage, *n.* shipping, esp. in terms of cargo capacity.

ton′sil, *n.* oval growth at the back of the throat. —**ton″sil·li′tis**, *n.*

ton·so′ri·al, *adj.* pertaining to barbering.

too, *adv.* **1.** also. **2.** excessively.

tool, *n.* **1.** object for shaping, fastening, etc. **2.** something or someone used. —*v.t.* **3.** shape with a tool.

toot, *v.i.* **1.** give a shrill whistle. —*n.* **2.** shrill whistle.

tooth, *n.*, *pl.* **teeth**. **1.** hard white growth used for biting. **2.** similar object in a gear, etc. —**tooth′ache″**, *n.* —**tooth′brush″**, *n.* —**toothed**, *adj.* —**tooth′less**, *adj.* —**tooth′pick″**, *n.* —**tooth′y**, *adj.*

tooth′some, *adj.* tasty.

top, *n.*, *v.t.*, **topped**, **topping**. *n.* **1.** uppermost point or part. **2.** spinning toy. —*v.t.* **3.** put a top on. **4.** remove a top from. **5.** surpass.

to′paz, *n.* yellow gem.

top′coat″, *n.* light overcoat.

top′-draw′er, *Informal.* first-rate. Also, **top′-flight′, top′-notch′.**

top′-heav″y, *adj.* liable to tip.

top′ic, *n.* subject of discussion. —**top′i·cal**, *adj.*

top′most″, *adj.* at the very top.

top′notch′, *adj.* *Informal.* among the best.

to·pog′ra·phy, *n.*, *pl.* **-phies**. **1.** study of the earth's surface. **2.** terrain. —**top″o·graph′i·cal, top″o·graph′ic**, *adj.* —**to·pog′ra·pher**, *n.*

top′ping, *n.* something put on top.

top′ple, *v.*, **-pled**, **-pling**. *v.t.*, *v.i.* overturn.

top′sail″, *n.* *Nautical.* second sail up.

top′soil″, *n.* fertile surface soil.

top′sy-tur′vy, *adv.*, *adj.* in disorder.

To′rah, *n.* Hebrew scriptures.

torch, *n.* flame-bearing object. —**torch′light″**, *n.*, *adj.*

tor′e·a·dor″, *n.* bullfighter.

tor·ment, *v.t.* (tor ment′) **1.** harass or torture. —*n.* (tor′ment) **2.** tormented state. **3.** something that torments. —**tor·men′tor, tor·men′ter**, *n.*

tor·na′do, *n.*, *pl.* **-does**, **-dos**. violent whirlwind.

tor·pe′do, *n.*, *pl.* **-does**, *v.t.*, **-does**, **-doing**. *n.* **1.** explosive water projectile. —*v.t.* **2.** hit with a torpedo.

tor'pid, *adj.* without energy. —**tor'pid·ly,** *adv.* —**tor'por, tor·pid'i·ty,** *n.*

torque, *n.* twisting force.

tor'rent, *n.* rush of fluid. —**tor·ren'tial,** *adj.*

tor'rid, *adj.* 1. hot. 2. **Torrid,** between the tropics on either side of the equator.

tor'sion, *n.* twisting. —**tor'sion·al,** *adj.*

tor'so, *n., pl.* -sos. trunk of the human body.

tort, *n. Law.* basis of a civil suit.

tor·til·la (tōr tē'ya), *n.* flat Mexican cake of corn meal.

tor'toise, *n.* land turtle.

tor'tu·ous, *adj.* winding; involved. —**tor' tu·ous·ly,** *adv.* —**tor'tu·ous·ness,** *n.*

tor'ture, *n., v.t.,* -tured, -turing. *n.* 1. application of severe pain, etc. —*v.t.* 2. subject to torture. —**tor'tur·er,** *n.*

toss, *v.t.* 1. throw lightly. 2. jerk upward. —*n.* 3. act or instance of tossing.

toss'up'', *n.* even chance.

tot, *n.* small child.

to'tal, *adj.* 1. being a sum. 2. complete. —*n.* 3. sum. —**to'tal·ly,** *adv.* —**to·tal' i·ty,** *n.*

to·tal''i·tar'i·an·ism, *n.* absolute control by one political group. —**to·tal''i· tar'i·an,** *n., adj.*

tote, *v.t.,* toted, toting. carry.

to'tem, *n.* natural object used as a clan symbol. —**to·tem'ic,** *adj.*

tot'ter, *v.i.* walk unsteadily.

touch, *v.t.* 1. tap, pat, or feel. 2. move emotionally. —*n.* 3. act or instance of touching. 4. distinctive manner. 5. slight amount. —**touch'ing,** *adj.* —**touch'ing·ly,** *adv.*

touch and go, precarious situation.

touch'down, *n.* football score.

touched, *adj.* 1. emotionally moved. 2. insane.

touch'stone'', *n.* test of genuineness or worth.

touch'y, *adj.,* -ier, -iest. readily hurt or annoyed. —**touch'i·ness,** *n.*

tough, *adj.* 1. resistant to injury. 2. enduring. 3. brutal. 4. difficult. —**tough' ness,** *n.* —**tough'en,** *v.t., v.i.*

tou·pee (tōō pā'), *n.* small wig worn esp. by men.

tour, *n.* 1. trip with many stops. —*v.t.* 2. make a tour through.

tour de force, *n., pl.* **tours de force.** example of high skill.

tour'ist, *n.* person on a pleasure tour. —**tour'ism,** *n.*

tour'na·ment, *n.* 1. knightly contest. 2. series of athletic contests.

tour'ni·quet, *n.* twisted device to stop bleeding.

tou'sle, *v.t.,* -sled, -sling. muss.

tout, *Informal. v.t.* 1. praise highly. 2. sell bets. —*n.* 3. person who touts.

tow, *v.t.* 1. pull with a line. —*n.* 2. act or

instance of towing. —**tow'line'', tow' rope'',** *n.* —**tow'path'',** *n.*

to·ward', *prep.* in the direction of. Also, **to·wards'.**

tow'el, *n.* drying cloth.

tow'er, *n.* 1. tall construction. —*v.i.* 2. stand high.

tow'er·ing, *adj.* 1. standing high. 2. violent.

town, *n.* 1. large community. 2. urban center. —**towns'man,** *n.* —**towns'-peo'' ple,** *n., pl.*

town'ship'', *n.* unit of local government.

tox'ic, *adj.* poisonous. —**tox·ic'i·ty,** *n.*

tox''i·col'o·gy, *n.* study of poisons. —**tox''i·col'o·gist,** *n.*

tox'in, *n.* poison from organisms.

toy, *n.* 1. something to play with. —*v.i.* 2. play; trifle.

trace, *n., v.t.,* **traced, tracing.** *n.* 1. faint sign or trail. —*v.t.* 2. follow the trail of. 3. copy by following the lines of. —**trace'a·ble,** *adj.* —**trac'er,** *n.* —**trac' ing,** *n.*

trac'er·y, *n., pl.* -ies. decorative frame in a window.

track, *n.* 1. trail or trace. 2. pair of rails, etc. used as a guide. —*v.t.* 3. follow or trace. —**track'less,** *adj.*

tract, *n.* 1. expanse of land. 2. series of bodily organs. 3. religious leaflet.

trac'ta·ble, *adj.* readily managed. —**trac' ta·bly,** *adv.* —**trac''ta·bil'i·ty,** *n.*

trac'tion, *n.* 1. pulling effort. 2. friction between a foot or wheel and a surface.

trac'tor, *n.* pulling vehicle.

trade, *v.,* **traded, trading,** *n., v.t.* 1. exchange. —*v.i.* 2. have business dealings. 3. make an exchange. —*n.* 4. buying and selling. 5. skilled occupation. 6. swap. —**trad'er,** *n.*

trade'-in'', *n.* return of a used object in partial payment for a new one.

trade'mark'', *n.* symbol of a business or product.

trade'off'', *n.* sacrifice of one advantage for another.

trades'man, *n.* 1. skilled worker. 2. merchant.

trade wind, tropical wind blowing toward the equator.

tra·di'tion, *n.* long-accepted custom or belief. —**tra·di'tion·al,** *adj.* —**tra·di' tion·al·ly,** *adv.* —**tra·di'tion·al·ist,** *n., adj.*

tra·duce', *v.t.,* -duced, -ducing. slander.

traf'fic, *n., v.i.,* -ficked, -ficking. *n.* 1. movement along roadways. 2. commerce. —*v.i.* 3. have dealings. —**traf' fick·er,** *n.*

trag'e·dy, *n., pl.* -ies. 1. drama ending unhappily. 2. disastrous event. —**tra· ge'di·an,** *n., fem.,* **tra·ge'di·enne''.** —**trag'ic, trag'i·cal,** *adj.* —**trag'i·cal· ly,** *adv.*

trail, *n.* **1.** mark left in passing. **2.** route, esp. in wild country. —*v.t.* **3.** trace. **4.** drag. —*v.i.* **5.** drag or grow along the ground.

trail'er, *n.* vehicle pulled by another.

train, *n.* **1.** string of railroad cars. **2.** trailing skirt or cape. **3.** connected series. **4.** procession. —*v.t.* **5.** educate for a purpose. **6.** exercise for sports. —**train'ee',** *n.* —**train'er,** *n.* —**train'ing,** *n.*

traipse, *v.i.* traipsed, traipsing. *Informal.* walk.

trait, *n.* distinctive quality.

trai'tor, *n.* betrayer of one's country. —**trai'tor·ous,** *adj.*

tra·jec'to·ry, *n., pl.* -ries. path of a missile.

tram, *n.* car on rails.

tram'mel, *n.* **1.** Usually trammels, hindrance or restraint. —*v.t.* **2.** hinder or restrain.

tramp, *v.i.* **1.** walk heavily. **2.** travel on foot. —*n.* **3.** vagrant. **4.** hike. **5.** unscheduled freighter.

tram'ple, *v.,* -pled, -pling. *v.i.* **1.** tread heavily. —*v.t.* **2.** crush under foot.

tram·po·line (tram′pə lēn″), *n.* stretched horizontal sheet used by tumblers.

trance, *n.* sleeplike or abstracted state.

tran'quil, *adj.* serene; relaxed. —**tran′quil·ly,** *adv.* —**tran·quil'i·ty,** *n.* —**tran'quil·ize″,** *v.t.* —**tran'quil·iz″er,** *n.*

trans·act', *v.t.* complete, as a business deal. —**trans·ac'tion,** *n.* —**trans·ac'tor,** *n.*

trans″at·lan'tic, *adj.* **1.** from across the Atlantic Ocean. **2.** across the Atlantic Ocean.

tran·scend', *v.t.* **1.** go outside the limits of. **2.** surpass. —**tran·scend'ent,** *adj.*

tran″scen·den'tal, *adj.* beyond the limits of the apparent world. —**tran″scen·den'tal·ism,** *n.* —**tran″scen·den'tal·ist,** *n., adj.*

trans″con·ti·nen'tal, *adj.* across a continent.

tran·scribe', *v.t.,* -scribed, -scribing. copy elsewhere or in another medium.

tran'script, *n.* copy of a document.

tran·scrip'tion, *n.* **1.** transcript. **2.** arrangement of a musical score. **3.** radio or television recording.

tran'sept, *n.* arm of a church crossing the nave.

trans·fer', *v.,* -ferred, -ferring, *n., v.t., v.i.* (trans fər′) **1.** move to another place. —*n.* (trans′fər) **2.** act or instance of transferring. **3.** authorization for transferring. —**trans·fer'a·ble,** *adj.* —**trans·fer'ence,** *n.*

trans·fig'ure, *v.t.,* -ured, -uring. make glorious. —**trans·fig″u·ra'tion,** *n.*

trans·fix', *v.t.* **1.** pierce. **2.** halt in one's tracks.

trans·form', *v.t., v.i.* change in nature.

—**trans″for·ma'tion,** *n.* —**trans·form'er,** *n.*

trans·fuse', *v.t.,* -fused, -fusing. **1.** instill. **2.** admit to a blood vessel. —**trans·fu'sion,** *n.*

trans·gress', *v.t.* **1.** sin against. **2.** go beyond. —**trans·gres'sion,** *n.* —**trans·gres'sor,** *n.*

tran'sient, *adj.* **1.** temporary. —*n.* **2.** temporary lodger. —**tran'sient·ly,** *adv.* —**tran'science, tran'scien·cy,** *n.*

tran·sis'tor, *n.* device controlling electrical current flow. —**tran·sis'tor·ize″,** *v.t.*

tran'sit, *n.* **1.** movement from place to place. **2.** public transportation.

tran·si'tion, *n.* gradual change of nature or condition. —**tran·si'tion·al,** *adj.*

tran'si·tive, *adj. Grammar.* taking a direct object.

tran'si·to″ry, *adj.* impermanent. —**tran′si·to″ri·ness,** *n.*

trans·late', *v.t.,* -lated, -lating. **1.** alter in language. **2.** alter in condition. —**trans·la'tion,** *n.* —**trans·la'tor,** *n.* —**trans·lat'a·ble,** *adj.*

trans·lit'er·ate″, *v.t.,* -ated, -ating. put into a different alphabet, etc. —**trans·lit″er·a'tion,** *n.*

trans·lu'cent, *adj.* passing light but not images. —**trans·lu'cence, trans·lu'cen·cy,** *n.*

trans·mi'grate, *v.i.,* -grated, -grating. enter a new body after death. —**trans″mi·gra'tion,** *n.*

trans·mis'sion, *n.* **1.** act or instance of transmitting. **2.** something transmitted. **3.** gear assembly.

trans·mit', *v.t.,* -mitted, -mitting. **1.** convey through a medium. **2.** send out in radio waves. **3.** hand down, as to a new generation. —**trans·mit'tal, trans·mit'tance,** *n.* —**trans·mit'ti·ble, trans·mit'ta·ble,** *adj.* —**trans·mit'ter,** *n.*

trans·mute', *v.t.,* -muted, -muting. alter in nature. —**trans″mu·ta'tion,** *n.* —**trans·mut'a·ble,** *adj.*

trans″o·ce·an'ic, *adj.* across the ocean.

tran'som, *n.* **1.** crosspiece. **2.** window over a door.

trans″pa·cif'ic, *adj.* **1.** from across the Pacific Ocean. **2.** across the Pacific Ocean.

trans·par'ent, *adj.* **1.** passing light and images. **2.** obvious. —**trans·par'ent·ly,** *adv.* —**trans·par'en·cy,** *n.*

tran·spire', *v.i.,* -spired, -spiring. **1.** become known. **2.** *Informal.* occur. —**tran″spi·ra'tion,** *n.*

trans·plant', *v.t.* **1.** plant in a new place. **2.** graft surgically. —*n.* **3.** act or instance of transplanting. —**trans″plan·ta'tion,** *n.*

trans·port', *v.t.* (trans port′) **1.** carry. —*n.* (trans′port) **2.** transportation. **3.**

state of rapture. **4.** carrier for troops.
—**trans″por·ta′tion,** *n.*

trans·pose′, *v.,* **-posed, -posing.** *v.t., v.i.*
change in order or position. —**trans″
po·si′tion,** *n.*

trans·sex′u·al, *n.* person who identifies
with the opposite sex.

trans·ship′, *v.t.,* **-shipped, -shipping.** put
on a new conveyance. —**trans·ship′
ment,** *n.*

trans·verse′, *adj.* crosswise. —**trans·
verse′ly,** *adv.*

trans·ves′tite, *n.* dresser in clothes for
the opposite sex.

trap, *n., v.t.,* **trapped, trapping.** *n.* **1.** device for catching animals. **2.** trick for
detection or capture. —*v.t.* **3.** catch. **4.**
adorn. —**trap′per,** *n.* —**trap′pings,** *n.,*
pl.

trap′door″, *n.* horizontal door.

tra·peze′, *n.* swing with a bar.

trap′e·zoid″, *n.* four-sided figure with
two parallel sides. —**trap″e·zoi′dal,**
adj.

trash, *n.* discarded matter. —**trash′y,** *adj.*

trau′ma, *n., pl.* **-mas, -mata.** bodily or
emotional shock. —**trau·mat′ic,** *adj.*
—**trau′ma·tize″,** *v.t.*

tra·vail′, *n.* agony.

trav′el, *v.i.,* **-eled** or **-elled, -eling** or
-elling, *n.* *v.i.* **1.** go on a journey. —*n.*
2. traveling, esp. for pleasure. —**trav′
el·er, trav′el·ler,** *n.*

trav·erse′, *v.t.,* **-ersed, -ersing.** pass
across.

trav′es·ty, *n., pl.* **-ties,** *v.t.,* **-tied, -tying.**
n. **1.** mocking imitation. —*v.t.* **2.** make
a travesty of.

trawl, *n.* **1.** dragged fish net. —*v.i.* **2.** use
a trawl. —**trawl′er,** *n.*

tray, *n.* shallow, broad receptacle.

treach′er·y, *n., pl.* **-ies.** betrayal of trust.
—**treach′er·ous,** *adj.*

tread, *v.,* **trod, trodden, treading.** *v.i.* **1.**
walk deliberately. —*v.t.* **2.** press,
make, etc. by treading. —*n.* **3.** manner
of treading. **4.** step. **5.** surface of a
wheel, tire, etc. that touches the
ground.

trea′dle, *n.* foot-operated lever.

trea′son, *n.* betrayal of one's country.
—**trea′son·a·ble, trea′son·ous,** *adj.*

treas′ure, *n., v.t.,* **-ured, -uring.** *n.* **1.** precious possession. —*v.t.* **2.** regard as a
treasure.

treas′ur·er, *n.* handler of funds.

treas′ure-trove″, *n.* discovered treasure.

treas′ur·y, *n., pl.* **-ies.** department or
place for storing money.

treat, *v.t.* **1.** act toward as specified. **2.**
handle as specified. **3.** give medical
care to. **4.** have as a guest. —*n.* **5.**
something offered a guest. **6.** source of
pleasure. —**treat′ment,** *n.*

trea′tise, *n.* paper on a subject.

trea′ty, *n., pl.* **-ties.** agreement between
nations.

tre′ble, *adj., v.t.,* **-bled, -bling.** *adj.* **1.** triple. **2.** high-pitched. —*v.t.* **3.** multiply
by three. —**treb′ly,** *adv.*

tree, *n., v.t.,* **treed, treeing.** *n.* **1.** tall plant
with a woody stem and branches.
—*v.t.* **2.** chase up a tree. —**tree′less,**
adj.

trek, *v.i.,* **trekked, trekking.** *n.* *v.i.* **1.**
travel with difficulty. —*n.* **2.** long, difficult journey.

trel′lis, *n.* frame for climbing plants.

trem′ble, *v.i.,* **-bled, -bling. 1.** shiver. **2.**
be in fear or awe.

tre·men′dous, *adj.* huge. —**tre·men′
dous·ly,** *adv.*

trem′o·lo″, *n., pl.* **-os.** wavering of a musical tone.

trem′or, *n.* quiver.

trem′u·lous, *adj.* timid.

trench, *n.* deep, narrow ditch.

trench′ant, *adj.* incisive.

trend, *n.* current style or tendency.

trep″i·da′tion, *n.* fear and doubt.

tres′pass, *v.i.* **1.** enter property without
right. —*n.* **2.** sin. —**tres′pas·ser,** *n.*

tress, *n.* lock of hair.

tres′tle, *n.* **1.** transverse frame. **2.** viaduct
on framed towers.

tri′ad, *n.* group of three.

tri′al, *n.* **1.** test, as for value. **2.** annoyance or source of annoyance. **3.** examination in a law court.

tri·an′gle, *n.* three-sided figure. —**tri·an′
gu·lar,** *adj.*

tribe, *n.* group of related persons under
one leader. —**trib′al,** *adj.* —**tribes′
man,** *n.*

trib″u·la′tion, *n.* distress.

tri·bu′nal, *n.* court of justice.

trib′une, *n.* speaking platform.

trib′u·tar″y, *adj., n., pl.* **-ies.** *adj.* **1.**
paying tribute. **2.** flowing into a larger
stream. —*n.* **3.** tributary stream or river.

trib′ute, *n.* **1.** compulsory payment. **2.** expression of gratitude or honor.

trice, *n.* instant.

trick, *n.* **1.** cunning or treacherous act.
—*v.t.* **2.** cheat. —**trick′er·y,** *n.* —**trick′
ster,** *n.*

trick′le, *v.i.,* **-led, -ling.** flow in a thin,
slow stream.

trick′y, *adj.,* **-ier, -iest. 1.** treacherous;
wily. **2.** challenging the skill or cunning.

tri′cy·cle, *n.* three-wheeled vehicle.

tri′dent, *n.* three-pronged spear.

tried, *adj.* proved, esp. as trustworthy.

tri′fle, *n., v.i.,* **-fled, -fling.** *n.* **1.** something of little importance. —*v.i.* **2.** talk
or act frivolously. —**tri′fler,** *n.*

tri′fling, *adj.* unimportant; insignificant.

tri′fo′′cals, *n.* spectacles with three focuses.

trig′ger, *n.* 1. lever for firing a gun. —*v.t.* 2. precipitate; cause to happen.

trig′′o·nom′e·try, *n.* mathematics based on the triangle. —**trig′′o·no·met′ric**, *adj.*

trill, *n.* 1. high, warbling sound. —*v.i.* 2. emit a trill.

tril′lion, *n.* one thousand billion.

tril′o·gy, *n., pl.* **-gies.** trio of related novels, etc.

trim, *v.t.,* **trimmed, trimming,** *n., adj.,* **trimmer, trimmest.** *v.t.* 1. make neat. 2. decorate. 3. balance. —*n.* 4. good condition. —*adj.* 5. neat. —**trim′ly**, *adv.* —**trim′mer**, *n.*

tri·mes′ter, *n.* third of an academic year.

trim′ming, *n.* something added, as a decoration.

trin′i·ty, *n., pl.* **-ties.** 1. set of three. 2. **the Trinity,** God as Father, Son, and Holy Spirit.

trin′ket, *n.* small ornament.

tri·o (trē′ō), *n., pl.* **-os.** group of three.

trip, *v.,* **tripped, tripping,** *n.* *v.i.* 1. stumble and lose balance. —*v.t.* 2. cause to stumble. 3. set in motion. —*n.* 4. act or instance of tripping. 5. journey.

tri·par′tite, *adj.* in three parts.

tripe, *n.* 1. edible part of an animal stomach. 2. *Informal.* drivel.

trip′ham′′mer, *n.* heavy mechanical hammer.

tri′ple, *adj., v.,* **-pled, -pling.** *adj.* 1. in three parts. 2. three times normal size. —*v.t., v.i.* 3. multiply three times. —**tri′ply**, *adv.*

tri′plet, *n.* one of three siblings born at the same time.

trip′li·cate, *n.* threefold form.

tri′pod, *n.* three-legged support.

tri·sect′, *v.t.* divide in three. —**tri·sec′tion**, *n.*

trite, *adj.,* **triter, tritest.** overly familiar. —**trite′ly**, *adv.* —**trite′ness**, *n.*

tri′umph, *n.* 1. victory. 2. delight in victory. —*v.i.* 3. be victorious. —**tri·um′phal**, *adj.* —**tri·um′phant**, *adj.*

tri·um′vi·rate, *n.* trio in power.

triv′et, *n.* stand for hot things.

triv′i·a, *n., pl.* trivial things.

triv′i·al, *adj.* petty and unimportant. —**triv′′i·al′i·ty**, *n.* —**triv′i·al·ly**, *adv.*

troll, *n.* supernatural cave dweller.

trol′ley, *n., pl.* **-leys.** 1. raised structure for collecting electricity. 2. streetcar with such a structure. 3. wheeled container.

trom·bone′, *n.* brass musical instrument. —**trom·bon′ist**, *n.*

troop, *n.* 1. uniformed group. —*v.i.* 2. move in a group. —**troop′er**, *n.*

tro′phy, *n., pl.* **-phies.** memento of victory.

trop′ic, *n.* 1. boundary of the Torrid Zone. 2. **tropics,** Torrid Zone or nearby areas. —*adj.* 3. Also, **trop′i·cal,** pertaining to the Torrid Zone.

tro′pism, *n. Biology.* response, as in growth, to stimuli.

trot, *v.i.,* **trotted, trotting,** *n.* *v.i.* 1. run at moderate speed. —*n.* 2. trotting gait. —**trot′ter**, *n.*

trou′ba·dour′′, *n.* medieval singer.

trou′ble, *n., v.,* **-bled, -bling.** *n.* 1. worry or exertion. 2. source of these. —*v.t.* 3. cause trouble to. —*v.i.* 4. go to trouble. —**trou′ble·some**, *adj.* —**trou′ble·mak′′er**, *n.*

trough, *n.* long, open container.

trounce, *v.t.,* **trounced, trouncing.** beat.

troupe, *n.* group of performers. —**troup′er**, *n.*

trou′sers, *n., pl.* pants.

trous′seau, *n., pl.* **-seaux, -seaus.** bride's clothing, etc.

trout, *n., pl.* **trout, trouts.** edible freshwater fish.

trow′el, *n.* spreading or scooping hand tool.

troy, *adj.* pertaining to a jeweler's weight with a twelve-ounce pound.

tru′ant, *n.* unauthorized absentee from school. —**tru′an·cy**, *n.*

truce, *n.* temporary suspension of hostilities.

truck, *n.* 1. freight motor vehicle. 2. hand cart for loads. —*v.t.* 3. carry by truck. —**truck′er**, *n.*

truck′le, *v.i.,* **-led, -ling.** be servilely submissive.

truc′u·lent, *adj.* fierce. —**truc′u·lent·ly**, *adv.* —**truc′u·lence**, *n.*

trudge, *v.i.,* **trudged, trudging,** *n.* *v.i.* 1. walk laboriously. —*n.* 2. laborious walk.

true, *adj.,* **truer, truest.** *adj.* 1. according with truth. 2. faithful. —**tru′ly**, *adv.* —**true′ness**, *n.*

tru′ism, *n.* tritely true statement.

trump, *n.* highest-ranking card.

trump′er·y, *n., pl.* **-ies.** worthlessly pretentious things.

trum′pet, *n.* brass musical wind instrument. —**trum′pet·er**, *n.*

trun′cate, *v.t.,* **-cated, -cating.** remove part of. —**trun·ca′tion**, *n.*

trun′cheon, *n.* club.

trun′dle, *v.t.,* **-dled, -dling.** roll out or along.

trunk, *n.* 1. large piece of luggage. 2. main stem of a tree. 3. body apart from head and limbs.

truss, *n.* 1. frame of triangular parts. 2. support for the ruptured. —*v.t.* 3. bind up. 4. support with a truss.

trust, *n.* 1. reliance; faith. 2. custody. 3. monopolistic combination. —*v.t.* 4. have reliance or faith in. —**trust'ful,** **trust'ing,** *adj.* —**trust'worth''y, trust'y,** *adj.*

trus·tee', *n.* person to whom property is entrusted. —**trus·tee'ship,** *n.*

trust'y, *adj.,* **-ier, -iest.** trustworthy.

truth, *n.* 1. that which is actually so. 2. accuracy. —**truth'ful,** *adj.* —**truth'ful·ly,** *adv.* —**truth'ful·ness,** *n.*

try, *v.t.,* **tried, trying.** *n. v.t.* 1. attempt. 2. test. 3. examine in a court of law. 4. annoy or afflict. —*n.* 5. attempt or test. —**try'ing,** *adj.*

try'out'', *n. Informal.* test operation.

tryst, *n.* lovers' appointment.

tsar, *n.* Slavic emperor.

tub, *n.* broad, deep vessel.

tu'ba, *n.* large brass wind musical instrument.

tub'by, *adj.,* **-bier, -biest.** chubby.

tube, *n.* hollow cylinder. —**tub'ing,** *n.* —**tub'u·lar,** *adj.*

tu'ber, *n.* swelling part of an underground plant stem. —**tu'ber·ous,** *adj.*

tu·ber''cu·lo'sis, *n.* illness with swelling lesions. —**tu·ber'cu·lar, tu·ber'cu·lous,** *adj.*

tuck, *v.t.* insert by pressing.

Tues'day, *n.* third day of the week.

tuft, *n.* cluster of fibers, threads, etc.

tug, *v.t.,* **tugged, tugging,** *n. v.t.* 1. pull forcefully. —*n.* 2. act or instance of tugging. —**tug'boat'',** *n.*

tu·i'tion, *n.* fee for teaching.

tu'lip, *n.* plant with a cup-shaped flower.

tum'ble, *v.i.,* **-bled, -bling.** 1. fall or roll helplessly. 2. perform acrobatics on a flat surface.

tum'bler, *n.* 1. drinking glass. 2. acrobat who tumbles.

tu'mid, *adj.* swollen.

tum'my, *n., pl.* **-mies.** *Informal.* stomach

tu'mor, *n.* abnormal growth.

tu'mult, *n.* commotion. —**tu·mul'tu·ous,** *adj.*

tun, *n.* large cask.

tu'na, *n., pl.* **-na, -nas.** large ocean fish.

tun'dra, *n.* barren Arctic plain.

tune, *n., v.t.,* **tuned, tuning.** *n.* 1. melody. 2. harmony. —*v.t.* 3. put in tune. —**tune'ful,** *adj.* —**tune'less,** *adj.*

tun'ic, *adj.* jacket, often belted.

tun'nel, *n., v.i.,* **-neled, -neling.** *n.* 1. route cut underground. —*v.i.* 2. dig a route.

tur'ban, *n.* headdress of wound cloth.

tur'bid, *adj.* cloudy or muddy. —**tur·bid'i·ty,** *n.*

tur'bine, *n.* rotary engine driven by the passing of a fluid.

tur'bo·jet'', *n.* jet engine using turbine-compressed air.

tur'bu·lent, *adj.* in disturbed motion. —**tur'bu·lence,** *n.*

tu·reen', *n.* covered soup container.

turf, *n.* earth held by grass roots. —**turf'y,** *adj.*

tur'gid, *adj.* pompously or excessively worded. —**tur'gid·ly,** *adv.* —**tur·gid'i·ty, tur·gid·ness,** *n.*

tur'key, *n.* large North American fowl.

tur'moil, *n.* confused activity.

turn, *v.t., v.i.* 1. change in direction. 2. change in nature. —*n.* 3. curve. 4. loop. 5. place in a sequence. 6. act toward another. —**turn'ing,** *n.*

turn'a·bout'', *n.* reversal of conditions.

turn'coat'', *n.* renegade.

tur'nip, *n.* edible root.

turn'out'', *n.* attendance at a meeting.

turn'o''ver, *n.* 1. rate of sale, replacement, etc. 2. baked dish of crust folded over filling.

turn'pike'', *n.* toll road.

turn'stile'', *n.* rotating gate.

turn'ta''ble, *n.* rotating platform.

tur'pen·tine'', *n.* oil from coniferous trees.

tur'pi·tude'', *n.* vileness.

tur'quoise, *n.* greenish-blue stone.

tur'ret, *n.* 1. small tower. 2. housing for cannon.

tur'tle, *n.* shell-encased reptile.

tusk, *n.* long, projecting tooth.

tus'sle, *n., v.i.,* **-sled, -sling.** struggle.

tu'te·lage, *n.* 1. guardianship. 2. education. —**tu'te·lar, tu'te·lar''y,** *adj.*

tu'tor, *n.* 1. private teacher. —*v.t.* 2. teach privately. —**tu·to'ri·al,** *adj., n.*

tux·e'do, *n.* semiformal evening suit.

TV, television.

twang, *n.* 1. sound of a plucked string. 2. nasal accent.

tweak, *v.t., n.* pinch with a twist.

tweed, *n.* rough woolen cloth.

tweet, *n., v.i.* chirp.

tweez'ers, *n., pl.* small pincers.

twelve, *n., adj.* ten plus two. —**twelfth,** *adj., n.*

twen'ty, *adj., n.* two times ten. —**twen'ti·eth,** *adj.*

twice, *adv.* two times.

twid'dle, *v.t.,* **-dled, -dling.** play with absently.

twig, *n.* tiny plant branch.

twi'light'', *n.* half-light, as between day and night.

twill, *n.* cloth with a diagonal pattern.

twin, *n.* 1. one of two siblings born at the same time. 2. exact match. —*adj.* 3. matching another or each other exactly.

twine, *n., v.,* **twined, twining.** *n.* 1. string. —*v.t., v.i.* 2. twist together.

twinge, *n.* stab of pain.

twin′kle, *v.i.,* **-kled, -kling,** *n.* *v.i.* 1. gleam intermittently. 2. show amusement. —*n.* 3. act or instance of twinkling.

twin′kling, *n.* instant.

twirl, *v.t., v.i.* rotate rapidly.

twist, *v.t.* 1. wind around, rotate, or bend into a helical form. 2. distort the actuality of. —*v.i.* 3. assume a twisted form. 4. squirm. —*n.* 5. act or instance of twisting.

twit, *v.t.,* **twitted, twitting.** address teasingly.

twitch, *v.i.* 1. jerk spasmodically. 2. pluck. —*n.* 3. spasmodic jerk.

twit′ter, *v.i.* chirp rapidly.

two, *n., adj.* one plus one. **—two′fold″,** *adj., adv.* **—two′some,** *n.*

two′-edged′, *adj.* interpretable two ways.

ty·coon′, *n.* man of great wealth and power.

type, *n., v.t.,* **typed, typing.** *n.* 1. variety; sort. 2. reproducible characters used in printing. —*v.t.* 3. classify. 4. produce with a typewriter.

type′writ″er, *n.* machine for producing letters by mechanical means.

ty′phoid, *n.* acute infectious disease.

ty·phoon′, *n.* violent storm of the west Pacific Ocean.

ty′phus, *n.* acute infectious disease.

typ′i·cal, *n.* 1. representative of a type. 2. customary. **—typ′i·cal·ly,** *adv.*

typ′i·fy″, *v.t.,* **-fied, -fying.** be typical of

typ′ist, *n.* user of typewriters.

ty·pog′ra·phy, *n.* art of composing and printing with type. **—ty″po·graph′ic,** *adj.* **—ty·pog′ra·pher,** *n.*

ty′rant, *n.* harsh, arbitrary ruler. **—tyr′an·ny,** *n.* **—ty·ran′ni·cal,** *adj.* **—tyr′an·nize″,** *v.i., v.t.*

ty′ro, *n., pl.* **-ros.** beginner; novice.

U

U, u, *n.* twenty-first letter of the English alphabet.

u·biq′ui·ty, *n.* presence everywhere simultaneously. **—u·biq′ui·tous,** *adj.*

ud′der, *n.* mammary gland of a cow.

ug′ly, *adj.,* **-lier, -liest.** 1. unattractive. 2. discomfiting; difficult. **—ug′li·ness,** *n.*

u·kase′, *n.* arbitrary command.

ul′cer, *n.* open break in tissue. **—ul′cer·ous,** *adj.* **—ul′cer·ate″,** *v.i., v.t.*

ul′na, *n.* large bone of the forearm. **—ul′nar,** *adj.*

ul·te′ri·or, *adj.* 1. further; beyond. 2. concealed; disguised.

ul′ti·mate, *adj.* 1. final; conclusive. 2. fundamental; basic. **—ul′ti·mate·ly,** *adv.*

ul″ti·ma′tum, *n., pl.* **-matums** or **-mata,** final, decisive demand.

ul′ti·mo, *adj.* of or occurring in the preceding month.

ul″tra·light, *n.* miniature aircraft for solo, powered flight.

ul″tra·ma·rine′, *adj.* deep blue.

ul″tra·vi′o·let, *adj.* beyond the visible spectrum at its violet end.

um′bel, *n.* cluster of flower with the stalks having a common center.

um′ber, *n.* reddish brown.

um·bil′i·cus, *n.* navel. **—um·bil′i·cal,** *adj.*

um′brage, *n.* resentment; pique.

um·brel′la, *n.* collapsible device with a fabric-covered frame, carried for protection against the weather.

um′pire, *n., v.t.,* **-pired, -piring.** *n.* 1. final authority; judge. —*v.t.* 2. to serve as umpire for.

un-, prefix indicating "not." **unable, unassuming, unavoidable, unaware, unbalanced, unbend, unborn, unbridled, uncertain, uncivil, unclean, unclothe, uncommon, unconcern, unconscious, uncork, undeniable, undeclared, undress, undue, unduly, uneasy, unequal, unerring, unexpected, unfailing, unfaithful, unfasten, unfit, unfold, unfortunate, unfriendly, ungodly, unhinge, unholy, unlike, unlock, unnatural, unpack, unroll, unscrew, unsettle, unshackle, unsightly, untangle, untouchable, untrue, untruth, untypical, unusual, unveil, unwell, unwind, unwise, unyoke.**

u″nan′i·mous, *adj.* totally agreed. **—u·na·nim′i·ty,** *n.* **—u″nan′i·mous·ly,** *adv.*

un″a·wares′, *adv.* not aware.

un·bo′som, *v.t.* disclose; reveal.

un·called′-for″, *adj.* unwarranted; unneeded.

un·can′ny, *adj.* unnatural; eerie.

un′cle, *n.* brother of one's mother or father, or husband of one's aunt.

Uncle Sam, the United States.

un·con′scion·a·ble, *adj.* excessive; unreasonable. **—un·con′scion·a·bly,** *adv.*

un·couth′, *adj.* lacking grace; clumsy.

unc′tion, *n.* consecration with oil.

unc′tu·ous, *adj.* 1. oily. 2. unpleasantly suave.

un′der, *prep., adj., adv.* 1. below; beneath. 2. less than. —*adj.* 3. lower.

un′der·brush″, *n.* low-growing forest shrubs and grass.

un′der·cov″er, *adj.* disguised; secret.

un′der·cut″, *v.t.,* **-cut, -cutting.** offer at a lower price than.

un′der·dog″, *n.* predicted loser.

un"der·es'ti·mate", *v.t.*, -ated, -ating. value or estimate too low.

un"der·go', *v.t.* -went, -gone, -going. endure; experience.

un·der·grad'u·ate, *n.* college student working toward a bachelor's degree.

un'der·ground", *adj.* 1. below the ground. 2. secret; confidential. —*adv.* 3. below the ground. —*n.* 4. secret army of resistance.

un'der·hand", *adj.* secret; sly. Also, un'der·hand"ed.

un'der·mine", *v.t.* -mind, -mining. weaken; sabotage.

un·der·neath', *prep., adv.* beneath.

un·der·stand', *v.t., v.i.* -stood, -standing. *v.t.* 1. comprehend; take the meaning of. —*v.i.* 2. sympathize. —un·der·stand'ing, *n., adj.*

un·der·stood', *adj.* assumed; agreed upon.

un'der·stud·y, *n., pl.* -dies. performer on call for emergencies.

un·der·take', *v.t.*, -took, taken. 1. set about; enter upon. 2. accept as an obligation.

un'der·tak"er, *n.* director of funerals.

un'der·world", *n.* world of criminals.

un'der·write", *v.t.* -wrote, -written, -writing. accept, as an expense or liability. —un'der·writ"er, *n.*

un"do', *v.t.* -did, -done, -doing. 1. unfasten. 2. nullify. 3. ruin.

un'du·late", *v.t., v.i.*, -lated, -lating. 1. move or form in waves. 2. fluctuate in pitch and cadence. —un"du·la'tion, *n.*

un·earth', *v.t.* discover; reveal.

un'guent, *n.* ointment; salve.

u·ni·corn, (yōō' ni korn), *n.* mythical horselike animal with a single horn.

u'ni·form", *adj.* 1. alike; similar. —*n.* 2. distinctive or stylized dress for a particular group. —*v.t.* 3. clothe with a uniform. —u·ni·form'i·ty, *n.*

u'ni·fy", *v.t.* -fied, -fying. make into a whole; unite. —u"ni·fi·ca'tion, *n.*

u·ni·lat'er·al, *adj.* one-sided.

un'ion, *n.* 1. act or instance of uniting. 2. labor group organized for mutual aid. —un'ion·ize", *v.t., v.i.*

Union Jack, British flag.

u"nique', *adj.* 1. single; only. 2. rare; unusual. —u·nique'ly, *adv.*

u'ni·son", *n.* agreement; harmony.

u'nit, *n.* single amount, item, etc.

u·nite', *v.t., v.i.*, -nited, -niting. join into one group or entity.

u'ni·ty, *n.* 1. state of being united; oneness. 2. agreement.

u"ni·ver'sal, *adj.* including all. —u"ni·ver·sal'i·ty, *n.*

u'ni·verse", *n.* entirety of physical creation.

u"ni·ver'si·ty, *n., pl.* -ties. large institution of higher learning.

un·kempt', *adj.* untidy; shabby; messy.

un·less', *conj., prep.* if not; except.

un·rav'el, *v.t.* 1. disentangle; undo. 2. solve.

un·rest', *n.* 1. uneasy state. 2. discontent.

un·ru'ly, *adj.* undisciplined; rebellious. —un·rul'i·ness *n.*

un·tie', *v.t.*, -tied, -tying. loosen or undo.

un·til', *conj., prep.* 1. up to the time when. 2. before.

un'to, *prep. Archaic.* to.

un·told', *adj.* vast; incalculable.

un·to·ward', *adj.* 1. improper. 2. adverse.

un·wield'y, *adj.* awkward; bulky.

un·wit'ting, *adj.* unintentional; inadvertent. —un·wit'ting·ly, *adv.*

un·wont"ed, *adj.* not usual; uncharacteristic.

up, *adv., adj., prep., v.t.*, -ped, -ping. *adv.* 1. to a higher level or location. 2. straight; erectly. 3. at bat. 4. awake; out of bed. 5. (computers) operating. —*prep.* 6. to a higher level or place in or on. —*v.t.* 7. increase.

up·braid', *v.t.* scold; chide.

up·heav"al, *n.* turmoil; unrest; agitation.

up·hold', *v.t.* -held, -holding. support; advocate.

up·hol'ster, *v.t.* furnish with padding and fabric covering. —up·hol'ster·er, *n.*

up'keep", *n.* maintenance; support.

up·lift, *v.t.* (up lift') 1. elevate; exalt. —*n.* (up'lift) 2. edification.

up·on', *prep.* on; onto.

up'per, *adj.* higher. —up'per·most", *adj.*

up'ris"ing, *n.* rebellion; revolt.

up'roar", *n.* tumult; din.

up·root", *v.t.* 1. to pull up by the roots. 2. displace from a home or homeland.

up·set, *v.*, -set, -setting, *adj., n. v.t.* (up set') 1. overturn. 2. defeat. 3. put in confusion or distress. —*v.i.* 4. be overturned. —*adj.* 5. distressed in mind. —*n.* (up'set") 6. act or instance of upsetting.

up'shot, *n.* final result.

up"stairs', *adj.* 1. situated on an upper floor. —*adv.* 2. to or on an upper floor. —*n.* 3. floor above a ground floor.

up'start", *n.* person of recent power or wealth.

up'-to-date', *adj.* latest; modern; current.

up'ward, *adv.* 1. Also, up'wards, to a higher level or place. —*adj.* 2. toward a higher level or place.

u·ra'ni·um, *n.* radioactive metallic element used as a source for atomic energy.

ur'ban, *adj.* pertaining to cities.

ur·bane′, *adj.* sophisticated; polite. —**ur·ban′i·ty**, *n.*

ur′chin, *n.* unkempt child; ragamuffin.

urge, *v.t.*, **urged, urging**, *n. v.t.* **1.** advocate. **2.** implore. —*n.* **3.** impulse; desire; longing.

ur′gent, *adj.* pressing; vital; crucial. —**ur′gen·cy**, *n.* —**ur′gent·ly**, *adv.*

u′ri·nate′, *v.i.* **-nated, -nating.** pass urine. —**u″ri·na′tion**, *n.*

u′rine, *n.* fluid waste from kidneys.

urn, *n.* vase.

us, *pron.* objective case of we.

us′age, *n.* **1.** custom. **2.** treatment; handling.

use, *v.t.*, **used, using**, *n. v.t.* (yōōz) **1.** employ or engage for a purpose. **2.** expend; consume. **3.** behave toward; treat. **4.** do regularly. **5.** accustom; habituate. —*n.* (yōōs) **6.** application; employment. **7.** value; service. —**us′a·ble**, *adj.* —**use′ful**, *adj.* —**use′less**, *adj.*

us″er-friend′′ly, *adj.* (computers) designed for ease of use.

ush′er, *n., v.t.* escort; guide.

u′su·al, *adj.* **1.** habitual; customary. **2.** ordinary; common. —**u′su·al·ly**, *adv.*

u·surp′, *v.t.* take or assume without right. —**u·surp′er**, *n.*

u′su·ry, *n.* lending of money at excessive interest. —**u′sur·er**, *n.*

u·ten′sil, *n.* implement or vessel useful esp. in the kitchen.

u′ter·us, *n.* female bodily organ in which fetuses develop.

u·til′i·tar′i·an, *adj.* practical; useful; functional.

u·til′i·ty, *n., pl.* **-ties. 1.** usefulness; function. **2.** service provided for public use.

u′ti·lize, *v.t.*, **-lized, -lizing.** make use of. —**u″ti·li·za′tion**, *n.*

ut′most″, *adj.* **1.** furthest. **2.** greatest.

u·to′pi·an, *adj.* impossibly ideal.

ut′ter, *v.t.* **1.** say; speak; enunciate. —*adj.* **2.** total; complete. —**ut′ter·ance**, *n.* —**ut′ter·ly**, *adv.*

u·vu·la (yōō′vyə lə), *n.* fleshy pendant lobe of the soft palate.

ux·o·ri·ous (ōōk sōr′i əs), *adj.* excessively fond of one's wife.

V

V, v, *n.* twenty-second letter of the English alphabet.

va′can·cy, *n., pl.* **-cies. 1.** state of being vacant. **2.** void. **3.** available rental space.

va′cant″, *adj.* **1.** empty; uninhabited. **2.** stupid; foolish. **3.** expressionless. —**va′cant″ly**, *adv.*

va′cate″, *v.* **-cated, -cating.** *v.t.* **1.** deprive of an occupant or incumbent. **2.** leave. **3.** void; annul. —*v.i.* **4.** vacate a tenancy, office, or post.

va·ca′tion, *n.* **1.** respite from duty or occupation. **2.** period of rest and relaxation. —*v.i.* **3.** take a vacation. —**va·ca′tion·er, va·ca′tion·ist**, *n.*

vac′ci·nate″, *v.t.*, **-nated, -nating.** inoculate with cowpox virus for immunity to smallpox. —**vac′′ci·na′tion**, *n.*

vac·cine (vak sēn′), *n.* substance used for vaccinating. —**vac′ci·nal**, *adj.*

vac·il·late (vas′ə lāt″), *v.i.* **-lated, -lating. 1.** sway; oscillate; fluctuate. **2.** waver; hesitate. —**vac′′il·la′tion**, *n.*

va·cu′i·ty, *n., pl.* **-ties. 1.** emptiness. **2.** emptyheadedness. —**vac′u·ous**, *adj.* —**vac′u·ous·ly**, *adv.*

vac′u·um, *n.* **1.** space devoid of matter. —*v.t.* **2.** use a vacuum cleaner on.

vag′a·bond″, *adj.* **1.** wandering; rootless. —*n.* **2.** person leading a vagabond life.

va′gar·y, *n., pl.* **-garies.** capricious action or notion.

va·gin·a (və jī′nə), *n.* canal in the female from the vulva to the uterus. —**vag′i·nal**, *adj.*

va′grant, *n.* **1.** wanderer, esp. without visible means of support. —*adj.* **2.** wandering; itinerant. **3.** random; wayward. —**va′gran·cy**, *n.*

vague, *adj.*, **vaguer, vaguest. 1.** not definite; imprecise. **2.** indistinct; blurred. —**vague′ly**, *adv.* —**vague′ness** *n.*

vain, *adj.* **1.** futile. **2.** conceited. —**vain′ly**, *adv.*

val·ance (văl′əns), *n.* drapery or frame disguising the top of a window.

vale, *n.* valley.

val·e·dic′tion, *n.* act of bidding farewell. —**val′′edic′to·ry**, *adj.*

va′lence, *n. Chemistry.* combining power of an element or radical.

val′en·tine, *n.* **1.** sentimental greeting on St. Valentine's Day. **2.** sweetheart chosen on St. Valentine's Day.

val·et, (val′it, val′ā), *n.* man's personal servant.

val′iant, *adj.* possessing valor; courageous. —**val′ian·tly**, *adv.*

va′lid, *adj.* **1.** reasonable. **2.** having legal force. —**va·lid′i·ty**, *n.* —**val′id·ly**, *adv.* —**val′i·date**, *v.t.*

va·lise (və lēs′), *n.* traveling bag; suitcase.

val′ley, *n.* long depression between mountains, plateaus, etc.

val′or, *n.* courage; bravery. —**val′o·rous**, *adj.* —**val′o·rous′′ly**, *adv.*

val′u·a·ble, *adj.* **1.** having worth or usefulness. —*n.* **2. valuables,** valuable possessions. —**val′u·a·bly,** *adv.*

val·u·a′tion, *n.* estimated value.

val′ue, *n., v.t.* **-ued, -ing.** *n.* **1.** importance; worth. **2.** relative worth. **3.** basic principle. —*v.t.* **4.** estimate the worth of. **5.** prize; esteem. —**val′ue·less,** *n.*

valve, *n.* device for regulating the flow of a fluid. —**val′vu·lar,** *adj.*

vamp, *n.* **1.** uppermost front part of a shoe, etc. **2.** seductive woman. **3.** repeated introductory musical passage. —*v.i.* **4.** play a musical vamp.

vam′pire″, *n.* **1.** corpse believed to rise and suck the blood of sleepers at night. **2.** Also, **vampire bat,** South American bat subsisting on blood.

van, *n.* **1.** foremost part; vanguard. **2.** enclosed truck.

van′dal, *n.* person who willfully damages property. —**van′dal·ism,** *n.* —**van′dal· ize,** *v.t.*

Vandyke, *n.* short, pointed, trimmed beard.

vane, *n.* blade rotated by moving air, steam, etc.

van′guard″, *n.* **1.** advance troops. **2.** forefront of an action, movement, or cause.

va·nil′la, *n.* extract of a tropical American orchid used in cookery.

van′ish, *v.i.* disappear.

van′i·ty, *n., pl.* **-ties.** inflated pride; conceit.

van′quish, *v.t.* defeat; conquer.

van′tage, *n.* position giving strategic advantage.

va′pid, *adj.* dull; uninteresting; flat. —**vap′id·ly,** *adv.* —**va·pid′i·ty,** *n.*

va′por, *n.* gaseous substance, as steam or mist. —**va′por·ous,** *adj.*

va′por·ize″, *v.,* **-ized, -izing.** *v.t., v.i.* turn into vapor. —**va″por·i·za′tion,** *n.* —**va′por·i″zer,** *n.*

var′i·a·ble, *adj.* **1.** changeable; fluctuating. **2.** inconstant; fickle. —**var″i·a· bil′i·ty,** *n.* —**var′i·a·bly,** *adv.*

var′i·ance, *n.* **1.** divergence. **2.** disagreement.

var′i·ant, *adj.* **1.** varying. **2.** altered in form. —*n.* **3.** variant form or structure.

var″i·a′tion, *n.* **1.** change; alteration. **2.** degree of change. **3.** elaboration of a musical theme. —**var″i·a′tion·al,** *adj.* —**var″i·a′tion·al·ly,** *adv.*

var′i·e·gate″, *v.t.,* **-gated, -gating. 1.** add different colors to; dapple. **2.** add variety to. —**var″i·e·gat′ed,** *adj.* —**var″i·e·ga′tion,** *n.*

va·ri′e·ty, *n., pl.* **-ties. 1.** diversity. **2.** assortment. **3.** category; kind; type. —**va·ri′e·tal,** *adj.*

va·ri′o·la, *n.* smallpox; cowpox.

var′i·ous, *adj.* **1.** several. **2.** diverse; different. —**var′i·ous·ly,** *adv.*

var′nish, *n.* **1.** resinous liquid preparation drying to a hard, glossy surface. **2.** outward appearance; gloss. —*v.t.* **3.** apply varnish to. **4.** gloss over; conceal.

var′y, *v.,* **varied, varying.** *v.t., v.i.* **1.** change; fluctuate. **2.** differ. —**var′i· ance,** *n.*

vase, *n.* ornamental vessel.

vas′sal, *n.* **1.** landholder subservient to a feudal lord. **2.** person under domination of another. —**vas′sal·age,** *n.*

vast, *adj.* enormous; huge; immense. —**vast′ly,** *adv.* —**vast′ness,** *n.*

vat, *n.* large vessel for holding fluids.

vaude′ville, *n.* stage entertainment with a series of acts. —**vaude·vil′lian,** *n.*

vault, *n.* **1.** arched structure forming a ceiling. **2.** space covered by such a structure. **3.** burial chamber. **4.** room or container for valuables. —*v.t.* **5.** form or cover with a vault. **6.** leap over. —*v.i.* **7.** perform a leap; jump.

vaunt, *v.i.* **1.** brag; boast. —*v.t.* **2.** call attention to boastfully. —*n.* **3.** boast.

VCR, video cassette recorder.

veal, *n.* flesh of a young calf.

veer, *v.i.* **1.** change direction or course. —*n.* **2.** act or instance of veering.

veg′e·ta·ble, *n.* **1.** partly edible plant. —*adj.* Also, **veg′e·tal. 2.** being a vegetable. **3.** pertaining to plants.

veg″e·tar′i·an, *n.* **1.** abstainer from meat. —*adj.* **2.** advocating the exclusion of meat in the diet. **3.** consisting solely of vegetables. —**veg″e·tar′i·an· ism,** *n.*

veg′e·tate″, *v.i.,* **-tated, -tating. 1.** grow in the manner of a plant. **2.** lead a passive life. —**veg′i·ta″tive,** *adj.*

ve′he·ment, *adj.* **1.** passionate; emotional; fervid. **2.** violent. —**ve′he·ment·ly,** *adj.* —**ve′he·mence,** *n.*

ve′hi·cle, *n.* **1.** inert medium containing an active agent. **2.** means of transporting or conveying. —**ve·hic′u·lar,** *adj.*

veil, *n.* **1.** net-like cloth for covering the face. **2.** outer covering of a nun's headdress. **3.** screen; cover-up. —*v.t.* **4.** cover with or as if with a veil.

vein, *n.* **1.** tubular vessel conveying blood within the body. **2.** tubular thickening in an insect wing or a leaf. **3.** stratum of mineral, ore, or ice. **4.** spirit; mood. —*v.t.* **5.** pattern with or as if with veins.

vel′lum, *n.* parchment.

ve·loc′i·ty, *n., pl.* **-ties.** speed.

vel′vet, *n.* fabric with a thick, short, soft pile. —**vel′vet·y,** *adj.*

ve′nal, *adj.* open to bribery or corruption; mercenary. —**ve′nal·ly,** *adv.* —**ve·nal′i·ty,** *n.*

vend, *v.t.* sell; peddle. —**ven′dor,** *n.*

ve·neer′, *n.* **1.** facing of fine material. **2.** outer appearance. —*v.t.* **3.** cover with or as with a veneer.

venerable

ven·er·a·ble, *adj.* worthy of or commanding reverence. —**ven·er·a·bil'i·ty,** *n.*

ven'er·ate", *v.t.,* **-ated, -ating.** respect deeply; worship; revere. —**ven"er·a'tion,** *n.*

ve·ne're·al, *adj.* relating to or resulting from sexual activity.

venge'ance, *n.* retaliation; retribution.

venge'ful, *adj.* seeking revenge; vindictive. —**venge'ful·ly,** *adv.*

ve'ni·al, *adj.* pardonable; forgivable. —**ve'nial·ly,** *adv.*

ven'i·son, *n.* deer meat.

ven'om, *n.* **1.** poisonous secretion. **2.** malice; spite. —**ven'om·ous,** *adj.*

vent, *n.* **1.** means of outlet or escape. —*v.t.* **2.** provide or serve as a vent. **3.** give free expression to.

ven'ti·late, *v.t.,* **-ated, -ating. 1.** provide with or expose to fresh air. **2.** express openly and freely. —**ven·ti·la'tion,** *n.*

ven·tril'o·quism, *n.* technique of projecting the voice so that it seems to emanate from a source other than the speaker. —**ven·tril'o·quist,** *n.*

ven'ture, *v.t.,* **-tured, -turing,** *n.* *v.t.* **1.** expose to hazard; risk. **2.** offer at risk of rejection. —*n.* **3.** challenging or risky undertaking. —**ven'ture·some,** **ven'tur·ous,** *adj.*

Ve'nus, *n.* **1.** goddess of love. **2.** second planet in distance from the sun.

ve·ra'cious, *adj.* openly honest; truthful. —**ve·ra'cious·ly,** *adj.* —**ve·rac'i·ty,** *n.*

ve·ran'da, *n.* an open portico attached to a building; porch. Also, **ve·ran'dah.**

verb, *n. Grammar.* part of speech indicating action, occurrence, being, etc.

ver'bal, *adj.* **1.** relating to or formed of words. **2.** oral; spoken. **3.** relating to or constituting a verb or form of a verb. —**ver'bal·ly,** *adv.*

ver'bal·ize", *v.,* **-ized, -izing.** *v.t.* **1.** express in words. —*v.i.* **2.** speak in words. —**ver"bal·i·za'tion,** *n.*

ver·ba'tim, *adv.* word for word; literally.

ver'bi·age, *n.* excess of words.

ver·bose', *adj.* wordy; loquacious. —**ver·bose'ness, ver·bos'i·ty,** *n.*

ver'dant, *adj.* green. —**ver'dant·ly,** *adj.* —**ver'dan·cy,** *n.*

ver'dict, *n.* decision.

ver'dure, *n.* **1.** greenery. **2.** greenness.

verge, *n., v.i.,* **verged, verging.** *n.* **1.** margin; edge. —*v.i.* **2.** border; surround. **3.** tend; incline.

ver'i·fy, *v.t.,* **-fied, -fying.** prove or ascertain the correctness of. —**ver·i·fi'a·ble,** *adj.* —**ver·i·fi·ca'tion,** *n.*

ver'i·ly, *adv.* truly.

ver"i·sim·il'i·tude, *n.* appearance of truth or reality.

ver'i·ta·ble, *adj.* true; genuine. —**ver'i·ta·bly,** *adj.*

ver'i·ty, *n., pl.* **-ties.** truth.

ver'min, *n., pl.* obnoxious animals or creatures collectively. —**ver'min·ous,** *adj.*

ver·nac'u·lar, *adj.* **1.** locally native. —*n.* **2.** language characteristic, esp. of a particular group or class.

ver'nal, *adj.* pertaining to spring.

ver'sa·tile, *adj.* changing tasks or activities easily. —**ver·sa·til'i·ty,** *n.*

verse, *n.* **1.** poetry. **2.** part of a poem, esp. when rhymed. **3.** passage from the Bible.

versed, *adj.* accomplished; skilled; knowledgeable.

ver·si·fy, *v.,* **-fied, -fying.** *v.t.* **1.** put into verse. —*v.i.* **2.** compose verse. —**ver"si·fi·ca'tion,** *n.* —**ver'si·fi"er,** *n.*

ver'sion, *n.* **1.** account. **2.** translation.

ver'te·bra, *n., pl.* **-bras, -brae.** segment of the spinal column. —**ver'te·bral,** *adj.*

ver'te·brate, *adj.* **1.** having vertebras. —*n.* **2.** creature having vertebras.

ver'ti·cal, *adj.* **1.** perpendicular to the horizon. —*n.* **2.** vertical plane, line, etc. —**ver'ti·cal·ly,** *adv.*

ver'ti·go", *n., pl.* **-gos.** dizziness.

ver'y, *adv., adj.,* **-ier, -iest.** *adv.* **1.** to a great extent. —*adj.* **2.** identical; actual. **3.** absolute.

ves'pers, *n., sing.* evening religious service.

ves'sel, *n.* **1.** ship, boat, etc. **2.** container for fluid. **3.** channel for blood.

vest, *n.* **1.** sleeveless garment worn under a coat or jacket. —*v.t.* **2.** put in possession or control of. **3.** endow with authority.

ves'ti·bule, *n.* antichamber. —**ves·ti'bu·lar,** *adj.*

ves'tige, *n.* remnant; trace. —**ves·tig'i·al,** *adj.*

vest'ment, *n.* gown; robe.

vest-pocket, *adj.* small enough for a pocket.

ves'try, *n., pl.* **-tries. 1.** auxiliary room of a church. **2.** church committee. —**ves'try·man,** *n.*

vet'er·an, *n.* **1.** person who has served, esp. in the military forces. —*adj.* **2.** greatly experienced.

vet'er·i·nar"y, *adj., n., pl.* **-ies.** *adj.* **1.** pertaining to the healing of animals. —*n.* **2.** Also, **vet"er·i·nar'i·an,** doctor for animals.

ve'to, *n., pl.* **-toes,** *v.t.,* **-toes, -toing.** *n.* **1.** power to reject, prohibit, or ignore. **2.** prohibition. —*v.t.* **3.** reject or prohibit by veto.

vex, *v.t.* **1.** irritate. **2.** trouble. —**vex"a'ti·ous,** *adj.* —**vex'ed·ly,** *adj.*

vexed, *adj.* controversial.

vi·a (vī'ə, vē'ə), *prep.* by way of.

vi'a·ble, *adj.* capable of or fit for living. —**vi'a·bly,** *adv.*

vi′a·duct″, *n*. long road bridge.

vi′and, *n*. item of food, esp. when very choice or tasty.

vi′brant, *adj*. 1. oscillating; fluctuating. 2. vigorous; energetic. —**vi′brant·ly**, *adj*. —**vi′bran·cy**, *n*.

vi′brate, *v*., **-brated, -brating**. *v.t*., *v.i*. 1. move rapidly back and forth. —*v.i*. 2. shiver. 3. resound. —**vi·bra′tion**, *n*. —**vi′bra·to″ry**, *adj*. —**vi·bra·tor**, *n*.

vic′ar, *n*. 1. parish priest. 2. representative of the pope or of a bishop. 3. **Vicar of Christ**, pope. —**vic′ar·ship″**, *n*.

vi·car′i·ous, *adj*. 1. serving in the place of another. 2. experienced in imagination only. —**vi·car″i·ous·ly**, *adv*. —**vi·car′i·ous·ness**, *n*.

vice, *n*. 1. moral depravity. 2. habitual personal shortcoming.

vice′-pres′i·dent, *n*. official next in rank below president. —**vice′-pres″i·den′tial**, *adj*. —**vice″-pres′i·den·cy**, *n*.

vice′roy, *n*. deputy sovereign; representative ruler. —**vice-re′gal**, *adj*.

vi′ce ver′sa, with the order changed; conversely.

vi·cin′i·ty, *n*., *pl*. **-ties**. local area; neighborhood.

vi′cious, *adj*. 1. depraved; immoral. 2. spiteful; malicious. 3. evil. —**vi′cious·ly**, *adv*. —**vi′cious·ness**, *n*.

vi·cis·si·tude (və sis′ə tōōd″), *n*. unpredictable change.

vic′tim, *n*. 1. sufferer from a force or action. 2. dupe. —**vic′tim·ize″**, *v.t*.

vic′tor, *n*. winner; conqueror.

vic′to·ry, *n*., *pl*. **-ries**. success in a contest; triumph. —**vic·to′ri·ous**, *adj*. —**vic·to′ri·ous·ly**, *adv*.

vict·ual (vi′təl), *n*. 1. **victuals**, food. —*v.t*. 2. provision.

vid″e·o, *n*., *adj*. 1. television. 2. a short, visual performance featuring a rock music soundtrack.

vid″e·o·tape′, *n*. electromagnetic tape for recording visual images.

vie, *v.i*. **vied, vying**. contend; compete.

view, *n*. 1. seeing; beholding. 2. area or range of vision. 3. landscape. 4. purpose. 5. opinion; attitude. —*v*. 6. look at; regard. —**view′er**, *n*. —**view′less**, *adj*.

vig′il, *n*. act of keeping awake and alert.

vig′i·lant, *adj*. alert; keenly aware. —**vig′i·lant·ly**, *adv*. —**vig′i·lance**, *n*.

vig′or, *n*. robust health, energy, or strength. —**vig′or·ous**, *adj*. —**vig′or·ous·ly**, *adv*.

vile, *adj*., **viler, vilest**. 1. of little account; mean. 2. nasty; contemptible. —**vile′ly**, *adv*. —**vile′ness**, *n*.

vil′i·fy″, *v.t*. **-fied, -fying**. denounce; defame. —**vil″i·fi·ca′tion**, *n*.

vil′la, *n*. country or suburban house.

vil′lage, *n*. small town; hamlet. —**vil′lag·er**, *n*.

vil′lain, *n*. wicked person; scoundrel. —**vil′lain·ous**, *adj*. —**vil′lain·y**, *n*.

vim, *n*. vigor; robustness.

vin′di·cate″, *v.t*. **-cated, -cating**. absolve from suspicion or doubt. —**vin″di·ca′tion**, *n*. —**vin′di·ca·ble**, *adj*.

vin·dic′tive, *adj*. holding a grudge. —**vin·dic′tive·ly**, *adj*. —**vin·dic′tive·ness**, *n*.

vine, *n*. slender, creeping or climbing plant.

vin′e·gar, *n*. sour fermented liquid. —**vin′e·gar·y**, *adj*.

vine·yard (vin′yərd), *n*. garden or plantation for the growth of vines.

vin′tage, *n*. 1. wine extracted from a single harvest of grapes. 2. harvest of grapes.

vi·o·la (vē ō′lə), *n*. stringed instrument with a pitch slightly below that of a violin.

vi′o·late″, *v.t*., **-lated, -lating**. 1. break; transgress. 2. desecrate. 3. rape. —**vi″o·la′tion**, *n*. —**vi′o·la″tor**, *n*.

vi′o·lent, *adj*. 1. physically aggressive. 2. severe; turbulent. —**vi′o·lent·ly**, *adv*. —**vi′o·lence**, *n*.

vi′o·let, *n*. 1. low-growing herb bearing purplish or bluish blossoms. 2. bluish purple.

vi·o·lin′, *n*. small, stringed musical instrument played with a bow. —**vi″o·lin′ist**, *n*.

vi″o·lon·cel′lo, *n*., *pl*. **-los**. cello. —**vi″o·lon·cel′list**, *n*.

vi′per, *n*. 1. venomous snake. 2. ill-tempered, malicious person. —**vi′per·ous**, *adj*.

vi·ra′go, *n*., *pl*. **-gos, -goes**. malicious woman; shrew; witch.

vir′gin, *n*. 1. sexually inexperienced person. —*adj*. 2. being a virgin. 3. unexplored, unexploited, etc. —**vir′gin·al**, *adj*.

vir′ile, *adj*. 1. capable of siring offspring. 2. vigorous; manly; potent. —**vi·ril′i·ty**, *n*.

vir′tu·al, *adj*. so in effect. —**vir′tu·al·ly**, *adv*.

vir′tue, *n*. 1. morality. 2. chastity. 3. merit. —**vir′tu·ous**, *adj*. —**vir′tu·ous·ly**, *adv*. —**vir′tu·ous·ness**, *n*.

vir″tu·o′so *n*., *pl*. **-sos, -si**. musician, etc., of outstanding skill. —**vir″tu·os′i·ty**, *n*.

vir′u·lent, *adj*. 1. poisonous; deadly. 2. hostile. —**vir′u·lence, vir′u·len·cy**, *n*. —**vir′u·lent·ly**, *adv*.

vi′rus, *adj*. infectious agency. —**vi′ral**, *adj*. —**vi′ral·ly**, *adv*.

vi·sa (vē′zə), *n*. endorsement to a passport.

vis′age, *n*. 1. face. 2. aspect; look.

vis·cer·a (vis'sər ə), *n., pl.* internal bodily organs. —**vis'cer·al,** *adj.*

vis·cid (vis'id), *adj.* sticky to the touch; tacky. Also, **vis'cous.** —**vis·cos'i·ty,** *n.*

vise, *n.* holding tool attached to a work bench, etc.

vis'i·ble, *adj.* **1.** capable of being seen. **2.** perceptible. —**vis'i·bly,** *adv.* —**vis·i·bil'i·ty,** *n.*

vi'sion, *n.* **1.** sense of sight. **2.** supernatural apprehension. **3.** foresight. —**vi'sion·al,** *adj.*

vi'sion·ar''y, *adj.* **1.** fanciful. **2.** apprehended by or as by supernatural means. **3.** unreal; fancied. —*n.* **4.** person seeing visions. **5.** impractical person; dreamer.

vi'sit, *v.t.* **1.** go to and stay briefly at. **2.** afflict. —*n.* **3.** brief stay, esp. as a guest. —**vis'i·tor,** *n.* —**vis'i·tant,** *adj.* —**vis''i·ta'tion,** *n.*

vi'sor, *n.* forward projecting part, as of a helmet or cap.

vis'ta, *n.* panoramic view.

vis'u·al, *adj.* pertaining to sight. —**vis'u·al·ly** *adj.*

vis'u·a·lize'', *v.t.,* **-ized, -izing.** obtain or create a picture or conception of. —**vis''u·al·i·za'tion,** *n.*

vi'tal, *adj.* **1.** pertaining to life or existence. **2.** extremely important. **3.** full of exuberance, creativity, etc. —**vi'tal·ly,** *adv.* —**vi·tal'i·ty,** *n.*

vi'ta·min, *n.* organic substance vital in small quantities to proper nutrition. —**vi''ta·min'ic,** *adj.*

vi·ti·ate (vish'i āt''), *v.t.,* **-ated, -ating.** **1.** impair. **2.** invalidate; negate. —**vi''ti·a'tion,** *n.*

vit're·ous, *adj.* glazed or glassy.

vit'ri·ol, *n.* sulfuric acid.

vit''ri·ol'ic, *adj.* **1.** pertaining to vitriol. **2.** caustic, as criticism.

vi·tu·per·ate (vī tōō' pər āt''), *v.t.,* **-ated, -ating.** **1.** criticize harshly or abusively. **2.** revile. —**vi·tu''per·a'tion,** *n.* —**vi·tu'per·a·tive,** *adj.*

vi·va'cious, *adj.* animated; lively. —**vi·va'cious·ly,** *adj.* —**vi·vac'i·ty, vi·va'cious·ness,** *n.*

viv'id, *adj.* **1.** bright; brilliant. **2.** intense. —**viv'id·ly,** *adj.* —**viv'id·ness,** *n.*

viv'i·sect'', *v.t.* dissect while alive. —**viv''i·sec'tion,** *n.* —**viv''i·sec'tion·ist,** *n.*

vix'en, *n.* **1.** female fox. **2.** mischievious girl or woman.

vo·cab'u·lar·y, *n., pl.* **-ies.** **1.** stock of words used by a person, people, or group. **2.** collection of words in alphabetical order.

vo'cal, *adj.* **1.** pertaining to the voice. **2.** pertaining to singing. **3.** articulate; outspoken. —**vo'cal·ly,** *adj.* —**vo'cal·ize,** *v.t., v.i.* —**vo''cal·i·za'tion,** *n.*

vo·ca'tion, *n.* profession; occupation. —**vo·ca'tion·al,** *adj.*

voc'a·tive, *adj.* **1.** relating to a grammatical case indicating person or thing addressed. —*n.* **2.** vocative case.

vo·cif·er·ate (vō sif'ər āt''), *v.,* **-ated, -ating.** *v.i., v.t.* shout. —**vo·cif''er·a'tion,** *n.* —**vo·cif''er·ous,** *adj.*

vogue, *n.* **1.** fashion; trend. **2.** popular favor or approval.

voice, *n., v.t.* **voiced, voicing.** *n.* **1.** sound uttered through the mouth. **2.** singing or speaking voice. **3.** expression. **4.** choice. **5.** right to express one's opinion. **6.** *Grammar.* verbal inflection indicating whether subject is acting or acted upon. —*v.t.* **7.** express; declare. —**voice'less,** *adj.*

void, *adj.* **1.** without legal power. **2.** useless; fruitless. **3.** empty; hollow. —*n.* **4.** empty or hollow space. —*v.t.* **5.** cancel; invalidate. —**void'a·ble,** *adj.* —**void'ance,** *n.*

vol'a·tile, *adj.* **1.** evaporating rapidly. **2.** energetic; lively. **3.** tending to erupt into violence. —**vol·a·til'i·ty,** *n.*

vol·ca'no, *n., pl.* **-noes, -nos.** mountain that ejects molten lava, rock, and steam. —**vol·can'ic,** *adj.* —**vol·can'i·cal·ly,** *adv.*

vo·li'tion, *n.* **1.** power of choosing or determining; will. **2.** act of willing. —**vo·li'tion·al,** *adj.*

vol'ley, *n., pl.* **-leys,** *v.t. n.* **1.** simultaneous discharge of a number of missiles. —*v.t.* **2.** fire in a volley.

volt, *n.* unit of electromotive force.

vol'u·ble, *adj.* fluent; talkative. —**vol'u·bly,** *adv.* —**vol·u·bil'i·ty,** *n.*

vol'ume, *n.* **1.** size in three dimensions. **2.** quantity; mass. **3.** degree of loudness. **4.** book.

vo·lu'mi·nous, *adj.* **1.** great in size or degree. **2.** consisting of or filling many books. —**vo·lu'min·ous·ly,** *adv.*

vol·un·tar''y, *adj.* **1.** performed or acted on by choice. **2.** controlled by the will. —**vol''un·tar'i·ly,** *adv.*

vol''un·teer', *v.t.* **1.** offer freely or spontaneously. —*v.i.* **2.** volunteer oneself. —*n.* **3.** person who volunteers.

vo·lup'tu·ous, *adj.* sensuous; sensual; luxurious. —**vo·lup'tu·ous·ly,** *adv.* —**vo·lup'tu·ous·ness,** *n.*

vom'it, *v.i.* **1.** disgorge the contents of the stomach through the mouth. —*v.t.* **2.** eject with force. —*n.* **3.** matter ejected by vomiting.

vo·ra'cious, *adj.* ravenous; greedy. —**vo·ra'cious·ly,** *adv.* —**vo·ra'ci·ty, vo·ra'cious·ness,** *n.*

vor'tex, *n., pl.* **-tices, -texes.** whirling mass drawing objects to a central cavity.

vote, *n., v.,* **voted, voting.** *n.* **1.** formal expression of opinion or choice, as by ballot. 2. right to such opinion or choice. 3. votes collectively. —*v.t.* 4. express or endorse by vote. —*v.i.* 5. cast one's vote. —**vot′er** *n.*

vouch, *v.i.* 1. give a guarantee or surety. 2. give personal assurance.

vouch′er, *n.* 1. person who vouches. 2. document certifying the occurrence of a transaction.

vouch·safe′, *v.t.,* -safed, -safing. permit; grant; allow.

vow, *n.* 1. pledge; solemn promise. —*v.t.* 2. promise solemnly; swear. —*v.i.* 3. make a vow.

vow′el, *n.* 1. speech sound made with the central part of the breath channel unblocked. 2. letter representing a vowel: *a, e, i, o, u* and sometimes *y.*

voy′age, *n., v.,* -aged, -aging. *n.* 1. an extended journey, esp. by sea. —*v.i.* 2. make a journey; travel. —*v.t.* 3. traverse; sail. —**voy′ag·er** *n.*

vul·can·ize″, *v.t.,* -ized, -izing. treat crude or synthetic rubber chemically to give it elasticity and strength. —**vul″can·i·za′tion,** *n.* —**vul′can·i″zer,** *n.*

vul′gar, *adj.* 1. lacking taste or breeding; unrefined. 2. ordinary; plebian. 3. ostentatiously showy. 4. indecent; obscene. 5. vernacular. —**vul′gar·ly,** *adv.* —**vul·gar′i·ty, vul′gar·ness,** *n.*

vul′ner·a·ble, *adj.* 1. capable of being physically or emotionally wounded. 2. open to damage or attack. —**vul′ner·a·bly,** *adv.* —**vul″ner·a·bil′i·ty,** *n.*

vul′ture, *n.* 1. large bird subsisting chiefly on carrion. 2. predatory or rapacious person. —**vul′tur·ous,** *adj.*

vul′va, *n., pl.* -vas, -vae. external female genital organs. —**vul′val, vul′var,** *adj.*

vy′ing, *adj.* competing; competitive.

W

W, w, *n.* twenty-third letter of the English alphabet.

wack′y, *adj.* -ier, -iest. *Informal.* odd, erratic, crazy. —**wack′i·ly,** *adv.* —**wack′i·ness,** *n.*

wad′dle, *v.i.,* -dled, -dling. *n. v.i.* 1. walk like a duck. —*n.* 2. waddling gait.

wade, *v.,* waded, wading. *v.i.* 1. walk through water. —*v.t.* 2. cross by wading. —**wad′er,** *n.*

wa′fer, *n.* 1. thin, crisp cracker or cookie.

2. thin disk of bread used in the Eucharist.

waf′fle, *n.* crisp batter cake baked in a double griddle.

waft, *v.t., v.i.* float through air or over water.

wag, *v.,* wagged, wagging. *n. v.t., v.i.* 1. shake in an arc. —*n.* 2. wit, joker. —**wag′ger·y,** *n.* —**wag′gish,** *adj.*

wage, *n., pl.* wages, *v.t.,* waged, waging. *n.* 1. pay. —*v.t.* 2. carry on, as war.

wa′ger, *n., v.t., v.i.* bet.

wag′gle, *v.,* -gled, -gling. *n. v.t., v.i.* 1. shake. —*n.* 2. shake.

wag′on, *n.* four-wheeled draft freight vehicle.

waif, *n.* homeless child or animal.

wail, *v.i., v.t.* 1. cry mournfully. —*n.* 2. mournful cry. —**wail′er,** *n.*

wain′scot, *n.* 1. woodwork along an interior wall. —*v.t.* 2. line with woodwork.

waist, *n.* part of the body between ribs and hips. —**waist′band″,** *n.* —**waist′line″,** *n.*

wait, *v.i.* 1. stop briefly; pause. 2. be in expectation. 3. be patient. 4. remain undone. 5. serve food, etc. —*n.* 6. act, instance, or period of waiting. 7. **in wait,** in ambush.

wait′er, *n.* 1. person who waits. 2. Also, *fem.,* **wait′ress,** server of diners.

waive, *v.t.,* waived, waiving. give up; relinquish.

waiv′er, *n.* document that relinquishes.

wake, *v.,* waked, or woke, woked or woken, waking. *v.i.* 1. awake. 2. be alert. —*v.t.* 3. arouse. —*n.* 4. vigil, as over a corpse. —**wake′ful,** *adj.* —**wake′ful·ly,** *adv.* —**wake′ful·ness,** *n.*

wale, *n., v.t.,* waled, waling. *n.* 1. welt as from a whip. —*v.t.* 2. mark with wales.

walk, *v.i.* 1. go on foot. —*v.t.* 2. cause to walk. 3. accompany on foot. —*n.* 4. act or instance of walking. 5. place for walking. —**walk′er,** *n.*

walk′ie-talk′ie, *n.* portable two-way radio.

wall, *n.* 1. upright enclosure. —*v.t.* 2. enclose or separate.

wall′board″, *n.* light material for covering interior walls or ceilings.

wal′let, *n.* pocket case for money, cards, etc.

wall′flow″er, *n. Informal.* 1. girl onlooker at a party. 2. sweet-scented flowering plant that sometimes grows on walls.

wal′lop, *v.t.* 1. beat or thrash. —*n.* 2. powerful blow.

wal′low, *v.i.* 1. roll about, as in mud. 2. indulge oneself. —*n.* 3. muddy area.

wall′pa″per, *n.* 1. decorative paper for

interior walls. —*v.t.* **2.** put wallpaper on.

Wall Street, U.S. financial world.

wal'nut'', *n.* edible nut from a northern tree.

wal'rus, *n.* large sea mammal with two tusks.

waltz, *n.* **1.** dance in three-quarter time. —*v.i.* **2.** dance a waltz. —*v.t.* **3.** *Informal.* lead briskly. —**waltz'er,** *n.*

wam'pum, *n.* shell beads used by North American Indians as money or ornaments.

wan, *adj.,* **wanner, wannest.** pale or sick-looking. —**wan'ly,** *adv.*

wand, *n.* rod with supposed magical power.

wan'der, *v.i.* **1.** move about aimlessly. **2.** stray. —*v.t.* **3.** travel over. —**wan'der·er,** *n.*

wan'der·lust'', *n.* desire to wander or travel.

wane, *v.i., n.,* **wane, waning.** *v.i.* **1.** grow dim, as the moon's light. **2.** decline in strength or power. —*n.* **3.** decrease or decline.

wan'gle, *v.t.,* **-gled, -gling.** *Informal.* get by scheming or persuasion.

want, *v.t.* **1.** wish for. **2.** desire, crave, demand. —*v.i.* **3.** be lacking or deficient. —*n.* **4.** something needed. **5.** deficiency or lack. —**want'ing,** *adj., prep.*

wan'ton, *adj.* **1.** gratuitous. **2.** sexually loose. —*n.* **3.** lascivious woman. —*v.t.* **4.** squander. —**wan'ton·ly,** *adv.* —**wan'ton·ness,** *n.*

wap'i·ti, *n., pl.* **-tis, -ti.** elk with wide antlers.

war, *n., v.i.,* **warred, warring.** *n.* **1.** armed conflict, as between nations. **2.** hostility or struggle. —*v.i.* **3.** be in conflict. —**war'fare'',** *n.* —**war'like,** *adj.*

war'ble, *v.,* **-bled, -bling,** *n.* *v.t., v.i.* **1.** sing with trills, as a bird. —*n.* **2.** warbling. —**war'bler,** *n.*

ward, *n.* **1.** administrative division of a city. **2.** division of a hospital. **3.** person under the care of a guardian. —*v.t.* **4.** repel or avert.

war'den, *n.* **1.** chief officer of a prison. **2.** person in charge of others or things, keeper.

ward'er, *n.* guard.

ward'robe'', *n.* **1.** collection of clothes. **2.** closet for clothes.

ward'room'', *n.* living and dining area for commissioned officers on a warship.

ware, *n.* goods for sale.

ware'house'', *n., v.t.,* **-housed, -housing.** *n.* **1.** storage building. —*v.t.* **2.** store in a warehouse.

war'head'', *n.* explosive front part of a bomb, missile, or torpedo.

war'horse'', *n.* **1.** veteran of many conflicts. **2.** overfamiliar concert number.

war'lock'', *n.* male with magical power; sorcerer.

war'lord'', *n.* military ruler.

warm, *adj.* **1.** having or giving moderate heat. **2.** friendly or affectionate. **3.** irritated or angry. —*v.t., v.i.* **4.** heat moderately. —**warm'ly,** *adv.* —**warmth, warm'ness,** *n.* —**warm'ish,** *adj.*

warm'heart'ed, *adj.* friendly; sympathetic.

war·mon·ger (wor'mun''gər), *n.* inciter of war.

warn, *v.t.* give notice of danger; caution. —**warn'ing,** *n., adj.*

warp, *n.* **1.** distortion. **2.** lengthwise threads in cloth. —*v.t., v.i.* **3.** distort.

war'rant, *n.* **1.** authorization, as by law. **2.** guarantee. —*v.t.* **3.** authorize. **4.** guarantee. —**war'rant·a·ble,** *adj.*

war'ran·ty, *n., pl.* **-ties.** guarantee on something sold.

war'ri·or, *n.* soldier.

wart, *n.* small hard protuberance on the skin. —**wart'y,** *adj.*

war'y, *adj.,* **warier, wariest.** cautious; watchful. —**war'i·ly,** *adv.* —**war'i·ness,** *n.*

was, *v.* 1st and 3rd person singular, past indicative of be.

wash, *v.t.* **1.** clean with or in water or a solution. **2.** flow over. —*v.i.* **3.** wash oneself. **4.** undergo washing. —*n.* **5.** washing, as of clothes. **6.** current behind a moving ship or plane. —**wash'a·ble,** *adj.* —**wash'board',** *n.* —**wash'bowl',** *n.* —**wash'cloth',** *n.* —**wash'stand',** *n.*

wash'er, *n.* **1.** washing machine. **2.** pierced disk for tightening a joint to prevent leakage, etc.

wash'out'', *n.* **1.** washing away of earth, soil, etc. **2.** *Informal.* failure.

WASP, *n.* white Anglo-Saxon Protestant. Also, **W.A.S.P., Wasp.**

wasp, *n.* stinging insect. —**wasp'ish,** *adj.*

was'sail (wos'əl), *n.* **1.** drinking or toasting a person's health, as with a spiced ale. **2.** drinking festivity. —*v.i., v.t.* **3.** toast.

waste, *v.,* **wasted, wasting,** *n., adj. v.t.* **1.** use up needlessly. **2.** ruin. —*v.i.* **3.** be used up gradually. —*n.* **4.** needless consumption or expenditure. **5.** unused remains. **6.** neglect. **7.** ruin. —*adj.* **8.** unused. —**waste'bas'ket,** *n.* —**waste'ful,** *adj.* —**waste'pa'per,** *n.*

wast·rel (wās'trəl), *n.* wasteful person; spendthrift.

watch, *v.i.* **1.** observe; be on the alert. —*v.t.* **2.** observe. **3.** guard or tend. —*n.* **4.** period of watching; observation. **5.** small timepiece worn on the person. —**watch'band,** *n.* —**watch'**

dog, *n.* —watch'ful, *adj.* —watch' man, *n.* —watch'tow'er, *n.*

watch'word'', *n.* 1. password. 2. motto; slogan.

wa'ter, *n.* 1. colorless, odorless liquid forming rain, rivers, etc. —*v.t.* 2. supply with water. —*v.i.* 3. dischargewater or tears. —wa'ter·y, *adj.*

wa'ter·bed'', *n.* heavy water-filled bag used as a bed.

water closet, toilet.

wa'ter·col''or, *n.* 1. pigment mixed with water. 2. painting with such pigments.

wa'ter·course'', *n.* channel for water, as a river, canal, etc.

wa'ter·fall'', *n.* steep fall of water, as over a precipice.

wa'ter·fowl'', *n.* water bird.

water glass, drinking glass.

water lily, aquatic plant with floating leaves and flowers.

wa'ter-logged'', *adj.* saturated with water.

wa'ter·mark'', *n.* 1. mark showing height of water, as of a river, etc. 2. manufacturer's impression on paper. —*v.t.* 3. mark with a watermark.

wa'ter·mel''on, *n.* large fruit with juicy, red pulp.

wa'ter·proof'', *adj.* 1. impervious to water. —*v.t.* 2. make waterproof.

wa'ter·shed'', *n.* 1. ridge between two drainage areas. 2. drainage area.

wa'ter-ski'', *v.,* -skied, -skiing, *n.* *v.i.* 1. skim over water on ski-like boards drawn by a line attached to a speedboat. —*n.* 2. short, broad board for water-skiing.

wa'ter·spout'', *n.* 1. pipe for discharging water. 2. tubelike column of air and water occurring over water.

water table, *n.* level below which the ground is saturated.

wa'ter·wheel'', *n.* mill wheel moved by water.

wa'ter·works'', *n.* plant for supplying water.

watt, *n.* unit of electric power. —watt' age, *n.*

wat'tle, *n.* 1. stakes interwoven with twigs, as for fences, walls, etc. 2. fleshy skin hanging from the throat or chin.

wave, *n., v.* waved, waving. *n.* 1. ridge. along the ocean's surface. 2. undulation. 3. movement back and forth, as of a hand or flag. —*v.i., v.t.,* 4. move to and fro. —*v.i.* 5. signal with the hand. —wav'y, *adj.*

wa'ver, *v.i.* 1. hesitate. 2. sway. —*n.* 3. wavering.

WAVES, *n.* W(omen) A(ppointed for) V(oluntary) E(mergency) S(ervice); women in the U.S. Navy.

wax, *n.* 1. readily melted, molded, and burned substance. —*v.t.* 2. treat with wax. —*v.i.* 3. increase, as the moon. 4. *Archaic.* become. —wax'en, *adj.* —wax'er, *n.* —wax'y, *adj.*

wax'wing'', *n.* crested bird with scarlet wings' ends.

way, *n.* 1. manner, custom, or fashion. 2. plan. 3. direction or route. 4. ways, tracks for launching a ship.

way'far''er, *n.* traveler or rover.

way'lay', *v.t.,* -laid, -laying. lie in wait for; ambush.

way'ward, *adj.* 1. willful. 2. capricious. —way'ward·ness, *n.*

we, *pron.* nominative plural of *I.*

weak, *adj.* 1. not strong physically. 2. lacking moral or mental strength. 3. easily broken. —weak'ly, *adj., adv.* —weak'en, *v.t., v.i.* —weak'ling, *n.* —weak'ness, *n.*

wealth, *n.* 1. abundance of money or property. 2. large and valuable amount. —wealth'y, *adj.*

wean, *v.t.* 1. accustom to food other than mother's milk. 2. cure of a dependency or delusion.

weap'on, *n.* instrument for fighting. —weap'on·ry, *n.*

wear, *v.,* wore, worn, wearing. *v.t.* 1. have on the body, as clothing. 2. diminish by use. —*v.i.* 3. deteriorate as through use. —*n.* 4. diminution or impairment through use. 5. clothing. —wear'a·ble, *adj.* —wear'er, *n.*

wea'ri·some, *adj.* tiresome.

wear'y, *adj.,* -rier, -riest, *v.t.,* -rying, -ried. *adj.* 1. very tired. 2. causing fatigue. —*v.t.* 3. tire. —wear'i·ly, *adv.* —wear'i·ness, *n.*

wea'sel, *n.* small, flesh-eating mammal.

weath'er, *n.* 1. condition of the sky. 2. storms, rains, etc. —*v.t.* 3. withstand. 4. expose to the weather. —*adj.* 5. toward the wind.

weath'er·beat''en, *adj.* showing the effect of weather.

weave, *v.,* wove, woven or weaved, weaving, *n.* *v.t.* 1. interlace threads, etc., as on a loom. 2. construct, as in the mind. —*v.i.* 3. become interlaced. —*n.* 4. type of weaving. —weav'er, *n.*

web, *n., v.t.,* webbed, webbing. *n.* 1. something woven. 2. network spun by spiders. 3. trap. —*v.t.* 4. join or cover,as by or with a web. —webbed, *adj.* —web'bing, *n.*

web'foot'', *n., pl.* -feet. foot with webbed toes. —web'-foot''ed, web'-toed'', *adj.*

wed, *v.,* wedded, wedded or wed, wedding. *v.t., v.i.* 1. marry. 2. join. —wed' ding, *n.*

wedge, *n., v.,* wedged, wedging. *n.* 1. object with two faces meeting at a sharp angle. —*v.t.* 2. force or fix with a wedge. —*v.i.* 3. become wedged.

wed'lock, *n.* state of marriage.

Wednes'day, *n.* fourth day of the week.

wee, *adj.* tiny.

weed, *n.* **1.** useless plant. —*v.i.* **2.** free from weeds. —**weed'er,** *n.* —**weed'y,** *adj.*

week, *n.* **1.** period of seven days, esp. starting from Sunday. **2.** working days of the week.

week'day", *n.* **1.** any day except Saturday or Sunday. —*adj.* **2.** pertaining to such days.

week'end", *n.* Saturday and Sunday.

week'ly, *adj., adv., n., pl.* **-lies.** *adj.* **1.** appearing or occurring once a week. **2.** lasting a week. —*adv.* **3.** every week. —*n.* **4.** weekly periodical.

weep, *v.i.,* **wept, weeping.** mourn or shed tears. —**weep'er,** *n.*

wee'vil, *n.* beetle destructive to grain, fruit, etc.

weigh, *v.t.* **1.** measure the heaviness of. **2.** consider carefully. —*v.i.* **3.** have significance. **4.** be a burden. —**weigh'er,** *n.*

weight, *n.* **1.** heaviness or pressure. **2.** burden, influence, or importance. —*v.t.* **3.** burden. —**weight'y,** *adj.* —**weight'i·ness,** *n.*

weird, *adj.* strange, uncanny, or queer. —**weird'ly,** *adv.* —**weird'ness,** *n.*

wel'come, *n., v.t.,* **-comed, -coming,** *adj.* *n.* **1.** friendly greeting. —*v.t.* **2.** greet with pleasure. —*adj.* **3.** happily or readily received. **4.** freely permitted.

weld, *v.t.* **1.** unite, as by heat or pressure. —*n.* **2.** welded joint. —**weld'er,** *n.*

wel'fare", *n.* **1.** well-being. **2.** aid for the poor.

well, *adv.,* **better, best,** *adj., n., v.i., interj.* *adv.* **1.** in a benevolent, good, or thorough manner. —*adj.* **2.** in good health. **3.** suitable. —*n.* **4.** opening in the earth as a source of water, oil, etc. —*v.i.* **5.** flow or gush. —*interj.* **6.** (exclamation denoting surprise or introducing a sentence).

well- prefix meaning "in a good or thorough manner." **well-accomplished, well-adjusted, well-aimed, well-argued, well-armed, well-arranged, well-attended, well-aware, well-behaved, well-built, well-considered, well-contented, well-controlled, well-developed, well-disciplined, well-documented, well-earned, well-educated, well-equipped, well-governed, well-hidden, well-justified, well-kept, well-liked, well-loved, well-managed, well-planned, well-prepared, well-protected, well-qualified, well-regulated, well-remembered, well-respected, well-satisfied, well-secured, well-situated, well-spent, well-stated, well-suited, well-taught, well-trained, well-traveled, well-treated, well-understood, well-used.**

well'-be'ing, *n.* state of being well and happy.

well'-bred', *adj.* with good manners.

well'-es·tab'lished, *adj.* settled; firmly in place.

well'-found'ed, *adj.* based on good reason. Also, **well'-ground'ed,** *adj.*

well'head", *n.* fountainhead; source.

well'-man'nered, *adj.* polite; courteous.

well'-mean'ing, *adj.* having good intentions. —**well'-meant',** *adj.*

well'-nigh', *adv.* almost.

well'-off', *adj.* **1.** in a good condition. **2.** prosperous.

well'-pre·served', *adj.* **1.** in good condition. **2.** youthful for one's age.

well'-round'ed, *adj.* **1.** having varied abilities. **2.** well-diversified.

well'-spo'ken, *adj.* speaking well or pleasantly.

well'spring", *n.* source.

well'-to-do', *adj.* wealthy.

well'-wish"er, *n.* person who wishes well to another.

welt, *n.* **1.** ridge or wale on the body from a blow. **2.** leather strip on the seam of a shoe. —*v.t.* **3.** beat soundly.

welt'er, *v.i.* **1.** roll or heave, as waves. **2.** wallow. —*n.* **3.** jumble or muddle.

wen, *n.* skin cyst or tumor.

wench, *n.* **1.** young woman. **2.** strumpet. —*v.i.* **3.** associate with promiscuous women.

went, *v.i.* past form of *go.*

were, *v.* past plural form of *be.*

were'wolf", *n., pl.* **-wolves.** person changed into a wolf.

west, *n.* **1.** compass point to the left of north. **2.** direction of such point. **3.** Also, **West,** the Occident. —*adj., adv.* **4.** toward or from the west. —**west'ern,** *adj.* —**west'ern·er,** *n.*

west'er·ly, *adj., adv.* **1.** from the west, as wind. **2.** toward the west.

west'ern·ize", *v.t.,* **-ized, -izing.** make Occidental in culture.

west'ward, *adj.* **1.** toward the west. —*adv.* **2.** Also, **west'wards, toward the west.** —*n.* **3.** westward direction.

wet, *adj.,* **wetter, wettest,** *n., v.* *adj.* **1.** covered with water or liquid. —*n.* **2.** water or moisture. —*v.t.* **3.** make wet. —*v.i.* **4.** become wet. —**wet'ness,** *n.*

whack, *Informal. v.t., v.i.* **1.** slap or strike. —*n.* **2.** sharp blow.

whale, *n., v.i.,* **whaled, whaling.** *n.* **1.** large sea mammal. —*v.i.* **2.** hunt whales. —**whal'er,** *n.*

whale'bone", *n.* elastic material in the upper jaw of some whales.

wharf, *n., pl.* **wharves.** pier or quay.

what, *pron., pl.* **what,** *adj., adv., interj.* *pron.* **1.** which one? **2.** that which. —*adj.* **3.** which kind of. —*adv.* **4.** how? **5.** partly. —*interj.* **6.** (exclamation of surprise).

what·ev′er, *pron.* 1. anything that. —*adj.* 2. of any kind.

what′not″, *n.* open cupboard, as for bric-a-brac.

wheal, *n.* small swelling, as from an insect bite.

wheat, *n.* cereal grass used in flour, etc.

whee′dle, *v.t.,* -dled, -dling. persuade by coaxing.

wheel, *n.* 1. rotating disk that transmits power or facilitates movement. —*v.t., v.i.* 2. move on wheels. 3. revolve.

wheel′bar″row, *n.* one-wheeled container for moving loads.

wheel′base″, *n.* distance between the front and rear wheel hubs of an automobile.

wheel′er-deal′er, *n. Informal.* person skillful in business deals.

wheeze, *v.i.,* wheezed, wheezing. *n. v.i.* 1. breathe with a whistling sound. —*n.* 2. a wheezing sound. —wheez′y, *adj.*

whelm, *v.t.* 1. submerge. 2. overwhelm.

whelp, *n.* 1. young of a dog, bear, etc. —*v.t., v.i.* 2. give birth to.

when, *adv.* 1. at what time? —*conj.* 2. at the time that. —*pron.* 3. what or which time.

whence, *adv.* from what place, cause, etc.

when·ev′er, *adv.* 1. when. —*conj.* 2. at whatever time.

where, *adv.* 1. at what place? 2. in what way? —*conj.* 3. at which place; wherever. —*pron.* 4. the place at which.

where′a·bouts″, *adv.* 1. where. —*n.* 2. location.

where·as′, *conj.* 1. considering that. 2. on the contrary.

where′fore″, *adv., conj.* for what.

where·in′, *conj.* in which.

where″up·on′, *conj.* upon which.

where′with·al″, *n.* means.

wher′ry, *n., pl.* -ries. light rowboat.

whet, *v.t.,* whetted, whetting. 1. sharpen. 2. stimulate, as the appetite. —whet′stone″, *n.*

wheth′er, *conj.* 1. if it is so that. 2. if either.

whey, *n.* water part of curdled milk.

which, *pron.* 1. what one? 2. that. —*adj.* 3. what one.

which·ev′er, *pron., adj.* 1. any. 2. regardless of which.

whiff, *n.* light odor or puff.

whif′fle·tree″, *n.* crossbar to which harness traces are fastened.

while, *n., conj., v.t.,* whiled, whiling. *n.* 1. time. —*conj.* 2. during the time that. 3. although. —*v.t.* 4. spend pleasantly, as time.

whim, *n.* sudden fancy; caprice. —whim′si·cal, *adj.* —whim′sy, *n.*

whine, *v.i.,* whined, whining. 1. complain childishly. 2. make a high-pitched, nasal sound. —whin′ing·ly, *adv.* —whin′y, *adj.*

whin′ny, *v.i.,* -nied, -nying, *n., pl.* -nies. neigh.

whip, *v.,* whipped, whipping, *n. v.t.* 1. strike or lash. —*v.i.* 2. move quickly. —*n.* 3. instrument for whipping.

whip′cord″, *n.* hard, braided cord.

whip′lash″, *n.* neck injury from jerking of the head as in an automobile accident.

whip′per·snap″per, *n.* presumptuous person.

whip′pet, *n.* fast dog.

whip′poor·will″, *n.* gray bird with nocturnal cry.

whir, *v.,* whirred, whirring, *n. v.i., v.t., n.* hum or buzz. Also, whirr.

whirl, *v.i., v.t.* 1. move or revolve rapidly. —*n.* 2. whirling movement. 3. uproar or confusion.

whirl′pool″, *n.* whirling current of water.

whirl′wind″, *n.* whirling current of air.

whisk, *v.t., v.i.* 1. brush with a quick motion. —*n.* 2. act or instance of whisking. —whisk′broom″, *n.*

whisk′er, *n.* 1. a facial hair. 2. long bristle, as on a cat.

whis′key, *n., pl.* -keys, -kies. liquor distilled from fermented grain. Also, whis′ky.

whis′per, *v.i., v.t.* 1. speak softly. 2. make a low rustling. —*n.* 3. act or instance of whispering.

whist, *n.* card game.

whis′tle, *v.i.,* -tled, -tling, *n. v.i.* 1. make a high-pitched sound through pursed lips. —*n.* 2. act or instance of whistling. 3. noise-making device using steam or air.

whit, *n.* small bit.

white, *adj.* 1. of the color of snow. 2. pale. 3. pure. —*n.* 4. opposite to black. 5. Caucasoid. —white′ness, *n.* —whit′ish, *adj.* —whit′en, *v.t., v.i.*

white elephant, 1. albino elephant. 2. awkward, useless possession.

white′fish″, *n.* edible lake fish.

White House, 1. residence of the U.S. president. 2. executive branch of the U.S. government.

white lie, small, pardonable lie.

white slave, woman forced into prostitution. —white slavery.

white′wash″, *n.* 1. mixture for whitening walls. —*v.t.* 2. apply whitewash to. 3. *Informal.* conceal the guilt of.

white′y, *Informal.* white person or people. Also, White′y, whit′y.

whith′er, *adv., conj. Archaic.* to what place.

whit′ing, *n.* 1. food fish. 2. chalk for paints.

whit′low, *n.* inflammation of a finger or toe.

whit′tle, *v.,* -tled, -tling. *v.t., v.i.* 1. cut or

carve, as from wood. —*v.t.* **2.** reduce the amount of.

whiz, *v.i.,* **whizzed, whizzing.** *n.* *v.i.* **1.** make a buzzing sound in motion. —*n.* **2.** such a sound. **3.** *Informal.* expert. Also, **whizz.**

who, *pron.* **1.** which person? **2.** person that.

whoa, *interj.* stop!

who·ev'er, *pron.* anyone that.

whole, *adj.* **1.** entire. **2.** intact. **3.** *Math.* not a fraction. —*n.* **4.** all the amount. —**whole'ly,** *adv.* —**whole'ness,** *n.*

whole'heart'ed, *adj.* enthusiastic; dedicated. —**whole'heart'ed·ly,** *adv.*

whole'sale'', *n., adj., v.,* **-saled, saling.** *n.* **1.** sale of goods in quantity, as to retailers. —*adj.* **2.** selling by wholesale. —*v.t., v.i.* **3.** sell wholesale. —**whole'sal'er,** *n.*

whole'some, *adj.* healthful, salutary. —**whole'some·ly,** *adv.* —**whole'some·ness,** *n.*

whom, *pron. Grammar.* objective case of who.

whoop, *n.* **1.** shout of joy. **2.** sound in whooping cough. —*v.t., v.i.* **3.** utter with whooping.

whop·per, *n. Informal.* **1.** something unusually large. **2.** outrageous lie. —**whop'ping,** *adj.*

whore, *n., v.i.,* **whored, whoring.** *n.* **1.** prostitute. —*v.i.* **2.** consort with whores. —**whor'ish,** *adj.*

whorl, *n.* spiral or circular arrangement.

whose, *pron. Grammar.* possessive case of who.

who'so·ev'er, *pron.* whoever.

why, *adv., n., pl.* **whys,** *interj. adv.* **1.** for what reason or cause. —*n.* **2.** reason, cause, or purpose. —*interj.* **3.** exclamation of surprise.

wick, *n.* length of fiber that absorbs fuel to burn.

wick'ed, *adj.* **1.** bad, evil. **2.** mischievous. —**wick'ed·ly,** *adv.* —**wick'ed·ness,** *n.*

wick'er, *n.* **1.** flexible twig. —*adj.* **2.** made of wicker. —**wick'er·work'',** *n.*

wick'et, *n.* **1.** small gate. **2.** upright frame used in cricket or croquet.

wide, *adj.,* **wider, widest.** *adj.* **1.** broad. —*adv.* **2.** far. —**wide'ly,** *adv.* —**wide'ness,** *n.* —**wid'en,** *v.t., v.i.* —**wide'spread',** *adj.*

wide'-a·wake', *adj.* alert.

widg'eon, *n.* fresh-water wild duck. Also, **wig'eon.**

wid'ow, *n.* **1.** unmarried woman whose husband has died. —*v.t.* **2.** make into a widow. Also, *masc.,* **wid'ow·er.** —**wid'ow·hood'',** *n.*

width, *n.* breadth.

wield, *v.t.* **1.** handle or manage. **2.** exercise, as authority or power. —**wield'er,** *n.*

wie'ner, *n.* frankfurter. Also, *Informal,* **wee'nie** or **wie'nie.**

wife, *n., pl.* **wives.** married woman. —**wife'less,** *adj.* —**wife'ly,** *adj.*

wig, *n., v.,* **wigged, wigging.** *n.* **1.** artificial hair piece. —*v.t.* **2.** furnish with a wig.

wig'gle, *v.,* **-gled, -gling.** *n. v.i., v.t.* **1.** move with quick motions from side to side. —*n.* **2.** act or instance of wiggling. —**wig'gly,** *adj.*

wig'wag'', *v.,* **-wagged, -wagging.** *n. v.t., v.i.* **1.** signal with swung flags. —*n.* **2.** act or instance of wigwagging.

wig'wam, *n.* American Indian hut.

wild, *adj.* **1.** uncivilized. **2.** uncontrollable. **3.** lacking restraint; dissolute. —*n.* **4.** desolate region. —**wild'ly,** *adv.* —**wild'ness,** *n.*

wild'cat'', *n., v.,* **-catted, -catting.** *n.* **1.** large, fierce feline. **2.** savage person. **3.** exploratory oil or gas well. —*v.i., v.t.* **4.** search for oil or gas.

wil'der·ness, *n.* uninhabited region.

wild'-goose' chase, search for a nonexistent thing.

wile, *n., v.t.,* **wiled, wiling.** *n.* **1.** sly trick. —*v.t.* **2.** beguile. **3. wile away,** pass leisurely, as time.

will, *n., v.,* **willed, willing.** *n.* **1.** power of conscious choice or action. **2.** determination. **3.** disposition toward another. **4.** legal document of one's wishes after death. —*v.i., v.t.* **5.** desire, wish, or want. **6.** bequeath by a will. —*auxiliary v.* **7.** am, is, or are about to. **8.** am, is, or are willing to. **9.** am, is, or are expected to. —**will·a·ble,** *adj.*

will'ful, *adj.* **1.** intentional. **2.** stubborn. Also, **wil'ful.** —**will'ful·ly,** *adv.* —**will'ful·ness,** *n.*

will'ing, *adj.* **1.** favorably inclined. **2.** cheerfully done. —**will'ing·ly,** *adv.* —**will'ing·ness,** *n.*

will''-o'-the-wisp', *n.* **1.** elusive light. **2.** anything that deludes.

wil'low, *n.* slender tree with flexible limbs and narrow leaves. —**wil'low·y,** *adj.*

wil'ly-nil'ly, *adv., adj.* whether willingly or not.

wilt, *v.i.* **1.** become limp or weak; droop. —*v.t.* **2.** cause to wilt. —*n.* **3.** wilted state.

wil'y, *adj.,* **-lier, -liest.** sly. —**wi'li·ness,** *n.*

win, *n., won, winning, n. v.i.* **1.** succeed. —*v.t.* **2.** gain, as a victory, favor, etc. **3.** influence. —*n.* **4.** victory.

wince, *v.i.,* **winced, wincing.** *n. v.i.* **1.** shrink, as from a blow or pain. —*n.* **2.** act or instance of wincing.

winch, *n.* **1.** crank. **2.** windlass. —*v.t.* **3.** hoist or haul by a winch.

wind *v.,* **wound, winding.** *n. v.t.* (wīnd) **1.** turn. —*v.i.* **2.** coil. **3.** make one's way, as along a path. —*n.* (wind) **4.** air in motion, as a gale. **5.** breath. **6.** intestinal gas. —**wind′er**, *n.* —**wind′y**, *adj.*

wind′bag″, *n. Informal.* empty talker.

wind′break″, *n.* shield against the wind.

wind′burn″, *n.* inflammation of the skin from the wind. —**wind′burned″**, *adj.*

wind′ed, *adj.* out of breath.

wind′fall, *n.* **1.** unexpected good fortune. **2.** something blown down by the wind.

wind instrument, musical instrument sounded by the breath.

wind′jam″mer, *n.* large sailing ship.

wind′lass, *n.* winch.

wind′mill″, *n.* wind-driven machine.

win′dow, *n.* opening in a wall for light, air, etc. —**win′dow·pane″**, *n.* —**win′dow·sill″**, *n.* —**window shade.**

window dressing, 1. store display. **2.** specious display.

wind′pipe″, *n.* trachea.

wind′row″, *n.* row of leaves, hay, etc.

wind′shield″, *n.* glass above and across a car's dashboard.

wind′up″, *n.* **1.** conclusion or end. **2.** *Baseball.* pitcher's arm and body movements before throwing.

wind′ward, *n.* **1.** direction from which the wind blows. —*adj.* **2.** moving to windward. —*adv.* **3.** toward the wind.

wine, *n., v.,* **wined, wining.** *n.* **1.** fermented juice from grapes, other fruits, or plants. —*v.i., v.t.* **2.** entertain with wine. —**win′y**, *adj.*

win′er·y, *n., pl.* **-ies.** wine-making place.

wing, *n.* **1.** organ for flight of birds, insects, bats, etc. **2.** supporting surface of an airplane. **3.** distinct section. —*v.t.* **4.** shoot in an arm or wing. —*v.i.* **5.** travel on wings. —**wing′ed**, *adj.* —**wing′less**, *adj.* —**wing′like**, *adj.* —**wing′tip″**, *n.*

wing′span″, *n.* distance between an airplane's wingtips.

wing′spread″, *n.* distance between the tips of extended wings.

wink, *v.i., v.t.* **1.** close and open quickly, as one eye. **2.** signal by winking. —*v.i.* **3.** shine or twinkle. —*n.* **4.** winking, as a signal. **5.** instant.

win′ner, *n.* person or thing that wins.

win′ning, *adj.* **1.** pleasing; charming. **2.** victorious. —*n.* **3.** Often **winnings,** something won, as money. —**win′ning·ly**, *adv.*

win′now, *v.t., v.i.* **1.** blow away from grain. **2.** separate.

win·o, *n., pl.* **-os.** *Informal.* alcoholic who drinks cheap wine.

win′some, *adj.* attractive. —**win′some·ly**, *adv.* —**win′some·ness**, *n.*

win′ter, *n.* **1.** cold season between autumn and spring. **2.** time like winter, as of decline, cold, etc. —*v.i.* **3.** spend the winter. —**win′ter·time″**, *n.* —**win′try**, **win′ter·y**, *adj.*

win′ter·green″, *n.* small evergreen aromatic shrub with white flowers.

win′ter·ize″, *v.t.,* **-ized, -izing.** prepare for winter.

wipe, *v.t.,* **wiped, wiping,** *n., v.t.* **1.** clean or rub. —*n.* **2.** act or instance of wiping. —**wip′er**, *n.*

wire, *n., v.,* **wired, wiring.** *n.* **1.** stringlike piece of metal. **2.** *Informal.* telegram. —*v.t.* **3.** install or bind with wire. —*v.t., v.i.* **4.** telegraph.

wire′hair″, *n.* fox terrier.

wire′less, *adj. Archaic.* pertaining to radio.

wire′tap″ping, *n.* listening secretly to the telephone calls of others.

wir′y, *adj.,* **-ier, -iest.** lean and tough.

wis′dom, *n.* **1.** knowledge and good judgment. **2.** wise teachings.

wisdom tooth, back molar.

wise, *adj.,* **wiser, wisest. 1.** showing knowledge and judgment. **2.** erudite or informed. **3.** *Informal.* insolent. —**wise′ly**, *adv.*

wise′a·cre, *n.* person who affects to have wisdom. Also, *Informal,* **wise guy.**

wise′crack″, *Informal. n.* **1.** flippant remark. —*v.i.* **2.** make wisecracks.

wish, *v.t.* **1.** want or desire. —*v.i.* **2.** yearn. —*n.* **3.** desire; longing. —**wish′er**, *n.* —**wish′ful**, *adj.* —**wish′ful·ly**, *adv.* —**wish′ful·ness**, *n.*

wish′bone″, *n.* forked breastbone of a bird.

wish′y-wash′y, *adj.* weak and vacillating.

wisp, *n.* thin film or strand. —**wisp′y**, *adj.*

wis·te′ri·a, *n.* climbing shrub with showy flowers.

wist′ful, *adj.* longing or yearning. —**wist′ful·ly**, *adv.* —**wist′ful·ness**, *n.*

wit, *n.* **1.** intelligence. **2.** cleverness of expression. **3.** person clever with words. —**wit′less**, *adj.* —**wit′less·ly**, *adv.* —**wit′ty**, *adj.* —**wit′ti·ly**, *adv.*

witch, *n.* **1.** woman with supposed supernatural power. **2.** ugly woman. —**witch′craft″**, *n.* —**witch′er·y**, *n.*

witch doctor, man who uses magic to cure sickness.

witch hazel, 1. shrub with yellow leaves. **2.** liquid extracted from it.

with, *prep.* **1.** accompanied by. **2.** characterized by. **3.** against. **4.** in regard to.

with·draw′, *v.,* **-drew, -drawn, -drawing.** *v.t.* **1.** take back. **2.** retract, as a statement, etc. —*v.i.* **3.** remove oneself. —**with·draw′al**, *n.*

withe, *n.* willow twig.

with′er, *v.t., v.i.* **1.** shrivel. —*v.t.* **2.** confuse and humiliate. —**with′er·ing·ly**, *adv.*

with′ers, *n. pl.* lower nape of the neck of a sheep, horse, etc.

with·hold′, *v.t.*, **-held, -holding. 1.** hold back. **2.** deduct, as taxes.

with·in′, *adv.* **1.** inside; indoors. —*prep.* **2.** inside. **3.** in the area of.

with·out′, *prep.* **1.** lacking; not with. **2.** outside. —*adv.* **3.** outside; externally.

with·stand′, *v.t.*, **-stood, -standing.** resist or oppose.

wit′ness, *n.* **1.** person who sees. **2.** testimony. —*v.t.* **3.** see. **4.** attest.

wit′ti·cism″, *n.* witty remark.

wit′ting, *adj.* knowing; intentional. —**wit′ting·ly**, *adv.*

wiz′ard, *n.* magician; sorcerer. —**wiz′ard·ry**, *n.*

wiz′ened, *adj.* withered.

wob′ble, *v.*, **-bled, -bling,** *n. v.i., v.t.* **1.** shake. —*n.* **2.** wobbling motion. —**wob′bly,** *adj.* —**wob′bli·ness,** *n.*

woe, *n.* **1.** grief. **2.** trouble. —*interj.* **3.** alas! —**woe′ful,** *adj.* —**woe′ful·ly,** *adv.* —**woe′ful·ness,** *n.*

woe′be·gone″, *adj.* showing woe. —**woe′be·gone″ness,** *n.*

wolf, *n., pl.* **wolves. 1.** wild, doglike mammal. **2.** *Informal.* man who flirts with women. **3.** cruel person. —*v.t.* **4.** devour greedily. —**wolf′hound″,** *n.* —**wolf′ish,** *adj.* —**wolf′like″,** *adj.*

wol″ver·ine′, *n.* stocky, carnivorous mammal.

wom′an, *n., pl.* **women.** female human being. —**wom′an·hood″,** *n.* —**wom′an·ish,** *adj.* —**wom′an·like″,** *adj.* —**wom′an·ly,** *adj.* —**wom′an·li·ness,** *n.*

wom′an·ize″, *v.* **-ized, -izing.** *v.t.* **1.** make effeminate. —*v.i.* **2.** pursue women habitually. —**wom′an·iz″er,** *n.*

womb, *n.* **1.** uterus. **2.** source of being.

won′der, *n.* **1.** awe or amazement. **2.** source of such an emotion. —*v.i.* **3.** be curious. **4.** be filled with wonder. —**won′der·ful,** *adj.* —**won′der·ful·ly,** *adv.* —**won′der·ing·ly,** *adv.* —**won′der·ment,** *n.* —**won′drous,** *adj.* —**won′drous·ly,** *adv.*

wont, *adj.* **1.** Also, **wont′ed,** accustomed. —*n.* **2.** habit.

won′t, *v.* contraction of *will not.*

woo, *v.i., v.t.* solicit for love or favor. —**woo′er,** *n.*

wood, *n.* **1.** hard substance beneath the bark of trees. **2.** Also, **woods,** forest. **3.** lumber. —*adj.* **4.** wooden; made of wood. —**wood′en,** *adj.* —**wood′en·ness,** *n.* —**wood′craft″,** *n.* —**wood′cut″ter,** *n.* —**wood′ed,** *adj.* —**wood′pile″,** *n.* —**wood′shed″,** *n.* —**woods′man,** *n.* —**woods′y,** *adj.* —**wood′y,** *adj.*

wood′bine″, *n.* honeysuckle or the Virginia creeper.

wood′chuck″, *n.* burrowing and hibernating marmot.

wood′cock″, *n.* snipelike game bird.

wood′cut′, *n.* **1.** carved block of wood. **2.** print from this block.

wood′en, *adj.* **1.** made of wood. **2.** without natural feeling or expression. —**wood′en·ly,** *adv.*

wood′land″, *n.* land covered with trees.

wood′peck″er, *n.* bird with a hard bill for pecking.

wood′wind″, *n.* musical non-brass wind instrument.

wood′work″, *n.* **1.** objects made of wood. **2.** wooden fittings of a house, as doors, moldings, etc. —**wood′work″er,** *n.* —**wood′work″ing,** *n.*

woof, *n.* cross-threads of a fabric.

woof′er, *n.* loudspeaker for reproducing low frequencies.

wool, *n.* **1.** soft, curly hair, as from sheep, goats, etc. **2.** yarn or garments made from such. —**wool′en, wool′len,** *adj.* —**wool′y, wool′ly,** *adj.* —**wool′i·ness, wool′li·ness,** *n.*

wool′gath″er·ing, *n.* absentmindedness or daydreaming.

wooz′y, *adj.*, **-ier, -iest.** *Informal.* muddled or dizzy. —**wooz′i·ly,** *adv.* —**wooz′i·ness,** *n.*

word, *n.* **1.** spoken or written sounds with meaning as a unit of language. **2. words,** speech or talk. **3.** promise or assurance. **4.** news or information. **5.** (computers) several bits of data treated as a unit. —*v.t.* **6.** express in words —**word″age,** *n.* —**word″ing,** *n.* —**word″less,** *adj.* —**word″y,** *adj.* —**word″i·ness,** *n.*

work, *n., v.,* **worked** or **wrought, working,** *n.* **1.** labor or toil. **2.** occupation. **3.** something on which one is working. —*v.i.* **4.** do work. **5.** act or operate. —*v.t.* **6.** manage or manipulate. **7.** solve. **8.** cultivate, as the soil. **9.** provoke or excite. —**work′a·ble,** *adj.* —**work′bench″,** *n.* —**work′book″,** *n.* —**work′er,** *n.* —**work′day″,** *n.* —**work′ing·man″,** *n.* —**work′man,** *n.* —**work′shop″,** *n.* —**work′week″,** *n.*

work′day″, *n.* **1.** day on which work is done. **2.** part of the day one works.

work′man·like″, *adj.* skillful.

work′man·ship″, *n.* **1.** workman's art or skill. **2.** quality of work.

work′out″, *n.* practice athletic session.

world, *n.* **1.** earth; universe. **2.** people; mankind. **3.** part of the earth. **4.** great quantity or extent. —**world′wide″,** *adj.*

world′ly, *adj.*, **-lier, -liest. 1.** secular. **2.** Also, **world′ly-wise′,** sophisticated. —**world′li·ness,** *n.*

worm, *n.* **1.** long, soft, legless, creeping animal. **2.** something like this creature. **3.** *Informal.* contemptible person. **4.**

worms, intestinal disease from parasitic worms. —*v.i.* **5.** move or act stealthily. —*v.t.* **6.** get by insidious efforts. **7.** free from worms. —**worm′y,** *adj.* **-ier, -iest.** —**worm′i·ness,** *n.*

worm′wood″, *n.* **1.** bitter, strong-smelling herb. **2.** something bitter or unpleasant.

worn, *adj.* **1.** used by wear, handling, etc. **2.** exhausted; tired. —**worn′-out′,** *adj.*

wor′ry, *v.,* **-ried, -rying,** *n., pl.* **-ies.** *v.i.* **1.** feel anxious. —*v.t.* **2.** make anxious. —*n.* **3.** anxiety. **4.** cause of anxiety. —**wor′ri·er,** *n.* —**wor′ri·some,** *adj.*

worse, *adj.* **1.** bad in a greater or higher degree. **2.** in poorer health. —*n.* **3.** that which is worse. —*adv.* **4.** in a worse manner. —**wors′en,** *v.t., v.i.*

wor′ship, *n., v.,* **-shiped,** or **-shipped, -shiping** or **-shipping.** *n.* **1.** reverence for a deity. **2.** admiration or love. —*v.t., v.i.* **3.** show religious reverence. —**wor′ship·er, wor′ship·per,** *n.* —**wor′ship·ful,** *adj.*

worst, *adj.* **1.** bad in the highest degree. **2.** least well. —*n.* **3.** that which is worst. —*adv.* **4.** in the worst manner. —*v.t.* **5.** beat; defeat.

wor·sted (wŏos′tid), *n.* **1.** firmly twisted wool yarn. **2.** garment made of it. —*adj.* **3.** consisting of worsted.

wort, *n.* infusion with malt before fermentation, as in making beer or mash.

worth, *n.* **1.** material value, as in money. **2.** importance; value. —*adj.* **3.** worthy of; justifying. **4.** having equal value. —**worth′less,** *adj.* —**worth′less·ness,** *n.*

worth′while′, *adj.* worthy of doing, etc.

worth′y, *adj.,* **-ier, -iest.** deserving. —**worth′i·ly,** *adv.* —**worth′i·ness,** *n.*

would, *auxiliary v.* (expressing condition, futurity, habitual action, or request).

would′-be″, *adj.* wishing or intending to be.

wound, *n.* **1.** physical injury. **2.** injury to feelings, sensibilities, etc. —*v.t.,* **3.** injure. —**wound′ed,** *adj., n., pl.*

wrack, *n.* ruin or destruction.

wraith, *n.* ghost.

wran′gle, *v.t., v.i.,* **-gled, -gling,** *n.* dispute. dispute.

wrap, *v.,* **wrapped** or **wrapt, wrapping,** *n.* *v.t., v.i.* **1.** wind or fold, as around something. —*v.t.* **2.** enclose or envelop. —*n.* **3.** outer garment wrapped around the body. —**wrap′ping,** *n.*

wrap′per, *n.* **1.** person who wraps. **2.** something wrapped around as a cover.

wrath, *n.* **1.** anger; rage. **2.** vengeance. —**wrath′ful,** *adj.* —**wrath′ful·ly,** *adv.*

wreak, *v.t.* inflict.

wreath, *n., pl.* **wreaths.** circular formation, as of flowers, etc.

wreathe, *v.t.,* **wreathed, wreathing. 1.** form into a wreath. **2.** encircle.

wreck, *n.* **1.** structure or object in ruins. **2.** run-down person. —*v.t.* **3.** tear down or destroy. —**wreck′age,** *n.* —**wreck′er,** *n.*

wren, *n.* small, active songbird.

wrench, *n.* **1.** sudden twist or pull, as to the arms, back, etc. **2.** sudden emotional strain. **3.** tool for turning bolts, etc. —*v.t., v.i.* **4.** turn suddenly. —*v.t.* **5.** overstrain or injure.

wrest, *v.t.* **1.** pull violently. **2.** usurp. —*n.* **3.** twist.

wres′tle, *v.,* **-tled, -tling.** *v.t.* **1.** grapple and attempt to throw down. —*v.i.* **2.** engage in wrestling. **3.** struggle. —**wrest′ler,** *n.*

wretch, *n.* **1.** unhappy person. **2.** despicable person.

wretch′ed, *adj.* **1.** pitiful. **2.** contemptible. **3.** worthless. —**wretch′ed·ly,** *adv.* —**wretch′ed·ness,** *n.*

wrig′gle, *v.i., n.,* **-gled, -gling.** *v.i.* **1.** squirm; twist and turn. —*n.* **2.** act or instance of wriggling. —**wrig′gly,** *adj.*

wright, *n.* constructor.

wring, *v.t.,* **wrung, wringing,** *n., v.t.* **1.** twist; press; squeeze. —*n.* **2.** act or instance of wringing. —**wring′er,** *n.*

wrin′kle, *n., v.,* **-kled, -kling.** *n.* **1.** ridge or furrow on a surface. **2.** ingenious trick or device. —*v.t., v.i.* **3.** crease or furrow. —**wrin′kly,** *adj.*

wrist, *n.* joint between the hand and forearm. —**wrist′band″,** *n.* —**wrist′watch″,** *n.*

writ, *n.* **1.** *Law.* formal legal order or document. **2.** something written.

write, *v.* **wrote, written, writing.** *v.i.* **1.** form letters, words, etc., as with a pen, pencil, etc. —*v.t.* **2.** compose. **3.** communicate with. —**writ′er,** *n.*

writhe, *v.,* **writhed, writhing,** *n. v.t., v.i.* **1.** squirm, twist, or bend, as in pain. —*n.* **2.** act or instance of writhing.

wrong, *adj.* **1.** not right or good. **2.** not truthful or factual. **3.** inappropriate. —*n.* **4.** injustice; evil. —*v.t.* **5.** do wrong to. —**wrong′ly,** *adv.* —**wrong′ness,** *n.* —**wrong′do″er,** *n.* —**wrong′do″ing,** *n.* —**wrong′ful,** *adj.* —**wrong′ful·ly,** *adv.*

wrong′head″ed, *adj.* deeply erroneous.

wroth, *adj. Archaic.* angry.

wrought, *adj.* **1.** worked. **2.** shaped by beating.

wrought′-up′, *adj.* upset; excited.

wry, *adj.,* **wrier, wriest. 1.** distorted or lopsided. **2.** misdirected or perverse. **3.** bitterly ironic. —**wry′ly,** *adv.* —**wry′ness,** *n.*

wurst, *n.* sausage.

X

X, x, *n.* twenty-fourth letter of the English alphabet.

xe·non (zē'non), *n.* chemically inactive gaseous element.

xen·o·pho·bi·a (zen''ə fō'bē ə), *n.* irrational fear of that which is foreign or strange. —**xen''o·pho'bic,** *adj.*

Xmas, *n.* Christmas.

x'-ray, *n.* **1.** electromagnetic radiation which penetrates solids. **2.** picture made by x-rays. —*v.t.* **3.** treat or photograph with x-rays.

xy·lem (zī'ləm), *n.* woody tissue of plants and trees.

xy'lo·phone'', *n.* musical instrument with wooden sounding bars struck by small hammers.

Y

Y, y, *n.* twenty-fifth letter of the English alphabet.

yacht, *n.* pleasure ship. —**yachts'man,** *n.*

ya·hoo', *n.* coarse or rowdy person.

Yah·weh (Yah'we), *n.* God of the Hebrews.

yak, *n.* long-haired Tibetan ox.

yam, *n.* edible potatolike root; sweet potato.

yam'mer, *v.i.,* **-mered, -mering. 1.** complain or whine. **2.** talk persistently; chatter.

yank, *v.t.,* *v.i.* **1.** pull strongly and abruptly. —*n.* **2.** strong, abrupt pull.

Yan'kee, *n.* native or inhabitant of the U.S., the northeastern U.S., or New England.

yap, *v.i.,* **yapped, yapping.** *n.* *v.i.* **1.** yelp; bark shrilly. —*n.* **2.** shrill bark.

yard, *n.* **1.** linear unit of measure equal to 3 feet. **2.** open area. **3.** long spar that supports a sail.

yard'age, *n.* amount in yards.

yard'stick'', *n.* one-yard measuring stick.

yarn, *n.* **1.** multi-stranded thread for sweaters, etc. **2.** story; tall tale.

yaw, *v.i.* **1.** deviate from a course. —*n.* **2.** deviation.

yawl, *n.* two-masted sailboat.

yawn, *v.i.* **1.** involuntarily open the mouth wide as from drowsiness. —*n.* **2.** act or instance of yawning.

yawp (yap), *v.i.,* *n.* *Informal.* yelp; squawk.

yea, *adv., n.* yes.

year, *n.* **1.** time period equal to 365 or 366 days. **2.** years, age. —**year'ly,** *adv., adj.*

year'ling, *n.* year-old animal.

yearn, *v.i.* **1.** desire earnestly or strongly. **2.** feel affection or tenderness. —**yearn'ing,** *n., adj.*

yeast, *n.* fungous substance used to leaven bread, etc.

yell, *v.i., n.* cry; shout.

yel'low, *n.* **1.** bright color of butter, etc. —*adj.* **2.** of the color yellow. **3.** *Informal.* cowardly; chicken.

yel'low fe'ver, *n.* tropical disease.

yelp, *v.i.* **1.** cry quickly or shrilly like a dog. —*n.* **2.** quick, sharp bark.

yen, *n.* *Informal.* desire; urge.

yeo·man (yō'mən), *n.* **1.** naval petty officer. **2.** small independent farmer. —*adj.* **3.** valiant.

yes, *adv., n.* (expression of assent, agreement or affirmation).

yes'ter·day, *adv., n.* day before today.

yet, *adv.* **1.** up to now. **2.** besides. **3.** nevertheless. **4.** eventually. —*conj.* **5.** but; still.

yew, *n.* coniferous evergreen tree or bush.

yield, *v.t., v.i.* **1.** produce. **2.** surrender. **3.** concede. —*v.i.* **4.** give way to force. —*n.* **5.** amount produced.

yo·del (yōd'əl), *v.,* **-deled, -deling,** *n.* *v.t., v.i.* **1.** shout or sing alternating falsetto with chest voice. —*n.* **2.** act or instance of yodeling.

yo'ga, *n.* **1.** Hindu philosophy teaching suppression of the body to free the soul. **2.** system of exercises for total bodily control.

yo·gi (yōg'ē) *n.* adherent of yoga.

yo'gurt, *n.* fermented milk food.

yoke, *n., v.,* **yoked, yoking,** *n.* **1.** device for joining oxen. **2.** pair, esp. of oxen. **3.** something oppressive. —*v.t.* **4.** put a yoke on.

yo'kel, *n.* rustic; bumpkin.

yolk, *n.* yellow part of the egg.

Yom Kip·pur (yom kē pōōr'), *n.* Jewish Day of Atonement.

yon'der, *adj., adv.* over there.

yore, *adv. adj.* *Archaic.* long ago.

you, *pron.* **1.** person or persons addressed. **2.** any person.

young, *adj.* **1.** in the early stages of life, etc. **2.** pertaining to youth. —*n.* **3.** children; young people. —**young'ish,** *adj.*

young'ster, *n.* child; youth.

your, *adj.* pertaining to you.

yours, *pron.,* belonging to you.

your·self', *pron.*, *pl.* **-selves. 1.** form of you used reflexively or emphatically. **2.** your true self.

youth, *n.* **1.** young state. **2.** child; young person. **—youth'ful**, *adj.* **—youth'ful·ly**, *adv.* **—youth'ful·ness**, *n.*

yowl, *v.i.*, *n.* howl.

yuc'ca, *n.* tropical American plant.

yule, *n.* Christmas.

yule'tide", *n.* Christmas season.

Z

Z, z, *n.* twenty-sixth letter of the English alphabet.

za'ny, *n.*, *pl.* **-nies**, *adj.* *n.* **1.** clown. **2.** silly person. **—adj. 3.** crazy; foolish.

zeal, *n.* intense or eager interest. **—zeal'ous**, *adj.* **—zeal'ous·ly**, *adv.* **—zeal'ous·ness**, *n.*

zeal·ot (zel'ot), *n.* enthusiast; fanatic. **—zeal'ot·ry**, *n.*

ze'bra, *n.* black and white striped horselike African mammal.

Zen, *n.* Buddhist sect.

ze'nith, *n.* **1.** celestial point directly overhead. **2.** highest point.

zeph'yr, *n.* mild or gentle breeze.

zep'pe·lin, *n.* large dirigible. Also, **Zep'pe·lin.**

ze'ro, *n.* **1.** numerical symbol, 0, denoting the absence of quantity. **2.** nothing.

zest, *n.* **1.** something enhancing enjoy-

ment. **2.** enjoyment. **—zest'ful**, *adj.* **—zest'ful·ly**, *adv.*

zig'zag", *n.*, *adj.*, *adv.*, *v.i.*, **-zagged, -zagging.** *n.* **1.** short sharp alternations in a line. **—adj.**, *adv.* **2.** with or having sharp back and forth turns. **—v.i. 3.** proceed in a zigzag.

zinc, *n.* bluish metallic element.

zing, *n.* **1.** sharp singing or whistling sound. **2.** vitality. **—v.i. 3.** move with or make a zinging sound.

zin'ni·a, *n.* colorful annual garden flower.

Zi'on·ism", *n.* political movement for re-establishment of the Jewish Biblical homeland. **—Zi'on·ist**, *n.*

zip, *v.*, **zipped, zipping**, *n.* *v.i.* **1.** act or move speedily or energetically. **—v.t. 2.** fasten with a zipper. **—n. 3.** energy.

zip'per, *n.* slide fastener with interlocking teeth.

zith'er, *n.* stringed musical instrument.

zo'di·ac, *n.* imaginary heavenly region including the paths of all planets except Pluto, with divisions for the twelve constellations.

zom'bi, *n.* reanimated dead body. Also, **zom'bie.**

zone, *n.*, *v.t.*, **zoned, zoning**. *n.* **1.** special area or region. **—v.t. 2.** mark off or arrange in zones.

zoo, *n.* park where animals are exhibited.

zo·ol'o·gy, *n.* study of animals. **—zo·o·log'i·cal**, *adj.* **—zo·ol'o·gist**, *n.*

zoom, *v.i.* **1.** move quickly with a humming sound. **2.** fly upward sharply and at great speed.

zuc·chi·ni (zo͞o kē'nē), *n.* green cylindrical summer squash.

zy·gote', *n.* fertilized egg cell.